Foundations of Physical Education, Exercise Science, and Sport

Jennifer L. Walton-Fisette
Kent State University

Deborah A. Wuest
Ithaca College

FOUNDATIONS OF PHYSICAL EDUCATION, EXERCISE SCIENCE, AND SPORT, TWENTY-FIRST EDITION

Published by McGraw Hill LLC, 1325 Avenue of the Americas, New York, NY 10019.

This book is printed on acid-free paper.

1 2 3 4 5 6 7 8 9 LCR 28 27 26 25 24 23

ISBN 978-1-264-46165-3 (bound edition)
MHID 1-264-46165-8 (bound edition)

ISBN 978-1-265-29404-5 (loose-leaf edition)
MHID 1-265-29404-6 (loose-leaf edition)

Product Developer: *Elisa Odoardi*
Marketing Manager: *Kim Schroeder-Freund*
Content Project Managers: *Lisa Bruflodt, Katie Reuter*
Buyer: *Rachel Hirschfield*
Content Licensing Specialist: *Melissa Homer*
Cover Image: *PHOTOCREO Michal Bednarek/Shutterstock*
Compositor: *Aptara®, Inc.*

Library of Congress Cataloging-in-Publication Data

Names: Walton-Fisette, Jennifer L., 1978- author. | Wuest, Deborah A., author.
Title: Foundations of physical education, exercise science, and sport / Jennifer L. Walton-Fisette, Kent State University, Deborah A. Wuest, Ithaca College.
Description: Twenty first edition. | Dubuque : McGraw Hill LLC, [2024] | Includes index.
Identifiers: LCCN 2022032185 (print) | LCCN 2022032186 (ebook) | ISBN 9781264461653 (hardcover) | ISBN 9781265294045 (spiral bound) | ISBN 9781265287054 (ebook) | ISBN 9781265301798 (ebook other)
Subjects: LCSH: Physical education and training. | Sports. | Physical education and training–Vocational guidance. | Sports–Vocational guidance.
Classification: LCC GV341 .W85 2024 (print) | LCC GV341 (ebook) | DDC 796.07–dc23
LC record available at https://lccn.loc.gov/2022032185
LC ebook record available at https://lccn.loc.gov/2022032186

mheducation.com/highered

Brief Contents

Part I
Nature and Scope of Physical Education, Exercise Science, and Sport 1

1 Meaning and Scope 2
2 Philosophy, Goals, and Objectives 25
3 Health and Physical Activity in Our Society 50

Part II
Foundations of Physical Education, Exercise Science, and Sport 75

4 Historical Foundations 76
5 Motor Behavior 114
6 Biomechanical Foundations 146
7 Exercise Physiology and Fitness 179
8 Sociological Foundations 219
9 Sport and Physical Activity Psychology 246
10 Physical Education Pedagogy 281

Part III
Careers and Professional Considerations 315

11 Career and Professional Development 316
12 Teaching and Coaching Careers 349
13 Fitness- and Health-Related Careers 386
14 Sport Management, Media, and Sport-Related Careers 410

Part IV
Future Professionals as Leaders and Advocates 435

15 Future Professionals as Leaders and Advocates 436

CONTENTS

Preface x
About the Authors xvi

PART I
Nature and Scope of Physical Education, Exercise Science, and Sport 1

CHAPTER 1

Meaning and Scope 2

Starting Your Journey–Exploring Your Social Identity and Systems of Meaning 3
Contemporary Physical Education, Exercise Science, and Sport Programs 4
Contemporary Physical Education, Exercise Science, and Sport Programs 5
Physical Education, Exercise Science, and Sport Defined 8
Physical Education, Exercise Science, and Sport 10
Allied Fields 16
Health 16
Recreation and Leisure 17
Dance 17
Growing as a Professional in Physical Education, Exercise Science, and Sport 18
Reading Research 18
Staying Up-to-Date with Technology 19

Summary 22

Discussion Questions 23

Self-Assessment Activities 24

References 24

CHAPTER 2

Philosophy, Goals, and Objectives 25

Philosophy 26
What Is Philosophy? 26
Branches of Philosophy 27
Major Philosophies 27
Modern Educational Philosophy 30
The Mind-Body Relationship 31
Philosophy of Sport and Physical Activity 32
Your Professional Philosophy 32
Goals and Objectives Defined 33
Goals of Physical Education, Exercise Science, and Sport 35
Learning Domains 35
Taxonomies 36
Cognitive Domain 36
Affective/Social Domain 39
Psychomotor Domain 42

Assessment of Learning 45
Assessment Defined 45
Purposes of Assessment 45

Summary 47

Discussion Questions 48

Self-Assessment Activities 49

References 49

CHAPTER 3

Health and Physical Activity in Our Society 50

Changing Demographics 50
Cultural Humility and Social Justice 52
Wellness Movement 54
Wellness and Health 54
Epidemiologic Shift 55
Chronic Disease in the United States 55
Health Goals of the Nation 56
Implications of the Wellness Movement 59
Fitness and Physical Activity Movement 60
Fitness and Physical Activity of Children and Youth 66
Fitness and Physical Activity of Adults 69
Implications of the Fitness and Physical Activity Movement 69

Summary 72

Discussion Questions 72

Self-Assessment Activities 73

References 73

PART II

Foundations of Physical Education, Exercise Science, and Sport 75

CHAPTER 4

Historical Foundations 76

Sport History 77
Definition and Scope 77
Historical Development 77
Areas of Study 78
Ancient Greece and Rome 78
Early Modern European Programs 79
Germany 79
Sweden 81
Denmark 81
Great Britain 82
Physical Education and Sport in the United States 82
Colonial Period (1607-1783) 82
National Period (1784-1861) 84
Civil War Period through 1900 85
Early Twentieth Century 90
World War I (1916-1919) 91
Golden Twenties (1920-1929) 93
Depression Years (1930-1939) 94
Mid-Twentieth Century (1940-1970) 96
Significant Recent Developments (1970-Present) 98
The Discipline 98
Disease Prevention and Health Promotion 99
School Physical Education 100
Physical Fitness and Participation in Physical Activity 101
The Growth of Sports 101
Girls and Women in Sports 102
Programs for Individuals with Disabilities 105
Olympics 108

Summary 111

Discussion Questions 111

Self-Assessment Activities 112

References 112

CHAPTER 5

Motor Behavior 114

Motor Behavior 114
Motor Learning and Motor Control 114
Definition and Scope 115
Areas of Study 116
Motor Learning Models 117
Performance Characteristics and Skill Learning 119

Stages of Learning 120
Factors Influencing Learning 122
Motor Learning Concepts 125
Motor Development 131
Definition and Scope 132
Areas of Study 132
Phases of Motor Development 132
Selected Fundamental Motor Skills 135
Development of Fundamental Motor Skills 139

Summary 143

Discussion Questions 144

Self-Assessment Activities 144

References 145

CHAPTER 6

Biomechanical Foundations 146

Kinesiology and Biomechanics 147
Definition and Scope 148
Growth of Biomechanics 148
Reasons for Studying Biomechanics 150
Major Areas of Study 154
Selected Biomechanical Terms Related to Human Motion 155
Mechanical Principles and Concepts Related to Movement 158
Stability 158
Motion 159
Leverage 161
Force 162
Biomechanical Analysis 165
Instruments and Techniques 165
Analysis 170
The Future 174

Summary 176

Discussion Questions 176

Self-Assessment Activities 177

References 177

CHAPTER 7

Exercise Physiology and Fitness 179

Exercise Physiology: An Overview 180
Definition 180
Areas of Study 180
Physical Fitness 181
Physical Activity, Physical Fitness, and Health 181
Fitness Development 186
Energy Production for Physical Activity 186
Principles of Fitness Training 187
FITT Formula 189
Health Fitness Components 190
Cardiorespiratory Endurance 191
Body Composition 195
Muscular Strength and Endurance 199
Flexibility 203
Designing an Exercise Program 206
Special Considerations for Fitness 206
Environmental Conditions and Fitness 206
Nutrition and Fitness 209
Performance-Enhancing Drugs 211

Summary 216

Discussion Questions 217

Self-Assessment Activities 217

References 218

CHAPTER 8

Sociological Foundations 219

Sociology of Sport 220
Definition and Scope 220
Areas of Study 221
Sport: A Definition 221
Sport and Organized Sport Activities 222
Conditions 222
Participation Motives 223
Sport in Educational Institutions 223
Interscholastic Sport 224
Intercollegiate Sport 226
Girls and Women in Sport 230
Racial Minorities in Sport 233

Sport for Children and Youth 237
Violence in Sport 239
Performance-Enhancing Substances in Sport 240

Summary 242

Discussion Questions 243

Self-Assessment Activities 244

References 244

CHAPTER 9

Sport and Physical Activity Psychology 246

Sport and Physical Activity Psychology 247
Definition and Scope 247
Areas of Study 247
Psychological Benefits of Physical Activity 249
Motivation 250
Exercise Adherence 252
Understanding Behavior Change 252
Promoting Adherence 256
Personality 257
Nature of Personality 258
Personality and Sport 258
Anxiety and Arousal 261
Nature of Anxiety and Arousal 261
Why Does Arousal Influence Performance? 261
Anxiety, Arousal, and Performance 262
Goal Setting 264
Types of Goals 264
How Goal Setting Works 264
Principles of Effective Goal Setting 265
Enhancing Performance through Self-Talk 267
Nature of Self-Talk 267
Types of Self-Talk 268
Application of Self-Talk 268
Modifying Self-Talk 269
Mental Imagery to Enhance Performance 270
Nature of Imagery 271
Uses of Imagery 272
Intervention Strategies 273
Mental Health of Athletes 274
Removing Barriers, Facilitating Mental Well-being 275
Supporting Athlete Mental Health 276
Your Role as a Professional 276

Summary 277

Discussion Questions 277

Self-Assessment Activities 278

References 279

CHAPTER 10

Physical Education Pedagogy 281

Physical Education Pedagogy: An Overview 282
Definition and Scope 282
Areas of Study 282
Standards-Based Education 283
Curriculum Development 285
Pedagogical Models 289
Skill Themes 289
Personal and Social Responsibility 289
Teaching Games for Understanding/Tactical Games Model 291
Sport Education 292
Fitness Education 294
Adventure-Based Learning 294
Outdoor Education 295
Activist Approaches 295
Pedagogies of Affect 296
Assessment and Accountability 297
Types of Assessment 297
Characteristics of Effective Teaching 300
Addressing Social Justice Issues in Physical Education 304
(Dis)ability 305
Gender 306
Body Issues 307
Race 307
Social Class 307
Sexuality 309

Summary 310

Discussion Questions 311

Self-Assessment Activities 311

References 312

PART III
Careers and Professional Considerations 315

CHAPTER 11

Career and Professional Development 316

Careers in Physical Education, Exercise Science, and Sport 317
Choosing a Career 320
Maximizing Professional Preparation 322
Attaining a Professional Position 330
Professionalism 335
Leadership 335
Advocacy 336
Accountability 337
Cultural Humility 337
Ethics 337
Role Modeling 339
Involvement and Continued Professional Development 339
Service 339
Professional Organizations in Physical Education, Exercise Science, and Sport 339
Why Belong to a Professional Organization? 340
Professional Organizations 341
Occupational Socialization and Self-Care 344

Summary 345

Discussion Questions 346

Self-Assessment Activities 347

References 347

CHAPTER 12

Teaching and Coaching Careers 349

Teaching and Coaching in Today's World 350
The Teaching Profession 352
Why Teach? 352
Rewards, Benefits, and Challenges of Teaching 352
Competencies for Teachers 354
Physical Education and Physical Activity Initiatives 355
Quality Physical Education 355
Connecting School and Community for the Well-Being of Students 358
Teaching Responsibilities 360
Teaching Careers 361
Teaching in the School Setting 361
Teaching in Nonschool Settings 367
Teaching Certification 370
Coaching Careers 371
Why Coach? 371
Rewards, Benefits, and Challenges of Coaching 372
Teaching and Coaching 373
Coaching Responsibilities 374
Securing a Coaching Position 375
Coaching Education and Certification 376
Burnout and Self-Care 377
Increasing Your Professional Marketability 379

Summary 382

Discussion Questions 383

Self-Assessment Activities 384

References 384

CHAPTER 13

Fitness- and Health-Related Careers 386

Fitness- and Exercise-Related Careers 387
Workplace Wellness Programs 389
Commercial and Community Fitness Programs 391

Personal Trainers 393
Health and Wellness Coaches 394
Strength and Conditioning Professionals 395
Rehabilitation Programs 396
Career Preparation 396
Health-Related Careers 399
Athletic Training 399
Wellness, Health Clubs, and Spas 401
Therapy-Related Careers 402
Dance/Movement Therapy 403
Therapeutic Recreation/Recreation Therapy 403
Physical Therapy 403
Chiropractic Care 404
Increasing Your Professional Marketability 405

Summary 407

Discussion Questions 407

Self-Assessment Activities 408

References 408

CHAPTER 14

Sport Management, Media, and Sport-Related Careers 410

Sport Management 411
Careers in Sport Management 413
Athletic Administration 413
Collegiate Recreation and Wellness 415
Workplace Recreation 416
Sport Facilities Management 416
Sport Retailing 418
Sport Marketing 419
Career Opportunities in Professional and Sport Organizations 420
Sport Analytics 421
Careers in Sport Media 421
Sport Broadcasting 421
Sportwriting and Journalism 422
Sport Photography 424
Sports Information 424
Web Development and Social Media 425
Performance and Other Sport Careers 425
Dance 425
Professional Athletics 426
Officiating 427
Sport Law and Agency 428
Entrepreneurship 428
Increasing Your Professional Marketability 430

Summary 431

Discussion Questions 432

Self-Assessment Activities 432

References 433

PART IV

Future Professionals as Leaders and Advocates 435

CHAPTER 15

Future Professionals as Leaders and Advocates 436

Leadership in Physical Activity 436
Leadership in Physical Education and Youth Sport 438
Advocacy 439
Current and Future Trends 441

Summary 443

Discussion Questions 443

Self-Assessment Activities 444

References 444

INDEX I-1

PREFACE

Was physical education or anatomy and physiology one of your favorite classes? Were you a high school athlete or did you play a club sport? Are you interested in fitness, physical activity, and sport? Most importantly, are you considering a career in a human movement field such as a physical education teacher, exercise specialist, personal trainer, or sport administrator? Then this text is for you! Come join us on this educational journey to learn about physical activity, physical education, and sport. We will provide you with the most up-to-date information while recognizing that the dynamic field of kinesiology and its disciplines are ever changing in this fast-paced, technology-driven society in which we live.

We will challenge you from the beginning of your career to commit to ongoing professional development and growth in your discipline. We encourage you to be advocates for physical activity and quality physical education, to value diversity and appreciate its many forms, and to work toward making opportunities to participate in physical activity available to all people throughout their lifespan. We hope that, as a young leader, you will work collaboratively with other dedicated professionals to address the issues facing us, the challenges ahead, and the realization of physical education, exercise science, and sport's potential to positively contribute to the lives of all people.

ORGANIZATION

The 15 chapters of this book are organized into four parts. Part I provides students with an orientation to the field of kinesiology along with the field's disciplines. Chapter 1 focuses on exploring your social identity and systems of meaning and the meaning and scope of contemporary physical education, exercise science, and sport. Emphasis is placed on understanding the scope of the disciplines and committing to professional development. In Chapter 2, students are introduced to the philosophy, goals, and objectives of physical education, exercise science, and sport. The last chapter in this part, Chapter 3, discusses the health and physical activity levels in our society, particularly in relation to the changing demographics, wellness movement, and fitness and physical activity movement.

In Part II, the historical foundations of the field and an overview of some of the disciplines are presented. The historical foundations are covered in Chapter 4, including our heritage from other countries and the significant influences on the growth of the field in the United States. In Chapter 5, an overview of motor behavior is provided. Chapter 6, biomechanics, is written by Dr. Deborah King, Ithaca College. Chapter 7 with its focus on exercise physiology and fitness follows. In Chapter 8, an overview of sport sociology is presented, and Chapter 9 provides information on sport and physical activity psychology. Chapter 10 focuses on physical education pedagogy and provides information on curriculum, pedagogy, and assessment.

Part III, which consists of four chapters, addresses professional considerations and career opportunities, including enhancing professional marketability. Chapter 11 focuses on professional development, including professional responsibilities, ethics, and certification. New to this edition is information on occupational socialization and self-care. Chapter 12, on teaching and coaching careers, shows how opportunities for these careers have broadened from the school setting and school-age population to nonschool settings and people of all ages. In Chapter 13, employment opportunities for professionals interested in fitness- and health-related careers are discussed. Careers in sport management, sport communication, performance, and other sport-related careers are described in Chapter 14.

Part IV explores how professionals can be leaders and advocates and looks ahead to the future. The final chapter, Chapter 15, addresses two key professional responsibilities: leadership and advocacy. The textbook closes with a discussion of current and future trends.

HIGHLIGHTS OF THIS EDITION

The twenty-first edition of *Foundations of Physical Education, Exercise Science, and Sport* continues its dual emphasis on providing students with an overview of disciplinary knowledge and encouraging them to explore the expanding career opportunities. This edition reflects the dynamic nature of the field today and is designed for use in introductory and foundations courses. Specifically, the most significant change in this edition is an explicit emphasis placed on social justice, diversity, and cultural humility. These concepts and issues have been a component of the text for some time; however, we have created social justice boxes in each chapter to highlight the salient social issues that are concerning and prevalent related to the chapter focus. We also invite the students to explore their social identities and systems of meaning starting in Chapter 1. We believe, as physical education, exercise science, and sport professionals, that students and future professionals need to be educated about issues related to social justice and social inequities.

The text continues its focus on the role of physical education, exercise science, and sport professionals in promoting lifespan participation in physical activity for all people. There is a need for culturally sensitive professionals to work with our increasingly diverse population. The responsibility of professionals to serve as advocates for historically underserved populations is stressed; this work is essential if our goal of lifespan involvement in physical activity for all is to be achieved.

Updated information and statistics are used to help students stay abreast of developments in the field. Additional key changes to this edition are highlighted below:

- A focus on current trends has been included in each chapter. Salient factors and issues related to each chapter that are currently hot topics are discussed.
- Expanded emphasis on social justice and the importance of professionals to infuse this theme within their professional practice.
- Updated information on using social media to network and advance one's career is included. Occupational socialization, self-care, and mental health are new additions to this text.
- New end-of-chapter Discussion Questions are added to this edition and can be used by instructors to engage students' critical thinking skills in the classroom.
- Several chapters have been restructured based on government reports and policies that have significant applications for professional practice, such as *2020–2025 Dietary Guidelines and MyPlate Recommendations, Gender and Race Report Card in Sports, SHAPE America Physical Education National Standards, Every Student Succeeds Act,* and *Whole School, Whole Community, Whole Child Model.*
- Because the future of physical education, exercise, and sport is closely related to the issues and challenges of today, this edition combines these

topics in one final chapter. This final chapter closes the textbook with an emphasis on leadership and advocacy and discusses future trends.

We hope that readers will gain knowledge and inspiration through the topics and issues discussed in this text. We hope that they will aspire to be future leaders and agents of change as physical education, exercise science, and sport professionals.

SUCCESSFUL FEATURES

The following pedagogical aids have been incorporated into this textbook:

Instructional Objectives. At the beginning of each chapter, the instructional objectives and competencies to be achieved by the students are listed. This identifies for the students the points that will be highlighted. Attainment of the objectives indicates the fulfillment of the chapter's intent.

Summaries. Each chapter ends with a brief review of the material covered, assisting the students in understanding and retaining the most salient points.

Discussion Questions. At the end of each chapter, discussion questions are provided to stimulate critical thinking. Students are encouraged to share their perspectives with their classmates and to explore different solutions to the problems and issues presented.

Internet Resources. Each chapter includes a *Get Connected* box, which lists Internet sites that provide up-to-date information about relevant topics. The self-assessment exercises include activities that draw on these Internet resources.

Self-Assessment Activities. Self-assessment activities are presented at the end of each chapter to enable students to check their comprehension of the chapter material. More activities using technology resources and tools are included.

References. Each chapter provides up-to-date references to allow students to gain further information about the subjects discussed in the chapter.

Photographs. Carefully chosen photographs have been used throughout the text to enhance the presentation of material and to illustrate key points.

Writing Style. Foundations of Physical Education, Exercise Science, and Sport has been written in a style that students find readable and that provides them with important insights into the foundations and the roles of physical education, exercise science, and sport in the world today. Students will find substantial information about the career and professional opportunities that exist for knowledgeable, dedicated, and well-prepared professionals committed to the promotion of lifespan involvement in physical activity for all people.

Mc Graw Hill connect®

The twenty-first edition of *Foundations of Physical Education, Exercise Science, and Sport* is now available online with Connect, McGraw Hill Education's integrated assignment and assessment platform. Connect also offers SmartBook® 2.0 for the new edition, which is an adaptive reading experience proven to improve grades and help students study more effectively. All the title's website and ancillary content is also available through Connect, including:

- an Instructor's Manual for each chapter;
- a full Test Bank of multiple-choice questions that test students on central concepts and ideas in each chapter;
- Lecture Slides for instructor use in class.

TEST BUILDER IN CONNECT

Available within Connect, Test Builder is a cloud-based tool that enables instructors to format tests that can be printed or administered within a learning management system (LMS). Test Builder offers a modern, streamlined interface for easy content configuration that matches course needs, without requiring a download.

Test Builder allows you to:

- access all test bank content from a particular title;
- easily pinpoint the most relevant content through robust filtering options;

- manipulate the order of questions or scramble questions and/or answers;
- pin questions to a specific location within a test;
- determine your preferred treatment of algorithmic questions;
- choose the layout and spacing;
- add instructions and configure default settings.

Test Builder provides a secure interface for better protection of content and allows for just-in-time updates to flow directly into assessments.

ACKNOWLEDGMENTS AND DEDICATIONS

The authors extend their appreciation to Dr. Deborah King, Ithaca College, for authoring Chapter 6. We also thank the reviewers for their thoughtful feedback. The reviewers of this edition include:

Elizabeth Ash
Morehead State University

David Perron
Bryan College

Victor Romano
Catawba College

Barbara Tyree
Valparaiso University

This textbook would not have been possible without the outstanding professionals at McGraw Hill who contributed in many ways to the completion of this project. We also extend our appreciation to our development editor, Amy Oline, for her patience and attention to detail, especially with the new online system!

In closing, the authors would like to acknowledge the people who helped support them throughout this endeavor.

Jennifer L. Walton-Fisette. This edition is dedicated to all of the professionals who stayed devoted to their disciplines and persevered throughout the pandemic to create educational experiences for their students, clients, and patients. Your commitment, care, and tenacity were noticed and meaningful to many. This book is also dedicated to my coauthor, Deb, who has been a great mentor and friend for many years. I marvel at her ability to see good in all, to have patience and fortitude through so much chaos, and continually mentors, supports, and advocates for others. Thank you for your dedication and heart, Deb.

Deborah Wuest. This edition is dedicated to my daughter, Meriber, who inspires me with her passion for the world's beautiful game–soccer or football as known globally. This book is also dedicated to my early-morning writing companions–my cats Evy, Sophie, Magic, and Casper and my dogs, Bella and Hank. They were great company and, in their honor, a portion of the proceeds of this edition will be donated to the SPCA. Most importantly, a special thank you to my coauthor, Jen. Jen continues to impress me with her enthusiasm for life, her passion for and leadership within the field, and her ongoing advocacy for social justice. Jen's commitment to social justice is reflected throughout this edition. I value our longstanding professional relationship and personal friendship.

Instructors

The Power of Connections

A complete course platform

Connect enables you to build deeper connections with your students through cohesive digital content and tools, creating engaging learning experiences. We are committed to providing you with the right resources and tools to support all your students along their personal learning journeys.

65%
Less Time Grading

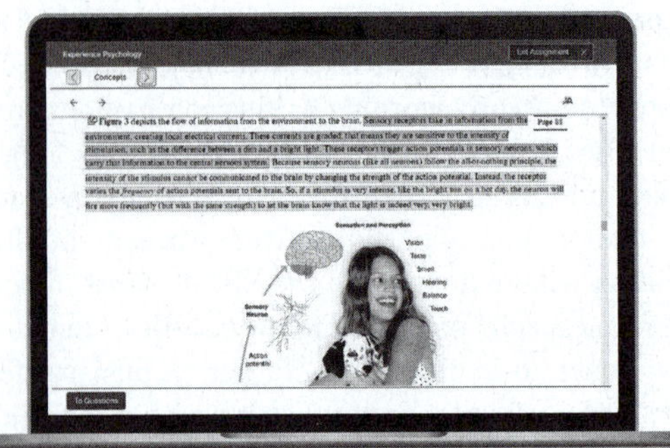

Laptop: Getty Images; Woman/dog: George Doyle/Getty Images

Every learner is unique

In Connect, instructors can assign an adaptive reading experience with SmartBook® 2.0. Rooted in advanced learning science principles, SmartBook 2.0 delivers each student a personalized experience, focusing students on their learning gaps, ensuring that the time they spend studying is time well-spent.
mheducation.com/highered/connect/smartbook

Affordable solutions, added value

Make technology work for you with LMS integration for single sign-on access, mobile access to the digital textbook, and reports to quickly show you how each of your students is doing. And with our Inclusive Access program, you can provide all these tools at the lowest available market price to your students. Ask your McGraw Hill representative for more information.

Solutions for your challenges

A product isn't a solution. Real solutions are affordable, reliable, and come with training and ongoing support when you need it and how you want it. Visit **supportateverystep.com** for videos and resources both you and your students can use throughout the term.

Students
Get Learning that Fits You

Effective tools for efficient studying

Connect is designed to help you be more productive with simple, flexible, intuitive tools that maximize your study time and meet your individual learning needs. Get learning that works for you with Connect.

Study anytime, anywhere

Download the free ReadAnywhere® app and access your online eBook, SmartBook® 2.0, or Adaptive Learning Assignments when it's convenient, even if you're offline. And since the app automatically syncs with your Connect account, all of your work is available every time you open it. Find out more at **mheducation.com/readanywhere**

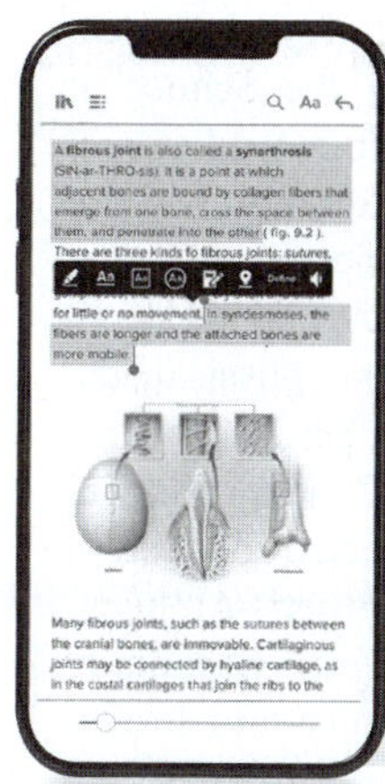

"I really liked this app—it made it easy to study when you don't have your text-book in front of you."

- Jordan Cunningham, Eastern Washington University

iPhone: Getty Images

Everything you need in one place

Your Connect course has everything you need—whether reading your digital eBook or completing assignments for class, Connect makes it easy to get your work done.

Learning for everyone

McGraw Hill works directly with Accessibility Services Departments and faculty to meet the learning needs of all students. Please contact your Accessibility Services Office and ask them to email accessibility@mheducation.com, or visit **mheducation.com/about/accessibility** for more information.

About the Authors

Jennifer L. Walton-Fisette is a Professor of Physical Education Teacher Education in the School of Teaching, Learning, and Curriculum Studies and the Director of Educator Preparation at Kent State University. Before taking this position in 2008, she taught physical education and health in Rhode Island. She obtained her B.S. degree in physical education from Rhode Island College, her M.S. degree in sport pedagogy from Ithaca College, and her Ed.D. in Physical Education Teacher Education from the University of Massachusetts-Amherst. Her teaching responsibilities include: Secondary Physical Education Content; Inquiry into Professional Practice; Development and Analysis of Game Performance; Introduction to Physical Education, Fitness, and Sport; Analysis of Motor Skills; Curriculum Development; and Forms of Inquiry, a doctoral course. Her scholarship throughout her career has produced more than 45 refereed journal publications, four books, and over 80 state, national, and international conference presentations, in the areas of curriculum, teaching, and learning; pedagogical practices and social justice issues related to physical education. Her current scholarship centers on social justice, equity, and policy issues within physical education at the K-12 and higher education levels.

Deborah A. Wuest is a professor in the Department of Health Promotion and Physical Education at Ithaca College, New York. She received her B.S. degree in physical education from SUNY Cortland, her M.S. degree in physical education from Indiana University, and her Ed.D. in Human Movement from Boston University. Deborah has over 50 years of teaching experience, has twice received Ithaca College's Charles C. Dana Award for Teaching Excellence, and most recently honored with the Ithaca College Faculty Excellence Award. Deborah teaches courses in the foundations of physical education, foundations of health sciences, stress management, coaching, and computer applications in health and physical education. She has coauthored textbooks on foundations of physical education, exercise science, and sport and secondary methods in physical education contributed to a textbook on humanism in coaching.

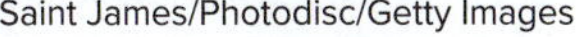

Saint James/Photodisc/Getty Images

Anthony Saint James/Photodisc/Getty Images

Mitch Hrdlicka/Photodisc/Getty Images

PART I

Nature and Scope of Physical Education, Exercise Science, and Sport

Part I introduces the reader to physical education, exercise science, and sport. The first chapter sets the stage for the reader to explore their social identities and systems of meaning and then provides an introduction to the specialized areas of study within physical education, exercise science, and sport. Chapter 1 concludes with a discussion of how to grow as a professional as current students and in their future career paths within kinesiology. Chapter 2 includes the influences of various philosophies on programs and provides the reader with information about the objectives and assessment of physical education, exercise science, and sport. Chapter 3 describes the contribution of physical education, exercise science, and sport to society and health, and the critical role of professionals delivering services to people of all ages.

Physical education, exercise science, and sport are representative of the growing and expanding field of kinesiology. The growth of this field is reflected in the expanding knowledge base and the development of specialized areas of study. The expansion of physical education, exercise science, and sport has created a diversity of career options for professionals.

Polka Dot Images/Getty Images

CHAPTER 1

Meaning and Scope

OBJECTIVES

After reading this chapter, students should be able to–

- Identify your social identities and systems of meaning and discuss how they will impact you as a future professional in the field of kinesiology.
- Define the following specialized areas of study: sport philosophy, sport history, sport sociology, sport and physical activity psychology, motor development, motor learning, biomechanics, exercise physiology, sports medicine/athletic training, physical education pedagogy, adapted physical activity/physical education, and sport management.
- Describe how the disciplines are interdisciplinary to the professions of physical education, exercise science, and sport relative to the field of kinesiology.
- Explain the relationship of physical education, exercise science, and sport to allied fields of study.
- Describe the different types of research reports and their application to physical education, exercise science, and sport.
- Identify social media resources that can inform the practice within the field of physical education, exercise science, and sport.

Our lives have been disrupted, challenged, and changed due to national and global experiences related to the COVID-19 pandemic, continued racial injustice, and political unrest. The pandemic has devastated many lives through loss of loved ones, worsened mental health issues, and/or not having the financial resources to support oneself or family. Systemic racism has permeated our country for hundreds of years. This came to the forefront when George Floyd was murdered in May 2020, which propelled thousands of protestors advocating for racial justice across all institutions (e.g., education, sport) as well as rallying against laws and policies that discriminate and oppress Black, people of color, and marginalized persons. The November 2020 Presidential election resulted in polarization in our country, creating a divide among the American people on a wide range of issues, including the pandemic and rights for marginalized folx. Such heaviness. Such hardship. Even a few years later.

You have come into adulthood during this challenging time. There is no doubt, in some way, you have been affected by one or more of these issues—and likely still are since there is no resolve. Yet, we have hope. Through all of this, we have exposed the importance of justice, equity, diversity, and inclusion (JEDI) of all people regardless of one's social identity—in all facets of our world. This includes our field of kinesiology as each of you intend to work with individuals in a human movement career path. This means that you will be working with individuals who are similar and different from you. You may be in charge of making decisions related to policies and practices, curriculum and instruction, and the planning and development of movement or sport-related tasks. Across these areas, there are many systems in place that perpetuate or focus on privileged people—particularly white, male, heterosexual, able-bodied individuals. How will you actively take action against these systemic and socially constructed issues to be equitable and just for all?

Phew. This is some heavy stuff here, especially if you are just starting out your collegiate career. How does this impact you as a future professional in physical education, exercise science, or sport? It is quite simple: You need to learn and grow into a professional that is equitable and just. This is not something that you do at the end of your program or learn on the job, this influences who you are—and becomes a part of your philosophy and what you value. In any interview, they will ask you what your philosophy of physical education, coaching, personal training, or sport management is. They will also ask how you work with others and what steps you will take to create equitable learning opportunities for those engaged in your programs. We want you to start working toward answering those questions along your time in the program. We want you to be prepared and develop into a professional that values and instills JEDI-related practices. We are here to help you along your journey.

Starting Your Journey—Exploring Your Social Identity and Systems of Meaning

The first step in this process is exploring and critically reflecting upon your social identity. Your social identity consists of how you identify related to your race, gender, sexuality, (dis)ability, social class, and religion, among others. See Figure 1-1 to help guide you in this exploration. After completing this chart (there are many other activities that you can complete to explore your social identities) ask yourself—how and why do you identify this way? Which

SOCIAL IDENTITY PROFILE

Social Identities	Examples of Social Identities	Your Identity
Race	Black, White, Indigenous, Asian/Pacific Islander, Latino/a, Native American, Biracial	
Gender	Woman, Man, Transgender, Non-binary	
Class	Poor, Working Class, Middle Class, Owning Class	
Physical/Mental/Developmental Ability	Non-Disabled, Disabled, Hidden	
Sexual Identity	Lesbian, Gay, Bisexual, Heterosexual, Questioning	
Religion	Catholic, Jewish, Protestant, Buddhist, Hindu, Muslim, Baptist, Evangelical	
Age	Young, Old, Middle-Aged	
Other		

Figure 1-1

Reflecting on Systems of Meaning

What is your comfort level with?

- A person who is a different racial, ethnic or cultural group?
- A person who believes you are incompetent?
- A person who is openly judgmental and critical of others?
- A person who speaks a different language?
- A person with a physical disability?
- A person who is abusing drugs or alcohol?
- A person who engages in recreational drug use?
- A person who was raised in a different social class than you?
- A person who practices a different religion than you?
- A person who is suicidal?
- A person who is loud and loves the attention of others?
- A person who is obese?
- A person who is always right and never asks for opinions?
- A person who believes women are not worthy of respect?
- A person who believes that abuse is acceptable in certain situations?
- A person who dislikes children?
- A person who is experiencing mental illness?
- A person who is having mental health issues?

Figure 1-2 Reflect on your Systems of Meaning. Adapted from Souers, K., & Hall, P. (2019).

identities are more salient to you compared to others and why? How have you been privileged, marginalized, and/or oppressed based on your social identities? This certainly is a lot to reflect upon and process, but it is necessary as you start to envision yourself as an educator, coach, or trainer.

The next step is to explore your systems of meaning (see Figure 1-2) related to your comfort level of people who may be similar or different from you. The key is to allow yourself to be honest and open. We all have biases and place judgment on others. None of us are free from this—we are human after all! Reflect on the question prompts and consider your level of comfort with each of those contexts and situations. What are your responses telling you about yourself and what you believe and value? This is all foundational work as you prepare to become a physical education, exercise science, and sport professional. Although it is important to engage in this process, now it is our hope that you will continue to critically reflect upon your social identities and how this positions you in the contexts in which you live and work as a professional in the field of kinesiology. Let us move forward in your exploration of becoming the professional you hope to be.

Contemporary Physical Education, Exercise Science, and Sport Programs

Contemporary physical education, exercise science, and sport have evolved from a common heritage—the traditional program of physical education designed to prepare teachers to serve children and youth in the school setting. Since the 1960s, the foundation, scope, and focus of our programs have grown and changed tremendously. As physical education expanded, new disciplines of study—exercise science and sport—emerged. Today physical education, exercise science, and sport professionals serve people of all social identities in diversity settings within the field of kinesiology.

Providing an overview of the entire field of kinesiology is, quite admittedly, a challenge as it is expanding and changing rapidly. This virtual explosion of knowledge has led to the development of new areas of study that are highly specialized and discrete and yet, at the same time, highly interrelated and vitally connected. Thus, in this text, we will refer to kinesiology with a specific emphasis placed on and within the disciplines of physical education, exercise science, and sport.

SOCIAL JUSTICE

Defining Social Justice: Advocacy, agency, and action directed toward (a) correcting disparities and inequities in all institutions across societies including education, health, law, politics, and so on, between majority (e.g., mostly white men) and minoritized people (e.g., African American citizens), especially those in poor communities, women, and persons with disabilities; and (b) empowering such marginalized people for meaningful, sustainable change (Harrison et al., 2021; Hodge & Clark, 2020; Hodge & Harrison, 2021).

Talking Points

- Physical activity initiatives and opportunities need to be provided to all individuals regardless of one's social identity and status (e.g., gender identity, race, sexual identity, (dis)ability, socioeconomic status, and age) if we want to increase physical activity levels and decrease chronic and hypokinetic diseases.
- All aspects of human movement need to be advocated for and supported rather than placing emphasis on judging and critiquing the level or type of an activity over others (e.g., playing a sport is better than walking or doing yoga).
- Emphasis needs to be placed on the interrelatedness of the disciplines and allied fields instead of the disciplines operating as silos or in competition with one another.
- Establishing a critical perspective through scientific-based research will allow professionals to make informed decisions that influence their clients, players, employees, or students.

We now know that leading a physically active lifestyle can help prevent disease and positively contribute to health and well-being throughout the lifespan. If the health of our nation is to improve, physical education, exercise science, and sport professionals must make certain that all people have access to programs, regardless of their age, race, ethnicity, gender, gender identity, sexual identity, ability/disability status, income, educational level, or geographic location. This is a challenge that awaits you as future professionals.

Career opportunities in physical education, exercise science, and sport range from teaching in the school setting to instructing in nonschool settings, such as leading group exercise classes in a community or corporate fitness setting.
Hero/Fancy/Corbis/Glow Images

CONTEMPORARY PHYSICAL EDUCATION, EXERCISE SCIENCE, AND SPORT PROGRAMS

The proliferation of physical education, exercise science, and sport programs during the last five decades has been remarkable. Programs have expanded from the traditional school setting to community, home, worksite, commercial, and medical settings. School-community partnerships bring sport instruction and fitness programs to adults in the community and offer increased opportunities for youth involvement. Community recreation programs offer a great variety of instruction and sport activities for people of all ages and abilities.

Millions of people purchase health club memberships or a wide array of exercise equipment to

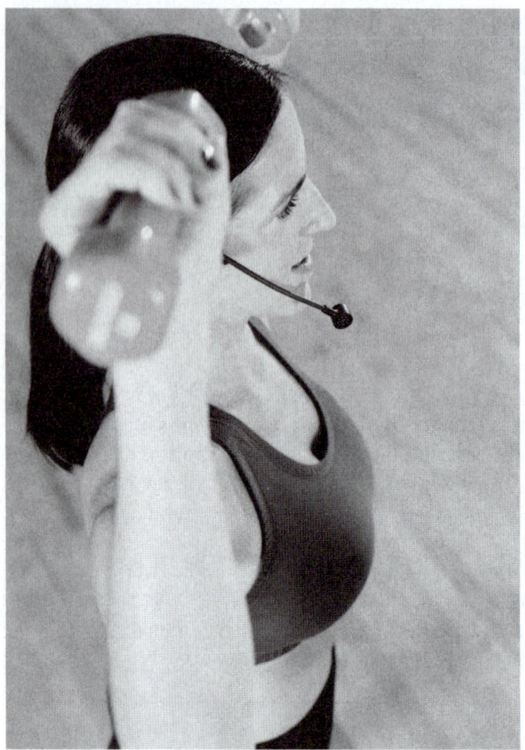
Ryan McVay/Getty Images

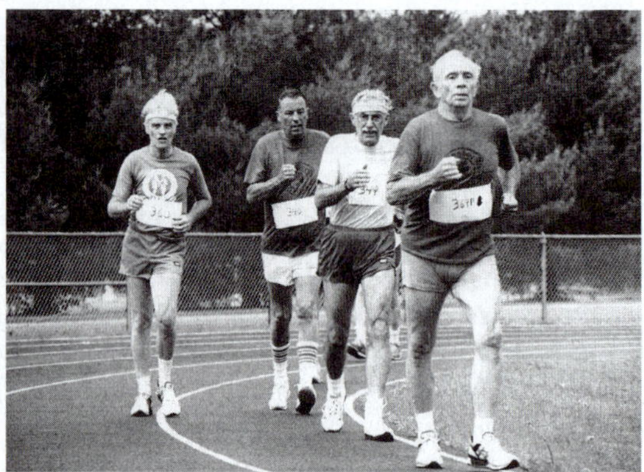
People of all ages enjoy athletic competition.
Sarah Rich

workout at home, especially during COVID-19. Corporations offer employees comprehensive onsite health promotion programs, encompassing a wide range of fitness activities as well as cardiac rehabilitation and nutritional counseling. Many worksites offer smoking cessation, stress management, and occupational safety courses to their employees, who find it convenient to fit these health-enhancing opportunities into their busy schedules. Hospitals sponsor cardiac rehabilitation programs and increasingly offer fitness programs to community members. Sports medicine clinics treat injured sport and fitness participants of all identities, no longer limiting their practice to the elite adult athlete.

People of all ages are seeking out sport opportunities in many different settings. A total of 56.1% of young people participate in youth sports.[1] Almost 8 million athletes participate in interscholastic sports and over 641,000 participate in intercollegiate sports.[2,3,4,5] Sport events such as Senior Games, running events, Tough Mudders, and master's swimming competitions involve millions of adults in sport competitions. Community recreational leagues provide increased opportunities for participation. Sport events such as the Super Bowl, Olympics, World Cup, and National Collegiate Athletic Association basketball tournament capture the enthusiasm of millions of spectators. Girls and women are participating in sports and physical activities in record numbers.

School physical education programs focus on promotion of lifespan involvement in physical activity. Students learn the skills, knowledge, and dispositions that will enable them to participate in various physical activities throughout their lives. At the collegiate level, young adults enroll in personal fitness and wellness courses, work out at fitness centers, and take part in recreational sports programs. Intercollegiate athletic programs for men and women continue to expand, involving more participants and attracting greater interest from the public.

COVID-19 prompted many to get outdoors and engage in physical activity, resulting in an increased public recognition that being active is good for your health. Several national reports, such as the *National Physical Activity Plan*,[6] *Healthy People 2030*,[7] and *The Physical Activity Guidelines*[8] present overwhelming evidence that people of all social identities can improve their health and quality of

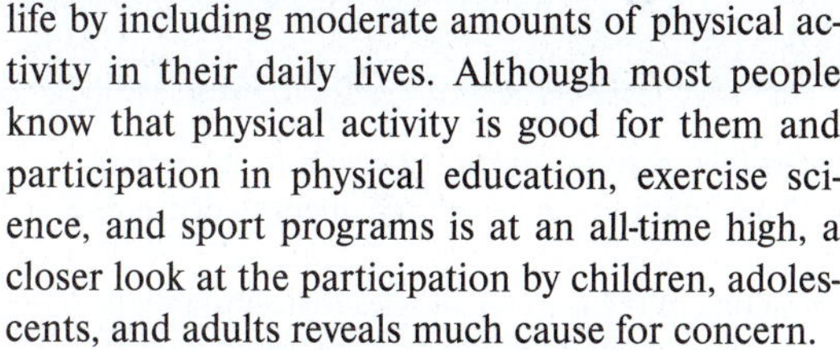

Patrick Byrd/mylife photos/Alamy Stock Photo

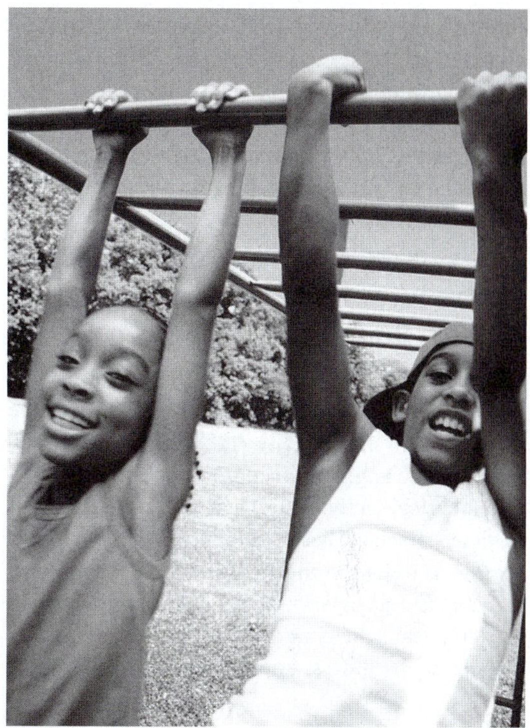

Maria Taglienti-Molinari/Brand X Pictures/Getty Images

life by including moderate amounts of physical activity in their daily lives. Although most people know that physical activity is good for them and participation in physical education, exercise science, and sport programs is at an all-time high, a closer look at the participation by children, adolescents, and adults reveals much cause for concern.

A primary reason that individuals across the lifespan may not engage in physical activity is due to the health disparities and fitness inequities among different population groups. Age, socioeconomic status, race, ethnicity, gender, educational attainment, and geographic location were found to influence physical activity levels. Inactivity is greatest among women, racial minorities, the economically and educationally disadvantaged, people with disabilities, and the aged.[7] These populations have less access to services and face other barriers to the adoption and maintenance of physically active lifestyles. Their limited opportunities for physical activity adversely affect their health, their quality of life, and, ultimately, their lifespan. This was significantly enhanced during COVID-19 in relation to individuals who had severe symptoms, were hospitalized, and/or lost their lives.

The main challenges facing professionals are increasing the level of physical activity by people across the nation and addressing inequities in physical activity opportunities. As physical education, exercise science, and sport professionals, we must make a greater commitment to reach out to these populations and involve them in our programs. We must address the specific barriers that inhibit the adoption and maintenance of physical activity by different population groups, utilize new approaches that are sensitive to the needs of increasingly diverse populations, and improve access by developing quality public programs in schools, recreation centers, worksites, and health care settings. All people have the right to good health and the opportunity to be physically active throughout their lifespan.

As you begin your professional career, make a commitment to service. Commit yourself to creating opportunities for all people–regardless of race, age, income, education, ethnicity, gender identity, sexual identity, geographic location, or ability–to enjoy and to benefit from lifespan participation in physical activity.

Physical Education, Exercise Science, and Sport Defined

Physical education, exercise science, and sport share a common focus–human movement or, more generally, physical activity. Yet, each discipline offers a unique approach as to how human movement and physical activity are learned, enhanced, or achieved. Each of these disciplines is defined in this section as well as in the Definitions of Terms box.

Physical education is an educational process that uses physical activity as a means to help individuals acquire skills, fitness, knowledge, and dispositions that contribute to their optimal development and well-being. In this definition, the term *education* refers to the ongoing process of learning that occurs throughout our lifespan. Education, just like physical education, takes place in a variety of settings and is not limited to a specific age group. Homeschooling, continuing education through distance learning, worksite health promotion programs, and preschools are just some of the expanded settings for education and physical education programs. Teachers today may be called instructors, leaders, directors, or facilitators. Today's students span the age range, from the very young exploring movement skills in a preschool program to the older adults learning how to play an activity through a community recreation program.

Most physical education programs focus on developing the whole person. Physical education includes the acquisition and refinement of motor skills, the development and maintenance of fitness for optimal health and well-being, the attainment of knowledge about physical activities, and the fostering of

DEFINITION OF TERMS

- Exercise–physical activity done for the purpose of getting fit that increases energy expenditure above baseline levels. Exercise is planned, structured, and repetitive. The duration, frequency, and intensity of exercise can be measured.
- Physical Activity–bodily movement produced by the contraction of the skeletal muscles that substantially increase energy expenditure above baseline level. As a broad term, it encompasses exercise, sport, dance, active games, activities of daily living, and active occupational tasks.
- Physical Education–subject matter taught in schools that provides K–12 students with opportunities to learn, and have meaningful content and appropriate instruction. Quality physical-education programs focus on increasing physical competence, health-related fitness, self-responsibility, and enjoyment of physical activity for all students so that they can be physically active for a lifetime.
- Physical Fitness–capacity of people to perform physical activities; set of attributes that allow individuals to carry out daily tasks without undue fatigue and have the energy to participate in a variety of physical activities; state of well-being associated with low risk of premature health problems.
- Sport–well-established, officially governed competitive physical activities in which participants are motivated by internal and external rewards.

Sources: Adapted from the President's Council on Fitness, Sports, and Nutrition. Definitions: Health, fitness, and physical activity. 2013 (www.fitness.gov); US Department of Health and Human Services. *Healthy People 2030* (www.healthypeople.gov); National Association for Sport and Physical Education. *Moving into the Future: National Standards for Physical Education* (2nd ed.). Reston, Va.: Author, 2004; and Coakley J. *Sport in Society: Issues and Controversies* (10th ed.). New York: McGraw Hill, 2009.

Exercise physiologists study the body's short- and long-term adaptations to exercise.

Mauro Grigollo/E+/Getty Images

positive dispositions and values conducive to lifelong learning and lifespan participation.

Within the last five decades, there has been an increase in the scholarly study of physical education. Research continues to expand our knowledge with respect to the preparation of physical education teachers, teacher effectiveness, teaching methods, models-based practice, improvement of student learning, and pedagogies that are equitable and just. It also provides us with new insights on coaches' and athletes' behaviors.

Exercise science is the scientific analysis of exercise or, more inclusively, physical activity. To study physical activity, exercise scientists draw upon scientific methods and theories from many different disciplines, such as biology, biochemistry, physics, and psychology. The application of science to the study of physical activity led to rapid expansion of the knowledge base of exercise science. As the knowledge base of exercise science grew, so did our understanding of the effects of physical activity on various systems of the body. The significant role that physical activity plays in preventing disease and promoting health became clearer. Exercise's value as a therapeutic modality in the treatment of disease and the rehabilitation of injuries became better known.

Exercise science is a very broad area of study, encompassing many different aspects of physical activity. Through research, scholars gain new insights into how people's movements develop and change across their lifespan and further expand their understanding of how people learn motor skills. Analysis of the performance of motor skills using biomechanics leads to improvement in skill efficiency and effectiveness. Researchers' exploration on the limits and capacities of performers has enabled athletes, of all abilities and identities, to perform at higher levels of achievement. The psychological effects of physical activity on well-being and strategies to enhance adherence to exercise and rehabilitation programs are some other areas of study within exercise science.

Sports are highly organized, competitive physical activities governed by rules. Rules standardize the competition and conditions so that individuals can compete fairly and achieve specified goals. Sports provide meaningful opportunities to demonstrate one's competence and to challenge one's limits. Competition can occur against an opponent or oneself.

People of all social identities engage in sports for enjoyment, personal satisfaction, and the opportunity to attain victory and/or obtain rewards. The level of competition ranges from recreational to elite sport. When sport is highly developed, governing bodies regulate sport and oversee its management. *Athletics* refers to highly organized, competitive sports engaged in by skillful participants. At this level, coaches play a significant role, athletes are highly skilled, specially trained officials ensure the fairness of the competition, records are kept, events are promoted through the media, and spectators assume an important role. Sports occupy a prominent position in our society.

Since the early 1970s, there has been an enormous interest in the scholarly study of sport. These sport studies have focused on the significant role of sport in our society, its tremendous impact on our culture, and its effects on the millions of people who play sports and the millions more who watch and read about them. Scholars study the philosophical, historical, sociological, and psychological dimensions of the sport experience. The growing popularity of sport and its prominent role in our society makes sport a vital area of study.

The realm of physical education, exercise science, and sport today embraces many different programs, diverse settings, and people of all social identities. This recent growth of physical education, exercise science, and sport has been accompanied by an increased interest in its scholarly study. This research has led to the development of specialized areas of knowledge. The subsequent increase in the breadth and depth of knowledge provides a foundation for professional practice. The expansion of physical education, exercise science, and sport has led to a tremendous growth of career opportunities for enthusiastic and committed professionals.

More and more individuals with disabilities are engaging in sports. Here athletes are playing quad rugby.

Image Source/Getty Images

Physical Education, Exercise Science, and Sport

Physical education, exercise science, and sport can be described with reference to their status as a profession. A *profession* is an occupation requiring specialized training in an intellectual field of study that is dedicated to the betterment of society through service to others. Professionals provide services to others through the application of knowledge and skills to improve people's well-being.

Physical educators, exercise scientists, and sport leaders possess a bachelor's degree and frequently pursue advanced study via graduate programs in the field. Their professional preparation programs include extensive study in the theoretical aspects of the field, skill and content knowledge development, and often practical experiences that allow them to apply their knowledge and use their skills under the guidance of qualified professionals. Additional requirements and certifications may be necessary to engage in professional practice.

Today there is increased recognition by society of the valuable contribution professionals in our field can make in the lives of others. Our commitment to promoting lifespan physical activity for all members of society benefits the health of the nation. The expansion of physical education, exercise science, and sport programs to different settings and the involvement of people of all social identities in our programs offer professionals increased opportunities to serve others and enhance their well-being.

The emergence of new professional opportunities has created a need for highly qualified professionals who possess a high level of skill, an appreciation and understanding of the needs of an increasingly diverse population, and a sound grasp of the knowledge of physical education, exercise science, and sport. Throughout the remainder of this text, the term *professionals* will be used in place of "physical educators, exercise scientists, and sport leaders."

The Academic Discipline

In the 1960s, the field of physical education advanced its status as an academic discipline. Henry[9] defines an *academic discipline* as

> an organized body of knowledge collectively embraced in a formal course of learning. The acquisition of such knowledge is assumed to be an adequate and worthy objective as such, without any demonstration or requirement of practical application. The content is theoretical and scholarly as distinguished from technical and professional.

An academic discipline has a focus, a conceptual framework that provides structure for the field, a unique scope in comparison to other fields, and distinct scholarly methods and modes of inquiry leading to the advancement of knowledge and indepth understanding. This body of knowledge is worthy of study for its own sake and does not need to have any immediate application to professional practice. Traditional academic disciplines include biology, psychology, philosophy, history, and mathematics.

The seminal point in the development of the discipline movement occurred in 1964 when Franklin Henry called for the "organization and study of the academic discipline herein called physical education."[9] His clarion call came at a time when forces in society were exerting pressure for educational reform, improved educational standards, and greater academic rigor in the preparation of teachers. Then, physical education teacher preparation programs focused on the application of knowledge and endured criticism for their lack of academic rigor, their emphasis on the learning of job-related skills, and their focus on activity-based courses, such as basketball or badminton.

Henry's call for an academic discipline stimulated greater scholarly activity by academicians at colleges and universities. Developing technologies, theoretical knowledge, and methods of scientific inquiry from other disciplines were directed to the study of physical education and increasingly to exercise and sport. The proliferation of research and generation of scholarship led to the development of specialized areas of study, commonly called *disciplines*.

People of all ages are frequenting fitness centers and health clubs. Many work out on a regular basis. Regular physical activity contributes to good health and overall quality of life.

Stephen Simpson/Stone/Getty Images

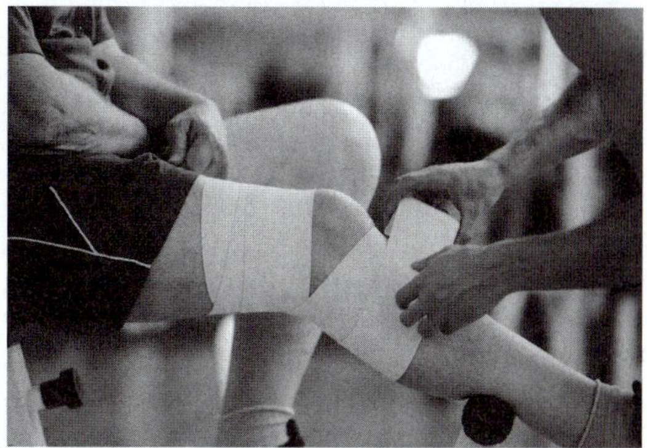

Athletic trainer helping athlete with rehabilitation.

DenisProduction.com/Shutterstock

Disciplines within Physical Education, Exercise Science, and Sport

The field of kinesiology has evolved into a variety of disciplines (see Table 1-1), many of which fall under the broader professional umbrellas of physical education, exercise science, and sport. The interdisciplinary nature of physical education, exercise science, and sport is evident from the disciplines identified and described in this section. Theories, principles, scientific methods, and modes of inquiry from many other academic disciplines were used by researchers and scholars in the development of these specialized areas of study. Knowledge and research methods from the hard sciences of biology, chemistry, physics, anatomy, physiology, and mathematics strongly influenced the development of the disciplines of exercise physiology and sport biomechanics. Psychology, sociology, history, and philosophy, often called the social sciences, formed the foundation for the development of sport and physical activity psychology, motor development, motor learning, sport sociology, sport history, and sport philosophy. The rehabilitation sciences, particularly physical therapy, exerted an important influence on the development of sports medicine, athletic training, and adapted physical activity. Educational research significantly affected the development of physical education pedagogy. In the discipline of sport management, the influence of management, law, business, communication, and marketing is evident.

TABLE 1-1 Career Opportunities within the Disciplines of Physical Education, Exercise Science, and Sport

Discipline	Career Opportunities
Exercise Physiology	Personal trainers, fitness directors, strength and conditioning specialists, group exercise instructor, cardiac and pulmonary rehabilitation specialists, and higher education faculty, physical therapists, and occupational therapists with advanced degrees.
Sport Medicine/Athletic Training	Sports medicine physician, athletic trainer, exercise physiologist, kinesiotherapist, physical therapist, nursing, doctor of osteopathy, and nutrition/dietetics.
Sport Biomechanics	Lab technician in gait analysis and strength and flexibility; researcher, designer, and tester of sport companies, interfaces, and athletes; higher education faculty (most require an advanced degree).
Sport Philosophy	Coach, sport journalist, and advanced degrees could lead to becoming a lawyer and higher education faculty.
Sport History	Sport historian, higher education faculty (advanced degree required).
Sport and Physical Activity Psychology	Academic, clinical, applied with sport teams and individuals participating in physical activity (advanced degree required).
Motor Development	Physical/adapted physical education teacher, coach, rehabilitation specialist.
Motor Learning	Physical/adapted physical education teacher, coach, rehabilitation specialist.
Sport Sociology	Coach, journalist, higher education faculty (advanced degree required).
Physical Education Pedagogy	Physical education teacher, coach.
Adapted Physical Activity/Physical Education	Physical/adapted physical education teacher, coach, adapted physical activity director.
Sport Management	Account or event coordinator/director, media and public relations specialist, sales representative, sport facility operations manager, sports marking director, sports information director, sport agent.

The growth of these disciplines broadens the scope of the field of kinesiology. Equally important, the interdependence between these growing areas offers us valuable knowledge and greater insight as we move toward the accomplishment of our goals. The disciplines are briefly described below.

Exercise physiology is the study of the effects of various physical demands, particularly exercise, on the structure and function of the body. The exercise physiologist is concerned with both short-term (acute) and long-term (chronic) adaptations of the various systems of the body to exercise. The effects of different exercise programs on the muscular and cardiorespiratory systems, the immune system, and the health status of different population groups such as children and the aged are just some areas of study within the field. Clinical exercise testing, design of rehabilitation programs for postcardiac patients, and planning of exercise programs to prevent cardiovascular disease are among the responsibilities of exercise physiologists. (See Chapter 7.)

Sports medicine/athletic training is concerned with the prevention, treatment, and rehabilitation of sports-related injuries. Athletic trainers' responsibilities are broader than just administering treatment to the injured athlete on the playing field. From the standpoint of prevention, the athletic trainer works with the coach to design conditioning programs for various phases of the season, to correctly fit protective equipment, and to promote the welfare of the athlete, such as counseling the athlete about proper nutrition. With respect to treatment and rehabilitation, the athletic trainer assesses injuries when they occur, administers first aid, works collaboratively with the physician to design a rehabilitation program, provides treatment, and oversees the athlete's rehabilitation. (See Chapter 13.)

Sport biomechanics applies the methods of physics and mechanics to the study of human motion and the motion of sport objects (e.g., a baseball or javelin). Biomechanists study the effect of various forces and laws (e.g., Newton's laws of motion) on the body and sport objects. The musculoskeletal system and the production of force, leverage, and stability are examined with respect to human movement and sport object motion (e.g., spinning across the circle to throw a discus). Analysis of movements with respect to efficiency and effectiveness is used to help individuals improve their performance. (See Chapter 6.)

Sport philosophy examines sport from many different perspectives. Sport philosophy encompasses the study of the nature of reality, the structure of knowledge in sport, ethical and moral questions, and the aesthetics of movement. Sport philosophers critically examine the meaning of sport for all participants involved and enjoin us to question our beliefs and assumptions about sport. Sport philosophers engage in systematic reflection, use logic as a tool to advance knowledge and arrive at decisions, and seek to understand the relationship between the mind and the body. Sport philosophers debate questions of ethics, morals, and values. (See Chapter 2.)

Sport history is the critical examination of the past, with a focus on events, people, and trends that influenced the development and direction of the field. History is concerned with the who, what, when, where, how, and why of sport.[10] These facts, when placed in the social context of the time, help us better understand the present and gain insight regarding the future. (See Chapter 4.)

Sport and physical activity psychology uses principles and scientific methods from psychology to study human behavior in sport.[10] Sport psychologists help athletes improve their "mental game," that is, develop and effectively apply skills and strategies

Biomechanists analyze the mechanical aspects of athletes' skill performance in order to help them improve.

SSGT, Jason M. Carter, USMC/DoD Media

that will enhance their performance. Achievement motivation, regulation of anxiety, self-confidence, rehabilitation adherence, cohesion, and leadership are among the topics studied by sport psychologists. Recently, physical activity psychology has attracted greater attention from researchers. Physical activity psychology is concerned with exercise addiction, adherence, and other psychological issues affecting the well-being of people who are physically active. (See Chapter 9.)

Motor development studies the factors that influence the development of abilities essential to movement. The motor development specialist uses longitudinal studies (i.e., studies that take place over a span of many years) to analyze the interaction of genetic and environmental factors that affect the ability of individuals to perform motor skills throughout their lifespan. The role of early movement experiences, heredity, and maturation on children's development of motor skills is an important focus of study. Professionals use theories of development to design appropriate movement experiences for people of all ages, identities, and abilities. (See Chapter 5.)

Motor learning is the study of changes in motor behavior that are primarily the result of practice and experience. The effect of the content, frequency, and timing of feedback on skill learning is a critical area of study. Motor learning is concerned with the stages an individual progresses through in moving from a beginner to a highly skilled performer. The most effective conditions for practicing skills, the use of reinforcement to enhance learning, and how to use information from the environment to modify performance are investigated by motor learning specialists. Motor control, intimately related to motor learning, is concerned with the neurophysiological and behavioral processes affecting the control of skilled movements. (See Chapter 5.)

Sport sociology is the study of the role of sport in society, its impact on participants in sport, and the relationship between sport and other societal institutions. Sport sociologists examine the influence of gender, race, and socioeconomic status on participation in sports and, more recently, physical activity. Drug abuse by athletes, aggression and violence, the effect of the media on sport, and

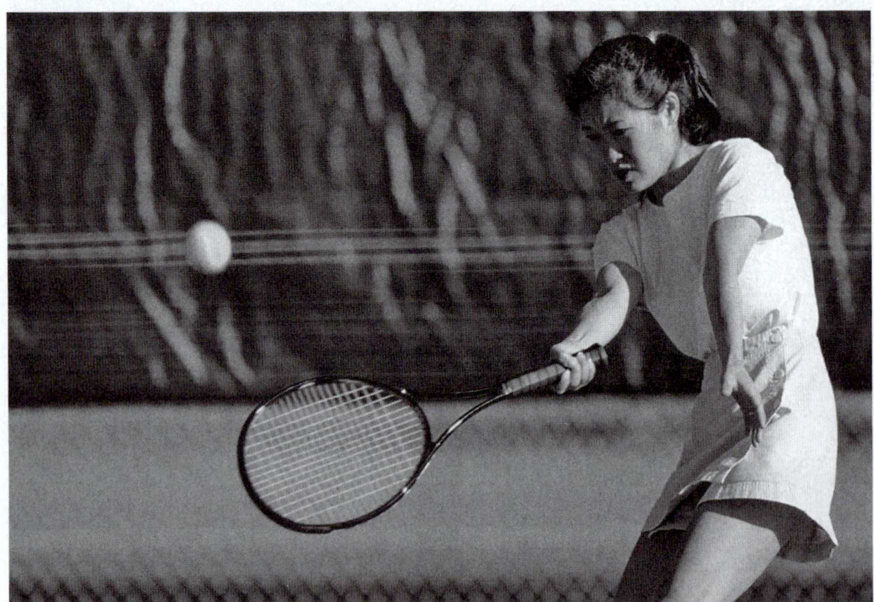

Sport psychologists help athletes achieve optimal levels of performance.

Karl Weatherly/Photodisc/Getty Images

player-coach relationships interest sport sociologists. The experiences of the millions of children involved in youth sport has also drawn the attention of sport sociologists. (See Chapter 8.)

Physical education pedagogy can be defined broadly to include the study of teaching and learning in school and nonschool settings. Physical education pedagogy studies how physical educators and sport leaders provide an effective learning environment, achieve desired learning goals, and assess program outcomes. Physical education pedagogy seeks to determine the characteristics and skills possessed by effective teachers and coaches and how these influence student/athlete activity and student/athlete learning. Curricular development, its implementation, and the preparation of teachers are major foci in physical education pedagogy. (See Chapter 10.)

Adapted physical activity/physical education is concerned with the preparation of teachers and sport leaders to provide programs and services for individuals with disabilities. Specialists modify activities and sport to enable people with different abilities to participate. By federal law, adapted physical educators have a role in designing an individualized educational plan (IEP) for students with disabilities so that they can participate to the fullest extent they are able in school physical education. Advocacy to secure services and leadership to create more opportunities in physical education and sport are important aspects of this field. (See Chapters 10 and 12.)

Sport management encompasses the many managerial aspects of sport. These include personnel management, budgeting, facility management, and programming. Other aspects of sport management are law, policy development, fundraising, and media relations. Knowledge from this area can be used by professionals in many different aspects of the sport enterprise, including interscholastic and intercollegiate sports, professional sports, fitness and health clubs, community sport and recreation programs, and sporting goods sales. (See Chapter 14.)

Physical education pedagogy studies the behaviors of teachers and coaches, identifying those who contribute to an effective learning environment.

Erik Isakson/Blend Images/Getty Images

Sport sociologists study the behavior of people in sport situations—athletes, coaches, and fans—as well as the impact of sport on the community.

Don Hammond/Design Pics

ALLIED FIELDS

Health, recreation and leisure, and dance are frequently referred to as allied fields. These allied fields share many purposes with physical education, exercise science, and sport, namely, the development of the total individual and concern for quality of life. However, the content of the subject matter of the allied fields and the methods used to accomplish their goals may vary from the subject matter and methods of physical education, exercise science, and sport.

Health

Health education concerns itself with the total well-being of the individual, encompassing physical, mental, social, emotional, occupational, and spiritual health. Three areas within health education are health instruction, provision of health services, and environmental health.

Health instruction focuses on teaching the basics of healthy living in many areas, including disease prevention, mental health, nutrition, physical fitness, stress management, and dealing with abuse of drugs and alcohol. Health service is concerned with developing and maintaining a satisfactory level of health for all people through services such as routine eye examinations, cholesterol and blood pressure monitoring, and cancer screening. Environmental health focuses on the development of healthful and safe environments where individuals are not needlessly exposed to hazards such as toxic chemicals and infectious materials.

Americans are becoming increasingly conscious of the instrumental role physical activity plays in one's health-related quality of life. Data supporting the health benefits of participation in appropriate physical activity on a regular basis continue to mount. Accrued benefits of regular physical activity include the prevention of coronary heart disease, hypertension, non-insulin-dependent diabetes mellitus, osteoporosis, obesity, and mental health problems.[7] Other benefits may include the reduction of the incidence of stroke and the maintenance of the functional independence of the elderly.[7] Additionally, it has been found that, on average, individuals who are physically active outlive individuals who are physically inactive.[7] The strong role regular and appropriate physical activity plays in the health and well-being of individuals further confirms the allied nature of health and physical education, exercise science, and sport.

Recreation and Leisure

Another allied field is recreation and leisure. Recreation and leisure are generally thought of as self-chosen activities that provide a means of revitalizing and refreshing one's body and spirit. The spectrum of activities ranges from active to passive and from group to individual in nature.

It is within recreation and leisure opportunities that individuals of all identities can simply play. The notion of play, whether formal or informal, is often lost after early childhood and youth. Ask yourself, when was the last time that you played? How do you feel when you simply play? Most often, individuals have fun and feel a sense of enjoyment when they are free to play, create their own games and activities, and have the opportunity to express themselves through physical movement (or other forms of play).

Schools, communities, and businesses offer a wide range of activities to meet the fitness and leisure needs of individuals. Worksite fitness programs, industrial sport leagues, commercial fitness programs, competitive recreational leagues, instructional clinics, and open facilities for drop-in recreation are increasing in number. During nonschool hours, school facilities are the site for various recreational offerings for people of all ages. Many individuals and families pursue recreational activities independently as well.

Therapeutic recreation focuses on providing a broad range of services for individuals of all ages who have disabilities. Through a diversity of interventions, the individual's quality of life is enhanced, the development of leisure skills is encouraged, and the integration of the individual into community recreational opportunities and life is emphasized.

Recreation and leisure can contribute to the quality of an individual's life. They provide opportunities for individuals to engage in freely chosen activities, including physical activities that will yield beneficial health outcomes, during their leisure time.

Dance

The third allied area is dance. Dance is a popular activity for people of all ages and is both a physical activity and a performing art that gives participants an opportunity for aesthetic expression through movement.

As a form of recreation, dance provides opportunities for enjoyment, self-expression, and relaxation. Dance also can be used as a form of therapy, providing opportunities for individuals to express their thoughts and feelings. It provides a means to cope with the various stresses placed on individuals. Dance is increasingly used as a means to develop fitness.

There are many forms of dance that are enjoyed by individuals–including ballet, ballroom, folk, clog, contemporary, salsa, hip-hop, square, and tap. Cultural heritage is reflected in and passed on through dance activities.

Health, recreation and leisure, and dance are allied fields to physical education, exercise science, and sport. The overall focus of these fields of endeavor is the development of the total individual and the enhancement of each person's quality of life. Attainment of these aims involves health promotion, pursuit of worthy leisure-time activities, and creative expression through dance. These experiences, coupled with the movement activities that compose the realm of physical education, exercise science, and sport, offer the potential to enhance the lives of people of all social identities. Fulfillment of this potential will depend on the quality of leadership provided by professionals in health, recreation and leisure, dance, physical education, exercise science, and sport.

Physical activity contributes to health and fitness throughout life. Bicycling is an excellent activity for people of all ages.

Ariel Skelley/Blend Images

GROWING AS A PROFESSIONAL IN PHYSICAL EDUCATION, EXERCISE SCIENCE, AND SPORT

As a future professional, it is important that you make a commitment to your discipline that goes well beyond your academic course work and practical experience. You might ask why it is important for professionals with bachelor's and graduate degrees to continue professional development throughout their careers. The primary reason is that our field and your specialized area of study is constantly changing, placing us in a position to continue our knowledge development based on the latest research, both scientific- and practitioner-based. Research findings create opportunities for professionals to inform, change, modify, and enhance their practice. If you do not want to be that professional that is deemed "old school," then it is your ethical duty to stay current in the latest research, practice, and technologies to provide your students, clients, and players with the most accurate and effective instruction and practice.

Do you believe everything that you hear and read or do you draw your own conclusions? How do you know what to believe or not to believe (i.e., what is fact and what is falsified interpretation)? In the first part of this text, we are going to educate you on how to read and critique research by guiding you through the 12 Steps to Understanding Research Reports (see box). In the Self-Assessment Activities found at the end of each chapter, a specific activity will be provided that centers on how to find research articles as well as the 12 steps as you learn how to read research reports found in professional journals. We will also emphasize how research can inform professional practice and provide you with opportunities to apply research findings to your future profession.

Reading Research

Before you begin to read research reports, it is important for you to understand research terminology that will provide different perspectives from which you will analyze and critique reports in professional

Adults can use a variety of physical activities to accumulate the recommended 30 minutes a day of moderate-intensity physical activity necessary for health benefits.

Fran Polito/Moment/Getty Images

journals. First, it is important to distinguish between scientific and practitioner-based research. *Scientific research* is based on a systematic approach to gathering information that potentially answers an investigated question, whereas *practitioner-based research* focuses on how to apply the information learned within your instruction or area of practice.

Second, research reports are usually based on two paradigms (i.e., types) of research: quantitative and qualitative. *Quantitative research* is based on numbers, primarily the statistical analysis of numeric data that were gathered. Quantitative reports typically describe, correlate, predict, or explain a hypothesis that was posed at the beginning of a study. In contrast to quantitative research, *qualitative research* answers questions through words, images, and sounds. The purpose of this research is to learn more about the social context in which the participants live, which is conducted through the lens and interpretation of the researcher(s).[11] As you read quantitative and qualitative reports, Silverman, Spirduso, and Locke[12] suggest that you attempt to answer five basic questions:

1. What is the report about?
2. How does the study fit into what is already known?
3. How was the study done?
4. What was found?
5. What do the results mean?

Quality research that is scientific- and practitioner-based within the quantitative and qualitative paradigms has the potential to provide the reader with new knowledge that can inform the practice of all professionals.

Staying Up-to-Date with Technology

In today's society, technology influences many aspects of our lives and will play an important role in your professional endeavors. Technology helps professionals stay abreast of new developments in

12 STEPS TO UNDERSTANDING RESEARCH REPORTS

Steps	Questions
Step 1–Citation	What is the name of the study, who is the author(s), and where and when was it published? Report the complete reference citation using APA format.
Step 2–Purpose and General Rationale	What was the purpose of the study and how did the author(s) make a case for its importance? Is the study quantitative or qualitative in nature?
Step 3–Fit and Specific Rationale	How does the topic of the study fit into the existing research literature, and how is that information used to make a specific case for the investigation?
Step 4–Participants	Who was studied (give number and characteristics), and how were they selected to participate in the study?
Step 5–Context	Where did the study take place? Describe important characteristics of the environment and setting (e.g., group demographics).
Step 6–Steps in Sequence	In the order performed, what were the major procedural steps in the study? Describe or diagram in a flowchart. Show a sequential order and any important relationships among the steps.
Step 7–Data Collection	What data sources were used (e.g., test scores, questionnaire responses, or frequency counts for a quantitative study or field notes, interview transcripts, photographs, or diaries for a qualitative study), how were the data collected, and what was the role of the author(s) throughout the process?
Step 8–Data Analysis	What form(s) of data analysis was used, and what specific questions was it designed to answer? What statistical operations and computer programs, if any, were employed?
Step 9–Results	What did the author(s) identify as the primary results (products or findings produced by the analysis of data)? In general, "what was going on there?"
Step 10–Conclusions	What did the author(s) assert about how the results in Step 9 responded to the purpose(s) established in Step 2, and how did the events and experiences of the entire study contribute to that conclusion?
Step 11–Cautions	What cautions does the author(s) raise about the study itself or about interpreting the results? Add here any of your own reservations, particularly those related to methods used to enhance validity and credibility (quantitative) or trustworthiness and believability (qualitative).
Step 12–Discussion and Application	What interesting facts or ideas did you learn from reading the report? Include here anything that was of value in regard to results, research designs and methods, references, data-collection instruments, history, useful arguments, or personal inspiration. How can the information learned be applied to improve professional practice? Or, what were the implications of this study for a practitioner?

Source: Adapted from Silverman S, Spirduso WW, and Locke LF. *Reading and Understanding Research* (4th ed.). Thousand Oaks, CA: Sage, 2016.

the field, facilitates communication among professionals, and plays a role in professional activities such as teaching, assessment, and research. This has certainly been brought to the forefront due to the COVID-19 pandemic causing many professionals to operate remotely/virtually.

Electronic databases such as ProQuest, Academic Search Premier, and SPORTDiscus provide ready access to professional journals. Really Simple Syndication (RSS), lets you subscribe and receive up-to-date information from online newspapers, some electronic journals, and government initiatives. Additionally, professionals can subscribe to updates from the U.S. Department of Health and Human Services (http://www.hhs.gov, click on the icon to subscribe to updates) to get the most current information and decisions on issues such as obesity, morbidity, nutrition, physical activity, and hypokinetic diseases. Smartphone applications can deliver this information directly to your fingertips.

Through the World Wide Web and the Internet, communication with other professionals can occur rapidly. E-mail is one of the most common ways to communicate. Real-time communication between professionals can occur using LinkedIn, instant messaging programs, and other applications, such as FaceTime, Zoom, and Skype, let professionals engage in phone and video chat. Live web conferencing programs, such as Adobe Connect, allow professionals to share presentations and multimedia from their desktops and receive feedback from other professionals. Although having such readily available information is convenient, you need to be critical consumers about the information that you get from the World Wide Web and the Internet. To help guide your critical analysis of web pages, see the Critiquing the Web box.

Social media, such as Instagram, Twitter, Facebook, Ning, and Tapped In (http://www.tappedin.org), lets professionals communicate with each

CRITIQUING THE WEB

These are tips for evaluating the quality of content on the web. In recent years, the web has become a rich environment of pages, blogs, wikis, social networking sites, free research services, media, and more. It can be a challenge to figure out which content to trust. This information will help you identify the type of site you are visiting and evaluate its content.

Here are a few general tips for evaluating content on the web. Check that the . . .

- author has expertise on the topic.
- source of the content is stated, whether original or borrowed, quoted, or imported from elsewhere, and that the content can be independently verified from other sources. This is especially important if you cannot check on the expertise of the author or if the author is not identified.
- level and depth of the information meets your needs.
- site is currently being maintained. Check for posting or editing dates.
- information is up-to-date.
- links are relevant and appropriate and in working order.
- site includes contact information.
- top-level domain in the site address is relevant to the focus of the material, for example, .edu for educational or research materials, .org for profit or nonprofit organizations, and .gov for government sources. Note that the top-level domain is not necessarily a primary indicator of site content. For example, some authors post their content on blog or wiki platforms hosted by companies with .com addresses.

Source: Adapted from: https://library.albany.edu/infolit/resource/evalweb

other, form groups around common interests, and readily exchange ideas. Blogging (e.g., Tumblr), the posting of commentary, video, and photos (e.g., Pinterest), gives professionals the opportunity to stay cognizant of current trends and issues as well as contribute to the discussion. Wikis, collaboratively built web pages, allow professionals to work together to develop new websites of professional interest. Social bookmarking sites, such as Digg, invite people to bookmark websites of interest, tag them with descriptors, and choose to share them with other people.

Sharing of ideas, best practices, and research is easy and convenient. Websites such as PE Central and PHE America invite professionals to voice their opinions, share lesson plans, and post best practices, while providing a multitude of resources. YouTube provides individuals all over the world with video clips that range from children engaged in daily activity to the latest fitness techniques. Consumers (i.e., you) need to analyze and critique the information to determine what is and is not accurate or appropriate practice.

Continuing your professional development is an important responsibility of professionals. Webinars and podcasts offer the opportunity to stay on top of professional development opportunities. Online courses and degrees allow you to continue your education without having to be physically present in a classroom or educational institution.

Current technology, as well as new and emerging technologies, means that it is easier for professionals to remain abreast of developments in the field. Communicating and collaborating with colleagues, sharing ideas and resources, and taking advantage of professional development opportunities are just some of the ways in which technology helps professionals fulfill their responsibilities.

CURRENT TRENDS: MOVING TOWARD THE FUTURE

- The disciplines within the field of kinesiology will continue to be interdisciplinary, yet also align with other areas within the medical, public health, and business fields.
- Advanced degrees are increasingly required for many professions within the disciplines.
- The disciplines of exercise physiology, sport medicine/athletic training, and sport management are rapidly expanding.
- Physical activity levels, nationally and worldwide, will continue to decline if access and opportunity are not provided to all individuals.
- Physical activity and health initiatives and policy will begin to make a positive impact on people's longevity and quality of life if they are equitable and just for all individuals regardless of social identity.
- Empirical research will continue to provide us with valuable information that will allow us to make informed decisions about our health and wellness.

SUMMARY

Our lives have been disrupted, challenged, and changed due to national and global experiences related to the COVID-19 pandemic, continued racial injustice, and political unrest. The pandemic has devastated many lives through loss of loved ones, worsened mental health issues, and/or not having the financial resources to support oneself or family. Through all of this, we have exposed the importance of justice, equity, diversity, and inclusion (JEDI) of all people regardless of one's social identity—in all facets of our world. An important step in this process is exploring and critically reflecting upon your social identity and systems of meaning. Your social identity consists of how you identify related to your race, gender, sexuality, (dis)ability, social class, religion, among others.

Contemporary physical education, exercise science, and sport are rapidly changing within the broader field of kinesiology and includes both disciplinary and professional dimensions. The discipline is the body of knowledge of the field. Scholars and researchers engage in activities designed to provide greater scientific understanding and insight. The professional dimension of the field focuses on providing services to people of all social identities in many different settings. Professionals use the body of knowledge and specialized skills to meet the unique needs of people and help them improve their health and quality of life. The growth of knowledge in physical education led to the change in the field to kinesiology as well as to specialized areas of study, such as sport and physical activity psychology, sport sociology, physical education pedagogy, sport philosophy, sport biomechanics, exercise physiology, motor development, motor learning, adapted physical activity/physical education, sport history, and sport management. Each practitioner should be knowledgeable about these specialized areas of study as well as appreciate their interrelatedness and their contribution to the discipline as a whole.

The field of kinesiology, and specific to this text, the professions of physical education, exercise science, and sport is continuously changing. To grow as a professional, it is important to stay up-to-date with the latest research, both scientific- and practitioner-based, and technological tools. Understanding research reports, learning about research findings, and utilizing the newest technology allow professionals the opportunity to provide equitable and just practices and instruction to students, clients, and athletes within physical education, exercise science, and sport programs.

DISCUSSION QUESTIONS

1. Reflect upon and discuss your social identity and systems of meaning. How will your identity influence you as a future professional? What potential biases, judgments, or concerns do you need to work through as you move forward in your program of study?
2. In this text, we have named kinesiology as the "field" and refer to physical education, exercise science, and sport as professions within this field. In today's society, should kinesiology be considered the field? Is there a different name that should be considered for the field of human movement and physical activity? Or, should there be multiple fields? Explain your reasoning behind your decision. What factors can you use to support your stance?
3. Of the disciplines, which one most closely aligns with your desired profession? Why have you chosen to go into that profession?

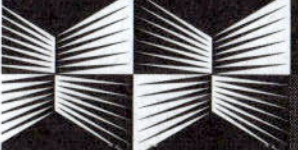

GET CONNECTED

Newsletters, RSS feeds, and podcasts are just some of the ways to stay abreast of current news, research, and developments related to physical education, exercise science, and sport.

U.S. Department of Health and Human Services–This site offers access to RSS feeds, podcasts, videos, and newsletters related to health. There are instructions on the site explaining how to watch, listen, or subscribe to a wide variety of information on health and physical activity.

https://www.hhs.gov/

American College of Sports Medicine–ACSM Fit Society electronic newsletter for the general public, focusing on popular health, sport, nutrition, and fitness topics.

https://www.acsm.org/ > Fit Society Page > sign up to subscribe.

PHE America Newsletter–sponsored by PHE America, this website offers a monthly newsletter and articles on a variety of topics, primarily related to the teaching of physical education and the promotion of active lifestyles. It also offers a directory of e-mailing lists and newsgroups for sport sciences, athletic training, wellness, and health.

http://www.pheamerica.org/

SELF-ASSESSMENT ACTIVITIES

These activities are designed to help you determine if you have mastered the materials and competencies presented in this chapter.

1. Complete the social identity profile (Figure 1-1). Then, reflect upon your social identities and how and why you identify this way. Describe which identities are more salient to you compared to others and why. Discuss how have you been privileged, marginalized, and/or oppressed based on your social identities.
2. Without consulting your text, describe the disciplines of the field of kinesiology. Discuss how these areas are interrelated. Use examples to illustrate why it is important to be knowledgeable about the various specialized areas within the discipline.
3. Refer to the 12 Steps to Understanding Research Reports box. Search for two scientific journals in which you can find research articles that focus on contemporary physical education, exercise science, and sport or one of the disciplines. Within these journals, you must be able to identify at least one original research article. This means that the authors of the article conducted the research study and are not referencing or analyzing data found in other research articles.
4. The Get Connected box lists resources for physical education, exercise science, and sport. Subscribe to a newsletter. Discuss the benefits the Internet offers to professionals in the field. For the semester, keep copies of your resources and summarize what you have learned at the end of the semester.

REFERENCES

1. Aspen Project Plays (2022). Youth sport facts: participation. https://www.aspenprojectplay.org/youth-sports/facts/participation-rates.
2. National Federation of State High School Associations. (2019). *2018–2019 high school athletics participation survey.* Retrieved from http://www.nfhs.org.
3. National Collegiate Athletic Association. (2022). *Membership.* Retrieved from http://www.ncaa.org.
4. National Association of Intercollegiate Athletics. (2022). Retrieved from http://www.naia.org.
5. National Junior College Athletic Association. (2022). Sponsors and partners. Retrieved from http://www.njcaa.org.
6. National Physical Activity Plan. (2016). Retrieved from http://www.physicalactivityplan.org/index.html.
7. US Department of Health and Human Services. (2020). *Healthy people 2030.* Retrieved from http://www.healthypeople.gov.
8. Office of Disease Prevention and Health Promotion. (2018). *2018 physical activity guidelines.* Retrieved from https://health.gov/paguidelines/.
9. Henry, F. M. (1964). Physical education: an academic discipline. *Journal of Health, Physical Education, and Recreation, 37*(7), 32–33.
10. Charles, J. M. (1996). Scholarship reconceptualized: the connectedness of kinesiology. *Quest 48,* 152–164.
11. Rossman, G. B. & Rallis, S. F. (2011). *Learning in the field: An introduction to qualitative research* (3rd ed.). Thousand Oaks, CA: Sage.
12. Silverman, S. J., Spirduso, W. W., & L. F. Locke. (2016). *Reading and understanding research* (4th ed.). Thousand Oaks, CA: Sage.

CHAPTER 2

PHILOSOPHY, GOALS, AND OBJECTIVES

Polka Dot Images/Getty Images

OBJECTIVES

After reading this chapter, students should be able to–

- Discuss key concepts of philosophy and their application to the disciplines within physical education, exercise science, and sport.
- Begin to develop a professional philosophy.
- Describe potential goals and objectives that can be developed within physical education, exercise science, and sport.
- Describe the cognitive, affective/social, and psychomotor learning domains and apply these domains to the different disciplines.
- Describe the purposes and the importance of assessment in physical education, exercise science, and sport.

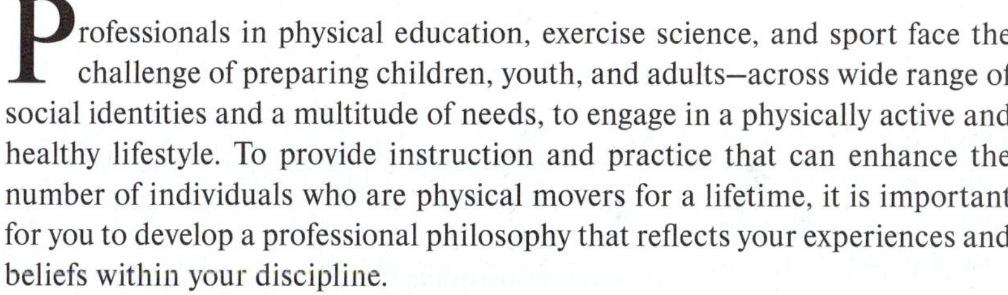

Professionals in physical education, exercise science, and sport face the challenge of preparing children, youth, and adults–across wide range of social identities and a multitude of needs, to engage in a physically active and healthy lifestyle. To provide instruction and practice that can enhance the number of individuals who are physical movers for a lifetime, it is important for you to develop a professional philosophy that reflects your experiences and beliefs within your discipline.

As discussed in Chapter 1, your social identities and systems of meaning influence your beliefs, what you value, and your lived experiences in all aspects of your life. It also influences your philosophy for the profession in which you aspire to do. At the onset of this chapter, we are asking you to continue to reflect on your social identities and systems of meaning and relate them to what will develop into your professional philosophy.

Your professional philosophy creates a framework (i.e., a way of thinking, a perspective) in which you formulate the goals and objectives of your program. As professionals, we must define the goals and objectives of our programs based on the context in which we work, whether in a corporate fitness center, cardiac rehabilitation program, or a community sports program. Clearly

SOCIAL JUSTICE

Talking Points

- Our professional philosophy is influenced by our social identities, systems of meaning, and personal lived experiences. Professionals, regardless of their philosophy, will need to be inclusive and sensitive to the wide variety of identities and experiences of the people with whom they work.
- Professionals within the field of kinesiology need to develop goals and objectives specific to each student, player, or client to best meet their goals and needs, while taking into consideration their identities, circumstances, access, and environment.
- Professionals should have the ability to meet all the diverse learning needs of their students, players, or clients to create equitable opportunities for them to succeed.

defined goals and objectives are essential if physical education, exercise science, and sport programs are designed to foster optimal human development, enhance health, and enrich the quality of life of all individuals.

Within this chapter, we will discuss the major philosophies; the philosophy of sport and physical activity; the goals and objectives of physical education, exercise science, and sport; the cognitive, affective/social, and psychomotor domains; and the implementation of assessment within instruction and practice.

PHILOSOPHY

The term *philosophy* can conjure up a variety of visions and reactions depending on the person. At that time, ask yourself, how do you respond when you hear the word philosophy? What is your current perspective about philosophy? How does philosophy play a role in your personal and professional lives?

What Is Philosophy?

Philosophy, derived from the Greek word *philosophia*, means "the love of wisdom."[1] Philosophers pursue the truth through the systematic investigation of reality, knowledge, meanings, and values. Philosophy is a system of values by which one lives and works. Your system of beliefs and values guides your conduct in both your personal life and professional life. Philosophy helps individuals address the problems that confront them through the use of critical thinking, logical analysis, and reflective appraisal. Our philosophy is greatly influenced by our lived experiences and those lived experiences are often dependent upon our social identities. Some of you have had to challenge and question the status quo and/or systems en route to developing your beliefs and values.

Questions that reflect the concerns of philosophers include the following:

- What is the role of human beings on this earth?
- What are the origin and nature of the universe?
- What constitutes good and evil and right and wrong?
- What constitutes truth?
- Is there a God?
- What relationship exists between mind and body or matter?

Are there additional questions you have philosophized about that are not listed? What were they? What brought you to philosophize about such topics? Throughout the remainder of the philosophy section, consider how these philosophies can relate to your personal life and future professional career.

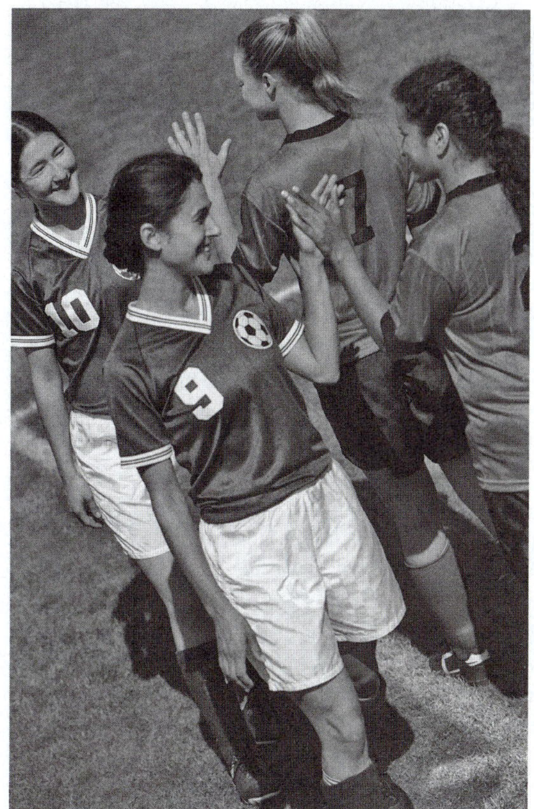

What does it mean to be a "good sport"?
PNC/Brand X Pictures/PunchStock

Branches of Philosophy

Philosophy's branches of study are generally divided into four domains: metaphysics, epistemology, logic, and axiology. *Metaphysics* seeks to address the ultimate nature of reality, that is, what is real and exists. Speculative in its approach, metaphysics may be used to understand the relationship between mind and body or the essential meaning of sport.

Epistemology is the branch of philosophy concerned with examining the nature of knowledge. It uses critical, analytical methods to examine the structure of knowledge, its origin, and its limits. This approach can help us define the nature of the discipline (i.e., body of knowledge) of physical education, exercise science, and sport.

Logic focuses on the examination of ideas in an orderly and systematic way. Logic uses a critical approach to study how ideas relate to each other and applies sound and reasoned judgment to decision making. Logic can help members of our field design sound research approaches or organize facts to document the contribution of physical activity to well-being.

Axiology examines the nature of values. Two extensions of axiology are ethics and aesthetics. *Ethics* is concerned with issues of right and wrong, responsibility, and standards of conduct. Speculative in nature, ethics examines moral values. Moral reasoning helps people determine what the right thing to do is in a given situation or circumstance. The development of character, the nature of fair play, and issues of justice are just a few of the ethical concerns of physical education, exercise science, and sport. *Aesthetics* is the study of the nature of beauty and art. The beauty of skilled movement and artistic expression through dance enable us to see movement as an art form.

These branches represent different aspects of philosophy. In developing a comprehensive philosophy for a discipline, such as physical education, exercise science, or sport, each of these areas is addressed. The Branches of Philosophy box highlights the focus of each branch, provides a typical general question that may be posed, and shows how these questions may be framed within the context of physical education, exercise science, and sport.

Major Philosophies

The six major philosophies that have been typically described with respect to their impact on physical education, exercise science, or sport are idealism, realism, pragmatism, naturalism, existentialism, and humanism. Although space precludes an extensive discussion of each philosophy, a brief overview of the basic tenets of each is provided, with suggestions of how they can potentially influence professionals in their work.

Idealism

As a philosophy, *idealism* emphasizes the mind as central to understanding and the critical role that reasoning plays in arriving at the truth. Under this

BRANCHES OF PHILOSOPHY

Branch	Focus	General Questions	Physical Education, Exercise Science, and Sport Questions
Metaphysics	Nature of reality	What is the meaning of existence? What is real?	What experiences in a physical education program will better enable the individual to meet the challenges of the real world?
Epistemology	Nature of knowledge and methods of obtaining knowledge	What is true?	What is the validity of the knowledge pertaining to physical activity and its influence on the development of the individual?
Logic	Systematic and orderly reasoning	What is the method of reasoning that will lead to the truth?	What process should a researcher use to determine the value of physical education to program participants?
Axiology	Aims and values of society	How do we determine what has value, and on what criteria is this judgment based?	What is the value of physical education programs to the individual?
Ethics	Issues of conduct, right and wrong	What is the highest standard of behavior each person should strive to attain?	How can sport be utilized to develop ethics?
Aesthetics	Nature of beauty and art	What is beauty?	Why are skilled performers' movements beautiful to view?

philosophy, values and ideals are held in high regard and are considered to be universal and absolute. Values and ideals do not change, regardless of circumstances.

Professionals who follow the tenets of idealism would emphasize the development of character, the importance of values, and the application of reasoning in their work. A youth sport coach who espoused the philosophy of idealism would promote the development of character and the ideals of sportspersonship among the athletes on their team over winning. A fitness leader who believed in the philosophy of idealism would place a high value on serving as a role model to their clients. A cardiac rehabilitation specialist who followed the tenets of idealism would solicit from their cardiac patient, a former runner, the meaning running held for them, understand the patient's desire to return to running, and work with the patient to develop a realistic rehabilitation program to accomplish this goal.

Realism

The philosophy of *realism* emphasizes the use of the scientific method to arrive at the truth. Reasoning and understanding the natural laws of nature are features of this philosophy. The total development of the person is important, and physical activity has an important role in this endeavor.

Philosophy influences athletes' attitudes toward winning and helps them interpret the meaning of success.

Larry William Associates/Fuse/Getty Images

An exercise physiologist who subscribed to the philosophy of realism would carefully evaluate the scientific evidence in order to better understand the contribution of different types of physical activity to health. Physical educators who believed in realism would incorporate frequent assessment procedures into their classes, so that their students would have a means to monitor their progress toward attainment of their goals. In accordance with this philosophical approach, coaches would select training techniques based on the scientific evidence of their effectiveness, and would use a systematic, progressive approach in designing practices.

Pragmatism

According to the philosophy of *pragmatism*, experiences–not ideals or realities–are the basis of truth. Because individuals experience different situations, reality differs from person to person. Thus, within this philosophical approach, whatever works in a given situation at a given time is seen as successful. Although pragmatists see truth as variable and rightness as individually determined, they emphasize social responsibility. Pragmatists emphasize problem solving, consideration of individuals' needs and interests, development of individuals' social skills, and cooperation.

A pragmatist conducting a community fitness program for older adults would design the program to meet their needs and interests. A college recreational sports director would be sure to include a variety of different activities in the program offerings, so that the students would be able to choose activities that were personally meaningful and enjoyable. A corporate worksite health promotion specialist who believed in the pragmatic approach may choose to incorporate Project Adventure problem-solving activities into a special program for middle managers; after the completion of the activities, they would ask them to share perceptions of their experiences while the specialist facilitated the discussion.

Naturalism

The belief that life is governed by the laws of nature is central to the philosophy of *naturalism*. Naturalism emphasizes the importance of considering each individual's level of growth and development in learning, and designing experiences that are congruent to the individual's needs. Self-direction, individualized learning, and competition against oneself are important in this approach. Play and outdoor activities provide beneficial opportunities for exploration and problem solving as a means of personal growth and learning.

Physical educators who believe in the philosophy of naturalism would use developmentally appropriate physical activities with their students at all levels of instruction, and individualized learning would be emphasized. Fitness leaders who adhere to the tenets of naturalism would encourage their program's participants to take advantage of opportunities to engage in outdoor pursuits during their leisure time as a means of incorporating physical activity into their lifestyle.

Existentialism

According to the *existentialist* philosophy, reality is determined by individuals' experiences. An individual's experiences and choices create a uniquely personal worldview and affect their perception of reality. Existentialism emphasizes the freedom of individuals to think as they choose and to make choices, but stresses that they must accept the consequences of their actions. Creativity, individuality, self-responsibility, and self-awareness are important aspects of this philosophy; learning experiences should reflect these attributes.

Under the existentialist philosophy, a sport psychologist would encourage an athlete to carefully reflect upon their experiences to identify the thoughts that led to poor performances. The sport psychologist would offer the athlete a variety of options to deal with these issues, allowing the athlete to choose among the alternatives. A coach who advocated for an existentialist philosophy would emphasize the athlete's responsibility in adhering to the established code of conduct. The coach may allow some individuality in dress, but would emphasize the athlete's responsibility in adhering to training rules. A physical educator would allow students to select from a variety of activities within the program, promoting reflection and individual responsibility for learning.

Humanism

A *humanistic* philosophy emphasizes the development of the full potential of each individual. Personal growth, self-actualization, and the development of values are central tenets of this philosophy. Treating students as individuals, valuing the dignity of each person, enhancing self-esteem, fostering personal and social development, and promoting self-responsibility are hallmarks of this approach. Within the realm of physical education, exercise science, and sport, humanism encourages a greater emphasis on meeting individual needs, and recognizes that one type of program is not suited for all individuals. The feelings, needs, goals, capabilities, and limitations of individuals should be carefully considered in conducting programs. For example, in corporate fitness, programs are designed to meet the needs of individual clients, assumption of responsibility for one's own health and fitness is stressed, and a holistic approach to health is emphasized.

Collectively, the beliefs and tenets of the traditional philosophies of idealism, realism, pragmatism, naturalism, existentialism, and humanism have influenced physical education, exercise science, and sport programs.

Modern Educational Philosophy

Today's educational philosophy reflects several influences. Most schools today follow an educational philosophy based on many of the beliefs advocated by John Dewey. John Dewey is recognized as the leader of the progressive education movement, and his ideas were influential in shaping American education.

Dewey's ideas of *progressive education* reflect a pragmatic orientation. Progressives believed that

CENTRAL BELIEFS UNDERLYING TRADITIONAL PHILOSOPHIES

Idealism	The mind interprets events and creates reality; truth and values are absolute and universally shared.
Realism	The physical world is the real world and it is governed by nature; science reveals the truth.
Pragmatism	Reality is determined by an individual's life experiences; the individual learns the truth through experiences.
Naturalism	Reality and life are governed by the laws of nature; the individual is more important than society.
Existentialism	Reality is based on human existence; individual experiences determine what is true.
Humanism	Reality and life consider humans to be of primary importance; personal growth, self-actualization, and the development of values are emphasized.

education was the avenue to improving the social conditions of society. Dewey's approach of "learning by doing" significantly changed the nature of American education. This child-centered approach to learning emphasized children taking an active role in their learning, as opposed to being passive recipients of knowledge conveyed to them by the teacher.[2]

Dewey also believed in the unity of the mind and the body. Educational activities were viewed as contributing to the development of the total person, not just the mind. The tenets of progressive education lent support to the inclusion of physical education in the school curriculum. Physical activity developed the physical goals of education, as well as contributing to its intellectual and social goals. This philosophy of education through the physical was to become one of the most important influences on twentieth-century physical education.[2]

The Mind-Body Relationship

What is the relationship between the mind and the body? Are they separate, independent entities? Or are the mind and body a unified, interdependent, dynamic organism? Philosophers have long debated these questions, resulting in varying answers and perspectives.

The belief that the mind and the body are separate entities is termed *dualism*. Dualism views the mind and the body as independent, with either the mind or the body being superior. Usually, dualists emphasize the superiority of the mind over the body, relegating the body to an inferior role. The reduction or elimination of school physical education programs in order to increase time for more "academic" pursuits reflects the emphasis on development of the mind at the expense of development of the body. There are other times in physical education, exercise science, and sport

Some sports, such as the martial arts, emphasize the development of the mind and spirit as well as the body.
Dave and Les Jacobs/Blend Images

programs when the emphasis is placed solely on the development of the body. When the development of the body is emphasized under this philosophical approach, this is referred to as *education of the physical*. As the mind and the body are separate entities, educating or developing the body has no effect on the mind.

In contrast to the dualist approach, *monism* views the mind and the body as a fused, unified entity. Because the mind and the body are viewed as a unified whole, neither one can be subservient to the other; physical activity is as important as intellectual activity. From this philosophic perspective, physical education is as important as the rest of the courses in the educational curriculum. When physical education, exercise science, and sport adopt this philosophical approach, physical activity is seen as a medium for the development of the total person. This approach of *education through the physical* is the most dominant force in contemporary physical education.

The monist, holistic approach is central to our mission of promoting lifespan participation in physical activity. Achievement of lifespan participation requires that professionals embrace the developmental approach to physical activity–that is, design physical activity programs to promote fitness and motor skills and to instill in participants an appreciation for the contribution of physical activity to one's total well-being.

Philosophy of Sport and Physical Activity

Sport philosophy emerged as a specialized area of study in the mid-1960s and into the 1970s. The definition, scope, and areas of study are discussed in this section.

Definition and Scope

Sport philosophy is the systematic and reflective study of the truth, meanings, and actions of sport. Sport philosophers use logic and reasoning to gain a broader understanding of how sport contributes to our lives, and to analyze the principles that guide our professional practices and actions. Sport philosophers study the values connected with sport, examine the relationship between the mind and body, and debate justice, equity, and ethical dilemmas. They call upon us as professionals to critically reflect upon our beliefs and assumptions about sport and challenge us to use our insight and knowledge for the well-being of others.

Areas of Study

As sport philosophy became more organized and sophisticated, philosophers undertook the investigation of a wider array of topics. Some of the questions sport philosophers may investigate include:

- How does one's social identities influence their ability to participate in sport?
- Why do some athletes risk permanent disability by continuing to participate in sport when injured?
- Why do adults persist in emphasizing winning in sport when children want to emphasize the fun elements associated with play?
- What is the relationship among play, work, and sport?
- How does athletic ability influence the meaning of sport for the participant? Are the values derived from participation in sport different for athletes of different abilities?
- How can opportunities to participate in physical activity be made more just and equitable?

The philosophies of physical activity and sport help us understand the meaning of movement and involvement to participants. This knowledge can help professionals make decisions and develop guidelines that will lead to a more positive experience for those involved. Sport philosophy offers us a systematic, reasoned approach to examining our beliefs, exploring the connections and relationships between our personal values, critically reflecting on societal values, and aligning our actions according to the goals and aims to be achieved.

Your Professional Philosophy

A professional philosophy is important for all physical educators, exercise scientists, and sport leaders. A professional philosophy will help you articulate the worth and value of the discipline and will influence the design and leadership of your programs. Your philosophy will be reflected in your actions as a professional, the manner in which you handle the responsibility of being a role model, and your behaviors toward and interactions with the people you serve. It is important to understand that your professional philosophy may emphasize the philosophies discussed in this chapter as well as the many others that this chapter did not address. However, your professional philosophy will primarily emphasize your beliefs and values within your chosen profession, which may align or be supported by a professional organization's vision or mission statement.

Your professional philosophy can serve as a guide in making equitable and ethical decisions as you confront many issues and problems within the field. When confronted with equitable and ethical decisions, you can use your professional philosophy to reflect on how you ought to act, what is right and wrong in the given situation, and what is just and unjust.

A professional philosophy will be helpful in addressing both societal and professional questions that may affect the conduct of your program, your actions as a professional, and the outcomes experienced by the people you are serving. Some general questions that a philosophy might help you address are:

- What has value in today's society?
- What is relevant to the needs of people today?
- What are some inequities in opportunity that must be addressed? And what is my commitment to social justice?

As a professional, you will be confronted with many questions that must be addressed. Some examples are:

- Should youth sport programs mandate equal playing time for all participants?
- Should intercollegiate athletes be required to maintain a certain grade point average to participate?
- Should employees be required to participate in a corporate fitness program in order to receive health benefits?
- Should certification be required of all health-and-fitness club employees? If so, what certification should be required?
- Does an athletic director have a right to mandate that no athletes have social-media accounts?

A well-developed professional philosophy gives you some guidance in resolving these and a multitude of other questions and issues you will face.

Developing your professional philosophy will be one of your major tasks as you continue your professional preparation. One of the most commonly asked questions of job candidates by employers is, "What is your professional philosophy?" Your professional philosophy will likely change as you learn more about the field, acquire more professional experience, and come to understand who you are as an individual. As you begin to develop your professional philosophy, it may be helpful to think about your personal philosophy (which will relate to your social identities and systems of meaning) and use those beliefs and values as a starting point. The guidelines presented in the Developing Your Professional Philosophy box will help you determine, define, and articulate your philosophy of physical education, exercise science, and sport. Collectively, professional philosophies and program goals and objectives within physical education, exercise science, and sport will be discussed.

Goals and Objectives Defined

Before we discuss the goals and objectives of physical education, exercise science, and sport, we will first define these terms. *Goals* are statements of purposes, intents, and aims that reflect desired accomplishments. Goals are expressed as general statements and are broad in their direction. They state long-term outcomes to be achieved by participants in the program.

Objectives are derived from goals. Objectives describe learning, specifically what individuals should know, do, or feel as a result of instruction. Objectives are more specific than goals. They are short-term statements of specific outcomes that build

DEVELOPING YOUR PROFESSIONAL PHILOSOPHY

Steps	Questions to Consider
1. Review your past experiences in physical education, exercise science, and sport.	What were some of your most outstanding experiences in this field? What were some of your most disheartening ones? Why? Is there a professional you particularly admire, one who served as a role model for you or even prompted your entry into this field? If so, what was their philosophy?
2. Read about the different philosophies.	What theories are compatible with your beliefs? What theories are at odds with them? How do these theories translate into practice? What are the characteristics of programs conducted from these philosophical perspectives?
3. Review the philosophies of leaders in physical education, exercise science, and sport.	After reviewing the philosophies of leaders in the field, which of their beliefs are compatible with yours and which are incompatible? Why?
4. Take advantage of opportunities you have during your professional preparation to talk to various professors about their philosophies.	What beliefs are evident in their teaching? As you critically examine your experiences during your professional preparation, do you ask yourself why things are the way they are? How could things change? How would these changes influence the philosophy of the program? Would these changes align with your professors' beliefs and philosophies?
5. Review the codes of conduct and ethical standards of various professional organizations.	Many physical education, exercise science, and sport professional organizations have standards of conduct that serve as guidelines for their members. What are the standards of conduct expected of professionals entering your prospective field? What are the expectations for service to the profession and to others?
6. Express your philosophy.	What are your current perspectives and beliefs about your prospective field? If you have previously written a professional philosophy, how has your philosophy changed or evolved? What factors influenced these changes?

cumulatively to reach a goal. Objectives can be stated in many different ways and vary in their degree of specificity. They can be stated with reference to general behavior or to specific outcomes. For example, one goal of *Healthy People 2030* is to increase life expectancy and for individuals to be free of preventable disease, disability, injury, and premature death.[3] A general objective that will contribute to this goal is increasing the number of people who engage in exercise to achieve cardiorespiratory fitness. A more specific objective related to physical activity is increasing from 15% to 30% the proportion of adults who engage regularly in moderate physical activity for at least 30 minutes per day.

Well-constructed objectives can take on many different forms and can be stated in many different ways. Most importantly, whatever the format, objectives should describe the behavior the individual will demonstrate when the desired outcome is achieved. When objectives are stated in terms that are measurable, they provide a means to assess the individual's progress toward the achievement of the goal.

Each individual's level of development should be considered in planning activities.
Deborah Wuest

Objectives may be developed for different areas of learning, that is, intellectual development, physical development, or social-emotional development. Objectives guide the development of assessment procedures and instructional experiences. They help professionals focus their efforts on the subject content that is most important for participants to learn.

GOALS OF PHYSICAL EDUCATION, EXERCISE SCIENCE, AND SPORT

An important goal for many physical education, exercise science, and sport leaders is the improvement of the well-being and quality of life of individuals who participate in our programs. We can accomplish this by socializing individuals into the role of participants who will make a long-term commitment to participation in enjoyable and meaningful physical activity and sport experiences. Our main purpose is to provide people with the skills, knowledge, and dispositions to participate in regular physical activity throughout their lifespan.

Contemporary physical education, exercise science, and sport programs are growing in popularity. These programs are diverse in content and varied in setting, and they serve people of all identities. What are the goals and objectives of these contemporary programs? What outcomes should participants in these programs achieve? These questions can be addressed by researching the professional organization of your discipline, such as the National Athletic Trainer's Association (www.nata.org), the North American Society for Sport Management (www.nassm.com), the American College of Sports Medicine (www.acsm.org), or the Society of Health and Physical Educators (www.shapeamerica.org) to name a few. Having an understanding of the professional goals of your discipline will help guide you in how to develop goals and learning objectives for your students, players, or clients.

LEARNING DOMAINS

Objectives for learning can be classified into multiple domains: cognitive (thinking), affective/social (feeling/interaction), and psychomotor (doing). The cognitive domain is concerned with the acquisition of knowledge and its application. The affective/social domain includes the promotion of values, the fostering of social skills, and the enhancement of emotional development. The psychomotor domain involves the development of motor skills and physical fitness.

It is critical that professionals consider all domains when planning learning experiences to meet individuals' needs. Separation of behaviors into domains simplifies the formulation of objectives. It enables us to more readily take into account individuals' levels of development in each domain as we design and conduct activities. However, these domains are interrelated and, as professionals, we must keep this at the forefront of our minds as we work with people in our programs.

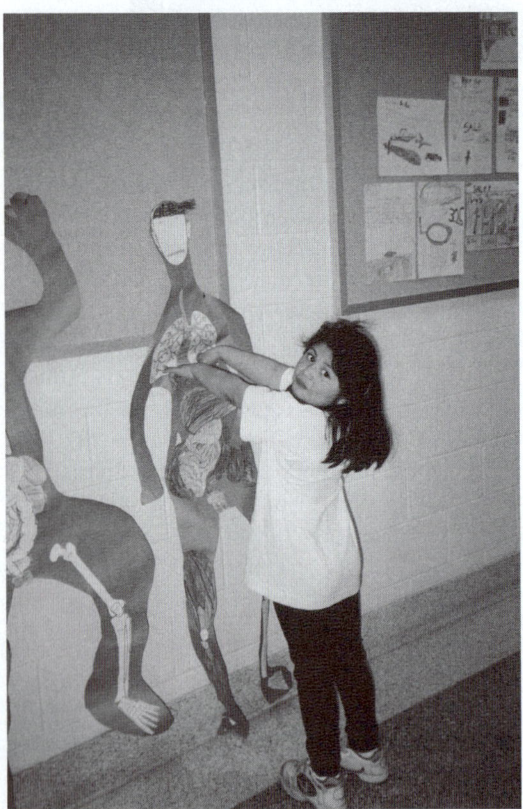

Physical education can help children understand the human body. This 8-year-old is pointing to the lungs, which she says "help you live and get air to run hard."

Sarah Rich

Education is a process of learning that can take place in many different settings. Physical education, exercise science, and sport programs contribute to the cognitive, affective/social, and psychomotor development of program participants. These programs involve people of all identities, from diverse contexts, and with many different goals. As we continue to expand our programs, we must actively seek to extend the opportunity for participation to all people, regardless of gender, race, ethnic and cultural background, and socioeconomic status.

Taxonomies

Taxonomies serve as a guide for professionals in planning for learning outcomes and achievement of the desired goals. A taxonomy organizes objectives in a progressive hierarchy, from low to high, using developmental theories as a basis for formulating those objectives. Behaviors at one level serve as the foundation and prerequisite for behaviors at a higher level. Stated more simply, lower-order objectives serve as stepping stones to the attainment of higher levels of achievement.

Taxonomies have been developed for each domain. These taxonomies offer guidelines for professionals in all fields/disciplines who work with people to enhance learning and promote human development.

Cognitive Domain

The cognitive domain is concerned with the acquisition of knowledge and the development of intellectual skills. Bloom and his colleagues originally developed a taxonomy of educational objectives for this domain in the 1950s, which was not revised until 2001 by Anderson and Krathwohl.[4] These objectives reflect an increase in complexity at each level of development. Remembering facts is the initial objective, and from this grows understanding and application of concepts, critical analysis, evaluation, and creating. (The Cognitive Domain box presents the objectives for this domain.)

Development of knowledge and understanding is an important objective for physical education, exercise science, and sport programs in all settings.

THE COGNITIVE DOMAIN

Category	Description	Application
1. Remembering	Ability to recall; retrieving relevant knowledge from long-term memory; represents lowest level of learning outcomes in cognitive domain.	**Physical Education**–What are the critical elements of the overhead clear in badminton? **Exercise Science**–What are the health-related components of fitness? **Sports Programs**–What are the primary rules of basketball?
2. Understanding	Constructing meaning of instructional materials (oral, written, and graphic); understanding without perceiving implications; interpret; translate; estimate; predict; represents lower level of cognitive domain.	**Physical Education**–Compare the critical elements of the overhead clear in badminton to the softball/baseball throw. **Exercise Science**–Compare the health and motor components of fitness. **Sports Programs**–How are the primary rules of basketball similar to soccer?
3. Applying	Ability to use learned information in new situations; can apply rules, methods, and concepts; can carry out or use a procedure in a given situation; higher level of understanding.	**Physical Education**–When is the best time to use the overhead clear in badminton? Why? **Exercise Science**–What exercises would you prescribe to a 40-year-old woman who is just starting to exercise? **Sports Programs**–On offense, the point guard has picked up her dribble and you are being defended by an opponent. What movement(s) could you do to create opportunities to get open?
4. Analyzing	To break down material into its component parts; organization and relationships between parts made clear; identifying; selecting; inferring; higher intellectual level.	**Physical Education**–In a game of badminton, your opponent consistently wins the point by landing the shuttle at the front of the court. Describe how you will adjust your game play to improve your opportunities to score. **Exercise Science**–Select cardiovascular exercises for a 55-year-old man who just had a minor heart attack. **Sports Programs**–In a basketball game, your opponent is scoring most of their points inside the key. Describe how you would change your defense to prevent your opponent from scoring.

(Continued)

THE COGNITIVE DOMAIN (*Continued*)

Category	Description	Application
5. Evaluating	Make judgments based on criteria and standards; second highest learning outcome because it contains elements of all other categories.	**Physical Education–**In a singles game of badminton, you lose by a score of 15-6. Reflect upon your game play and explain what tactics and strategies your opponent utilized to win the game and describe what skills, tactics, and strategies you need to work on to improve your game performance. **Exercise Science–**How will you adjust your client's workout based on the following information from a pre- and postassessment: increase in 1 rep max on the bench press by 20 pounds, flexibility did not improve, and resting heart rate lowered 2 beats/minute. **Sports Programs–**Throughout the season thus far, your team is averaging 20 turnovers/game. Create drills your team can practice that have the potential to decrease the number of turnovers per game.
6. Creating	Put elements together to form a coherent or functional whole; reorganize elements into a new pattern or structure.	**Physical Education–**In a singles badminton tournament, you will face the same opponent that you lost to in last year's tournament. Design a game plan as to how you will approach all aspects of the match. For example, if your opponent has a powerful first serve, how will you position yourself to return the ball or if your opponent approaches the net after the second return, where will you place your shot on the court? **Exercise Science–**Your client (from above) approaches you and wants to change his goals. He decides that he wants to train for a Tough Mudder and would like you to create a program to prepare for this event, which is 4 months away. **Sports Programs–**Your team is going to face a new opponent for the first time. You and your team study film of their previous games. Create a game plan as to how you are going to stop their high-tempo, fast-break offense.

Our programs are concerned with educating individuals about the many dimensions of human movement, including the knowledge within our discipline.

Professionals in all settings need to place more emphasis on the scientific principles and concepts underlying the performance of various activities. Physical activities are not performed in a vacuum. As such, instructors should continually provide appropriate knowledge and information for participants and encourage them to question what they are doing. "Why should I exercise regularly? How will this exercise contribute to the rehabilitation of my knee? Why is warming up before exercising important? How can I get more distance for my golf drive? What can I do to throw the ball farther? Why is it important to play by the rules? Why are my experiences different from others?" Participants should be provided with more opportunities to think, to apply problem-solving skills to physical activity situations, to experience situations that allow for creativity and individual expression, and to question, critique, and challenge inequities and injustices within our discipline.

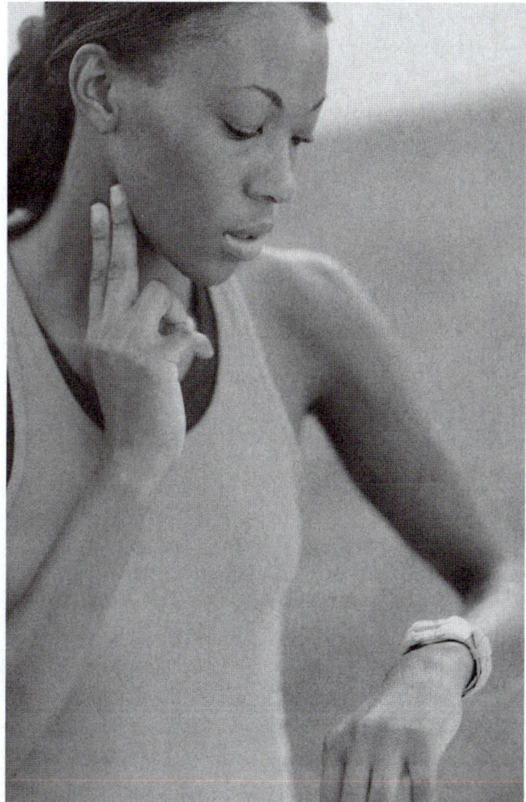

Knowing how to monitor your heart rate, calculate your training zone, and modify your fitness program to meet your individual needs are cognitive outcomes that can be achieved in programs.

Laura Doss/Fancy Collection/SuperStock

Professionals can also use fitness activities to stimulate cognitive development. Students can self-analyze their fitness levels, identify areas of improvement, apply their knowledge to design an individualized exercise program, and evaluate their progress regularly, adjusting their program as needed. These cognitive skills of analysis, identification, application, evaluation, and creating contribute to the goal of preparing individuals to be lifelong learners. These activities also give these individuals the skills to modify their fitness programs during their adult lives as their needs change, a critical feature of lifespan involvement.

Affective/Social Domain

Many factors influence individuals' learning, including their feelings about themselves, the learning experience, and the subject. Most recently, the COVID-19 pandemic has negatively affected many people's mental health. Whether that is due to isolation and lack of social engagement, financial struggles, or being burnt out from numerous years of limitations, difficulties, and challenges. The likelihood of this affecting people of all identities for years to come is relatively high. These circumstances, among many others, showcase the importance and need to focus on the affective/social domain. Relating to affective domain, we utilize Krathwohl and associates taxonomy for the affective domain.[5] This taxonomy reflects the development of values, appreciations, attitudes, and character. As individuals progress through the levels within this domain, they move from a concern about themselves to a value structure that embraces concern for others. At the highest level, their internalized values directly influence their choices and actions. Affective development also encompasses social and emotional development. (The objectives are shown in the Affective/Social Domain box.)

THE AFFECTIVE/SOCIAL DOMAIN

Category	Description	Application
1. Receiving	Sensitivity to the existence of certain events or stimuli; awareness; willingness to receive or attend to phenomena.	**PE**–Students follow the teacher's directions. **Ex Sci**–A cardiologist listens to her patient to describe their symptoms. **Sport**–Players choose to shake hands with the opposing team after a win or loss.
2. Responding	Active attention to stimuli; reacting to a situation beyond mere perception; responding overtly.	**PE**–Students choose to use rock-paper-scissors to decide whether the ball was in or out in a game instead of arguing the call. **Ex Sci**–A client questions the benefits and potential side effects of a new fad diet. **Sport**–A player practices hitting in the batting cages before and after the team's actual practice on a daily basis.
3. Valuing	Assigning worth to stimuli or phenomena; placing a value on events; characteristics of a belief or attitude; appreciation.	**PE**–Students voluntarily participate in physical activity outside of school. **Ex Sci**–Elderly participants create a walking club in their neighborhood for social and physical development. **Sport**–Players demonstrate fair play and good sportspersonship to their coaches, teammates, and opponents.
4. Organizing	Internalizing values and organizing them into a system; determining interrelationship among values; arranging values in hierarchical form; comparing, relating, and synthesizing values.	**PE**–Students accept responsibility for their own behavior. **Ex Sci**–Individuals accept a physical therapist's guidelines as to when they can return to competition. **Sport**–A player recognizes his or her own abilities, limitations, and values and develops realistic aspirations of how he or she can contribute to the team.
5. Characterizing by a value or complex	Acting in accordance with internalized values; behaving consistently with accepted values and integrating them into personality.	**PE**–Students appreciate and value the opportunity to collaborate and socialize with their classmates as they problem-solve how to accomplish a challenge or task successfully. **Ex Sci**–Individuals commit to 30 minutes of daily physical activity to enhance their health and decrease stress levels. **Sport**–Players choose to eat healthy and work hard to increase their performance instead of taking performance-enhancing drugs.

All people have certain basic social needs. These include feelings of belonging, recognition, self-respect, and love. Fulfillment of these needs contributes to social development. Physical education, exercise science, and sport programs can help participants meet some of these social needs. For example, elderly participants who join an exercise program typically benefit not only physically but also socially, deriving pleasure from meeting with their group regularly and forming new friendships. Such interactions help to diminish the feelings of isolation experienced by many elderly who live alone.

Promotion of a positive self-concept and enhancement of feelings of self-worth and self-respect are desired outcomes associated with this domain. One way that physical education, exercise science, and sport activities can contribute to these outcomes is to provide opportunities for individuals to develop competence in physical skills and to challenge themselves to attain new levels of achievement and realistic goals. Experiences should be structured to allow for meaningful success for all involved. Individuals who perceive themselves as competent and have confidence in themselves as movers are more likely to seek involvement in physical activities.

The development of positive attitudes and appreciation for the contributions that engaging in regular physical activity makes to lifelong health and well-being are outcomes that physical education, exercise science, and sport professionals are increasingly emphasizing. Knowledge of the benefits of physical activity and the development of the skills to participate in various activities are not, in and of themselves, sufficient to promote lifespan involvement. If we are to achieve our goal of promoting regular physical activity, we must instill in participants the motivation to lead a healthy, active lifestyle. Our programs should help participants appreciate the contribution that physical activity can make to their health, performance, and rewarding use of leisure time.

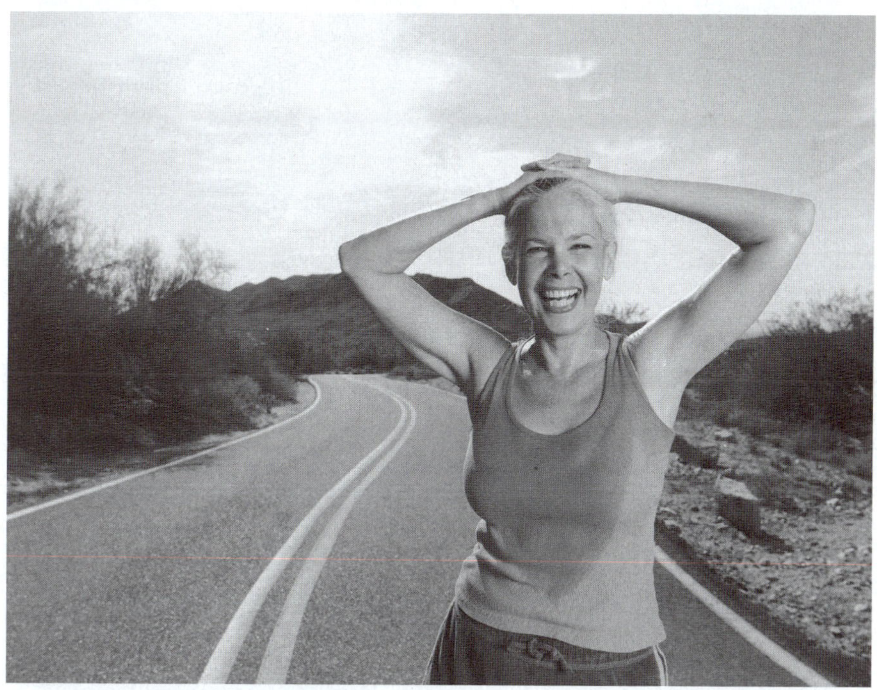

Valuing physical activity for enjoyment and challenge is an example of an affective outcome.

Dave and Les Jacobs/Blend Images

Professionals can promote social responsibility, an important component of good citizenship. Hellison[6] developed a model to promote responsibility that has been successfully used with at-risk students in both school- and community-based programs. This model emphasizes personal growth through self-control, involvement, goal setting, and assisting others. Success, personal awareness, problem solving, and self-reflection are also incorporated within this model. This approach and other thoughtfully designed instructional experiences can do much to promote the development of socially acceptable values.

Professionals must also give careful thought to the influence of their own behaviors, values, and actions on their program participants. How important is it for professionals to practice what they preach? Professionals who aspire to promote affective and social development must carefully weigh this question. As leaders, they serve as models for participants. Consideration for the needs and feelings of others, respect for each individual, and enthusiasm for physical activity are some behaviors physical educators, exercise science, and sport professionals should exhibit if they want to promote the same behaviors within their participants.

Psychomotor Domain

Developed by Dave, the taxonomy of objectives in the psychomotor domain shows a progression of development that provides the foundation for programs of physical activities.[7] The lower-order objectives focus on the acquisition of basic movements and perceptual abilities. The higher-order objectives emphasize the development of fitness and highly skilled movements, as well as increased creativity in the use of these movements. (The Psychomotor Domain box lists the objectives of this domain.)

The acquisition of motor skills is one focus of the psychomotor domain.
Racheal Grazias/Shutterstock

THE PSYCHOMOTOR DOMAIN

Category	Description	Application
1. Imitation	Observing and patterning behavior after someone else, perhaps with low-quality performance.	**PE**–After the physical education teacher demonstrates the shooting technique in basketball, the students imitate her performance without a ball, then with a ball in self-space before they can shoot at the basket. **Ex Sci**–Members of a yoga class follow the instructor's directions as they move from a Downward Dog into a Warrior II pose. **Sport**–A volleyball coach demonstrates the approach to the spike and then has his players repeatedly perform the same approach (without a ball) before they participate in a spiking drill.
2. Manipulation	Ability to perform certain actions by following instructions and practicing.	**PE**–In a basketball shooting drill, the students shoot from self-selected distances (marked by poly spots) without a defender for 10 minutes at the beginning of each class period. **Ex Sci**–Members of a yoga class make up their own warm-up pattern, which consists of four different poses, at the start of each class. **Sport**–A softball coach demonstrates a soft toss drill to the team so that the players can work on their hand-eye coordination. The players get into six small groups and perform the same drill following the coach's instructions.
3. Precision	Refining; becoming more exact, with few apparent errors.	**PE**–Students repeatedly practice their gymnastics routine until it has seamless transitions and solid beginning and ending poses, and each movement has appropriate body alignment. **Ex Sci**–A client practices keeping her body straight and bending her elbows at a 90-degree angle as she attempts 10 traditional push-ups daily. **Sport**–A golfer reviews video clips of his putting technique. He adjusts the speed of his backswing as he hits golf balls from the same distance with the goal of getting 40 out of 50 into the cup.
4. Articulation	Coordinating a series of actions; achieving harmony and internal consistency.	**PE**–Students create a line dance that aligns to the beat of the music. **Ex Sci**–As a warm-up, a client jumps rope for 3 minutes consecutively without tripping over the rope or stopping due to fatigue. **Sport**–During a baseball game, the defensive team completes a perfect relay from right field to get the runner out at home.
5. Naturalization	Performing at a high level automatically, without needing to think much about it.	**PE**–During a soccer game, students move without the ball to create space and get open to receive a pass from their teammates. **Ex Sci**–A runner records negative splits over a 10-mile course without checking the time after each mile. **Sport**–A quarterback changes the offensive play call after noticing that the defense is setting up to blitz.

Motor Skill Development

The development of motor skills is sometimes referred to as the development of neuromuscular or psychomotor skills because effective movement depends on the harmonious working together of the muscular and nervous systems. The acquisition and refinement of motor skills essential for everyday activities such as posture and lifting and for movement in a variety of physical activities, such as dance, sports, aquatics, or outdoor pursuits, are important outcomes of motor skill development. The development of motor skills focuses on helping individuals learn how to move effectively to accomplish specific goals efficiently, that is, with as little expenditure of energy as possible.

Motor skill development is a sequential process that occurs throughout one's lifespan. Infants possess reflexive, involuntary movements that are replaced with voluntary movements as they mature. Fundamental movements, such as running and throwing, begin to develop in early childhood around the time the child can walk independently. These fundamental motor skills progress through various stages, such as imitation and manipulation, leading to the mature form of the skill. As children progress through these stages, they exhibit a greater degree of competency in their movements, the movements become more precise, and fewer errors occur.

Fundamental movements form the basis for the development of specialized motor and sport skills in the later childhood years. Fundamental movements such as running, kicking, trapping, and dodging now can be articulated and applied to a sport such as soccer. Movements such as running, striking, and sliding can be incorporated into a game of tennis. In these situations, increased demands are placed on the individual with respect to form, speed, accuracy, and complexity of skill performance. If we are to achieve our goal of lifespan participation in physical activity, careful attention must be paid to the development of each individual's motor skills. As our programs expand to meet the needs of people of all identities, from preschoolers to the elderly, we must be prepared to promote the acquisition and refinement of motor skills in diverse populations.

Sports, aquatics, and dance give individuals enjoyable activities for use during their free time. They offer a pleasurable means to relax after work and are popular recreational pursuits on the weekends. Development of motor skills for participation in sport and recreational activities is important for all people, including individuals with disabilities. Professionals in all settings must be prepared to teach individuals with a diversity of needs and to modify activities and instructional strategies to be appropriate to the abilities of the individuals with whom they are working. Challenging activities that lead to skill development and meaningful participation are essential to providing a positive learning experience for all individuals, including those with special needs.

Physical Fitness Development

The evidence supporting the contribution of physical activity and health-related fitness to well-being and quality of life is overwhelming. Development and maintenance of physical fitness has long been heralded as one of the most important outcomes of school physical education programs. Fitness promotion is the focus of many nonschool physical education, exercise science, and sport programs as well.

A progressive, systematic approach to the development of physical fitness should be used. First and foremost, the program should consider the needs of the individual. Based on these needs, the program should be designed to accomplish the desired outcomes. Careful attention should be given to helping individuals identify and develop proficiency in activities that are enjoyable and meaningful to them while contributing to the attainment of fitness. This will encourage individuals to make these activities an integral part of their lifestyle.

If we are to accomplish our objectives related to physical fitness, a multifaceted approach is needed. Obviously, we must teach exercises and activities that promote fitness. However, this is not enough. Through our programs, individuals must acquire the knowledge to design and modify their fitness program to meet their changing needs. Moreover, our

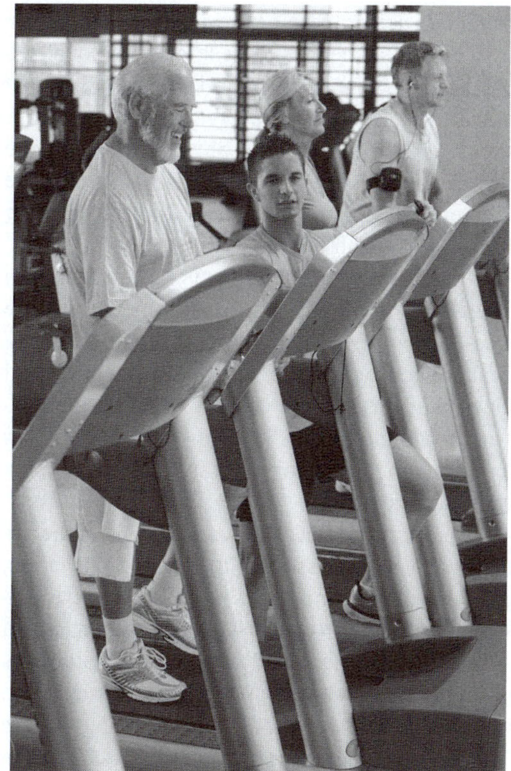

Improving fitness is an important goal of many worksite health promotion programs.

Bounce/Cultura/Getty Images

programs must instill within each individual the desire to make fitness a lifelong pursuit, the enjoyment of physical activity, and the appreciation of the value of leading a healthy, active lifestyle.

ASSESSMENT OF LEARNING

How do professionals determine whether the participants in their physical education, exercise science, and sport programs have achieved the stated objectives? How do we diagnose the needs of the individuals engaged in our programs? How do participants know when they have accomplished their goals? What changes can we make in our programs to be more effective? How can we show the worth of our programs in this era of accountability? How can we, as professionals, enhance our own abilities to meet the needs of participants in our programs? Assessment enables us to answer these and many other important questions.

Assessment should be a dynamic, ongoing process integrated into programs and viewed as an essential, crucial element of any program. The development of quality physical education, exercise science, and sport programs requires establishing clear goals, assessing participants' needs, setting specific objectives, planning learning experiences, providing effective instruction, and evaluating the outcomes.

Assessment can yield important information about participants' progress, program quality, instructional practices, and the effectiveness of professionals. Evaluation promotes accountability. Participants are accountable for their performance and professionals are accountable for participants' achievements. Today more than ever, demonstrating the worth and value of our programs is critical. Assessment is central to this purpose because it provides meaningful information about learning and achievement related to goals, objectives, and outcomes across the learning domains.

Assessment Defined

Assessment is the process of gathering information to learn what participants know and are able to do, in order to determine their progress toward achievement of goals and objectives. *Measurement* is the process of gathering information or collecting data. *Evaluation* is the process of interpreting the information or data.

Assessment encompasses a variety of measurement, evaluation, and assessment techniques that have as their primary purpose the gathering and interpretation of information. This information is used to make decisions that will enhance the outcomes achieved and the experiences of participants in physical education, exercise science, and sport programs.

Purposes of Assessment

The main purposes of assessment include diagnosis, placement, monitoring of progress, determination of achievement, motivation, program improvement,

ASSESSMENT

Assessment is the process of gathering information to learn what participants know and are able to do in order to determine their progress toward achievement of goals and objectives.

Purposes of Assessment

- Diagnosis
- Placement
- Monitoring of progress
- Determination of achievement
- Motivation
- Program improvement
- Evaluation of leadership effectiveness

and evaluation of instructor effectiveness. (See the Assessment box for a definition and list of purposes of assessment.)

Diagnosis is one of the most important uses of assessment. Diagnostic procedures can be used to identify individuals' strengths and weaknesses, levels of abilities, and developmental status in the various domains. When working with children with disabilities, the adapted physical activity specialist may use the Test of Gross Motor Development 3 (TGMD-3) to measure children's locomotor and object control motor development. A sport psychologist working with an intercollegiate athletic team to improve its performance uses several survey tests to find out athletes' satisfaction, perception of team climate, attentional styles, and leadership roles. Additional knowledge gleaned from interviews of the athletes and coaches and from personal observation of the team during practice and games helps the sport psychologist identify factors limiting the team's achievement.

Exercise and physical activity prescription uses diagnostic information to design programs to meet identified needs. A cardiac rehabilitation specialist uses the results of an exercise stress test to prescribe an exercise program for the postcardiac patient. A personal trainer reviews the various assessments of a client's fitness level, nutritional status, and lifestyle habits, and then designs an individualized wellness program for the client. Working with the athlete's physician, an athletic trainer plans a program of exercise to restore the full range of motion to an athlete who is recovering from a rotator cuff injury.

Classification, or placement of individuals into groups based on their abilities, is another purpose of assessment. For children with disabilities, assessment influences their educational placement and the type of services they receive. Sport activity instructors commonly assign people to ability groups for instruction, believing that same-ability grouping facilitates learning.

Determination of achievement is one of the primary purposes of assessment. Physical education, exercise science, and sport programs involve purposeful activity directed toward the attainment of certain goals. Have the program participants achieved the stated objectives? Without assessment, how would we know whether our participants have achieved the desired objectives? Assessment can provide an indicator of achievement at the end of a program. When assessment is done at both the beginning and the end of the program, improvement can be seen. Incorporation of various assessment techniques throughout the program allows for the tracking of participants' progress.

Another purpose of assessment is program evaluation. Assessment can provide evidence of the effectiveness of the program. Corporate fitness directors can document the progress and concomitant health gains made by employees enrolled in the program. This lets the employer know whether the program is beneficial to the employees and whether the investment in the program has yielded cost savings. This more global approach can also be used to improve the program. From this perspective, items such as program content, progression of instructional experiences, administration and organization, facilities and equipment, and time allocation are addressed as part of the overall program assessment. This enables professionals to make improvements in their programs to heighten their effectiveness.

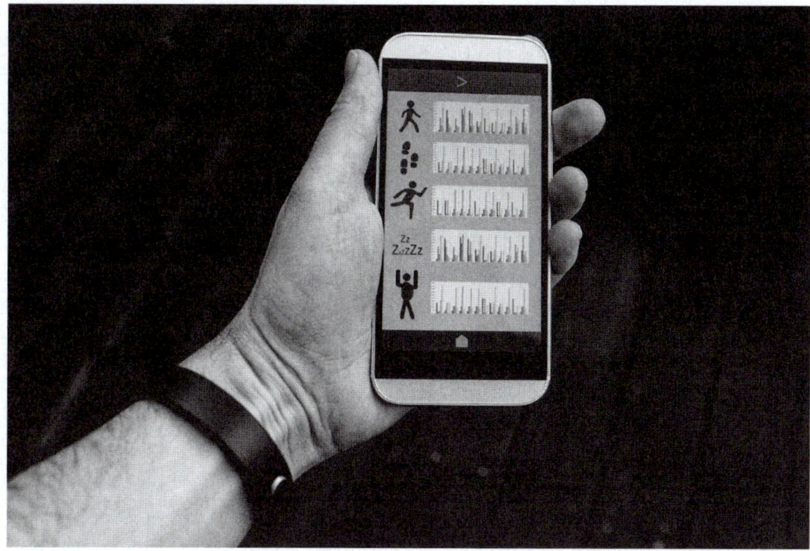

Smart-phone apps and fitness tracker wristbands are increasing in popularity. This technology makes it easier for people to monitor their workout and self-assess their fitness status.
mikkelwilliam/iStock/Getty Images

Professionals who care deeply about their professional endeavors reflect upon all the information gathered via the assessment process to improve their own effectiveness. They might ask themselves, "Are there any changes that I can make in my presentation? Is the order of the instructional tasks the best sequence to enhance participants' developments? Do I need to give participants more guidance?" These and other questions can help professionals enhance their effectiveness and thus influence the outcomes of the participants in their programs.

CURRENT TRENDS: MOVING TOWARD THE FUTURE

- As disciplines within the field of kinesiology continue to evolve, a wider range of professional philosophies will be developed to guide current and future professionals.
- National health and physical activity goals, such as those that form the foundation of *Healthy People 2030* and the National Physical Activity Plan, will provide broad and specific guidelines for individuals across the lifespan on how to lead a healthy and physically active lifestyle.
- Smart-phone apps and physical activity wristbands are increasing individuals' interest in their physical activity levels as the apps and watches provide immediate access to their fitness outcomes.

SUMMARY

Philosophy is influenced by our social identities and systems of meaning and is critical to our endeavors. The major branches of philosophy include metaphysics, epistemology, logic, axiology, ethics, and aesthetics. Philosophies such as idealism, realism, pragmatism, naturalism, existentialism, and humanism have influenced the nature and practice of physical education, exercise science, and sport programs. Over the years, the philosophy

of education through the physical has significantly influenced the design and conduct of our programs.
Sport philosophy emerged as a specialized area of study in the mid-1960s and 1970s. As this area grew, emphasis shifted from philosophical issues associated with physical education in schools to the study of sport. Sport philosophers use logic and critical reasoning to study the meaning of physical activity and the mind-body relationship. As this discipline matured, the philosophical study of physical activity broadened.

Each professional should develop their own philosophy. One's philosophy influences the goals and objectives or outcomes sought from one's programs and the methods by which these goals and objectives are attained. Goals are broad statements of aims that reflect desired accomplishments. Objectives are more specific statements of outcomes that build progressively to the achievement of the goals.

Human behavior is often described with reference to learning domains: cognitive, affective/social, and psychomotor domains. Taxonomies organize the objectives associated with each domain into hierarchies. These taxonomies guide professionals in designing programs to meet the needs of their participants. Physical education, exercise science, and sport programs contribute in many ways to learning in these three domains.

Assessment of learning is critical in physical education, exercise science, and sport. Assessment is a continual process that serves many purposes. These include diagnosis, prescription, classification, determination of achievement, documentation of progress, enhancement of motivation, program improvement, and professional development. There are many types of assessment methods for professionals to utilize.

Chapter 3 will discuss the role of physical education, exercise science, and sport in our society.

Discussion Questions

1. Of the six major philosophies, which one do you identify with the most? Why do you identify with this philosophy? How does this philosophy align with your social identities and systems of meaning? How do you think your philosophical perspective can impact you as a future professional?
2. As a physical educator, exercise scientist, or sport leader, how do you develop goals and objectives for your program? How do these goals and objectives align with your professional philosophy?
3. Describe how assessment aligns with program goals and objectives. What assessments would you use to learn whether your students, clients, or players have met the goals and objectives?

GET CONNECTED

Cooper Institute–information about the Fitnessgram and Activitygram assessments, fitness resources, and research.

http://www.cooperinstitute.org/

International Association for the Philosophy of Sport–the website for the organization offers access to resources related to the philosophy of sport, including a blog of current news.

http://www.iaps.net/ > Resources

Society of Health and Physical Education (SHAPE) America–SHAPE America offers information about national standards for physical education as well as coaches, codes of conduct for sport and physical education, and position papers related to philosophical issues such as fitness for physical activity professionals and the use of physical activity for punishment. The national standards were revised in 2014.

https://www.shapeamerica.org/

Self-Assessment Activities

These activities are designed to help you determine whether you have mastered the material and competencies presented in this chapter.

1. Compare the characteristics of physical education, exercise science, and sport programs guided by each of the major philosophies: idealism, realism, pragmatism, naturalism, existentialism, and humanism.
2. Using the Developing Your Professional Philosophy box, attempt to write your philosophy of physical education, exercise science, or sport. Reflect on your social identities, systems of meaning, and lived experiences; review various philosophies; and take time to talk with some of your professors about their philosophy.
3. Reflect on your experiences in youth, interscholastic, and intercollegiate sport. How did these experiences contribute to your development in the cognitive, affective/social, and psychomotor domains? What changes could have been made in the programs to further enhance your development in each of the domains?
4. Refer to the 12 Steps to Understanding Research Reports box located in Chapter 1. Before you complete a 12 Step, first select an original research article (quantitative or qualitative) of a topic of your interest. Describe how and why you selected this article as well as why it is considered an original research article.

References

1. Mechikoff, R. A. (2013). *A history and philosophy of sport and physical education: From ancient civilizations to the modern world* (6th ed.). New York, NY: McGraw Hill.
2. Siedentop, D., & van der Mars, H. (2011). *Introduction to physical education, fitness, and sport* (8th ed.). New York, NY: McGraw Hill.
3. U.S. Department of Health and Human Services. (2020). *Healthy people 2030.* Washington, D.C.: U.S. Government Printing Office.
4. Anderson L. W., & Krathwohl, D. A. (2011). *Taxonomy for learning, teaching and assessing: A revision of Bloom's taxonomy of educational objectives.* New York, NY: Longman.
5. Krathwohl, D. R., Bloom, B. S., & Masia, B. B. (1964). *Taxonomy of educational objectives, handbook II: Affective domain.* New York, NY: David McKay.
6. Hellison, D. R. (2010). *Teaching personal and social responsibility through physical activity* (3rd ed.). Champaign, IL: Human Kinetics.
7. Dave, R. H. (1970). Psychomotor levels. In R. J. Armstrong (Ed.), *Developing and writing behavioral objectives* (p. 33). Tucson, AZ: Educational Innovators Press.

Polka Dot Images/Getty Images

CHAPTER 3

HEALTH AND PHYSICAL ACTIVITY IN OUR SOCIETY

OBJECTIVES

After reading this chapter, students should be able to–

- Describe the changing demographics of the United States and their implications for physical education, exercise science, and sport.
- Explain the importance and need for professionals in physical education, exercise science, and sport in the promotion of health and the attainment of wellness.
- Identify and discuss the physical activity of people of all identities and the implications for professionals in physical education, exercise science, and sport.

Societal trends influence professions and professionals in physical education, exercise science, and sport. One significant trend is the changing demographics of our population. Our society is more culturally diverse than at any other time in its history. This diversity will become even greater as we move farther into the twenty-first century. Two other societal trends that hold implications for physical education, exercise science, and sport are the wellness and fitness and physical activity movements. The wellness movement emphasizes the individual's potential opportunity to make informed choices that will lead to an optimal state of health. Disease prevention and health promotion are the cornerstones of this movement. In the fitness and physical activity movement, participation in physical activity by people of all social identities is encouraged. There is substantial evidence to support the value of leading a physically active lifestyle across the lifespan.

CHANGING DEMOGRAPHICS

The United States is in the midst of demographic changes that will profoundly influence our future as a nation and will greatly affect the nature and conduct of physical education, exercise science, and sport programs.[1,2] Our growing diversity requires that we–as physical educators, exercise scientists, and sport

SOCIAL JUSTICE

Talking Points

- Professionals will need to develop and engage in cultural humility when working with individuals who have different social identities and cultural backgrounds and experiences as you.
- Individuals with a higher socioeconomic status have the financial means to purchase a health club membership and/or fitness equipment to improve their health, whereas people who cannot afford such luxuries have limited access and opportunity and have a more difficult time taking care of their overall wellness.
- Community access to physical activity opportunities need to be made available to all individuals regardless of geographic location (urban, rural, suburban), social status, age, race, and ethnicity.
- Sport is prominent in the US culture for youth, adolescents, and young adults; particularly those who can afford to partake in such sport programs. Affordable sport programs, in a variety of communities, need to be offered across all age groups.

leaders–be able to work effectively in cross-cultural situations. Changes within and among different population groups, such as children and older adults, determine the demand for education, health care, facilities, and other services that meet the needs of different segments of the population. This, in turn, will influence job opportunities, funding for services, and the nature and conduct of programs designed to serve these populations.

As a nation, our cultural diversity continues to grow. The surge in immigration increased our diversity tremendously. The 2020 census data revealed that 18% of the population was of Hispanic and Latino origin, and 82% of the population was non-Hispanic.[1] With respect to non-Hispanic races, 72.3% of the population was white, 12.7% of the population was Black or African American, 0.8% American Indian or Alaskan Native, 5.6% Asian, and 0.2% Native Hawaiian and other Pacific Islanders.[1] A total of 3.3% of the population identified themselves as multiracial. It is predicted that by 2060, the US population will grow to 404 million, 50% of which will be of non-Hispanic white origin.[1] Despite this growing population, by 2030, one out of every five Americans will be 65 and older; the number of children will be less than the older adult population for the first time, and the US population will continue to grow, but at a slower than ever before.[1] Immigration will impact the growing population. The Hispanic population is the fastest growing of any racial and ethnic group, and it is estimated that 27.5% of the population will be Hispanic by the year 2060.[1]

Dramatic racial and ethnic changes are expected in the school-age population. In 2015, 73% of public school students were non-white Hispanic. Black and Hispanic students accounted for 14.4% and 26%, respectively, of public school enrollment.[3] The changes in the racial and ethnic composition of student enrollments have altered the diversity of language and culture in the nation's schools. In 2018, 10.2% of all students, or 5 million, were identified as English Language Learners.[4] There are several school systems in the United States where more than 100 languages are spoken by the students. The variety in culture and language enriches the learning environment while at the same time creating great challenges for the schools.

Socioeconomic status exerts a significant influence on many aspects of an individual's life, including health status, educational attainment, and future employment. Poverty is associated with poor health outcomes for all identities, including higher rates of mortality. Unfortunately, many adults and children live in poverty today, and poverty rates vary by race, gender, age, ethnicity, family composition, and

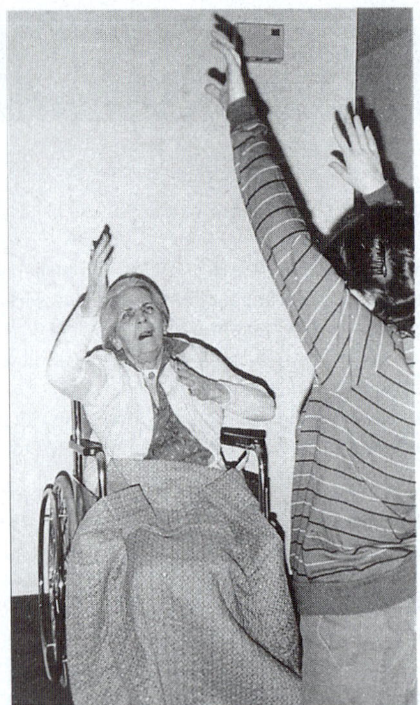

Participation in appropriate exercise can help elderly people increase their flexibility.
Sarah Rich

employment. Poverty level differs by the size of the household. The 2022 poverty guideline was an annual income of $13,590 for a single person and $27,750 for a family of four.[1] In 2019, 11.4% of the population lived below the poverty level. The poverty rate for white non-Hispanics was 7.3%, for Blacks 18.8%, for Hispanics 15.7%, and for Asians and Pacific Islanders 7.3%.*

The 2020 census demonstrated how our society continues to become more culturally diverse across all demographic groupings. This increase in cultural diversity will have implications on our physical education, exercise science, and sport programs. For the first time in over a century, our life expectancy has decreased, which has certainly been impacted by the extensive number of deaths due to COVID-19. The population of children will remain stable; however, our country as a whole will continue to get older, and poverty rates will remain daunting if our economic disparity does not narrow across class stratifications. Over the next few decades, our country will continue to see a shift in the demographics of our population, which will continue to increase our cultural diversity.

Cultural Humility and Social Justice

The many demographic changes that are occurring in the twenty-first century present professionals with great challenges and with extraordinary opportunities. As we reflect on these demographic and societal changes, we must ask ourselves what we can do to provide opportunities for participation in physical activity for all people. How can we involve a greater number of older people in our programs? How can we design programs that are sensitive to the values and needs of different racial and ethnic populations? How can we provide access to our programs for individuals living in poverty? How do we reach underserved populations, and, most importantly, what is our commitment to doing so? Attainment of our goal of lifespan participation in physical activity for all people requires that we do much more than we are currently doing to reach people of all ages, socioeconomic backgrounds, and different population groups.

DeSensi defines cultural diversity as the

> differences associated with gender, race, national origin, ethnicity, social class, religion, age, and ability/disability, but it can also be extended to include differences in personality, sexual orientation, veteran status, physical appearance, marital status, and parental status.[5]

DeSensi's broad definition embraces many different groups. As you reflect on this definition, do you feel prepared to work with culturally diverse populations, whether in a school, community, sport, health care, or private setting? Do you consider yourself culturally competent, and do you demonstrate cultural humility?

Culture plays a complex, significant role in the health and well-being of people of all identities. Culture influences an individual's health, beliefs, behaviors, activities, access to care, adherence to programs, and treatment outcomes. Communication between

---

*US Census Bureau (2022). United States poverty rates. Retrieved on February 15, 2022 from: https://aspe.hhs.gov/topics/poverty-economic-mobility/poverty-guidelines.

the professional and the client/player/student is influenced by cultural norms, including norms related to language and usage, eye contact, personal space, expression of symptoms and concerns, openness or extent of disclosure, and degree of formality in the interaction. As health is significantly influenced by cultural beliefs, cultural issues should be a major consideration in the design and implementation of health promotion and prevention services, including physical activity programs.

As you work toward being inclusive and equitable to all people regardless of their social identities, it is important to continuously reflect on your social identity and systems of meaning (see Chapter 1). This self-reflective process, along with self-evaluation and self-critique related to your interactions, experiences, beliefs, and biases toward people of similar and different culture and social identities, is referred to as cultural humility.[6] At this stage in your life and career, you may be just beginning your self-reflective process of how you are positioned within our society. You might be discussing topics of diversity, social issues, privilege, and marginalization for the first time in your life. Yet, as a future professional, it will be important that you take this cultural knowledge and become an advocate and activist for those who may be less fortunate than you, and who experience social inequalities and need your help to create change. This advocacy and works toward action are moving toward equity and justice. This is one of the challenges we will continue to face as professionals in our ever-changing world, and engaging in cultural humility will allow us to engage with the people with whom we work and educate.

When professionals practice culturally humility, they design and implement programs that appropriately serve people of diverse cultures in a manner that affirms participants' worth and dignity. Programs incorporate the values, traditions, and customs of the cultural group. Members of the cultural group are involved in meaningful ways in the creation and conduct of the health promotion or disease prevention program. Professionals respect individual rights, use effective communication skills that convey respect and sensitivity, and appreciate how diversity enriches our lives. When the culture of a specific population group or community is incorporated into programs, professionals are more likely to be effective in their efforts.

Cultural humility is important for coaches because it can enhance coach and player relationships and the level of comfort an individual feels on a team, which can ultimately influence performance.

Fuse/Getty Images

As a professional in the field, you need to recognize how culture and one's social identity influences their beliefs, behavior, and overall worldview. This recognition will help you work with individuals from different identities and backgrounds. For example, according to the National Collegiate Athletic Association (NCAA), in 2021, 78% of men and women coaches across all three divisions were white. Only 40% of head coaches were women. Furthermore, 90% of athletic directors were white, and 10% were female. These statistics inform us that minorities continue to be underrepresented in a sporting institution where many of the players do not have the same racial and gender identity as those who are leading them, which may bring to life cultural differences among these individuals.[7]

Within the school setting, there is a lot of diversity among students. However, there is significantly less diversity among faculty and staff. Currently, in the elementary and secondary schools, 53% of students are racial minorities. Yet, in 2017–2018, 79% of teachers were white.[8] Given the diversity inherent in the school setting, it is important that physical educators have the opportunity to develop the skills to work successfully with students with different social identities.

According to Burden, Hodge, O'Bryant, and Harrison, physical education professional preparation programs have a "responsibility to implement diversity training such that novice teachers are trained and socialized with culturally relevant content knowledge, pedagogy and management skills and multiple experiences teaching culturally, linguistically, and ethnically diverse learners."[9] Such training is critical if we are to achieve our goal of eliminating disparities in physical activity levels, improve the health of participants in our programs, and socialize our learners into being physically active throughout their lifespan.

WELLNESS MOVEMENT

Over the past 60 years, we have experienced tremendous changes in our approach to health, seen dramatic shifts in life expectancy, and acquired a greater understanding of the causes of diseases. Nationally, we have seen a growing emphasis on disease prevention and health promotion. These changes will be discussed throughout this section, as they have important implications for physical education, exercise science, and sport professionals and programs.

Wellness and Health

The wellness philosophy reflects a change from our traditional approach to health–freedom from disease. From this perspective, if an individual was not ill, they were considered healthy. However, in 1947, the World Health Organization (WHO) defined health as a "state of complete physical, mental, and social well-being and not merely the absence of disease and infirmity."[10] The WHO definition offered a broader, multidimensional perspective of health than the traditional freedom-from-illness approach.

In the latter part of the twentieth century, the holistic approach to health grew in popularity. Holistic health focuses on the whole person and encompasses the intellectual and spiritual dimensions of health in addition to the physical, mental, and social dimensions included in the WHO definition. From the holistic point of view, individuals who are healthy have achieved a high level of wellness.

Wellness is a state of optimal health and well-being. It is living life to the fullest and striving to achieve one's potential as a person. It is a state of being in which the individual's physical, emotional, social, mental, spiritual, and environmental aspects of health are in balance. See the Wellness Definitions box for definitions of each aspect of health.

WELLNESS DEFINITIONS

Physical	Refers to how one's body functions, freedom from disease, being active on a regular basis, following sound nutritional practices, maintaining a healthy body weight, and getting sufficient sleep.
Emotional	Enhances well-being through acceptance of one's feelings, appropriately expressing a wide range of emotions, and effectively managing stress.
Social	Emphasizes developing of interpersonal skills and healthy, fulfilling relationships as well as contributing to the welfare of others and one's community.
Mental	Is characterized by sound decision making skills, intellectual growth, and high self-esteem.
Spiritual	Reflects a sense of purpose in life and living in accordance with one's beliefs and values.
Environmental	Encompasses where an individual lives and works, including amount of noise, level of pollution, availability of safe places to walk, and type of housing.

Wellness emphasizes individuals' taking personal responsibility for their health and understanding how the choices they make impact their well-being. Many lifestyle choices we make, whether smoking tobacco or working out on a regular basis, influence our health and well-being, both on a daily scale and across our lifespan. However, while focusing on individual responsibility, the wellness approach to health recognizes that a multitude of forces–societal, genetic, environmental, and personal–interact to affect one's health. Living conditions, heredity, and societal issues such as poverty, access to education, and discrimination expose the inequities that are experienced by many and exert a significant influence on one's well-being.

Epidemiologic Shift

In the twentieth century, there was a gradual epidemiologic transition from infectious to chronic diseases as the leading causes of death. In 1900, the leading causes of death were influenza, pneumonia, tuberculosis, and gastrointestinal problems (e.g., diarrhea). Life expectancy was 47.3 years.

Half a century later, in 1950, life expectancy had drastically increased to 68 years due to the development of antibiotics, the availability of vaccines, and improvements in housing, sanitation, food and water supplies, and diet. In 2020, average life expectancy was 77 years.[11] Currently, the leading causes of death are chronic diseases, specifically heart disease, cancer, and stroke. However, in 2020, a new leading cause of death was COVID-19. It is likely that COVID-19 will also be a leading cause of death for 2021 and potentially 2022.[12]

As this epidemiologic shift from infectious to chronic diseases occurred, the role of risk factors in disease occurrence and early mortality received greater attention because those factors increase the likelihood of disease and health problems. Risk factors can be categorized as nonmodifiable or modifiable. Nonmodifiable risk factors are age, gender, race, ethnicity, and heredity. Modifiable risk factors include smoking, physical inactivity, diet, obesity, sun exposure, and alcohol use, to name a few. Modifiable risk factors are controllable. For some individuals, the choices we make and the habits we develop can influence our health and longevity. It is important to note that some healthy choices and habits are not always an option. More and more evidence shows that an individual's lifestyle influences the occurrence of chronic diseases such as heart disease, cancer, or diabetes.

Chronic Disease in the United States

In the United States, the Centers for Disease Control and Prevention (CDC) reports that "chronic diseases–such as cardiovascular disease (primarily heart disease and stroke), cancer, and diabetes–are among the most prevalent, costly, and preventable of all health problems.[12] See Figure 3-1 for the leading causes of death.

Two of the most prevalent chronic diseases are cardiovascular disease and cancer, the number one and two causes of death in the United States. Cardiovascular disease, which includes coronary and congestive heart disease, stroke, and hypertensive disease, is the number one killer of adults in the United States. Physical inactivity, poor nutrition, obesity, and tobacco and alcohol use contribute to cardiovascular disease.[13] Sedentary people have nearly twice the risk of cardiovascular disease as those who are active.[13] Smokers have twice as much risk of cardiovascular disease as nonsmokers.[13] Although the risk for inactivity and smoking is similar, the prevalence of inactivity in the nation is greater than the incidence of smoking. Cancer is the number two cause of death in the United States. According to the American Cancer Society, many of the 602,350 cancer deaths are related to poor nutrition, physical inactivity, overweight and obesity, and other lifestyle factors.[14] The top four modifiable causes of death in the United States are lack of physical activity, poor nutrition, tobacco use, and excessive alcohol consumption.[13] Addressing these modifiable risk factors will lead to improvement in the health of the nation.

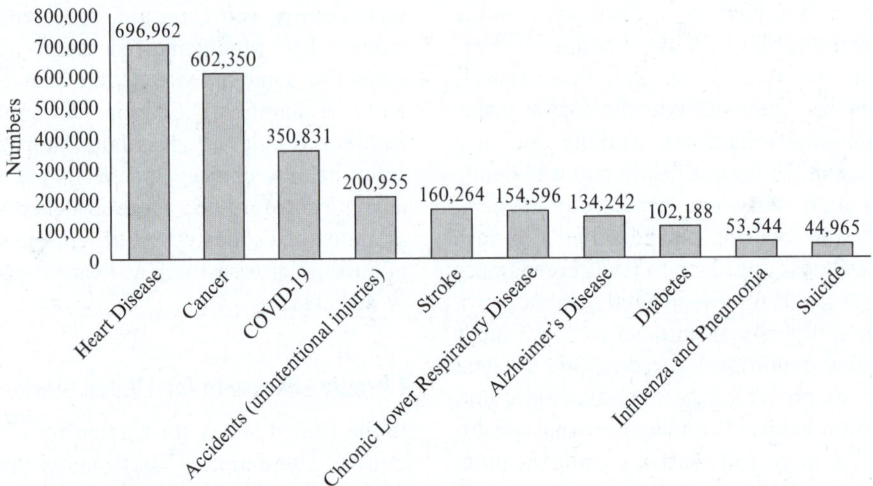

Figure 3-1 Leading causes of death in the United States in 2020.

Source: Data from the National Center for Health Statistics, February 2022.

Health Goals of the Nation

During the 1980s and 1990s, societal interest in promoting health and preventing disease increased. The accumulation of evidence supported the fact that changes in behavior could reduce individuals' risk of disease, increase their span of healthy life, and improve their quality of life. This evidence stimulated the growth of national disease prevention and health promotion initiatives.

The latest report, *Healthy People 2030*,[15] stresses improvement of the health of the nation through a comprehensive approach that emphasizes health promotion and disease prevention. The underlying premise of *Healthy People 2030* is that everyone in our society lives long, healthy lives.[15]

Have the national Healthy People initiatives been successful? These past four decades have seen dramatic progress in improving the nation's health. Infant mortality rates significantly declined, childhood vaccinations rose to an all-time high, and death rates for coronary heart disease and stroke decreased.[15] Yet, heart disease remains the nation's number one killer. Diabetes continues to be a serious health problem, and all too often mental health disorders go undiagnosed and untreated.[15] Too many people still smoke, obesity among children and adults continues to rise, and too few people eat a balanced diet and are physically active enough to gain health benefits. Yes, for some people, this is attributed to personal choice, but for many, it is due to poverty and lack of access to healthy foods and safe spaces to exercise. *Healthy People 2030* is a blueprint for improving the health of individuals and the health status of the nation.

In the United States, the National Health and Nutrition Examination Survey (NHANES), conducted periodically since 1960, tracks the prevalence of overweight and obese youths and adults. The NHANES results indicate that overweight and obesity among adults have risen to an all-time high (see Figure 3-2). In 2017–2018, 42.5% of adults were obese in the United States, which is a dramatic increase from the 1970s, when 14.6% of adults were obese.[16] These statistics signify the incline in obesity over the past 40 years, particularly the staggering increase in the proportion of obese adults, which has more than doubled.

Obesity among children and adolescents has also reached a record high, about 19.3% (see Figure 3-3). In 2017–2018, it was estimated that 13.4% of children aged 2 to 5, 20.3% of children aged 6 to 11, and 21.2% of adolescents aged 12 to 19 were

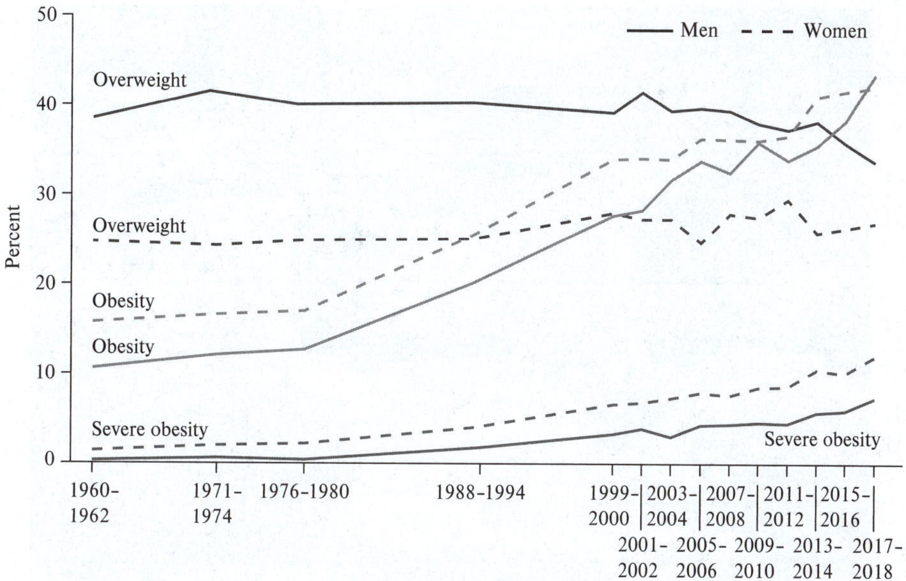

Figure 3-2 Obesity trends among US adults: BMI ≥ 30, or about 30 pounds overweight for 5′4″ person.
Source: Behavioral Risk Factor Surveillance System, CDC, 1990, 2000, 2010.

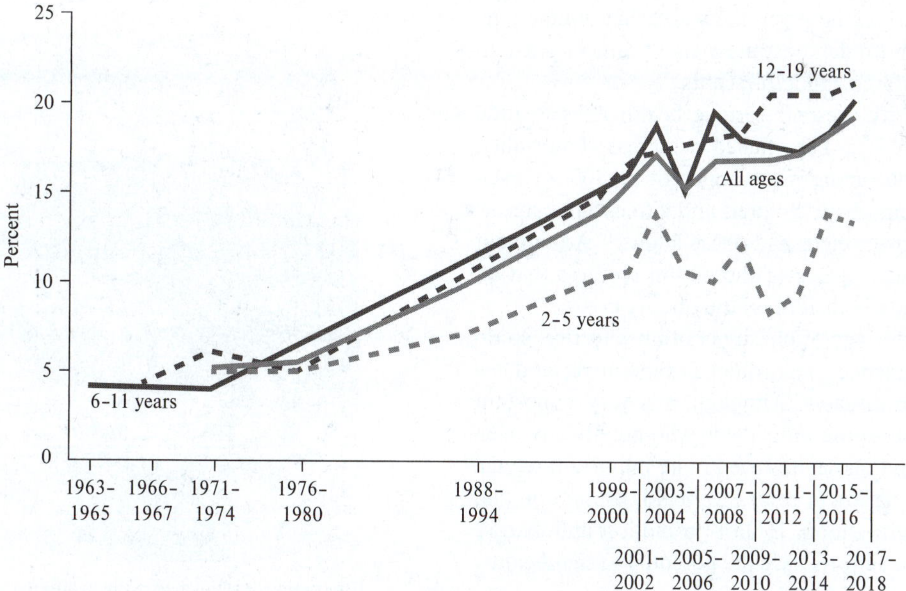

Figure 3-3 Percentage of children and adolescents with obesity: 2018.
Source: National Center for Health Statistics.

Fast foods and large portion sizes contribute to the increase in obesity in our society.
John Flournoy/McGraw Hill

obese.* The biggest and most concerning change that has occurred with children and adolescents' weight is that in 2003–2004, the results were based on *overweight*; however, the staggering numbers reported above demonstrate a significant increase in *obese* children and adolescents.

Obesity presents serious health risks to individuals and has been linked to increased mortality. This is becoming more apparent as 80% of overweight and obese children and adolescents are becoming overweight and obese adults.[16] Attainment of the health goals of the nation requires that efforts be made to address the obesity crisis.

As the rate of obesity continues to rise, so do the prevalence of chronic, degenerative, and hypokinetic diseases. Although it is very important to educate those individuals who are already overweight and obese, it is even more important to educate our nation in regard to health promotion and disease prevention. Health promotion and disease prevention efforts have the potential to significantly constrain the enormous and rapidly escalating cost of health care in the United States. In 1999, health care expenditures totaled $1.2 trillion and

*Centers for Disease Control and Prevention. (2022). Childhood obesity facts. https://www.cdc.gov/obesity/data/childhood.html.

Being physically active early in life helps build lifelong habits.
Jennifer L. Walton-Fisette

consumed more than 13% of the US gross national product (GNP), more than any other industrialized nation.[17] Most recently, in 2018, health care expenditures reached $3.6 trillion.[17]

A focused effort is needed if the *Healthy People 2030* objectives and recommendations are to be met. Americans show limited progress in achieving previous goals, objectives, and recommendations suggested by *Healthy People* and calls to action from the nation's administration. As you will see in the next section on physical activity and fitness, too many people across social identities are inactive, fail to achieve the recommended amount of regular physical activity, make unhealthy food choices, and are overweight or obese. This is cause for great concern as we continue in the second decade of the twenty-first century.

Implications of the Wellness Movement

Physical education, exercise science, and sport programs provide an avenue for people of all social identities to be active and to acquire the skills, knowledge, and values conducive to leading a physically active lifestyle. If the health of the nation is to be improved, effective use must be made up of school health and physical education programs. The schools provide an efficient means to reach over 50 million students a year. As professionals, we must be strong, passionate spokespeople on behalf of physical education and sport. The decline in the number of children participating in daily physical education must be reversed. Quality programs are critical to this effort. The inclusion of physical education as an integral component of a comprehensive school physical activity program is another approach to increasing physical education programs. During these impressionable years, much can be done by schools and parents working together to lay the groundwork for healthy living as an adult.

The school setting also offers a means to reach adults. Over 5 million adults are employed by the schools in both instructional and noninstructional positions. More schools are offering worksite health promotion programs, similar to those found in corporations, to their employees. These programs often encompass fitness promotion, skill development, and health education.

The use of the school as a community center has not reached its full potential. Although more schools are opening their doors to the community during evening hours, on the weekend, and during the summer, many schools remain unused and others underutilized. The use of the school as a community center would enable us to reach adults and offer a diversity of programs to meet their needs. Moreover, school-based adult programs offer a means to bring physical activity and sport experiences to adults who lack the financial resources to join a fitness club or do not have a program at their worksite. They provide an avenue to reach people within the community. Programs can be designed to focus on the needs of people of all ages, ranging from young adults to the older adults, at a minimal cost. Other programs can be started that foster family participation, emphasizing children and parents participating in activities together.

Worksite health promotion programs have grown tremendously. Many worksite programs have increased their scope of offerings from just a fitness program to include an array of different activities. Programs vary but may include fitness programs, recreation activities, and health promotion programs such as cancer and hypertension screening, nutritional counseling, smoking

Physical education plays a critical role in educating millions of children on the skills and knowledge to be physically activity for a lifetime.

FatCamera/CEFutcher/iStockphoto/Getty Images

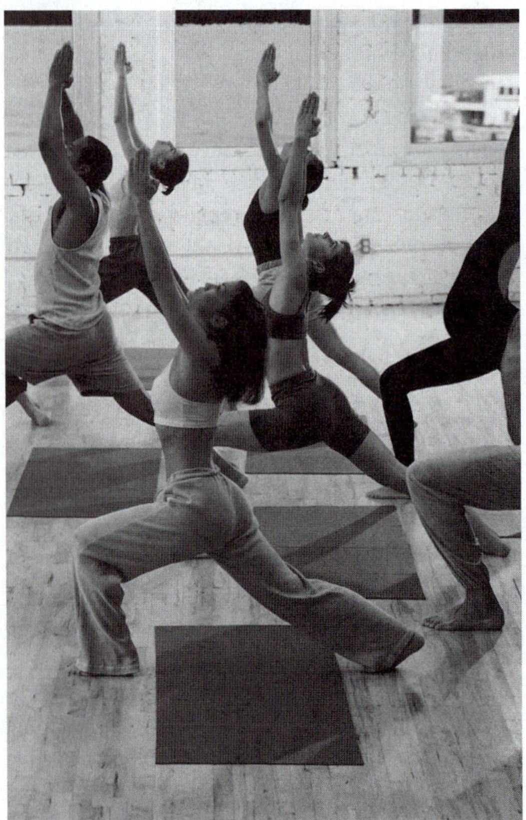

Selecting activities that are enjoyable is a good approach to developing health-fitness components.
Ryan McVay/Photodisc/Getty Images

cessation, and mental health. Another change is that businesses have moved from viewing these programs as the perks of upper management to making these programs available to employees at all levels. This growth of programs has led to an increase in career opportunities in this sector.

Commercial fitness clubs and community agency programs, such as those at the YMCA, are growing. Although these programs were initially targeted toward adults, they are now reaching out to the elderly and preschool children. These programs provide instruction in skills, encourage the development of fitness, offer education, and strive to promote regular participation.

FITNESS AND PHYSICAL ACTIVITY MOVEMENT

The fitness and physical activity movement, which began as a trend in the 1970s, has over five decades later grown to be an enduring feature of our society. People of all social identities are participating in fitness and sport activities to an extent not witnessed before in this country.

However, when data about participation are closely examined, the widespread extent of physical activity and fitness in American society is not supported. As previously stated, available data show that many children and adults are leading sedentary lives.

In 1996, *Physical Activity and Health: The Surgeon General's Report* was released.[18] This landmark document convincingly set forth the contribution physical activity can make to the health and lives of all people. The contribution of physical activity to health continues to be the primary focus of the most recent *Physical Activity Guidelines for Americans* (2018)[19] and the US National Physical Activity Plan (2016).[20]

Several key messages are presented in these documents:

- People of all ages can benefit from physical activity.
- People can improve their health by engaging in a moderate amount of physical activity on a regular basis.
- Greater health benefits can be achieved by increasing the amount of physical activity, through changing the duration, frequency, or intensity of effort.

The *Physical Activity Guidelines for Americans* (see box)[18] recommend that children, adolescents, and adults engage in moderate to vigorous physical activity each week. Children and adolescents (aged 6 to 17) are recommended to engage in 60 minutes of moderate physical activity daily and vigorous physical activity three times a week. It is also recommended that they engage in muscle- and bone-strengthening activity 3 days a week. Adults (aged 18 to 64) are recommended to

NATIONAL PHYSICAL ACTIVITY PLAN 2016 STRATEGIES

Business and Industry

Strategy 1: Businesses should provide employees opportunities and incentives to adopt and maintain a physically active lifestyle.

Strategy 2: Businesses should engage in cross-sectoral partnerships to promote physical activity within the workplace, and such efforts should extend to local communities and geographic regions.

Strategy 3: Professional and scientific societies should create and widely disseminate a concise, powerful, and compelling business case for investment in physical activity promotion.

Strategy 4: Professional and scientific societies should develop and advocate for policies that promote physical activity in workplace settings.

Strategy 5: Physical activity and public health professionals should support the development and deployment of surveillance systems that monitor physical activity in US workers and physical activity promotion efforts in US workplaces.

Community, Recreation, Fitness, and Parks

Strategy 1: Communities should develop new, and enhance existing, community recreation, fitness, and park programs that provide and promote healthy physical activity opportunities for diverse users across the lifespan.

Strategy 2: Communities should improve availability of and access to safe, clean, and affordable community recreation, fitness, and park facilities to support physical activity for all residents.

Strategy 3: Community recreation and park organizations, the fitness industry, and private business should recruit, train, and retain a diverse group of leaders, staff, and volunteers to promote, organize, lead, and advocate for initiatives that encourage physical activity in their communities.

Strategy 4: Community recreation and park organizations, the fitness industry, and private business should advocate for increased and sustainable funding and resources to create new, or enhance existing, physical activity facilities and services in areas of high need.

Strategy 5: Community recreation and park organizations and the for-profit and not-for-profit fitness industry should improve monitoring and evaluation of participation in community-based physical activity programs to gauge their effectiveness in promoting increased levels of physical activity for all.

Education

Strategy 1: States and school districts should adopt policies that support implementation of the Comprehensive School Physical Activity Program model.

Strategy 2: Schools should provide high-quality physical education programs.

Strategy 3: Providers of after-school, holiday, and vacation programs for children and youth should adopt policies and practices that ensure that participants are appropriately physically active.

Strategy 4: States should adopt standards for childcare and early childhood education programs to ensure that children ages 0 to 5 years are appropriately physically active.

Strategy 5: Colleges and universities should provide students and employees with opportunities and incentives to adopt and maintain physically active lifestyles.

Strategy 6: Educational institutions should provide preservice professional training and in-service professional development programs that prepare educators to deliver effective physical activity programs for students of all types.

Strategy 7: Professional and scientific organizations should develop and advocate for policies that promote physical activity among all students.

(Continued)

NATIONAL PHYSICAL ACTIVITY PLAN 2016 STRATEGIES (*Continued*)

Faith-Based Settings

Strategy 1: Faith-based organizations should identify effective applications of their health ministries to promote physical activity.

Strategy 2: Faith-based organizations should establish partnerships with organizations from other sectors to promote physical activity in a manner that is consistent with their values, beliefs, and practices.

Strategy 3: Large faith-based organizations should institutionalize physical activity promotion programs for their employees.

Strategy 4: Large faith-based organizations should identify or develop marketing materials tailored for faith community leaders to enhance their perceptions of the value of physical activity.

Strategy 5: Physical activity and public health organizations should partner with faith-based organizations in developing and delivering physical activity programs that are accessible to and tailored for diverse groups of constituents.

Strategy 6: Physical activity and public health organizations should create and maintain an electronic resource for faith-based organizations to access evidence-based programs and best practices for promoting physical activity in faith-based settings.

Health Care

Strategy 1: Health care systems should increase the priority of physical activity assessment, advice, and promotion.

Strategy 2: Health care systems and professional societies should establish the spectrum of physical inactivity to insufficient physical activity as a treatable and preventable condition with profound health and cost implications.

Strategy 3: Health care systems should partner with other sectors to promote access to evidence-based physical activity–related services and to reduce health disparities.

Strategy 4: Universities, postgraduate training programs, and professional societies should include basic physical activity education in the training of all health care professionals.

Mass Media

Strategy 1: Government health agencies, in collaboration with national nonprofit health organizations, should launch a national physical activity campaign to educate individuals about effective behavioral strategies for increasing physical activity.

Strategy 2: Physical activity professionals should partner with communication experts to develop mass communication messages and a standardized "brand" for promoting physical activity that is consistent with current federal physical activity guidelines.

Strategy 3: Professionals in physical activity and public health should inform mass media professionals about the effects of physical activity on health and on effective strategies for increasing physical activity at the individual and community levels.

Strategy 4: Professionals in physical activity and public health should optimize application of social media and emerging technologies in media campaigns to promote physical activity.

Public Health

Strategy 1: Public health organizations should develop and maintain a workforce with competence and expertise in physical activity and health and that has ethnic, cultural, and gender diversity.

Strategy 2: Public health agencies should create, maintain, and leverage cross-sectoral partnerships and coalitions that implement evidence-based strategies to promote physical activity.

(Continued)

NATIONAL PHYSICAL ACTIVITY PLAN 2016 STRATEGIES (*Continued*)

Strategy 3: Nonprofit public health organizations should engage in policy development and advocacy to elevate the priority of physical activity in public health practice, policy, and research.

Strategy 4: Public health agencies should expand monitoring of policy and environmental determinants of physical activity and the levels of physical activity in communities (surveillance), and should monitor implementation of public health approaches to promoting active lifestyles (evaluation).

Strategy 5: Public health organizations should disseminate tools and resources important to promoting physical activity, including resources that address the burden of disease due to inactivity, the implementation of evidence-based interventions, and funding opportunities for physical activity initiatives.

Strategy 6: Public health agencies should invest equitably in physical activity, commensurate with its impact on disease prevention and health promotion.

Sport

Strategy 1: Sports organizations should collaborate to establish a national policy that emphasizes the importance of sports as a vehicle for promoting and sustaining a physically active population.

Strategy 2: Sports organizations should establish an entity that can serve as a central resource to unify and strengthen stakeholders in the sports sector.

Strategy 3: Leaders in multiple sectors should expand access to recreational spaces and quality sports programming while focusing on eliminating disparities in access based on race, ethnicity, gender, disability, socioeconomic status, geography, age, and sexual orientation.

Strategy 4: Sports organizations should adopt policies and practices that promote physical activity, health, participant growth, and development of physical literacy.

Strategy 5: Sports organizations should ensure that sports programs are conducted in a manner that minimizes the risk of sports-related injuries and illnesses.

Strategy 6: Public health agencies, in collaboration with sports organizations, should develop and implement a comprehensive surveillance system for monitoring sports participation in all segments of the population.

Strategy 7: Coaches, game officials, parents, and caregivers should create safe and inclusive environments for sports participation that promote physical activity and health for youth and adult participants.

Strategy 8: Sports organizations should use advances in technology to enhance the quality of the sport experience for participants.

Transportation, Land Use, and Community Design

Strategy 1: Community planners should integrate active design principles into land-use, transportation, community, and economic development planning processes.

Strategy 2: Communities should change zoning laws to require or favor mixed-use developments that place common destinations within walking and bicycling distance of most residents and incorporate designated open space suitable for physical activity.

Strategy 3: Physical activity and public health organizations should advocate for funding and policies that increase active transportation and physical activity through greater investment in bicycle and pedestrian infrastructure and transit.

Strategy 4: Transportation and public health agencies should invest in and institutionalize the collection of data to inform policy and to measure the impacts of active transportation on physical activity, population health, and health equity.

Strategy 5: Transportation and public health agencies should implement initiatives to encourage, reward, and require more walking, bicycling, and transit use for routine transportation.

Source: National Physical Activity Plan, 2016, www.physicalactivityplan.org/.

engage in moderate-intensity exercise (150–300 minutes a week), vigorous-intensity aerobic physical activity (75–150 minutes a week), or an equivalent combination of moderate- and vigorous-intensity aerobic physical activity each week. Adults should also partake in muscle-strengthening activities twice a week.

The recommendation to include moderate-to-vigorous-intensity physical activity as part of one's daily schedule represents an effort to broaden the scope of physical activity recommendations. It is hoped that with additional opportunities to engage in beneficial physical activity, more people will participate. While participation in some cases is not of

PHYSICAL ACTIVITY GUIDELINES FOR AMERICANS 2018

Key Guidelines for Preschool-Aged Children

- Preschool-aged children (ages 3 through 5 years) should be physically active throughout the day to enhance growth and development.
- Adult caregivers of preschool-aged children should encourage active play that includes a variety of activity types.

Key Guidelines for Children and Adolescents

- It is important to provide young people opportunities and encouragement to participate in physical activities that are appropriate for their age, that are enjoyable, and that offer variety.
- Children and adolescents ages 6 through 17 years should do 60 minutes (1 hour) or more of moderate-to-vigorous physical activity daily:
  - Aerobic: Most of the 60 minutes or more per day should be either moderate or vigorous-intensity aerobic physical activity and should include vigorous intensity physical activity on at least 3 days a week.
  - Muscle-strengthening: As part of their 60 minutes or more of daily physical activity, children and adolescents should include muscle-strengthening physical activity on at least 3 days a week.
  - Bone-strengthening: As part of their 60 minutes or more of daily physical activity, children and adolescents should include bone-strengthening physical activity on at least 3 days a week.

Key Guidelines for Adults

- Adults should move more and sit less throughout the day. Some physical activity is better than none. Adults who sit less and do any amount of moderate-to-vigorous physical activity gain some health benefits.
- For substantial health benefits, adults should do at least 150 minutes (2 hours and 30 minutes) to 300 minutes (5 hours) a week of moderate intensity, or 75 minutes (1 hour and 15 minutes) to 150 minutes (2 hours and 30 minutes) a week of vigorous-intensity aerobic physical activity, or an equivalent combination of moderate- and vigorous-intensity aerobic activity. Preferably, aerobic activity should be spread throughout the week.
- Additional health benefits are gained by engaging in physical activity beyond the equivalent of 300 minutes (5 hours) of moderate-intensity physical activity a week.
- Adults should also do muscle-strengthening activities of moderate or greater intensity and that involve all major muscle groups on 2 or more days a week, as these activities provide additional health benefits.

Key Guidelines for Older Adults

The key guidelines for adults also apply to older adults. In addition, the following key guidelines are just for older adults:

- As part of their weekly physical activity, older adults should do multicomponent physical activity that includes balance training as well as aerobic and muscle strengthening activities.
- Older adults should determine their level of effort for physical activity relative to their level of fitness.

(Continued)

PHYSICAL ACTIVITY GUIDELINES FOR AMERICANS 2018 (*Continued*)

- Older adults with chronic conditions should understand whether and how their conditions affect their ability to do regular physical activity safely.
- When older adults cannot do 150 minutes of moderate-intensity aerobic activity a week because of chronic conditions, they should be as physically active as their abilities and conditions allow.

Key Guidelines for Women During Pregnancy and the Postpartum Period

- Women should do at least 150 minutes (2 hours and 30 minutes) of moderate-intensity aerobic activity a week during pregnancy and the postpartum period. Preferably, aerobic activity should be spread throughout the week.
- Women who habitually engaged in vigorous-intensity aerobic activity or who were physically active before pregnancy can continue these activities during pregnancy and the postpartum period.
- Women who are pregnant should be under the care of a health care provider who can monitor the progress of the pregnancy. Women who are pregnant can consult their health care provider about whether or how to adjust their physical activity during pregnancy and after the baby is born.

Key Guidelines for Adults with Chronic Health Conditions and Adults with Disabilities

- Adults with chronic conditions or disabilities, who are able, should do at least 150 minutes (2 hours and 30 minutes) to 300 minutes (5 hours) a week of moderate intensity, or 75 minutes (1 hour and 15 minutes) to 150 minutes (2 hours and 30 minutes) a week of vigorous-intensity aerobic physical activity, or an equivalent combination of moderate- and vigorous-intensity aerobic activity. Preferably, aerobic activity should be spread throughout the week.
- Adults with chronic conditions or disabilities, who are able, should also do muscle-strengthening activities of moderate or greater intensity and that involve all major muscle groups on 2 or more days a week, as these activities provide additional health benefits.
- When adults with chronic conditions or disabilities are not able to meet the above key guidelines, they should engage in regular physical activity according to their abilities and should avoid inactivity.
- Adults with chronic conditions or symptoms should be under the care of a health care provider. People with chronic conditions can consult a health care professional or physical activity specialist about the types and amounts of activity appropriate for their abilities and chronic conditions.

Key Guidelines for Safe Physical Activity

To do physical activity safely and reduce risk of injuries and other adverse events, people should:

- Understand the risks yet be confident that physical activity can be safe for almost everyone.
- Choose types of physical activity that are appropriate for their current fitness level and health goals, because some activities are safer than others.
- Increase physical activity gradually over time to meet key guidelines or health goals. Inactive people should "start low and go slow" by starting with lower intensity activities and gradually increasing how often and how long activities are done.
- Protect themselves by using appropriate gear and sports equipment, choosing safe environments, following rules and policies, and making sensible choices about when, where, and how to be active.
- Be under the care of a health care provider if they have chronic conditions or symptoms. People with chronic conditions and symptoms can consult a health care professional or physical activity specialist about the types and amounts of activity appropriate for them.

Source: https://health.gov/paguidelines/second-edition/.

sufficient intensity to develop cardiorespiratory fitness, being physically active does yield health benefits.

The emphasis on moderate-to-vigorous physical activity and the focus on integration of physical activity into one's lifestyle offer additional opportunities for sedentary individuals to improve their health through participation in physical activities that are enjoyable and personally meaningful, and fit more easily into their daily schedules. Healthy lifestyle patterns, including regular physical activity, should be developed when people are young. These lifestyle patterns can then be carried into adulthood, reducing the risk of disease. People who regularly participate in moderate amounts of physical activity can live longer, healthier lives. The most recent National Physical Activity Plan (NPAP) provides strategies and tactics for individuals across the lifespan on how to be physically active. These strategies and tactics are within societal sectors such as Business and Industry; Community Recreation, Fitness, and Parks; Education; Faith-Based Settings; Health Care; Mass Media; Sport; Public Health; and Transportation, Land Use, and Community Design (see the NPAP box to learn more about the strategies under each of these societal sectors). The NPAP's vision is that all Americans will become physically active and that we will have safe spaces that encourage and support us in doing so.[20]

Fitness and Physical Activity of Children and Youth

It is difficult to arrive at a clear picture of the fitness status and physical activity patterns of the nation's children and youth. The historical shift from performance-related to health-related fitness, the growing emphasis on the accrual of moderate to vigorous physical activity, and the variability in procedures

Sit-ups are often used as part of a health fitness assessment.

Ken Karp/McGraw Hill

Since physical activity patterns are formed in childhood, children should spend less time watching TV and being on their computers, tablets, and smartphones and instead be encouraged to be physically active each day.

Jamie Grill/JGI/Blend Images

involved in testing and sampling of subjects contribute to the difficulty. There has been no large-scale fitness testing of children and youth since the 1980s. However, there is sufficient information to help us understand that we, as physical education, exercise science, and sport professionals, need to do much more to help children and youth lead a more active lifestyle.

The 2019 Youth Risk Behavior Surveillance System (YRBSS) surveyed over 13,000 students to assess the presence of health risk factors.[21] The results offer us insight into the youths' physical activity patterns and their physical education experiences. The students completed questions on their participation in physical activity during the 7 days preceding the survey. The 2019 YRBSS revealed:

- 23.2% of the students were physically active for 60 minutes or more a day on all 7 days, meeting the recommended physical activity guidelines for health. Males were more active than females, 30.9% versus 15.4%. White adolescents were the most active (25.6%) compared to Black (21.1%) and Hispanic (20.9%) who were the least active.
- 16.5% of students met both aerobic and muscle-strengthening physical activity guidelines. More females were inactive than males (10.1% versus 23.1%). Black students were the most inactive (13.4%). The 2019 YRBSS survey results demonstrate a slight decrease in high school students' engagement in physical activity across gender and racial groups even for 1 day from 13.8% in 2011 to 17% in 2019.
- Being on the computer and watching television reduces the time to be active: 46.1% of students played video or computer games or used the computer for something nonschool-related, and

Skills learned at an early age can provide the foundation for lifelong pursuits.

Left: BananaStock/Alamy Stock Photo; Right: Digital Vision/Getty Images

19.8% watched television for 3 or more hours a day on an average school day. Computer usage among high school students, across racial and gender identities, continues to rise, whereas television usage has decreased over recent years.

The NHANES surveys provide us with additional information about the occurrence of overweight among children and adolescents. The results support previously mentioned statistics from the Centers for Disease Control and Prevention that overweight among children and adolescents has reached a record high and its prevalence has increased from 40 years ago. Collectively, the findings from the YRBSS and the NHANES indicate that too many of our nation's children and youth are inactive and overweight, particularly during their adolescent years, when they reduce their physical activity engagement. Yet, it is very important to note that for many of these adolescents, it is not in their control as they navigate a plethora of inequities and circumstances that prohibit them from being physically active.

Physical education, exercise science, and sport professionals should collaborate with policy makers, teachers, parents, and community members to develop and maintain quality physical activity programs in the schools and in the community. The emphasis should be on enjoyable participation in physical activity. A diverse range of noncompetitive and competitive activities appropriate for different ages and abilities should be offered. Children and youth need opportunities to learn skills, knowledge, and dispositions to lead a physically active lifestyle. Special efforts must be made to encourage and sustain participation by marginalized populations. Quality programs, however, are not enough; programs need to be accessible. Affordable programs remove some socioeconomic barriers to participation, and when programs are offered where children and youth live, participation will likely increase. It is vital for physical activity and health to be central in young people's lives, and we need to remove barriers that limit their engagement in physical activity.

Fitness is important for all people. These adults, in wheelchairs, are playing a game of volleyball at a local gymnasium.

Realistic Reflections

Fitness and Physical Activity of Adults

Based on averaged data from the Behavior Risk Factor Surveillance System from 2017 through 2020, 25.3% of adults do not participate in regular leisure-time physical activity. Overall, non-Hispanic Asian adults (20.1%) had the lowest prevalence of physical inactivity outside of work followed by non-Hispanic White (23.0%), non-Hispanic American Indian/Alaska Native (29.1%), non-Hispanic Black (30.0%), and Hispanic adults (32.1%). According to the 2018 National Health Interview Survey, about 23.2% of adults engaged in regular physical activity during their leisure time in both health component areas of aerobic and muscle strengthening; 53.3% be the aerobic physical activity recommendations.[22] More males (27.7%) than females (20.9%) engaged in both health components.

Understanding the level of adult participation in our society is challenging. The picture of participation in our society is quite perplexing and often contradictory–health club memberships are booming, fitness and sports participation appears to be growing, yet overweight, obesity, and physical inactivity have reached an all-time high. It is important to understand the nuances of the statistics and requirements as to what the CDC considers overweight, obese, and physically active. As critical consumers, it is important to question and critique the data-gathering techniques and measurements as to whether they truly demonstrate peoples' health and physical activity.

Implications of the Fitness and Physical Activity Movement

Although many Americans are not exercising vigorously with sufficient frequency, intensity, and duration to maintain an adequate level of health-related fitness, many people are making a commitment to incorporate moderate physical activity into their lifestyle. Furthermore, the increased documentation of the positive relationship between adequate levels of health-related fitness and wellness offers strong support for physical education, exercise science, and sport programs. It also emphasizes the need for fitness and physical activity programs to reach all individuals of our society, regardless of gender, race, educational level, occupation, economic status, and community setting. As

Health club membership continues to rise. Treadmills remain a popular means of working out.

Nice One Productions/Fuse/Flame/Getty Images

Daily, moderate physical activity is important for all members of the family.

Ariel Skelley/Blend Images

professionals, we must capitalize on the interest in fitness and its contribution to health to promote and secure funding for our programs.

Findings relative to the physical activity levels of the nation's youth show an urgent need for the fitness and physical activity movement to reach the children and youth of our nation. Schools should emphasize lifelong fitness, and this education should begin early in life. School-based programs must teach students the skills for lifetime participation and foster an appreciation for the value of fitness and physical activity in maintaining an optimal state of well-being. Fitness education should also be extended to parents and families. Parent and family roles in shaping their children's physical activity habits should be recognized, and professionals should involve parents in creating positive physical activity patterns. Because much of children's and youth's physical activity takes place outside of the school setting, school and community physical activity programs should be closely coordinated so that the maximum benefits are derived from participation. The NPAP as well as the most recent *Physical Activity Guidelines for Americans 2018* have developed guidelines for school and community programs to promote physical activity among the nation's youth.[19] These guidelines make it clear that promoting lifelong physical activity requires a coordinated effort among the home, school, and community. (See the guidelines and plans in the National Physical Activity Plan and the *Physical Activity Guidelines for Americans Key Recommendations* boxes.) Moreover, it emphasizes the inclusion of physical education as part of a comprehensive school-wide approach to promote well-being.

Professionals who are equitable and espouse cultural humility are needed to design and implement programs that are sensitive to the needs and values of different population groups, such as racial and ethnic minorities, females, and the aged. Health promotion and disease prevention programs are most effective when they incorporate the cultural beliefs and practices of the targeted population. Not only must we make a special effort to encourage marginalized populations to be more active, but we must also recognize and address the barriers that serve to limit participation in physical activity.

Barriers such as cultural beliefs, financial constraints, physical limitations, and unsafe neighborhoods influence participation in physical activity. Prejudice and discrimination needlessly limit opportunities. Addressing disparities in participation and inequities in opportunities requires that professionals make a commitment to challenging the status quo and working to increase opportunities for marginalized populations. Equity-oriented physical educators, exercise scientists, and sport leaders are needed if we are going to achieve our goal of lifespan involvement in physical activity for all people.

This is true for serving both children and adults. Family members are important role models for physical activity involvement. However, an increasing number of children in single-parent families, many of whom are at risk for poor school outcomes, may not have the parental or familial support for involvement. Besides fitness promotion, structured physical fitness programs can affect many risk factors associated with the problems of at-risk youth. Properly designed and led by committed leaders, programs can increase well-being, enhance self-esteem, and teach important life skills such as goal setting, planning, and values development.[23]

Socioeconomic status is a significant influence on participation in physical activity. Individuals who come from affluent backgrounds have greater involvement than those from less affluent circumstances. They have more disposable income they can use to support their involvement in fitness and sports. Children, youth, and adults from lower economic strata have fewer resources available. Their limited resources–money, energy, and time–must be spent on securing the necessities of life: food, shelter, clothing, safety, and medical care. There is little left for the less crucial activities of life such as exercise and sports. Even access to physical activity programs that are affordable may be difficult for those living in low-income neighborhoods. The relatively poor health of people in lower socioeconomic groups may also limit their participation. Compared to those who are wealthier, those who are poor have less control over their lives, encounter greater stress, receive less social support from others, and must deal with the realization that they are deprived. As professionals, we must understand these inequities, the strong feelings they evoke, and the strategies that can be effectively employed to change this situation.

Historically, the most widely available opportunities for participation have been in the public sector in schools, community recreation programs such as youth soccer and football, and public facilities such as parks and swimming pools. As the shift toward private opportunities continues, efforts must be directed at expanding public sector opportunities and making them available to people of all socioeconomic classes. Offering low-cost programs and reduced fees for those unable to pay will allow individuals from low-income groups to participate. However, reducing fees may not be sufficient. For example, one city pool lowered its fees for children but found that did little to increase the number of participants from lower-income families. When the city offered free bus transportation to the pool, participation increased. Not only must opportunities be provided, but steps must be taken to ensure that people can access these opportunities. Even in the public sector, fees may limit participation.

A large segment of our population is over 50, and that segment is growing rapidly. Because of the remarkable increases in longevity and the growing awareness that some of the risks associated with disease and disability can be reduced, health promotion is emerging as a significant theme in geriatrics.

Professionals can contribute in many different ways to the promotion of physical activity by older adults. Exercise physiologists and other professionals are needed to conduct high-quality programs for older adults in many different settings, such as in the community, retirement spaces, worksites, schools, assisted living facilities, senior citizen centers, health and sport clubs, hospital wellness programs, and other settings easily accessible to the older population. A greater effort must be made to assist individuals in selecting physical activity options that match their interests, lifestyles, and functional abilities as well as identifying avenues to pursue them. Educating medical and other health care professionals about the value of physical activity and disseminating information about "best practice" programs that can be replicated in other settings is a role that professionals can capably undertake.

Regular moderate physical activity can yield important health benefits for people of all ages.
Ariel Skelley/Blend Images

A concerted effort by professionals must be made to reach all segments of the population and to give them the necessary skills, knowledge, and attitudes to develop and maintain adequate levels of health-related fitness. We must sustain participation by that small segment of society, the individuals who exercise vigorously enough to maintain an adequate level of health-related fitness. We must encourage the people who engage in moderate physical activity to upgrade the intensity of their efforts to achieve the full benefits of appropriate vigorous exercise. Finally, we must reach out to those individuals who exercise irregularly, if at all, and help them begin to incorporate physical activity into their lives. Accomplishment of these goals requires committed, qualified professionals and a diversity of programs conducted in a variety of settings and targeted to all segments of the population.

CURRENT TRENDS: MOVING TOWARD THE FUTURE

- Life expectancy has slowly declined over recent years, and current generations are predicted to not live as long as their parents. Getting individuals physically active and educated on appropriate health behaviors can prevent hypokinetic diseases and a decrease in life expectancy.
- The US educational system will continue to become more diverse, and white students will make up less than 50% of the school population.
- Technology offers benefits and barriers to our health. One barrier is that children choose to be on their computers instead of being physically active.

SUMMARY

Professions within physical education, exercise science, and sport in our society are influenced by societal trends. One significant trend is the changing demographics of our population. Our society is more culturally diverse than at any point in its history, and the diversity will increase as we move farther into the twenty-first century. Our society is becoming older; it is estimated that the number of people aged 65 and older will equate to 20% of the population by 2030. The number of people with disabilities continues to grow. The structure of the family is changing. Too many Americans live in poverty; poverty is associated with poor health and educational outcomes. As physical educators, exercise scientists, and sport leaders, we must be committed to providing opportunities for lifelong involvement in physical activity for all people. Cultural humility and equity are important in working with people from diverse population groups to adopt and maintain a physically active lifestyle.

The wellness and fitness and physical activity movements also hold several implications for physical education, exercise science, and sport. The wellness movement emphasizes health promotion and disease prevention through lifestyle modification and individual responsibility for one's own health. Fitness and physical activity are integral parts of a healthy lifestyle. The evidence supporting the contribution of physical activity to health continues to mount. *Healthy People 2030*, the *Physical Activity Guidelines for Americans 2018*, and the *National Physical Activity Plan* document the significant role physical activity plays in promoting well-being. Within the past few decades, there has been a tremendous surge of interest in fitness and physical activity. However, when participation patterns are examined, too many children and adults lead a sedentary lifestyle. Professionals need to increase their efforts to involve people in physical activity, which includes removing barriers and creating more equitable opportunities so more individuals can be involved and active.

DISCUSSION QUESTIONS

1. Today's society is more culturally diverse than ever before. Describe the benefits and barriers you may encounter as you educate diverse individuals across all populations. How does the cultural diversity in the United States influence the overall health and well-being of the entire population?
2. *Healthy People 2030*, the *Physical Activity Guidelines for Americans 2018*, and the *National Physical Activity Plan* have developed goals and objectives to decrease the number of chronic, degenerative, and hypokinetic diseases. What steps and/or initiatives can physical education, exercise science, and sport professionals implement for students, clients, and players to meet these goals and objectives? How will we know if they have met the goals and objectives?
3. Do you consider yourself to have a high level of wellness? Why or why not? How did you determine whether you have a high level of wellness or not?
4. Many children, youth, adults, and older adults are inactive. How can you create equitable opportunities for individuals, regardless of social identity, to be physically active?

GET CONNECTED

Centers for Disease Control and Prevention–presents information on a variety of health status indicators, including news, health information, and statistics. This site offers access to *Morbidity and Mortality Weekly Report.*

http://www.cdc.gov

Healthy People 2030–this site offers information about the nation's health goals, leading health indicators, and specific objectives in different areas, including physical activity.

http://www.healthypeople.gov

USA.gov–provides links to federal and state agencies including the U.S. Census Bureau, as well as agencies dealing with health, nutrition, and recreation.

http://www.usa.gov

U.S. Department of Health and Human Services, Office of Minority Health–highlights minority health initiatives and provides links to minority health resources, including *Healthy Minorities, Healthier America*, a newsletter on reducing disparities in health.

http://minorityhealth.hhs.gov

SELF-ASSESSMENT ACTIVITIES

These activities are designed to help you determine if you have mastered the material and competencies presented in this chapter.

1. You have been invited to speak to a community group on the role of physical activity in the promotion of health and the attainment of wellness. Prepare a short speech reflecting the contribution of physical education, exercise science, and sport to a healthy lifestyle. Use the information provided in the Get Connected box or reference list to locate current information about the value of physical activity.
2. For each of the *Healthy People 2030* objectives for physical activity and fitness, strategies and tactics based on the *National Physical Activity Plan*, or the strategies suggested by the *Physical Activity Guidelines for Americans 2018*, provide specific examples of how physical education, exercise science, and sport programs can help in their attainment.
3. As can be seen from the information on changing demographics, our society is becoming more diverse. What specific steps can physical education, exercise science, and sport professionals take to reach marginalized populations? If what ways do you espouse culturally humility and actively strive for equity to work with our nation's increasingly diverse populations?
4. Compare and contrast the United States' health and physical activity levels with other countries throughout the world. Document and analyze this data addressing how the health and physical activity levels are similar and different.
5. Refer to the 12 Steps to Understanding Research Reports box in Chapter 1. Complete all 12 steps utilizing the same article you selected in Chapter 2.

REFERENCES

1. US Census Bureau. (2022). 2020 Census. Retrieved February 15, 2022, from https://www.census.gov/programs-surveys/decennial-census/decade/2020/2020-census-main.html.
2. National Center for Educational Statistics. (n.d.). Retrieved April 3, 2019, from nces.ed.gov.
3. National Center for Education Statistics. (2022). Race and ethnic enrollment in public schools.

Retrieved February 15, 2022: https://nces.ed.gov/programs/coe/indicator/cga.

4. National Center for Education Statistics. (2022). English language learners in public schools. Retrieved February 15, 2022: https://nces.ed.gov/programs/coe/indicator/cgf.
5. DeSensi, J. T. (1995). Understanding multiculturalism and valuing diversity: A theoretical perspective. *Quest 47*, 34–43.
6. Cervantes, C. M., & Clark, L. (2020). Cultural humility in physical education teacher education: A missing piece in developing a new generation of socially just physical education teachers. *Quest, 72*(1), 57–71.
7. The Institute for Diversity and Ethics in Sport. (2022). The 2020 racial and gender report card. Retrieved February 15, 2022 from https://www.tidesport.org/college.
8. National Center for Educational Statistics. (2016). Characteristics of public school teachers. Retrieved February 14, 2022, from https://nces.ed.gov/programs/coe/indicator/clr.
9. Burden, J. W. Jr., Hodge, S. R., O'Bryant, C. P., & Harrison, L. Jr.. (2004). From colorblindness to intercultural sensitivity: Infusing diversity training in PETE programs. *Quest, 56,* 173–189.
10. World Health Organization. (1947). Constitution of the World Health Organization. *Chronicle of the World Health Organization, 1,* 29–43.
11. National Center for Health Statistics (2020). Mortality in the United States, 2020. https://www.cdc.gov/nchs/products/databriefs/db427.htm#Key_finding.
12. Centers for Disease Control and Prevention. (2022). Leading causes of death for 2020. https://www.cdc.gov/nchs/fastats/deaths.htm.
13. Centers for Disease Control and Prevention. (2019). Heart disease behavior. Retrieved April 3, 2019, from http://www.cdc.gov/heartdisease/behavior.htm.
14. American Cancer Society. (2013). Cancer facts & figures 2013. Atlanta, GA: Author. Retrieved April 3, 2019, from https://www.cancer.org/content/dam/cancer-org/research/cancer-facts-and-statistics/annual-cancer-facts-and-figures/2013/cancer-facts-and-figures-2013.pdf.
15. US Department of Health and Human Services. (2020). *Healthy people 2030.* Washington, DC: US Government Printing Office. https://health.gov/healthypeople.
16. Centers for Disease Control and Prevention (2022). Childhood obesity facts. https://www.cdc.gov/obesity/data/childhood.html.
17. National Center for Health Statistics. (2022). Healthy expenditures, 2018. https://www.cdc.gov/nchs/fastats/health-expenditures.htm.
18. US Department of Health and Human Services. (1996). Physical activity and health: A report of the surgeon general. Atlanta, GA: US Department of Health and Human Services, Centers for Disease Control and Prevention, National Center for Chronic Disease.
19. US Department of Health and Human Services. (2018). Physical activity guidelines for Americans, 2018. Retrieved April 3, 2019, from http://www.health.gov/paguidelines.
20. National Physical Activity Plan. (2016). Retrieved April 3, 2019, from http://physicalactivityplan.org/docs/2016NPAP_Finalforwebsite.pdf.
21. Centers for Disease Control and Prevention. (2022). Youth risk behavior surveillance–United States, 2019. https://www.cdc.gov/healthyyouth/data/yrbs.
22. National Center for Health Statistics. (2022). Exercise and physical activity. https://www.cdc.gov/nchs/fastats/exercise.htm.
23. Harris, J. C. (1996). Enhancing quality of life in low-income neighborhoods: Developing equity oriented individuals. *Quest, 48,* 366–377.

ʻ Saint James/Photodisc/Getty Images

Anthony Saint James/Photodisc/Getty Images

Mitch Hrdlicka/Photodisc/Getty Images

II

Foundations of Physical Education, Exercise Science, and Sport

In Part I, physical education, exercise science, and sport were defined and their philosophy and objectives discussed. Part II builds on that knowledge by discussing the foundations of physical education, exercise science, and sport. Part II begins with a discussion of the historical foundations of physical education, exercise science, and sport in Chapter 4. Chapter 5 provides an overview of motor behavior. Chapters 6, 7, 8, 9, and 10 present the biomechanical, physiological, sociological, and psychological bases from which physical education, exercise science, and sport derive their principles and concepts. These areas of study are the major sciences or disciplines of the field–namely, exercise physiology, motor behavior, sport and exercise psychology, sport sociology, biomechanics, and physical education pedagogy. The principles and concepts discussed in these chapters introduce the professional to the knowledge needed to plan and conduct meaningful programs in physical education, exercise science, and sport.

Polka Dot Images/Getty Images

CHAPTER 4

HISTORICAL FOUNDATIONS

OBJECTIVES

After reading this chapter, students should be able to–

- Identify events that served as catalysts for the growth of physical education, exercise science, and sport.
- Identify some of the outstanding leaders in physical education, exercise science, and sport over the course of history and the contributions each made to the field.
- Discuss recent developments in physical education, exercise science, and sport.
- Draw implications from the discussion of history of principles that will guide the professional future of physical education, exercise science, and sport.

Physical education, exercise science, and sport in the United States is built on a rich heritage. Our programs today have been influenced by philosophies, practices, and sports from other cultures, but particularly the programs of ancient Greece, Rome, Great Britain, Sweden, and Germany. Events in the United States–such as colonialism, the expanding frontier, the Great Depression, the growth of public school education, urbanization, and technology–have affected the growth and direction of our field. Within the United States, dynamic, visionary leaders advanced the scope and status of physical education, exercise science, and sport. This chapter provides a brief overview of the history of physical education, exercise science, and sport from ancient times to recent developments. Space limitations preclude a more detailed approach. Generally, the terms *physical education* and *sport* are used in reference to early historical developments, with physical education typically used to refer to school-based programs and sport used to refer to organized, competitive contests. It is only in the latter decades of the twentieth century that the term *exercise science* emerged.

History enlightens us–it enables us to understand how physical education, exercise science, and sport have been shaped by the leaders and events of the past. History guides us–it suggests future possibilities and courses of action that might be most effective in the years to come. History is a scholarly field of study, focusing on the study of change over time. Historians engage in descriptive and interpretive research.

SOCIAL JUSTICE

Talking Points

- Professionals will need to be inclusive of individuals with special needs as they participate in physical education classes as well as sport and physical activity events.
- Systemic racism needs to be addressed and dismantled across policies, procedures, and practices.
- Women athletes should receive equal pay to men athletes in all sports.

The interpretive perspective seeks to explain the significance of historical events within the historical and social context of the time. History expands our understanding of society as well as physical education, exercise science, and sport.

SPORT HISTORY

Sport history emerged as a discipline within the realm of physical education, exercise science, and sport in the late 1960s and early 1970s. Its definition, scope, historical development, and areas of study are discussed in this section.

Definition and Scope

Sport historians examine the historical development of sport. They describe and analyze the actions and behaviors of leaders, examine and interpret significant events, study the evolution of organizations, and explore the emergence of trends. It is difficult to appreciate the evolution of sport without understanding the practices, philosophies, and beliefs that were popular at the time. Sport historians are interested in how the past has shaped sport as we experience it today.

Historical Development

There has long been an interest in the history of sport. Early works on the history of sport typically were descriptive in nature, describing the development of a specific sport (e.g., baseball), chronicling the contributions of a leader to physical education (e.g., Dudley Sargent), or documenting certain events (e.g., the development of the forerunner to the American Alliance for Health, Physical Education, Recreation, and Dance). However, as interest in the history of sport grew, more interpretive analytical studies were undertaken. These interpretive studies, which incorporated information about the historical and social context of the time, greatly enriched our understanding of sport.

Struna reports that prior to the 1960s, much of the research on sport history was produced by scholars in departments of history.[1] Physical educators who conducted historical studies were more narrow in their approach, focusing on activities and individuals who had a role in shaping physical education. By the 1980s, Struna found that this trend had reversed. Many of the leading sport historians were faculty in departments of exercise and sport science.[1] Additionally, scholars from other fields besides history and physical education, such as the humanities and anthropology, began to investigate sport.

As sport history grew as a fertile area of research, sport historians undertook a wider range of questions. Throughout the 1970s, historians focused primarily on describing and explaining organized, competitive sport; its evolution; and its programs. However, as the discipline grew, a wider range of questions were addressed, using more analytical approaches. As Struna points out, historians came to understand that "modern" sport–organized, competitive physical contests–needs to be interpreted in light of the context in which it was created. Historians need to understand that sport is constructed by a particular group of people during a particular time. This understanding has elicited a wider range of questions–not only about the history of sport, but also about the context in which it developed.

With the growth of interest in the history of sport, in 1972, the North American Society for Sport History (NASSH) held its first meeting. NASSH provides a central forum for sport history scholars from all disciplines to exchange ideas and share their work. NASSH's *Journal of Sport History* is recognized as one of the preeminent publications in the field and provides a means for scholars to disseminate their research.[1] Other journals that provide avenues for sport history research are the *Canadian Journal of History of Sport and Physical Education,* the *International Journal of Sport History, Sport History Review,* and the *Journal of Olympic History.*

Areas of Study

As sport history grew as a specialized area of study, sport historians sought to investigate a wider array of topics within the realm of sport, including physical education, dance, play, conceptions of the body, sport, and exercise. Sport historians also came to recognize that many groups–such as racial and ethnic minorities and females–have been overlooked in historical research on sport. Some of the questions sport historians may investigate include:

- How did urbanization influence the development of sports in America?
- How did the sport activities of Native Americans influence the recreational pursuits of the early colonists?
- How did segregation influence the participation of blacks in sports?
- What factors contributed to the establishment of the National Collegiate Athletic Association?

As Mechikoff and Estes point out, history often provides us with an illuminating perspective.[2] It helps us understand why we think and act the way we do and gives us some idea about what may happen in the future.[2] Sport history helps physical education, exercise science, and sport professionals gain a greater understanding of the events, forces, and leaders that shaped the field of today, and offers us guidance for our behaviors and actions in the future.

ANCIENT GREECE AND ROME

One profound influence on the development of physical education and sport was the civilization of ancient Greece (prehistoric times–338 B.C.). The city-states of ancient Greece, particularly Athens, placed a high value on physical activity, viewing sport, exercise, and fitness as integral to education and life. The Greek ideal stressed the unity of the mind, body, and spirit. Reflecting this principle, Greek education encompassed both intellectual and physical development. The expression "a sound mind in a sound body" exemplifies this belief. Gymnasiums served as centers for intellectual discussions as well as sport instruction and physical training. Males received instruction in physical activities, such as wrestling, running, and jumping. Development of the body was valued, and the Greeks engaged in training to develop their physiques. The guiding principle of Athenian society, *arête*–the pursuit of excellence–encouraged individuals to push themselves to achieve the highest extent possible.

In honor of the gods, Greeks held festivals, where sporting events gave Greek men the opportunity to demonstrate the beauty of their physique as well as their athletic abilities. The most renowned of these festivals was the Olympic Games, held in honor of Zeus, the chief god. Beginning around 776 B.C., the Olympic Games were held every 4 years and featured music, feasting, and athletic contests spanning at least 5 days. The Olympic Games were so important that the frequently warring city-states declared a truce so that contestants from all city-states could safely travel and participate in the games.

During the ancient Roman period (500–527 B.C.), physical activity was also regarded with importance, although its role was different than in Greece. Being fit and having athletic prowess were important to

This Greek vase, called an *amphora*, was found in eastern Greece and dates to about 550–525 B.C.

Leemage/Universal Images Group/Getty Images

Rome's military success. Males received training in many physical activities, such as archery, wrestling, riding, and fencing. Strength development was important so that the men could be successful in defending the state and waging war as Rome sought to expand its empire.

After Rome conquered Greece, Greek gymnastics were introduced to the population, but were not popular. Romans preferred professional sports, often blood sports such as gladiatorial contests, men fighting wild animals, and men fighting each other to the death. Spectators enjoyed these and other events, such as chariot races. Feasting and drinking bouts, in conjunction with little physical activity, led to the decline of the Roman population's fitness. Ultimately, the Roman Empire came to an end, with the poor physical condition of its citizens one of the contributing factors in its decline.

The programs of ancient Greece, in particular, influenced physical education programs in the United States. The Greek ideal of the unity of the mind and body is reflected in many physical education programs today. The development of the body and the pursuit of excellence stand as the motive for many who welcome the challenge of competition at their own level and who value achievement over winning.

EARLY MODERN EUROPEAN PROGRAMS

During the late 1700s and 1800s, early modern Europe experienced the rising tide of nationalism. Against this backdrop, physical education programs in Germany, Sweden, and Great Britain developed and expanded. During the 1800s, proponents of these programs introduced them to the United States.

Germany

During the early modern European period, physical education in Germany focused on the development of strong citizens through programs in the schools and community associations. Physical education leaders of the time, such as Johann Bernhard Basedow (1723-1790), Johann Christoph Friedrich Guts Muths (1759-1839), and Adolph Spiess (1810-1858), were instrumental in promoting

Drawing of a *Turnplatz*, a German exercise ground that included equipment for jumping, vaulting, balancing, climbing, and running.

historic-maps/akg-images/The Image Works

Associations of gymnasts called *Turnverein* were still popular in the 1920s. At right, members of the Durlach Turnverein are shown.
Deborah Wuest

school gymnastics. Their programs focused on exercises and instruction in activities such as gymnastics, games, marching, running, and wrestling. These leaders believed that physical education deserved a place in the school curriculum.

In 1779, Basedow founded the Philanthropinium, a school for boys located at Dessau. The curriculum of the school was guided by the philosophy of naturalism, and he designed his program to meet the individual needs of his students. Physical activity played an important part in the daily program of all students; 3 hours a day were devoted to sport instruction and recreation activities and 2 hours a day to manual labor such as gardening. This was the first school in modern Europe that admitted boys from all classes and that included physical education as part of the educational curriculum.

Guts Muths was an instructor in physical education at the Schnepfenthal Educational Institute, founded by Christian Gotthilf Salzmann (1744–1811). The school's program was greatly influenced by Basedow's naturalistic philosophy and incorporated many of his physical activities into the curriculum. As an instructor there for 50 years, Guts Muths developed an extensive program of outdoor gymnastics, which included tumbling, vaulting, the horizontal bar, and rope ladders. Three to four hours a day were devoted to physical activity. Because of his outstanding contributions, Guts Muths is often referred to as one of the founders of modern physical education in Germany.

Friedrich Ludwig Jahn (1778–1852) developed the *Turnverein* movement, associations of gymnasts, in an effort to strengthen the country's youth. During his lifetime, Napoleon overran Germany. In hopes of contributing to the effort to free Germany from Napoleonic control and reunify the country, Jahn designed a gymnastics program to improve the fitness of German boys. In 1811, near Berlin, the first *Turnplatz*, an outdoor exercise area, was established. The *Turnplatz* had equipment for jumping, vaulting, balancing, and climbing. Here the gymnasts, known as turners, practiced on the apparatus. Running, wrestling, and calisthenics helped the boys become strong and fit. Jahn emphasized nationalism, building strong youth for the defense of Germany.

Jahn's system of gymnastics expanded throughout Germany. *Turnvereins* were formed in many cities. As Germans immigrated to the United States, they formed *Turnvereins* where they settled. Proponents of the German system of gymnastics promoted their system in the United States during the 1800s.

Adolph Spiess advocated for the inclusion of gymnastics within the school curriculum. In the 1840s, influenced by the teachings of Guts Muths and Jahn, Spiess developed a system of school gymnastics and persuaded German officials to incorporate gymnastics into schools' curriculum. He believed that schools should be interested in the total growth of the child, which included intellectual and physical development, and that gymnastics should receive the same consideration as other subjects such as math and language. Spiess developed progressions for different grades, different ability levels, and different genders. Sport, marching, and gymnastics accompanied by music were included in the curriculum. Discipline and obedience were emphasized.

Sweden

During the early 1800s, gymnastics in Sweden was influenced by nationalism. Per Henrik Ling (1776–1839) played a major role in the development of gymnastics during this time. In 1814, Ling assumed the directorship of the Royal Gymnastics Central Institute, Stockholm. At the institute, he developed a training program for military men who emphasized exercises that stressed mass drills and movements from position to position on command and in a prescribed, progressive sequence. Ling developed exercise apparatus, including stall bars, vaulting boxes, and oblique ropes.

In addition to his program of military gymnastics, Ling is credited with the development of medical, educational, and aesthetics gymnastics. He used the sciences of anatomy and physiology to examine the effects of physical activity on the body; this emphasis on the scientific approach stands as one of Ling's greatest contributions to physical education. This understanding aided Ling in designing a program of medical and therapeutic exercises, with the goal of restoring health to injured parts of the body and helping the weak regain their strength. His program of educational gymnastics laid the foundation for physical education in the schools. His aesthetic gymnastics emphasized the expression of feelings and thoughts through movement. An advocate of teacher training, Ling believed instructors of gymnastics needed to know proper techniques and have an understanding of the effect of exercises on the body. Ling's gymnastics became known as the Swedish system. Although the Swedish system of gymnastics used apparatus and emphasized precise movements in response to commands, it was less formal and strenuous than the German and Danish systems.

Hjalmar Frederik Ling (1820–1886), Per Ling's son, is recognized for his significant role in developing educational gymnastics. In 1861, Hjalmar Ling was put in charge of the educational gymnastics program at the Royal Gymnastics Central Institute, where he directed the program for 18 years. Ling developed written curriculum guides for elementary- and secondary-school gymnastics programs for both girls and boys, which included exercises arranged in progression by difficulty. From these tables of exercises, teachers could select and sequence exercises according to the age, ability, and needs of their students. His father's systematic and progressive approach to exercise was reflected in the Day's Order, a series of daily exercises for schoolchildren that move in sequence from head to toe.

Denmark

In the early 1800s, Danish gymnastics was also influenced by nationalism. Franz Nachtegall (1777–1847) played a significant role in shaping physical education programs in Denmark and is regarded as the father of Danish physical education. In 1799, Nachtegall opened a private outdoor gymnasium in Copenhagen, the first to be devoted to physical training. His curriculum was influenced by the work of Guts Muths. In 1804, Nachtegall was appointed by the Danish king to serve as the director of a training school for teachers of gymnastics in the army. In 1809, Nachtegall began working with Danish public schools to incorporate physical education into their curriculum for boys, at the elementary and secondary levels. In 1821, Nachtegall was appointed director of gymnastics for Denmark and given authority over both civilian and military gymnastics. Danish programs of gymnastics emphasized fitness and strength, with formalized exercises performed on command and little individual expression allowed. Danish gymnastics used hanging ropes and ladders, poles for climbing, beams for balancing, and wooden horses for vaulting.

Great Britain

Great Britain during the early 1800s took a different approach to physical education. While other European countries stressed organized programs of gymnastics, Great Britain emphasized programs of organized games and sports. Sports have a long, rich heritage in Great Britain. Swimming, rowing, archery, riding, hockey, quoits, tennis, golf, football (soccer), and cricket were played prior to the 1800s.

Sport and recreational pursuits in Great Britain during this time were clearly divided among class lines or by socioeconomic status. Sports that required little equipment, such as football (soccer) and boxing, were popular among the working class. Sports such as cricket and rugby found popularity among the upper-class men, many of whom had played such sports at their private boarding schools. In addition to their love of sports, amateurism and its emphasis on playing for the love of the game is a lasting British legacy.

One of the leaders of physical education in Great Britain was Archibald Maclaren (1820–1884). Maclaren had a background in both sports and medicine. He believed that it was important to treat physical training as a science. Maclaren recognized that physical action is an antidote for tension, nervousness, and fatigue from hard work. He noted that the recreational exercise found in games and sport is not enough in itself for growing boys and girls and that physical exercise is essential to optimum growth and development.

Maclaren believed that both physical training and intellectual development were important. The mind and body represent a "oneness" in human beings and sustain and support each other. Maclaren stated that exercises should be adapted to an individual's level of fitness and that exercises should be progressive in nature.

During the early and mid-1800s, the philosophy of muscular Christianity developed and grew in popularity. Following the Reformation in the sixteenth century, Protestant sects, including the Puritans, enacted rigid prohibitions against participation in many physical activities and sports. Participation was viewed as sinful. Muscular Christianity argued that sports activities provided a means to teach and reinforce moral values and virtues, thus serving to build character.

Proponents of muscular Christianity suggested that physical weakness reflected moral and spiritual weakness; thus, engaging in physical activities and sport to develop the body reflected one's commitment to developing desirable Christian qualities. Other advocates of muscular Christianity believed that the body was the soul's temple and, as Christians, individuals were obligated to care for their physical being. Muscular Christianity—engaging in sport to build moral character—helped reconcile sport and religion. The philosophy of muscular Christianity greatly influenced English educational institutions, which came to promote the inclusion of sport in schools as a means to develop fair play, honor, and self-discipline among students and to prepare students for life.

PHYSICAL EDUCATION AND SPORT IN THE UNITED STATES

The growth of physical education and sport in the United States was influenced by European ideals, systems of gymnastics (exercises), and philosophies. In more recent years, there has been a greater incorporation of activities and beliefs from ancient Asian cultures, such as yoga, the martial arts, mindfulness, and the beliefs about the relationship between the mind, body, and spirit.

Colonial Period (1607-1783)

Colonists coming from Europe to settle in the New World found Native Americans leading a very active existence. Native Americans hunted, fished, canoed, ran from place to place, and engaged in a multitude of physical activities as they sought food, built shelters, and communicated with other tribes. Young men had to successfully complete a series of challenging physical tests in order to become warriors. Various forms of physical activity were included within their rituals (i.e., burial services, fertility-based ceremonies, and medicinal rites), which were performed in an effort to influence the religious forces they believed directed their lives.[3] Sport, dance, and dramatic enactments were incorporated into Native American festive celebrations and engaged in as forms of relaxation. Prior to major competitions, there was a period of preparation of the mind, body, and spirit. According to Ray, games and sport played important roles in the lives of Native Americans; they promoted group identity, served as an outlet for creativity, and offered opportunities for individual recognition.[4]

Tribal differences in culture and lifestyle influenced the physical activity of Native Americans, although there were many similarities in the games and sports of tribes across North America. Men, women, and children participated in various sports and games, with some activities being relegated to certain age groups or genders, while others were enjoyed by both males and females or adults and children.[4]

Physical prowess, cunning, coordination, skill, speed, and endurance were valued. Baggataway (lacrosse) was popular, and rituals often surrounded the game. The game was also used as a means to settle disputes. Rules and playing equipment varied

EUROPEAN CONTRIBUTORS–PHYSICAL EDUCATION, 1700s-1800s

Johann Bernhard Basedow (1723-1790)	Germany	Naturalism guided his development of physical education curriculum; program designed to meet individual needs; activities included dancing, fencing, riding, running, jumping, wrestling, swimming, skating, games, gymnastics, and marching.
Johann Christoph Friedrich Guts Muths (1759-1839)	Germany	Naturalism influenced design of program; extensive program of outdoor gymnastics, using exercises and apparatus; wrote *Gymnastics for the Young and Games;* founder of modern physical education in Germany.
Friedrich Ludwig Jahn (1778-1852)	Germany	Nationalism motivated establishment of *Turnverein* associations; program of gymnastics designed to build strong and fit youth and men with the goal of reunification of Germany.
Adolph Spiess (1810-1858)	Germany	Promoted gymnastics as part of the school's curriculum, as important as other school subjects for both girls and boys; required trained teachers; program emphasized discipline and included variety of activities–marching, free exercise, and gymnastics to music.
Per Henrik Ling (1776-1839)	Sweden	Gymnastics training program for military using directed drills and exercises; therapeutic gymnastics to restore health; massage; emphasized the educational and aesthetic aspects of gymnastics; teacher training.
Hjalmar Fredrik Ling (1820-1886)	Sweden	Promoted educational gymnastics; incorporation of physical education in the curriculum of schools.
Franz Nachtegall (1777-1847)	Denmark	Incorporated gymnastics into Danish schools; gymnastics teacher training for schools and for military.
Archibald Maclaren (1820-1884)	Great Britain	Emphasis on role of physical activity in health; contribution of physical activity to growth and development; organized sports and games; outdoor activities.

by tribe. Shinny, a game similar to field hockey, in which a stick was used to propel a ball into a goal, was played by both males and females. Footraces often extended over many miles and allowed members of the tribe to demonstrate their speed and endurance. Swimming, canoeing, archery, various types of ball games, and games of chance were other popular activities among Native Americans.

When the first colonists from Europe arrived in North America, they were confronted with harsh conditions and focused their efforts primarily on survival. When they were not working, they engaged in recreational activities that varied according to their heritage, their religious beliefs, and the area of the country in which they settled. In the New England area, religious beliefs led to prohibitions against many physical activities. The Puritans saw pleasurable physical activities, such as dance and many games, as leading to sin and eternal damnation. Hard work, stern discipline, austerity, and frugality were thought to be secrets to eternal life and blessedness.

People in other sections of the nation, however, brought the knowledge and desire for various types of sport with them from their native countries. The Dutch in New York liked to engage in sports such as skating, coasting, hunting, fishing, and their favorite, bowling. In Virginia, many kinds of sports were popular, such as running, boxing, wrestling, horse racing, cockfights, fox hunts, and later, cricket and football.

Education during this time period was limited. Children attended academies that focused their efforts on helping students attain some degree of proficiency in the basic subjects of reading, writing, and arithmetic. Although advanced educational institutions existed, few students continued their education beyond the elementary level. Physical education was not part of the school curriculum. Recreational games and sports provided a diversion from hard work and allowed opportunities for socializing.

National Period (1784-1861)

During the national period, interest in education grew, and more schools were established for both females and males. The growth of female seminaries (private schools) increased educational opportunities for women. During the 1800s, free public education began to slowly become available for girls and boys, although opportunities for secondary school and college education were limited. In the 1820s and 1830s, physical education began to be incorporated into school curricula.

During the 1820s, German gymnastics was introduced to the United States by German immigrants. In 1825, Charles Beck (1798-1866), a turner, introduced Jahn's gymnastic program of exercise and apparatus to his students at the Round Hill School in Northampton, MA. Beck built an outdoor gymnasium and started the first school gymnastics program. In 1826, Charles Follen (1796-1840) organized exercise classes, based on the German system, for students at Harvard University.

Catharine Beecher (1800-1878) was the director of the Hartford Female Seminary in Connecticut, an institution of higher education for young women. In 1828, she developed and implemented a program of physical education within the educational curriculum of the school. The program consisted of calisthenics performed to music. These exercises included Swedish gymnastics and were designed to improve the health and vitality of her students and to prepare them more fully for their future role as homemakers and mothers. She was among the first to advocate for the inclusion of daily physical activities into the public schools.

In the 1840s, many Germans immigrated to the United States, fleeing from the unstable political situation in Germany. The Germans brought with them their customs, and within a short period of time, *Turnvereins* began to be established. In 1851, in Philadelphia, the first national Turnfest was held. Turners from New York, Boston, Cincinnati, Brooklyn, Utica, and Newark engaged in this competition. As Germans moved westward to settle, they established *Turnverein* societies in their communities.

During the early to mid-1800s, more schools and colleges opened their doors to both males and females. Gymnasiums and swimming pools were constructed, increasing opportunities for participation. Intercollegiate athletics began during this period of time. In 1852, the first intercollegiate competition

Wand drills were an important part of physical education program activities in the 1890s.
Historic Maps/ullstein bild/Getty Images

occurred. A crew race between Harvard and Yale was held, with Harvard winning the race. Intercollegiate athletics would begin to assume an increasingly prominent role on college campuses.

Sports participation grew as settlers became more established and religious prohibitions relaxed. Horse racing and footraces were popular. Baseball, which had evolved from the English sport of rounders, was "invented" in 1839. Rowing was a popular, and competitive, pastime. One of the favorite activities, however, was gambling on sport events.

Civil War Period through 1900

Many outstanding leaders with new ideas influenced the development of physical education and sport during the Civil War period and the late 1800s. Physical education was increasingly included in the schools, and sports grew in popularity.

In 1860, Dioclesian Lewis (1823-1886) developed the Lewis system of "light" gymnastics and introduced it to men, women, and children living in Boston. Exercises to improve the cardiovascular system were performed to music. Posture and flexibility exercises and light apparatus, such as wands, Indian clubs, and beanbags, were incorporated into his program. In 1861, Lewis established the Normal Institute for Physical Education in Boston to prepare teachers. Courses in anatomy and physiology, hygiene, and gymnastics comprised the 10-week professional preparation program. This was the first teacher training program in the United States.

Edward Hitchcock (1828-1911) and Dudley Sargent (1849-1924), both of whom were physicians, were central figures in the development of college physical education programs. In 1861, Hitchcock was named the director of health and hygiene at Amherst College. In this position, Hitchcock was responsible for the physical development and health of the students. Physical education classes consisted of developmental exercises performed using horizontal bars, rings, ropes, ladders, Indian clubs, vaulting horses, and weights. Marching and calisthenics were included within the curriculum, as were some sports skills. To monitor the progress of his students, Hitchcock used anthropometric or bodily measurements (e.g., height, weight, and chest girth), before and after the completion of training. Hitchcock is recognized for his pioneering work using the scientific approach in physical education.

Girls' physical education class in 1908.
Mark Jay Goebel/Mark Goebel Photo Gallery/Archive Photos/Getty Images

In 1879, Sargent was appointed director of the new Hemenway Gymnasium at Harvard University. Students who elected to take physical education received a medical examination and underwent a battery of anthropometric tests as the basis for an individually prescribed conditioning program. Sargent developed specially designed exercise equipment, which the students used in conjunction with carefully selected German and Swedish gymnastic exercises to work out. Students were also encouraged to participate in sports, such as baseball, fencing, and rowing. In 1881, Sargent founded the Sanatory Gymnasium, a school to prepare physical education teachers to utilize his scientific and comprehensive approach to physical education. Later this school became the Sargent School for Physical Education, and today it is the Sargent College of Boston University.

Delphine Hanna (1854–1941) attended Sargent's school and received training in his approach to physical education. In 1885, Hanna accepted a teaching position at Oberlin College, where she taught until 1921. In 1903, Hanna was promoted to full professor, the first woman in the United States to be a full professor of physical education. Hanna's training program for prospective teachers eventually evolved into one of the first professional preparation programs for physical education. Among her students were future physical education leaders Thomas Wood and Luther Gulick.

During the 1880s, the complete Swedish system of gymnastics was introduced in the United States and became popular in the eastern section of the country. Hartvig Nissen (1855–1924) pioneered this effort. In 1883, he began teaching Swedish gymnastics at the Swedish Health Institute in Washington, D.C., and later continued his teaching in Boston. In Boston, he assumed a leadership role in directing physical training for the Boston public school system and promoted the adoption of Swedish gymnastics. Baron Nils Posse (1862–1895), graduate of the Royal Central Institute of Gymnastics, came to

Boston in 1885 and began teaching Swedish gymnastics. Bostonian philanthropist Mary Hemenway became an advocate of the Swedish system and wanted to have schoolchildren reap the benefits of this program. The Swedish system soon eclipsed the German system in popularity in the East, but the German system remained more prevalent in the Midwest.

The late 1880s were marked by considerable debate among physical educators regarding which system of gymnastics should serve as the curriculum in American schools. This controversy is often referred to as the "Battle of the Systems." Advocates for each system–the German, Swedish, and various systems developed by Americans (e.g., Hitchcock, Sargent)–articulated the merits of their system and advanced reasons why that particular system should be the national curriculum of the schools. In 1889, a pivotal point occurred in the development of the American system of physical education–the Boston Conference on Physical Training.

Organized and led by Mary Hemenway, with the assistance of Amy Morris Homans, the Boston Conference brought together prominent leaders in physical education to discuss and evaluate the various systems. The conference was significant because it stimulated discussion about the purpose of American Physical Education and which program would best serve the needs of the American people. No consensus was reached about which system should be the national curriculum. Nils Posse suggested that what was needed was an American system designed for the American people.

The growth of physical education was encouraged by the efforts of the turners. The *Turnvereins* took an active role in promoting physical education, advocating for its inclusion in the schools. To prepare teachers for their system, the turners in 1866 established the North American Gymnastic Union in New York City. The curriculum of this 1-year program, which expanded to a 2-year program in 1885, included physical education, anatomy, gymnastics instruction, and teaching methodology.

Another stimulus to the growth of physical education during this time was the Young Men's Christian Association (YMCA), founded in London in 1844. The first YMCA opened in the United States in 1851. Because of the interest in gymnastics and other health-promoting activities, the YMCAs added physical education after the Civil War. To ensure qualified teachers for the association's programs, in 1885, the YMCA International Training School was founded in Springfield, MA; this school later became Springfield College. Luther Gulick (1865-1918) played an instrumental role in the YMCA Training School for over 15 years, and he designed the YMCA logo, an equilateral triangle stressing the unity of the body, mind, and spirit and reflecting the importance of developing the whole person–physically, mentally, and spiritually.

At the close of the century, there was greater recognition of the value of physical education to educational progress. Organized physical education programs began to appear as part of the curriculum in elementary and secondary schools in the 1850s. California was the first state to require schools to offer physical education, in 1866, followed by Ohio in 1892. In 1881, the acceptance of physical education grew when the National Education Association recognized physical education as a curricular area. In 1893, Anita J. Turner was the first black physical education teacher in Washington, D.C.'s black school system, where she fought for gender and racial equity and provided a well-rounded educational experience for her students, including girls.[5]

A significant step in the development of physical education was the founding, in 1885, of the Association for the Advancement of Physical Education (AAPE). William Anderson (1860-1947), a teacher at Adelphi Academy in Brooklyn, was interested in learning more about how other physical education professionals were teaching and structuring their programs. He organized a meeting at Adelphi Academy and invited professionals in the field. Dr. Edward Hitchcock served as the first president of AAPE. When the group met again in 1886, they changed their name to the American Association for the Advancement of Physical Education (AAAPE). This organization was the forerunner of the American Alliance for Health, Physical Education, Recreation, and Dance (AAHPERD), which remained as an organization for over 125 years. Today, this association is called the Society of Health and Physical Educators (or SHAPE America). It should be noted that many professionals initially involved in AAPE were physicians and held M.D. degrees. They supported physical education because of the beneficial health effects it provided. It is important to note that these professionals were primarily white males. However, Dr. E. Lavonia Allison advocated for black student involvement, justice, and equity and conducted physical education curriculum research in the national organization.[5]

During the mid- to late 1800s, considerable progress occurred in the growth of organized sports. Tennis was introduced in 1874, and in 1880, the United States Lawn Tennis Association was organized. Golf was played in the United States in the late 1880s, and in 1894, the United States Golfing Association was formed. Bowling had been popular since the time of the early Dutch settlers in New York, but it was not until 1895 that the American Bowling Congress was organized. Basketball, one of the few sports originating in the United States, was invented by James Naismith in 1891. Some other sports that became popular during this period are wrestling, boxing, volleyball, skating, skiing, lacrosse, handball, archery, track, soccer, squash, football, and swimming. In 1879, the National Association of Amateur Athletics of America was developed, from which the American Athletic Union (AAU) was later formed.

The AAU has played an instrumental role in the participation of the United States in the Olympic Games. A pedagogist, Baron Pierre de Coubertin, was attracted to the idea of using sport as a means to develop pride and honor among the youth of France. An idealist, Coubertin saw that the Olympics could embody the ideals to which he ascribed: amateurism, fair play, good competition, promotion of goodwill, and fostering of understanding among athletes of the world.

Upon returning from the United States to France in 1892, he proposed the reestablishment of the Olympic Games to the governing athletic organization. At an international meeting of amateur athletic associations in Paris in 1894, Coubertin was successful in establishing the modern Olympics; he nurtured their growth as the first president of the newly created International Olympic Committee.

The first modern Olympics were held in Athens in 1896. A small delegation of American athletes, organized by history professor William Sloane, participated in the Athens Olympics. Participation was limited to males and to 28 events in four sports: track and field, gymnastics, target shooting, and fencing. From the first modern games in 1896, the Olympics grew in scope and popularity to become the events that they are today.

Intercollegiate athletics grew during this time period. Williams and Amherst played the first intercollegiate baseball game in 1859, and Rutgers and Princeton the first football game in 1869. Other intercollegiate contests soon followed in tennis, swimming, basketball, squash, and soccer. Although mostly males participated in athletics, opportunities were available for women. For example, in 1896, the first intercollegiate women's basketball game was held, with teams from the University of California and Stanford University competing.

Initially, intercollegiate athletics were organized and directed primarily by the students. Athletics were viewed by school administrators and faculty as extracurricular activities because they were not perceived as central to the educational mission of the university. However, as athletics grew in popularity and prominence, problems and abuses became more frequent. Faculty raised concerns about student athletes' academic performance, eligibility, commercialization, payment of athletes, and overemphasis on athletics at the expense of academics.

To address these and related concerns and to control its future growth, faculty and administrators became involved in the governance of athletics. Faculty athletic committees were formed on campus, with Harvard University establishing the first committee in 1892. The next step in assumption of faculty control was the development of university associations to govern athletics. In 1895, the Intercollegiate Conference of Faculty Representatives was formed. Comprising faculty representatives from seven Midwestern institutions, it established

US LEADERS–PHYSICAL EDUCATION, 1800s-1900s

Charles Beck (1798-1866)	Introduced Jahn's program of gymnastics to students at Round Hill School, MA (1825-1830).
Charles Follen (1796-1840)	Organized exercise classes, based on the German system, for students at Harvard College (1826-1828).
Catharine Beecher (1800-1878)	Director of Hartford Female Seminary in Connecticut (1824); developed a program of calisthenics performed to music; physical activity important for women's health.
Dioclesian Lewis (1823-1886)	Developed system of "light" gymnastics using handheld apparatus; established Normal Institute for Physical Education in Boston to train teachers (1861); first teacher preparation program in the United States.
Edward Hitchcock (1828-1911)	Director of hygiene and physical education at Amherst College (1861-1911); pioneered the use of anthropometric measurements to evaluate effectiveness of training; first president of the Association for the Advancement of Physical Education (1885).
Dudley Sargent (1849-1924)	Director of Hemenway Gymnasium at Harvard College (1879); used anthropometric measurements to develop individualized conditioning programs for students; founded forerunner to Sargent College for Physical Education to prepare physical education teachers (1881).
Anita J. Turner	First black female physical education teacher in 1893 in Washington, D.C.'s Black public system. She was an advocate for gender and racial equity and justice throughout her career and included girls in her teaching.
Delphine Hanna (1854-1941)	Taught at Oberlin College (1885-1921); in 1903 promoted to full professor, the first woman full professor in physical education; developed anthropometric measurement tables for women; established a professional preparation program for physical education (1892).
George Fitz (1860-1934)	Stressed the importance of basing physical education programs on scientific principles, not assumptions; established physiological laboratory at Harvard University, where he and his students conducted research on physiological effects of physical activity (1892).
Hartvig Nissen (1855-1924)	A pioneer in the promotion of Swedish system of gymnastics in the United States; taught at Swedish Health Institute in Washington, D.C. (1883); served as assistant and later director of physical training for the Boston public school system, where he influenced the adoption of Swedish gymnastics (1891-1900).
Baron Nils Posse (1862-1895)	Leader in the promotion of Swedish system of gymnastics in the United States (1885); helped establish the Boston Normal School of Gymnastics to train teachers in Swedish system (1889).
Amy Morris Homans (1848-1933)	Director of the Boston Normal School of Gymnastics (1889); played an influential role in getting the Boston public school system to adopt the Swedish system of gymnastics (1890).
Luther Gulick (1865-1918)	Played a significant role in the development of the YMCA as an instructor and later superintendent of the YMCA International Training School in Springfield, Mass.; designed the YMCA logo, with the triangle representing unity of the mind, body, and spirit.
William Anderson (1860-1947)	Played an instrumental role in the founding of the Association for the Advancement of Physical Education (1885); had an interest in sharing information about teaching physical education and learning about different programs; director of physical training at Adelphi Academy in Brooklyn.

eligibility requirements for students pertaining to enrollment and academic performance, imposed limits on athletic financial aid, and developed guidelines for the employment and retention of coaches. This conference, which later became the Big Ten, was the forerunner of other conferences established throughout the country to govern intercollegiate athletics and to define its role in university life.

Opportunities for women to participate in sport were limited by the social constraints of the time. Women's sports consisted of those in which they could participate and continue to be ladylike; Victorian sensibilities and contemporary standards of morality led to women's participating in activities in which they could be fully dressed and not break out in a sweat. Individual sport activities, such as archery, were acceptable. As physical education programs grew in the schools, more women became interested in participating in a wider range of physical activities. Women's team sports, such as basketball, became popular around the turn of the century; however, some schools and members of the public discouraged women's participation.

Around 1870, the high-wheeler bike, with a huge front wheel about 5 feet tall and a small rear wheel, became popular. However, the bike was rather unstable, and riders were prone to frequent accidents. Around 1886, the safety bicycle, the forerunner of today's bicycle, was invented, and both males and females began to ride in great numbers. The popularity of the bicycle led to changes in women's attire; women began dressing in ways that allowed for more freedom of movement and enabled greater participation in a wide variety of physical activities. (It is important to realize that during this time, women had not yet gained the right to vote.)

Opportunities for blacks to participate in sports were also limited by societal constraints. After slaves were freed following the Civil War, they engaged in a variety of sports, with baseball, boxing, and horse racing being the most popular. A rising tide of racism in the late 1800s led to the passage of "Jim Crow" laws that resulted in the segregation of blacks and whites in many areas of life, including schools, playgrounds, and sports. The banning of competition between blacks and whites led to the formation of separate sport leagues and college athletic conferences. This segregation continued through the 1900s, and integration in many sports did not occur until after World War II. Major league baseball remained segregated until 1946. For women, this was extended further until the enactment of Title IX in 1972. A year after this gender equality law, Dr. Doris R. Corbett-Johnson, a black woman, developed the first women's intercollegiate athletic program and was the first head women's basketball coach at Howard University.[5]

Early Twentieth Century

The early twentieth century marked a significant period of growth and development for both physical education and sport. Physical education changed its focus from a narrow emphasis on systems of gymnastics, exercise regimes, and calisthenics to a broader focus that encompassed games, sports, aquatics, dance, and outdoor activities. The "new physical education" developed, which emphasized a program of activities and the contribution of physical education to the total education of the individual. Physical education leaders debated whether physical education should emphasize education *of* the physical or education *through* the physical. Physical education teacher training programs grew in number, and graduate degrees in physical education began to be awarded with greater frequency.

Sport became increasingly organized during this time and grew tremendously in popularity. Extensive programs were established in schools and universities, and recreation programs flourished. Intercollegiate athletics were brought under more rigid academic control. Intramurals became more popular as the emphasis on sports for all gained momentum.

During the first decade of the twentieth century, Luther Gulick continued to promote play as important to the development of children. He played an

Ina Gittings, a student at the University of Nebraska, pole vaulting in 1905.
Courtesy of SHAPE America

instrumental role in the formation of the Playground Association of America in 1906, which sought to promote the development of urban and rural playgrounds, and served as its first president. By 1930, the Playground Association had evolved into the National Recreation Association.

Physical education began to change in scope. At the forefront of this change was Thomas Denison Wood (1864–1951), who advocated the development of a new program of physical education that would enhance the development of the whole individual through participation in play, games, sports, and outdoor activities.

His program was first introduced under the title "natural gymnastics," but later became known as the "new physical education."

Robert Tait McKenzie (1867–1938), physician, physical educator, and noted artist-sculptor, was on the faculty of McGill University (Canada) from 1891 to 1904 and the University of Pennsylvania from 1904 to 1931. McKenzie worked to help develop physical education programs for individuals with disabilities.

World War I (1916–1919)

World War I started in 1914, and the United States' entry in 1918 had a critical impact on the nation and education. The Selective Service Act of 1917 called to service all men between the ages of 18 and 25.

Social forces were also at work during this period. The emancipation of women was furthered by passage of the Nineteenth Amendment. Women also began to show interest in sport and physical education, as well as in other fields formerly considered to be off-limits.

During World War I, many physical educators, such as Dudley Sargent, Luther Gulick, and R. Tait McKenzie, contributed their services to the armed forces. Women physical educators were also active

Students participate in play day at the John Muir School in 1924.
Courtesy of SHAPE America

Girls playing basketball in 1915.
Mark Jay Goebel/Mark Goebel Photo Gallery/Archive Photos/Getty Images

in conditioning programs in communities and industries at home. When the war ended, the public had an opportunity to study the medical examiner's report for the men who had been called to military duty. One-third of the men were found physically unfit for armed service, and many more were physically inept.

Golden Twenties (1920-1929)

Many advances in physical education occurred during the Twenties that had a profound influence on physical education for decades to come. The "new physical education" began to take shape during this period, influenced by the leading progressive education theorists of the time, including John Dewey. Clark Hetherington's (1870-1942) philosophy of physical education was influenced by Wood's beliefs and his "natural gymnastics" approach. In 1910, Hetherington articulated the four objectives of physical education as organic development (fitness), psychomotor development (skill), character development (social), and intellectual development (mental). Hetherington, like Wood, believed that physical education had a broader purpose than the development of the physical aspects of the individual, which was the popular approach of the times. Hetherington is often credited with inventing the phrase "new physical education" to describe the changing emphasis of the field that was initially described by Wood.

Rosalind Cassidy (1895-1980) was also an advocate of "education through the physical"—a philosophy that guides the development of physical education programs that could contribute to the development of the whole person. Jesse F. Williams (1886-1966) and Jay B. Nash (1886-1965) also advocated for "education through the physical." Williams set forth beliefs, based on the unity of the mind and body, that social responsibility and moral values can be developed through physical education and that athletics could play a vital role in creating socially responsive citizens. Nash strongly believed in the value of recreation and thought that through experiences such as camping, individuals would gain both an appreciation of nature and an understanding of the principles of democracy. In his view, the physical education curriculum should be designed to prepare students to use their leisure time in a worthy manner.

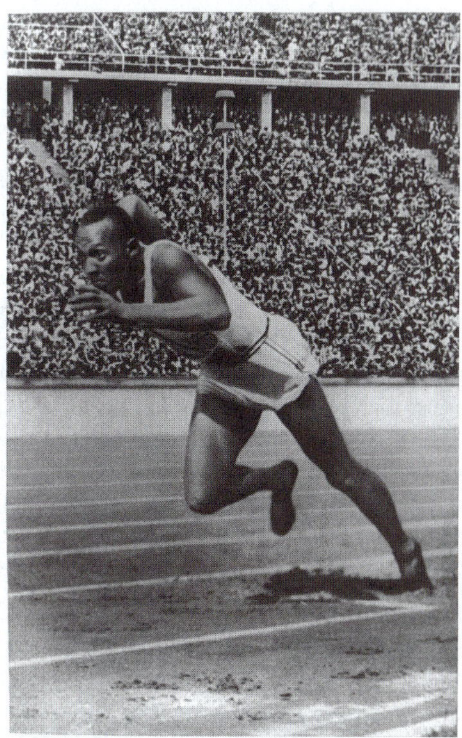

Jesse Owens won four gold medals in the 1936 Olympics, hosted in Berlin, Germany. Adolf Hitler sought to use the Games to promote Aryan racial superiority. Owens's wins in the 100 meters, 200 meters, long jump, and as part of the 4 × 100 meter relay countered Hitler's efforts.

Library of Congress Prints & Photographs Division [LC-USZ62-27663]

The 1920s and 1930s marked a time when an increasing emphasis was placed on defining the scientific basis of physical education. Measurement was used as a means of grouping students, assessing achievement, prescribing exercises, and motivating performance. Some leaders argued that it was important to be able to demonstrate outcomes and identify which programs of exercise yielded beneficial results. The growth of doctoral programs in physical education also stimulated an interest in research. In 1924, the Teachers College of Columbia University and New York University offered the first doctoral degrees in physical education, and other programs began to develop around the country as well. In 1930, the American Physical Education Association published the *Research Quarterly,* now called the *Research Quarterly for Exercise and Sport.*

Many problems arose in regard to college athletics. As a result, the Carnegie Foundation provided a grant, in 1923, for a study of intercollegiate athletics practices in American colleges and universities. This report was published in 1929 under the title *American College Athletics.* The report denounced athletics as being professional rather than amateur in nature and as a means of public entertainment and commercialization. Problems such as recruiting and subsidizing athletes were also exposed.

During this period, intramural athletic programs increased in colleges and universities. Women's programs experienced an increase in the number of staff, hours required for student participation, activities offered, and physical education buildings in use.

Depression Years (1930–1939)

The 1929 stock market crash ushered in the Great Depression, which affected education. Unemployment and poverty reigned. Health and physical education had a difficult time surviving in many communities.

During the period of economic depression in the United States, many gains achieved by physical education in the schools of the nation were lost. Budgets were cut back, and programs in many cases were either dropped or downgraded. Between 1932 and 1934, an estimated 40% of the physical

Women playing archery in the early 1900s.
Chronos Dokumentarfilm GmbH/ullstein bild/Getty Images

education programs were dropped completely. Legislative moves were made in several states, such as Illinois and California, to do away with the physical education requirement.

Another development during the Depression years was that physical educators became more involved in recreation programs in the agencies and projects concerned with unemployed people. The national association, recognizing the increased interest in recreation, voted to change its title to include the word *recreation*–the American Association for Health, Physical Education, and Recreation.

One of the leaders of this time was Charles McCloy (1886-1959). He advocated "education of the physical," espousing the belief that school physical education's unique contribution to the education of the individual is organic and psychomotor development. According to McCloy, school physical education programs should focus their efforts on promoting fitness and teaching sports skills. Furthermore, McCloy recognized the importance of physical educators being able to document results and measure progress using scientific data.

US LEADERS–PHYSICAL EDUCATION, 1900-1940

Thomas Dennison Wood (1864-1951)	Presented his vision for the "new education" at the International Conference on Education (1893); coauthored *The New Physical Education: A Program of Naturalized Activities for Education toward Citizenship* with Cassidy (1927); his program of "natural gymnastics" came to be known as the "new physical education."
Robert Tait McKenzie (1867-1938)	Physician, physical educator, artist, and sculptor; worked to develop physical education programs for individuals with disabilities; wrote *Exercise in Education and Medicine* (1910); created hundreds of sculptures of athletes engaged in sporting events.
Clark Hetherington (1870-1942)	Articulated the four objectives of physical education as organic development, psychomotor development, character development, and intellectual development. Credited with the phrase "new physical education" to describe the changing emphasis advocated by Wood.
Rosalind Cassidy (1895-1980)	A prolific writer, promoted the "new physical education" in *The New Physical Education: A Program of Naturalized Activities for Education toward Citizenship*, coauthored with Wood; advocated for the "education through the physical" approach to teaching physical education.
Jesse F. Williams (1886-1966)	Advocate of "education through the physical" philosophy of physical education; stressed the development of social responsibility and moral values through physical education and athletics.
Jay B. Nash (1886-1965)	Believed physical education should give students the ability to use their leisure time in a worthy manner and should teach them recreational skills they can use for enjoyment throughout their lifetime.
Charles McCloy (1886-1959)	Was active in research and measurement, including anthropometry; advocated "education of the physical" philosophy; believed physical education's primary objectives are the development of organic vigor and skills.

Interscholastic athletic programs continued to grow and in some situations dominated physical education programs and created many educational problems. The National Association of Intercollegiate Basketball was established in 1940 for the purpose of providing an association for the smaller colleges. It changed its name in 1952 to the National Association of Intercollegiate Athletics. In 1937, representatives of the Junior Colleges of California met for the purpose of forming the National Junior College Athletic Association.

Intramural athletics continued to grow in colleges and universities. Women's athletic associations also increased in number. The principles that guided such programs were established largely during the early years by the National Section of Women's Athletics.

Mid-Twentieth Century (1940–1970)

During the middle of the twentieth century, physical education and sport programs grew, in part, due to World War II [see the Mid-Twentieth Century (1940–1970) box for significant events]. Selective Service examinations of drafted men indicated that they were not in sound condition. This helped stimulate the development of physical training programs in branches of the armed forces, and President Franklin Roosevelt appointed John P. Kelly as the national director of physical training. The importance of fitness and its role in the national defense were highlighted by the establishment of a Division of Physical Fitness within the US Office of Defense Health and Welfare Services.

The war years had their impact on physical education programs in schools and colleges. At all levels, there was an emphasis on more formalized conditioning programs, with the goal of improving the fitness of children and youth. Girls and women as well as boys and men were involved in their programs.

Another significant event occurred in December 1953, when the *Journal of Health, Physical Education, and Recreation* published an article entitled "Muscular Fitness and Health." The article reported the results of the Kraus-Weber Minimal Muscular Fitness Tests given to European and American children. Nearly 60% of the American children had failed, compared with only 9% of the European children. The fitness test primarily mea-

MID-TWENTIETH CENTURY (1940–1970)

1942 The Division of Physical Fitness was established within the US Office of Defense Health and Welfare Services.

1950 The National Athletic Trainer's Association (NATA) was founded.

1953 President Eisenhower established the President's Council on Youth Fitness due to the low scores of American children on the Kraus-Weber Minimal Muscular Fitness Test. The council evolved into the current President's Council on Fitness, Sports, and Nutrition.

1953 The National Conference on Program Planning in Game and Sports for Boys and Girls of Elementary School Age brought professionals together to discuss the value of organized games and sport for children younger than high school age.

1954 The Federation of Sports Medicine was founded, which later became the American College of Sports Medicine (ACSM).

1956 The intramural movement at the collegiate level was supported by the National Conference on Intramural Sports for College Men and Women.

1964 The first National Institute on Girls' Sports was held.

1968 The Special Olympics was founded.

sured flexibility and abdominal strength. Nevertheless, the condition of the American children was cause for concern. This concern eventually led President Eisenhower to establish the President's Council on Youth Fitness, the forerunner to the current President's Council on Fitness, Sports, and Nutrition.

A significant teacher shortage during and following the war led to an increase in professional preparation programs in colleges and universities. Early leaders in physical education were physicians, not physical educators. As the number of professional preparation programs in physical education grew, physical educators assumed many of the leadership roles. In 1954, a group of 11 physicians founded the Federation of Sports Medicine, which later became the American College of Sports Medicine (ACSM).

As sports programs expanded and participation increased, qualified individuals were needed to treat injured athletes and to design programs to prevent injuries. Physical educators, coaches, and other individuals stepped forward to fulfill these responsibilities, working as athletic trainers. In 1950, the National Athletic Trainers' Association (NATA) was founded.

Promoting participation of girls and women in competitive sports at both the high school and college levels was the result of several events during this time. In 1964, the first National Institute on Girls' Sports was held, with conference participants discussing ways to encourage more girls and women to participate in sports. The Division for Girls' and Women's Sports (DGWS) of AAHPERD played an important role in developing guidelines for girls' and women's participation. Another effort

American physical education leaders William Anderson and Amy Morris Homans.

(both): Courtesy of SHAPE America

included becoming involved in the Olympic development movement as a means to promote more opportunities. These and many other efforts, as well as the societal changes of those times, were all steps that led to a movement to increase opportunities in competitive sports by girls and women.

Another significant development during this time was the increased emphasis placed on including sports within the physical education curriculum that could be played throughout a person's lifetime for enjoyment and fitness. The Lifetime Sports Foundation, begun in 1965, was instrumental in providing leadership in this area. School and college physical education programs changed to include a greater emphasis on teaching activities such as bowling, tennis, golf, and badminton.

While sports were being promoted at the high school and college levels, there was controversy regarding sports for children below the high school level. The 1953 National Conference on Program Planning in Game and Sports for Boys and Girls of Elementary School Age brought together professionals in medicine, education, recreation, and other child-focus fields to discuss the value of organized games and sport for children that young. Two conference recommendations were that programs of games and sports be based on the developmental level of children, with no contact sports allowed for children under 12 years of age, and that competition be recognized as inherent in the growth and development of the child; whether it would be beneficial or harmful would depend on a multitude of factors.

During this time period, physical educators became more convinced that students with special needs, such as individuals who have physical or developmental disabilities, would benefit from participation in physical education and sport. The growth of participation opportunities for individuals with disabilities increased during this time. One significant event was the founding of the Special Olympics in 1968. Since its inception, the Special Olympics has provided competitive sport opportunities for individuals with intellectual disabilities. Adapted physical education received increased attention, with courses being included in the physical education professional preparation curriculum.

Research in physical education continued to develop during this time. The former Research Council of AAHPERD, established in 1952, focused on promoting research along strategic lines, providing assistance to researchers through dissemination of materials, and synthesizing research in professional areas. Studies were conducted in areas such as exercise physiology, motor learning, sociology of sport, and physical education pedagogy.

SIGNIFICANT RECENT DEVELOPMENTS (1970-PRESENT)

Physical education, exercise science, and sport currently is in one of its most exciting eras. So many changes have occurred since 1970 that include the disciplinary movement, the quest for identity, the emergence of the disciplines, new directions in professional preparation, and increased career opportunities in these dynamic fields. The national emphasis on disease prevention and health promotion, and increasing evidence of the positive relationship between physical activity and health, have stimulated participation by people of all identities and created new opportunities within the realm of physical education, exercise science, and sport. Sport participation at all levels and within all segments of the population has exploded. Legislation has increased opportunities for girls and women in sports and for people with disabilities. The Olympics have experienced a period of growth, withstood politicization, and emerged as a commercial venture of huge proportions. Technology has contributed in many ways to the continued growth of physical education, exercise science, and sport. Many of these recent developments are included within other chapters.

The Discipline

The disciplinary movement is generally acknowledged to have begun with Franklin Henry's 1964 clarion call for the study of the academic discipline of physical education.[6] It is only since the 1970s, however, that the body of knowledge composing the discipline of physical education, exercise science, and sport has grown rapidly. Expanded and rigorous research efforts by dedicated academicians, coupled with improvements in technology, have contributed to the explosion of knowledge. Specialized areas of study or disciplines such as exercise physiology, exercise and sport psychology, and motor learning have emerged (see Chapter 1).

The disciplinary movement that has been evolving since the 1970s led to considerable debate about the best name for our field of endeavor. The traditional name of physical education was perceived by some as too narrow and as failing to convey the expanding scholarly interest in sport. In 1989, the prestigious American Academy of Physical Education voted to change its name to the American Academy of Kinesiology and Physical Education and recommended *kinesiology* as the title of the field. Other popular names were physical education and sport, exercise science, and exercise and sport science. In 1994, Ziegler reported that *physical education and sport* was the most widely used title for the field worldwide.[7] As the disciplinary movement continued to grow in the 1970s and 1980s, departments of physical education in colleges and universities changed their name in an effort to more accurately convey the nature of their work. In 1997, in the United States, there were more than 150 different names for departments in higher education.[8]

Physical education, exercise science, and sport programs have expanded from serving school- and college-age populations to serving people of all ages–from preschoolers to the elderly. Expansion of programs from the traditional school setting to non-school settings such as community centers and corporate fitness centers has occurred at an increasing rate. Private-sector programs in the health enhancement and leisure services industries have grown, creating a diversity of career opportunities for well-prepared individuals. The American College of Sports Medicine (ACSM), the National Athletic Trainers' Association (NATA), the National Strength and Conditioning Association (NSCA), and the Aerobics and Fitness Association of America (AFAA) offer certification programs for professionals. (Professional preparation programs and career opportunities are discussed in Part III.)

Participation by individuals with disabilities in competitive and recreational opportunities continues to grow in the discipline of adapted physical activity. Modified equipment and advances in prosthetics contribute to increase activity for individuals with physical disabilities.

Realistic Reflections

One milestone in this period was the celebration in 1985 by the American Alliance for Health, Physical Education, Recreation, and Dance (AAHPERD) of the one hundredth anniversary of its founding as the American Association for the Advancement of Physical Education.

Disease Prevention and Health Promotion

One of the most significant changes in society during these past decades is the increased emphasis on disease prevention and health promotion. As disease prevention and health promotion initiatives grew, greater attention was directed at helping individuals improve their health by incorporating health-enhancing behaviors into their lifestyle. At this time, there was an emerging consensus of epidemiologists, experts in exercise science, and health professionals, as well as a growing body of evidence, that supported the contribution of physical activity to health and well-being. Over the past six decades, six national health reports titled

Healthy People (1979, 1980, 1990, 2000, 2010, 2020),[9] clearly identified the contribution that physical activity could make to well-being. These reports established specific objectives to be accomplished by physical education, exercise science, and sport, the attainment of which would lead to the improvement of the health of the nation.

The landmark 1996 report *Physical Activity and Health: A Report of the Surgeon General*[10] and the 2010 *Surgeon General's Vision for a Healthy and Fit Nation*[11] affirmed the contribution of physical activity to the attainment and maintenance of health. These reports on physical activity and health emphasized that many Americans can substantially improve their health and quality of life by including moderate to vigorous physical activity in their daily lives. The goal of these national calls to action is to improve the health of the nation; this offers a tremendous challenge to all members of our field as we attempt to provide access and opportunities so that all individuals can engage in healthy life practices.

School Physical Education

Public health initiatives since 1970 have emphasized the critical role that school physical education programs can play in helping children acquire the skills, knowledge, and dispositions to be active throughout their lives. These decades have been marked by efforts to promote physical education and advocacy on behalf of quality physical education in the schools.

In 1971, the Physical Education Public Information Project (PEPI) was begun to inform the public, educators, and policy makers about the value of physical education. PEPI emphasized that "physical education is health insurance."[12] In 1986, the National Association for Sport and Physical Education (NASPE), an association of AAHPERD, defined the characteristics of a "physically educated person."[13] In 1995 and again in 2004, NASPE published *Moving into the Future: National Standards for Physical Education–A Guide to Content and Assessment.*[14,15] For the first time in the United States, this document offered physical educators a national framework to guide the development of their physical education curricula. In 2014, SHAPE America developed the third edition of the national standards for physical education, including grade-level outcomes for the first time.[16]

Periodic surveys such as SHAPE America's (formerly AAHPERD) Shape of the Nation and the CDC's Youth Risk Behavior Surveillance System (YRBSS) provide information about the status of physical education in the nation's schools. The first Shape of the Nation survey, conducted in 1987,[17] revealed that only one state, Illinois, required daily physical education for kindergarten through 12th grade. In 2015, only Oregon and the District of Columbia met the national recommendations for weekly time in physical education at the elementary and middle school levels.[18] Only 24 states require physical education to be included in students' grade point average, 30 states allow exemptions and waivers for physical education time or credit requirements, and 31 states permit the substitution of other activities for physical education class and/or requirements for graduation.[18]

The national standards and health reports such as *Healthy People 2030* called for increasing daily quality physical education for all students. School physical education is regarded as a key setting to increase the physical activity of children and youth as well as lay the foundation for a lifetime of physical activity. Yet despite the recognition that physical education can make a significant contribution to students' health, physical educators are facing tremendous pressures to justify their programs. Increasing pressures for academic reform have led to efforts to make more time in the curriculum for educational core classes and reduction in time for "extras" such as art, music, and physical education (see Chapter 10). Furthermore, physical educators have reported tremendous pressure to justify their programs due to fiscal constraints.

As the twenty-first century progresses, greater efforts must be directed at promoting physical education as an educational core course, an integral part of the school curriculum for children and youth in all grades.

Physical Fitness and Participation in Physical Activity

The fitness movement began as a trend in the 1970s and has continued to expand. Many people of all ages lead an active lifestyle, engaging in activities such as running, biking, walking, and weight training. While it may appear that America is an active nation, studies report that too many adults engage in no physical activity during their leisure time (see Chapter 3). As we create more access and opportunities to a wider range of individuals, the hope is that more and more people will lead healthier lives.

Starting in the 1970s, there was a gradual shift from an emphasis on performance-related fitness to one on health-related fitness. During the 1970s and 1980s, as the emphasis on disease prevention and health promotion grew, the contribution of fitness to health gained increased recognition. Physical inactivity was linked to disease. To improve health, it was recommended that people engage in fitness activities on a regular basis.

At this time, there was a similar shift in fitness development and testing in the schools. In 1980, AAHPERD inaugurated the Health-Related Physical Fitness Test.[19] This test was designed to measure the fitness components associated with health. In 1988, AAHPERD introduced a new fitness test and educational program entitled Physical Best.[20] Physical Best emphasized not only the physical dimension of fitness but the cognitive and affective dimensions as well. The educational component was designed to help teachers assist students in attaining desirable fitness habits through individualized goal setting, motivational techniques, and encouragement of participation in physical activities outside the school setting. In 1994, AAHPERD and the Cooper Institute for Aerobic Research (CIAR) announced an agreement to collaborate on youth fitness testing and education. AAHPERD agreed to adopt CIAR's Prudential Fitnessgram system for testing and assessment of youth fitness. In 2012, the President's Council on Fitness, Sport, and Nutrition, formerly the President's Council on Physical Fitness, adopted the Cooper Institute Fitnessgram. SHAPE is currently endorsing Fitnessgram, which is being used in physical education programs throughout the country.

Sales of sports equipment have increased dramatically during the 80s, 90s, and 2000s, creating many new career opportunities in sports retailing.

Lakov Filimonov/Shutterstock

As researchers continued to investigate the relationship among fitness, physical activity, and health, they found that health-related benefits could be obtained at more moderate-intensity levels of activity than previously realized. In 1995, guidelines for physical activity reflecting this finding were issued by the CDC, the ACSM, and the National Institutes of Health (NIH) Consensus Development Conference on Physical Activity and Cardiovascular Health, recommending that all population groups should accumulate at least 30 minutes a day of moderate-intensity physical activity.[10] The new recommendations also emphasized that greater benefits would accrue by engaging in moderate-intensity activities for a greater period of time or participating in more vigorous physical activity.[10]

The Growth of Sports

Participation in sport has experienced phenomenal growth at all levels since the 1970s. Participation by children and youth involved in organized sport activities outside the school setting, under the guidance of public or private agencies, has grown tremendously. It is estimated that children and youth sports involve millions of children and adult volunteer coaches. Additionally, thousands of paid coaches work primarily in private sports clubs with elite performers.

Participation in interscholastic sports has grown from 3,960,932 boys and girls in 1971 to almost 8 million in 2018–2019.[21] Recently, there has been an increased trend toward specialization in a specific sport at an early age. A youth may play on the school soccer team in the fall, participate in an indoor soccer recreational league in the winter, play spring soccer, and then attend soccer camp in the summer. Some school districts, facing budgetary difficulties, have instituted "pay-to-play" plans in which athletes are charged fees to participate. Considerable concern has been raised that these fees will limit participation and disproportionately affect students from lower socioeconomic groups. The National Federation of State High School Associations opposes this practice, stating that sports have educational value and therefore students should have access to them as part of their educational experience.

At the collegiate level, participation in sports has increased as well. The National Collegiate Athletic Association (NCAA) reported that during the 1989–1990 academic year, 266,268 collegians participated in intercollegiate athletics; in 2021–2022, over 504,000 collegians participated.[22] Seventy seven thousand more collegiate athletes participate at the over 250 schools that are members of the National Association of Intercollegiate Athletes (NAIA)[23] and 60,000 more athletes are governed by the National Junior College Athletic Association (NJCAA).[24] Moreover, during this time, sport has emerged as big business in NCAA Division I schools. Media revenues for televising football and basketball games and tournaments have reached millions of dollars. For example, Division 1 men's basketball champion television and marketing rights equates to $844.3 million and in 2016 received an 8-year extension totally $8.8 billion.[25]

Participation in recreational leagues (e.g., softball, soccer, volleyball) and road races by adults has increased enormously as well. Master's programs in swimming and track and field, the National Senior Games, the National Olympic Festival, and state games such as the Empire State Games engage people of all ages in various levels of competition in a multitude of sports.

Professional sports have also increased during this time. Since the 1970s, expansion has resulted in the addition of many professional hockey, football, basketball, soccer, and baseball teams. Salaries of professionals have increased dramatically; multimillion dollar contracts have become increasingly common.

The past decade has seen the growth of professional basketball opportunities for women. The Women's National Basketball Association (WNBA), backed by the National Basketball Association, began its inaugural season in 1997. The Women's United Soccer Association (WUSA), the women's professional soccer league, played its first season in 2001. Unfortunately, due to financial issues, the league suspended its operations in 2003, yet the Women's National Team has been a success for decades. The number of women participating in professional sports, such as the Ladies Professional Golf Association (LPGA), has grown tremendously. Male and female athletes in both tennis and golf now compete for prizes worth millions of dollars; in both, the winnings are equal for men and women. In 2022, this monetary equality was given to both the men's and women's soccer national teams.

Girls and Women in Sports

Since the 1970s, participation by girls and women in sports has grown rapidly. The dramatic increase in participation was enhanced by the changing attitudes toward women in society and by the passage of Title IX of the Education Amendments of 1972. The Title IX law specifically states, "No person in the United States shall on the basis of sex be excluded from participation in, be denied the benefits of, or be subjected to discrimination under any educational program or activity receiving Federal financial assistance."[26] Over the past 50 years, this educational law has had wide-ranging effects on physical education and athletic programs in the United States.

One major reason Title IX came into existence was to ensure that girls and women receive the same (i.e., equal) rights as boys and men. Testimony before congressional committees prior to the enactment of this legislation showed that girls and women were being discriminated against in many educational programs, including physical education and athletics.

Participation in sports by girls and women has risen dramatically since the enactment of Title IX. According to the National Federation of State High School Associations, during 1971, the year before Title IX legislation, 3,366,000 boys and 294,000 girls competed in interscholastic sports in the United States. In 2018-2019, the federation reported that 4,534,758 boys and 3,402,733 girls took part in interscholastic sports.[21] Participation by women at the intercollegiate level also showed substantial increases. For example, according to the NCAA, 32,000 women competed in intercollegiate sports in 1972, whereas in 2020-2021, 222,920 women competed.[27] (These figures include only NCAA-sponsored championship sports; thus, the number of participants is greater than reported here.)

Title IX mandates certain provisions for physical education and athletic programs. With respect to physical education, no discrimination can occur in program offerings, quality of teachers, and availability and quality of facilities and equipment. Physical education classes must be organized on a coeducational basis. However, classes may be separated by sex for contact sports such as wrestling, basketball, and football. Also, within classes, students may be grouped in a variety of ways except by sex; however, depending on the form of groupings created, without the intent of grouping by sex, there is the potential that same-sex groupings may result.

Title IX also caused changes in the conduct of athletic programs. Separate teams for men and women or a coeducational team must be provided in schools and colleges. For example, if only one team is organized in a particular school for a sport, such as swimming, then students of both sexes must be permitted to try out for the team. Both sexes in educational institutions must be provided with equal opportunities for equipment and supplies, use of facilities for practice and games, medical and training services, coaching and academic tutoring, travel allowances, housing and dining facilities, compensation of coaches, financial assistance, and publicity. Equal aggregate expenditures are not required; however, equal opportunities for men and women are mandated.

There have also been changes since 1972 in the governance of women's intercollegiate sports. The Association of Intercollegiate Athletics for Women (AIAW), founded in 1972, initially was the governing body for women's intercollegiate sports. The AIAW established policies and procedures governing competition and conducted national championships for women's intercollegiate sports. The NCAA used its vast financial resources to entice teams to leave the AIAW, which led to the demise of the AIAW. In 1982, the NCAA and the NAIA assumed the governance of intercollegiate sports for women at all NCAA and NAIA institutions.

Throughout its history, many challenges to Title IX have been heard by the courts. In 1984, the United States Supreme Court ruled 6-3 in *Grove City College v. Bell* that Title IX should be regarded as program specific. In essence, this narrow interpretation of Title IX held that only programs directly receiving federal aid were required to comply with Title IX, not the institution as a whole. Before this ruling, Title IX was interpreted broadly; that is, institutions receiving any federal funds were required to comply with Title IX in all institution activities. Since athletic programs typically receive little, if any, direct federal funding, the threat of losing funding for noncompliance and nonsupport of women's athletics is without substance. While some institutions remained deeply committed to women's athletics, the fear existed that some institutions, without the threat of penalties for noncompliance, would allow women's athletics to stagnate or even to become victims of budgetary cutbacks.

In 1988, the Civil Rights Restoration Act superseded the 1984 Supreme Court ruling. Once again, Title IX was interpreted broadly and its applicability to athletics was reinstated. In 1991, the Office of Civil Rights announced that investigation of Title IX athletic complaints would be one of the office's priorities.

TITLE IX–SELECTED HISTORICAL DEVELOPMENTS

"No person in the United States shall, on the basis of sex, be excluded from participation in, be denied the benefits of, or be subjected to discrimination under any education program or activity receiving Federal financial assistance." –Title IX of the Education Amendments of 1972, U.S. Department of Education

1972 Title IX of the Education Amendments of 1972 prohibits sex discrimination in any educational program or activity receiving federal financial assistance, including employment, admission to college programs (e.g., science, math, medicine, law), and standardized testing; prohibits sexual harassment. This changes conduct of physical education classes and opens up opportunities for girls and women in intercollegiate and interscholastic sports.

1975 US Department of Health, Education, and Welfare clarifies policies relative to intercollegiate athletics. Three areas are identified for compliance: accommodation of students' interests and abilities, financial aid, and programmatic support.

1980 US Department of Education gives oversight for Title IX to the Office of Civil Rights (OCR).

1984 Supreme Court, in *Grove City College v. Bell*, rules that Title IX is program specific. Only programs or activities that receive direct federal funding need to comply with Title IX; narrow interpretation of Title IX.

1988 Civil Rights Restoration Act supersedes 1984 Supreme Court ruling in *Grove City College v. Bell.* All educational institutions receiving federal financial assistance, whether direct or indirect, must comply with Title IX; broad interpretation of Title IX.

1992 Supreme Court, in *Franklin v. Gwinnett County Public Schools*, rules that plaintiffs may receive monetary damages when an educational institution intentionally violates Title IX.

1992 National Collegiate Athletic Association (NCAA) publishes its first Gender Equity Study; annual reports required.

1994 Equity in Athletics Disclosure Act requires all higher education institutions to disclose information on participation and budgets for men's and women's intercollegiate sports; annual report available to the public.

1996 OCR issues clarifications about how institutions can demonstrate accommodating interests and needs of underrepresented gender; three-prong test–proportionality, history of progress, and accommodation of interests.

2002 US Secretary of Education establishes 15-member Commission on Opportunities in Athletics (COA) charged with reviewing Title IX to ensure that both males and females have equal opportunities to participate in athletics.

2003 OCR provides further clarification regarding compliance, including the use of proportionality as part of the three-prong test for assessing participation opportunities; COA issues report.

2005 Supreme Court, in *Jackson v. Birmingham Board of Education*, accords individuals who suffer retaliation as a result of reporting Title IX violations the right to sue the institution; protects "whistle-blowers."

2010 OCR overturns the policy that allowed colleges and universities to use a survey to demonstrate that they were meeting the athletic interests and abilities of women on campus. The policy allowed institutions to equate lack of response with a lack of interest in athletics; policy change will require educational institutions to use other data sources, in addition to the surveys, to learn students' athletic interests.

Sources: Women's Sports Foundation (www.womenssportsfoundation.org); Curtis M and Grant CHB. Gender Equity in Sports. Updated February 23, 2006 (http://bailiwick.lib.uiowa.edu/ge); Thomas K. "Rule Change Takes Aim at Loophole in Title IX." *New York Times,* April 19, 2010 (www.nytimes.com/2010/04/20/sports/20titleix.html); Dougherty J. "Biden Announces Change in Title IX Women's Sports Policy." Cable News Network (CNN), April 20, 2010 (http://edition.cnn.com2010/POLITICS/04/20/biden.title.ix/index.html?hpt=Sbin).

Since 2016, protection for transgender students and athletes have been at the center of policy guidance documents–first in favor and then opposed. Most recently in 2021, policies were amended to protect from discrimination against gender identity and sexual orientation.[28]

Title IX has led to dramatic changes in the conduct of physical education and athletic programs and to significant increases in participation by girls and women within these programs. (See the Title IX–Selected Historical Developments box.) However, the impact of Title IX has been limited by several factors, including gender biases, limited budgets, inadequate facilities, lack of qualified leadership (i.e., coaches), and resistance to change. Although equal opportunity is mandated by law and great strides have occurred within the last decades, much still needs to be accomplished within both physical education and athletic programs to achieve equity.

Programs for Individuals with Disabilities

In recent years, many judicial decisions and legislative acts have supported the rights of individuals with disabilities to have the same opportunities as other individuals. These mandates have resulted in significant changes in the conduct of physical education and athletic programs for individuals with disabilities. The rights of people with disabilities in programs for which schools and other sponsoring organizations receive federal funds were guaranteed by Section 504 of the Rehabilitation Act of 1973.

The most widely known law related to education for people with disabilities is the Education of All Handicapped Children Act of 1975. This law provided a free and appropriate education for children aged 3 to 21. Section 121a.307 of the regulations stated that physical education services were to be made available to every child with a disability. All educational services are to be provided for students with disabilities in the least restrictive environment. In essence, this means that a child with a disability is placed in a special class, or mainstreamed into a regular class, or moved between the two environments as dictated by their abilities and capabilities. Furthermore, the school assumes the responsibility of providing the necessary adjunct services to ensure that students with disabilities perform to their optimum capacity, whether they are integrated into a regular program or left in a special class. Each child with disabilities must have an individualized educational plan (IEP).

In 1990, the Individuals with Disabilities Education Act (IDEA) was passed. Among its mandates was a requirement that all references to "handicapped children" be changed to "children with disabilities." It mandated that transitional services be provided to students as early as 14 and no later than 16 years of age. Transitional services are a coordinated set of activities designed to help

Wheelchair basketball at the 2004 Paralympic Games in Athens.
Sarah Rich

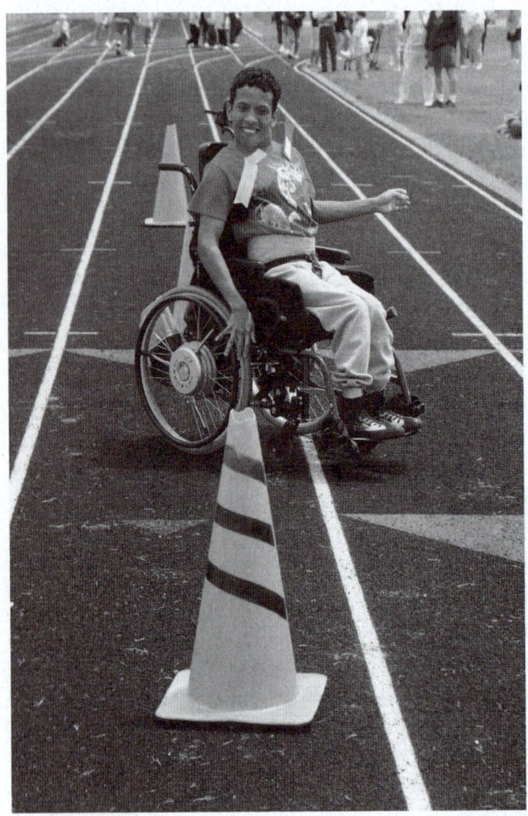

A young man receives numerous ribbons after competing in Special Olympics events.
Ilene MacDonald/Alamy Stock Photo

students with disabilities make the transition from school to postschool life in the community. For example, if fitness development was part of the IEP, then linkages need to be created between the school and local fitness programs. IDEA also provides more opportunities for children with disabilities to receive assistive technologies to improve their abilities. For example, students can get racing wheelchairs or other specialized equipment that would enhance their ability to participate. Children with disabilities must have the opportunity to participate in extracurricular activities and services, such as athletics, intramurals, and the art club.

IDEA stated that physical education and sport must be available to every child who is receiving a free and appropriate education. Each student with a disability must be afforded the opportunity to participate in a regular physical education program with children who do not have a disability unless the child is enrolled full time in a separate facility or needs a specially designed physical education program. The philosophy, known as inclusion, is based on the rights of children with disabilities, regardless of severity, to attend their home schools and participate in the regular educational setting rather than be isolated from their peers in special programs. An alternative approach is the use of the least restrictive environment. The least restrictive environment places a child in the educational setting that is most appropriate for a person's abilities and developmental level. The environment can range from full inclusion in the regular setting to special programs in a self-contained setting. Regardless of the approach, it is important that children with disabilities have individualized programs that are appropriate for their developmental levels and that optimize their potential.

Federal legislation directed toward improving conditions for people with disabilities and meeting their educational needs has caused many changes. Schools are now required to provide physical education, intramurals, recreational programs, and athletic programs for students with disabilities. Adapted physical education programs have expanded. Teachers have had to learn different strategies to enhance learning opportunities for students with disabilities participating in regular physical education classes. Facilities have been altered and modified to meet the needs of the disabled.

In 1990, a landmark law, the Americans with Disabilities Act (ADA) was passed. This law sought to end discrimination against individuals of all ages with disabilities and to remove barriers to their integration into the economic and social mainstream of American life. Five areas are addressed by the law: employment, public accommodations, public services, transportation, and telecommunications. The ADA mandates that all facilities, including recreational and sport facilities, must provide equal access and equal services to individuals with disabilities. This law opens playgrounds, swimming pools, gymnasiums, and health spas, for example,

SIGNIFICANT LEGISLATION FOR INDIVIDUALS WITH DISABILITIES IMPACTING PHYSICAL EDUCATION AND SPORTS

Year	Legislation	Description
1973	Rehabilitation Act of 1973–Section 504	Prohibits discrimination against individuals with disabilities. Mandates equal opportunities and access to programs receiving federal assistance. Includes physical education, intramurals, and athletics in the school setting.
1975	Education of All Handicapped Children Act	Requires that children aged 3 to 21 who have disabilities receive a free and appropriate education in the least restrictive environment. Includes provision for physical education.
1978	Amateur Sports Act	Charges the United States Olympic Committee to provide assistance to amateur athletic programs and to expand opportunities for meaningful competition for individuals with disabilities.
1986	Education for All Handicapped Children Amendments	Mandates educational services for infants (up to 2 years old) with special needs and expanded services for 3- to 5-year-olds with special needs. Includes physical education.
1990	Individuals with Disabilities Education Act	Mandates that all references to "handicapped children" be changed to "children with disabilities." Students with disabilities have the right to free and appropriate education; they must have opportunity to participate in general school curriculum and extracurricular activities, such as athletics. Requires transitional services for adolescents to help them transition from school to life after school, for example, forging linkages from physical education programs to community physical activity programs.
1990	Americans with Disabilities Act	Seeks to end discrimination against people of all ages who have disabilities and to involve them in the mainstream of society. Addresses employment, public accommodations, public services, transportation, and telecommunications. Increases access to recreational and sport opportunities.
1998	Olympic and Amateur Sports Act	Affiliates Paralympics with United States Olympic Committee; Paralympics governed in similar fashion as other Olympic sports.

to individuals with disabilities, increasing their opportunities to participate in fitness and sport activities.

Since the 1970s, the number of individuals with disabilities participating in competitive sports has increased. The Amateur Sports Act of 1978 charged the United States Olympic Committee (USOC) to encourage provisions for sporting opportunities for the disabled, specifically to expand participation by individuals with disabilities in programs of athletic competition for able-bodied individuals. This charge served as the impetus for the formation of the Committee on Sports for the Disabled in 1983. In 1998, the Olympic and Amateur Sports Act was passed, amending the Amateur Sports Act. The new act strengthened the rights of athletes to compete, encouraged the growth of disabled sports, and provided for the Paralympics to be affiliated with the USOC, similar in fashion to other sport governing agencies.

Advances in equipment design have helped athletes with disabilities to train and compete in physical activity and competitive sports.

Realistic Reflections

Participation in national and international competitions and games by athletes with specific disabilities continues to rise. Competitions include the Paralympics, Special Olympics, World Games for the Deaf, and World Wheelchair Games, to name a few.

Olympics

In 1996, the centennial Olympic Games were held in Atlanta, Georgia. In the 100 years since their rebirth in 1896, the Olympics had evolved into an event of global magnitude. In the 1896 Olympics held in Athens, 311 athletes from 11 nations competed. In Atlanta, 10,750 athletes from 197 nations competed.

The modern Olympic Games, organized originally with the idealistic goal of fostering understanding among the people of the world, have become an instrument for political goals. Ideological differences have exerted a profound influence on the conduct of the games. The 1936 Olympic Summer Games, held in Berlin, were used by Adolf Hitler to further the Nazi ideology of Aryan supremacy. The Germans invested considerable resources in order to stage the most spectacular Olympics in history and to train the German athletes, all of whom typified the Nazi Aryan ideal. The German athletes won 89 medals, more than any other country in the games. The United States won 66 medals, four by the African American athlete Jesse Owens, who set three world and Olympic records. Owens's phenomenal performance refuted the Nazi theory of Aryan supremacy.

The 1972 Munich Olympics were marked by terrorism. Eight armed Arab guerrillas entered the Olympic Village complex occupied by the Israelis; a day later, 11 Israelis, 5 terrorists, and 1 German policeman were dead. Millions of people around the world mourned the slain athletes. After a memorial ceremony, the Munich Olympics continued.

Social and political issues led to boycotts at the 1976 Summer Olympics in Montreal over the issue of representation of China and the issue of apartheid. The United States led a boycott of the 1980 Summer Olympics in Moscow in protest of the Soviet Union's

MODERN SUMMER OLYMPIC GAMES

Year	Location	Countries	Athletes	Sports	Events
1896	Athens, Greece	12	176	9	43
1900	Paris, France	29	1,224	20	95
1920	Antwerp, Belgium	29	2,675	25	160
1932	Los Angeles, United States	41	1,876	18	126
1948	London, Great Britain	59	4,369	21	149
1964	Tokyo, Japan	93	5,136	21	163
1972	Munich, West Germany	121	7,113	23	195
1988	Seoul, South Korea	159	8,453	27	237
1996	Atlanta, United States	197	10,329	31	271
2004	Athens, Greece	201	10,558	34	301
2008	Beijing, China	204	10,902	34	303
2012	London, United Kingdom	204	10,820	26	302
2016	Rio de Janeiro, Brazil	205	11,544	28	306
2020*	Tokyo, Japan	206	11,417	33	339

Source: Data retrieved from Sports Reference, LLC, http://www.sports-reference.com/olympics/summer/ and https://www.statista.com/topics/1730/olympic-summer-games/.

*Due to the COVID-19 pandemic, the 2020 Summer Olympic Games was played in summer 2021.

invasion of Afghanistan. The Soviet Union, in turn, led a boycott of the 1984 Summer Olympics in Los Angeles, claiming that the United States had to adhere to the Olympic ideals. The 1988 Summer Olympics in Seoul, Korea, saw Americans and Soviets competing. The International Olympic Committee took a strong position against drug "doping." Canadian sprinter Ben Johnson tested positive for steroid use after winning the 100 meters, and American Carl Lewis was then awarded the gold medal.

Several monumental events in the early 1990s, such as the collapses of the Berlin Wall and the Soviet Union, had a significant impact on the world and the Olympics. In 1992, the Germans competed in Barcelona as a unified team, and athletes from the former Soviet Union competed as part of the Commonwealth of Independent States. South Africa competed for the first time in decades, and the Baltic states participated as independent countries for the first time since World War II. As more countries began to be more open about paying their athletes for their performances, the issue of amateurism became a moot point. Professional athletes began to participate in the games in increased numbers. Public attention was focused on the United States's basketball "Dream Team," which largely comprised professionals such as Michael Jordan, David Robinson, and Larry Bird.

The Winter Games also flourished during this time, mirroring the changes seen in the Summer Games. In the early 1990s, the International Olympic Committee voted to stagger the Winter and Summer Games in a 2-year rotation instead of a 4-year rotation. This started with the 1994 Winter Games in Lillehammer, Norway. It was believed that, given the high degree of public interest in the Olympics, the public would embrace this change.

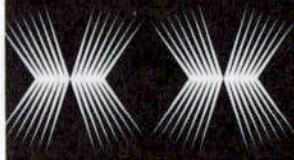

FOCUS ON CAREER: Sport History

PROFESSIONAL ORGANIZATIONS

- International Society for the History of Physical Education and Sport
- North American Society for Sport History (NASSH)

PROFESSIONAL JOURNALS

- *Canadian Journal of History of Sport and Physical Education*
- *The International Journal of the History of Sport*
- *Journal of Olympic History*
- *Journal of Sport History*
- *Sport History Review*

There would also be an economic benefit to the International Olympic Committee if the games were held every 2 years rather than every 4.

Over the past 100-plus years, the Olympic Games have developed into athletic contests that represent hundreds of nations and thousands of athletes from all over the world (see the Modern Olympic Summer Games box). New events have been added to the Summer and Winter Games, such as skate boarding, women's wrestling and ice hockey, beach volleyball, and free style skiing.

Participation by women has increased during these past decades. Women's softball in 1996 and women's ice hockey in 1998 are just two of the new sports added to the Games. In 1998, following the Winter Games in Nagano, Japan, the International Olympic Committee stated that no new events would be added to the competition unless a comparable event could be added for women. The 2020 Summer Olympics (played in 2021) included 174 events for women, the most in Olympic history.

The Paralympics are an international Olympic competition for people with disabilities. The disability categories are amputee, cerebral palsy, intellectual disability, *les autres,* vision-impaired, and wheelchair. In the early 1990s, the International Olympic Committee mandated that the Paralympics would be the responsibility of the same country that hosted the Olympic Games. The same venues would be used, and the Paralympics would take place immediately following the closing of the Olympic Games. The 2020 Paralympics in Tokyo, Japan involved 4,403 athletes (1,853 women) representing 162 countries. The athletes participated in 539 events in 22 sports.[29]

In recent years, the Olympics have been used as a means to further political ideologies. The line between amateurism and professionalism has disappeared. Commercialization has reached new heights and continues to grow. The Olympics have become an embedded component of our global culture.

CURRENT TRENDS: MOVING TOWARD THE FUTURE

- Women's participation in sport will continue to rise at the interscholastic, intercollegiate, professional, and Olympic levels.
- Individuals with special needs will be provided increased opportunities to participate in physical education, sporting, and physical activity events.
- Major changes will be made in policies, procedures, and practices for more racial equity in sport and physical education.

SUMMARY

History provides the foundation for the field of physical education, exercise science, and sport. Many of our programs and activities today have been shaped by our heritage. Studying history also provides an appreciation for other cultures and the role of physical activity in these societies.

An adage states that "history tends to repeat itself." Recurring themes are apparent throughout the history of physical education, exercise science, and sport. For example, wars frequently served as the impetus for societies to intensify their physical education program or to justify its existence. Physical fitness was promoted among the populace to prepare for these war efforts.

However, studying history allows us to understand more fully many of the changes that have occurred in our field. The impact of different philosophies on the content and structure of physical education, exercise science, and sport programs, and changes in the nature and importance of objectives, can be discerned throughout the years. It is important to be aware of the events that served as catalysts and deterrents to the growth of physical education, exercise science, and sport. By understanding the history of physical education, exercise science, and sport, a professional can better understand the nature of the field, appreciate the significant developments of today, and project trends for the future.

DISCUSSION QUESTIONS

1. How has physical education changed and developed over the past 250 years?
2. During each time period discussed in the chapter, how did societal movements and events influence sport, fitness, and physical education?
3. How have the Olympics and Paralympics changed and developed over time? What factors influenced the changes?
4. How has Title IX influenced the participation of girls and women in physical education and sport? Has the intent of the law, to provide equal opportunities for men and women, been upheld?

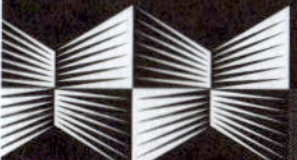

GET CONNECTED

Amateur Athletic Foundation of Los Angeles–offers access to the history of the Olympics and sports, including a wonderful catalog of art and artifacts; research articles on children and the media, gender, and sport; the *Journal of Olympic History*; and the *Journal of Sport History*.

https://la84.org/

HickokSports.com–contains information about the history of specific sports and biographies of athletes from many different sports and times.

North American Society for Sport History–provides access to NASSH news, related sites, and the *Journal of Sport History*.

https://www.nassh.org/

Smithsonian Museum–focuses on significant events in sport and the social context in which they occurred. The site includes information about different athletes and their contributions to changing the game or removing barriers, key sports events, the Olympics, and resources.

https://www.si.edu/learn-explore

SELF-ASSESSMENT ACTIVITIES

These activities are designed to help you determine if you have mastered the materials and competencies presented in this chapter.

1. Describe events that served as catalysts for the growth of physical education, exercise science, and sport, and events that served as deterrents to the growth of physical education, exercise science, and sport throughout history.
2. Using the information provided in the Get Connected box, explore the history of the Olympic Games or other sports.
3. Project future developments for physical education, exercise science, and sport based on historical events, including events from both early and recent times.
4. Using the MyHistro mapping tool at www.myhistro.com, develop a timeline of the salient events throughout history specific to your discipline.

REFERENCES

1. Struna, N. L. (1997). Sport history. In J. D. Massengale & R. A. Swanson (Eds.), *The history of exercise and sport science* (pp. 143–180). Champaign, IL: Human Kinetics.
2. Mechikoff, R. A., & Estes, S. G. (2009). *A history and philosophy of physical education and sport: From ancient civilizations to the modern world* (5th ed.). New York, NY: WCB/McGraw Hill.
3. Salter, M. (1997). Play in ritual: An ethnohistorical overview of native North America. *Stadion, 3*(2), 230–243.
4. Ray, H. L. (1970, June 14). Let's have a friendly game of war. *Quest, 14,* 28–41.
5. Blackshear, T. B. & Culp, B. (2022). The Hidden Figures of physical education: Black women who paved the way in PE. Momentum, winter issue.
6. Henry, F. M. (1964). Physical education: An academic discipline. *Journal of Health, Physical Education, and Recreation, 37*(7), 32–69.
7. Ziegler, E. F. (1994). *Physical education and kinesiology in North America: professional and scholarly foundations.* Champaign, IL: Stipes.
8. Ziegler, E. F. (1997). From one image to a sharper one! *Physical Educator, 54*(2), 72–77.
9. US Department of Health and Human Services. (2020). *Healthy people 2030.* Washington, DC: US Government Printing Office. Retrieved from http://www.healthypeople.gov.
10. US National Center for Chronic Disease Prevention and Health Promotion & President's Council on Physical Fitness and Sports. (1996). *Physical activity and health: A report of the Surgeon General.* Atlanta, Ga: US Dept. of Health and Human Services, Centers for Disease Control and Prevention, National Center for Chronic Disease Prevention and Health Promotion.
11. US Department of Health and Human Services. (2010). *The surgeon general's vision for a healthy and fit nation.* Retrieved from http://www.surgeongeneral.gov.
12. Biles, F. (1971). The physical education public information project. *Journal of Health, Physical Education, Recreation, 41*(7), 53–55.
13. National Association for Sport and Physical Education. (1990). *Definition of a physically educated person: Outcomes of quality physical education programs.* Reston, VA: AAHPERD.
14. National Association for Sport and Physical Education. (1995). *Moving into the future: National standards for physical education–A guide to content and assessment.* St. Louis, MO: Mosby.
15. National Association for Sport and Physical Education. (2004). *Moving into the future: National standards for physical education* (2nd ed.). Reston, VA: AAHPERD.

16. National Association for Sport and Physical Education. (1993). *Shape of the nation 1993.* Reston, VA: AAHPERD.
17. SHAPE America. (2014). *National standards & grade-level outcomes for K-12 physical education.* Champaign, IL: Human Kinetics.
18. SHAPE America. (2016). *Shape of the national report: Status of physical education in the USA.* Reston, VA: AAHPERD.
19. American Alliance for Health, Physical Education, Recreation, and Dance. (1980). *Health-related fitness test.* Reston, VA: AAHPERD.
20. American Alliance for Health, Physical Education, Recreation, and Dance. (1988). *Physical best.* Reston, VA: AAHPERD.
21. National Federation of State High School Associations. (2022). *2018-2019 high school athletics participation survey.* Retrieved from http://www.nfhs.org.
22. National Collegiate Athletic Association. (2022). *Membership.* Retrieved from http://www.ncaa.org.
23. National Association of Intercollegiate Athletes. (2022). Retrieved from www.naia.org.
24. National Junior College Athletic Association. (2022). *Sponsors and partners.* Retrieved from http://www.njcaa.org.
25. National Collegiate Athletic Association. (2022). *About us: Resources and finances.* Retrieved from http://www.ncaa.org/about/resources/finances.
26. Education Amendments Act of 1972, 20 U.S.C. §§1681-1688 (1972).
27. Statista. (2021). Number of student athletes in the United States in 2020, by gender. https://www.statista.com/statistics/1098761/student-athletes-by-gender/.
28. Women's Sports Foundation. (2022). History of Title IX. https://www.womenssportsfoundation.org/advocacy/history-of-title-ix/.
29. International Paralympic Committee. (2022). *Paralympic games 2020.* Retrieved from https://www.paralympic.org/tokyo-2020.

Polka Dot Images/Getty Images

CHAPTER 5

MOTOR BEHAVIOR

OBJECTIVES

After reading this chapter, students should be able to—

- Define motor behavior, motor development, motor control, and motor learning, and understand the influence of readiness, motivation, reinforcement, and individual differences on the learning of motor skills.
- Understand selected models of motor learning, characteristics of performance, and the stages of learning and be able to draw implications for instruction.
- Apply to the teaching of motor skills selected concepts of motor learning such as feedback, design of practice, and transfer.
- Describe the fundamental movements and their development.

Motor behavior is a broad umbrella term used to encompass the areas of motor control, motor learning, and motor development. This chapter provides a short introduction to motor behavior. In this chapter, the terms *teacher* and *learner* are used in their broadest sense to encompass physical education, exercise science, and sport professionals (teachers) who provide instruction to people of all ages (learners) in a diversity of settings.

MOTOR BEHAVIOR

One of the primary concerns of physical education, exercise science, and sport professionals is the learning and refinement of motor skills. Motor behavior is concerned with the acquisition and control of motor skills across the lifespan.[1] Motor behavior encompasses three areas: motor learning, motor control, and motor development. All of these areas, although highly specialized, are interrelated. Although researchers in these areas focus on slightly different questions, a more highly integrated approach to research is often seen.

MOTOR LEARNING AND MOTOR CONTROL

Motor learning and motor control are interrelated. The definition and scope of these specialized areas of study and areas of study are briefly described in this section.

SOCIAL JUSTICE

Talking Points

- Beliefs about growth and development as well as physical activity vary from culture to culture. As professionals, it is important we understand how these cultural beliefs influence the acquisition of motor skills and participation in physical activity by people of all ages.
- Although many today view engagement in physical activity by older adults as positive and contributing to good health, some older adults face discrimination and lack of opportunity to participate as a result of ageism.
- We need to be more aware of the challenges individuals with disabilities face in the learning of motor skills, particularly those individuals who have disabilities affecting their senses. Since the senses play a prominent role in learning, we must find ways to address these challenges and help individuals reach their potential.
- As physical education programs in the schools are cut back to address academics, efforts must be made to ensure that all children and youth have access to opportunities within the community to develop their fundamental motor skills, providing them with a strong foundation for future participation in physical activity.

Definition and Scope

Motor learning is the study of the acquisition of motor skills as a result of practice and experience. *Learning* is defined as a relatively permanent change in behavior or performance as a result of practice or experience. Learning is inferred from changes in the performance. For example, an instructor determines whether an individual has learned a tennis serve by observing and assessing the individual's performance. As the individual receives instruction and practices, performance of the tennis serve should improve–that is, become more consistent, effective, and efficient. You would then infer from the individual's performance that learning had occurred.

Motor skills range in scope from simple skills, such as learning to walk, to highly complex skills, such as those shown by an elite gymnast performing intricate tumbling passes as part of a floor exercise routine. Motor learning can involving the acquisition of new skills–learning to bat in cricket–or the relearning of skills after an injury or illness, such as relearning how to walk again after a stroke. Understanding how feedback, practice, and individual differences influence the acquisition and retention of motor skills is one of the primary goals of motor learning.[1]

Intimately related to the area of motor learning is motor control. Motor control is the study of the neurophysiological and behavioral processes affecting the control of skilled movements. Researchers in motor control are interested in the processes underlying the learning and performance of motor skills, such as how the nervous system works with the muscular system to produce and coordinate movement. Understanding how environmental information is used to plan and adjust movements is an important aspect of motor control.[1]

MOTOR BEHAVIOR

Motor Learning–the study of the acquisition of motor skills as a result of practice and experience.

Motor Control–the study of the neurophysiological and behavioral processes affecting the control of skilled movements.

Motor Development–the study of the origins of and changes in movement behavior throughout the lifespan.

With practice, motor performance becomes more efficient, effective, and consistent.

Kelly Redinger/Design Pics

Areas of Study

Many topics have captured the interest of researchers. Researchers in motor learning have investigated the effectiveness of various types of practice, the impact of different types of feedback on motor performance, the use of cognitive strategies to improve performance, reaction time, and transfer of learning–how skills learned in one setting can enhance or hinder learning in another setting. Some researchers have focused their efforts on understanding motor problems in special populations–such as postural and coordination control in the aging. Motor control researchers have tried to determine how movements are coordinated, how the sequence of our behaviors is controlled, and how information obtained from the environment is used to plan and modify movements.

Researchers in motor learning and motor control may address questions such as these:

- How do the type and frequency of feedback impact skill acquisition?
- How does the structure of practice influence the retention of skills?

- How does skill performance change as beginners move from novice to advanced levels of performance?
- How does the aging process affect motor control? How do specific diseases, such as Parkinson's disease, affect an individual's ability to perform motor skills?
- When teaching a skill such as serving in tennis or pitching, should you first emphasize speed or accuracy?
- How do differences in individuals' learning styles influence their ability to learn motor skills?

Advances in technology and a greater emphasis on cross-disciplinary research help further our understanding of how motor skills are learned and controlled.

Motor Learning Models

Many theories have been advanced to explain the process by which motor skills are learned and controlled. These theories help researchers formulate models to illustrate how learning occurs. Models developed from these theories serve as frameworks for professionals. They help professionals design and implement learning experiences for participants in their programs. The information processing model and the dynamical systems model are two of the several models that have been used to describe motor skill acquisition and performance.

Information Processing Model

In its simplest form, the information processing theory explains motor learning in terms of cognition and the processing of information. The information processing model consists of four components or processes: input, decision making, output, and feedback. This model is illustrated in Figure 5-1.

Input is the process of obtaining information from the environment. This information is obtained through the senses. Visual, auditory, kinesthetic, and other sensory information is transmitted through the nervous system to the brain where the process of *decision making* occurs.

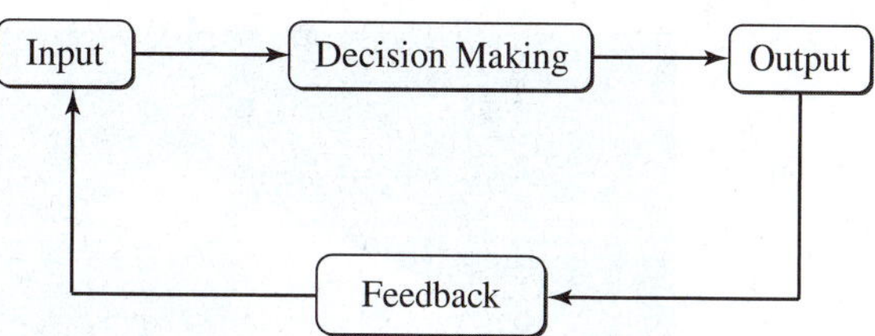

Figure 5-1 Information processing model.

During this step, the input is processed; that is, it is sifted, evaluated, and interpreted. Relevant environmental cues are identified. Using this current information and relevant past experiences stored in memory, the individual selects an appropriate response. A decision is reached about what movement to make. The response is organized; a "motor program" that will control the response is retrieved from memory. The muscles are directed to contract in proper order, with the proper amount of force and with the correct timing to produce the desired movement. The response and its execution are the *output*.

Feedback is information about the performance of the movement and its quality, appropriateness, or outcome. This information can be used to provide input for making ongoing adjustments in performance or to modify the next skill attempt. The knowledge gained from feedback can be used to improve the decision making process as well as the succeeding output. As individuals become more adept at performing the skill, often they also become more skilled at using the feedback to improve the performance.

Teachers can use this model to design practices that facilitate individuals' opportunity to learn through appropriate structuring of the learning environment. The teacher must give learners appropriate input through the careful selection of teaching methods, materials, and procedures. The teacher must help learners understand the goal of the movement and then distinguish between relevant and irrelevant information or cues with respect to that goal, drawing the learners' attention to cues essential for the decision making process and teaching the learners to disregard the irrelevant ones.

Fencing is a sport that requires rapid processing of information as well as split-second decision making skills.
Lawrence M. Sawyer/J&L Images/Photodisc/Getty Images

Next, the teacher can help learners become wise decision makers. This can be accomplished by helping learners evaluate their past experiences, by explaining the "why" of underlying skills and strategies, by instructing learners on how to use the available feedback, and by making sure that the learners are attending to the right cues and interpreting the information correctly. The use of proper progressions and provision of appropriate and sufficient practice opportunities can help learners' development.

Finally, the teacher can help learners by providing feedback about the learners' performance and communicating this information to learners in an understandable way. Additionally, the teacher must draw the learners' attention to the feedback available during the execution of the skill as well as the information regarding the outcome of the performance. This information can provide the basis for adjustments in learners' movements.

As you can see from the information processing model, the senses play a critical role in motor learning and performance. Vision is one of the most important senses for gathering information or input from the environment to use for decision making. An area of study that is gaining increasing emphasis is sports vision training. *Sports vision training* combines vision science, motor learning, biomechanics, sport psychology, and neuroanatomy to help individuals improve their performance.[2]

Dynamical Systems Model

The dynamical systems theory explains human movement as the result of the interaction between three systems: the individual or the organism, the environment, and the task. Characteristics of each system interact to influence movement.[3,4] Based on this theory, the dynamical systems model is shown in Figure 5-2.

Individual characteristics encompass the anatomical and physiological systems, heredity, height, weight, previous experiences, fitness status, motivation, and a host of other characteristics such as perceptual skills and attention. These are the individual differences that professionals take into account in designing movement experiences to learn new skills or improve performance.

The environment reflects the context in which the learning or performing is taking place. This could include physical characteristics such as the weather or space, or sociocultural characteristics such as competition or peer pressure. The teacher is an important part of the environment and can

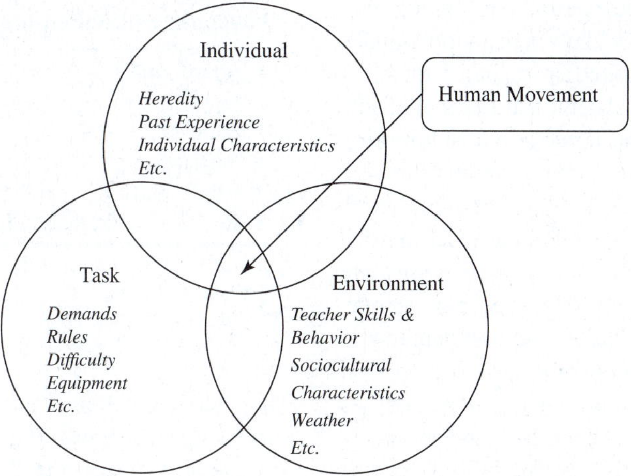

Figure 5-2 Dynamical systems model.

exert a tremendous influence on learning.[3] Teachers' skill in presenting the task, structuring the progressions, creating a positive learning environment, directing learners' attention to relevant cues, and providing feedback to learners are just a few of the characteristics that interact with individual differences and the task to influence learning.[4]

The characteristics of the task must also be considered as part of the dynamical system interaction. Task characteristics reflect the demands of the task; for example, does the skill place a premium on speed, accuracy, or both? The task difficulty needs to be considered as well. Another factor is the nature of the task. Does the skill require making adjustments to individuals in the environment, such as in dribbling a ball down the field in soccer, or is the environment stable, as in archery? The rules of a sport or game and the boundaries in which it is conducted are also task characteristics that must be considered.

Professionals involved in the teaching of human movement skills need to consider the interaction of all three systems–individual, environment, and task–in designing learning experiences to develop skills. The environment and task systems are the most easily manipulated by the teacher to facilitate the acquisition and development of motor skills.[3] Additionally, failure to consider the characteristics of one of the systems, such as the maturity or fitness level of the individual, can hinder the acquisition of skills and limit performance. As a professional, it is important to realize the dynamic nature of this interaction and consider aspects of all systems in planning for learning.

As you can see from these brief descriptions of the information processing model and the dynamical systems model, human movement is an exceedingly complex phenomenon. Theories and the models developed from them give us some insight into understanding human movement and offer professionals guidance for developing and improving a wide variety of movements and skills. Advances in technology, increasingly sophisticated research methodology, and interdisciplinary approaches hold great promise for enhancing our understanding of motor skill acquisition and control.

An understanding of the manner in which individuals learn skills can help professionals make the learning process more effective and more enjoyable–that is, less frustrating for learners. Because we infer learning from performance, it is important to know what performance characteristics are indicative of learning.

Performance Characteristics and Skill Learning

Performance is defined as an observable behavior. Learning, a change in the capability of an individual to perform a skill, is inferred from performance.

If you were teaching a new motor skill, such as batting a cricket ball, you could observe an individual's performance and judge whether or not learning had occurred. If the individual demonstrated a relatively permanent improvement in performance following practice or experience, you could say that the individual has learned the skill. Magill and Anderson describe six performance characteristics associated with skill learning.[5] These characteristics are improvement, consistency, stability, persistence, adaptability, and reduction of attention demand.

Improved performance of a skill over a period of time indicates that learning has occurred. As learning progresses, the skill performance becomes more consistent. There is less variability from one performance attempt to the next. The individual's performance becomes more stable as learning occurs, with the individual less affected by internal concerns like anxiety or external conditions such as crowd noise or weather. As learning continues, the performance becomes more persistent, that is, lasting over longer periods of time.

Another performance characteristic is adaptability. As a skill is learned, the individual becomes more adept at modifying the skill to changing conditions, whether they are internal conditions such as heightened level of anxiety, or external conditions, such as being confronted with different types of defenses in a basketball game. This term may also be referred to generalizability defined as the ability of the individual to modify the skill to adapt to changing demands in the environment.

The last characteristic of a performance that reflects learning is the reduction in attention demands. As an individual becomes more skilled, there is less need to concentrate on how to perform the skill, freeing up the individual's attention to focus on other events in the environment. For example, at first, when learning to be a goalkeeper in soccer, the individual has to concentrate on how to catch the ball and how to punt it. Once the individual becomes more capable in these skills, more attention can be directed to strategy, such as cutting down the angle of the attacking player or organizing the team's defenders.

As individuals acquire motor skills, their performance improves and becomes more consistent. They become better at performing the skill under varying and changing conditions, and reduce their attentional focus on the skill itself, enabling them to focus on environment. We can infer from these performance changes that learning has occurred. Professionals must also be aware that learning occurs in stages.

Performance Characteristics and Skill Learning

- Improvement
- Consistency
- Stability
- Persistence
- Adaptability
- Reduction in Attention Demands

Source: Magill R and Anderson D. *Motor Learning and Control: Concepts and Applications* (12th ed.). New York: McGraw Hill, 2021.

Stages of Learning

As an individual learns motor skills and makes the transition from unskilled to skilled performer, the individual progresses through several stages. Many different models have been developed to explain the stages associated with the skill acquisition process. One of them, developed by Fitts and Posner, identified three stages of learning: the cognitive stage, the associative stage, and the autonomous stage.[6] The teacher must be cognizant of the characteristics of the learner at each stage to plan for instruction. Different instructional strategies and techniques are required at each stage to make practice more effective. (See Table 5-1.)

Cognitive Stage

The first stage of learning is the cognitive stage. During this stage, the learner is trying to understand the nature goal of the activity to be learned. The learner might be concerned with such questions as "How do I stand?" "How do I hold the tennis racquet?" "How do you score in this game?" "What is the sequence of actions in this swimming stroke?" The learner also needs to pay close attention to the information provided by the instructor;

TABLE 5-1 Characteristics Associated with Stages of Learning

Cognitive	Associative	Autonomous
Learner's focus		
Cognitive understanding of the goal of the skill	Concentration on temporal aspects or timing of movements	Concentration on use of the skill in performance situations, use of strategies
Concentration on spatial aspects or sequence of skill components		
Performance characteristics		
Lacking smoothness, inefficient, variable, large number of gross errors	Smoother, less variable, more efficient, reduction of extraneous movements, fewer and reduced range of errors	Smooth, efficient, highly refined and well organized spatially and temporally, adaptable to environmental demands
Teacher's focus		
Provide overview of nature of skill and goal, feedback on intent of skill, information and demonstration of skill, cognitive understanding	Direct learner's attention to critical cues and feedback available; provide numerous practice opportunities; accommodate individual differences	Focus on refinement of response, consistency for closed skills and flexibility for open skills, use of skill in performance situations, feedback for refinement of movements

this includes verbal directions as well as visual information, perhaps from demonstration of a skill or a videotape of a performer executing this skill. After analyzing this information, the learner formulates a plan of action based on an understanding of the task and the specific directions provided by the instructor. Formulating a plan of action is referred to as establishing a motor plan or an executive plan. A high level of concentration on the task is required as the learner tries to put together the various parts of the skill in the correct sequence.

As the learner makes initial attempts at performing the skill, the performance is characterized by a large number of errors, usually gross in nature, and a great deal of variability. To improve skill performance, the learner needs specific feedback from the instructor, communicated in understandable terms. For example, someone just learning the tennis forehand must concentrate on moving to the correct position on the court, the grip of the racquet, the stance, turning the body, keeping an eye on the ball, making contact with the ball with the head of the racquet so that it goes over the net, shifting the body's weight, following through, and returning to ready position. The beginner at times will hit the ball over the net; with the next attempt, the learner might hit the ball into the net or out of the court or miss the ball entirely. The learner's actions, although performed in the correct sequence, may lack the smooth, polished look and the consistency of a highly skilled performer.

Associative Stage

The second stage is the associative stage. At this point, the basics of the skill have been learned and the learner concentrates on refining the skill. During this stage, the learner works on mastering the timing needed for the skill; the learner's performance looks smoother. Fewer errors are committed, and the same type of error tends to recur. The learner is also aware of some of the more obvious errors he or she is making in executing the task and can use this information to adjust subsequent performance. The tennis player learning the forehand may notice more success in getting the ball over the net and inside the boundaries of the court, although he or she cannot place the ball with any assurance. The player may notice a frequent failure to follow through after contacting the ball, but he or she is not aware that the angle of the racquet face needs adjustment. The instructor can provide the learner with additional instruction focusing on specific actions and point out relevant cues.

Autonomous Stage

The third stage is the autonomous stage. This stage of learning is reached after much practice. The learner can perform the skill consistently with few errors. The skill is well coordinated and may appear to be performed effortlessly. During this stage, the skill has become almost automatic. The learner does not have to pay attention to every aspect of the skill; he or she can perform the skill without consciously thinking about it at all. The tennis player no longer has to concentrate on the fundamentals of the skill; instead, his or her focus can be directed to placing the ball in the court, varying the speed of the shot, placing spin on the ball, or executing game tactics. The learner also becomes more skilled at detecting errors and making adjustments, in a sense becoming his or her own teacher.

Individuals do not proceed through these stages at the same rate. It may also be difficult at times to identify what stage an individual is in. To plan practices to promote effective learning professionals need to be cognizant of the characteristics and the needs of the learner in the various stages. Professionals also need to be aware of changes in performance characteristics that indicate learning is occurring and plan their instruction accordingly.

Factors Influencing Learning

To create an effective learning situation, teachers must be cognizant the myriad of factors that influence learning. Four of these factors–readiness, motivation, reinforcement, and individual differences–will be discussed.

Highly skilled performers exemplify the autonomous stage of learning.

Lawrence M. Sawyer/J&L Images/Photodisc/Getty Images

Readiness

Successful acquisition of new information or skills depends on the individual's level of readiness. *Readiness* can be defined in terms of physiological and psychological factors influencing an individual's ability and willingness to learn. Physiological readiness in children is the development of the necessary strength, flexibility, and endurance, as well as development of the various organ systems, to such a degree that children can control their bodies in physical activities. Psychological readiness refers to the learner's state of mind. One's feeling or attitude toward learning a particular skill–in other words, the desire and willingness to learn–will affect one's acquisition of that particular skill. To create an effective learning environment, the teacher must keep in mind the individual's physiological and psychological readiness.

Teachers planning learning activities must be cognizant of the individual's cognitive, affective, and physical characteristics as well as the individual's past experiences. The teacher should structure the learning experience so that the individual experiences success rather than the frustration that may come from trying to learn a task that is too difficult or beyond the individual's ability at that time. The teacher may need to modify the task to make it either easier or more challenging. For example, many youth baseball and softball teams let younger children hit the ball off a batting tee rather than hit a pitched ball. This adjustment was made because younger children were having difficulty tracking and successfully hitting a moving object. In being allowed to hit the ball while it was stationary–sitting atop a batting tee–the children were able to practice the skill of striking an object, or batting, and experience success. Adjusting the learning task to the individual's ability requires consideration of the individual's physiological readiness. Planning learning experiences that promote success enhances the individual's psychological readiness to learn.

Motivation

Motivation is a basic factor in learning. The term *motivation* refers to a condition within an individual who initiates activity directed toward a goal. The study of motivation focuses on the causes of behavior, specifically those factors that influence the initiation, maintenance, and intensity of behavior.

Learning experiences should be appropriate for the participant's abilities.

Ilene MacDonald/Alamy Stock Photo

Needs and drives form the basic framework for motivation. When individuals sense an unfulfilled need, they are moved to do something about it. This desire prompts people to seek a solution to the recognized need through an appropriate line of action. This line of action may require practice, effort, mastery of knowledge, or other behavior to be successful. For example, an individual who is hungry becomes motivated to seek food, whereas at the cognitive level, the individual who wants to pass a certification desires to acquire the necessary knowledge.

Motivation refers to an individual's general arousal to action. It might be thought of as the desire or drive a person must have to achieve a goal to satisfy a particular need. The term *need* refers to an internalized deficiency of the organism. The need might be physiological or psychological in nature. The term *drive* refers to the concept of the stimulus for action. Motivation, for example, might be associated with the drive to exercise to satisfy the need to keep the body healthy. The motivating factor might be internal, resulting from the individual's own desire to be fit, or it might be the result of some outside force, such as peer pressure to be thin.

Although motives are internal in nature, they may be affected by external influences. However, it is common to describe an individual's motives as being either internal or external. Motives such as the desire to develop one's body, to have fun, or to test one's limits are examples of internal motives for learning. The desire to win awards, to appease parental pressures for participation, or to win money are examples of external motives for participation. For example, some employees may decide to participate in a workplace fitness program because of their desire to enhance their health status (internal motivation); on the other hand, other employees may participate because they were wanted to earn the monetary bonuses offered to those who successfully engaged in the program (external motivation). Internal motivation is more conducive to positive learning and performance and sustained participation than external motivation.

Professionals should be aware of the motives for the individual's participation not only differ but may also change. For example, as previously mentioned, motives for participation in the workplace fitness program vary. Some participants may be internally motivated to join, while others might be externally motivated and perhaps even reluctant to participate in the activities. During the course of the program, however, the externally motivated participants may develop an internal motivation. The change could result because professionals made the program challenging, meaningful, and satisfying to the employees. As a consequence, the once reluctant employees may become an enthusiastic participant in the program.

Teachers' actions can have a positive effect on the individual's motivation. In a physical education and sport program, not all individuals will be motivated to the same extent to learn new skills; in fact, some individuals may not be motivated to learn at all. Teachers can enhance an individual's motivation for learning through goal setting, that is, establishing challenging, albeit attainable, goals for the individual. Motivation can also be enhanced by structuring the learning environment for success and by making the learning experience positive and enjoyable. An individual's level of motivation may also be enhanced through reinforcement.

Reinforcement

Professionals can use reinforcement to promote the development of skills and desirable behaviors. *Reinforcement* is using events, actions, and behaviors to increase the likelihood of a certain response (e.g., a skill or a behavior) recurring.

Reinforcement may be positive or negative. Reinforcement is considered positive when it is given following the desired response, and it is deemed negative when it is withheld following a desired response. Teachers providing encouragement, praise, or recognition of effort following successful execution of a skill is an example of positive reinforcement. Such an acknowledgment of an individual's success not only will serve to reinforce correct skill performance but will also likely motivate the individual to continue efforts to master the skill. If teachers belittle an individual's unsuccessful effort to perform a skill and discontinue this behavior when the individual successfully executes the skill, the teacher is using negative reinforcement.

Two types of reinforcers are tangible and intangible. Tangible reinforcers are material items such as a medal or money. Intangible reinforcers include verbal praise, a pat on the back, or a nod of approval. Think about the reinforcement you have received for your efforts and whether they were tangible or intangible in nature. For reinforcement to be effective, it must be meaningful to, important to, or desired by the recipient.

Reinforcement, motivation, readiness, and development are important factors influencing learning. Another important consideration in planning for learning is individual differences.

Individual Differences

In any learning situation, be it with children or adults, the teacher must strive to provide optimal learning experiences for all participants. As a teacher, this means committing to learning about the uniqueness of each learner. Race, gender, culture, and socioeconomic status are just a few differences that can influence the prior physical activity experiences individuals bring to the learning situation. Our increasingly diverse society means that some individuals are bilingual, with English being their second language. Thus, teachers need to take into account differences in language abilities when instructing their learners. Differences in physical abilities, including fitness levels, influence physical activity instruction. Some individuals possess a high degree of fitness or skill in a certain area, such as tennis, whereas others might have lower levels of fitness and no prior experience with the sport. Personality differences must also be considered. Some individuals are eager to try new skills and see learning a new skill as a challenge, while others are reluctant or intimidated by the prospect of learning something new. Some individuals are highly self-motivated to learn, while others might need more support and encouragement.

Differences in preferred learning styles hold implications for the manner in which the skills and activities are to be taught. Some individuals learn

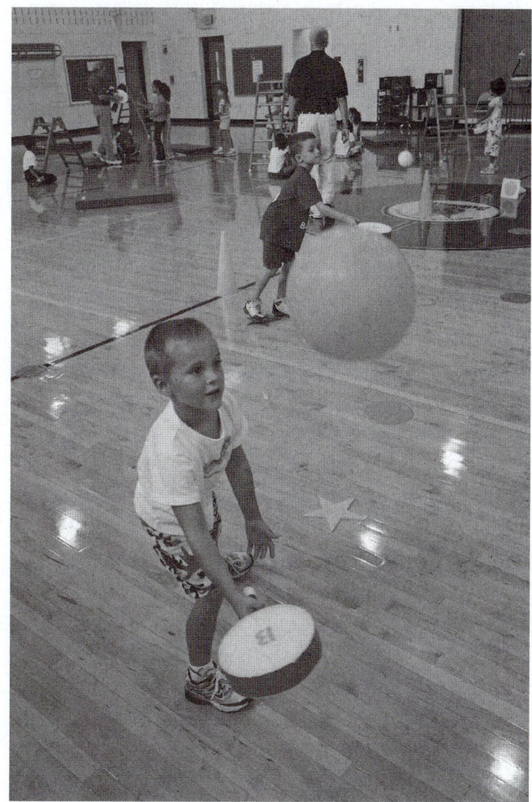

Elementary children work with paddles and different size objects to develop eye-hand coordination.

Lars A. Niki/McGraw Hill

best by listening to the instruction, while others find it more effective to observe a skilled demonstration. Some individuals prefer to work in groups, while others prefer to learn more independently. Teachers should include a variety of learning experiences to accommodate differences in learning styles. By differentiating instruction, teachers strive to match learning opportunities to individual learners to elicit optimal levels of learning for each individual. Accomplishing this requires careful planning and commitment on the part of the teachers. It is not an easy task to design learning experiences for a diversity of abilities, but it is not impossible. One of the first steps is taking time to learn about each individual's uniqueness, areas of strength, and areas where additional support might be needed for the individual to achieve success. Having a wide repertoire of teaching styles and approaches helps teachers vary instruction to meet individuals' needs.

Motor Learning Concepts

In planning for motor learning, the professional must consider a learner's level of readiness, development, individual characteristics, motivation, and need for reinforcement. At this point, it will be helpful to consider additional concepts, factors, and conditions that promote the learning of motor skills and improve performance.

1. *Practice sessions should be structured to promote optimal conditions for learning*. Practices should be organized so that distracting elements are eliminated from the setting. The instructor should ensure that the proper mental set has been established in the mind of the learner, the proper facilities and equipment are available, the learner has the proper background to understand the material being presented, and conditions are such that a challenging learning situation exists.

Much research has been done on the organization of practice. The design of practice should consider the nature of the task to be learned, the characteristics of the learner, the energy costs of the tasks, and safety. Practice sessions should be structured to maximize the number of opportunities learners have to practice the task. Using small groups, incorporation of stations, and providing an array of relevant activities helps teachers maximize practice opportunities.

2. *Learners must understand the task to be learned*. Helping the learner acquire a cognitive understanding of the nature of the task to be learned is one of the first steps in the learning process. As previously discussed in the stages of learning, the learner must establish an executive or motor plan for action; this involves understanding the nature of the task, analyzing the task, demands, and devising techniques to achieve the task goal. This conception of the task, or image, serves as a guide for the learner's initial attempts.

Typically, learners have been helped to establish an image of the task or skill through verbal instructions provided by the teacher. However, the teacher may overuse instructions when faced with the task of describing a complex movement. Too many instructions may overwhelm learners, and in an effort to cope with the avalanche of information about what to do and when to do it, learners may disregard much of the information. Instructions should focus on key elements of the task.

Succinct, accurate instructions in conjunction with other techniques such as demonstrations or watching videos of performers may be more useful than instructions alone in helping the learner understand the task. Demonstrations of the skill allow the learner to form an image of the task. The teacher can use instructions to call the learner's attention to the critical components of the skill. During the learner's initial performances of the task, the learner can model the performance exhibited. Children frequently learn skills on their own by imitating or modeling the performance of others. Teachers may also use videos of skilled performers to provide a model for performance.

3. *The nature of the skill or task to be learned should be considered when designing practice.* Skills can be classified in a variety of ways. To facilitate learning, practices should be appropriate to the type of skill to be learned.

One popular skill classification continuum, closed/open, is based on the predictability of the environment in which the skill is performed and the extent to which the performer can control the performance situation. The continuum ranges from predictable to unpredictable. (See Figure 5-3.)

Skills performed in a predictable, stable environment are classified as closed skills. The environment remains the same during the skill performance. Performers are self-paced; they choose when to initiate the skill in the relatively stable environment. Driving a golf ball off a tee, executing a forward 2½ somersault dive from the 3-meter springboard, performing a floor exercise routine in gymnastics, and shooting a foul shot in basketball are examples of closed skills. When instructing closed skills, response consistency should be the goal.

Open skills are skills that are performed in an unpredictable environment. The environment is variable. Performers must continually modify and adapt their responses to the ever-changing environment. Performers must consider external conditions and adapt their skill to them. Shooting a goal during a soccer game, hitting a tennis backhand during a match, and dribbling down the basketball court to execute a layup are examples of open skills. When teaching open skills, teachers should focus on response flexibility, adapting the skill to changing conditions.

Because this classification falls on a continuum, some skills may be placed more toward the middle of the continuum rather than at either end. For example, archery is a self-paced sport, with the

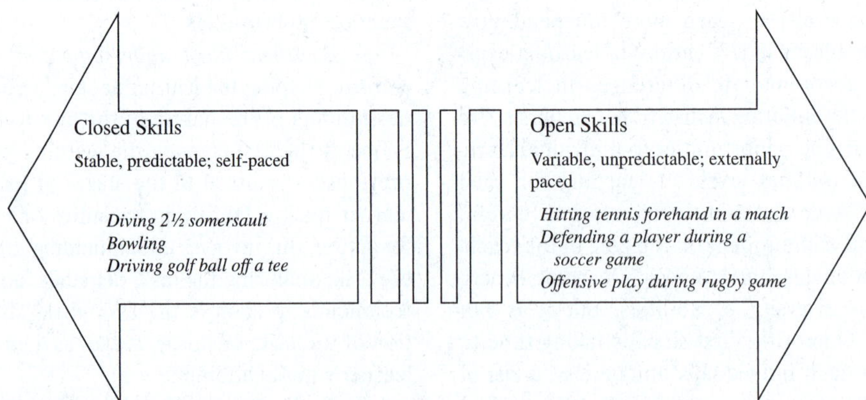

Figure 5-3 Motor skill classification: Open versus closed skills.

archer shooting at a target a set distance away. However, in order to be successful, the archer must take into account environmental conditions, such as the wind, and make modifications to the performance accordingly.

Teachers design of practice should reflect the nature of the skill and the conditions under which the skill will eventually be performed. In practicing closed skills, where the environment remains relatively stable during the performance of the skill, teachers should emphasize achieving consistency of movement. With open skills, the changing environment requires individuals to make alterations in performance to adjust to the changing conditions (e.g., movements of opponents and teammates, speed, and direction of the ball). Thus, practice should be variable, with individuals exposed to a variety of situations similar to those they will actually encounter when performing the skill.

During the initial stages of teaching an open skill, the teacher may structure the environment to be stable (closed) to make learning easier for the beginner. For instance, in learning to bat a pitched ball, the teacher may start the performer out hitting a ball off a batting tee; then the teacher may use a pitching machine set to pitch a ball at a certain speed and height. Finally, the performer is given the opportunity to hit balls thrown by a pitcher and must then learn how to adjust the bat's swing to the varying speeds and heights of the ball. Thus, while open skills may be practiced under closed conditions initially, once the performer is ready, open conditions should prevail.

4. *The nature of the task and the background of the learner should be considered in deciding whether to teach the skill by the whole or the part method.* The instructor must decide whether to teach a skill as a whole or to break it down into its component parts. For example, do you teach a skill such as the front crawl stroke as a whole, or do you break the stroke down and teach it by parts–arm action, leg action, and breathing? What about the jump shot in basketball? Or the tennis serve? If the learner is highly skilled and has had previous experience in the sport, is the whole or the part method better?

This area has been much researched, but the findings are somewhat confusing. At the risk of generalizing, the instructor should teach a highly complex task as parts. Parts should consist of individual, discrete skills. Tasks in which the skill components are highly interrelated, such as the jump shot in basketball, should be taught as a whole. Highly skilled learners with previous experience in the sport will probably be able to learn effectively if the whole method is used. Lesser-skilled learners or individuals with short attention spans, such as young children, may find it easier to learn if taught by the part method. It appears that all learners benefit from seeing a demonstration of the whole skill; this may enhance the organization of the information provided to the learner and the learner's understanding of the goal of the skill.

If the teacher were to teach the high jump by the part method, the learners would be taught the approach (run to the bar); then they would be taught the jump; next, they would be taught the landing. After all components had been taught, the learners would practice the total skill.

Another option is to use the progressive part method, which consists of initially teaching the first two parts of the skill, combining these two parts into a whole, teaching a third part, then connecting this to the first two parts, and so on. For example, the first two sequences in a dance routine would be taught and practiced, then the third sequence taught; then the third sequence would be added to the first two sequences, and all three sequences practiced together. This process of progressively adding parts of a skill is continued until the entire skill is learned.

In summary, the structure of the task–both its complexity and organization–and the characteristics of the learner must be considered in selecting methods of instruction.

5. *Whether speed or accuracy should be emphasized in learning a skill depends on the requirements of the skill.* Teachers are often required to make a judgment as to whether speed or accuracy should be emphasized in the initial stages of learning a skill. For example, a highly skilled tennis player tries to serve the ball with as much velocity as possible into the service court. When teaching the tennis serve,

should the teacher emphasize speed, accuracy, or both speed and accuracy? When teaching pitching, should the teacher emphasize throwing the ball as fast as possible, getting the ball into the strike zone all the time, or pitching the ball into the strike zone as fast and as often as possible? This dilemma—whether to emphasize speed or accuracy—is often referred to as a speed-accuracy trade-off. In essence, to perform the skill as accurately as possible means that the performer will have to sacrifice some speed and perform the skill more slowly. Attainment of maximum speed or velocity in performing a skill is at the expense of accuracy. When both speed and accuracy are desired, both qualities will decrease.

Different sport skills have different speed and accuracy requirements. Pitching a ball or performing a tennis serve requires a high degree of both speed and accuracy. In throwing the javelin, speed is more important than accuracy, whereas in the tennis drop shot, accuracy in terms of court placement is more important than speed. The teacher must understand the requirements of the task and design practices accordingly.

Teachers must decide whether to emphasize speed or accuracy when teaching a skill that requires both elements.
Carson Granci/Design Pics/SuperStock

The research seems to suggest that skills should be practiced as they are to be performed. This advice is relatively straightforward when the skill emphasizes either speed or accuracy. For example, based on the research findings, speed should be emphasized in teaching the javelin throw, and accuracy emphasized in the tennis drop shot. However, what about skills that place a premium on being both fast and accurate, such as pitching a ball or executing a tennis serve? The research suggests that when both speed and accuracy are of paramount concern, both variables should receive equal and simultaneous emphasis. The rationale is that mastery is sacrificed when an individual practices a motor skill at slower speed than is needed in the game situation, because the person must readjust to the faster situation. The teacher should understand the speed and accuracy demands of a skill and structure practices so that the learner can practice the skill as it is to be ultimately performed.

6. *Transfer of learning can facilitate the learning of motor skills.* The influence of a previously learned skill on the learning or performance of a new skill is called transfer of learning. The influence exerted may be positive or negative. When a previous experience or skill aids in the learning of a new skill, positive transfer occurs. For example, students who play tennis may find it easier to learn other racquet sports such as pickleball, squash, tennis, racquetball, and badminton because both skills require the use of the racquet and similar stokes, although there are some differences in techniques. Transfer, however, is not automatic. Teachers should teach for transfer, pointing out similarities between the tasks and identifying where some adjustments might be needed.

Teachers must also be aware of negative transfer. Negative transfer occurs when a previously learned skill interferes with the learning of a new skill. For example, individuals being introduced to the game of golf for the first time might experience difficulty in swinging the club because of their previous experience in another skill such as softball or baseball. In such cases, the expression often heard is, "You're swinging the golf club like a baseball bat."

Physical educators and coaches seek to transfer the skills and strategies learned in practice sessions to actual game situations. To this end, they strive to make their drills as much like a game as possible, or they make an effort in the practice environment to familiarize their team with situations it may encounter in the game. For example, during practice sessions before a basketball game, coaches may have their substitutes imitate the actions of the opponents so that the varsity team is familiar with the opponents' style of play on the night of the game.

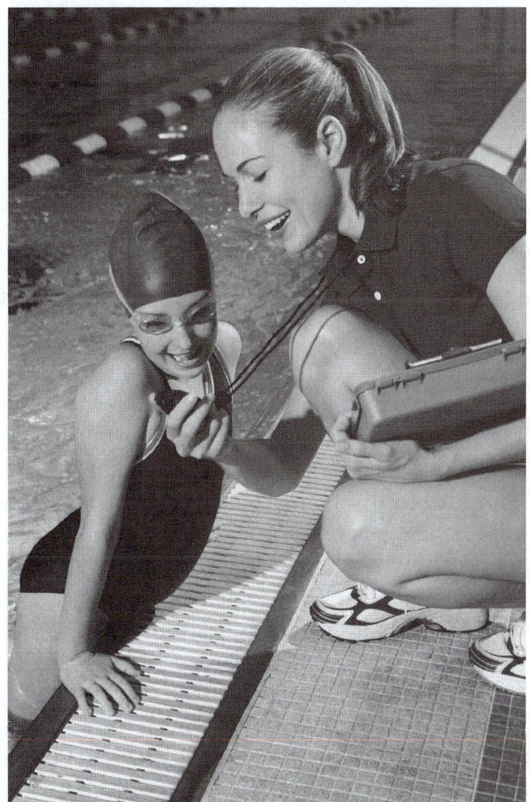

Feedback serves several functions. It provides information to correct performance, helps reinforce learners' efforts, and offers encouragement and motivation.

ThinkStock/age fotostock

Transfer may either facilitate or hinder the acquisition of a skill. Teachers need to be aware of the principles of transfer so that they can use positive transfer to promote skill learning and enhance performance and can readily counteract the effects of negative transfer.

7. *Feedback can play an important role in learning.* One of the most critical factors affecting learning is feedback. Feedback is information about an individual's performance. Feedback can serve several functions. It provides learners with information about their performance. Using this information, learners can make adjustments in their response prior to the next attempt. Second, feedback can serve to reinforce learners' efforts, strengthening the correct response. Finally, feedback may also serve to motivate learners by providing information about their progress.

Feedback may be classified in many ways. Feedback for error correction may focus on the outcome of the movement or the movement itself. Knowledge of results provides information about the effects of the movement on the environment, information that tells the learner whether or not the goal of the movement was achieved. Knowledge of performance provides information about the movement itself. The learner's awareness and feelings about how correctly the movement was executed in relation to the intended movement is knowledge of performance. For example, in shooting a foul shot in basketball, the player can readily see if the goal of the movement–putting the ball in the basket–was attained. This is knowledge of results. However, the player may know even before the ball goes in the basket that the shot will be good because the movement "felt right." This is knowledge of performance. Knowledge of performance depends on the learner being sensitive to the "feelings" associated with correct and incorrect performance; in other words, the learner becomes aware of what feels right and what feels wrong. Changes in performance occur as the learner compares information about the outcome with the desired outcome and information about performance with the intended movement. The learner then adjusts the performance accordingly until the correct response is achieved.

Feedback may also be classified according to its source or according to when it is presented to the learner. Feedback may be described as intrinsic when the source of the information is the outcome of the task or skill itself.[7] Scoring an ace with a tennis serve, having the shot go slightly wide of the goal in soccer, and scoring on a foul shot in basketball are examples of intrinsic feedback. Information from external sources such as an instructor, friend, or video is classified as extrinsic or augmented feedback.[7] When the learner receives information during the performance of the skill, this feedback is referred to as concurrent. Feedback given after the performance is completed is called terminal feedback. Often, feedback is a combination of information from various sources. For example, comments from the teacher during the learner's performance provide the learner with extrinsic concurrent feedback. A soccer player seeing the kicked ball go in the goal receives intrinsic terminal feedback.

How can professionals use feedback effectively? The most effective use of feedback includes both general and specific information. One simple method to guide professionals in giving feedback is the use of a "feedback sandwich."[8] The feedback sandwich combines all three functions of feedback: reinforcement, information, and motivation. For example, "Good job, Robin. With your elbow in line, you will always have good alignment when shooting the basketball. Keep up the good work." Professionals should plan for specific feedback. Feedback should be positive and relate to teaching cues. The feedback sandwich offers professionals a guide to increase the meaningfulness and effectiveness of their feedback.

8. *Learners may experience plateaus in performance.* The extent to which an individual has learned a skill can be inferred from his or her performance. When learning a new skill, an individual may initially demonstrate a sharp improvement in performance. This may be followed by a plateau, or a period in which little or no progress is made. Finally, additional practice results in further improvements in performance.

The plateau may occur for a variety of reasons, such as loss of interest and lack of motivation, failure to grasp a clear concept of the goal to be attained, lack of attention to the proper cues or attention to irrelevant cues, preparation for a transition from fundamental skills to more complex skills in the learning process, or poor learning conditions. Teachers should be cognizant of the plateaus and the conditions under which learners make little or no apparent progress in the activity. They should be especially careful not to introduce certain concepts or skills too rapidly, without allowing sufficient time for their mastery. It is helpful to watch for certain physical deterrents to progress, such as fatigue or lack of strength. Some individuals cannot go beyond a given point because of physiological limits with respect to speed, endurance, or other physical characteristics. Often, however, it is not physiological limits but rather psychological limits that must be overcome. By implementing techniques to enhance learners' interest and enthusiasm, these limits can be overcome.

9. *Self-analysis should be developed.* During the early periods of instruction when the basic techniques of the skill are being learned, learners need frequent instruction and help from the teacher. However, as the skill is mastered, learners should rely less on the teacher's help and more on internal resources. Good teachers help their learners to be their own teacher. This involves providing learners with opportunities for self-criticism and analysis. Learners need to know how to detect errors and how to correct them. By helping learners become aware of their performance and techniques by which it can be improved, teachers promote independent and lifelong learning.

Today, the ease of videotaping via a tablet or smartphone and the development of apps to review performance not only help teachers provide feedback to learners, but also make it easier for learners to self-analyze their performance. Apps such as Coach's Eye, Hudl, and Dartfish, to name a few, enable the teacher or learner to play back the video of their performance, tag certain sections for review, and analyze performance in relationship to desired form. Some apps compare an individual's performance to that of an expert, making it easier to identify needed changes in skill performance.

GUIDELINES FOR PHYSICAL ACTIVITY INSTRUCTION

1. Use models of motor learning to assist in the planning of learning experiences.
2. Match the type of instruction to the individual's stage of learning.
3. Consider the individual's level of readiness when teaching new skills and information.
4. Plan instructional experiences that take into account the individual's level of development in all three domains–cognitive, affective, and psychomotor.
5. Use the powerful influence of motivation to facilitate learning.
6. Provide positive reinforcement to strengthen desirable responses.
7. Take individual differences into account when teaching by selecting approaches that accommodate a diversity of abilities and needs.
8. Structure practice sessions to promote optimal conditions for learning.
9. Help individuals gain an understanding of the task to be learned and its requirements.
10. Consider the nature of the skill or task when designing practice sessions.
11. Evaluate the task demands and assess the learner's background in deciding whether to use the whole or part method to teach a skill.
12. Study the requirements of the skill to determine whether speed or accuracy should be emphasized in teaching.
13. Facilitate learning by using positive transfer.
14. Incorporate appropriate meaningful feedback to help individuals correct their performance, motivate them, and reinforce their efforts.
15. Be prepared to deal with plateaus in performance.
16. Assist individuals in developing self-analysis skills.
17. Provide strong leadership that contributes to the attainment of the desired objectives.

Smart equipment and associated apps provide the user with feedback relative to performance. Smart equipment use small sensors, wireless technology, and apps to capture information about an individual's performance. Tennis rackets, bats, golf clubs, and basketballs are just a few pieces of smart equipment becoming increasingly available and more affordable. With the smart tennis racquet, sensors track the movement of the racquet as well as where the ball hits the strings, the amount of spin, and how hard the ball was hit. This information is wirelessly transmitted to the smart-phone app, which displays the information in easy-to-understand diagrams. The app can track the length of the game, providing the player with information about the total shots, hits, and misses.[9] Smart equipment and apps allow individuals to self-analyze their performance and monitor their learning.

10. *Leadership influences how much learning will take place*. Teachers should make sure that their learners have a clear idea of the goal or objective to be accomplished. Practices should be designed to maximize learners' opportunities to perform the skill and minimize unproductive activities such as waiting. Teachers should be continually alert to detect correct and incorrect responses and encourage correct performance. Learners motivation can be enhanced by providing them with opportunities to experience success and by presenting meaningful activities. Learning activities should be appropriate to learners' level of understanding and be cognizant of individual differences. Teachers should use their leadership to promote participants' learning. The Guidelines for Physical Activity Instruction box summarizes motor learning concepts that will improve performance.

Chapters 10 and 12 provide more information about teaching. Different approaches and strategies related to teaching and learning are discussed within these chapters.

MOTOR DEVELOPMENT

Motor development is encompassed within the broad area of motor behavior. The definition and scope of motor development as well as areas of study are briefly described in this section.

Definition and Scope

Motor development is the study of the origins of and changes in movement behavior throughout the lifespan. Gallahue, Ozmun, and Goodway define motor development as the "progressive change in motor behavior throughout the life cycle brought about by interaction among the requirements of the movement task, the biology of the individual, and the conditions of the learning environment."[10] Payne and Issacs define motor development as a "lifelong process involving the progressions and regressions in our movement ability as we pass through life."[11] They point out that motor development is complex and to fully understand motor development we must understand the ongoing interaction between the cognitive, affective, and psychomotor domains throughout our lifespan.

According to Gallahue and his colleagues, the study of motor development can be undertaken from both a process and a product approach. From the process perspective, "motor development involves the study of the underlying biological, environmental, and task demands that influence change in motor behavior from infancy through older adulthood."[10] From the product perspective, "motor development may be regarded as descriptive or normative change over time and is typically viewed as age-related changes in motor behavior and motor performance."[10]

Areas of Study

Many broad areas of study fall within motor development, including the influence of age on the acquisition of skills and the development of theories to serve as a framework for our understanding of how movements are developed and controlled. Specialists in motor development may investigate questions such as these:

- What are the hereditary and environmental factors most significantly associated with obesity?
- At what age can children safely engage in resistance training?
- How does socioeconomic status affect the development of motor skills?
- What are the developmental stages individuals go through as they acquire fundamental motor skills? What factors affect the rate of development?
- How does early sensory stimulation affect the development of motor skills?
- How does the wearing of shoes or different types of shoes influence the development of walking?
- What are the changes in motor skill development experienced across the lifespan?

Because physical education, exercise science, and sport professionals are concerned with helping individuals of all ages acquire and improve their motor skills, motor development, from both its theoretical and applied perspectives, is important to professionals in our fields.

Phases of Motor Development

The study of motor development emphasizes consideration of a multitude of factors that influence all aspects of development across the lifespan. Development is a highly interrelated process. The study of motor development must not be undertaken in isolation but rather grounded in the study of the total developmental process of humans across the lifespan. It requires consideration of the interaction of both the cognitive and affective domains of behavior on motor development as well as the impact of a vast array of individual and environmental factors.

Gallahue developed and continues to refine an hourglass model (see Figure 5-4) to illustrate how development is a continuous process, beginning at conception and continuing throughout the lifespan, ceasing at death.[10] In our hourglass is the "stuff of life: 'sand.'" He views sand entering our hourglass from two containers, which symbolize the hereditary and environmental contributions to the process of development. The heredity container has a lid, reflecting that at conception our genetic makeup is determined; thus, the amount of sand in that container is fixed. The second container, the environment, has no lid; thus, more sand can be added to it from the environment and sand poured into our hourglass.

During the early reflexive (in utero to about 1 year of age) and rudimentary movement (birth to about 2 years of age) phases of motor development, the sand pours into the hourglass primarily from the heredity container. During the first 2 years of life, the sequential progression of motor development is highly predictable. For example, with the

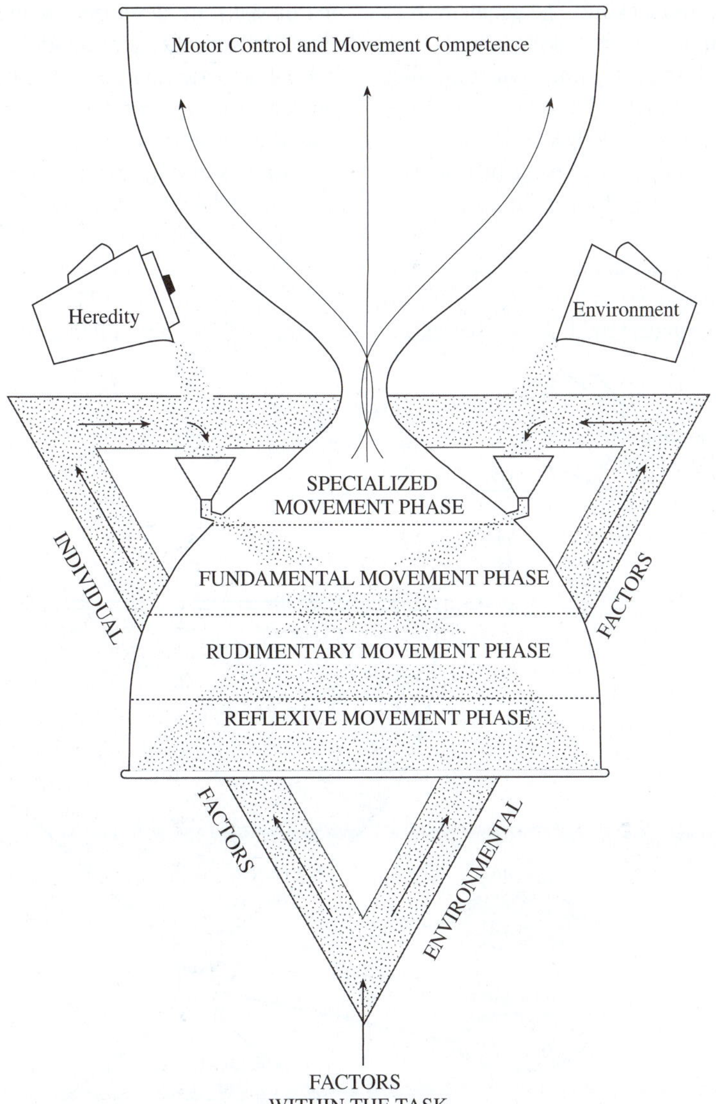

Figure 5-4 Gallahue's model of lifespan motor development.

Gallahue DL and Ozmun JC. *Understanding Motor Development: Infants, Children, Adolescents, Adults* (5th ed.). New York, NY: McGraw Hill, 2012.

rudimentary movements, children learn to sit before they stand and stand before they walk. However, there is considerable variability in the rates at which children acquire these rudimentary skills. This variability in motor skill acquisition occurs throughout life. Motor skill acquisition is enhanced when individuals–infants, children, adolescents, and adults–receive additional opportunities for practice, encouragement, and instruction in an environment conducive to learning. When these opportunities are absent or limited, acquisition of motor skills is inhibited. The rate of acquisition is also influenced by the nature and the requirements of the task.

During the fundamental movement phase (ages 2 to 7), children begin to develop the fundamental movement skills, such as running, jumping, throwing, catching, and kicking. The acquisition of these fundamental movement skills can be described as moving through separate, but somewhat overlapping, stages: initial, emerging elementary, and proficient (these are briefly described later). Encouragement, instruction, and plentiful opportunities for practice are crucial for children to move through these stages.

Acquisition of specialized movement skills, from about ages 7 to 10 and older, is influenced by the attainment of mature, fundamental skills. Specialized motor skills are developed, refined, and combined; these skills are used for activities of daily living, recreational activities, and sports. These skills have improved form, greater accuracy, and better control than the fundamental motor skills.

After showing how our movements are developed, Gallahue then portrays the hourglass as turning over at some point in our lives; sand begins to pour out, typically in our late teens and early twenties.[10] (See Figure 5-5.) The time for the "turnover" is quite variable and influenced more by social and

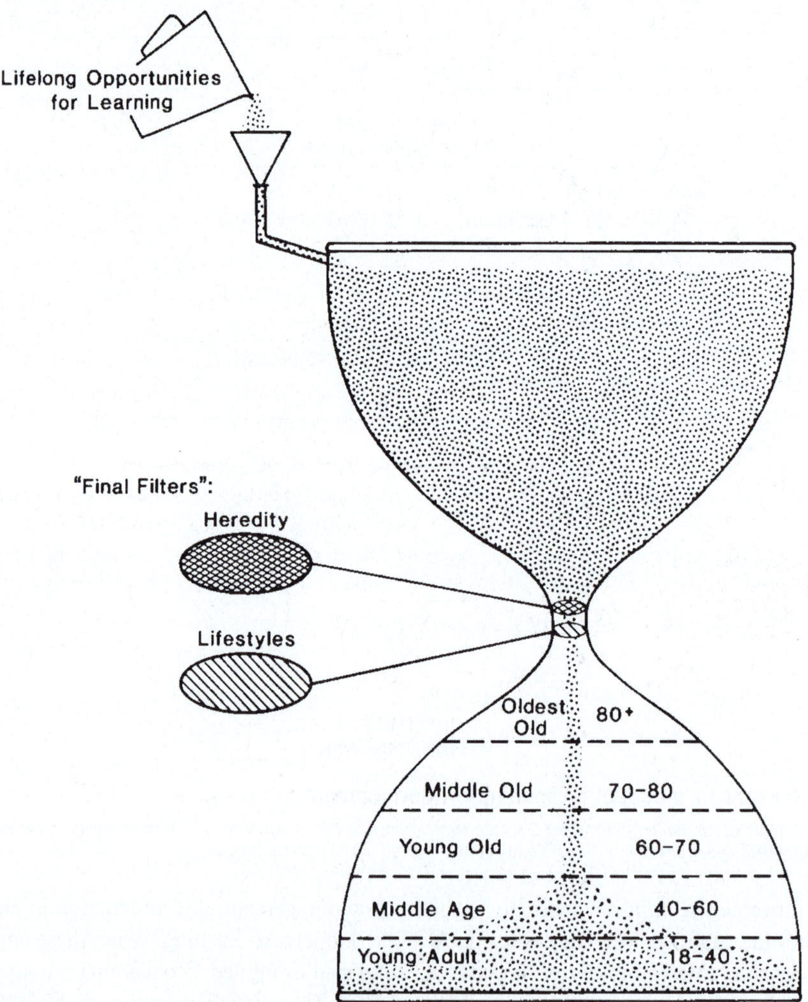

Figure 5-5 Emptying the overturned hourglass of life.

Gallahue DL and Ozmun JC. *Understanding Motor Development: Infants, Children, Adolescents, Adults* (5th ed.). New York, NY: McGraw Hill, 2012.

cultural factors than by physical factors. Sand falls through two filters–the heredity filter and the lifestyles filter. Filters can be dense, allowing sand to go through slowly, or very porous, in which case sand will pass through rapidly.

The heredity filter represents our inherited predispositions, whether they are toward longevity or coronary heart disease. Sand also passes through the lifestyles filter, which is environmentally based and over which we have some degree of control. Physical fitness, nutritional status, physical activity, stress resistance, and spiritual well-being influence the density and, hence, the rate at which sand falls through this filter. Although we cannot stop the sand from flowing through the hourglass–that is, the aging process–we can control the rate at which it falls by as much as 40%. Gallahue describes the wonderful opportunities that we as professionals in these fields have to help people add more sand to their hourglass and to develop "lifestyles filters" that will slow the rate at which sand falls through the hourglass.[10] He points out that even when the hourglass is overturned and sand is flowing through to the bottom, we can still take advantage of many opportunities for continued development and activity, thereby adding more sand to our hourglass and increasing our longevity.[10]

FUNDAMENTAL MOTOR SKILLS

Locomotor Skills	Nonlocomotor Skills	Manipulative Skills
Walk	Bend and stretch	Throw
Run	Twist and turn	Catch
Jump and land	Push and pull	Strike
Hop	Swing and sway	Dribble
Leap		Kick
Slide		Volley
Gallop		
Skip		
Dodge		

Selected Fundamental Motor Skills

Fundamental motor skills encompass a broad range of skills that form the foundation for successful participation in games, sports, dance, and fitness activities. These skills can be categorized into locomotor, nonlocomotor, and manipulative skills. Locomotor skills are those in which the body moves through space, including running, jumping, and sliding. Nonlocomotor skills, or axial movements, are typically done from a relatively stationary position, using a stable base of support. Generally performed in place, nonlocomotor skills include bending, stretching, and pushing. Manipulative skills are skills used in handling objects; throwing, catching, striking, and kicking are examples of manipulative skills.

Fundamental motor skills are combined to create the specialized movement necessary in many activities. For example, the softball throw requires a combination of sliding (locomotor skill) and throwing (manipulative skills) and twisting (nonlocomotor skill). The triple jump in track is a combination of a hop, step, and jump. Other specialized sport skills require more complex combinations of movements.

The next section contains a brief analysis of selected locomotor, nonlocomotor, and manipulative motor skills. As children learn the skills, they should also acquire knowledge of the critical elements important to skill performance. This knowledge increases children's understanding of the technique and forms the foundation for future learning.

Locomotor Movements

Locomotor skills refer to those skills that enable individuals to move themselves from one point to another point. The following locomotor skills are discussed: walking, running, jumping (for distance and height), hopping, leaping, skipping, sliding, and galloping. These are the skills most commonly used by elementary schoolchildren. Opportunities for students to explore and use these skills by themselves and in combination with nonlocomotor movements create a sufficient foundation for more complex movement skills.

Fundamental motor skills are the foundation for skills used in many different sports activities.

(Upper left): Jana Fernow/Westend61/Getty Images; (Upper right): Ingram Publishing; (Bottom left): U.S. Air Force photo by John Van Winkle; (Bottom right): Doug Menuez/Forrester Images/Photodisc/Getty Images

Walking Walking involves the transfer of weight from one foot to the other while moving. The weight of the body is transferred in a forward direction from the heel to the ball of the foot and then to the toes. The feet should move parallel to each other, with the toes pointing straight ahead. One foot is in contact with the ground at all times; this is the support foot. The body is erect, with the head up. The arm action is coordinated with leg action; the opposite arm and leg move in the same direction. These movements should be rhythmical and natural.

Running Running is similar to walking in several ways. However, some critical differences exist. In running, the movement is faster. The stride is longer, the flexion and extension of the legs are greater, and there is a momentary period of flight when the body is not supported at all. The body leans slightly forward to place the center of gravity above the front foot in the stride. The arms swing forward and back, opposing the legs, and contribute power to the movement.

Jumping Jumping varies according to the goal of the task. Jumping for distance and jumping for height are common skills. The standing long jump, for example, is done by bending the knees and lowering the upper body into a crouched position. As the body rocks back on the feet, the arms are brought down and beyond the hips. At takeoff, the forward and upward swing of the arms is coordinated with the powerful extension of both the feet and legs. The body is propelled forward as if reaching for an object in front of the body. The knees bend in midair so that the feet do not touch the ground prematurely. The landing is on the feet, with the knees bending to absorb the impact and the body falling forward.

Hopping Hopping involves forcefully pushing off the ground from one foot, a brief suspension in the air, and landing on the same foot. The push-off from the ground is made from the toes and the ball of the foot (supporting foot), with the knee of the opposite foot bent and that foot off the ground (nonsupporting foot). The arms are thrust upward to aid in body lift. The landing is on the toes, ball, and heel of the foot in that order. The knee is bent slightly to help absorb the shock of the landing. To aid in balance, the arms and nonsupporting foot are used. Hopping should be practiced with both feet.

Leaping Similar to the run, a leap is a long step forward to cover distance or to go over an obstacle. It is an exaggerated running step, with the stride longer and the body projected higher in the air. In the leap, the toes of the takeoff foot leave the floor last, and the landing is on the ball of the opposite foot. The arms should be extended upward and forward to give added lift to the body during the leap. Often, the legs are extended in the air. Before the execution of the leap, usually, a short run is taken to gain momentum for the leap itself.

Skipping A skip is a combination of a step and a hop, with feet alternating after each step-hop. A long step is taken on one foot, followed by a hop on the same foot, and then a step with the opposite foot, again followed by a hop. Balance is aided by swinging the arms in opposition to the legs.

Sliding A slide is a sideways movement in which the weight of the body is shifted in the direction of the slide. In a slide to the right, the right foot steps sideways (leading foot); then the left foot (trailing foot) is quickly drawn close to the right foot. Weight is shifted from the leading foot to the trailing foot. The same foot continues to lead in sliding movements. The body maintains an upright posture and the arms are used for balance. The legs should not be crossed. The slide should be practiced in both directions.

Galloping Galloping is similar to sliding, but the movement is performed in a forward direction. One foot leads in the forward direction (leading foot). After a step by the leading foot, the rear or trailing foot is brought quickly forward and close to the lead foot. The stepping leg is always the lead leg. Opportunities to lead with the right foot and with the left foot should be included in practicing the gallop.

Nonlocomotor Movements

Nonlocomotor movements are generally performed using a stable base of support. The nonlocomotor movement skills discussed are bending, stretching, twisting, turning, pushing, pulling, and swinging. Generally, they are performed in place and can be done from a variety of body positions (e.g., standing or sitting). They can also be combined with locomotor movements.

Bending and Stretching Bending is a movement occurring at the joints of the body in which body parts are brought closer together. For example, by bending the body at the hips to touch the toes, a person is decreasing the angle between the upper and lower body at the hip joint. This is called flexion. Bending movements may be in several directions: for example, forward, backward, sideways, or in a circular motion. The range of bending movements is determined by the type of joint at which the movement occurs. Ball-and-socket joints permit the greatest movement. Hip joints and shoulder joints are examples of ball-and-socket joints. Hinge joints permit only backward and forward movements. The knee joint is a hinge joint.

A stretch is an extension or hyperextension at the joints of the body. Stretching is the opposite of bending. In movements such as the wrist cock before a throw, hyperextension is needed to give added impetus to the throw.

Bending and stretching are necessary to maintain flexibility–the full range of movement about a joint. Bending and stretching are common to most of the activities of daily life (e.g., dressing and bathing), and they are very important to physical education activities.

Twisting and Turning Twisting is a rotation of the body or a body part around its axis while maintaining a fixed base of support. Twisting movements can take place at the neck, shoulders, spine, hips, ankles, and wrist. The body can be in different positions, for example, standing or lying down. As in bending and stretching movements, the range of a twisting movement is determined by the type of joint.

Turning generally refers to a rotation of the body around in space. When the body is turned, the base of support is shifted from one position to another. Jumping up and landing facing the opposite direction and pivoting are examples of turns. A twisting action is typically used to initiate a turn. Turns should be practiced in both directions, left and right or clockwise and counterclockwise.

Pushing and Pulling Pushing is a forceful action directed toward increasing the distance between the body and an object. A push can be used to move an object away from the body or the body away from an object. Pushing an opponent away in a wrestling match and a box across the floor are two examples of pushing. Proper body position enhances the effectiveness of a push. A forward stride position enlarges the body's base of support, and bending the knees lowers the center of gravity and increases the body's stability. Proper body alignment helps prevent back injuries.

Pulling is a forceful action designed to decrease the distance between the body and an object. A pull brings the body and the object closer together. As in pushing, widening the base of support and lowering the center of gravity increase effectiveness. In a tug-of-war, participants widen their base of support and dig their heels in as they try to pull their opponents across the dividing line. Partner resistance exercises and rowing use both pushing and pulling. Steady, controlled movements are recommended for both pulling and pushing.

Swinging A swing is a circular or pendular movement of a body part or of the entire body around a stationary center point. The center point may be a joint, such as the shoulder in swinging the arm, or an outside axis, such as the swing on a high bar. Swinging movements should be continuous, rhythmical, and free flowing.

Manipulative Skills

Manipulative skills involve the propulsion and control of objects. The body is used to apply force to an object and to absorb force when receiving or controlling an object. The manipulative skills of throwing, catching, kicking, and striking are briefly described.

Throwing Throwing an object may involve the use of the underhand, sidearm, or overhand pattern. Because the overhand throwing pattern is most frequently employed by children and adults, this movement will be described.

When throwing, the ball is held in the fingers of the throwing hand. As the throwing action is initiated, the ball is brought back and the body rotates so that the opposite side is toward the target. Weight is transferred back to the foot on the same side as the throwing hand. The arm is bent at the elbow, and the elbow leads slightly as the arm is brought forward for the throw. As the arm accelerates, a step forward onto the opposite foot is taken and the hips rotate forward. The arm quickly extends, the wrist snaps, and the ball is released. The arm follows in the direction of the throw, coming down and across the body.

Catching Catching involves the use of hands to stop and gain control of an object. As the object approaches, the individual makes a judgment about where it can be intercepted and moves to a location directly in line with the object, placing the hands in a position for effective reception. The eyes follow the flight of the object, and both hands reach out toward it. The object is grasped by the hands and pulled in by the arms and hands toward the body to absorb the object's force.

Kicking Kicking is imparting force to an object by the foot and the leg. The kicking of a stationary object is the foundation for the kicking of a moving object and for punting.

In kicking, the supporting foot is placed alongside the object. The kicking leg, knee bent, moving freely from the hip, swings through an arc toward the object. As the foot contacts the object, the knee is extended and the body leans back for balance. The kicking leg follows through, continuing its movement toward the direction of the flight of the object. The arms, relaxed, move in opposition to the legs. The eyes focus on the object throughout the kick.

Striking Striking involves using a body part (e.g., hand) or an implement (e.g., paddle, racquet, and bat) to apply force to a stationary or moving object. The length, size, and weight of the implement as well as characteristics of the object being struck influence the nature of the movement pattern. Kicking, described earlier, is also considered a striking task.

For the striking action typically seen in batting, the body is positioned perpendicular to the line of flight of the oncoming ball. The feet are placed in a forward-backward stride position, approximately shoulder width apart. The trunk is rotated back, the weight is shifted to the rear foot, and a backswing is taken. The flight of the ball is followed by the eyes until just before making contact. Body weight is shifted onto the forward foot in the direction of the intended flight of the ball. With the hips leading, the hips and trunk are rotated in the same direction as the weight shift. Arms move forward into contact, and the follow-through action occurs in the direction of the line of flight.

Fundamental motor skills are the foundation for the development of specialized game, sport, dance, and fitness activities. These skills are the building blocks for the future. Acquisition of skills for lifetime participation begins with the mastery of these fundamental motor skills. All children, the skilled and the unskilled, need sufficient opportunities and a variety of experiences to master these important movement basics. (See references for more information on the development of motor skills.)

Development of Fundamental Motor Skills

Motor development specialists are interested in children's acquisition of fundamental motor skills. Two ways that skill development has been studied are through the sequences approach and through the use of the dynamical systems model.[10] In studying the development of these skills, researchers have used a process or a product approach.[10] The process approach describes how a movement is performed, such as whether or not the child performing the overhand throw steps toward the target with the foot opposite the throwing arm. The product approach focuses on the outcome of the movement, such as how far was the ball kicked, whether or not a target was hit, or was the basket made or not.

The developmental sequences approach to understanding how fundamental motor skills are acquired involves placing descriptions of the common movement patterns of each skill on a continuum of sorts, ranging from the inefficient and ineffective patterns to efficient and proficient patterns of movement. Stages or steps along the continuum help identify where each child is in relation to developing the proficient form of the skill. These stages are referred to as initial, emerging elementary, and proficient.[11]

The initial stage, stage 1, is the most inefficient, and marks the beginning efforts of performance of the fundamental skill. This stage is often characterized by poor spatial and temporal integration of movements comprising the skill. The movements exhibit improper sequencing of parts of the skill, little body rotation, sometimes exaggerated use of the body, poor rhythm, and difficulties in coordination.

The emerging elementary stage can encompass multiple stages (2 through 4), with the number of these stages depending on the developmental sequence and specific skill. These emerging stages reflect the time needed to develop different aspects of the skill being learned. In this stage, we see greater control and rhythmical coordination of the movements. The spatial and temporal elements of the movements are better synchronized, and the movement is better coordinated. The movements are still restricted or exaggerated, and the mechanical principles are not consistently applied to the performance.

The proficient or final stage, stage 5, reflects the mechanically efficient performance of the skill. The stage is marked by increased mechanical efficiency, enhanced coordination, and improved control of the movements. Increases in size and strength contribute to greater force production.

The developmental sequences approach can focus either on the total body sequences or on the component sequences.[11] The total body sequences method of studying development involves describing the movement patterns for the total body, and then based on that description, making a determination of the child's stage of development. The component sequences approach describes how the movements of critical segments of the body, like the legs or arms, change as the child becomes more proficient.

With respect to the overhand throw, the total body sequence approach, as shown in Figure 5-6, illustrates how the movement patterns of the body change as proficiency is achieved. As the child becomes more proficient, there is greater mechanical efficiency; greater preparation for the throw, with the throwing arm and opposite leg working in opposition; greater trunk rotation; more force generation; and an incorporation of a follow-through.

The component sequences approach for the overhand throw focuses on the changes in five critical components of the skill: the step, arm backswing, trunk, humerus, and forearm. Critical developmental characteristics are then assessed to determine what stage is being exhibited. In terms of the overhand throw, for the component of trunk rotation, there are three developmental steps: step 1—no trunk rotation or forward-back movement, step 2—upper trunk rotation or total "block" rotation, with the trunk moving as a whole unit, and step 3—differentiated rotation, with the trunk segments moving in sequence. The development level of the child would then be rated as to whether he or she was at step 1, 2, or 3 for this particular component. All the components would be rated, to create a comprehensive picture of the child's development of this particular skill.[10]

The developmental sequences, total body and component, used to examine the development of fundamental motor skills are based on stage theory. Four of the key principles of stage theory hold that children proceed through the stages of development in the same order, without skipping a stage or changing the order, and there is no regression.[10] While the principles of stage theory accurately reflect the acquisition of fundamental skills by many children, researchers found that children learn these skills in a more variable manner than accounted for by these principles.[10] They skip stages, achieve the stages in different order, and experience regression at times. To address this variability and other shortcomings associated with stage theory, researchers turned to dynamical systems theory to explain motor development.

As discussed earlier in the chapter, dynamical systems theory explains that movements are influenced by the interaction of the individual, task, and the environment. In essence, these factors influence the movement pattern children exhibit. For example, if the task is to kick a ball a certain distance, the child selects a movement pattern to accomplish the task

Initial Stage	Emerging Elementary Stages			Proficient Stage
Stage 1	Stage 2	Stage 3	Stage 4	Stage 5
"Chop" Vertical windup "Chop" throw Feet stationary No spinal rotation	"Sling shot" Horizontal windup "Sling shot throw" Block rotation Follow-through across body	"Ipsilateral step" High windup Ipsilateral step Little spinal rotation Follow-through across body	"Contralateral step" High windup Contralateral step Little spinal rotation Follow-through across body	"Windup" Downward arc windup Contralateral step Segmented body rotation Arm-leg follow-through

Figure 5-6 Developmental sequence of throwing.

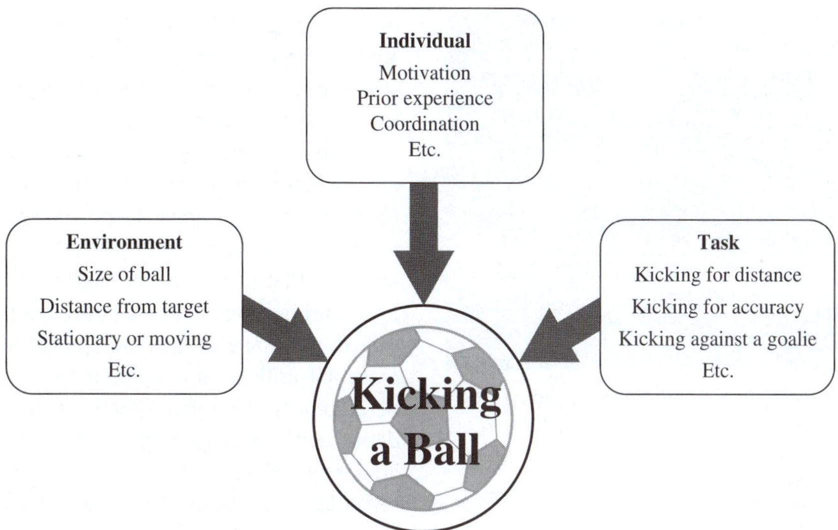

Figure 5-7 Dynamical systems and kicking performance.

(see Figure 5-7). In this scenario, even if the child is at the proficient stage of kicking, if asked to kick a ball a short distance, the child may choose to use a movement pattern that is not as efficient, but yet capable of accomplishing the task. When asked to kick the ball a much farther distance, the child may display a more efficient and proficient pattern that will enable the task to be accomplished. Therefore, one of the goals of motor development is to provide children with a wide array of movement options from which they can select to accomplish a particular task.

Development of proficiency in the fundamental motor skills is enhanced when plentiful opportunities for practice are provided, along with instruction and encouragement opportunities that would be available through a developmentally appropriate quality elementary physical education program. Elementary physical educators have a critical role in the development of competency in the fundamental motor skills. Spessato, Gabbard, and Valentini studied the relationship of motor competence and body mass index (BMI) on elementary school children's physical activity during physical education classes.[12] They found that motor competence was related to the amount of physical activity engaged in by students, but there was no significant relationship between BMI and physical activity. The researchers suggested that children who are competent in motor skills are more active during class. Developing motor competency, especially for children with high BMI, can influence their participation and further skill development. Additionally, failure to acquire the proficient form of the skill adversely impacts the development of more specialized skills in the later years.

Clark points out that poorly developed motor skills serve as a "proficiency barrier" to the development of more sport-specific skills in the later years, be it adolescence or adulthood.[13] A strong motor skills foundation provides for new movement opportunities later in life, whether sport or recreational in nature, such as skiing, rock climbing, and tennis. Another, perhaps unintended, consequence of poorly developed motor skills is that children and youth may lack self-efficacy regarding their motor performance. The lack of confidence in themselves as movers may make it less likely that they will participate in physical activity when older.

Sport specialization is a growing trend in youth sports, both globally and in the United States. Sport specialization is the focusing on a single sport at an early age to the exclusion of participation in other sports or activities. Sport specialization typically involves year-round training, often includes playing on multiple teams in the selected sport, and usually involves engaging in high-level competitions throughout the year.[14,15] Professionals have raised concerns

Elementary physical education programs should provide plenty of opportunities for children to develop their fundamental motor skills.

Lars A. Niki/McGraw Hill

that sport specialization increases youths' risk for overuse injuries and burnout.[14,15] With respect to motor development, one of the concerns is that youths who specialize early in a sport may not develop competency in a wide variety of fundamental motor skills.[14,15,16]

Attainment of physical literacy is one of the primary outcomes of contemporary physical education programs. Succinctly stated, "physical literacy is the ability, confidence, and desire to be physically active for life."[17] The attainment of competency in the fundamental movement skills is important to the achievement of these outcomes as these skills provide the framework for continued development of physical literacy. Competency in the fundamental motor skills provides the foundation for later development of more specific sport skills, lifetime physical activities, and participation in fitness activities.

An instructional climate that focuses on mastery promotes the development of physical literacy.[18] A mastery-oriented learning environment challenges students and nurtures their development. Teaching strategies that incorporate well-designed and sequential tasks, provide for inclusion of conceptual concepts, and feature ongoing corrective feedback and meaningful assessments contribute to the development of physical literacy. Opportunities for students to set and achieve personal goals, the use of challenging tasks that invite student engagement, and fostering a learning climate where effort and hard work are valued contribute to the development of physical literacy. Of critical importance is the support for the development of positive affective outcomes.[19] Confidence and motivation are viewed as integral to the attainment of physical literacy. Perceived confidence, self-efficacy, and ability to see oneself as a participating in physical activity and leading an active lifestyle is one of the cornerstones of physical literacy.

In focusing on this outcome, it is important to address inequities in opportunities to achieve physical literacy. We know that students from low-income families, who are racial and ethnic minorities, girls, and those with disabilities, are typically disadvantaged with respect to these opportunities. It is important to address these inequities during the elementary years, for if this gap is not addressed, surely it will widen. Physical literacy is important for all students.

Diversification, which is focusing on a variety of experiences in games and sports, helps children and youth develop competency in many of the fundamental motor skills that serve as the foundation for future activities in sports.[13,16] Youths who specialize early in a sport demonstrate proficiency in the skills associated with their sport but may not achieve proficiency in other fundamental skills. Elite soccer players may have highly developed skills of

FOCUS ON CAREER: Motor Behavior and Movement

PROFESSIONAL ORGANIZATIONS	• North American Society for the Psychology of Sport and Physical Activity (NASPSPA) (http://www.naspspa.com)
PROFESSIONAL JOURNALS	• *Journal of Motor Behavior* • *Journal of Teaching in Physical Education*

running, agility, kicking, and foot dribbling, honed by coaches through many hours of practice.[16] However, they may lack proficiency in other skills such as throwing and striking, necessary in other sports such as softball.[16] This lack of development of the fundamental skills may lead to youths encountering a proficiency barrier, limiting their opportunities to become skill performers in other sports.[14,15,16] The more skills people develop early in life, the more choices they have in their later years when deciding which activities to pursue for enjoyment and to remain active throughout their lifespan.

This chapter is designed to provide a brief overview of some of the concepts and concerns in the realm of motor behavior. An understanding of how individuals learn motor skills will help professionals design experiences to promote effective learning. Promoting effective learning is a concern of professionals working in both school and nonschool settings. In the school setting, for example, elementary school physical educators are concerned with helping children master fundamental motor skills, high school teachers focus their efforts on assisting students in acquiring skills in a variety of lifetime sports, and coaches spend countless hours helping their athletes refine the skills necessary for high-level performance. In the nonschool setting, athletic trainers may help injured athletes regain efficient motor patterns, while exercise leaders in a corporate or community program may help adults attain proficiency in such lifetime sports as golf or tennis. Thus, understanding how learning occurs and can be facilitated is important foundational knowledge for professionals to possess. The manners in which individuals control their movements (motor control) and the impact of development (motor development) on learning are also important considerations in designing learning experiences.

CURRENT TRENDS: MOVING TOWARD THE FUTURE

- More sophisticated technology will play an increasing role in helping us understand the neurophysiological processes of how people learn and control their movements.
- We will learn more about the physiological, neurological, psychological, and sociological changes associated with aging, enabling us to better help the older population remain physical activity throughout their lifespan.
- As sport specialization increases, school physical education becomes an important venue to help ensure that youths who specialize in one sport achieve proficiency in all the fundamental motor skills, not just those required by their sport.

SUMMARY

Motor behavior is a broad term, encompassing motor control, motor learning, and motor development. Motor control is the study of the neural mechanisms and processes by which movements are learned and controlled. Motor learning is the acquisition of motor skills as a consequence of practice and experience. Motor development is the study of the origins and changes in movement behavior throughout the lifespan.

Many theories and models have been advanced to describe learning. One theory is the information processing model. According to this model, learning and performance of skills can be described as a series of information processing tasks consisting of input, decision making, output, and feedback. Another theory is the dynamical systems model. This model explains the learning and performance of motor skills as the interaction between the individual, the environment, and the task. Individuals pass through three stages when learning a motor skill: cognitive, associative, and autonomic. Learning is influenced by readiness, motivation, reinforcement, and individual differences. To facilitate motor learning, physical education, exercise science, and sport professionals should incorporate concepts from motor learning into the design of their practices.

Fundamental motor skills form the foundation for learning more complex skills used in games, sports, dance, and a host of physical activities. In developing these fundamental skills, individuals move through three stages: initial, emerging elementary, and proficient. Professionals should understand how motor skills develop so that they can design learning experiences to facilitate their acquisition and promote physical literacy. The developmental sequences approach and the dynamical systems approach have been used to explain how fundamental motor skills are developed.

DISCUSSION QUESTIONS

1. Reflect on your physical education classes in elementary and secondary school. Can you recall a student who exhibited poor motor skills? Can you think of a student who possessed well-developed motor skills? Based on what you recall, how does motor skill ability influence participation in physical education? Try to think about social and emotional consequences of being poorly or highly skilled as well as the effects on participation.
2. How is individuals' failure to achieve mature forms of fundamental motor skill a proficiency barrier for the learning of more advanced sports skills? How might this affect their participation in lifespan physical activity?
3. Reflect on Gallahue's hourglass model of motor development. What specific strategies can professionals use to help individuals add more "sand" to their hourglass, thereby prolonging the time those individuals can enjoy being physically active?
4. Clark, in an article on the importance of motor literacy, suggests that children who do not possess motor literacy are "left behind" just as children who do not possess reading or math literacy are "left behind." Do you agree or disagree with this statement? [For more information, see Clark, J. E. (2007). On the problem of motor skill development, *JOPERD 78*(5), 39–40.]
5. More and more children and youths are specializing in one sport at an early age. What are the advantages and disadvantages of specialization? If you participated in youth sports, discuss the impact of such programs on your own skill development.

GET CONNECTED

North American Society for Psychology of Sport and Physical Activity (NASPSPA)–organization for those with interests in different aspects of motor behavior and sport psychology. It sponsors two journals, the *Journal of Motor Learning and Development* and the *Journal of Sport & Exercise Psychology*.

https://www.naspspa.com/

Neuroscience for Kids–Although written for a younger population, this site provides a wealth of information on the brain, nervous system, and neurological disorders. Access the link to information for high schoolers and older students to see an array of information on various topics.

http://faculty.washington.edu/chudler/neurok.html

Society for Neuroscience–offers a wealth of information, including the core concepts of neuroscience, neuroscience in the news, and an online book, *Brain Facts,* with a section on movement.

https://www.sfn.org/

SELF-ASSESSMENT ACTIVITIES

These activities are designed to help you determine if you have mastered the material and competencies presented in this chapter.

1. You are a teacher in the school setting, a sport instructor in a community setting working with senior citizens, or a fitness leader in a corporate fitness program working with adults. How would you incorporate each of the following concepts into your program: readiness, reinforcement, motivation, and individual differences?

2. Explain how you would use either the information processing model of learning or the dynamical systems model to enhance an individual's acquisition of a skill.
3. Review the list of motor learning concepts that promote the learning of motor skills and improve the performance. Select five of those concepts and illustrate how you would apply them to the teaching of a fundamental skill or sports skill.
4. Research physical literacy. Discuss strategies to promote physical literacy, with a focus on underserved populations. What can be done to ensure the gaps in physical literacy among different population groups is reduced, not widened?

REFERENCES

1. Thomas, K.T., Gu, X., & Thomas, J.R. (2022). Motor behavior. In D. V. Knudson & T. A. Brusseau (Eds.), *Introduction to kinesiology: Studying physical activity* (6th ed.). Champaign, IL: Human Kinetics.
2. Knudson, D., & Kluka, D. A. (1997). The impact of vision and vision training on sport performance. *Journal of Physical Education, Recreation and Dance, 68*(4), 17-24.
3. Garcia, C., & Garcia, L. (2006). A motor-development and motor-learning perspective. *Journal of Physical Education, Recreation and Dance, 77*(8), 31-34.
4. Rukavina, P. B., & Foxworth, K. R. (2009). Using motor-learning theory to design more effective instruction. *Journal of Physical Education, Recreation and Dance, 80*(3), 17-23, 27.
5. Magill, R. A., & Anderson, D. (2021). *Motor learning and control: Concepts and applications* (12th ed.). New York, NY: McGraw Hill.
6. Fitts, P. A., & Posner, M. J. (1967). *Human performance.* Belmont, CA: Brooks/Cole.
7. Rink, J. E. (2020). *Teaching physical education for learning* (8th ed.). New York, NY: McGraw Hill.
8. Docheff, D. M. (1990). The feedback sandwich. *Journal of Physical Education, Recreation and Dance, 61*(9), 17-18.
9. Kelly, H. (2014, December 31). Smart sports equipment turns phones into coaches. Retrieved April 29, 2019, from http://www.cnn.com/2014/11/28/tech/innovation/smart-sports-equipment/.
10. Gallahue, G. L., Ozmun, J. L., & Goodway, J. D. (2012). *Understanding motor development: Infants, children, adolescents, adults* (7th ed.). New York, NY: McGraw Hill.
11. Payne, V. G., & Isaacs, L. D. (2016). *Human motor development: A lifespan approach* (9th ed.). Scottsdale, AZ: Holcomb Hathaway.
12. Spessato, B. C., Gabbard, C., & Valentini, N. (2013). The role of motor competency and body Page 151 mass index in children's activity levels in physical education classes. *Journal of Teaching in Physical Education, 32*, 118-130.
13. Clark, J. E. (2007). On the problem of motor skill development. *Journal of Physical Education, Recreation and Dance, 78*(5), 39-40.
14. Meyer, G. D., Jayanthi, N., DiFiori, J. P., Faigenbaum, A. D., Kiefer, A. D., Logerstedt, D., & Mitcheli, L. J. (2015). Sports specialization. Part I: Does early sports specialization increase negative outcomes and reduce the opportunity for success in young athletes? *Sports Health, 7*, 437-442.
15. Meyer, G. D., Jayanthi, N., DiFiori, J. P., Faigenbaum, A. D., Kiefer, A. D., Logerstedt, D., & Mitcheli, L. J. (2016). Sports specialization. Part II: Alternative solutions to early sport specialization in youth athletes. *Sports Health, 8*, 65-73.
16. Branta, C. F. (2010). Sport specialization: Developmental and learning issues. *Journal of Physical Education, Recreation & Dance, 81*(8), 19-28.
17. Aspen Institute. (2015). Physical literacy in the United States: A model, strategic plan and call to action. Retrieved April 29, 2019, from http://plreport.projectplay.us/.
18. Chepko, S., & Doan, R. (2015). Teaching for skill mastery. *Journal of Physical Education, Recreation and Dance, 86*(7), 9-13.
19. Roetert, E. P., Kriellaars, D., Ellenbecker, T. S., & Richardson, C. (2017). Preparing students for a physically literate life. *Journal of Physical Education, Recreation and Dance, 88*(1), 57-62.

Polka Dot Images/Getty Images

CHAPTER 6

BIOMECHANICAL FOUNDATIONS

OBJECTIVES

After reading this chapter, students should be able to–

- Define the term *biomechanics* and articulate its relationship to kinesiology.
- Identify the value of biomechanics for physical education, exercise science, and sport professionals.
- Understand some of the terminology associated with biomechanics.
- Describe selected mechanical principles and concepts and illustrate their application of these principles and concepts to human movement and sport.
- Describe some of the techniques and technologies used to analyze motion.

Understanding the factors that govern human movement is essential for physical education, exercise science, and sport professionals. As professionals, we are concerned with helping individuals learn how to move efficiently and effectively. In elementary physical education classes, the teacher is concerned with helping students learn fundamental motor skills such as throwing and running, which provide a foundation for learning more advanced sport skills. In competitive athletics, where the difference between winning and losing may be one hundredth of a second or a fraction of a centimeter, a coach may use scientific methods such as high-speed videography, computer simulation, and wearable technology to fine-tune an athlete's form.

Weekend golfers, seeking to break par, request the assistance of golf pros to eliminate a troublesome slice from their swing. The golf pro may use a smartphone or mobile device with an app like Dartfish to make a video of the golfer's performance, annotate it, record comments, and then share the video with the golfer to help the golfer see what changes in stroke mechanics are needed. The athletic trainer rehabilitating an athlete recovering from shoulder surgery uses knowledge of the range of motion of this joint to help develop an effective rehabilitation program. The adapted physical educator

SOCIAL JUSTICE

Talking Points

- Concepts such as force and power (e.g., jumping ability) are sometimes racially stigmatized; this stigmatization needs to be eliminated in sport.
- The potential for biomechanics to create the means for individuals with physical disabilities, amputations, or spinal cord injuries to participate in physical activity and sport is huge and warrants greater attention from professionals.

analyzes the gait of a child with cerebral palsy in order to select and, if necessary modify, physical activities to meet the child's needs. A strength and conditioning specialist closely monitors a client lifting weights to ensure that the exercise is being performed properly through the range of motion. These examples show how professionals use the scientific knowledge of human motion from the realms of kinesiology and biomechanics to help individuals move safely, efficiently, and effectively.

KINESIOLOGY AND BIOMECHANICS

The study of human movement is the focus of kinesiology and biomechanics. *Kinesiology* is the scientific study of human movement. The term *kinesiology* is derived from the Greek *kinesi*, meaning "motion." Defined more broadly, kinesiology is used by some professionals as an umbrella term to encompass the disciplines that emerged from physical education in the 1970s. In this chapter, the term *kinesiology* will be used in a more narrow, traditional sense to refer to the anatomical and physiological study of human movement. To understand human movement fully, one needs an understanding of body movement or kinesiology.

Kinesiology involves the study of the skeletal framework, the structure of muscles and their functions, the action of the joints, and the neuromuscular basis of movement. Kinesiology helps us appreciate the intricacies and wonder of human motion. Hamilton, Weimar, and Luttgens write,

> One who gives it any thought whatever cannot help being impressed not only by the beauty of human motion but also by its apparently infinite possibilities, its meaningfulness, its orderliness, its adaptability to the surrounding environment. Nothing is haphazard; nothing is left to chance. Every study that participates in the movement of the body does so according to physical and physiological principles.[1]

Kinesiology helps us see human motion through new eyes and gain a greater appreciation for human movement.

Professionals in many occupations study kinesiology in order to learn how to improve performance by analyzing the movements of the body and applying the principles of movement to their work. Three important purposes for the study of kinesiology are safety, effectiveness, and efficiency.[1] As professionals, we strive to design and lead physical activities so that our participants can learn and perform safely, with optimum effectiveness, and efficiently, that is, with just the right amount of effort required for success.

Kinesiology helps prepare physical education, exercise science, and sport professionals to teach fundamental motor skills and specialized sport skills to people of all ages, as a means of optimizing performance. Kinesiology offers professionals a

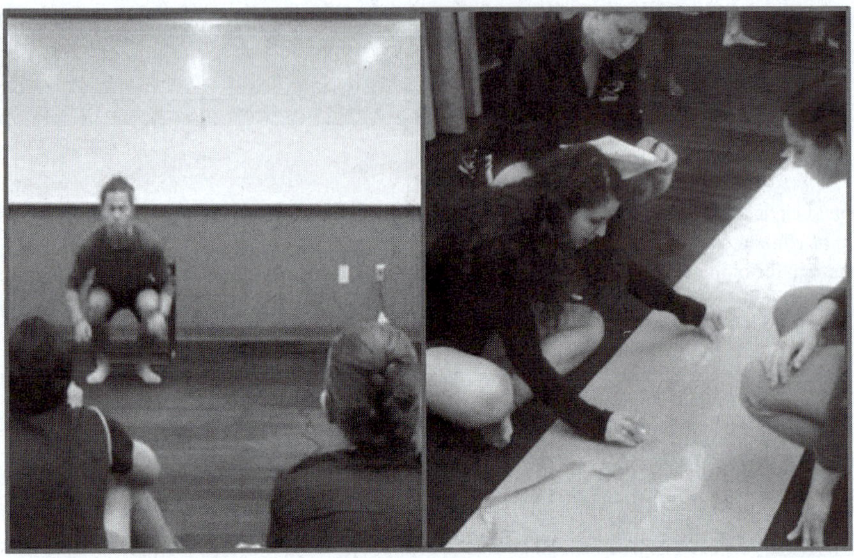

In kinesiology, students learn about the structure and function of the musculoskeletal system in relationship to human movement. Here, students are analyzing lower extremity landing mechanics by observing drop vertical jumps and evaluating gait by measuring stride length and step width. Students also learn to take anthropometric measurements, perform manual muscle testing, and break down sport skills into individual joint motions and muscle actions.
Deborah King

background from which to evaluate motor skills and how they affect the body.

Definition and Scope

Biomechanics focuses on the application of the scientific principles of mechanics to understand movements and actions of human bodies and sport implements (e.g., a tennis racquet). The term *biomechanics* can be better understood by examining the derivation of the word. *Bio* is from Greek and refers to life or living things, and *mechanics* refers to the field of Newtonian mechanics and the forces that act on bodies in motion. Biomechanists study how various forces affect human motion and how movements can be improved in terms of efficiency and effectiveness.

Kinesiology and biomechanics are integrally related. An understanding of how the body moves, including the function and actions of the joints, muscles, and bony structure, is essential to the understanding of biomechanics. In order to effectively study the influences of forces on motion–biomechanics–one must be knowledgeable about the actions of the joints and the muscles that cause these forces; this is the realm of kinesiology. Both kinesiology and biomechanics are fundamental to understanding human movement and to helping individuals attain their fullest potential.

The principles of biomechanics can be applied in many fields of study outside of physical education, exercise science, and sport. These include biology, physiology, engineering, ergonomics, robotics, prosthetics, military science, physical and occupational therapy, and medicine.

Growth of Biomechanics

Biomechanics has a long, rich history, beginning with the Ancient Greeks. Aristotle (384–322 B.C.) is thought to have been one of the first scholars to study the muscles and motions of the human body,

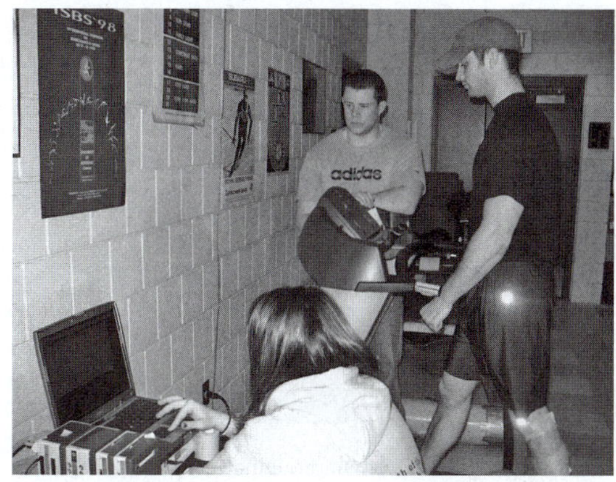

In biomechanics, students study the movements of athletes to improve performance and reduce injury. Here, three students are measuring the electrical activity of the calf muscle during walking using surface electromyography. They also have reflective markers on the joints of the lower extremity to measure motions of the ankle and knee during walking. Reflective markers are often used when doing motion capture or video analysis of human movement.

Deborah King

which he described in his book *De Moto Animalium* (*On the Movement of Animals*).[2]

In the early development of biomechanics in the United States, starting in the late 1800s, the term *kinesiology* was used to refer to the science of applying mechanics to the study of movement.[3] Atwater credits Nils Posse as the first to use the term kinesiology.[4] Posse wrote *The Special Kinesiology of Educational Gymnastics,* published in 1894. Until the 1960s, the terms kinesiology and biomechanics were used interchangeably.

Wilkerson describes the 1960s as the beginning of a new era in the development and growth of biomechanics–the emergence from physical education of biomechanics as a subdiscipline. During this time, the term *biomechanics* started to slowly replace the term *kinesiology* and was used more frequently to describe the scientific application of mechanics to the study of human movement. There was a greater emphasis on the study of both the anatomical and mechanical aspects of human movement. Advances in technology, instrumentation, and methodology contributed to the proliferation of research during this time and the emergence of biomechanics as an area of specialization.

The study of biomechanics is essential for those professionals engaged in the study of human movement and who aspire to work with individuals to develop and improve their motor performance. The *Guidelines for Undergraduate Biomechanics* recommends competencies that you should attain through your course work to work successfully in the field. As an undergraduate, through your course work in biomechanics, you should acquire the ability to

> 1. observe and describe a variety of movement patterns accurately; 2. determine the basic anatomical and mechanical factors associated with the performance of a variety of observed movements; 3. evaluate the suitability of a performer's technique with reference to the task at hand; and 4. identify factors that limit performance and establish a priority for change in those factors most likely to lead to improvement in performance for a variety of movements.[5]

The growth of biomechanics during these past few decades has led to the development of specialized areas of study. Biomechanists may specialize in a particular sport, such as swimming, or focus their research on a specific topic, such as footwear. Other biomechanists choose to direct their attention to more clinical concerns, such as prosthetic design and injury prevention. Some other areas of specialization are gait and posture analysis and computer simulation.

Biomechanics enables professionals to analyze human movement scientifically, increasing their ability to help individuals move safely, efficiently, and effectively to achieve their movement goals. There is a growing trend within the fields of exercise and sport sciences to refer to biomechanics as *sport biomechanics.* There is also a greater interest in using biomechanics to work not only with elite athletes, but also with people of all abilities, to strengthen and improve their performance of a variety of movement tasks.

Cyclists and wheelchair racers, like this Boston Marathoner, have benefited greatly from improvements in equipment design and research designed to help them streamline and refine their body position to improve performance.

Left: Aaron Roeth; Right: Lawrence M. Sawyer/J&L Images/PhotoDisc/Getty Images

Reasons for Studying Biomechanics

Many professionals can profit from the study of biomechanics. To be effective as practitioners, physical educators, exercise science, and sport professionals should have an understanding of the principles of biomechanics. Knowledge of biomechanics will provide the professional with a better understanding of the human body and the various internal and external forces that affect human movement, as well as the forces that act on object motion. This, in turn, will enable professionals to be better instructors, coaches, and leaders of the many motor activities and skills engaged in by participants in their programs.

Biomechanics is often at the forefront of changes in technique and technology. A great example in the early history of sport biomechanics is in the sport of swimming. In the late 1960s and early 1970s, James Counsilman, author of *The Science of Swimming*, worked with biomechanists to study the forces involved in propulsion in swimming.[6] In 1971, Brown and Counsilman filmed swimmers wearing lights on their hands as they swam in a darkened pool.[7] This allowed the pattern of the swimmers' hands to be identified and their actions carefully studied. It was found that the traditional technique of a straight arm pull was not as efficient as a curved arm pull technique that created lift forces.[7] At the time of this research, it was thought that the lift forces created by the curved arm pull were essential for creating propulsion and optimizing swim technique. However, astute observers of Olympians over the last decade will notice two arm pull styles are still being used. As research in swimming has advanced with the aid of computer modeling, the mechanics of both strokes reveal that the curved or "S-arm" pull is better for middle or long distances when stroke efficiency is a main concern.[8] The hand movement pattern of elite swimmers in the "S-stroke" creates a vortex that circulates and generates lift force used for propulsion.[8] The deep catch, straighter "I-stroke" arm pull works well for sprint distances where power is favored over energy conservation.[8] A different type of vortex is formed in the "I-stroke" that creates a drag force coming off the hand creating a strong propulsive force.[8]

Exciting new advances in swimming technique and technology are inevitable as scientists and coaches continue to increase their understanding of swimming biomechanics. In 2007, the international governing body for swimming announced possible changes to the starting blocks, which included an adjustable incline with a wedge at the back.[9] To determine how the block design would affect start performance, biomechanists studied propulsion time, takeoff velocity, and power using instrumented starting blocks. Results revealed that the incline provided modest improvements in start performance.[9]

Early adopter of V-technique in ski jumping.
Danny Iacob/Shutterstock

Since 2009, starting blocks at international competitions all incorporated this new design.

Innovations by athletes have also advanced biomechanics research. Athletes have created new techniques that have led to higher levels of performance, for example, in high jumping and ski jumping. Until the late 1960s, high jumpers approached the bar from an angle, thrust an arm and a leg up and over, then executed a kick, and the body "rolled" over the bar. In 1968, high jumper Dick Fosbury, utilizing his unorthodox flop style of jumping, won the gold medal at the Olympic Games in Mexico. The "Fosbury Flop" style of jumping used a curved approach to the bar with the jumper going over backward in a twisting lay-back of the body. Within 10 years, the traditional, long-used roll style of jumping was replaced by the flop style and records soared to new heights.

The sport of ski jumping was revolutionized in the late 1980s and early 1990s when Jan Boklov repeatedly won competitions using a "V-style" flight position.[10] Despite low style points, his jumps had such great distance that by 1992, all medalists at the Albertville Olympic Games used the V-style. The V-style optimizes lift force during flight allowing the ski jumpers to sail down the hill farther. This technique is still in use today and has been perfected through wind tunnel research and computer simulation.[10]

Some other professionals within the field who use the principles of biomechanics to improve an individual's movements and skill performance are adapted physical educators, athletic trainers, and exercise leaders. Knowledge of kinesiology and biomechanics helps these professionals design and conduct programs to enhance individual movement skills. Biomechanics helps professionals make sure that individuals are moving safely, effectively, and efficiently, with consideration given to the unique needs of individuals.

There are many specialized areas of study within biomechanics. Developmental biomechanics focuses on studying movement patterns and how they change across the lifespan, from infancy to old age and with people with disabilities. Especially with the aged, an understanding of the biomechanical principles involved in activities of daily living, such as walking, climbing stairs, lifting, and carrying, is important in designing activities to enable individuals to remain independent and able to care for their needs. For example, researchers are studying individuals with osteoarthritis to identify risk factors for developing this degenerative disease, which affects over 31 million Americans, predominantly those over the age of 65. Results from current research suggest that individuals with knee osteoarthritis often have altered gait biomechanics.[11,12,13,14] It is not yet known if the atypical gait patterns predispose individuals to knee osteoarthritis or if these patterns develop over the course of the disease, but researchers continue to make progress toward understanding the cause and developing preventative guidelines for this debilitating disease.[12,13,14]

The biomechanics of exercise is another specialized area of study. Exercise should be based on both physiological and biomechanical principles. Professionals can use biomechanical principles of exercise to make sure that individuals are performing the exercise correctly and achieving maximum benefits. For example, poor lifting technique can increase loads at the knee or low back. One of the more popular strength exercises, the back squat, is often taught only in parallel to reduce loads on the knee; however, this advice is controversial. A recent study suggests that due to knee anatomy as well as less weight lifted during deep squats, as compared to parallel squats, that knee loads are not higher when performed past parallel.[15] As long as proper lower extremity alignment is maintained along with proper spine curvature, speed may be a more important factor than depth in controlling joint loading. Front squats are also an alternative for those concerned about knee joint loading. Because of different loads lifted as well as different kinematics in the front squat, knee compressive forces are reduced compared to back squats with similar training stimulus to the lower extremity muscles.[16] Professionals should stay abreast of current research in strength training techniques to prevent unnecessary injuries and optimize training benefits.

Clinical biomechanics is the study of the prevention of injury or diseases that result in movement disorders and the rehabilitation of people who are injured or have a movement disorder disease or disability. This helps professionals understand the cause of injury or disease and how the injury or disease has altered the normal movement pattern of individuals. This information is then used to design injury prevention and rehabilitation programs to help individuals move optimally within their constraints and to restore normal function when possible. Athletes at risk for and recovering from anterior cruciate ligament (ACL) injury have benefited from biomechanical research designed to identify at-risk athletes and develop prerehabilitation and rehabilitation programs. Several coach-friendly screening tools, such as the Landing Error Scoring System (LESS)[17] and the ACL nomogram,[18] rely on visual observation or video analysis of athletes performing certain movement skills and result in a score estimating the athlete's risk for incurring an ACL injury. For athletes who do suffer an ACL injury, re-injury is a concern and occurs in 6–25% of athletes with reconstructed ACLs.[19] Current research suggests that athletes with reconstructed ACLs have altered biomechanics including increased knee valgus and asymmetrical knee extension moments during common sports movement skills (running, jumping, and cutting) up to 2 years following surgery.[19] These altered biomechanics are thought to be one risk factor for the high re-injury rates. Promising research in both preoperative rehabilitation[20] and targeted neuromuscular training postoperative rehabilitation[19] will hopefully lower the re-injury rate in the near future.

Equipment design is a growing area of biomechanics. Changes in equipment can lead to dramatic increases in performance. One of the most significant changes can be seen the speed skating. The speed skating event at the 1998 Nagano Olympics served as a showcase for new technology: the clap skate. The Dutch-invented clap skate, with its hinged blade, redefined record times. With conventional skates, the skater primarily uses the quadriceps with little calf muscle involvement and pushes through the back half of the skate. The clap skates use a hinge-and-spring mechanism to attach the front of the skate boot to the blade. The heel is not attached to the blade; thus, when the foot is raised above the ice, the blade snaps back to the heel, making the characteristic clapping noise. The clap skate allows the skater to use the calf muscles, making the push more powerful. The blade also remains on the ice for a longer time, allowing for a longer stride and greater speed. Since its introduction, the skate has been modified and refined to enhance its performance characteristics.

Biomechanics is an important component of concussion research, providing significant contributions to concussion identification and prevention. Helmet or head accelerometers are used by some sports teams to collect head impact data during games and practices.[21] These data help researchers understand the types of and magnitude of acceleration the head experiences during sport skills. Combining this data with concussion data from the players helps researchers better understand the biomechanics of mild traumatic brain injury (mTBI).[21] Biomechanists are also involved in helmet design. While helmets are designed to reduce the risk of skull fractures, not prevent concussions, recent focus has been on designing helmets to reduce concussions in athletes. Biomechanists also work with sports medicine professionals to design effective concussion screening programs. One interesting research area uses virtual reality to challenge multiple senses of an athlete while collecting data on spatial navigation, balance, and attention.[22,23] Results suggest virtual reality tests have promise for detecting lingering deficits in concussed athletes who are clinically asymptotic.[22,23]

Biomechanists are also involved in the testing of new fabrics, evaluating them in terms of their potential to contribute to performance. New fabrics, developed after years of testing, help competitors in several different sports decrease their times by reducing water or air resistance. In the 2000 Olympic Games in Sydney, swimmers wore new bodysuits created out of a special material that offered less resistance through the water than human skin. Modeled on a shark's skin, Speedo's Fastskin material helped competitors shave seconds off their times, critical in a sport where the difference between winning and finishing second can be as little as one hundredth of a second.[24] In the 2002 Winter Olympic Games, similar suits, Nike's Swift Skin, and Descente Vortex suits, were worn by speed skaters. Extensive testing went into the development of these fabrics, designed to decrease friction, and consequently, improve the performance. Biomechanists and other sport scientists continually work to modify textiles and designs in hopes of greater performances. Prior to the 2008 Beijing Olympics, Speedo introduced the LZR Racer made from elastane, nylon, and polyurethane.[25] The suit repelled water and reduced drag significantly.[25]

The tight compression and improved buoyancy helped swimmers maintain a more hydrodynamic position even while fatigued.[26] Twenty-five world records were broken in Beijing; 23 from swimmers wearing the LZR suit.[27] Critics termed these new suits and others like them "technological doping," and swimming's international governing body, FINA, issued new regulations in 2010 regarding swimsuit manufacturing.[27]

With similar concerns as FINA, the Federation Internationale de Ski (FIS) closely regulates ski jumping suits. Only 40 liters of air are allowed to pass through the fabric to control the amount of air the suit holds and limit "buoyancy."[28] In 2011, FIS required suits to be skin tight, with no more than 2 centimeters of loose fabric, to eliminate extra surface area that increases distance due to greater lift.[28]

Biomechanists are continually researching running technique to improve performance and reduce injuries. In the early 2000s, barefoot running became popular, inspiring the development of minimalist running shoes aimed at allowing runners to reproduce barefoot running biomechanics while wearing running shoes. Barefoot running typically alters the foot strike pattern of runners, creating a forefoot strike with the ankle in slight plantarflexion and shorter quicker steps.[29] These altered mechanics are being researched to learn how they relate to injuries and performance in runners. Runners who use a forefoot strike pattern may experience lower impact force and lower injury rates for some overuse injuries than those with a rear foot strike, though results are not equivocal and much research is still needed.[30] Interestingly, while barefoot and minimalist running were becoming the focus of biomechanical research, in 2010, Hoka introduced ultralight "maximally" cushioned running shoes with other shoe companies soon following.[31] The ultracushioned shoes are designed to reduce peak impact forces using the materials and structure of the shoe, while minimalist shoes are designed to reduce peak impact forces by encouraging the runner to adopt a forefoot strike and use his or her muscles to absorb the impact forces. With the ever-increasing popularity of running and a high overuse injury rate, look for continued biomechanical research on running mechanics and footwear.[31] An understanding of the way the body works, knowledge of the demands of the sport, and the ability to apply biomechanical principles are important in equipment design.

The application of biomechanical principles is not limited to the realm of physical education, exercise science, and sport. Biomechanists working in industry use this information to ensure safe working conditions for and efficient performance from

Physical education, exercise science, and sport professionals, when helping individuals perform exercises, should make sure that each movement is performed correctly and conforms to accepted biomechanical principles. This is important for safety reasons as well as to help ensure that the individual achieves the desired benefits.

Deborah King

workers. In medicine, orthopedists use biomechanics to evaluate how pathological conditions affect movement or to assess the suitability of prosthetic devices for patients. As the field of biomechanics continues to expand, its contribution to our understanding of human movement will become even more significant.

Major Areas of Study

Biomechanics is concerned with two major areas of study. The first area is biological in nature, as implied in the term *biomechanics.* Motion or movement involves biological aspects of the human body, including the skeletal and muscular systems. For example, bones, muscles, and nerves work together in producing motion. A muscle receives a signal from a nerve, causing a contraction. The muscle contraction creates force, which acts on a bone. The bone works as a lever, amplifying motion and allowing us to perform motions such as walking, throwing, and jumping. It is not possible to understand motor skill development without first knowing about biological aspects underlying human movement, such as joint action, anatomical structures, and muscular forces.

The second major area of study in biomechanics relates to mechanics. This area of study is important because it utilizes the laws and principles of Newtonian mechanics and applies them to human motion and movement. Biomechanics is also concerned with object motion. The study of mechanics includes *statics*, or the study of factors relating to nonmoving systems, such as those that contribute to stability and balance. It also includes *dynamics*, or the study of mechanical factors that relate to systems in motion. In turn, dynamics can involve a *kinematic* or *kinetic* approach. Kinematics is concerned with describing motion and includes the study of time and space factors in motion such as velocity and acceleration. Kinetics is concerned with understanding the cause of motion and includes the study of forces such as gravity and muscles that act on a system.

Research in biomechanics is concerned with studying movement and factors that influence performance. The kinds of questions that may be studied are listed here:

- How do running motions change as children develop?
- How do forces summate to produce maximum power in the tennis serve?
- What are the movement patterns of world-class hurdlers?
- How can athletic shoes be designed to reduce injuries on artificial turf?
- What is the wrist action of elite wheelchair marathon athletes?
- What is the optimal design of the javelin?
- What are the critical performance elements of throwing? Of various fundamental motor skills? Of various sport skills? What are the common errors associated with the performance of these skills, and how can they best be remediated? How do the mechanics of these fundamental motor skills change with age?
- Which techniques are best for increasing the range of motion after reconstructive surgery of the shoulder?
- What is the best body position for swimming the butterfly stroke?
- Is a specific brand of rowing ergometer safe to use? Can individuals of all fitness levels effectively use this piece of fitness equipment? Are the benefits claimed by the manufacturer for its use accurate?

These are only a few of the questions that can be addressed through biomechanical research techniques. In answering these questions, researchers measure such factors as joint angles and muscle activity, force production, and linear and angular acceleration. The next section presents selected biomechanical terms.

SELECTED BIOMECHANICAL TERMS RELATED TO HUMAN MOTION

Biomechanics has a specialized scientific vocabulary that describes the relationship between force and motion. As previously defined, kinematics is concerned with understanding the spatial and temporal characteristics of human movement, that is, the direction of the motion and the time involved in executing the motion. Important terms related to kinematics include *velocity*, *acceleration*, *angular velocity*, and *angular acceleration*. Understanding the relationship between linear and angular motions is also a very important part of kinematics. Kinetics is concerned with the forces that cause, modify, or inhibit motion. Terms related to kinetics are *mass*, *force*, *pressure*, *gravity*, *friction*, *work*, *power*, *energy*, and *torque*. (See Table 6-1.)

Velocity refers to the speed and direction of a body and involves the change of position of a body per unit of time. Because bodies in motion are continually changing position, the degree to which the body's position changes within a definite time span is measured to determine its velocity. For example, the velocity of a baseball from the time it leaves the pitcher's hand to the time it arrives in the catcher's glove can be measured in this manner.

Acceleration refers to the change in velocity over time. An individual playing basketball, for example, can add positive acceleration when dribbling toward the basket on a fast break, or the player can change pace and slow down (decelerate) to permit another player to move into position to serve as a screen.

Angular velocity is the angle that is rotated in a given unit of time. *Angular acceleration* refers to the change of angular velocity for a unit of time. For example, when a bowling ball is rolled down a lane, its angular velocity can be computed mathematically in terms of revolutions per second. The angular acceleration, on the other hand, occurs after the bowling ball is released and the ball actually starts

TABLE 6-1 Selected Biomechanical Terms

Kinematics–study of space and time factors in motion, such as velocity and acceleration
Kinetics–study of forces that act on a system, such as gravity and muscles
Velocity–change in the speed or direction of a body per unit of time
Acceleration–change in velocity
Angular velocity–angle that is rotated in a given unit of time
Angular acceleration–change in angular velocity for a given unit of time
Mass–amount of matter possessed by an object
Force–any action that changes or tends to change the motion of an object; described in terms of magnitude and direction
Pressure–ratio of force to the area over which the force is applied
Gravity–force that accelerates all objects vertically toward the center of the earth
Center of gravity–point at which all of an object's mass is balanced at a specific moment
Friction–force that occurs when surfaces come in contact with each other
Work–force that is applied to a body through a distance and in the direction of the force
Power–amount of work accomplished in one unit of time
Energy–capacity of a body to perform work
Torque–twisting, turning, or rotary force applied to the production of angular acceleration

rolling, instead of sliding, which occurs immediately on release.

The relationship between linear and angular motions of body parts should be understood. Northrip, Logan, and McKinney cite the following examples: (1) a throwing motion involves angular velocity of the wrist joint, which helps to determine throwing speed; and (2) kicking a football involves the angular velocity of the kicker's ankle joint, which helps to determine kicking performance.[32] The final linear velocity that results in both cases is achieved as the sum of many angular motions at the body joints. Because most body movements are rotational movements at the body's joints, to achieve the best results in skill performance, it is necessary to integrate linear and angular motions.

Mass is the amount of matter possessed by an object. Mass is a measure of the object's inertia, that is, the resistance of the object to efforts made to move it and, once it has begun to move, to change its motion. The mass of an object influences the amount of force needed to produce acceleration. The greater the mass, the larger the force needed. For example, in track and field, a larger force would be needed to accelerate a 16-pound shot (mass = 7.2 kilograms) than a 12-pound shot (mass = 5.45 kilograms).

Force is any action that changes or tends to change the motion of an object. Forces have both a magnitude (i.e., size) and a direction. Forces on the body can occur internally, such as when a muscle contracts and exerts forces on the bone to which it is attached. External forces such as gravity also act on the body.

Pressure refers to the ratio of force to the area over which the force is applied. For example, 16-ounce boxing gloves will distribute a given force over a larger surface area than 12-ounce boxing gloves, thus reducing pressure. In this case, distributing the pressure will ensure less chance of injury from blows when the 16-ounce gloves are used.

Gravity is a natural force that pulls all objects toward the center of the earth. An important feature of gravitational pull is that it always occurs through the center of mass of an object. In the human body, the center of mass is known as the *center of gravity*. The center of gravity is the point at which all of the body's mass seems to be located and the point about which an object would balance. The position of the center of gravity is constantly changing during movement. It can be either within or outside the body, depending on the shape of the body. It always shifts in the direction of movement or the additional weight. When human beings stand erect with their hands at their sides, the center of gravity is located at the level of the hips. Athletes can use their knowledge about the center of gravity to better their skills. For example, the basketball player during a jump ball swings both arms forward and upward to assist in gaining height. Once in the air, the player allows one arm to drop to his or her side and strives to get maximum reach with the other arm. By dropping one arm to the side, the player can reach farther beyond the center of gravity than with two arms overhead.

Friction is a force that occurs when surfaces come in contact and results when the surfaces move past each other. The roughness of the surfaces and the amount of force pressing them together, normal force, influence the amount of friction. The rougher the surface and the greater the normal force, the greater the magnitude of friction. Friction plays an important role in traction. Traction is important to athletes. The ability of athletes to make quick turns, change direction rapidly, stop, and propel themselves forward without losing footing depends on having the right amount of traction.[32] Shoe manufacturers design shoes to provide athletes with the right amount of traction for the specific sport, playing surface, and weather conditions.[32] Reduction of friction is important in sports such as skating and skiing, where the ability to glide over ice and snow is critical to performance.[32]

Work refers to a force that is applied to a body through a distance and in the direction of the force. An individual who bench-presses 240 pounds through 2 feet is doing work. The direction of the motion is the same as the direction of the force, and therefore, the total amount of work is determined by multiplying 240 pounds by 2 feet, which equals 480 foot-pounds of work for each repetition.

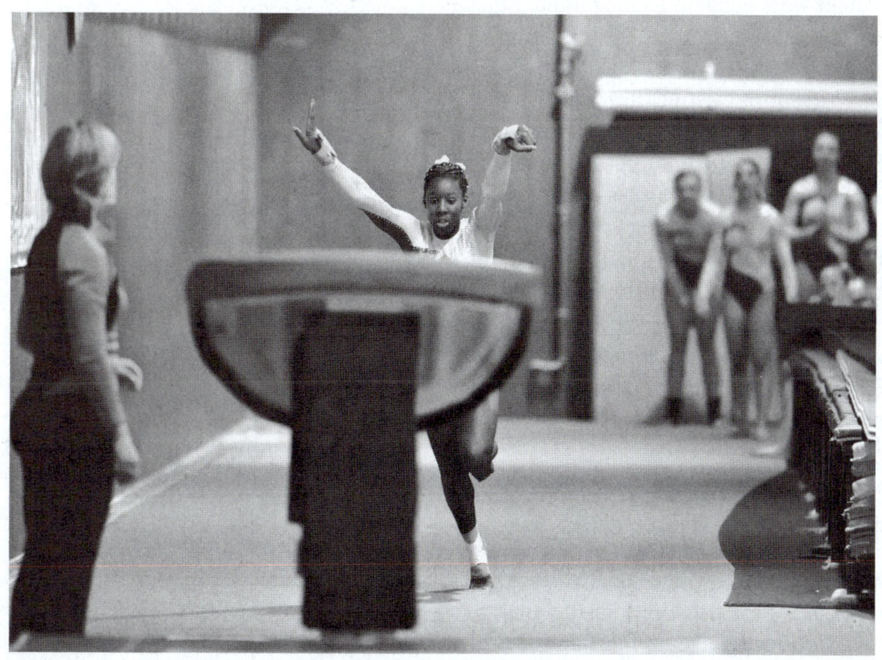

Understanding the principles of biomechanics can assist gymnasts in improving their performance.

Brian McEntire/iStock/Getty Images

Power is the amount of work accomplished in one unit of time. For example, a person performs a certain task, such as running, and exerts a certain amount of horsepower to perform the task in a given amount of time. To exert twice as much horsepower, the runner would have to perform the same task and accomplish the same amount of work (i.e., run the same distance) in half the amount of time.

Energy relates to the capacity of a body to perform work. Two types of energy used in biomechanics are (1) kinetic energy, the energy a body has because it is moving (such as a skier whose weight and velocity determine kinetic energy), and (2) potential energy, the energy that accrues as a result of the position that a body occupies relative to the earth's surface. The weight of the body and its height above the surface are used to determine potential energy. For example, a diver at the peak of a dive has the capacity to do work because of his or her position relative to the earth's surface. When he or she falls toward the water, the weight of the body does work equal to its magnitude times the distance the body moves in the direction of force.

Torque represents a twisting, turning, or rotary force related to the production of angular acceleration and is contrasted with the force necessary to produce linear acceleration. Muscles create torque as they rotate our limbs or body parts. For example, pronator teres produces torque about the radioulnar joint to create pronation. The production of torque is essential in gymnastics because of the many movements required in routines that use apparatus such as the high bar, parallel bars, uneven parallel bars, and rings.

MECHANICAL PRINCIPLES AND CONCEPTS RELATED TO MOVEMENT

Movements are governed by mechanical principles. Biomechanists use these principles in the analysis of movement. To illustrate some mechanical principles, selected principles and concepts relating to stability, motion, leverage, and force are presented in this section.

Stability

Stability is an important factor in all movement skills. It is related to equilibrium and balance. When all the forces acting on the body are counterbalanced by equal and opposite forces so that the sum of the forces equals zero, equilibrium is maintained. A state of equilibrium occurs when the body's center of gravity is over its base of support and the line of gravity (a line drawn from the center of the gravity to the center of the earth) falls within the base. The base of support of the body is the area outlined when all the points in contact with the ground are connected. The greater the body surface in contact with the ground, the larger the base of support. Thus, a sitting position has a larger base of support than a standing position. A stance that places four points of the body in contact with the ground, rather than just two points as in standing, typically increases the base of support.

Stability is the body's ability to return to a position of equilibrium after it has been displaced. The greater the body's stability, the more difficult it is to affect its equilibrium.

Static equilibrium occurs when the center of gravity is in a stable position (e.g., when one is sitting or performing a handstand in gymnastics). Dynamic equilibrium is a state in which the center of gravity is in motion (e.g., when one is running or performing a cartwheel in gymnastics). In sport and movement terminology, stability is often referred to as balance. The body's ability to maintain stability or balance is governed by three primary principles.

Principle

The lower the center of gravity is to the base of support, the greater the stability. When performing activities that require stability, individuals should lower their center of gravity. In running, for example, individuals can stop more efficiently and quickly if they bend their knees, thereby lowering the center of gravity, and place their feet in a forward stride position. Other examples include a wrestler taking a semicrouched position and a football lineman assuming a three-point stance.

Principle

The nearer the center of gravity is to the center of the base of support, the more stable the body. When the center of gravity extends beyond the boundaries of the base of support, balance is lost. Keeping the body's weight centered over the base of support helps promote stability. However, in activities where the objective is to move quickly in one direction, shifting the weight in the direction of the movement can aid performance. For example, in starting a sprint race, the runners will lean forward to get out of the starting blocks quickly.

Some activities, such as walking on a balance beam, have a small base of support. It is very easy to lose one's balance in these types of activities. When balance is lost while performing on the balance beam, the arm or leg on the opposite side from which the person is leaning is used to control the person's angular momentum and try to prevent a fall.

Principle

The wider the base of support is, the greater the stability. Widening the base of support helps achieve greater stability. When standing, for example, spreading the feet in the direction of movement adds stability. Using both hands and feet to create the base of support increases stability as is seen in a four-point stance in football.

Tai Chi has been found to improve balance in the elderly. The wide base of support offers the instructor stability as she leads the class through the movement.

Sarah Rich

To increase stability in situations when receiving or applying force, the direction of the force must be considered. When receiving either a fast-moving object or a heavy force, widen the base of support in the direction from which the force is coming. When applying a force, widen the base in the direction from which the force is to be applied.

Motion

Motion implies movement. Motion can be classified as linear or rotary; the human body usually employs a combination of both. The rotary action of the legs used to propel the body in a linear direction is an example.

Linear Motion

Linear motion refers to movement in a straight line and from one point to another. In running, for example, the body should be kept on a straight line from start to finish. Also, the foot and arm movements should be back and forth in straight lines rather than from side to side across the body.

Rotary Motion

Rotary motion consists of movement of a body about a center of rotation, called the axis. In most human movements, rotary motion is converted into linear motion. The speed of rotation can be increased when the radius of rotation is shortened. Conversely, the speed of rotation can be decreased when the radius of rotation is increased. Examples include tucking the head when performing tumbling stunts, to increase the rotation of the body, and holding the arms out when executing a turn on the toes on ice, to slow the body.

To have motion, the equilibrium of a body must be destroyed or upset. Equilibrium is upset when the forces acting on a body become unbalanced. A force is required to start a body in motion, to slow it down, to stop it, to change the direction of its motion, or to make it move faster. Everything that moves is governed by the laws of motion formulated by Sir Isaac Newton. These laws describe

DID YOU KNOW?

1. Softball batters generally have about two one hundredths of a second less to decide to swing at a fast ball than baseball players. Top pitch speeds (in mph) in softball reach the low 70s, while top speeds in baseball are in the high 90s. However, since the distance to the plate is shorter in softball, at these speeds, softball batters have about 0.417 second before the ball reaches the plate, while baseball players have about 0.437 second.
2. The title of fastest man or woman in the world goes to the world record holder in the 100-meter dash. Currently, Usain Bolt holds that honor for men, with a time of 9.58 seconds and an average speed of 23.8 mph. Florence Griffith Joyner holds the women's title at 10.49 seconds, running an average speed of 21.3 mph. These are just their average speeds; sprinters reach top speeds above 25 mph.
3. The fastest recorded spin in figure skating is 240 rpm, done by Ronald Robertson. That is four revolutions per second. Nathalie Krieg holds the record for longest spin, spinning for 3 minutes and 20 seconds.
4. The current record holder in heavy weight lifting, Hossein Rezazadeh, lifted 263 kilograms (579 pounds) in the clean and jerk. He is 6 feet 1 inch and weighs 345 pounds. While that is truly impressive, Om Yun-chol, coming in at 123 pounds and 5 feet tall, holds the world record in the 56-kilogram class with a clean and jerk of 171 kilograms (376 pounds). He lifted three times his body weight!
5. Ski jumpers reach speeds in excess of 60 mph before they leave the ramp and fly through the air for 5 seconds. On a "large hill," a ski jumper will start on top of a ramp that is typically over 33 meters (436 feet) above the landing area at the bottom of the hill. The skier glides down this 100-meter (320 feet) ramp before taking off and flying over 145 meters (475 feet) in the air–farther than the length of a football field.

how things move and make it possible to predict the motion of an object.

Newton's First Law

The law of inertia states that a body at rest will remain at rest and a body in motion will remain in motion at the same speed and in the same direction unless acted on by some outside force.

For a movement to occur, a force must act on a body sufficiently to overcome that object's inertia. If the applied force is less than the resistive force offered by the object, motion will not occur. Once an object is in motion, it will take less force to maintain its speed and direction (i.e., momentum). For example, it takes an individual more effort to start pedaling a bicycle to get it under way than it does to maintain speed once the bicycle is moving. The heavier the object and the faster it is moving, the more force that is required to overcome its moving inertia or to absorb its momentum, assuming that the time used to absorb its momentum is kept constant. In football, an opponent will exert more force to stop a massive, fast-moving lineman than to stop the lighter-weight and slower-moving quarterback.

Newton's Second Law

The law of acceleration states that a change in velocity (i.e., acceleration) of an object is directly proportional to the force producing it and inversely proportional to the object's mass. If two unequal forces are applied to objects of equal mass, the object that has the greater force applied will accelerate quicker. Conversely, if two equal forces are applied to objects of different masses, the smaller mass will accelerate quicker. For example, in shot putting, the athlete who is stronger and thus able to expend more force will toss the 12-pound shot farther than an athlete who possesses less strength. Also, an athlete will find that more force is needed to propel a 16-pound shot than a 12-pound shot.

Newton's Third Law

The law of action and reaction states that for every action, there is an equal and opposite reaction.

Bouncing on a trampoline and springing from a diving board are examples of the law of action and reaction. The more force one exerts on the downward bounce, the higher the bounce or spring into the air. The thrust against the water in swimming is another example of an equal and opposite reaction–the water pushes the swimmer forward with a force equal to the force exerted by the swimmer on the backward thrust of the strokes.

Leverage

Efficient body movement is made possible through a system of levers. A lever is a mechanical device used to produce a turning motion about a fixed point, called an *axis*. A lever consists of a fulcrum (the center or axis of rotation), a force arm (the distance from the fulcrum to the point of application of force), and a weight or resistance arm (the distance from the fulcrum to the weight on which the force is acting). The bones of the body act as levers, the joints act as the fulcrums, and the force to move the bone or lever about the joint or fulcrum is produced by the contraction of the muscles.

Three types of levers are determined by the relationship of the fulcrum (axis), the weight, and the point of application of force. In a *first-class lever*, the fulcrum is located between the weight and point of application of force. In a *second-class lever*, the weight is between the fulcrum and the force. In a *third-class lever*, the force is between the fulcrum and the weight.

Levers enable one to gain a mechanical advantage by producing either strength or range of motion and speed. First-class levers may produce either strength or speed, unless the fulcrum is in the middle of the force and weight, which produces a balanced condition. Second-class levers produce strength, and third-class levers favor range of motion and speed. The movements of the body are produced mostly through third-class levers. In third-class levers, the point of application of the force (produced by the muscles) is located between

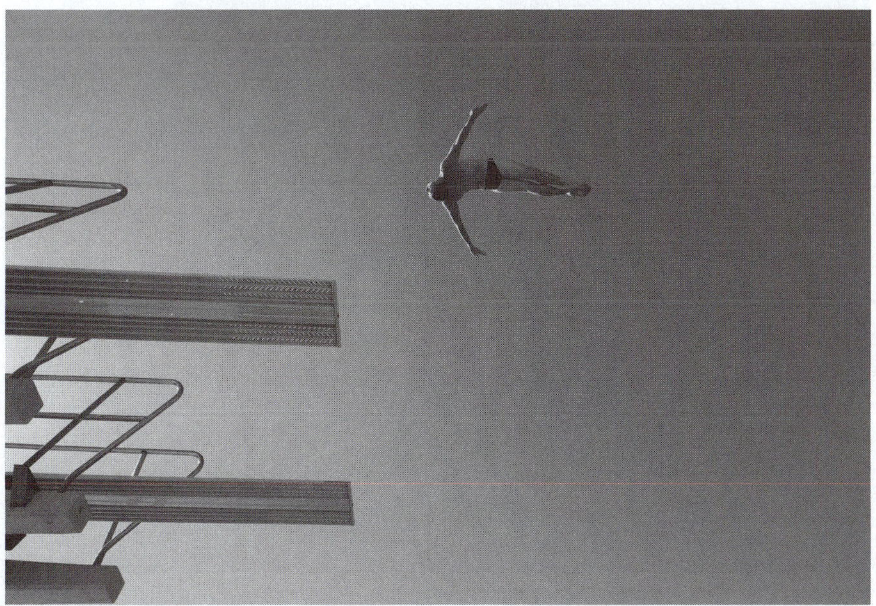

Understanding Newton's laws is important in attaining optimal performance.

sirtravelalot/Shutterstock

the fulcrum (the joint) and the resistance (the object to be moved).

The length of the force arm, distance from the axis to the active or applied force, is the key to producing either force or range of motion and speed. If great force is desired, the force arm should be as long as possible. If range of motion and great speed are desired, the resistive arm, the distance from the axis to the weight, should be lengthened. The internal levers of the body cannot be controlled in regard to the length of the force arm. However, when using implements such as bats and racquets, a person can choke up on a bat and decrease the resistance arm. With the axis closer to the center of mass of the bat, the bat is easier to swing, and thus, the batter should realize an increase in angular velocity. The smaller resistance arm decreases the linear distance through which the end of the bat travels, and depending on the change in angular velocity, this could have a positive or negative effect on linear bat speed. However, this strategy typically results in faster bat speeds. When using an implement to produce greater force or speed, the size and the length of the implement must match the strength of the person who is handling the implement.

Concepts

1. Levers are used to gain a mechanical advantage by producing either speed or force.
2. Greater speed is produced by lengthening the resistance arm, and greater force is produced by lengthening the force arm.

Force

Force is the effect that one body has on another. It is invisible, but it is always present when motion occurs. It should be pointed out, however, that there can be force without motion. An example of a force in which no motion is evident is the push against a wall by a person. The wall does not move, although great force might be exerted. Another example occurs when two arm wrestlers are pushing against each other with equal force and their arms remain relatively motionless.

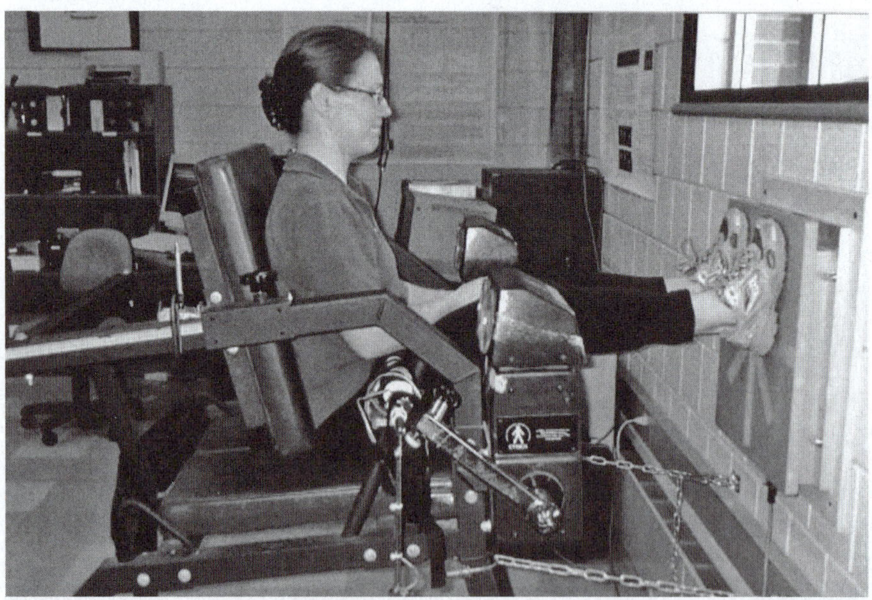

Leg press strength is being measured with a force plate attached to a wall. The force plate is connected to a computer where peak force and rate of force developed are displayed.

Deborah King

Professionals should be aware of the principles relating to the production, application, and absorption of force when they teach movement activities.

Production of Force

Body force is produced by the actions of muscles. The stronger the muscles, the more force the body is capable of producing. However, the force of the muscle group or groups must be applied in the same direction and in proper sequence to realize the greatest force. In the high jump, for example, the body should be lowered on the last step before the jump. This lowering of the body will enable the jumper to contract the muscles under optimal conditions to create power. The upward movement of the arms will give added force to the jump when coordinated with the upward push from the legs. It should be remembered that the principles of stability and the laws of motion must be observed in the performance of the high jump if the greatest height is to be attained.

Force must also be generated to propel objects. The same principles apply as mentioned above. In the swing of a softball bat, the application of force is possible because of the production of force by multiple muscle groups in a coordinated manner. For maximum force, the body should be rotated at the hips, shoulders, arms, and hands in a sequential order. The summation of these forces will produce the greatest momentum. A follow-through is necessary both to avoid jerky movements, decelerating prior to contact, and to reduce the possibility of injury to the muscles or tendons.

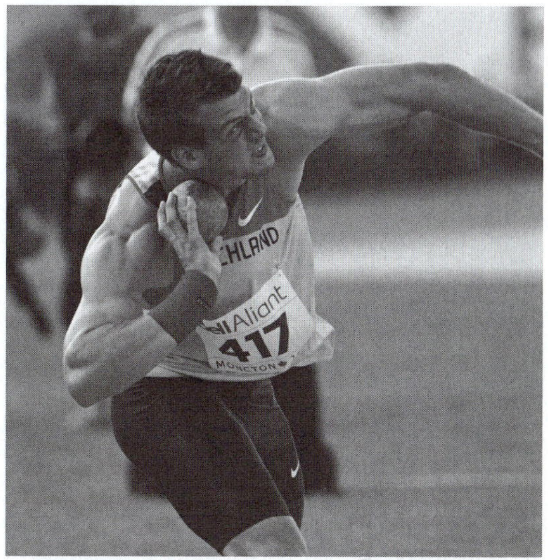

Force production is a critical component in many sports such as shot putting.
Jamie Roach/Shutterstock

Application of Force

The force of an object is most effective when it is applied in the direction that the object is to travel. Many activities in sport involve the projection of the body or another type of object into the air. To project an object or the body forward most efficiently, the force should be applied through the center of mass of the object and in a forward direction. To move the body upward, the force should be directed upward through the center of the body. The example of the vertical jump will illustrate this principle. Force from the legs must be applied to the ground such that the upward reaction force from the ground is directed through the center of the body. If the jumper leans forward or sideways when pushing off from the ground, the force will cause rotation and forward or sideways motion instead of purely vertical motion, and the jumper will not jump as high.

When someone throws an object, the following three main factors are of concern: (1) the speed of the throw, (2) the distance of the throw, and (3) the direction that the object will travel.

The speed of the throw depends on the speed of the hand at the moment of release of the object. The speed of the arm can be increased by lengthening it to its fullest, taking a step in the direction of the throw, shifting the weight properly, starting force generation with the lower body, and using optimally sequenced rotations of the pelvis through the arm (called kinetic chain). These movements must be done in a continuous motion to maintain momentum. If an implement such as a bat or paddle is used, it becomes an extension of the arm; therefore, the same principle applies.

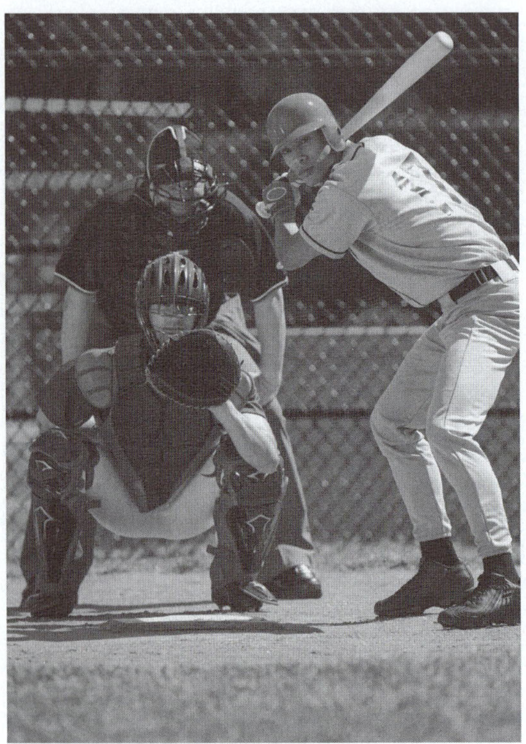

Absorption of force is important in catching objects. The catcher's mitt, which distributes the force over a greater area, and the action of giving with the catch help absorb the force of the pitched ball.

Tetra Images/Alamy Stock Photo

The distance of the throw will be affected by the pull of gravity and air resistance. The distance that an object will travel, therefore, depends on the angle of release in addition to the force imparted in the throw. Given a constant release velocity, an object will go farthest when released at 45 degrees. This represents a compromise between releasing an object at a large angle and having it remain in the air but not go very far because of wind resistance, and releasing the object at a smaller angle where the pull of gravity will keep it from traveling very far.

The direction or accuracy of the throw depends on the point of release of the object. In making the overhand throw in softball, for example, the hand should travel in the straightest line possible toward the target, on both the backswing and the follow-through.

In addition to gravity and air resistance, the flight of thrown and batted objects is also affected by the spin of the object. The object will travel in the direction of the spin.

Absorption of Force

Many instances occur when persons must receive or absorb force. Examples include absorbing the force of a thrown object, as in catching a football or softball, landing after a jump, and trapping a soccer ball. The impact of the force should be gradually reduced, and it should be spread over as large an area as possible. Therefore, when someone catches a ball, the arms should be extended to meet the ball. During the catch, the hand and arms should give with the catch. When landing from a jump, the person should bend the hips, knees, and ankles to gradually reduce the kinetic energy of the jump, thereby reducing the momentum. The feet must also be spread slightly to create a larger area of impact (base).

Concepts

1. The more muscles that are used, the greater the force that is produced (provided, of course, that they are working together).
2. The more elasticity or stretch a muscle is capable of, the more force it can supply. Each working muscle should be stretched fully to produce the greatest force.
3. When objects are moved, the weight of the objects should be pushed or pulled through the center and in the direction that they are to be moved.
4. When objects are kicked, hit, or thrown, the force of the muscles should be used in a sequential manner. For example, the order in throwing should be trunk rotation, shoulder, upper arm, lower arm, hand, and fingers.
5. When body parts (arms and legs) or implements such as bats and paddles are used, they should be extended completely when making contact with an object to be propelled.
6. When receiving or absorbing the force from an object (as in catching a ball), a fall, or a

kick, the largest possible area should be used to absorb the force. For example, the student should use two hands to catch a hard-thrown ball; more area will be available to absorb the force of the ball.
7. The absorption of force should be spread out as long as possible by recoiling or giving at the joints involved in the movement.

To analyze an individual's motor performance, professionals need to be cognizant of the principles governing movement. Selected principles pertaining to stability, motion, leverage, and force were discussed in this section. Professionals are also concerned with such concepts as friction, aerodynamics, hydrodynamics, and ball spin and rebound in the evaluation of performance. An understanding of both biomechanics and kinesiology provides the professional with a foundation for understanding and analyzing human movement.

BIOMECHANICAL ANALYSIS

Various instruments and techniques are used by biomechanists to study and analyze motion. Improvements in instrumentation coupled with advances in computers and microchip technology have greatly assisted biomechanists in their endeavors. Additionally, the development of better and more creative methods of using these instruments has greatly enhanced the understanding of human movement and the ability to improve the performance.[33] These tools include computers, anthropometry, timing devices, motion capture, videography, electrogoniometry, electromyography (EMG), dynamography, and telemetry. Sometimes, researchers use wind tunnels. These tools, as well as visual observation, can be used to perform quantitative and qualitative analysis of human movement.

Instruments and Techniques

Computers play an important role in biomechanical research. Biomechanical analysis requires dealing with prodigious amounts of data. The use of computers in dealing with such data is a necessity. Additionally, much of the instrumentation used in biomechanical research is linked to a computer. Much of the analysis of information can be performed online so that the results can be available almost instantly.

Computers can also be used to simulate movements. Simulation requires the use of mathematical formulas to develop models of a specific movement. Then, this computer model can be used to assist biomechanists in determining the effects of certain modifications in the movement or certain variables on performance. For example, simulation can address such questions as, "What is the effect of altering the takeoff position of a dive on the subsequent performance?" Or, "How does air resistance affect a skier's performance?" This approach helps researchers determine how a performance can be improved.

Comparisons of the optimal or ideal performance and an individual's actual performance are enhanced through the use of computer technology. The computer is used to generate graphic representations of the ideal performance and the actual performance. The drawing of the actual performance is compiled from analysis of the films of the performer. These graphic representations of the ideal performance and an individual's actual performance can then be compared. This helps to detect errors and identify strategies to improve the performance. Computers offer biomechanists tremendous assistance in understanding human movements.

Motion capture and high-speed imaging are two of the basic tools employed in biomechanical research. Sophisticated cameras are used to capture an individual's performance on a computer. These high-speed cameras capture details of movements that may escape the unaided eye of the professional observing the performer's movements. It is possible to measure such things as the speed, angle, range, and sequence of moving segments. Motion capture provides graphic representations of the movement, which can be completed in real time, while the performance is taking place, or postcapture via computer processing. Completion of mathematical calculations based on information provided from the computer model is an essential part of movement analysis. This process is greatly speeded and simplified through the use of computers. Motion capture is used not only for biomechanical analysis, but also by the motion picture and video game industries for computer animation. High-speed imaging utilizes sophisticated cameras to capture performances either on digital media, such as memory cards and sticks, or directly to a computer, via Wi-Fi or Bluetooth. Immediate feedback is available to the performer, coach, or practitioner via a computer or mobile device with slow-motion and stop-action capabilities to aid in the study of the performance.

Many software applications allow stop-action sequences of movement to be displayed. This enables sequential pictures of key body positions to be seen at once. For example, the path of the various body segments of a forehand stroke in tennis can be displayed to analyze the player's execution of the stroke. This facilitates the analysis of the individual's movements. With this technique, one person's execution of a movement skill (e.g., the forehand tennis stroke or the wrist action used) can be compared with that of another person or the ideal performance.

Videography is the use of video devices to record an individual's performance. Almost all video equipment are digital, which greatly eases the use of video for performance evaluation. Unlike motion capture systems, video is relatively inexpensive, easy to use, and readily available to practitioners. With today's technology, most mobile devices have video cameras that are sufficient for analyzing many human movements. In the cases of fast-moving skills where high frame rates are important, practitioners may want to purchase a high-speed video camera, though some smartphones currently come with a high-speed video option. The ability to directly play back what has been recorded allows for immediate viewing by the analyst and prompt feedback to the performer. This is one of the most inexpensive high-technology systems for the analysis of movement. Advances in technology have led to better-quality cameras, sophisticated playback capabilities that yield greater clarity of still and stop-action images, and user-friendly software applications for simple and inexpensive video analysis of human movement. Many mobile devices have cameras that can be used for video playback and analysis with applications available in every price range and with features ranging from simple frame-by-frame playback to angle and velocity measurements.

Anthropometry is concerned with the measurement of the human body. The length, width, diameter, circumference (girth), and surface area of the body and its segments are measured. Correct identification of anatomical landmarks is crucial to obtaining accurate measurements. Information about the structure of the human body is used to calculate the forces acting on the joints of the body and the forces produced by movement. Information about the structure of an individual's body is important in developing computer models of performance.

Timing devices or chronoscopes are used to record speeds of body movements. Some types of timing devices are stopwatches, digital timers, counters, switch mats, photoelectric cells, and real-time computer clocks. The chronoscope is started at a preselected point in time, typically the initiation of a movement, and then stopped at a preselected time, such as the completion of a movement. The speed of movement is then calculated. Radar guns can also be used to provide instantaneous information about speed. Some timing systems can be used for agility training and testing and can be programmed to measure an athlete's reaction to visual or audio cues. Many timing systems are fully integrated with mobile technology allowing for easy storage and tracking of athlete performances.

Electrogoniometry is a technique that can be used to provide information about the angles of the joint as part of a total motion pattern. Another term for an electrogoniometer is an elgon. An elgon works like a goniometer (see Chapter 7 for information about the use of goniometers to measure flexibility) but uses electrical devices such as potentiometers to measure the degrees of movement at a joint. This information can be transferred directly to a computer, recording paper, or oscilloscope. For

ATHLETES TURN TO TECHNOLOGY

In the digital era, as video cameras have become smaller, cheaper, and easier to use, many coaches and trainers are adding digital video to their coaching methods. Using any digital camcorder or mobile device (though cameras that have a high-speed shutter and frame rates are best for sports), coaches can take video clips of their athletes and break down the skill in slow motion, view the skill side by side with another athlete, or even compare different views of a skill–all using readily available sports analysis software. Coaches can also add audio or text comments and highlight specific techniques using drawing tools. Many mobile applications are free, with other applications and software programs available for purchase. For information on different sports analysis applications and programs, try: www.dartfish.com, www.hudl.com, www.powerchalk.com, www.kinovea.org, www.allsportsystems.com, www.siliconcoach.com, and v1sports.com. New software applications become available almost daily, so check the web and try free demos to determine which works best for you.

In addition to video, many companies make technology for specific sports to help analyze movement. Golf swing analyzers, for example, are available that attach to your club and communicate with your mobile

Deborah King

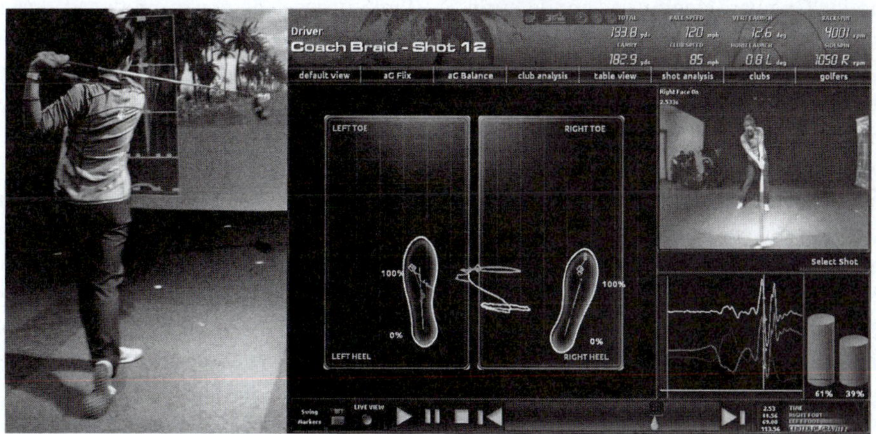

Ground reaction force and center of pressure of a golfer's swing superimposed with two different video views of the swing.

Deborah King

(Continued)

ATHLETES TURN TO TECHNOLOGY (*Continued*)

device providing information on variables such as club head speed, swing plane, and face angle.

The example screen shot from an app measuring shaft angle at impact from an accelerometer attached to the club. On the app, golfers can view their swing from different angles. Many companies make accelerometers and apps for baseball, softball, golf, and tennis, all with the goal of helping coaches and athletes fine-tune their performances.

In addition to video cameras, apps, and accelerometers, in some sports, athletes have access to computer simulators. In golf, for example, some indoor golf ranges and golf clubs have golf simulators that provide a detailed swing analysis. The golf simulator may include high-speed video of the club, multiple views of the golfer, as well as ground reaction forces and center of pressure. In the accompanying photo, a golfer is standing on turf on top of two force plates and swinging a ball at a projected driving range. On the projection screen, the golfer sees the trajectory of ball's flight as well as the distance of the shot. On the computer monitor, we see a front-view video at impact along with a detailed analysis of the weighting under her feet and the path of the center of pressure. We can see that the back spin was 4,001 rpm and the ball speed was 120 mph. At impact, she has 61% of her weight on the front foot and 39% on the back foot. The diamonds on the left and right footprints represent the location of the center of pressure under her feet at impact. We see that during the address position, her weight was back toward her heels, but at impact, the weight has shifted forward under the ball of her left foot and toes of her right foot.

example, this instrument would permit the study of the knee-joint action when a particular skill, such as walking or running, is executed. It can also measure range of motion, angular velocity, and acceleration. Electrogoniometry may be particularly useful when combined with EMG.

EMG is used to measure the electrical activity produced by a muscle or muscle group. When properly processed, this measurement serves as an approximate indicator of the amount of force being developed by a muscle. This provides a means to observe the involvement of a particular muscle or muscle group in a movement. Surface electrodes are placed over the muscle or muscle group, or fine wire electrodes are inserted into the muscle to be observed. Electrical impulses from muscle activity are then processed, recorded, and displayed. EMG may be used in conjunction with electrogoniometry. The electroencephalograph (EEG) provides the researcher with information on how the brain influences motor activity (this is studied within the realm of motor control).

Dynamography is a technique used to measure force, torque, or power produced during a movement. Isokinetic dynamometers are used to measure joint torque and power output in research and clinical settings. Strain gauges, load cells, piezoelectric, and other devices have been incorporated into equipment such as athletic footwear insoles, bicycle pedals, and uneven parallel bars to measure the force produced by the performers using this equipment. Power meters are now available for cyclists and runners to monitor power output over the course of a ride or run. Another device that is used to measure force is the force platform. Force platforms can be built into the floor to measure forces such as those associated with a foot striking the floor during walking. They can also be designed to measure force production by athletes during sprint starts, pole vaulting, and gymnastics.

Telemetry involves the wireless recording of various aspects of movement. Almost all mobile devices come standard with Bluetooth and Wi-Fi, forms of telemetry, and allow data to be sent from one device to another without wires or cables. Telemetry systems can be used to transmit information about heart rate or joint angles (electrogoniometry) during a performance. A distinct advantage of this technique is that it permits movement data to be recorded without encumbering the performer with wires and other equipment that can hinder performance. Some companies are making data logging systems that enable data from sensors to be stored on memory cards used in small data recording and storage units worn by the performer. Telemetry and data logging technology has greatly increased the mobility of performers during data collection as well as the number of activities that can be studied. Wearable technologies including accelerometers, GPS, heart rate monitors, temperature sensors, and much more are increasingly available to provide real-time feedback to mobile devices allowing coaches and athletes to monitor many aspects of performance.

Wind tunnels are used in many ways to improve athletes' performance. Nike used a wind tunnel to measure air resistance during the development of their Swift Skin,[24] and Speedo used one for the development of the LZR Racer suit.[25] Wind tunnels are used to determine whether equipment design can be improved: for example, whether the shape of a new helmet for cycling or a change in the composition of a bike wheel actually reduces air resistance. Reducing air resistance helps athletes achieve better times in their sports.

Skiers and sliders (such as bobsledders or lugers) use the wind tunnel to refine their movements for optimum efficiency and speed. These athletes experiment with various body positions inside the wind tunnel. Researchers, including biomechanists, analyze the video of the athletes to provide information about the aerodynamics of each position. Sometimes, special force-measuring devices are used to provide additional information to assist in the identification of the optimum body position. Working together, researchers, coaches, and athletes use this information to assist athletes in making form adjustments that will lead to optimum performance.

Advances in computers and instrumentation as well as the manner in which they are used have contributed much to the understanding of human movement. For example, the intersection of biomechanics and biofeedback has stimulated the development of new devices to improve sport. *Biofeedback* is the provision of information about a physiological or biomechanical parameter, such as heart rate or acceleration, to an individual. The individual then uses this information to modify his

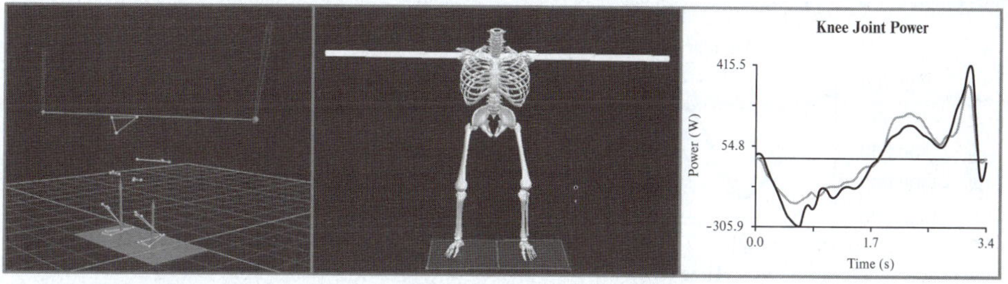

Three-dimensional motion capture is used to track the motions of the body and create computer models that are used to do a biomechanical analysis of the motion. In this example, ground reaction forces and kinematics were used to calculate left and right knee joint power output in a back squat. Motion-capture data, displayed as a stick figure, were used to make a skeletal model, from which knee joint power was calculated.

Deborah King

or her response. Wearable technologies such as those by Fitbit, Apple, Garmin, Polar, and Jawbone all provide biofeedback to athletes.

Analysis

Quantitative and qualitative methods can be used to analyze human movement. *Quantitative analysis* uses many of the techniques described previously to provide specific numerical information about the movement being studied. Specific information, for example, about the joint angles during movement, the force generated, and the speed of movement is provided (see Figure 6-1). Quantitative analyses are used predominantly in research efforts and are increasingly incorporated in clinical diagnoses, treatment, and rehabilitation, and as part of the overall training program of elite athletes to help them optimize their performance (e.g., biomechanists work with elite athletes at the U.S. Olympic Training Center in Colorado Springs, Colorado.). With advances in technology, quantitative analyses of performance are becoming more readily available to recreational athletes via sports medicine clinics, sports performance and fitness facilities, and even wearable technology.

Qualitative analysis also provides important information about the movement being studied. Qualitative analysis relies most commonly on visual evaluation of the movement. Qualitative analysis goes beyond generalized statements about performance, such as whether it was successful or not. Qualitative analysis can provide rich detail about the performer's movements, such as the release of the ball did not take place at the optimal angle.[34] An individual's performance can also be compared with another individual's performance or against a standardized model.

Qualitative analysis is most commonly used by practitioners. It offers practitioners who may not have access to sophisticated equipment or have the background to employ advanced techniques a method to effectively analyze an individual's movements. Biomechanical analysis can be used by athletic trainers

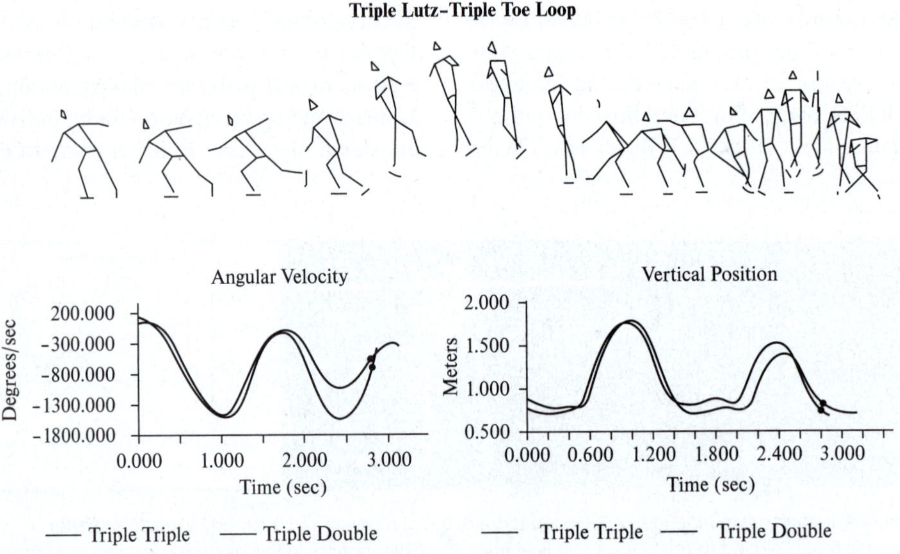

Figure 6-1 In biomechanics, movements of athletes are studied to improve the performance as well as reduce the occurrence of injury. Here, a computer model of a triple lutz–triple toe loop in figure skating is displayed, while the jump height and angular velocity of the triple lutz–triple toe loop are compared to those of a triple lutz–double toe loop.

in designing a rehabilitation program, by physical educators in conducting an evaluation of fundamental motor skills, and by exercise leaders in ensuring that clients perform each exercise correctly.

Teachers and coaches can use biomechanical analysis to improve students' and athletes' performance of sport skills. Additionally, teachers and coaches are often faced with the task of evaluating several performers of diverse skill levels in a short period of time. The use of video and slow-motion/stop-action playback can be useful to the practitioner in assessing an individual's performance. Mobile devices, such as smartphones and tablets, and the many applications available for them, have made video analysis increasingly available to professionals. Inexpensive apps for these devices let professionals create videos and analyze the performance of their program's participants. The video can be played back slow motion and annotated, identifying areas where improvements can be made. Videos can be compared side by side, comments recorded, and both shared with the participants. The use of apps makes video analysis of the performance, whether in classes, during practices, or when working out, much easier than in the past and much more affordable.

If video equipment is not available, then the professional must rely directly on his or her observations of the individual's performance. Whether the professional is using video or directly observing the individual's performance, the professional should keep in mind relevant biomechanical principles, have a mental image of the ideal performance of the skill being observed, and thoroughly understand the nature of the skill being performed. As an observer, the professional should be objective and proceed in a systematic fashion.

Knudson suggests that professionals use a comprehensive approach when performing qualitative analysis of motor skills to intervene to improve performance.[35] Rather than focusing solely on error detection and provision of corrections, or limiting themselves to biomechanical factors, professionals should take a more holistic and interdisciplinary approach, using many of the exercise and sport sciences as they design an intervention to improve the performance. Knudson's four-step approach includes preparation, observation, evaluation/diagnosis, and intervention.[35] Accuracy and consistency are important in conducting qualitative assessment.

During preparation, professionals must gather information about the movement to be analyzed and about the performer. What are the critical features of the movement? What are the abilities of the performer? Knudson encourages professionals to strive to increase their knowledge of human movement by being students of movement, studying movements and factors that influence the performance.[35]

Analysis of the kinematics of movement must be combined with observational experiences to accurately perceive critical features of movement. It is important to correctly select the critical features of the movement that are necessary for optimal performance. These critical features determine whether a movement is safe, efficient, and effective. Knowledge of biomechanics helps professionals determine which are the critical features of a skill.

Professionals benefit from a systematic approach to observation. The traditional approach emphasizes observing critical features based on the temporal phases of a skill–preparation, action, and follow-through.[35] Other professionals prefer a more holistic approach, watching several trials of a skill in order to form an overall impression of performance and then focusing on critical features.[36]

Accurate diagnosis requires determining the underlying strengths and weaknesses of the performance. Here the movement is analyzed relative to the predefined critical features.

In the intervention phase, the professional might find it beneficial to focus the performer's attention on one critical feature of the movement, rather than overwhelming the performer with multiple corrections. Knudson suggests that the professionals identify the intervention that would create the most improvement in performance and is the least difficult for the performer to implement.[35] It is also critical to convey the feedback in a manner that is easily understood by the performer.[36]

Consistency is another important aspect of qualitative analysis. According to Knudson, multiple observations of the performer improve the consistency and reliability of the analysis.[35] Consistency

USING SCIENCE TO IMPROVE TRAINING

To be competitive, athletes in many sports are turning to sports science to give them an extra edge. In biomechanics, force plates are often used to assess strength and power capabilities of athletes. Depending on the testing protocol, athletes may perform different combinations of squat jumps, countermovement jumps, and drop jumps with and without an external load while ground reaction forces are being measured. Scientists then examine the forces, looking at variables such as peak force produced, rate of force developed, contact time, and peak power. Jump height is also calculated from the ground reaction force. These variables help the sports scientists diagnose the lower extremity strength and power status of the athletes, helping fine-tune the athletes' training programs for the future.

Squat jumps reflect concentric force producing capabilities of the lower extremity. Countermovement jumps add an eccentric/stretch-shortening cycle to jump performance at moderate speed. The difference in jump height between these two jumps is sometimes used to reflect an athlete's ability to utilize the stretch shorten cycle under slow movements or low loads. Lastly, drop jumps reflect reactive and ballistic characteristics of strength and power at very high speeds. Reactive strength is often calculated from drop jumps and is used to assess an athlete's ability to produce force under high loads and rapid muscle stretch that is important in sports such as the long jump. Each of these areas of strength and power is trained with different exercise regimens, such as exercises with heavy loads, exercises using moderate resistance moved as quickly as possible, and plyometric exercises. Athletes in sports including gymnastics, weight lifting,

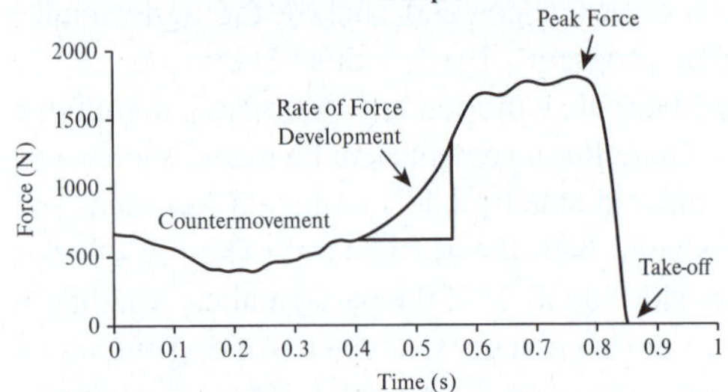

Deborah King

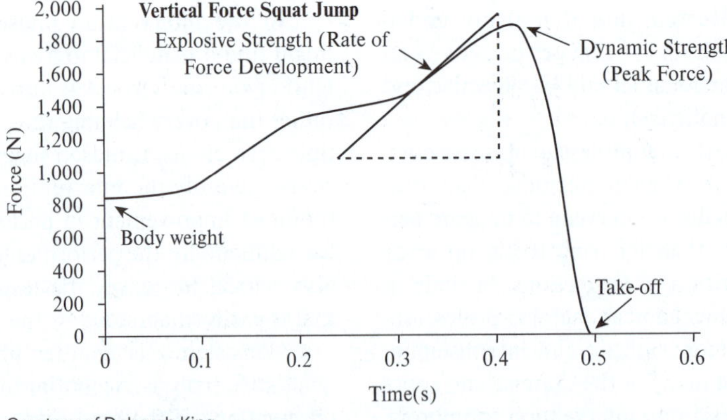

Courtesy of Deborah King

(Continued)

USING SCIENCE TO IMPROVE TRAINING (*Continued*)

bobsledding, track and field, and figure skating use the results of this testing to fine-tune their training programs. This type of testing is frequently done at strength testing centers for Olympic hopefuls.

Here is an example of a force tracing for a squat jump. In a squat jump, the athlete starts at a knee bend and then explodes straight upward. Several of the measures that can be obtained from the force profile are indicated on the graph, such as maximum dynamic strength (peak force) and explosive strength (rate of force development). In a drop jump, the athlete steps off a box and then explodes upward upon landing as shown in the picture below. The graph shows the athlete's vertical ground reaction force. From this force curve, the athlete's reactive strength index (0.83) was calculated.

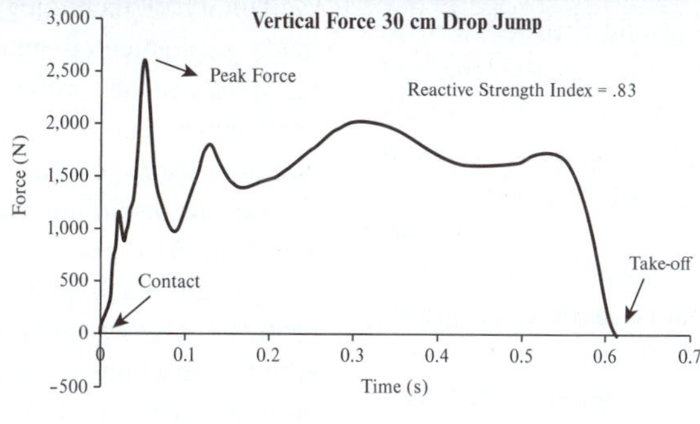

Deborah King

is further enhanced when the critical features have been precisely and clearly defined.

Hudson offers a method of analysis based on 10 core biomechanical concepts that is appropriate for professionals in an instructional setting. Six of the concepts pertain to essentially all human movements: range of motion, speed of motion, number of segments, nature of the segments (plane of movement), balance, and coordination.[37] Four of the concepts more commonly apply when projectiles are used: extension at release/contact, compactness, path of projection, and spin.[37] When observing an individual's performance, a professional can assess each relevant concept using a

CORE BIOMECHANICAL CONCEPTS

Range of motion
Speed of motion
Number of segments
Nature of segments
Balance
Coordination
Compactness
Extension at release/contact
Path of projection
Spin

Source: Hudson, J.L. (2006). Applied biomechanics in an instructional setting. *JOPERD, 77*(8), 25–27.

qualitative or quantitative approach. Multiple observations are useful in assessing performance.

Hudson notes that the key to this observational strategy is deciding which core concept is the best point for intervention.[37] Does the individual need to increase or decrease the range of motion when executing a football pass? Does the coordination of certain body segments need to be simultaneous or sequential when the individual is performing the triple jump? Does the javelin thrower need to change the angle of release to increase the length of the throw? Using core concepts as the basis of observation helps professionals make decisions about how to best intervene to improve the performance.

Physical education, exercise science, and sport professionals use qualitative analysis in many different ways to help participants in their programs move safely, efficiently, and effectively. Developing skills in qualitative analysis requires an understanding of biomechanical principles and the ability to accurately and consistently observe, assess, and prescribe strategies to improve the performer's movement, whether the movement is a sport skill, a specific exercise, or a task of daily living.

The Future

Technology will continue to drive the advancement of knowledge. To answer future questions, Adrian and Cooper assert that "we must use basic concepts about what is known to pose the questions of the future and create more effective, safe, and rewarding human movement."[33]

Adrian and Cooper state that mathematical modeling of the anatomical characteristics of individuals, coupled with computer simulation techniques, enables biomechanists to make predictions of performance as well as to develop new and advanced performance techniques.[33] Expertise in mathematics, anatomy, physiology, physics, and computers is necessary to take advantage of these approaches. Data collected via the tools of motion capture, high-speed imaging, dynamography, electrogoniometry, EMG, and accelerometry form the foundation for modeling and are entered into the computer, which analyzes the data using various software packages. Simulations allow movements to be varied with respect to speed, timing, range of motion, and environment. Through simulations, these changes in movement variables can be explored and determinations can be made about the optimization of performance and its safety. Computer-assisted drawing, design programs, and three-dimensional (3-D) printing can expedite the design of equipment.

Advances in the analysis of human movement continue to be made at a rapid pace. The increased availability of technology at a decreased cost has made sophisticated analyses readily available to teachers, coaches, athletic trainers, athletes, fitness participants, and practitioners. The use of multidisciplinary teams, composed of sport scientists from the various disciplines, facilitates the integration of data from multiple sources, enhancing our comprehension and enabling physical education and sport professionals to work more effectively with students, athletes, and individuals of all ages seeking to move more efficiently and effectively. The integration of biomechanics with motor development can increase our understanding of movement across the lifespan and enable us to more readily design solutions to remediate problems and safely advance the motor performance of people of all ages and abilities.

Expert profiling and simulations advance the frontier of knowledge and lead to improvements in performance. Worldwide databases make data available to interested researchers throughout the world. These databases allow for diagnosis of movement

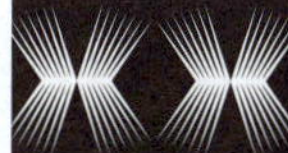

FOCUS ON CAREER: Biomechanics

PROFESSIONAL ORGANIZATIONS

- American Society of Biomechanics (http://www.asbweb.org)
- International Society of Biomechanics (http://isbweb.org/)
- International Society of Biomechanics in Sports (http://www.isbs.org/)
- International Sports Engineering Association (http://www.sportsengineering.org)

PROFESSIONAL JOURNALS

- *Clinical Biomechanics*
- *Journal of Applied Biomechanics*
- *Journal of Biomechanics*
- *Research Quarterly for Exercise and Sport*
- *Sports Biomechanics*
- *Sports Engineering*

problems, profiling, and collaborative research ventures. The increasingly sophisticated technology associated with virtual reality offers new opportunities for analysis and improvement of performance.

As we move further into the twenty-first century, another exciting trend is the shift in the population that biomechanists study and with whom they work.[3] Wilkerson suggests that in the future, we will see a great emphasis on research on women and the elderly, two populations that were not studied in the past.[3] Additionally, there will be a shift toward studying people with a wider range of abilities and in a greater array of settings; our research will expand from a focus on the elite athlete to a broader focus on people not only participating in sports but carrying out their tasks of daily living. A current example is the use of biomechanics to study complications of obesity such as tendonitis, foot pain, and osteoarthritis.

Current research suggests that older adults affected by obesity have a higher prevalence of foot pain impacting walking speed and quality of life.[38] Given that this population is rapidly growing at all age levels, this is an important area for continued research. Physical activity plays an important role in attaining and maintaining a healthy body composition. Understanding how being overweight or obese affects movement efficiency, effectiveness, and safety is critical if we as professionals are to help this population become more active.

CURRENT TRENDS: MOVING TOWARD THE FUTURE

- Further advances in smart apps, wearable devices and clothing, smart implements, and video technology will enable individuals as well as professionals to more quickly and easily analyze performance.
- The growth of 3-D printing technology will enable the design of shoes, equipment, and wearable technology to fit specific individual characteristics and needs.
- The growth and increasingly sophisticated technology associated with virtual reality offers exciting possibilities for the analysis and improvement of performance.
- Biomechanists will increasingly work as part of multidisciplinary teams with other sport scientists to enhance the movement of people of all ages and abilities.

SUMMARY

Understanding the factors that govern human movement is essential for physical education, exercise science, and sport professionals. Professionals are concerned with helping individuals optimize their movements. To accomplish this task, they need to thoroughly understand the mechanical principles that regulate movement. The analysis of human movement and sport movement using the principles of physics and mechanics is called biomechanics.

Biomechanics is concerned with two major areas of study. The first area focuses on the anatomical aspects of movement, while the second area concerns itself with the mechanical aspects of movement. Needless to say, these areas are closely related. Biomechanists have a specialized scientific vocabulary to describe their area of study. The terms *power, acceleration, velocity, mass, pressure, friction, work, energy, angular velocity, acceleration, torque,* and *gravity* are defined in this chapter. Selected biomechanical principles and concepts pertaining to stability, motion, leverage, and force are explained and illustrated.

Within the last 15 years, improvements in instrumentation and its application have been numerous, which has greatly expanded the knowledge base. Although the practitioner may not have access to much of the specialized equipment used by the biomechanist researcher, the practitioner can use available technology–such as video, wearable technology, mobile apps, or direct observation–to analyze performance. Understanding the principles of biomechanics is essential in improving individuals' performance.

DISCUSSION QUESTIONS

1. How are kinesiology and biomechanics different and integrally related? Do professionals *have* to have knowledge and understanding of both kinesiology and biomechanics? How can each discipline impact the movement of athletes, clients, and students?
2. In small groups, discuss experiences you have had (as a professional or as an athlete, client, or student) with sport, exercise, or rehabilitation biomechanics. What assessments or techniques were conducted? How did the analyses of these assessments or techniques transfer into improved movement or performance?
3. Discuss how your motion in performing a specific sport activity has changed since you were a child (e.g., running, throwing a football, swimming, and driving a golf ball)? What contributed to these changes?

GET CONNECTED

International Sports Engineering Association–offers access to sports engineers as well as serving as a global forum for dissemination of information related to sports engineering and technology.

http://www.sportsengineering.org

Exploratorium: Sport Science–designed for children, but includes many activities that use principles from biomechanics, such as application of biomechanical principles to skateboarding, baseball, and hockey.

https://www.exploratorium.edu/explore/sport-science

Science Friday–designed for teachers and students, offers video clips explaining the science behind winter Olympic sports.

https://www.sciencefriday.com/spotlights/winter-olympics/

Dartfish Blog–information about Dartfish video analysis and biomechanics, including case studies.

https://blog.dartfish.com

SELF-ASSESSMENT ACTIVITIES

These activities are designed to help you determine if you have mastered the materials and competencies presented in this chapter.

1. Write a short essay of 250 words on the worth of biomechanical knowledge to the practitioner in physical education, exercise science, and sport. Write the essay from the perspective of a practitioner in a career that you are considering for the future–that is, teacher, coach, athletic trainer, exercise physiologist, or sports broadcaster.
2. Explain and illustrate the meaning of each of the following terms: power, acceleration, velocity, mass, pressure, friction, work, energy, torque, and center of gravity.
3. Using a sport with which you are familiar, illustrate principles and concepts relating to stability, motion, leverage, and force.
4. If you own or have access to a smartphone or tablet, either Apple or Android, research apps that are available for the video analysis of performance. If time permits, make a video of a classmate performing a skill and use the app to analyze the performance.

REFERENCES

1. Hamilton, N., Weimar, W., & Luttgens, K. (2012). *Kinesiology: Scientific basis of human motion* (12th ed.). New York: McGraw Hill.
2. Martin, R. B. (1999, October). A genealogy of biomechanics. Presented at the annual conference of the American Society of Biomechanics, University of Pittsburgh, Pittsburgh, PA.
3. Wilkerson, J. D. (1997). Biomechanics. In J. D. Massengale & R. A. Swanson (Eds.), *The history of exercise and sport science* (pp. 321–366). Champaign, IL: Human Kinetics.
4. Atwater, A. E. (1980). Kinesiology/biomechanics: Perspectives and trends. *Research Quarterly for Exercise and Sport, 51*, 193–218.
5. SHAPE America–Society of Health and Physical Educators. (2018). *Guidelines for undergraduate biomechanics* (4th ed.). [Guidance Document]. Reston, VA: Author.
6. Counsilman, J. E. (1968). *The science of swimming.* Englewood Cliffs, NJ: Prentice Hall.
7. Brown, R. M., & Counsilman, J. E. (1971). The role of lift in propelling swimmers. In J. Cooper (Ed.), *Biomechanics*. Chicago, IL: Athletic Institute.
8. Mullen, I. (2016). Should you use a S- or I-pull in your freestyle stroke? *Swimming Science.* Retrieved from https://www.swimmingscience.net/.
9. Vint, P., & Russel, M. (2011). Effects of start block design on swim start performance. USA Swimming, Coaching Education Library. Retrieved from https://www.usaswimming.org/.
10. Spector, D. (2014). *Why ski jumpers hold their skis in a V-shape.* Business Insiders: Science.
11. Lynn, S. K., Reid, S. M., & Costigan, P. A. (2007). The influence of gait pattern on signs and symptoms of knee osteoarthritis in older adults over a 5–11 year follow-up period: A case study analysis. *The Knee, 14*, 22–28.
12. Hurwitz, D. E., Sumner, D. R., Adriacchi, T. P., & Sugar, D. A. (1998). Dynamic knee loads during gait predict proximal tibial bone distribution. *Journal of Biomechanics, 31*, 423–430.
13. Miyazaki, T., Wada, M., Kawahara, H., Sata, M., Baba, H., & Simada, S. (2002). Dynamic loads at baseline can predict radiographic disease progression in medial compartment knee osteoarthritis. *Annals of the Rheumatic Diseases, 61*, 617–622.
14. Weidenhielm, L., Svennson, O. K., & Brotsom, S. A. (1992). Change of adduction moment about the hip, knee and ankle joints after high tibial osteotomy in osteoarthritis of the knee. *Clinical Biomechanics, 7*, 177–180.
15. Hartmann, H., Wirth, K., & Klusemann, M. (2013). Analysis of the load on the knee joint and vertebral column with changes in squatting depth and weight load. *Sports Medicine, 43*, 993–1008.

16. Gullet, J. C., Tillman, M. D., Gutierres, G. M., & Chow, J. W. (2009). A biomechanical comparison of back and front squats in healthy trained individuals. *Journal of Strength and Conditioning Research, 23*, 284–292.
17. Padua, D., Marshall, S., Boling, M., Thigpen, C., Garrett Jr, W., & Butler, A. (2009). The Landing Error Scoring System (LESS) is a valid and reliable clinical assessment tool of jump-landing biomechanics: The JUMP-ACL study. *American Journal of Sports Medicine, 37*, 1996–2002.
18. Myer, G. D., Ford, K. R., & Hewett, T. E. (2011). New method to identify athletes at high risk of ACL injury using clinic-based measurements and freeware computer analysis. *British Journal of Sports Medicine, 45*, 238–244.
19. Bien, D. P., & Dubuque , T. J. (2015). Considerations for late stage ACL rehabilitation and return to sport to limit re-injury risk and maximize athletic performance. *International Journal of Sports Physical Therapy, 10,* 256–271.
20. Eitzen, I., Moksnes, H., Snyder-Mackler, L., & Risberg, M. A. (2010). A progressive 5-week exercise therapy program leads to significant improvement in knee function early after anterior cruciate ligament injury. *Journal of Orthopedic and Sports Physical Therapy, 40*, 705–721.
21. Guskiewicz, K., & Mihalik, J. (2011). Biomechanics of sport concussion: Quest for the elusive injury threshold. *Exercise & Sport Sciences Reviews, 39,* 4–11.
22. Teel, E., Gay, M., Johnson, B., & Slobounov, S. (2016). Determining sensitivity/specificity of virtual reality-based neuropsychological tool for detecting residual abnormalities following sport-related concussion. *Neuropsychology, 30*, 474–483.
23. Teel, E., Gay, M., Arnot, P. A., & Slobounov, S. (2016). Differential sensitivity between a virtual reality balance module and clinically used concussion balance modalities. *Clinical Journal of Sport Medicine, 26*, 162–166.
24. Boyle, A. (2002, February 1). The high-tech race for Olympic gold. Retrieved April 15, 2019, from http://www.nbcnews.com/id/3079010/ns/technology_and_science/t/high-tech-race-olympic-gold/#.XLSygehKjZs.
25. Naughton, K. (2008, June 20). Speedo: Making a splash. *Newsweek*. Retrieved April 15, 2019, from http://www.newsweek.com/2008/06/20/making-a-splash.html.
26. Kessel, A. (2008, November 23). Born slippy. *Observer*. Retrieved April 15, 2019, from http://www.guardian.co.uk/sport/2008/nov/23/swimming-olympics2008.
27. Charette, R. (2009, July 27). FINA proposes banning high-tech swim suits. *IIEEE Spectrum: The Risk Factor*. Retrieved April 15, 2019, from spectrum.ieee.org/riskfactor/computing/it/fina-proposes-banning-hightech-swim-suits.
28. Elliot, D. (2014). The fine line between innovation and "technological doping". *CBS NEWS, Winter Olympics 2014*. Retrieved April 15, 2019, from http://www.cbsnews.com/news/winter-olympics-2014-the-fine-line-between-innovation-and-technological-doping/.
29. Squadrone, R., & Gallozzi, C. (2009). Biomechanical and physiological comparison of barefoot and two shod conditions in experienced barefoot runners. *Journal of Sports Medicine and Physical Fitness, 49*, 6–13.
30. Knapik, J., Orr, R., Pope, R., & Grier, T. (2016). Injuries and footwear (part 2): Minimalist running shoes. *Journal of Special Operations Medicine: A Peer Reviewed Journal for SOF Medical Professionals, 16,* 89–96.
31. Davis, J. (2015). Are you more or less prone to injuries with maximalist shoes? *Runners Connect*. Retrieved April 17, 2019, from https://runnersconnect.net/more-less-injuries-maximalist/.
32. Northrip, J., Logan, G. A., & McKinney, W. (1979). *Introduction to biomechanical analysis of sport* (2nd ed.). Dubuque, IA: William C. Brown.
33. Adrian, M. J., & Cooper, J. M. (1987). *The biomechanics of human movement*. Dubuque, IA: Benchmark Press.
34. Hall, S. (2019). *Basic biomechanics* (8th ed.). New York, NY: McGraw Hill.
35 Knudson, D. (2000). What can professionals qualitatively analyze? *Journal of Physical Education, Research, and Dance, 71*(2), 19–23.
36. Bartlett, R. (2007). *Introduction to sport biomechanics: Analyzing human movement patterns* (2nd ed.) NY: Routledge.
37. Hudson, J. L. (2006). Applied biomechanics in an instructional setting. *Journal of Physical Education, Research, and Dance, 77*(8), 25–27.
38. Mickle, K. & Steele, J. (2015). Obese older adults suffer foot pain and foot-related functional limitations. *Gait & Posture, 42*, 442–447.

C H A P T E R 7

EXERCISE PHYSIOLOGY AND FITNESS

Polka Dot Images/Getty Images

O B J E C T I V E S

After reading this chapter, students should be able to–

- Define and explain the importance of exercise physiology.
- Identify and describe the components of health- and performance/skill-related fitness.
- Explain the principles and guidelines for designing fitness programs.
- Use the FITT formula to design a fitness program.
- Describe other factors related to fitness and performance, including environmental conditions, nutrition, and performance-enhancing drugs.

Exercise physiology is the study of the body's responses and its adaptation to the stress of exercise. Exercise physiologists are concerned with investigating both the immediate (acute) and the long-term (chronic) effects of exercise on all aspects of body functioning. These effects include the responses of the muscular system, the action of the nervous system during physical activity, the adjustments of the respiratory system, and the dynamics of the cardiovascular system. One major area of study for exercise physiologists is the description and explanation of the myriad of functional changes caused by exercise sessions of variable frequency, intensity, and duration.

Professionals, whether teachers in a school or nonschool setting, coaches, fitness leaders employed in a commercial club, or exercise physiologists working in a corporate fitness setting or a hospital, must understand the body's responses to exercise. Knowledge of the principles governing different types of training programs and the guidelines to be followed in constructing an exercise prescription enables professionals to design programs to meet each individual's physical activity needs and goals.

SOCIAL JUSTICE

Talking Points

- Exercise plans should be developed to meet the needs of each individual, regardless of gender, race, ethnicity, socioeconomic status, (dis)ability, or sexual identity.
- Educating individuals about "body fat" is imperative to reduce fat phobia of many individuals who have biases and prejudices based on a person's body size.
- Healthy and nutritious food and beverage options should be provided to all individuals regardless of socioeconomic status and home residence (i.e., urban, suburban, and rural).

EXERCISE PHYSIOLOGY: AN OVERVIEW

Exercise physiology is one of the most rapidly growing areas of specialization within the disciplines of physical education, exercise science, and sport. The definition, historical development, and areas of study and scope are discussed in this section.

Definition

Exercise physiology is the study of the effects of exercise on the body. Specifically, exercise physiology is concerned with the body's responses and adaptations to exercise, ranging from the system level to the subcellular level. These modifications can be short-term–that is, lasting only for the duration of the activity–or long-term–present as long as the activity is continued on a regular basis.

As a discipline, exercise physiology is one of the largest and most popular areas of study within the realm of physical education, exercise science, and sport. Today, the depth and breadth of knowledge in exercise physiology are growing rapidly because of the proliferation of research, which is facilitated by increasingly sophisticated technology and by the widespread interest of professionals in this discipline.

Areas of Study

Exercise physiology encompasses a broad range of topics. Examples of some areas of study are:

- effects of various exercise programs on the systems of the body, including circulatory, respiratory, nervous, skeletal, muscular, and endocrine systems;
- relationship of energy metabolism to performance;
- effects of various environmental factors–such as temperature, humidity, altitude, pollutants, and different environments (e.g., in space or undersea)–on physiological responses to exercise and performance;
- effects of individual differences–such as age, gender, initial level of fitness, or disability–on fitness development and performance;
- effectiveness of various rehabilitation programs on the recovery of injured athletes, on diseased individuals, and on individuals with disabilities;
- effects of performance-enhancing drugs on performance;
- health and therapeutic benefits to be gained from engaging in appropriate levels of physical activity.

The application of knowledge from the realm of exercise physiology appears to focus predominantly on studying the effects of physical activity and exercise on the body. Two primary areas of application can be discerned: first, the enhancement of fitness, promotion of health, and prevention of disease; and second, the improvement and refinement of motor performance, especially in sport. The principles of exercise physiology can be used to improve and maintain both health-related and performance/skill-related fitness. As in the other disciplines of physical education, exercise science, and sport, there is a growing emphasis on research and application across the lifespan, from the very young to the aged.

Knowledge of and skills associated with exercise physiology are used in many different ways by professionals. Physical education teachers help children set and attain fitness goals, both in physical education class and through participation in physical activity outside the school. Coaches typically use training guidelines to help their athletes achieve high levels of fitness essential for performance in specific sports. Cardiac rehabilitation specialists work in hospitals, clinics, worksites, or community settings, enhancing the fitness of post-heart attack patients, performing fitness evaluations, and leading preventive programs. Fitness professionals in private clubs, community programs, and corporate settings design, conduct, and evaluate fitness programs for people of all ages. Strength training specialists work with professional, intercollegiate, and interscholastic athletes and in rehabilitation. Athletic trainers develop preventative and rehabilitation programs for injured athletes.

Given the depth and breadth of the discipline, it is difficult within the limitations of this chapter to provide a worthy introduction to the area. Therefore, it was decided to focus on one area of exercise physiology–fitness–and approach it from an applied perspective. It is hoped that this approach will allow students enrolled in this introductory course to gain insight into the discipline of exercise physiology and be able to relate the information they are learning to their own experiences with exercise, fitness, and performance.

Physical Fitness

Physical fitness is the ability of the body's systems to function efficiently and effectively. There are two types of fitness components, health-related and performance/skill-related, which enable all individuals to develop their fitness levels. The Definitions of Physical Fitness Components box on page 182 identifies and defines the health and skill performance components.

Health fitness is important for all individuals throughout their lifespan. The achievement and maintenance of those qualities necessary for an individual to function efficiently and to enhance their health through the prevention and remediation of disease are the central focus of health fitness.

Performance-related or *skill-related physical fitness* emphasizes the development of those qualities that enhance the performance of physical activities such as sport. Performance-related fitness focuses on individuals' ability to improve their sport-related skills and become more efficient in their overall performance. Moreover, performance-related fitness is specific to the sport or activity in which individuals engage. Different degrees of performance-related fitness components are needed, depending on the specific motor activity. For example, the degree of power, agility, and speed needed by a football player are different from those required by a tennis player, though both individuals need these qualities to perform at an optimal level.

Fitness, be it health- or performance/skill-related, must be viewed in relation to an individual's characteristics (e.g., age, health status, occupation, and preferences), needs, and goals, and the tasks that must be performed. Most individuals possess certain levels of each of the health- and performance/skill-related fitness components. The extent to which each quality is developed depends on the individual. A weekend tennis player needs a different level of physical fitness than a competitive wheelchair marathoner; a 70-year-old grandparent requires a different level of fitness than the 10-year-old grandchild. Professionals charged with the responsibility of designing and conducting fitness programs should ask the program participants about their goals.

Physical Activity, Physical Fitness, and Health

Today, the effects of physical activity and fitness on the health status of the individual are a major area of research in exercise physiology. A major threat

DEFINITIONS OF PHYSICAL FITNESS COMPONENTS

Fitness Component	Definition
Health-Related Components	
Body composition	Amount of body fat relative to fat-free content, expressed as a percentage
Cardiorespiratory endurance	Maximum functional capacity of the cardiorespiratory system to sustain work or physical activity involving large muscle groups over an extended period
Flexibility	Range of movement possible at a joint or joints
Muscular endurance	Ability of a muscle or muscle group to repeat muscular contractions against a force or to sustain a contraction over time
Muscular strength	Maximum amount of force that can be exerted by a muscle or muscle group against a resistance during a single contraction
Skill-Related Components	
Agility	Ability to change direction rapidly with control
Balance	Ability to maintain equilibrium while stationary or moving
Coordination	Ability to execute movements smoothly and efficiently
Power	Ability to produce force at a fast speed; a combination of strength and speed usually applied during a short period
Reaction time	Time elapsed between the administration of a stimulus and the body's response to the stimulus
Speed	Ability to move the body quickly

to the health and well-being of Americans is chronic diseases, many of which can be categorized as hypokinetic diseases. *Hypokinetic diseases* are caused by insufficient physical activity, often in conjunction with inappropriate dietary practices. Coronary heart disease, hypertension, osteoporosis, noninsulin-dependent diabetes, chronic back pain, and obesity are examples of hypokinetic diseases.

Health Risk Factors

Researchers have identified risk factors that contribute to chronic diseases, such as heart disease and cancer–the major causes of death in the United States today. The causes of these diseases are a complex interaction of biological, environmental, and behavioral factors. Inherited and biological factors, such as gender, race, age, and inherited susceptibility to disease, cannot be changed. However, other risk factors associated with the environment and behavior may be amenable to change, reducing the individual's risk for disease.

Environmental factors, which include physical (e.g., air quality) and socioeconomic (e.g., poverty) factors, are associated with poor health outcomes. While they can be changed, people may face obstacles in doing so. For example, it is difficult to move above the poverty line, especially in troubled economic times; however, people can take an active role in their community to bring about change. They can speak out for clean air, support community-based health initiatives, and reduce their interactions with environments that are unhealthy.

Behavioral factors, such as smoking, physical inactivity, and poor nutrition, reflect individual behavior choices. These factors can be changed by individuals taking personal responsibility for their health and reducing the presence of chronic disease factors in their lifestyle. Taking responsibility for eating healthy, incorporating physical activity into one's lifestyle, and using alcohol only in moderation are steps individuals can take to reduce their risk factors and enhance their overall level of health.

Physical inactivity has been identified as a risk factor for several diseases. Individuals who lead a sedentary–that is, physically inactive–life have increased risk of morbidity and mortality from a number of chronic diseases.[1,2,3] One striking example is the relationship between physical activity and coronary heart disease. Individuals who are inactive have almost twice the risk of coronary heart disease as those who are active.[1,2,3]

Dose-Response Debate

There continues to be an ongoing debate about the amount of physical activity necessary to achieve these desired health outcomes. The *dose-response* debate centers on questions such as: "What kind of activity should be performed? How long does the workout need to be? How much effort or intensity should the activity require? How frequently should physical activity be performed to achieve health benefits?" The *dose* refers to the total amount of energy expended in physical activity; the *response* refers to the changes that occur as a result of being physically active.

The consensus of the Centers for Disease Control and Prevention (CDC),[3] the US Department of Health and Human Services (HHS),[4] and the National Physical Activity Plan (NPAP)[5] is that regular engagement in physical activity can yield substantial health benefits, particularly in the reduction of morbidity and mortality rates. Based on evidence gathered, it is recommended that adults engage in 150 minutes per week of moderate-intensity physical activity or 75 minutes of vigorous physical activity.[3,4,5] Moderate-intensity physical activity means you are working hard enough to raise your heart rate and break a sweat, yet still are able to carry on a conversation in activities such as biking (less than 10 mph), walking briskly, or ballroom dancing. In vigorous physical activity, such as running, swimming laps, or hiking uphill, you will not be able to say more than a few words without pausing for a breath. In addition to aerobic activity, the CDC,[3] HHS,[4] and NPAP[5] recommend that you engage in muscle strengthening exercises on 2 or more days a week that work all the major muscle groups. Individuals who incorporate this dose, or level of physical activity, into their lifestyle will reap substantial health benefits and reduce their risk for disease. Additional health benefits can be gained through greater amounts of physical activity than the recommended dose.[3,4,5]

For those individuals who have difficulty fitting 30 minutes of continuous physical activity in their busy daily schedule, they can satisfy the guidelines by accumulating 30 minutes of physical activity over the course of the day. Bouts of three 10-minute or two 15-minute sessions of physical activity throughout the day are sufficient to meet the recommended guidelines.

Moderate-intensity physical activities should be incorporated into individuals' daily routine and become an integral part of their lifestyle. The recommendations for children aged 6–17 should be physically active at least 60 minutes a day and up to several hours a day, broken up into several sessions.[3,4,5] Intermittent moderate-to-vigorous physical activity should be encouraged and long periods of inactivity discouraged.

The physical activity pyramid (see Figure 7-1) is helpful in understanding the different types of physical activities and their benefits.[6] The first level of the pyramid reflects lifetime physical activity that is associated with health benefits, chronic disease reduction, and reduced risk of premature death. Levels 2 and 3 reflect guidelines for development of cardiorespiratory fitness, flexibility, and muscle fitness. Level 4 indicates that some rest and inactivity are important, but too much inactivity results in low levels of fitness and poor health.

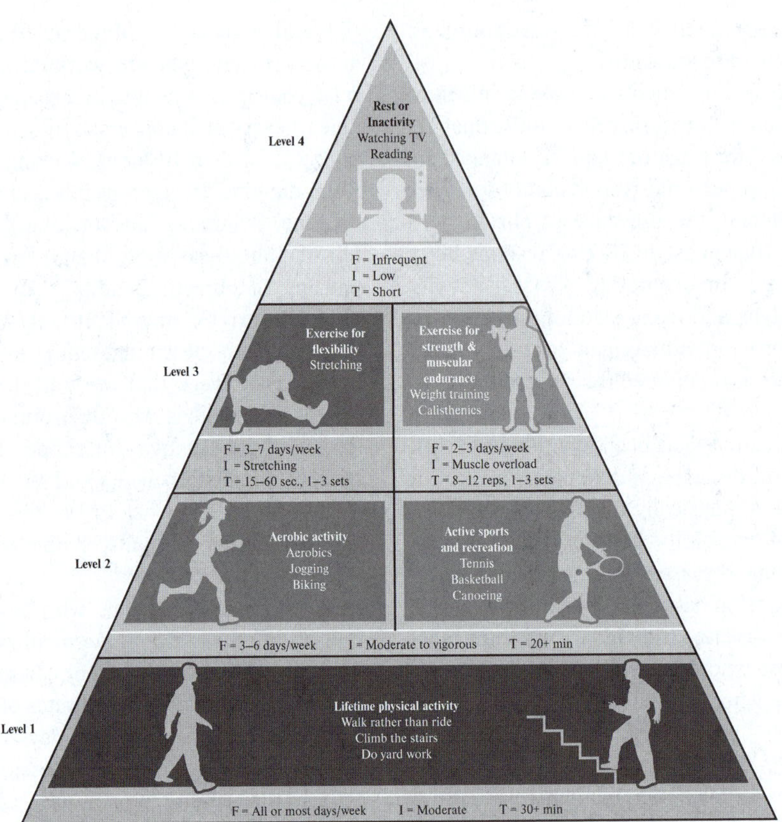

Figure 7-1 The physical activity pyramid.

Source: Powers, S., and E. Howley. *Exercise Physiology: Theory and Application to Fitness and Performance*, 8th ed. New York: McGraw Hill, 2012.

Health Benefits

Physical activity has been associated with a myriad of health benefits. Enhanced cardiovascular function is one health benefit of physical activity because it helps reduce the risk of heart disease. Benefits include a more efficient level of cardiovascular function, stronger heart muscles, lower heart rate, reduced blood pressure, increased oxygen-carrying capacity of the blood, and improved coronary and peripheral circulation. Resistance to atherosclerosis is improved as desirable serum cholesterol levels are maintained, low-density lipids are reduced, and protective high-density lipids are increased. Thus, the risk of a heart attack is lessened, and the chances of surviving a heart attack are increased. Physical activity can also help reduce other risk factors associated with cardiovascular disease such as obesity and hypertension.

Muscular strength, muscular endurance, and flexibility also are important to good health. Millions of Americans suffer from problems with low-back pain. Many of these problems can be attributed to muscular weakness and imbalance, which, in turn, can be attributed to inactivity or participation in inappropriate activities. Millions of elderly and individuals with disabilities may have trouble performing tasks of daily living because of insufficient development of these fitness components. Regular and appropriate physical activity can help these individuals achieve functional

Cycling classes are a popular fitness offering at employee fitness centers, community programs, and fitness clubs.
wavebreakmedia/Shutterstock

independence. Reduced risk of muscle and joint injury is also a positive outcome of regular and appropriate activity.

The value of physical activity is not limited only to the body; it also contributes to sound mental health. It may help alleviate mental illness and reduce susceptibility to depression and anxiety. Being active can help individuals withstand and manage stress more effectively. Many people find that exercising provides a release from tensions and makes them feel better. Regular participation in physical activity can contribute to the development of a positive self-concept and greater self-esteem. It enhances self-confidence, emotional stability, assertiveness, independence, and self-control.

Socialization is another benefit of participation in exercise and physical activities. Sports, recreational activities, and exercise groups offer opportunities to fulfill the desire to belong to a group as well as the desire for recognition. These are important psychosocial needs.

Health fitness can also contribute to increased work efficiency. Individuals who are fit have more energy, which contributes to greater productivity and efficiency of both physical and mental tasks. More energy is available for recreational activities and leisure-time pursuits. Fit individuals can also better withstand fatigue. Physical exercise can improve one's sleeping patterns.

Health fitness can improve overall general motor performance. Physical activities associated with daily living as well as sport skills can be performed more efficiently by individuals who are fit. Additionally, fit individuals recover more quickly from vigorous exercise and work than do unfit individuals. Physical activity enhances one's appearance and posture through the development of proper muscle tone, greater flexibility, and an enhanced sense of well-being.

Regular exercise can help mitigate the debilitating effects of old age. To be most effective in mitigating the effects of aging, the integration of regular physical activity into one's lifestyle should begin early in life. Individuals who remain active and physically fit throughout their life will retain a more desirable level of cardiovascular health, muscular strength, muscular endurance, flexibility, and body composition.

FITNESS DEVELOPMENT

In order to plan a fitness program, professionals must have knowledge of how energy is produced for physical activity. Understanding energy demands helps in structuring the fitness program to achieve desired results. Principles of fitness training offer guidance for program planning. In developing fitness programs, the frequency, intensity, time, and type of physical activity must be specified.

Energy Production for Physical Activity

Energy is necessary for the performance of physical activity, whether it is physical activity associated with the activities of daily living, moderate-intensity activity to improve health, exercise to improve fitness, participation in sports for recreation, or involvement in highly competitive athletics. Muscles must produce energy to move. Metabolism is the sum of all chemical reactions in the body, including energy production and energy utilization.

Energy for muscular contraction is produced from the breakdown of food we eat; food serves as a fuel source for the body. Protein, carbohydrates, and fat, macronutrients from food, are broken down via a series of processes to three main molecules–amino acids, glucose, and fatty acids. These molecules, in turn, are delivered via the bloodstream to the cells. In the cells, through a series of chemical reactions, *adenosine triphosphate* (*ATP*), is created. ATP is used as energy to perform muscular activity.

There are two major ways that energy, specifically ATP, is generated for activity: the anaerobic system and the aerobic system. *Anaerobic* means without oxygen; *aerobic* means with oxygen. With and without oxygen does not mean to hold one's breath or to breathe; rather, without oxygen means that a person does not need more oxygen than what is needed at rest. With oxygen means a person needs additional oxygen than what is needed at rest. The type of task performed, specifically the duration of the activity and its intensity (or the rate at which energy is expended), determines which energy system will contribute the majority of the energy required. (See Table 7-1.)

The anaerobic system provides energy for tasks that demand a high rate of energy expenditure for a short period of time–for example, the 100-yard dash, 50-yard freestyle swim sprint, or shot put–or in events where power–that is, quick, explosive movements–is necessary, such as gymnastics or football.[7] This system uses ATP and other necessary molecules for the chemical reactions that are stored in the muscle cells. When these small stores of ATP are used up, the body then uses stored glycogen as an energy source. Glycogen is broken down to glucose, which is then metabolized within the muscle cells to generate ATP for muscle contraction. Because body fuels can be metabolized to produce small amounts of ATP for energy without

TABLE 7-1 Energy Systems Used

Energy System	Length of Time	Type of Activity
Anaerobic	6–60 seconds	Any type of sprint (running, swimming, cycling) Short-duration, explosive activities
Combined systems	1–3 minutes	Medium-distance activities (400 and 800 meters) Intermittent sports activities
Aerobic	More than 3 minutes	Long-distance events Long-duration intermittent sport activities

Source: Prentice, W. *Fitness and Wellness for Life,* 6th ed. New York: McGraw Hill, 1999.

the use of oxygen, this is referred to as anaerobic metabolism. The anaerobic system can support high-intensity exercise for only about 1 minute. One product of anaerobic energy production is lactic acid, which accumulates in the muscles and contributes to fatigue.

When exercise continues for a prolonged time, the aerobic system provides the energy for physical activity. Physical activities requiring a lower rate of energy expenditure over a longer time, such as jogging 5 miles, cross-country skiing 10 kilometers, or engaging in a basketball game, use aerobic metabolism to supply the energy. For performing aerobic activities, a constant supply of oxygen is required by the muscles performing the work. Oxygen is used as part of a more complex process to generate ATP from carbohydrates and fats. The aerobic system is tremendously efficient at extracting ATP from the food nutrient molecules and without producing fatiguing by-products such as lactic acid.

In many activities, these systems function simultaneously. For example, many physical activities that would be considered aerobic in nature, such as basketball, soccer, racquetball, and long-distance events (e.g., running, cycling), include an anaerobic component. These activities require periodic bursts of speed or power, such as sprinting up the court for a long pass, accelerating past an opponent to an open space, and sprinting toward the finish line.

The anaerobic and aerobic systems of the body can be improved through training. Anaerobic training typically involves alternating high-intensity activity with rest periods of varying lengths; the number of repetitions in this cycle depends on the goal of the training. Anaerobic training increases the ability to do anaerobic work, tolerance for lactic acid, and muscle size. In contrast, aerobic training generally involves exercising at a lower intensity for a longer amount of time. Aerobic training improves the capacity of the body to transport and use oxygen, to generate ATP aerobically, and to utilize carbohydrates and stored fats for energy production. Aerobic training improves the function of the cardiovascular system. Understanding the different energy systems is important in developing, implementing, and evaluating training programs to improve fitness.

Principles of Fitness Training

Guidelines are provided for professionals in the discipline of exercise physiology to use when planning and conducting programs to improve fitness. Several physiological and behavioral factors must be taken into account if the sought-after benefits–improvement and maintenance of fitness–are to be realized.

1. **Principle of overload.** To gain improvements in health and fitness, an individual must perform more than their normal amount of exercise. An increased demand or workload (i.e., overload) must be placed on the body for benefits to occur. The body's adaptation to this increased workload leads to changes in fitness levels. For example, if improvement in muscular strength is the goal, the muscles must be exercised with a greater weight than normal.
2. **Principle of specificity.** The specificity principle indicates the need for an individual to perform a specific type of exercise to improve each fitness component or improve fitness of a specific body part.[8] Simply put, training must occur with the specific muscle or body part the person is attempting to improve.[9] Therefore, training programs should be designed and overload applied with specific goals in mind. For example, stretching exercises will have little impact on cardiorespiratory fitness, and weight training exercises such as squats and lunges build fitness in the legs, not in the arms. Professionals must understand individuals' fitness goals and sport demands to design fitness programs specifically to achieve these aims.
3. **Principle of progression.** Overload should be applied gradually and steadily increased (i.e., progressed) for best results. As the body adapts to the overload, the overload should be systematically increased by altering the frequency, duration, or intensity of the

exercise. An individual training to gain cardiorespiratory endurance may begin an exercise program by jogging 2 miles at a moderate intensity. The next week the individual would increase the distance to 2½ miles while still working at the same level of intensity. Week after week, the overload would be adjusted until the desired level of fitness was attained. Programs should be carefully monitored so that the individual is challenged by the workout but not overwhelmed.

4. **Principle of diminishing returns.** According to the dose-response relationship, as the dose or amount of physical activity increases, the gains accrued increase accordingly. As individuals become fitter, the benefits they receive from working out may not be as great as when they initially started. For example, sedentary individuals or those just beginning a fitness program tend to record the greatest magnitude of changes for small doses of physical activity. However, as these individuals become fitter, the gains achieved become less and less, even though physical activity is increased. This occurs as individuals approach their limits of adaptability. When improvements become less, or even diminish, maintenance of fitness becomes important.
5. **Principle of variation.** Having variation in a training program maintains individuals' interest and provides a change of pace while still making progress toward desired goals. Variation helps alleviate boredom and overcome plateaus or periods where there seems to be little progress. Manipulating the intensity of exercise, its duration, or its type can introduce variability into the program. Alternating hard workouts with easier workouts and running in different locations within the community are some ways to introduce variability into the individual's fitness program.
6. **Principle of reversibility.** The phrase "use it or lose it" sums up this important principle. Inactivity or disuse leads to a gradual erosion of the benefits achieved through overload. Gains in fitness begin to erode in as little as 2 weeks after cessation of training. Cardiorespiratory gains deteriorate most quickly and can disappear within 5–10 weeks of inactivity.[7] Strength gains erode more slowly; some strength gains remain for 6 months to 1 year after cessation of training.[7] To retain current fitness levels, individuals must continue to be active. However, less physical activity is needed to maintain fitness than was required to achieve it. Therefore, individuals can reduce their level of physical activity through modifications in the frequency, intensity, or duration of exercise.
7. **Principle of individuality.** Individuals respond differently to exercise. Individuals will differ in their rates of improvement and their potential levels of achievement. Heredity exerts a strong influence on fitness attainment. Heart and lung size, muscle fiber types, and physique are all influenced by heredity. Age, maturation, motivation, nutrition, and initial level of fitness also influence individuals' response to training. Individuals' activity preferences exert an important influence on their continued engagement in physical activity. Consideration of individual differences and tailoring the exercise program to these needs contributes to individuals' adherence to their fitness program.
8. **Principle of recovery.** The body needs time to adapt to the demands placed on it. Incorporating time for rest into the fitness program aids the body in this effort. Many individuals integrate recovery into their training by alternating the types of activities performed or by varying the muscle groups being trained. For example, an individual may work 1 day on improving upper body strength and devote the next day's training to working lower body strength. Researchers have also found that working out 7 days of the week increases the risk of injury.
9. **Principle of safety.** Safety is of paramount concern in designing a fitness program. Before starting a program, individuals should

have a thorough medical screening. This is particularly critical when special conditions exist, such as beginning an exercise program after a long period of inactivity or for rehabilitation after a heart attack. Special medical conditions, such as diabetes, require careful monitoring to ensure the safety of the individual. Additionally, individuals should be warned of the proper precautions to take when exercising in special weather conditions, such as intense heat, high humidity, or extreme cold. Finally, individuals should learn how to monitor carefully their responses to exercise and report any unusual occurrences (e.g., excessive breathlessness) to the professional conducting the program or to a physician.

Many adults exercise with sufficient intensity, duration, and frequency to realize health benefits.

Tom Grill/Corbis/Getty Images

FITT Formula

When professionals prescribe an exercise program for an individual, they must specify the frequency, intensity, time, and type of exercise. These variables are used in constructing an exercise prescription or program for an individual.

Each fitness component has a specific threshold of training that must be achieved. The *threshold of training* is the minimum level of exercise needed to achieve desired benefits.[6] The *target zone* begins at the threshold of training and defines the upper limits of training and the optimal level of exercise.[6] Exercise beyond the upper limit may be counterproductive.

Frequency refers to the number of exercise sessions per week–for example, three to five times per week. Achieving and maintaining health fitness requires that the individual exercise on a regular basis.

Intensity is the degree of effort or exertion put forth by the individual during exercise. It is how hard a person works. For example, the intensity of effort put forth by a runner can be described as 80% of their maximum effort (measured by heart rate), and the effort put forth during strength training can be described as weight lifted–for example, 80 pounds.

Time is the duration of the length of the activity, such as 40 minutes of exercise. Time is how long an exercise must be performed to be effective.

Type is the mode of exercise being performed. Since fitness development is specific, different types of activities build different components of fitness. Activities such as jogging, rowing, bicycling, stretching, and weight training are types of exercise that can be used to realize specific fitness gains. The selection of the type of exercise should be guided by the fitness goal to be achieved.

The acronym FITT can be used to help remember these prescriptive variables. These exercise variables are interrelated and can be manipulated to produce an exercise program appropriate to an individual's needs and to the outcomes wanted. For example, cardiorespiratory improvement can be realized by jogging (type) at 70% effort (intensity)

GUIDELINES FOR DEVELOPING HEALTH-RELATED FITNESS

Cardiorespiratory endurance

- Frequency: 3–5 days per week
- Intensity: 55%/65–90% of maximal heart rate or 40%/50–85% of heart rate reserve*
- Time: 20–60 minutes
- Type: Aerobic activity

Muscular strength and endurance

- Frequency: 3 days per week
- Intensity: Strength requires high resistance, 1–8 repetitions
  Endurance requires low resistance, 8–20 repetitions
- Time: 1–5 sets
- Type: Isotonic or progressive resistance exercises; can also use isometric and isokinetic exercises

Flexibility

- Frequency: Most days of the week
- Intensity: Stretch past the normal length until resistance is felt
- Time: Hold the stretch 5–10 seconds initially, building to 30–60 seconds
- Type: Static, dynamic, or contract-relax techniques

Body composition

- Maintain present level of physical activity and reduce caloric intake
- Maintain present level of caloric intake and increase level of physical activity
- Reduce caloric intake and increase level of physical activity
- Eat a diet low in fat

*ACSM guidelines[4] state that lower intensity values—that is, 55–64% of maximal heart rate or 40–49% of heart rate reserve—may be appropriate for those individuals who are unfit.

for 40 minutes (time) five times a week (frequency). Individuals who are just starting a program to improve their fitness may be more successful if they exercise at a lower intensity for a longer session. (See the Guidelines for Developing Health-Related Fitness box for specific criteria of the FITT principle.)

HEALTH FITNESS COMPONENTS

The components of health fitness include cardiorespiratory endurance, body composition, muscular strength and endurance, and flexibility. In this section, each fitness component is defined, its relationship to health delineated, methods to improve

Triathletes train to develop high levels of fitness and skill in several sports.

Traian Olinici/Shutterstock

GENERAL TRAINING PRINCIPLES

FITT Formula and Training Load	Principles
• Frequency–exercise sessions per week • Intensity–degree of effort or exertion • Time–duration of activity • Type–type of activity • Threshold of training–minimum level of activity needed to achieve desired benefits • Target zone–amount of physical activity needed to achieve desired benefits; range defined by the threshold of training and the upper limit of training	• Overload • Specificity • Progression • Diminishing returns • Variation • Reversibility • Individuality • Recovery • Safety

the fitness component discussed, and techniques to measure the component identified.

Cardiorespiratory Endurance

Cardiorespiratory endurance is the body's ability to deliver oxygen effectively to the working muscles so that an individual can perform physical activity. Efficient functioning of the cardiovascular system (i.e., heart and blood vessels) and the respiratory system (i.e., lungs) is essential for the distribution of oxygen and nutrients and removal of wastes from the body.

The performance of sustained vigorous physical activities is influenced by the efficiency of the cardiorespiratory system. The more efficient the system, the greater the amount of physical activity an individual can perform before fatigue and exhaustion occur. Performance diminishes greatly when sufficient oxygen cannot be provided by the cardiorespiratory system to the working muscles.

Cardiorespiratory endurance is regarded as the most important component of health fitness. Because of the benefits derived from improved cardiorespiratory function–such as the potential for reducing the risk of cardiovascular disease, improving work capacity, and providing greater resistance to fatigue–this component, if properly developed, can make a major contribution to an individual's health.

Cardiorespiratory endurance is concerned with the aerobic efficiency of the body. Aerobic efficiency is the body's ability to supply fuel and oxygen to the muscles. One of the major factors influencing aerobic efficiency is the capacity of the heart to pump blood. A well-conditioned heart is able to exert greater force with each heartbeat; consequently, a larger volume of blood is pumped through the arteries and throughout the body.

Another important factor in cardiorespiratory endurance is the efficiency of the lungs. The amount of oxygen that can be supplied to working muscles is a limiting factor in the performance. When demands for oxygen increase, such as during strenuous exercise, the body's ability to take in and provide oxygen to the working muscles is an important determinant of the amount of work that can be performed. The greater the body's ability to take in and deliver oxygen, the longer a person can exercise before fatigue and exhaustion occur. Thus, individuals who have well developed circulatory and respiratory systems can deliver more oxygen and therefore can exercise for a longer period.

Many benefits have been attributed to aerobic exercise. Aerobic exercise is activity that can be sustained for an extended period without building an oxygen debt in the muscles. Bicycling, jogging, skipping rope, rowing, walking, cross-country skiing, and swimming are some examples of aerobic activities. The benefits of aerobic exercise include the ability to use more oxygen during strenuous exercise, a lower heart rate at work, the production of less lactic acid, and greater endurance. Aerobic exercise improves the efficiency of the heart and reduces blood pressure.

Cardiorespiratory fitness can be improved and maintained through a well-planned program of exercise that follows the FITT formula.

Frequency. The American College of Sports Medicine (ACSM) recommends three to five exercise sessions per week for minimal improvement in cardiorespiratory fitness. Individuals may choose to work out more often; however, the body must have time to recover from the effects of exercise. Exercising every other day and following a strenuous workout day with a less strenuous recovery day are strategies individuals can implement to allow the body to recover.

Intensity. During exercise, heart rate changes in proportion to the energy requirements of the task. As the energy requirements increase, there is a corresponding increase in heart rate. Thus, heart rate can be used to monitor the intensity of exercise. (See the Measuring Your Heart Rate box.) Because heart rate slows within 1 minute following exercise, it is often recommended that the pulse be

MEASURING YOUR HEART RATE

You can determine your heart rate by counting the frequency with which your heart contracts in a period of time and converting this to the standard measure in beats per minute. Make sure you press just firmly enough to feel the pulse. If you press too hard, it may interfere with the rhythm.

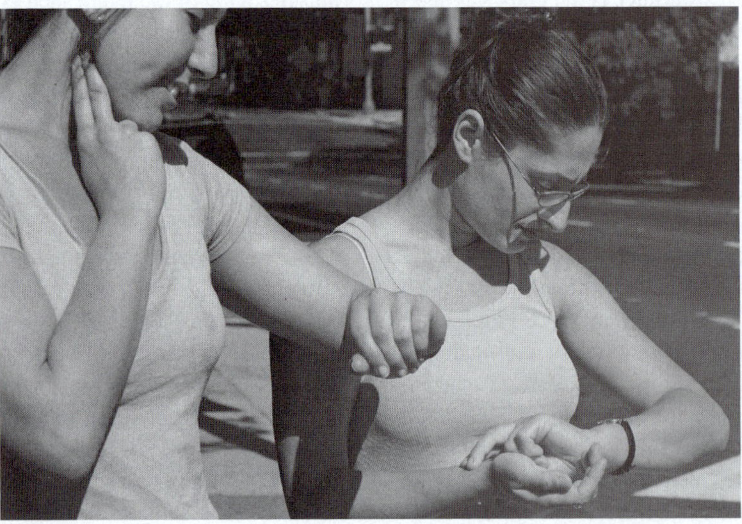

John Flournoy/McGraw Hill

Your pulse can be easily detected over the carotid artery in the front side of the neck.
You can also detect your pulse by placing a finger or fingers on your lower arm near the base of the thumb.

monitored for 10 seconds and then multiplied by 6 (or monitored for 6 seconds and multiplied by 10) to determine beats per minute. For an accurate reading, the heart rate should be monitored within 15 seconds of the cessation of exercise.

Exercising at the proper intensity is essential for a safe and effective workout. Intensity can be controlled by speeding or slowing the pace of exercise. To realize training benefits, the intensity of the exercise must be regulated so that the heart rate is elevated to a predetermined level and maintained within a certain range. This level is called the threshold of training and the range is called the THR zone.

The ACSM recommends that individuals who desire to develop and maintain cardiorespiratory fitness should exercise at one of the following intensity levels:

- 55/65%–90% of maximal heart rate (HR_{max})
- 40%/50%–85% of heart rate reserve (HRR)
- Maximum oxygen uptake reserve (VO_2R)

The lower intensities, 55–64% of HR_{max} and 40–49% of HRR, are most appropriate for individuals who have a low level of fitness.[10]

Maximal heart rate (HR_{max}) is estimated to be 220 beats per minute. Maximal heart rate is related to age; as individuals age, their maximal heart rate decreases. HR_{max} is calculated by the following formula:

$$HR_{max} = 220 - \text{age}$$

Heart rate reserve (HRR) is the difference or range between resting heart rate (RHR) and maximal heart rate (HR_{max}). HRR is calculated by the following formula:

$$HRR = HR_{max} - RHR$$

There are several formulas that can be used to calculate a target heart rate (THR) to monitor the intensity of exercise. One way is to calculate a percentage of HR_{max}. This can be done by using the following quick and simple formula:

$$THR = (\text{Target Intensity})(HR_{max})$$

Another method to calculate THR is to use a formula based on HRR. This method, commonly called the Karvonen equation, takes into account the individual's RHR and provides a more accurate estimation than the HR_{max} formula. This formula is

$$THR = (\text{Target Intensity})(HR_{max} - RHR) + RHR$$

The use of these calculations is shown in the Examples for Calculations of Heart Rate for Training Zone Using HR_{max} and HRR Methods box.

Time. The ACSM recommends 20–60 minutes of continuous aerobic activity. This amount can be accumulated during one or more sessions throughout the day. The exercise sessions should be a minimum of 10 minutes in duration.[10]

The intensity and duration of the activity are critical to achieving and maintaining fitness. Generally, as the intensity of the activity increases, its duration decreases; conversely, as intensity decreases, the duration of the activity increases. Typically, for the development of health-related cardiorespiratory endurance, lower intensities and longer durations are recommended. It is important to remember, however, that both the intensity and duration of the activity must meet minimum requirements for fitness development to occur.

Type. Aerobic activities should be used to develop cardiorespiratory endurance. Aerobic activities are those in which a sufficient amount of oxygen is available to meet the body's demands. During the performance of these activities, the

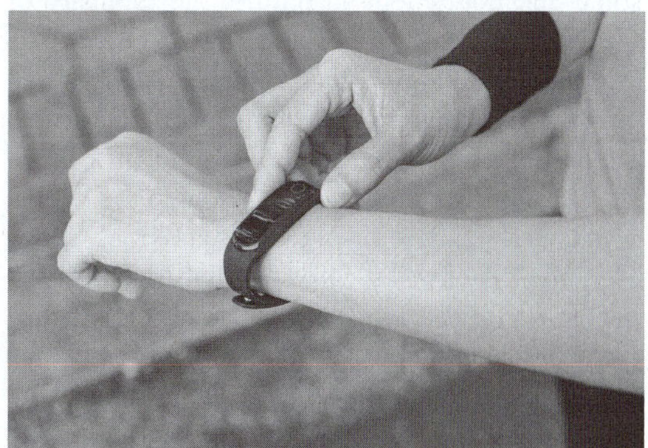

Fitness watches are used by some people to more closely monitor their training, which can be logged on smartphones.

Sasils/Shutterstock

EXAMPLES FOR CALCULATIONS OF HEART RATE FOR TRAINING ZONE USING HR_{MAX} AND HRR METHODS

A 20-year-old has an RHR of 70 beats per minute (bpm). Calculate the training zone–the threshold and upper limits for training. If the person wants to train at an intensity of 65%, calculate the THR.

	Maximal Heart Rate (HR_{max})	Heart Rate Reserve (HRR)
Formula	THR = (Target Intensity)(HR_{max})	THR = (Target Intensity) (HR_{max} − RHR) + RHR
HR_{max}	HR_{max} = (220 − age) = 200 bpm	HR_{max} = (220 − age) = 200 bpm
Threshold of training	THR = (55%)(200) = 110 bpm	THR = (40%)(200 − 70) + 70 = 122 bpm
Upper limit target zone	THR = (90%)(200) = 180 bpm	THR = (85%)(200 − 70) + 70 = 181 bpm
Training at 65% intensity	THR = (65%)(200) = 130 bpm	THR = (65%)(200 − 70) + 70 = 155 bpm

Practice calculating training heart rates using different ages, intensities, and RHRs. What patterns do you notice?

heart rate is maintained at an elevated level for an extended period. These activities typically involve vigorous and repetitive whole-body or large muscle movements that are sustained for an extended period, such as jogging, running, walking, swimming, cycling, rowing, aerobic dance, and cross-country skiing. Because these activities are somewhat continuous in nature, the intensity of the workload can be easily regulated by controlling the pace. Intermittent activities such as racquetball, basketball, and tennis involve various intensities of effort during the course of the activity. Thus, it is more difficult to regulate the degree of effort expended during these activities. However, these activities can contribute to the improvement of cardiorespiratory endurance if they are of sufficient intensity.

Cardiorespiratory fitness can be measured. The best method to determine the level of cardiorespiratory functioning is to measure maximum oxygen consumption. The more oxygen the body is able to deliver and use, the more work the body is able to perform before becoming fatigued. Maximum oxygen consumption is the greatest rate at which the oxygen is processed and used by the body.

Measurement of maximum oxygen consumption requires a sophisticated laboratory setting and well-trained personnel to monitor carefully the performance of the individual during the test. This testing is usually done on an individual basis. Following prescribed test protocols, the individual exercises on a treadmill or bicycle ergometer and breathes through a specially designed mouthpiece. Various physiological and metabolic parameters are monitored, such as heart rate, respiration rate, and rate of oxygen consumption. The exercise task is made progressively more difficult until no further increase in oxygen consumption is noted; this point is considered to be the maximum oxygen intake for the task. Although this test yields highly accurate information, it is expensive and time-consuming, and requires sophisticated equipment and highly trained personnel.

There are a variety of other methods that can be used to provide a good estimate of cardiorespiratory endurance. The most commonly used tests are

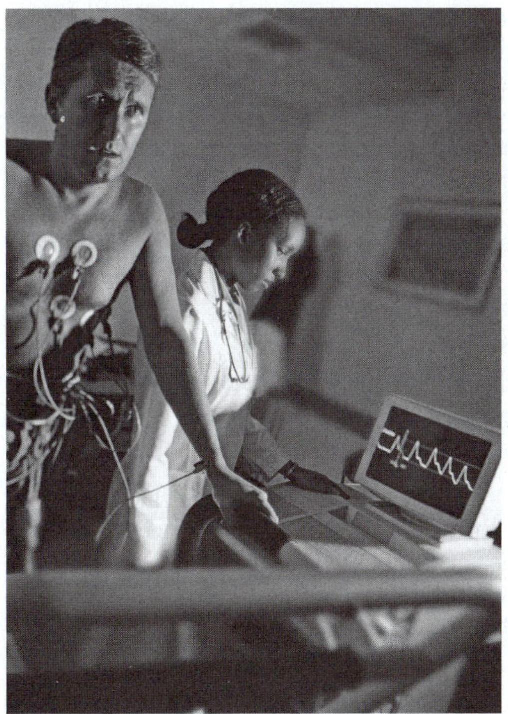

Exercise stress tests provide important information about cardiovascular fitness.

Stockbyte/Getty Images

the timed 1½- or 1-mile run/walk, the Pacer test (for children and adolescents), and the Harvard step test. These tests are most often used in school and community fitness programs. When these tests are properly conducted, results can be used to accurately estimate maximum oxygen consumption and provide an indicator of cardiorespiratory fitness.

Body Composition

Body composition is a description of the body in terms of muscle, bone, fat, and other elements. With respect to health fitness, it refers to the percentage of body weight composed of fat as compared with fat-free or lean tissue. Having a high percentage of body fat is a serious deterrent to fitness and health.

Height and weight tables traditionally have been used to determine desirable body weight. However, over recent years, body mass index (BMI) has been the primary assessment to identify whether a person is underweight, normal, overweight, or obese.

Although BMI has been statistically proven to be valid and reliable and is endorsed by the Centers for Disease Control and Prevention (CDC),[11] some individuals could be classified as overweight according to the BMI calculations. However, when their body composition is examined, the excess weight is attributable to muscular development, and their overall percentage of body fat is quite low (e.g., a professional football player can weigh 250 pounds or more, yet have only 12% body fat or less). The important consideration with respect to health fitness therefore is not weight but proportion of fat to lean tissue.

The average percentage of body fat is 18% for men and 23% for women. The percentage of body fat should not be less than 3% in men and 12% in women (the higher percentage for women is necessary for protection of the reproductive organs).[10] Extremely low percentages of body fat are hazardous to one's health. It is highly important that professionals and the public realize that a certain amount of adipose tissue or fat is essential for the body to function. Body fat also serves to protect internal organs. *The goal of fitness programs is not eliminating body fat, but helping individuals attain desirable levels of body fat.*

As previously stated, the CDC has adopted the use of the BMI to determine if an individual is at risk for poor health outcomes due to overweight or obesity.[11] The formula for calculating BMI is:

$$\text{BMI} = (\text{Weight in pounds}/[\text{Height in inches} \times \text{Height in inches}]) \times 703$$

An online calculator can be found at https://www.cdc.gov/healthyweight/assessing/bmi/adult_bmi/english_bmi_calculator/bmi_calculator.html to compute your BMI. For most people, BMI more closely correlates with total body fat than the traditional height-weight tables and provides a clearer indication of disease risk.[11] However, one limitation of BMI is that it overestimates the degree of fatness of very muscular individuals.

According to the CDC Guidelines, for adults, overweight is defined as a BMI between 25 and 30 and obesity is defined as a BMI of 30 or greater.[11] For children and adolescents, overweight is defined as a BMI between the 85th and 95th percentile for age and sex; equal to or greater than the 95th percentile is considered obese, based on the revised CDC growth charts.[12]

Overweight and obesity are associated with increased risk for coronary heart disease, type 2 diabetes, certain types of cancer, low-back pain, respiratory problems, and musculoskeletal disorders such as knee osteoarthritis. Additionally, overweight and obese individuals may experience social stigmatization, discrimination, and poor body image.[13]

Body composition is influenced by nutrition and physical activity. Although body composition is genetically related to body type (see Body Types box), the nature and amount of food consumed and the extent of participation in physical activity exert a profound influence on body composition. Poor nutritional practices may contribute to an unfavorable body composition. Eating more calories than needed and consuming a high-fat diet lead to high percentages of body fat. Sedentary individuals have lower levels of caloric expenditure.

Energy balance is important to achieving a favorable body composition. The relationship between food intake and energy expenditure is critical. This relationship is often referred to as energy or caloric balance:

Energy or caloric balance = Number of calories taken into the body as food − Number of calories expended

Energy is expended through three processes: (1) basal metabolism, or maintenance of essential life functions; (2) work, which is any activity requiring more energy than sleeping and includes exercise; and (3) excretion of bodily wastes.

BODY TYPES

Ectomorph	Mesomorph	Endomorph
Skinny, linear/ruler appearance	Naturally lean	Smooth, round body
Lightly muscled	Naturally muscular	Gains muscle easily, but tends to be underdeveloped
Small joints/bones	Medium size joints/bones	Medium/large joints/bones
Low body fat (without exercising or following low calorie diets)	Naturally strong	High levels of body fat (may be overweight)
Small shoulders, chest, and buttocks	Broad/square shoulders	Small shoulders, high waist, and large hips creating a pear-shaped physique
Long arms and legs	Body fat evenly distributed	Difficult to keep lost body fat off
Difficulty gaining weight	Losing fat is easy	Slow metabolic rate
Fast and efficient metabolism	Efficient metabolism	Attacks of tiredness/fatigue
Hyperactive	Gaining muscle easy	Lose weight slowly
Difficulty gaining muscle	Responds quickly to exercise	

Source: Muscle and Strength, https://www.muscleandstrength.com/articles/body-types-ectomorph-mesomorph-endomorph.html.

A neutral balance occurs when the caloric intake is equal to the caloric expenditure. Under these circumstances, body weight is maintained. When a positive balance exists–that is, when more calories are consumed than expended–the excess is stored as fat and body weight increases. A negative balance occurs when more calories are expended than consumed; this results in weight loss. Weight control requires maintaining the appropriate energy or caloric balance.

Body composition can be improved. Individuals who have an unhealthy percentage of body fat can reduce it by modifying their lifestyle. Fat loss can be accomplished by several means: (1) consuming fewer calories through dieting, (2) increasing caloric expenditure by increasing the amount of exercise, and (3) combining a moderate decrease in caloric consumption with a moderate increase in exercise or caloric expenditure.

Exercise increasingly is being recognized as a critical component of fat loss. Often, those desiring to lose fat focus on counting the number of calories consumed and neglect the exercise component. Exercise can aid in fat loss in several ways: (1) it can increase caloric expenditures; (2) it can suppress appetite and thereby contribute to reduction in caloric intake; (3) it can increase the metabolic rate for some time after vigorous exercise, thereby permitting extra calories to be burned; and (4) it can contribute to health fitness. Also, because sedentary living contributes to poor body composition, incorporation of regular appropriate exercise into one's lifestyle helps to successfully manage one's body composition.

Note that individuals who desire to gain weight should focus on increasing lean body mass (muscle) rather than body fat. This can be accomplished by following a sound muscle training program in conjunction with an appropriate increase in caloric intake to realize a gain of 1–2 pounds per week. Failure to incorporate muscle training as part of a total fitness program will result in excess calories being converted to fat. Thus, even though the weight gain is achieved, the percentage of body fat may be less than optimal. Therefore, a weight gaining program should combine a reasonable increase in caloric intake and a well-planned muscle training program to achieve an optimal body composition.

Sound practices should be followed in losing fat. Experts suggest the following guidelines regarding fat loss:

1. Prolonged fasting and diets that severely restrict calories are medically dangerous. These programs result in loss of large amounts of water, electrolytes, minerals, glycogen stores, and other fat-free tissue, with a minimal amount of fat loss.
2. Moderate caloric restriction is desirable, such as consuming 500 calories less than the usual daily intake. It is important that the minimum caloric intake does not go below 1,200 calories per day for a woman and 1,400 calories per day for a man, and that sound nutritional practices are followed.
3. Appropriate regular exercise of the large muscles assists in the maintenance of fat-free tissue, including muscle mass and bone density, and results in the loss of weight, primarily in the form of fat.
4. A program should be comprehensive in nature and include a nutritionally sound, low-fat diet with mild caloric restriction, regular and appropriate exercise to increase caloric expenditure, and behavior modification. Weight loss should not exceed 2 pounds per week.
5. Maintenance of proper weight and desirable body composition requires a lifetime commitment to proper eating habits and regular physical activity.

A word of caution: Some individuals become obsessed with weight loss, dieting, and exercise. This obsession can, in conjunction with a host of other factors, contribute to the development of an eating disorder. Two common eating disorders are anorexia nervosa and bulimia.

Anorexia nervosa is a disease in which a person develops a psychological aversion to food, resulting in a pathologic weight loss. Bulimia involves recurrent episodes of bin ge eating and subsequent purging by self-induced vomiting, use of laxatives, and/or excessive exercising. These disorders pose a severe threat to health and require professional treatment.

Body composition can be measured. Several methods can be used to determine the percentage of body fat. One of the most accurate methods is hydrostatic weighing. This involves weighing an individual on land and then in an underwater tank. Body density is then determined, and this information is used to calculate the percentage of lean body weight and body fat. This technique is used most often in exercise physiology laboratories and hospitals. It requires expensive equipment and is time-consuming, thus is not practical for use with large groups of people.

Air displacement plethysmography, also known as the Bod Pod, offers another means of assessment of body composition. Similar to hydrostatic weighing, the Bod Pod uses air instead of water. A person sits in the enclosed chamber (pod) and computerized sensors measure the amount of air displaced by the person's body. This approach offers similar accuracy to underwater weighing without requiring a person be submerged in water. It is easy to use, but its cost limits its availability. This technique is used most often in exercise physiology laboratories or clinical settings.

Dual-energy X-ray absorptiometry (DXA) is an extremely accurate way to assess body composition. This technique requires that the individuals lie on a table, while a machine, using two energy sources, scans alongside the body. This procedure yields an estimate of the body's density as well as information about the amounts of fat stored in different parts of the body. DXA is now considered the gold standard for measurement of body composition. Because it is extremely accurate, DXA estimates of

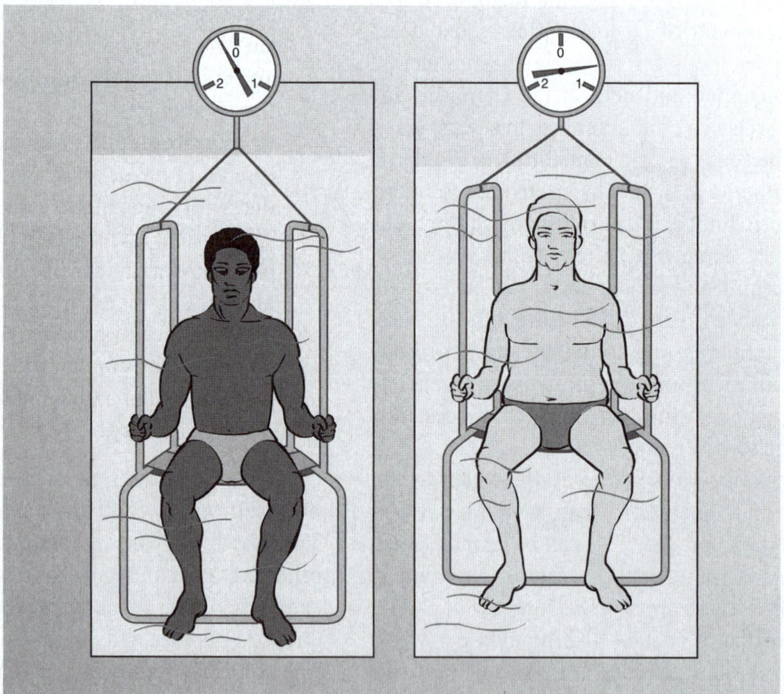

Underwater weighing is a sophisticated, accurate technique used to determine body composition. In this illustration, the underwater weighing technique demonstrates two individuals with the same height and weight, but different body composition.

Source: Powers, S., and E. Howley. *Exercise Physiology: Theory and Application to Fitness and Performance* (8th ed.). New York: McGraw Hill, 2012.

body composition can serve as a criterion by which other techniques, such as skinfolds, can be compared. Assessment of body composition with this technique is typically performed in exercise physiology research laboratories or in clinical settings.

Bioelectrical impedance analysis is a popular way to assess body composition. Electrodes are attached to an individual's body at the wrist and ankle, and a low-level electrical current is sent through the body. The resistance to the flow of the current as it passes through the body is measured. Because muscle tissue has a greater water content than fat tissue, it conducts electricity better and offers less resistance to the current. The resistance to the current is greater when there is a high percentage of body fat. The resistance to the current and body size is used to estimate the percentage of body fat. There are also scales that incorporate the same principles to provide estimates of body fatness; the individual stands on a metal plate atop the scale and the resistance to the flow of the current is measured. Bioelectrical impedance analysis can be performed relatively quickly, making it easy to use in field-based settings or to screen large groups of people.

Of the alternative approaches to measurement, the most common is the use of skinfold measurements. Skinfold measurements are taken from several selected sites, such as the triceps, subscapular, and thigh, with skinfold calipers. Formulas are then used to calculate the percentage of body fat. This method is relatively inexpensive, can be used with large groups of people, and produces accurate information when performed by well-trained individuals.

Professionals need to be cognizant of the limitations associated with the various measures of body composition. It is important to recognize circumstances under which results may be misleading, such as when the body composition values are affected by an individual's hydration status or when an individual is overweight due to having a high muscle mass rather than being overfat. Errors such as these may result in individuals being classified as obese or unfit, when they are actually healthy and fit. Professionals should make sure they know how to administer the assessment correctly and can interpret the results accurately.

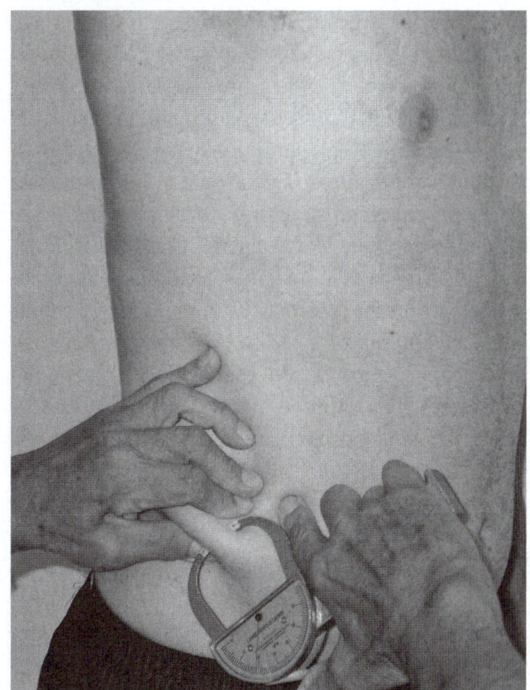

Skinfold caliper used to help calculate a person's percentage of body fat.

Connie Mueller/McGraw Hill

Muscular Strength and Endurance

Muscular strength is the ability of a muscle or muscle group to exert force against a resistance. Specifically, it is the maximum amount of force that a muscle or muscle group can apply against a resistance in a single effort.

The ability of a muscle or muscle group to exert force repeatedly is known as muscular endurance. Muscular endurance also refers to the capacity of a muscle or muscle group to sustain a contractive state over a period of time.

Different muscles in the body can have different levels of strength and endurance. Moreover, muscles used more frequently are stronger and have greater endurance than muscles used less frequently. When muscles are not used, strength and endurance decrease.

Muscular strength and endurance are important to good health. They contribute to the maintenance of proper posture and the improvement of personal appearance. Because strong muscles provide better protection for body joints, the risk of joint injuries is decreased. Millions of Americans suffer from low-back pain. Weak abdominal muscles and poor flexibility contribute to this problem. Strengthening the appropriate muscles and developing increased flexibility can help alleviate this condition.

High levels of muscular strength and endurance are important for athletes. Strength is a critical element of sport performance. Strength training for sport must be specifically related to the particular characteristics required for performance of the sport. Thus, the strength training of a sprinter will differ markedly from that of a shot putter, which will be different from that of a gymnast. For effective performance, each athlete requires the development of a high level of strength in specific muscles or muscle groups.

Strength combines with other physical elements to enhance the quality of performance. Many movements in sport require an explosive effort during execution. When force is generated quickly, the movement is known as a *power movement*. Power is critical to successful performance in many sports today, and proper strength training can enhance this component.

Isometric, isotonic, and isokinetic exercises can be used to develop muscular strength and endurance. Body movements depend on the contraction of muscles. As a muscle contracts, tension is created within the muscle and the muscle shortens, lengthens, or remains the same.

Isometric exercises. A muscle contracts isometrically when it exerts force against an immovable resistance. Although tension develops within the muscle, the length of the muscle remains relatively constant and there is little to no movement on the joint. This is referred to as a *static contraction*. For example, stand in a doorway and place the palms of your hands at shoulder height against the frame. Push with all your might and feel the tension develop in your muscles. Even if you contract your muscles to their maximum, it is impossible for you to move the resistance, in this case, the door frame.

Another approach to performing isometric contractions is to contract one muscle against another

Three types of muscle fitness exercises: (A) isotonic, (B) isometric, and (C) isokinetic.

Source: Corbin, C. B., G. Welk, W. R. Corbin, and K. A. Welk. *Concepts of Fitness and Wellness: A Comprehensive Lifestyle Approach,* 9th ed. New York: McGraw Hill, 2010.

muscle, applying an equal and opposite force; in this case, the opposing muscle serves as a resistance. For example, raise your arms to shoulder height and place your palms together. Push against your palms as you contract your muscles. There should be no movement as your muscles work against one another.

When one is performing isometric exercises, it is suggested that the muscles generate a maximum force for 5 seconds, with the contraction repeated 5–10 times each day. Isometrics offer the advantage of not requiring any equipment; any immovable object or your own body serves as the resistance. One frequently cited disadvantage of isometric exercise is that strength is developed at only a specific joint angle, not through the entire range of motion. Isometric exercises are most often used to develop strength at a specific joint angle to enhance a particular movement or for injury rehabilitation.

Isotonic exercises. Isotonic contractions occur when force is generated while the muscle is changing in length. For example, to lift a weight from its starting point when performing a biceps curl, the biceps muscle must contract and shorten in length. This is called a *concentric contraction.* To control the weight as it is lowered back to the starting position, the biceps muscle continues to contract while gradually lengthening. This is referred to as an *eccentric contraction.* When exercising isotonically, it is essential to use both concentric and eccentric contractions for the greatest improvement to occur and also to exercise through the range of motion.

One problem associated with isotonic training is that the force applied to the weight varies throughout the range of motion. This is attributable to the effects of gravity and the system of levers within the body. Once the initial resistance is overcome, lifting the weight can be easy or difficult, depending on the position of the weight relative to the body. Thus, the muscles are not working at or near their maximum effort throughout the range of motion.

Common forms of isotonic exercise equipment are free weights, barbells, dumbbells, and various machines. Some isotonic exercise machines have been designed specifically to vary the resistance throughout the range of motion. This permits the muscles to exert their maximum effort throughout the entire range of motion.

Isotonic exercises are probably the most popular means of developing strength and endurance. Millions of people use this approach to achieve and maintain desired levels of muscular development.

Isokinetic exercises. When one is performing isokinetic exercises, the length of the muscle changes while the contraction is performed at a constant velocity. Isokinetic devices such as the Cybex are designed so that the resistance can be moved only at a certain speed, regardless of the amount of force applied. The speed at which the resistance can be moved is the key to this exercise approach. Because isokinetic machines can be expensive, they are most often used in the diagnosis and treatment of various injuries.

Muscular strength and endurance can be improved. Many different methods of training can be effective to develop these fitness components. Although weight training is not necessary to realize gains in muscular strength and endurance, this approach is popular with many people. The term *progressive resistance exercise* is commonly used to denote weight training programs that involve working out against a resistance that is progressively increased as the muscle adapts to the workload or resistance.

When planning a training program, one must consider the weight used per lift, the number of repetitions per set, the number of sets per workout, and the number of workouts per week. (For more information, see the Definitions for Muscular Strength and Endurance Training box.) Because there are so many weight training programs available, only general guidelines with respect to frequency, intensity, and duration will be presented.

Frequency. The training program must include time for the muscles to rest and recover from the workout while adapting to a higher physiological level. The same muscle group should not be worked

DEFINITIONS FOR MUSCULAR STRENGTH AND ENDURANCE TRAINING

Resistance	Workload or weight being moved.
Repetition maximum (RM)	Maximum force that can be exerted or maximum weight of resistance lifted in a single effort; the intensity of the workout can be expressed as a percentage of 1 RM (e.g., if a person can bench-press 200 pounds, 80% of 1 RM would be 160 pounds).
Repetition	Performance of a designated movement or exercise pattern through the full range of motion.
Set	Number of repetitions performed without a rest.

on successive days. Recommended frequency plans are a full-body workout every other day; alternate lower- and upper-body workouts; and working each muscle group 1 or 2 days per week.

Intensity. The intensity of the workout refers to the extent to which the muscles are overloaded. Overload can be accomplished by any combination of the following: increasing the resistance or weight lifted, increasing the number of repetitions per set, increasing the number of sets per workout, increasing or decreasing the speed at which the repetition is performed, and decreasing the time of rest between sets. Programs can be designed to develop strength, endurance, or both, depending on the number of repetitions and the amount of resistance selected (see Figure 7-2).

Time. The duration of the training program depends on the person's level of fitness, fitness goals, equipment available, and time available to work out. One to three sets are often completed of each

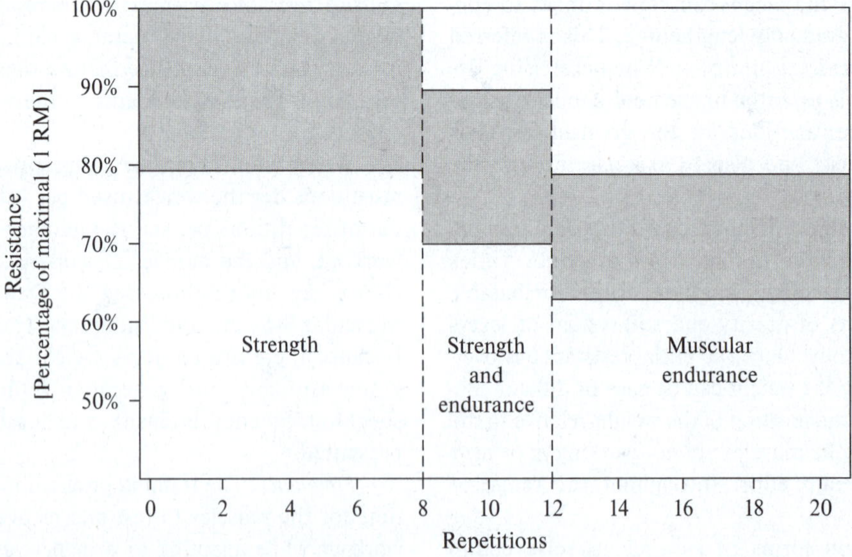

Figure 7-2 Guidelines for developing strength and muscular endurance.

exercise. The amount of rest between each set varies according to the individual's program. It is recommended to change a strength and endurance program every 8–12 weeks to provide variability to the muscles and continue to apply overload.

Muscular strength and endurance can be measured. Because muscular strength and endurance are specific to each muscle or muscle group, the level of development can vary among the various muscles or muscle groups. Therefore, the strength and endurance of each muscle or muscle group must be measured.

Strength can be measured isometrically by using a dynamometer. As muscle contraction occurs, the force is transmitted to the instrument and can be recorded (e.g., the hand dynamometer can be used to determine grip strength). Strength can be measured isotonically by determining the maximum amount of weight that can be moved once through the designated range of motion (e.g., bench press); this is 1 repetition maximum or 1 RM.

Endurance can be measured by determining the number of repetitions of a particular movement that can be performed continuously (e.g., the number of repetitions of the bench press that can be performed with a designated resistance) or the number of repetitions performed within a specified period of time (e.g., the number of sit-ups that can be performed in 1 minute). Endurance can also be determined by measuring the time a specific contraction can be sustained (e.g., how long a static push-up can be held).

Flexibility

Flexibility can be defined as the maximum range of motion possible at a joint–that is, the extent of movement possible about a joint without undue strain. Although it is one of the most important fitness components, it is often overlooked, and consequently, its development is neglected.

The extent of movement possible at a joint is influenced by the structure of the joint. For example, the elbow and the knee are hinge joints, allowing movement in one direction only; flexion (bending) and extension (straightening) are the only movements possible. In contrast, the shoulder and hip are ball-and-socket joints; this joint structure allows movement in many directions, usually with a greater range than the hinge joint. Soft tissues such as muscles, tendons, and ligaments greatly influence the range of movement possible at a joint. Flexibility is affected by the length that a muscle can stretch (i.e., its elasticity). When muscles are not used, they tend to become shorter and tighter, thus reducing the joint's range of motion.

Flexibility is essential to performing everyday tasks and is also a critical component in the performance of many sport activities. Activities such as gymnastics, wrestling, yoga, swimming, karate, and dance place a premium on flexibility. Limited flexibility decreases the efficiency with which everyday and sport activities can be performed.

Flexibility is important to good health. Flexibility is important for maintaining good posture. Poor postural alignment can cause pain and limit one's ability to move freely.

Flexibility can help prevent low-back pain. This condition is caused by poor muscle development and poor flexibility. Improving muscle development and flexibility in conjunction with using proper care in sitting, standing, and lifting objects can help alleviate this condition.

Flexibility is also important for preventing muscle injuries. Poor flexibility can contribute to uncoordinated and awkward movements, thus increasing the potential for injury. Muscle soreness and body stiffness following vigorous physical activity can be alleviated by using a good stretching program to develop flexibility both before and after an activity session.

Flexibility is important for the performance of physical activities. Flexibility is important to the performance of even the simplest everyday activities. Imagine how difficult it would be to get dressed without adequate flexibility. Developing and maintaining flexibility are critical to helping elderly people be functionally independent. Some physical conditions, such as arthritis or cerebral palsy, severely restrict flexibility. Improving flexibility to the greatest degree possible, given one's capabilities, can have a significant impact on one's quality of life–even to the extent of allowing a dependent individual to become functionally independent.

Athletes recognize the importance of flexibility in sport performance. Adequate flexibility can enhance performance capabilities by allowing the athlete to stretch and reach further, to generate more force when kicking or throwing an object, and to change positions more quickly and efficiently. Poor flexibility can adversely affect the performance. For example, a sprinter may have a shorter stride length and less speed because tight hamstring muscles can adversely affect their ability to flex the hip joint. Because certain sports require an extremely high degree of flexibility for successful performance, stretching exercises to enhance flexibility are typically included as part of an athlete's warm-up and cooldown activities. These activities enhance the elasticity of the muscles and thus help reduce the likelihood of injury and muscle soreness.

Decreased flexibility can be caused by many factors. People who are active tend to have better flexibility than those who are sedentary. When muscles are not used, they tend to become shorter, tighter, and less elastic. Consequently, flexibility decreases. Age is another factor that influences the extent of flexibility. It is important to encourage people to remain active as they grow older so that the effects of aging on fitness will be minimized.

Muscle tension can affect flexibility. Individuals who experience prolonged stress often respond by bracing or tensing the muscles in their neck, shoulders, and upper back. This tightens the muscles for long periods, thus reducing flexibility. Muscle imbalance can also restrict flexibility. When weight training, for example, if an individual strengthens one group of muscles around a joint while neglecting the development of the opposing group (e.g., the quadriceps muscle group in the front of the thigh is strengthened but the hamstring muscle group in the back of the thigh is not), flexibility will be decreased. Therefore, to ensure maximal flexibility when weight training, it is important to perform each exercise correctly, through the full range of motion, and develop opposing muscle groups.

To be successful, athletes must develop the fitness components required by their sports.

Top: bikeriderlondon/Shutterstock; Middle: Comstock Images; Bottom: Datacraft Co Ltd/imagenavi/Getty Images

Flexibility can be improved. Flexibility can be improved through a stretching program. Because flexibility is specific to each joint, improvement and maintenance of flexibility require a program that incorporates specific exercises for the major joints of the body. Flexibility exercises can be performed using ballistic, static, contract-relax, or dynamic stretching techniques.

Ballistic stretching. This dynamic method uses the momentum generated from repeated bouncing movements to stretch the muscle. Although it is effective, most experts do not recommend this technique because it may overstretch the muscle and cause soreness or injury. However, many athletes use this method.

Static stretching. An extremely popular and effective technique, static stretching, involves gently and slowly moving into the stretch position and holding it for a certain period of time. Movement should take place through the full range of motion until a little tension or tightness is felt in the muscle or muscle group. As the muscle relaxes, the stretch should be extended and held again. Stretching should not be painful. Care must be taken not to force the joint to move too far, which could cause an injury. Stretches should be held from 10 to 30 seconds and a minimum of five repetitions performed for each exercise. Flexibility exercises should be performed at least three to five times a week. If flexibility at a particular joint is extremely poor, a daily stretching program can be recommended. Flexibility exercises should also be performed at the start and end of a workout.

Contract-relax technique. When one is performing stretching exercises, it is important that the muscles involved are relaxed. The contract-relax technique facilitates the relaxation of muscles. Muscles are arranged in pairs; when one contracts, the opposing muscle in the pair relaxes (e.g., when the quadriceps muscles contract, the hamstring muscles relax). When one uses this technique to develop flexibility, the muscle opposite the one to be stretched is contracted for at least 5 seconds. This relaxes the muscle to be stretched. To apply this technique to the development of hamstring flexibility, an individual would contract the quadriceps muscles, thus relaxing the hamstrings. This technique allows the stretch to be performed through a greater range of motion.

Dynamic stretching. Dynamic stretching, or active stretching, is often used to warm up the muscles before engaging in physical activity and sport performance. Dynamic stretching increases the blood flow and range of motion and warms up the

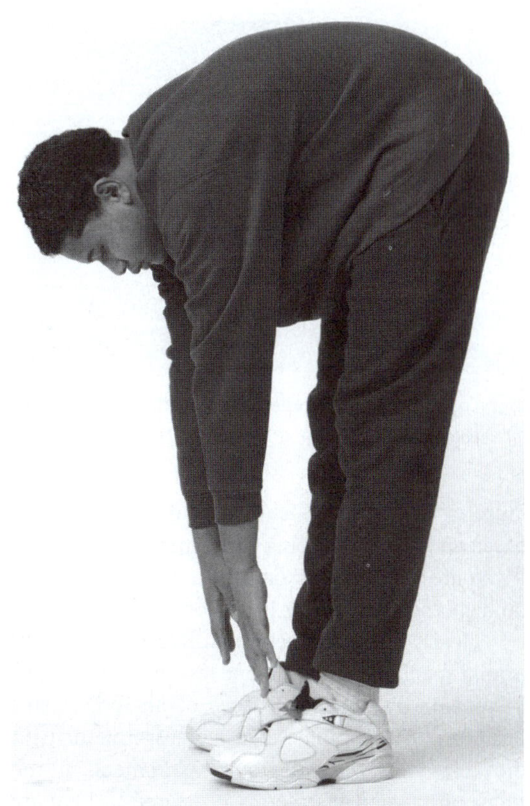

The standing straight-leg toe touch is an example of a ballistic exercise, which is not recommended by experts. The sitting hamstring stretch is safer and can be performed using static stretching or the contract-relax technique.

Top: Ken Karp/McGraw Hill; Bottom: Stockbyte/PunchStock/Getty Images

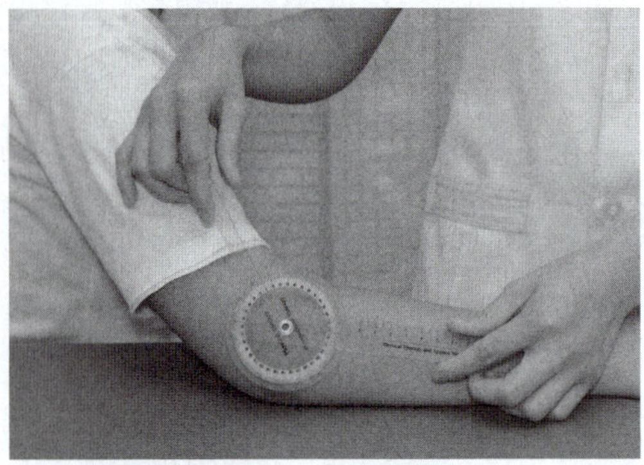

A goniometer is used to measure the angle at the elbow.
Praisaeng/Shutterstock

muscles. Dynamic stretches should be determined based on the activity being performed. For example, if you are about to run or sprint, you may want to do high knee raises, kick backs, or walking lunges.

Flexibility can be measured. Because flexibility is joint specific, there is no one test that can be used to provide an overall measure of an individual's flexibility. The goniometer, a large protractor with movable arms, provides a measurement of the range of movement in terms of degrees. There are also a number of other tests that have been developed to measure movement at certain joints and require little equipment to perform. For example, the sit-and-reach test is used to assess the flexibility of the lower back and hamstring muscles.

DESIGNING AN EXERCISE PROGRAM

The interactive nature of the exercise components allows for the design of exercise programs to meet individuals' needs. Personal characteristics such as fitness status, medical status, and age must be considered when prescribing exercise. Medical conditions such as heart disease, diabetes, and asthma must be taken into account when designing an exercise program. Appropriate modifications must be made to selected exercises to ensure participants' safety.

The next consideration in planning an exercise program is the participant's fitness needs and goals. The program must be designed to provide opportunities for the development of the fitness component the participant desires to improve. Selected activities should be specific to the goal.

Enjoyment is another critical factor in the selection of exercises. Adherence to the training program is enhanced when the participant enjoys the prescribed exercise. Activities should allow participants to achieve the desired fitness goals while maintaining interest and enjoyment. Individuals who find an activity enjoyable will be more likely to continue the exercise long enough to realize desired fitness improvements and to incorporate exercise into their lifestyle to maintain these improvements.

Achievement of a desirable level of fitness is a significant concern, but attention must also be directed to educating participants about the principles of designing a personal exercise program, assessing their own fitness, and resolving personal fitness problems. People need to take charge of their own lives and assume responsibility for their level of fitness. See the Designing an Exercise Program box for a guideline to developing their own exercise plan.

SPECIAL CONSIDERATIONS FOR FITNESS

There are many different factors that should be considered in conducting fitness programs, such as environmental conditions, nutrition, and performance-enhancing drugs (PEDs). These factors will be discussed in this section.

Environmental Conditions and Fitness

Participants' safety should always be the primary concern of professionals conducting fitness programs. Extreme caution must be used when exercising in hot, humid weather. The body's normal temperature is 98.6 degrees Fahrenheit. During exercise, as the body's temperature rises, several methods are used by the body to cool itself. As you exercise, you perspire or sweat, and the evaporation of the sweat keeps the body temperature within normal limits. When it is hot and humidity reaches 65% or higher, heat loss through evaporation is less effective, and the body's ability to dissipate heat is

DESIGNING AN EXERCISE PROGRAM

STEP 1: Set goals that are realistic (are they attainable?) and measurable (can they be assessed?).

- General goals (e.g., lose weight, run a 5K)
- Specific goals (based on health-related or motor performance components of fitness)

STEP 2: Establish a timeline to accomplish general and specific goals (include start and end dates).

STEP 3: Develop a physical activity program based on goals.

FITT Guidelines	Cardiorespiratory Endurance	Flexibility	Muscular Strength	Muscular Endurance	Other
Frequency					
Intensity					
Time					
Type					
Location					

Number of Overall Minutes Participating in Physical Activity							
Monday	Tuesday	Wednesday	Thursday	Friday	Saturday	Sunday	Weekly Total

impaired.[14] Additionally, excessive sweating and lack of fluid replacement can lead to dehydration. A person who is dehydrated stops sweating, and evaporation no longer cools the body. Heat-related problems such as heat cramps, heat exhaustion, and heat stroke can occur under hot and humid conditions.

Heat cramps are muscle cramps, typically in the muscles most used in exercise. Heat exhaustion is characterized by muscle cramps, weakness, dizziness, disorientation, nausea, elevated temperature, profuse sweating, rapid pulse, and collapse. Heat stroke is a life-threatening emergency. The symptoms include a sudden collapse, unconsciousness, rapid pulse, relatively dry skin from lack of sweating, and a core body temperature of 106 degrees Fahrenheit or higher.

To prevent heat-related problems, use caution when exercising in hot, humid weather. Be sure to drink plenty of fluids before, during, and after exercise to replace fluids lost through evaporation. Water and commercial sport drinks such as Gatorade and Powerade are good for replenishing fluids. Exercise during the coolest part of the day, either early in the morning or later in the evening. On extremely hot and humid days, participants should consider decreasing the intensity of their workout to reduce heat stress. Other considerations may involve canceling the workout or exercising indoors in a cool environment. It is also important to take time to acclimatize the body to the hot and humid weather. Acclimatization occurs usually in 5–7 days.[14]

Cold weather also requires precautions during exercise. Conserving heat is a major concern when exercising in cold weather. Hypothermia, the breakdown of the body's ability to produce heat, can occur when the weather is between 50 and 60 degrees Fahrenheit and it is damp and windy. Hypothermia occurs when the body temperature drops below 95 degrees Fahrenheit. Shivering and loss of coordination initially occur. As the body's temperature drops further, shivering stops, muscles stiffen, and unconsciousness occurs. This is a medical emergency, and first aid efforts should focus on raising the body's temperature and seeking immediate medical attention.

Extreme cold can also lead to frostbite. To prevent cold-related problems, participants should be aware of the conditions that contribute to hypothermia. Before exercising, individuals should check both the temperature and wind chill to determine whether it would be dangerous to exercise. Dress properly for exercise in cold weather. Hats should be worn to reduce the loss of body heat through the head. Several light layers of clothing should be worn so that the body temperature can be more easily regulated. Try to avoid getting wet in cold weather, which increases the risk for hypothermia. To prevent frostbite, wear a mask, gloves, and a hat. Be sure to take time to gradually acclimatize to exercising in the cold. In extreme conditions, consider canceling or limiting workouts or moving to an activity that can be performed indoors.

Environmental conditions pose challenges to individuals seeking to work out on a regular basis. It is important to be aware of the current weather conditions, the risks they pose, and the adaptations necessary to exercise safely. Maintaining the

There is a wide range of fitness equipment available to meet the needs of a variety of individuals at local fitness centers, including those in a wheelchair.

Realistic Reflections

core body temperature, taking time to gradually acclimatize to conditions, following safety precautions, and using common sense can help reduce the health risks associated with exercising under conditions of extreme heat, humidity, or cold.

Nutrition and Fitness

Nutrition plays an important role in enhancing fitness and health. The central focus of nutrition is the study of food requirements for the production of energy and the regulation of bodily processes.

What we eat can affect our health, growth, and development, and ability to perform various activities that fill our lives. In terms of health fitness, the foods we consume directly affect our body composition and the energy we have available to engage in physical activity. The energy derived from food is measured in kilocalories, which are commonly referred to as calories. Regulating one's energy balance by carefully monitoring caloric consumption and expenditure is important in achieving a desirable level of health fitness. Individuals must also consume sufficient calories so that they have the energy necessary for work and to lead a physically active lifestyle.

A nutrient is a basic substance that is used by the body to sustain vital processes such as the repair and regulation of cellular functions and the production of energy. The six major categories of nutrients are carbohydrates, fats, proteins, vitamins, minerals, and water. Carbohydrates, proteins, and fats–the three macronutrients–provide the energy required for muscular work. They also have a critical role in the maintenance of body tissues and the regulation of their functions.

Vitamins and minerals have no caloric value. Although they are required only in small amounts, they are essential to body functioning. Vitamins are needed for normal growth and development. Vitamins do not provide energy directly, but play a critical role in releasing energy from the foods that are consumed. Minerals are essential to the regulation and performance of such body functions as the maintenance of water balance and skeletal muscle contraction.

Water is the most basic of all the nutrients–it is necessary to sustain life. As the most abundant of all the nutrients in the body, water accounts for approximately 60% of the body's weight. Water is necessary for all of the chemical processes performed by the body. It is essential for such functions as energy production, digestion, temperature regulation, and elimination of the by-products of metabolism.

Maintaining a proper water balance is crucial. Insufficient water causes dehydration; severe dehydration can lead to death. People who are physically active should carefully monitor their water intake to ensure that an adequate fluid balance is maintained. This is particularly critical for individuals who exercise in a hot, humid environment. Exercising under these conditions typically causes excessive sweating and subsequently large losses of water.

The USDA *Dietary Guidelines for Americans*, published in 2020, provides advice to Americans on making healthful food choices.[15] Refer to the *Dietary Guidelines for Americans, 2020–2025* box. The current guidelines build on previous editions as well as highlight three important additions: (1) recognition that diet-related chronic diseases are prevalent among Americans and pose a major health problem, (2) a focus on dietary patterns, and (3) a focus on a lifespan approach from infant and toddlers to older age. The four primary guidelines across the lifespan focus on the following:

- Follow a healthy dietary pattern at every life stage.
- Customize and enjoy nutrient-dense food and beverage choices to reflect personal preferences, cultural traditions, and budgetary considerations.
- Focus on meeting food group needs with nutrient-dense foods and beverages, and stay within calorie limits.
- Limit food and beverages higher in added sugars, saturated fat, and sodium, and limit alcoholic beverages.

Additionally, the guidelines include recommendations for specific ethnic groups and special populations, such as pregnant and lactating women, children, and adults with hypertension.

DIETARY GUIDELINES FOR AMERICANS, 2020–2025

Guidelines

1. **Follow a healthy eating pattern at every life stage.** At every life stage—infancy, toddlerhood, childhood, adolescence, adulthood, pregnancy, lactation, and older adulthood—it is never too early or too late to eat healthfully.
2. **Customize and enjoy nutrient-dense food and beverage choices to reflect personal preferences, cultural traditions, and budgetary considerations.** A healthy dietary pattern can benefit all individuals regardless of age, race, or ethnicity, or current health status. The *Dietary Guidelines* provides a framework intended to be customized to individual needs and preferences, as well as the foodways of the diverse cultures in the United States.
3. **Focus on meeting food group needs with nutrient-dense foods and beverages, and stay within calorie limits.** Nutrient-dense foods provide vitamins, minerals, and other health-promoting components and have no or little added sugars, saturated fat, and sodium. A healthy dietary pattern consists of nutrient-dense forms of foods and beverages across all food groups, in recommended amounts, and within calorie limits.

   Core elements that make up a healthy dietary pattern include:

   - **Vegetables of all types**—dark green; red and orange; beans, peas, and lentils; starchy; and other vegetables
   - **Fruits**—whole fruit
   - **Grains**—at least half of which are whole grain
   - **Dairy**—including fat-free or low-fat milk, yogurt, and cheese, and/or lactose-free versions and fortified soy beverages and yogurt as alternatives
   - **Protein foods**—including lean meats, poultry, and eggs; seafood; beans, peas, and lentils; and nuts, seeds, and soy products
   - **Oils**—including vegetable oils and oils in food, such as seafood and nuts
4. **Limit foods and beverages higher in added sugars, saturated fat, and sodium, and limit alcoholic beverages.** A small amount of added sugars, saturated fat, or sodium can be added to nutrient-dense foods and beverages to help meet food group recommendations, but foods and beverages high in these components should be limited.
   - **Added sugars**—Less than 10% of calories per day starting at age 2. Avoid foods and beverages with added sugars for those younger than age 2.
   - **Saturated fat**—Less than 10% of calories per day starting at age 2.
   - **Sodium**—Less than 2,300 milligrams per day—and even less for children younger than age 14.
   - **Alcoholic beverages**—Adults of legal drinking age can choose not to drink, or to drink in moderation by limiting intake to two drinks or less in a day for men and one drink or less in a day for women, when alcohol is consumed. Drinking less is better for health than drinking more. There are some adults who should not drink alcohol, such as women who are pregnant.

Individuals should use the USDA MyPlate and the DASH (Dietary Approaches to Stop Hypertension) Eating Plan to help them integrate dietary recommendations into their lifestyle. MyPlate (see Figure 7-3) provides a personalized approach to healthy eating and physical activity. MyPlate is divided into sections of approximately 30% grains, 30% vegetables, 20% fruits, and 20% protein, accompanied by a smaller circle representing dairy, such as a glass of low-fat/nonfat milk or a yogurt cup.[16] Oils and fats should be consumed in moderation. The specific amount that should

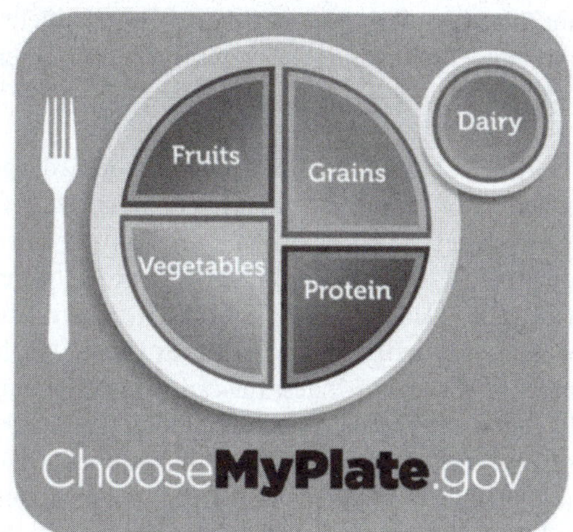

Figure 7-3 MyPlate–Daily food recommendations.

U.S. Department of Agriculture

be consumed depends on the individual's age, sex, and level of physical activity.[16] Physical activity is integral to good health and should be performed on a daily basis. MyPlate strives to offer a personalized approach to healthful eating, providing a wide array of options for individuals to incorporate into their life.

Performance-Enhancing Drugs

The issue of PEDs has been a consistent, salient concern within all levels of sport performance. Athletes take PEDs with the hope of improving their athletic performance. PEDs, also referred to as ergogenic aids, can include a variety of forms of drugs, such as anabolic, stimulants, endurance enhancement, nootropics, adaptogens, painkillers, sedatives, blood boosters, gene doping, and human biomolecules. Some of these PEDs are allowed in interscholastic, intercollegiate, professional, and Olympic competitions. In this text, we will focus on PEDs such as caffeine, carbohydrate loading, doping, supplemental drinks, creatine, and anabolic steroids.

Exercise physiologists study the effects of legal PEDs on an individual's physiologic state as well as the individual's performance. For example, they investigate the effects of different amounts or doses of the substance, the impact on both short- and long-term performance, and whether the effect is different for trained or untrained individuals.[6] They also consider whether the PED works better for power or endurance tasks and whether it has an impact on fine or gross motor tasks.[6]

Caffeine

Caffeine, a stimulant, is found in a variety of foods, drinks, and over-the-counter products. The International Olympic Committee (IOC) classifies caffeine as a restricted drug, allowing its use up to a urine level of 12 micrograms per milliliter, which is about four to seven cups of coffee. Caffeine is absorbed rapidly from the gastrointestinal tract, rising to a significant level in the blood about 15 minutes after consumption, with the peak concentration about 45–60 minutes after ingestion. Given this, an athlete wanting a boost in performance from caffeine needs to consume it about an hour before the event. Ingestion of the equivalent of about two cups of coffee has been shown to have a performance-enhancing effect.

Caffeine enhances the function of skeletal muscle, increasing tension development. It stimulates the sympathetic nervous system, which typically leads to increased alertness and decreased perception of fatigue. Research suggests that caffeine can increase endurance performance. However, the performance-enhancing effect is variable and influenced by the dose and the amount of caffeine the athlete typically consumes. Athletes who do not regularly consume products with caffeine typically see more pronounced performance-enhancing effects than athletes who are regular consumers of caffeine. Additionally, athletes who abstain from caffeine for a period of days prior to its use have more pronounced effects.

Some side effects associated with the use of caffeine include very rapid heart rate, diuresis, insomnia, nervousness, diarrhea, and anxiety. Athletes who choose to use this PED should be careful to monitor their dosage, modify the dose to take into account their pattern of caffeine consumption, and be cognizant of the side effects.

Carbohydrate Loading

Carbohydrate loading, or glycogenic supercompensation, is a practice followed by athletes who compete in endurance events lasting 60–90 minutes or longer. Carbohydrates perform a critical role in the production of energy in the body. They are converted to glycogen and are stored in the liver and muscles. Blood glucose, a by-product of the breakdown of carbohydrates, is also important to energy production. Muscle glycogen stores are used for muscle energy metabolism, and the liver's store of glycogen is used to replace blood glucose. During prolonged exercise, the stores of glycogen decline to very low levels, contributing to muscle fatigue, performance decrement, and exhaustion.

In an effort to maximize performance, endurance athletes practice carbohydrate loading before an event. By modifying their diet to eat more complex carbohydrates than normal, athletes hope to store additional glycogen in their muscles and liver, sometimes up to four times the usual level. During competition, athletes draw on these additional stores to delay fatigue and to maintain their race pace for a longer time. In addition to modifying their diet, athletes also change their training regimen to ensure that their glycogen stores are at capacity.

There are several approaches to carbohydrate loading. One approach requires athletes to begin the process of carbohydrate loading 7 days prior to competition. Both athletes' training and diet are modified. Seven days prior to competition, athletes deplete their muscle glycogen stores by training to exhaustion. Hard training continues for the next 3 days, followed by 3 days of rest prior to competition. In addition to altering their training schedule, athletes modify their diet. Typically, on the first day when training to exhaustion occurs, athletes consume a diet consisting of about 50% carbohydrates. During the other three hard training days, a diet high in fat and protein is eaten. The 3 days before competition, on the rest days, athletes consume a diet consisting of about 90% carbohydrates. On the day of the event, athletes eat a high-carbohydrate meal, typically consuming complex carbohydrates such as grains, pasta, rice, or bagels. Not all athletes find this approach to be beneficial. Some athletes have difficulty handling the extremes in diet. Other athletes are uncomfortable stopping their training 3 days before their competition.

Researchers determined that a modified approach could be successfully used to maximize glycogen stores.[6] This approach does not require athletes to exercise to exhaustion in order to deplete their glycogen stores, nor does it require athletes to eat extremely low or extremely high amounts of carbohydrates. Instead, athletes gradually reduce the intensity and duration of their workouts on the days preceding competition while modifying their diet to increase their carbohydrates to 70%. For example, 5 days before the event, athletes would decrease their workout time from 90 to 40 minutes, while eating a 50% carbohydrate diet. After 2 days, workout time again is reduced, this time from 40 to 20 minutes, while carbohydrate consumption is increased to 70%. The day prior to competition, athletes rest and continue to consume the 70% carbohydrate diet. This approach has been found to be effective in increasing glycogen stores and enhancing performance.

During the meal prior to the event, it is recommended that athletes consume between 1 and 5 grams of carbohydrate per kilogram of body weight and athletes should eat from 1 to 4 hours before exercise.[6] The meal should be easily digestible carbohydrate, but, if it is taken 1 hour before exercise, it should be in liquid form. Prior to trying carbohydrate loading before a competition, the athlete should test the procedure during practice. It should also be noted that following strenuous exercise, athletes can hasten their recovery by consuming carbohydrates.

Hydration, Energy, and Sports Drinks

During exercise, heat is dissipated by the body to minimize the increase in body core temperature. Researchers have found that in hot weather as much as 2.8 liters per hour can be lost in sweat.[6] In events of long duration, such as a marathon, some runners can lose as much as 8% of their body weight.[6] In addition to loss of water, electrolytes that are critical to the normal function of the body are lost. Levels of electrolytes such as sodium, calcium, chloride, and potassium decrease. The loss of fluid and electrolytes adversely affects cellular functions. If these fluids and electrolytes are not replaced, significant health problems could arise, such as heat stroke, and performance decrement will occur.

Fluid replacement during exercise is associated with lower heart rate, body core temperature, and levels of perceived exertion. The ease of fluid replacement depends on the activity. During intermittent activities such as soccer or football, it is easier for an athlete to replace lost fluid and electrolytes. During prolonged activities, such as marathon running, fluid replacement typically occurs on the go.

Water is often regarded as the natural choice for fluid replacement. It is readily available and inexpensive. It is generally recommended that 4–6 ounces of water be consumed for every 15–20 minutes of exercise, especially during prolonged exercise and conditions of high heat and humidity.[6] One problem associated with using water to rehydrate is that oftentimes athletes do not drink enough water to adequately replace the fluids. To some athletes, it is not as palatable as some of the other fluid-replacement beverages, so they drink an insufficient quantity. Another problem with drinking water to rehydrate is that it does not contain electrolytes or carbohydrates.

Sports drinks are popular for maintaining hydration. Sports drinks are designed to enhance performance through replacement of lost electrolytes and supplying of additional carbohydrates to replenish glucose stores. Researchers have found that sports drinks containing 6–8% carbohydrates are well tolerated by athletes and provide extra energy to enhance the performance.[6] Because of the variety of flavors and types (e.g., more, less, no sugar) offered, athletes find drinking sports drinks more appealing than drinking water.

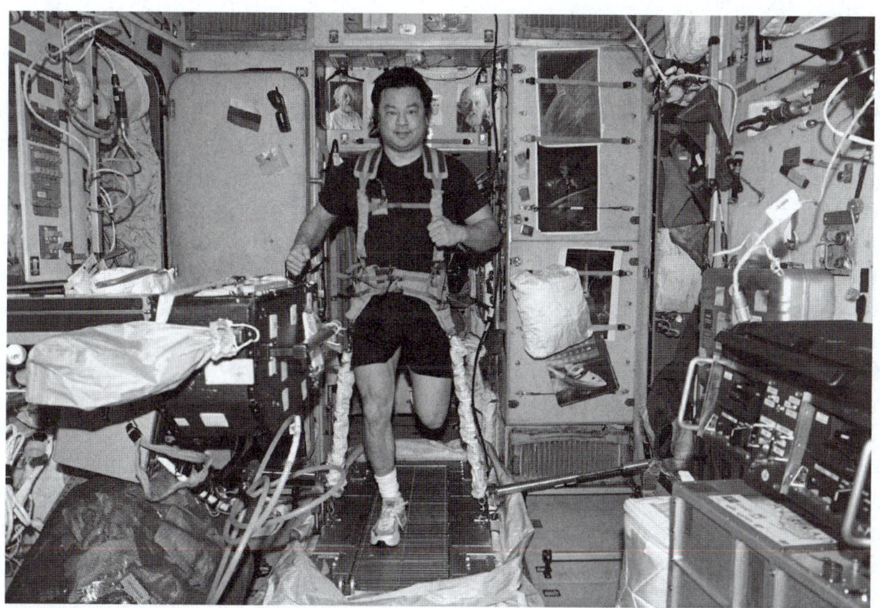

Maintaining fitness in space requires special considerations to deal with the effects of zero gravity, such as the bungee harness to allow the astronaut to work out on the treadmill.
NASA

Fluid replacement during exercise reduces athletes' heart rate and body temperature as well as athletes' perception of exertion. The greater the rate of fluid intake, the lower the athletes' responses.[6] Additionally, drink temperature influences absorption rate; cold drinks are absorbed more rapidly than warm drinks.[6] For exercise lasting less than 60 minutes, replacement of fluids using water is adequate. However, when exercise lasts longer than an hour, drinks should contain sodium, chloride, and carbohydrates.

Creatine

Many individuals use nutritional supplements in hopes of enhancing their athletic performance. One popular supplement used to improve the performance in events placing a premium on strength or power is creatine, commonly known as phosphocreatine.

Phosphocreatine in skeletal muscle is important to the production of adenosine triphosphate (ATP), a critical source of energy in high-intensity brief exercise lasting less than 5 seconds. Sprinting 50 meters in track, explosive events such as high jumping, short bursts of speed in soccer, and rapid weight lifting movements rely on this energy source. During these intense efforts, phosphocreatine is depleted, reducing the rate of ATP production.

Phosphocreatine is a limiting factor in short-term, high-intensity events. In an effort to increase stores of muscle phosphocreatine and have more fuel available to support short, high-intensity activity, many athletes have used creatine supplementation. Additionally, many athletes use creatine supplementation in conjunction with a resistance training program to maximize their muscular strength and increase their fat-free mass.

Compared to other supplements, there has been much research on the efficacy of creatine as a PED.[17] Research findings have been varied, with some supporting creatine's effectiveness as a PED in brief, high-intensity events, while other studies find less evidence to support anecdotal claims.[17] There is also less evidence that creatine supplementation can enhance performance in events lasting more than 90 seconds.[17] The ACSM's position is that creatine supplementation enhances exercise performance in events involving short periods of extremely powerful activity, especially during repeated efforts.[17] Additionally, research has shown individual variability in the supplement's effects, with some individuals benefiting more than others from its use.[17]

Typically, athletes go through a loading phase in which they try to maximize the amount of phosphocreatine in their muscles. Creatine is typically loaded with 20 grams per day for 5 days followed by a maintenance dose of 2 or more grams daily. Although 5-day loading is typical, 2 days of loading has also been used. A loading dose of 9 grams per day for 6 days has also been used. Some sources suggest that, instead of acutely loading, similar results can be obtained with 3 grams per day for 28 days.[17] This phase is sufficient to saturate the muscles and maximize the amount of phosphocreatine available for ATP production. However, in addition to using creatine supplementation prior to an event to improve performance, athletes use it to maximize the effects of their training, often in the off-season. Many athletes continue supplementation for weeks or months, ingesting several grams of creatine a day. During this phase, they engage in intense training to increase muscle strength, muscle size, and body mass.[17] Creatine supplementation allows athletes to train at higher workloads, enabling them to perform more repetitions per set of a given exercise and to recover more quickly between exercise sets.[17]

Little research has been conducted on the short- and long-term effects of oral creatine supplementation. Some athletes have experienced muscle cramping, excessive water retention, and gastrointestinal disturbances from supplementation. However, overall, it appears that creatine supplementation for up to 8 weeks does not produce major health risks.[17] More research is needed on the long-term effects of supplementation.

Anabolic-Androgenic Steroids

Anabolic-androgenic steroids are synthetic forms of testosterone, the primary male sex hormone.

Development of strength is one reason athletes use PEDs.
maradon 333/Shutterstock

Testosterone secreted by the testes is responsible for the development of masculine characteristics seen in adolescents and continued into adulthood. Testosterone functions both androgenically–stimulating the growth of male characteristics–and anabolically–promoting the growth of tissue, muscle mass, weight, and bone.[6]

Synthetic forms of testosterone were developed by scientists who sought to maximize the anabolic effects and minimize the androgenic effects.[6] The ability of steroids to develop muscle mass and strength soon attracted the attention of athletes. Athletes began to take steroids and use heavy resistance-training programs in an effort to acquire significant strength gains.

Even though illegal, steroid use by athletes continues. Athletes and others, including adolescents, use anabolic steroids to enhance performance and improve physical appearance. Anabolic steroids are taken orally or injected. Typically, dosages are taken daily in cycles of weeks or months, then stopped, for a period of time, and then resumed. Sometimes, in an effort to obtain maximum gains while minimizing the negative effects, users combine several different types of steroids, a process referred to as stacking. Steroid abuse is most prevalent in sports where the premium is placed on strength. Power lifting, throwing events in track and field, American football, and baseball are sports in which athletes may seek to gain an advantage through the use of steroids.

Adverse side effects associated with chronic steroid use include increased risk of heart disease, liver tumors and cancer, increased cholesterol, and hypertension. Psychological effects of use include mood swings and aggressive behavior. In males, side effects include male-pattern baldness, acne, and voice deepening. Males also experience a decrease in testicular function, including a decrease in sperm production, and gynecomastia (breast development). Females taking steroids may experience irreversible voice deepening, enlarged clitoris, increased facial hair, decreased breast size, increased libido, increased appetite, and menstrual irregularities as outcomes of chronic steroid use in females. Adolescent users risk a decrease in their ultimate height. Adolescents' long bones are still growing, and if they abuse steroids, the growth plates of these bones may cease growing prematurely.

The use of PEDs can take many forms, be it mechanical, psychological, physiological, or pharmacological. Some PEDs have been shown to be beneficial through research, while others gain popularity through anecdotal evidence. Users of PEDs need to be careful to understand the correct manner of usage, whether it is legal or not, and the associated health consequences.

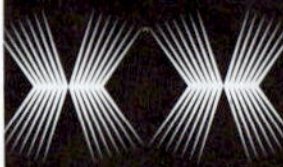

FOCUS ON CAREER: Exercise Physiology

PROFESSIONAL ORGANIZATIONS

- American College of Sports Medicine
- American Physiological Society
- National Strength and Conditioning Association

PROFESSIONAL JOURNALS

- *American Journal of Physiology*
- *Clinical Exercise Physiology*
- *Exercise and Sport Sciences Reviews*
- *International Journal of Sport Nutrition and Exercise Metabolism*
- *Journal of Aging and Physical Activity*
- *Journal of Applied Physiology*
- *Journal of Strength and Conditioning Research*
- *Medicine and Science in Sports and Exercise*
- *The Physician and Sports Medicine*
- *Research Quarterly for Exercise and Sport*
- *Strength and Conditioning Journal*

CURRENT TRENDS: MOVING TOWARD THE FUTURE

- PEDs, energy drinks, and other ergogenic aids, both legal and illegal, will be developed to help improve sport performance.
- Technological advances will provide for more efficient assessment of performance, whether that be a measurement of VO_2 max or calculating heart rate and target heart rate zone.
- Exercise science and exercise physiology will continue to be a prominent discipline within kinesiology as our population continues to get older and athletes continue to utilize scientific advances for improvement.

SUMMARY

Exercise physiology is the study of the effects of exercise on the body, ranging from the level of the system (e.g., cardiovascular system) to the subcellular (e.g., production of ATP for energy) level. Exercise physiologists are interested in both the acute and chronic adaptations of the body to exercise. Professionals in physical education, exercise science, and sport build on this foundational knowledge in many different ways. Knowledge from exercise physiology is used to design effective fitness programs for people of all ages, abilities, and identities to guide the development and implementation of cardiac rehabilitation programs, to plan programs to help children and youths incorporate physical activity into their life, to conduct training programs for elite athletes, and to structure rehabilitation programs for injured athletes and exercise enthusiasts.

A major concern of the exercise physiologist is fitness development, maintenance, evaluation, and outcomes. Within the profession, interest has increased in health-related fitness as opposed to performance-/skill-related fitness. The components of health-related and performance-/skill-related fitness are different, and the extent to which these components are developed depends on individuals' goals. The health-fitness components are cardiorespiratory endurance, body composition, muscular strength and endurance, and flexibility.

Attainment of desirable levels of these components can enhance one's health and well-being. Individuals who are unfit are at increased risk for disease.

Many health benefits are derived from physical fitness and the incorporation of physical activity into one's lifestyle. Physical education, exercise science, and sport professionals should follow medical guidelines and sound training principles in developing and implementing physical fitness programs. Professionals should be aware of contributors to fitness, such as sound nutritional practices.

Another area of study for exercise physiologists is performance-enhancing drugs. These PEDs–such as caffeine, creatine, sports drinks, carbohydrate loading, and steroids–are used in an attempt to improve the performance.

Discussion Questions

1. How would the dose-response debate and FITT formula influence the design of an exercise program for a 35-year-old man who is inactive and wants to lose 10 pounds?
2. How do you assess individuals' health-related components of fitness? Why is it important to assess their levels of fitness? What should professionals do based on the results?
3. How do individuals who want to (a) maintain weight, (b) lose weight, or (c) gain weight need to adjust their nutrition and exercise programs?
4. Should anabolic steroids remain illegal and be banned by all sport governing bodies? Why or why not?

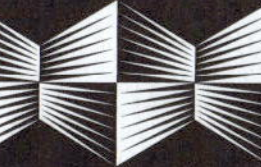

GET CONNECTED

American College of Sports Medicine–offers access to position papers and a free newsletter, *Fit Society Page*, as well as information about certification and upcoming conferences.

http://www.acsm.org

The Athlete Project–serves as a resource for those interested in sport and exercise sciences. Comprehensive information is provided on several topics, including exercise physiology, sport biomechanics, ergonomics, and coaching.

https://tapathlete.com/

Gatorade Sports Science Institute–gives you the opportunity to see sports science in action by touring the lab, as well as access to papers on hydration, nutrition, training, and performance.

https://www.gssiweb.org/en

President's Council on Fitness, Sports, and Nutrition–offers the latest research via the *Council Research Digest*, access to all publications via their Resources and Grants, and resources for physical education, exercise science, and sport professionals.

https://www.hhs.gov/fitness/index.html

Self-Assessment Activities

These activities are designed to help you determine if you have mastered the material and competencies presented in this chapter.

1. Define exercise physiology and discuss its importance to professionals in physical education, exercise science, and sport. Investigate one of the areas of study in exercise physiology and write a short paper on a selected topic of interest to you.
2. Using the information provided in the Get Connected box, access the ACSM site and review one of the

position papers. What new insights did you gain? How can you use this information as a professional? Or access the President's Council on Fitness, Sports, and Nutrition site and read the latest *Research Digest*. What are the implications of this research for professionals?

3. In a short paper, discuss how an individual's lifestyle and habits may be a deterrent to a state of fitness and health. What rationale would you use to persuade a friend or relative who was tired all the time, feeling overwhelmed by stress, and overweight to start a physical fitness program? What reasons may be offered for not being active? How could you counter these reasons?
4. Research information on the variety of performance-enhancing drugs available to individuals aspiring to improve their performance. Prepare a short presentation on a selected PED, including mechanism of effect, claims for use, research on efficacy, legality of the aid, and other related areas.
5. Go to https://www.myplate.gov/. Take the quiz on the home page. Then explore the life stages. Based on the recommendations for young adults, how would you describe your diet? Are you currently meeting the *Dietary Guidelines for Americans 2020–2025*? Describe how you would use the *Dietary Guidelines and MyPlate* to educate others about healthful eating.

REFERENCES

1. US Department of Health and Human Services. (2010). *Improving health.* Washington, DC: US Government Printing Office.
2. US Department of Health and Human Services. (2010). *Surgeon general's vision for a healthy and fit nation.* Rockville, MD: Author.
3. Centers for Disease Control and Prevention. (2016). Heart disease fact sheet. Retrieved April 3, 2019, from http://www.cdc.gov/HeartDisease/facts.htm.
4. US Department of Health and Human Services. (2018). 2018 physical activity guidelines for Americans. Retrieved April 3, 2019, from http://www.health.gov/paguidelines.
5. National Physical Activity Plan. (2016). Retrieved April 3, 2019, from http://www.physicalactivityplan.org/index.html.
6. Powers, S., & Howley, E. (2012). *Exercise physiology: Theory and application to fitness and performance* (8th ed.). New York, NY: McGraw Hill.
7. Prentice, W. (2011). *Get fit, stay fit* (6th ed.). New York, NY: McGraw Hill.
8. Corbin, C. B., Welk, G., Corbin, W. R., & Welk, K. A. (2010). *Concepts of fitness and wellness: A comprehensive lifestyle approach* (9th ed.). New York, NY: McGraw Hill.
9. Hoeger, W. W. K., & Hoeger, S. A. (2013). *Principles and labs for fitness and wellness* (12th ed.). Belmont, CA: Wadsworth.
10. Hoeger, W. W. K., & Hoeger, S. A. (2013). *Lifetime physical fitness and wellness: A personalized program* (12th ed.). Belmont, CA: Wadsworth.
11. Centers for Disease Control and Prevention. (2017). *Defining adult overweight and obesity.* Retrieved April 3, 2019, from http://www.cdc.gov/obesity/adult/defining.html.
12. Centers for Disease Control and Prevention. (2018). *About child & teen BMI.* Retrieved April 3, 2019, from http://www.cdc.gov/healthyweight/assessing/bmi/childrens_bmi/about_childrens_bmi.html.
13. US Department of Health and Human Services. (2013). *The surgeon general's call to action to prevent and decrease overweight and obesity.* Retrieved April 3, 2019, from https://www.ncbi.nlm.nih.gov/books/NBK44206/.
14. Prentice, W. E. (1999). *Fitness and wellness for life* (6th ed.). New York, NY: McGraw Hill.
15. US Department of Health and Human Services and US Department of Agriculture. (2020). *Dietary guidelines for Americans 2020–2025.* https://www.dietaryguidelines.gov/.
16. US Department of Agriculture. (2022). *MyPlate.* https://www.myplate.gov/.
17. National Institutes of Health. (2018). U.S. National Library of Medicine: MedlinePlus–Creatine. Retrieved April 3, 2019, from http://www.nlm.nih.gov/medlineplus/druginfo/natural/873.html.

C H A P T E R 8

Sociological Foundations

Polka Dot Images/Getty Images

O B J E C T I V E S

After reading this chapter, students should be able to–

- Show how sport is a socializing force in American culture.
- Discuss the nature and scope of sport.
- Trace the growth of sport in educational institutions in the United States and the attitude of educators toward this growth.
- Know the dimensions of concerns in sport today, including girls and women, children, racial minorities, violence, and the use of performance-enhancing substances.

Sport is an important part of this nation's culture and other cultures throughout the world. It captures social media headlines, holds television viewers' attention, produces millions of dollars a year in revenue for entrepreneurs, and even impacts international affairs.

Sport exerts a strong influence on many aspects of the American lifestyle. Millions of Americans are glued to their chairs when featured baseball, football, basketball, National Association for Stock Car Auto Racing (NASCAR), and golf contests are scheduled to be televised. Advertisers target large percentages of their promotional budgets to buy airtime during sporting events to sell their wares. For example, an average 30-second advertisement during the 2021 Super Bowl sold for $6.5 million.[1] Professional sports teams attract millions of spectators each year. Professional teams spend astronomical sums to obtain the best talent to sustain spectator support and interest and to ensure a profitable year for management.

The big business of sport has also influenced the nature of college and high school sport. Schools and colleges, in an effort to field the best teams, may compromise their academic standards. It is not uncommon for academically outstanding colleges to be more widely recognized for the feats of their athletic teams.

SOCIAL JUSTICE

Talking Points

- Systemic racism needs to be addressed and changes need to be made for racial justice to be central across all sports.
- Sporting opportunities for girls and women have significantly increased since 1972. However, in the coming decade, women need more opportunities to be head coaches, athletic trainers, and sport and conditioning coaches and to hold administrative positions, such as athletic directors.
- Women should be paid equivalent to men.
- Athletes, regardless of gender, race, sexual identity, ethnicity, etc., need to take a stand for equality and justice for all.
- An increase in sporting opportunities for individuals with disabilities must be provided at all sport levels. There has been a decline over the past decade.

Within the last 10 years, the number of sport participants in our society has increased dramatically. Millions of people of all social identities participate in a diversity of sport activities. Because of the social, political, legal, and educational influence of sport on cultures, it is important to examine this phenomenon.

SOCIOLOGY OF SPORT

Sport influences and is influenced by social institutions such as economics, family, education, politics, religion, mass media, and popular culture. Coakley notes that sport, as a social phenomenon, has "meanings that go far beyond score and performance statistics. Sports are related to the social and cultural contexts in which we live."[2] The prominence and pervasiveness of sport in American culture and its institutional nature led to its study from a sociological perspective. The definition, scope, and areas of study are discussed in this section.

Definition and Scope

Sociology is concerned with the study of people, groups, institutions, and human activities in terms of social behavior and social order within society. It is a science interested in such institutions of society as religion, family, government, education, and leisure. Sociologists are also concerned with the influence of social institutions on the individual; the social behavior and human relations that occur within a group or an institution and how they influence the behavior of the individual; and the interrelationships between the various institutions within a society, such as sport and education or religion and government.

As a medium that permeates nearly every important aspect of life, sport has led some professionals to believe that it should receive intensive study, particularly as it affects the behavior of human beings and institutions as they form the total social and cultural context of society. Sport sociology focuses on examining the relationship between sport and society. Coakley[3] lists the major goals of sport sociology to be an understanding of the following:

- The factors underlying the creation and organization of sports.
- The relationship between sport and other aspects of society, such as family, education, politics, the economy, the media, and religion.
- The influence of sport and sport participation on individuals' beliefs about equity, gender, race, ethnicity, disability, and other societal issues.
- The social dynamics within the sport setting, such as organizational structure, group actions, and interaction patterns.

- The influence of cultural, structural, and situational factors on the nature of sport and the sport experience.
- The social processes associated with sport, including competition, socialization, conflict, and change.

Sport sociologists challenge us to critically examine our common and perhaps sacrosanct assumptions about sport, to scrutinize sport from different perspectives, and to understand social problems and social issues associated with sport (e.g., relationship between wealth and opportunity in sport). Sport sociologists examine societal forces that lead to change in sport (e.g., increased opportunities for women and changing conceptions of gender roles). Increasingly, sport sociologists seek to take a more active role in changing the status quo; they identify problems in sport and encourage changes that would transform sport and lead to equitable opportunities and promote human well-being (e.g., inequalities of opportunities experienced by racial and ethnic groups).

The emphasis on being number one is so strong in the United States that oftentimes other values derived from participation in sport get forgotten.

Digital Vision/Getty Images

Areas of Study

Sport sociologists use sociological research strategies to study the behavior of individuals and groups within the sport milieu. Some questions sport sociologists might address are:

- Does sport help minorities, including people of color and women, become more fully integrated into society? How does participation in sport affect the social and economic status of minorities?
- How do the mass media affect sport?
- How are politics and sport related? Religion and sport? The economic status of the community or the country and sport?
- How does interscholastic and intercollegiate sport influence the academic achievement of its participants?
- How do coaches influence the lives of their athletes?

Before a discussion of several areas of concern to sport sociologists, it may be helpful to define sport and discuss its nature and scope.

SPORT: A DEFINITION

In order to study sport in a systematic manner, it is necessary to develop a specific definition of sport. Such a definition has traditionally, by its very nature, been limiting and restrictive. Yet, it provides a focus and a shared perspective by which to understand the relationship of sport to society.

In 2009, Coakley defined sports as follows:

> Sports are well-established, officially governed competitive physical activities in which participants are motivated by internal and external rewards.[2]

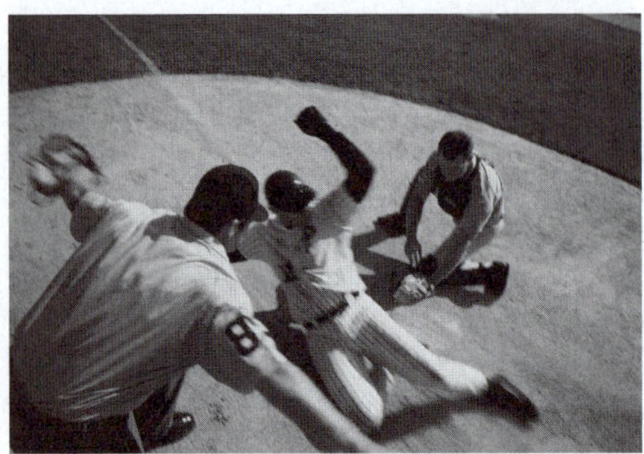

Sport is said to be institutionalized when there are standardization and enforcement of the rules, emphasis on organization, and a formal approach to skill development.

Purestock/SuperStock

This definition refers to what is popularly known as organized sport activities, particularly in the United States, which can be exclusionary to many individuals who want to engage in sport-related activities. On the basis of this definition, three often-asked questions can be addressed: (1) What kinds of activities can be classified as sport? (2) Under what circumstances can participation in activities be considered sport? (3) What characterizes the involvement of participants in sport?

More recently, sport sociologists have shifted their focus from organized sport and are placing more emphasis on "physical culture." Physical culture is more inclusive as "all forms of movement and physical activities that people in particular social worlds create, sustain, and regularly include in their collective lives."[4] Based on this wide-ranged definition, it leaves it up to individuals and organizations of sport to define "sport." How do you define sport, and what is your basis for this definition and perspective?

Sport and Organized Sport Activities

What physical activities can be considered sport? Jogging? Chess? Auto racing? Weight lifting? Are participants in a pickup basketball game engaged in sport even though their activity is different in nature from the game professionals play? Are these simply sport under the physical culture definition or sport in relation to organized sport?

Sport requires that participants use relatively complex physical skills, physical prowess, and/or vigorous physical exertion. Because these terms can be conceptualized as part of a continuum, at times it is difficult to make the distinction between physical and nonphysical skills, between complex and simple motor requirements, and between vigorous and nonvigorous activities. Because these terms are not quantified, determining what is complex physical activity and what is not can be a difficult task. Furthermore, not all physical activities involving complex physical skills or vigorous physical exertion are classified as (organized) sport. The circumstances and conditions under which these physical activities take place must be considered when classifying a physical activity as sport.

Conditions

The circumstances or context in which participation in physical activities occurs can be designated as ranging from informal and unstructured to formal and structured. For instance, compare the nature of a playground pickup game of basketball with a scheduled game between two professional teams. The individuals involved in both situations are playing basketball, but the nature and consequences of these games are different. Thus, the question is: Are both groups of individuals engaged in sport? Organized sport?

When some sport sociologists discuss sport, they are referring to physical activity that involves competition conducted under formal and organized conditions. Given this perspective, friends engaged in an informal game of basketball are not participating in sport, whereas athletes participating on the professional teams are participating in sport. From this sociological point of view, sport involves competitive physical activity that is institutionalized. However, other sport sociologists would argue against this view if they describe sport from a physical culture perspective.

According to sociologists, *institutionalization* is a standardized pattern or set of behaviors sustained over a period of time and from one situation to another. Thus, competitive physical activity can be considered sport when it becomes institutionalized. Institutionalization occurs when there is standardization and enforcement of the rules governing the activity, emphasis on organization and the technical aspects of the activity (e.g., training, use of strategies, specialization, and definition of the roles of players and coaches), and a formalized approach to skill development (e.g., use of experts to provide instruction).

Participation Motives

Sport depends on maintaining a balance between intrinsic and extrinsic motivations. When the intrinsic satisfaction of being involved coexists with extrinsic concern for external rewards (e.g., money, medals, approval from parents or a coach), sport occurs. The balance does not have to be 50–50, but when one source of motivation begins to greatly outweigh the other, changes occur in the nature of the activity and the experience of the participants. When participants' intrinsic motives prevail, the organization and structure of physical activity become one of play. When participants' extrinsic motives such as championships or money prevail, physical activity changes from sport to what is often referred to as spectacle or work. It should be noted that during the course of a single sport event, participants may shift back and forth from intrinsic to extrinsic sources of motivation. At times, participants may be absorbed in the flow of the action and revel in the satisfaction of being involved. Moments later, they may be motivated by the desire to win a medal or receive the adulation of the crowd; the play spirit becomes replaced with the desire to reap external rewards.

According to Coakley, an alternative approach to defining sport strives to understand sports within the social and cultural contexts of particular societies. Two key questions guide this approach: "What activities do people in a particular group or society identify as sports? Whose sports count the most in a group or society when it comes to obtaining support and resources?"[2] This approach serves as a focal point for sport sociologists to scientifically examine the role of sports in people's lives and within a particular society.

The sociology of sport has grown tremendously over the past four decades. Because of space limitations, an overview of only a few topics can be presented in this chapter. This chapter includes interscholastic and intercollegiate sport, girls and women in sport, minorities in sport, children and youth sport, violence in sport, and performance-enhancing substances in sport.

SPORT IN EDUCATIONAL INSTITUTIONS

In the United States, organized sports are accepted as an integral part of the extracurricular offerings of schools and colleges. Since the initial inclusion of athletics in educational institutions in the late 1800s, concerns were raised about the educational worth of athletics and its relevancy to the educational mission of the schools.

Despite some criticism about the educational merits of interscholastic and intercollegiate athletics, they continue to grow in popularity. The National Federation of State High School Associations (NFHS) Athletic Participation report for 2018–2019 revealed that participation in high school athletics was 7,937,491, a decline from the previous 2 years.[5] (See Figure 8-1.) Opportunities for students with disabilities to participate in adapted sports continue to slowly increase. More schools offer adapted sports such as basketball, bowling, floor hockey, softball, soccer, and track and field. However, school offerings and participation numbers are low–about 3,000 athletes.[2] Efforts need to be made to increase the opportunities for individuals with disabilities to participate in sport.

Participation at the collegiate level has also experienced strong growth. In 2015–2016, the National Collegiate Athletic Association (NCAA), the largest governing body of athletics, reported that over 504,000 athletes participated in intercollegiate athletics.[6] Note that these NCAA participation figures represent only those athletes who participate in sports in which the NCAA sponsors championships. Thus, many more participate in

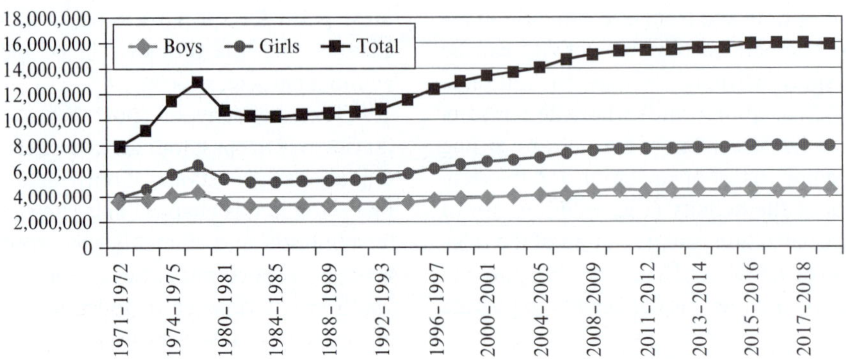

Figure 8-1 Participation in high school athletics by girls and boys, 1971–2019.

Source: Data from National Federation of State High School Athletic Associations. High School Athletics Participation Survey, 2018–2019.

nonchampionship NCAA sports as well as engage in sports in community college and non-NCAA member institutions.

Interscholastic and intercollegiate sports play an important role in our American culture, a role not limited to the participants or coaches involved in the experience. Because athletics plays such an important role in our society, it is interesting to examine some of the sociological implications of the phenomenon.

Interscholastic Sport

Interscholastic sport is viewed by many, including the NFHS, as an integral part of the educational experience for high school students and, increasingly, middle school students as well.

While there is widespread support for interscholastic athletics, there has also been much criticism of these programs. Proponents of interscholastic athletics cite their valuable contributions to the educational mission of the schools. Critics take the position that sport interferes with the attainment of educational goals.

Participation in interscholastic sport can benefit students in several ways. Participation in sport can help students develop a high level of physical fitness and attain a high degree of proficiency in selected sport skills and knowledge of various aspects of the game. Other benefits of participation include the development of sportspersonship, cooperation, leadership, and loyalty. Sport can provide opportunities for personal growth, pave the way for the development of friendships, develop decision making and critical thinking skills, teach self-discipline and commitment, enhance self-esteem and personal status, and promote the acceptance of others regardless of race or social identities.

Since the advent of Title IX in 1972, girls' and women's sports have grown in popularity. The University of Connecticut basketball players autograph photos for their fans prior to their 2004 NCAA championship appearance.

Sarah Rich

However, whether participation in sport enhances academic achievement is a very complex and debatable question. When viewed as a group, high school athletes generally have better grade point averages (GPAs) and express more interest in higher education than their nonathletic peers.[2] It is important to note, however, that such differences are typically small. It is also difficult to isolate the influence of sport participation from other factors known to influence academic achievement, such as family background, economic status, support and encouragement from others, and individual characteristics.

It is important to note that in many schools across the country, interscholastic sport programs are in serious need of reform. Some programs have little relevancy to the education process. Critics of interscholastic sport also denounce the overemphasis on winning, restriction of opportunities for students, and eligibility requirements for participation. Concern has also been voiced pertaining to drug abuse, soaring costs, pressures from parents and community supporters, and coaches' behavior.

Overemphasis on winning is one of the most frequently voiced criticisms of interscholastic sport. This disproportionate emphasis is reflected in the increased specialization in one sport, the participation of injured athletes, the subversion of the educational process, and the dependence of coaches' jobs on their win–loss records.

Compared to 10 years ago, more high school athletes are foregoing multisport competition and specializing in one sport.[7] While in the past, athletes would compete in fall, winter, and spring sports, there is a continued trend to compete in only one sport all year. Increasingly, athletes engage in conditioning programs and informal practices for their chosen sport in the off-season and attend specialized sport camps and play in community leagues during the summer. Proponents of sport specialization stress that such an emphasis is needed to develop proficiency in advanced skills, refine strategies, remain competitive with other teams, and increase an athlete's chances of receiving college grants-in-aid. Critics argue that specialization limits athletes' development, denying them opportunities to develop skills in other activities, participate with other athletes, and learn from other coaches. Athletes who specialize may be exploited by coaches seeking to win; they are subjected to overuse injuries; are at risk for athletic burnout (i.e., are tired and emotionally exhausted from participating); and may drop out of the sport, often near the point of reaching their fullest potential.

In an effort to win, coaches may resort to undesirable behaviors. They may pressure athletes to practice and play when injured. In an effort to maintain player eligibility, coaches may steer athletes toward easier courses, pressure teachers to pass athletes, or, in some cases, alter athletes' grades.

Winning is overemphasized when teachers are hired or fired based on their coaching win-loss records rather than their abilities as educators. Good teachers have been fired because of poor coaching records, and poor teachers have been retained because of their outstanding coaching accomplishments. If interscholastic sport is to realize its educational potential, it is important that winning be kept in perspective. The educational goals of learning and development should be emphasized, not the win-loss record.

The restricted number of opportunities for participation is another criticism of interscholastic sports. Schools typically have both a varsity and a junior varsity team in a variety of sports, although larger schools also may have freshman and reserve teams. Thus, when a given school offers both a varsity and a junior varsity basketball team for boys and for girls, perhaps as few as 48 students will have the opportunity to participate. Many students who are less skilled are excluded, despite their love of the game, and often no other scholastic sport opportunities are provided for them. Furthermore, in addition to consuming a great deal of the time and energy of physical education teachers, interscholastic sport teams utilize monies, facilities, equipment, and other resources that could be used for general participation (e.g., intramurals). In addition, even though federal legislation has mandated that boys and girls must have equal opportunities, often the informal support and commitment so necessary to develop and maintain quality programs for females is lacking.

Academic requirements for eligibility are also a controversial issue. Most high schools require that students meet certain academic standards to be eligible to participate in extracurricular activities, including sports. These standards often exceed the criteria required to stay in school. Many states have adopted "no pass, no play" policies, setting forth even more stringent requirements for athletes to maintain their eligibility. These requirements vary, but typically the policy bars participation of those individuals who do not pass all of their courses or who fail to maintain a certain GPA during a marking period.

Advocates of this policy believe that establishing stringent standards for participation in sport programs will have a positive effect on athletes' academic performance. In order to maintain their eligibility, athletes will be motivated to pursue their studies. Critics of this policy point out that students who stay in school mainly to play sports now find themselves ineligible and may drop out of school.

Eligibility standards may be appropriate if sport is an extracurricular activity and participation is a privilege to be earned. If, however, sport is an integral part of the educational experience–if it has educational value–then is it appropriate to deny this experience to any student? If participation in interscholastic athletics contributes to educational goals, if the experience can promote learning and foster personal development, why should any student be denied this opportunity?

One of the most serious problems in the secondary schools is drug abuse. Much media attention has been focused on the use of performance-enhancing drugs, such as anabolic steroids, in professional, international, and intercollegiate sports. However, such drug use is a concern in interscholastic sports as well. When anabolic steroids are taken in amounts far exceeding the recommended dosage (megadoses) and coupled with intense physical workouts, anabolic steroids can build muscle and enhance performance. The side effects associated with such large dosages are serious and lead to irreparable damage. Coaches must also be prepared to address the use of supplements, such as creatine, and other serious issues, including the use of tobacco, alcohol, and illegal drugs such as marijuana, amphetamines, prescription drugs, opiates, heroin, and cocaine.

Soaring costs are increasingly becoming a concern in interscholastic athletics. Rising costs for injury and liability insurance as well as costs associated with providing programs for girls and for students with disabilities have caused some schools to reduce the scope of their athletic programs or require athletes to pay in order to participate. A "pay-to-play" policy requires students who desire to participate in sports to pay for the opportunity. Critics have decried this policy because it discriminates against students who cannot afford to pay. Some schools and communities, in response, have made provisions so that economically disadvantaged students can participate in the athletic program. However, few of these students choose to participate.

Intercollegiate Sport

Given the tremendous diversity of intercollegiate sport programs, it is easy to understand how the nature of the intercollegiate sport experience for participants can vary greatly from school to school and within each program. The number of sports offered by a school can range from as few as 10 teams to as many as 25 different teams for men and women.[8] In smaller institutions, the athletic program may be part of and funded by the physical education department, the coaches may have faculty teaching status, and one individual may serve as the coach for two or more teams. In contrast, at larger institutions, separate athletic departments exist; athletics has its own budget and may generate substantial revenue from gate receipts and contributions; coaches have no teaching status; and an individual coaches only one sport. Program philosophies vary as well; in some institutions, the educational nature of intercollegiate sport is emphasized, while in other institutions, sport is seen as big business.

Financial assistance for athletes varies and may be directly influenced by the skill of the athlete. Some schools offer no athletic scholarships; financial assistance is based solely on financial need. Other schools offer athletes a full scholarship that covers all expenses for tuition, room, board, fees, and books. Still other schools may offer partial assistance to athletes, such as providing a tuition waiver. Given the tremendous diversity of intercollegiate sport programs, it is reasonable to believe that the nature of the intercollegiate sport experience for participants varies widely throughout the United States.

Intercollegiate sport is regulated by three primary governing bodies: the NCAA, the National Association of Intercollegiate Athletics (NAIA), and the National Junior College Athletic Association (NJCAA). These associations attempt to administer intercollegiate athletic programs in accordance with educational principles.

The NCAA is the largest, most powerful governing body in intercollegiate athletics. The NCAA is divided into five divisions based on the characteristics of their athletic program.[9] Division I includes 350 schools and is divided into three divisions, which are Division I-FBS (Football Bowl Subdivision), Division I-FCS (NCAA Football Championship Subdivision), and Division I that does not include any football programs. Division I "big-time" programs typically highlight football or men's basketball, because of their potential to generate revenue, often in the millions of dollars for successful programs. Divisions II and III are composed of over 300 and 450 schools, respectively.[9]

Athletes who participate in the big Division I programs generally possess a higher level of athletic talent, face a greater time commitment to their sport, receive full athletic scholarships (for certain sports such as football and basketball), experience a greater amount of travel, and benefit from greater media exposure. Pressures to have a winning program are often immense, and the consequences of winning and losing are usually much greater. Economic survival for these programs frequently depends on their ability to generate revenue through gate receipts, contributions, and, increasingly, television contracts. Winning teams generate interest among fans, which increases gate receipts, which, in turn, provides more money to hire coaches with proven winning records to raise the athletic program to even greater heights. Commercialism and entertainment dominate; educational goals are de-emphasized and often subverted, and athletics is transformed into a business and entertainment venture.

As with interscholastic sport, overemphasis on winning can lead to the subordination of educational goals. Such goals as sportspersonship, character development, and social development may be abandoned when winning becomes the most important objective. Desire and pressure to win may lead to the subversion or violation of rules in an effort to recruit the best athletes and maintain their eligibility.

The academic achievement of intercollegiate athletes is a major concern. There are many student-athletes who exemplify the true meaning of the word–they have combined sports and academics successfully. In many colleges and universities, the academic achievements of athletes are comparable to those of their nonathlete peers. Studies have shown that the academic performance of athletes on women's teams, NCAA Division III teams, and other nonrevenue-generating teams is comparable to other college students.

There are, however, many instances in which the term *student-athlete* is truly a misnomer; in these cases, athletics is given a much higher priority than academics. This is particularly true of student-athletes in the big-time programs. Athletes in these programs, especially those in revenue-generating sports such as football and basketball, face considerable demands on their time and energy that can interfere with their academic work.

Some athletes in big-time programs can successfully balance the time-consuming demands of athletics with the rigorous demands of academics and excel in both areas. However, sometimes, the pressures on coaches to win translate into pressure to keep athletes eligible. Focusing attention on eligibility rather than on learning can lead to many abuses. Coaches may recruit athletes who lack the academic preparation needed to succeed at the challenges of college. They counsel athletes into taking easy courses, pressure professors to give them good grades, and encourage athletes to enroll in majors that require little academic effort. Unfortunately, progress toward a degree is not monitored as closely as is maintenance of athletic eligibility. Additionally, because many black athletes are from rural and inner-city schools, where quality education programs are often lacking, a higher proportion of black athletes is affected.

In 1990, the US Congress passed a law requiring all colleges and universities to make public the graduation rates of their athletes, starting in 1991. However, even the availability of this information makes it difficult to get a true picture of the graduation rates of athletes. Additionally, the formula used by the US government, often referred to as the federal formula, is often criticized for failing to take into account students who transfer to another institution or who leave school to play on a professional team.

The graduation rates are based on individuals who received an athletic scholarship and who graduated within 6 years of initial college entry. The data show that Division I athletes with athletic grants graduate at a similar rate to the collective student body; the graduation rate for female athletes is higher than for male athletes and other female students; black male and female athletes graduate at a higher rate than the overall black student body, yet at a lower rate than white athletes; graduation rates are lowest in the revenue-producing sports of football and basketball; and black athletes are more likely to leave school with a GPA lower than 2.0.[10]

To address the shortcomings in the calculation of the federal graduation rate, the NCAA developed the graduation success rate (GSR). The GSR takes into account students who have transferred or not returned for a variety of reasons (e.g., financial circumstances or going professional), but left the institution in good academic standing (note that this does not mean that they were on track for their degree). This is thought by the NCAA to be a more accurate reflection of the academic success of their athletes. Unlike the federal rate, rates are not calculated for the general student body, so no comparisons can be made up of the student-athletes' academic performance to that of the general student body.

Another effort to address the academic concerns associated with big-time revenue-producing sports is the establishment of a minimum academic progress rate (APR). This rule, passed in 2004, applies to more than 5,700 Division I teams. APR is based on academic eligibility, retention, and academic success (GSR) of student-athletes and is calculated each semester.[11] A team receives one point for every athlete who is academically eligible and 1 point for each athlete who remains enrolled in school.[11] The highest APR score is 1,000 points.[12] Teams that fail to achieve a minimum score of 925 can lose one or more of their allocated scholarships, depending on how far below 925 they score.[11] A score of 925 reflects a graduation rate of about 50%.[11]

Another effort by the NCAA to improve the academic performance of athletes in Division I and II teams focuses on player eligibility, both initially as a freshman and then as a continuing student. Beginning in 2016, to compete as a freshman, a student must have graduated from high school, completed a minimum of 16 core courses (math, English, science, etc.) with a minimum GPA of 2.3 in each of the courses, and earned a qualifying score on either the ACT or SAT test.[13]

By setting initial eligibility standards, the NCAA hoped to send a strong message to high school administrators, coaches, and athletes that academic achievement was a prerequisite for participation in Division I and II athletics. It was further hoped that initial eligibility rules would help colleges and universities break the habit of recruiting athletes who had neither the academic background nor the potential to graduate within a 5-year period. It also provides first-year athletes who need a year to strengthen their academic abilities without the added pressures and time commitments associated with participation in sports.

The initial eligibility rules are controversial. Critics charge that they discriminate against economically disadvantaged students who were not fortunate enough to receive a strong high school preparation for college and those who do not have the resources to pay for commercial test preparation courses or to retake the standardized tests.

Continuing eligibility requires the student-athletes to make progress toward graduation. The NCAA's 40-60-80 rule requires steady progress toward completion of graduation requirements and the attainment of a specified GPA to remain eligible to compete. By the end of their second year, athletes must complete 40% of their graduation requirements with a GPA of at least 1.8.[14] At the conclusion of their third year, athletes must have completed 60% of the requirements with a GPA of at least 1.9.[14] Eighty percent of the requirements must be completed with a GPA of at least 2.0 by the end of the fourth year for athletes to remain eligible to compete.[14]

The long-term effectiveness of these academic reform measures remains to be seen. It is hoped that they will lead to an increased emphasis on academic achievement for athletes at both the high school and college levels. It appears that these measures are steps toward restoring much-needed academic integrity to intercollegiate athletic programs.

Several other problems beset big-time intercollegiate sport, including the fact that sport has become big business. This commercialism has led to financial concerns receiving a greater priority than the education and personal development of the athletes. Television contracts increase the pressure to have a winning program in order to reap greater financial benefits. Media coverage of sport continues to grow. The NCAA's recent contract with CBS–$10.8 billion for 14 years, from 2011 to 2024–for the Division I men's basketball championship, reflects the tremendous interest in the commercial value of intercollegiate sport.[15] Almost 80% of the NCAA's revenue comes from television rights.

There has been increased concern about the exploitation of athletes. Some intercollegiate athletes can generate millions of dollars for their institution, but the only compensation, for some, permitted under NCAA rules is tuition, room, board, books, and fees. Even at the most expensive institutions, when the total cost of the athletic scholarship is divided by the number of hours athletes are required to devote to their sport, the pay per hour is low. Although critics say that it is difficult to place a value on the benefits of a college education, oftentimes athletes are strongly encouraged to focus their energies and efforts on sports instead of academics. Recently, the NCAA approved policy that centers on the NIL of collegiate athletes. The rules associated with this policy include:

- Individuals can engage in NIL activities that are consistent with the law of the state where the school is located. Colleges and universities may be a resource for state law questions.
- Individuals can use a professional services provider for NIL activities.
- College athletes who attend a school in a state without an NIL law can engage in NIL activity without violating NCAA rules related to NIL.
- State law and schools/conferences may impose reporting requirements.

Several other issues in intercollegiate sport must be addressed. The media have increased the public's awareness of recruiting violations. Illegal recruiting practices, such as cash payments to prospective athletes, must be stopped. Drug abuse is also a problem. Athletes, in an effort to enhance their performance, may abuse such drugs as amphetamines and anabolic steroids. Although drug testing policies and procedures have become more stringent, methods to mask the use of drugs have become more clever. The effect of win–loss records on the retention of coaches, the role of coaches within institutions of higher education, and the role of alumni and other influential supporters in the hiring and firing of coaches must be carefully evaluated and monitored.

To help combat some of these issues, the Knight Commission on Intercollegiate Athletics was formulated to develop, promote, and lead transformational change that prioritizes the education, health, safety, and success of college athletes.[16] The impact the Knight Commission has over recent years includes:

- More than 88% of college athletes receive degrees.
- At least **50%** of a team's players must be on track to graduate in order for the team to be eligible for postseason championships.
- Between 2019 and 2032, more than **$1.1 billion** will be rewarded to institutions for the academic and graduation success of their teams.

Current initiatives of the Knight Commission include:

- Transforming the NCAA D-I Model Series.
- Achieving racial equity in college sports.
- Name, image, and likeness (NIL).
- College Athletics Financial Information (CAFI) database.

Like interscholastic sport, intercollegiate sport has the potential to contribute to the educational goals of the institutions that sponsor it. Whether these educational goals are attained depends on the leadership. When winning is overemphasized, commercialism is rampant, and athletes are exploited (since a limited number of student-athletes will benefit from the NIL policy), the educational relevance of these programs is called into question. When winning is placed in perspective, when academic achievement is strongly supported, and when athletes are encouraged and given opportunities to develop to their fullest potential, then the educational mission of intercollegiate athletics will be fulfilled.

GIRLS AND WOMEN IN SPORT

Prior to the 1970s, opportunities for girls and women to compete in sports were limited. Over the past 50 years, there has been a dramatic increase in girls' and women's participation in sports. This increase is visible at all levels of competition–the Olympics, professional, amateur, intercollegiate, interscholastic, and youth.

Federal legislation, specifically Title IX of the Education Amendments of 1972, was one of the most influential factors contributing to the increase in participation of girls and women in the United States, because it mandated equal treatment for women and men in programs receiving federal assistance. Because Title IX is politically controversial and the guidelines are complex, implementation and enforcement of this law are difficult. After its implementation, access to sport opportunities for women increased. However, it should be noted that only programs directly receiving federal aid are required to comply with the Title IX regulations, not whole institutions. Because athletic programs typically receive little if any direct federal funding, the threat of losing funding for noncompliance and nonsupport of women's athletics is not a substantial one.

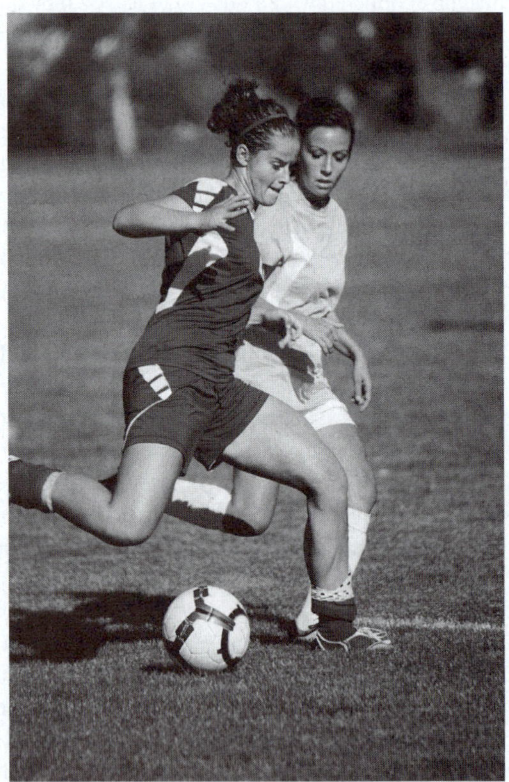

Since Title IX, sports opportunities for girls and women have increased. Sports are no longer just for fathers and sons.

Kirk Strickland/E+/Getty Images

Over the years, many colleges and universities have had issues about complying with Title IX. The Office of Civil Rights in 1979 developed a three-pronged test, the Effective Accommodation Test, which was clarified in 1996 to determine if an institution is in compliance. A school must meet one of these three tests to be within the law:

1. *Proportionality.* Are the opportunities for males and females substantially proportionate to the school's full-time undergraduate enrollment?
2. *History and continued practice.* Even though a school has a disproportionate number of male athletes, as long as the school is adding more women's sports and has added one recently, generally within the last 3 years, the school would probably be considered in compliance.
3. *Accommodation of interests and abilities.* If a school can demonstrate that its women do not have enough ability or interest to sustain additional teams, the school would be considered in compliance. However, if there are club teams playing sports, this could indicate to the court that there is sufficient interest to support another team.

The growth of participation by girls in interscholastic sport following the passage of Title IX can be seen in Figure 8-1. At the intercollegiate level, there has been an increase in the number of teams for women, the hiring of qualified coaches, and the offering of athletic scholarships to outstanding high school women athletes. In 1972, 32,000 women competed in intercollegiate sports; the NCAA reported that 222,920 women participated in its athletic programs in 2019-2020.[6] Spectator interest in women's sports has grown as well, which has resulted in increased attendance at games. For example, NCAA women's basketball attendance for the 2019-2020 season surpassed 11 million for the 12th straight year.[17] In the late 1990s and early 2000s, television coverage of women's sports increased to 6.3%; however, there has been a continuous decline in women's sports coverage since 2004.[18] In 2009, men's sports received 96.3% of airtime compared to 1.6% of women's sports.[18] Even the "ticker" included on ESPN and other sport networks only dedicate 3.6% of coverage to women.[18]

Professional opportunities for women are also increasing. In 1996, the Women's National Basketball Association (WNBA) was organized, offering elite women athletes the opportunity to continue to participate in their sport. The WNBA has 12 teams, is organized into two conferences, and attracted over 1.5 million spectators during the 2017 season, which was the highest total in 5 years.[19]

Professional women's soccer leagues have not survived in the United States; however, the women's national team is ranked number 1 in the world and has won numerous World Cups as recently as 2019, which was the most watched soccer match ever with over 260 million live viewers! Despite their success, women soccer players make only a quarter of what men soccer players do, even though the U.S. men's soccer team is ranked lower and generates less in revenue.[20] However, in 2022, the U.S. National Women's team won a $24 million equal pay settlement that will pave the way for equal pay among the women and men's national soccer teams.

Key legislation, the women's movement, the fitness movement, and increased visibility accorded female athletes who have done much to expand opportunities for women in sport. However, while opportunities for girls and women in athletics have increased tremendously over the past five decades, whether participation rates will continue to grow for women depends to a great extent on the expansion of opportunities for involvement and the support and encouragement of female athletic endeavors.

In spite of the passage of Title IX and improvements in opportunities, sex discrimination is still a feature of many athletic programs. New laws are often met with resistance and questions are raised about how to implement them. The most recent controversy is over trans women participating in women sports–both in Title IX legislation and sporting organizations. In 2022, Lia Thomas was the first openly trans women to with a Division I championship (in swimming) raising questions and debates as to whether trans women should be allowed to compete in women divisions.

Based upon history, people tend to be reluctant to change the status quo. Individuals with a vested interest in maintaining the status quo may use their power and control of financial resources to thwart the progress of women's programs. Women across the nation at all levels of competition are still denied fair treatment. Such discrimination can be as blatant as the refusal to fund a program. But inequality often occurs in less noticeable forms, such as the provision of quality equipment, supplies, and uniforms; the assignment of games and practice time; the use of facilities and locker rooms; the allocation of equal funds for travel and the availability of travel opportunities; the access to quality coaches, size of coaching staff, and compensation of coaches; the opportunity to receive support services such as academic tutoring; the administration of medical and training services; and the publicity accorded to individual athletes and the team.

Despite Title IX prohibitions against discrimination, women still do not receive equitable treatment in sport. Furthermore, violations of Title IX are often not prosecuted vigorously. Commitment, time, and effort are needed to ensure compliance with the law and ensure that the spirit of the law becomes an integral part of athletic programs at all levels.

Today there are fewer female coaches for women's sports than in the years following the passage of Title IX. Despite the fact that women's sport programs have increased, the proportion of women in coaching and athletic administrative positions has declined. For example, at the intercollegiate level, the percentage of female coaches of women's sport programs decreased from 90% in 1970 to 41.3% in 2021. And although men serve as head coaches for 58.7% of women's teams, only 4–6.8% of the head coaches of men's teams are women (sadly this stat is doubled from 2014).[21] In 1972, 90% of women's intercollegiate athletic programs were headed by female athletic administrators. In 2021,[21] 14% of Division I director of athletics positions were held by women; about one-third of the associate director and assistant director positions were held by women; and one-third of head athletic trainers were women. These stats are alarming enough collectively, but it is even more concerning the small percentage of women of color that hold any of these positions in collegiate sport.

Reasons for the underrepresentation of women and women of color in these positions have been debated widely, and the results of the research are confusing. However, one reason that is frequently cited is the lack of well-qualified women coaches and administrators. Recently, several programs have been implemented in the United States to recruit and train more women coaches. It is also important to note that the lack of visibility of women coaches and administrators within the sport structure provides few role models for females who aspire to careers in these areas. Other reasons include the persistence of traditional stereotypes of women and resistance of those in power, predominantly men, to providing opportunities for women.

More opportunities for both men and women to participate in sports can be achieved by reducing excessive funding of sports rather than denying opportunities to participate. This could be achieved in many different ways, such as holding the line on spending in men's sports, generating new revenue sources to support women's sports, and decreasing excessive spending by limiting squad sizes, decreasing the number of scholarships, or trimming excesses from existing budgets, such as teams spending the night in hotels before a home game. Remember that Title IX prohibits discrimination on the basis of sex, and that federal regulations require that both men and women be provided with equitable opportunities, including opportunities to participate in intercollegiate athletics.

Events of the past 50 years have served to increase opportunities for participation by women in sport at all levels. However, while progress has been made, continued increases in participation by women and women of color will depend on eliminating barriers to involvement such as financial constraints, less-than-full compliance with Title IX, lack of women coaches and administrators, and minimization of women's accomplishments.

Qualified and committed leadership is needed to change the structure of sport programs in order to reduce inequities and to further eliminate barriers to participation so that all individuals, regardless of gender, can enjoy the benefits of sport.

RACIAL MINORITIES IN SPORT

Sport is often extolled as an avenue by which to transcend differences in race and cultural backgrounds. It has been said, for example, that "sport is color-blind"–that on the playing field a person is recognized for ability alone, and rewards are given without regard to race and class. The widely televised performances of black and Hispanic male athletes in such sports as baseball, basketball, track and field, boxing, and football suggest to millions of viewers that sport is relatively free of the prejudice and discrimination often found in other areas of society. Despite a commonly held belief that sport allows individuals to accept one another on the basis of their physical competence, close scrutiny of the sport phenomena reveals that sport organizations are typically characterized by the same patterns of prejudice and discrimination found in the surrounding society. Most recently, during the 2016 NFL season, Colin Kaepernick of the San Francisco 49ers, chose to kneel during the national anthem because he did not want to support a song and tradition that was prejudiced against blacks and other minorities. Other athletes at both the professional and collegiate levels supported Kaepernick's mission to expose racial discrimination in the United States. However, despite this support, Kaepernick has not been hired on any NFL team since his display of activism. In 2019, Kaepernick reached an undisclosed financial settlement with the NFL. Furthermore, in 2022, Brian Flores, former head coach of the Miami Dolphins, sued the NFL and three teams due to racial discrimination.

Historically, sport in the United States has been characterized by racism and prejudice. While blacks and other minorities have a rich history of sport participation, prior to the 1950s, minorities were rarely given access to mainstream sport competition in the professional leagues, colleges and universities, and schools. Members of minorities organized their own leagues and competed within them; for example, blacks had their own basketball and baseball leagues. The integration of professional sport did not occur until 1946, when Jackie Robinson "broke the color barrier" by playing for the then Brooklyn Dodgers. Integration of intercollegiate sports occurred later and was particularly slow to occur in the South. The US Supreme Court's decision in *Brown v. Board of Education* in 1954, as well as the civil rights movement of the 1970s, slowly led to the integration of schools and the opening of doors to sports for minorities.

Currently, the participation of black athletes remains concentrated in a few sports such as football and basketball. These sports typically require no expensive equipment or training, have coaches readily available through the public schools, and offer visible role models to aspiring athletes. Black athletes are underrepresented in such sports as volleyball, swimming, hockey, gymnastics, soccer, golf, and tennis. The expenses increasingly required for many of these sports, such as private lessons and elite coaching, expensive equipment, funds for travel, and club memberships, as well as the virtual lack of role models in these sports, discourage minority participation. Participation by black women has been very limited, and accomplishments of black women athletes are typically accorded little attention. In the 2016 Olympics in Rio de Janeiro, three African American women made history by winning gold medals: Simone Biles (gymnastics), Simone Manuel (swimming), and Michelle Carter (shot put).

Minority men and women are significantly underrepresented in coaching and managerial positions in sports at all levels. For over 20 years, Dr. Richard Lapchick has authored a Racial and Gender Report Card (RGRC) that provides comprehensive analysis of opportunities for women and minorities in sports. College and professional sports organizations are assigned a grade, ranging from A+ to F, based on their hiring practices. Grades are given for gender, race, and both combined. An A for race is based on a 30% minimum for people of color and an A for gender requires 45%. Professional sports studied include the National Football League (NFL), National Basketball Association (NBA), Women's National Basketball Association (WNBA), Major League Baseball (MLB), and Major League Soccer (MLS). In 2020, the NBA and WNBA set the industry standard by receiving an A− and A+, respectively, for their combined grade for race and gender hiring practices.[22] The WNBA's A+ combined score continued with the highest grade in the history of the RGRC for the third year in a row. College sport received the lowest combined grade of C+, with a C+ in racial hiring and B in gender hiring (these scores were reversed in 2018). See the 2020 Racial and Gender Report Card box for additional grades. These grades are comprehensive of the hiring practices; however, the grades and scores are further broken down into categories such as coaches (head, assistant) and front office (general manager, team vice presidents, senior administration, etc.). We encourage you to go to the RGRC website (https://www.tidesport.org/racial-gender-report-card) and complete the second self-assessment activity at the end of the chapter.

Collectively, findings indicate that professional and collegiate sport teams are making some strides in hiring minorities and women, yet scores in both race and gender depreciated in many of the sports

2020 RACIAL AND GENDER REPORT CARD

League	Combined	Race	Gender
NBA	A+	A−	B
NFL	B−	B+	C
MLB	B	B+	C
MLS	B	A	C−
WNBA	A+	A+	A+
College Sport	C+	C+	B

Source: Lapchick, R. E. 2020 Racial and Gender Report Card. The Institute for Diversity and Ethics in Sport, 2022, http://www.tidesport.org/.

over the past 2 years. There have been more, but not many, opportunities for minorities and women to occupy powerful, decision making positions within sports. White men continue to occupy positions of power, at both coaching and administrative levels, within professional and collegiate sports. While there has been some progress in providing opportunities for women and minorities in intercollegiate sport, it is evident that much more needs to be accomplished.

The impact of societal beliefs about different racial and ethnic groups can be seen in the pattern of positions and roles played by athletes from different racial and ethnic backgrounds. Coakley uses the term *race ideology* to refer to a "web of ideas and beliefs that people use to give meaning to skin color and evaluate people and forms of social organization in terms of racial classifications."[2]

In some team sports, such as baseball, football, and women's volleyball, players from certain racial or ethnic groups are disproportionately represented at certain positions, in a phenomenon known as *stacking*. For example, in professional baseball, black and Latino players are most heavily concentrated in the outfield positions, whereas white players are concentrated at the positions of pitcher, catcher, and in the infield. Whites are disproportionately represented in positions requiring leadership, dependability, and decision making skills, while black players are overrepresented in positions requiring speed, agility, and quick reactions.[2] In women's intercollegiate volleyball, blacks are disproportionately represented at spiker, while whites are overrepresented at setter and bumper.[2]

Stacking patterns are widespread and occur in other sports and in countries throughout the world (e.g., in British soccer, black West Indians and Africans are overrepresented in the wide forward position, while white players are overrepresented at the goalie and midfielder positions).[2]

Stacking reflects stereotypical beliefs about different racial and ethnic groups–for example, that blacks are better jumpers, while whites are smarter and better leaders. Although stacking is one of the most studied topics in sociology of sport, there are

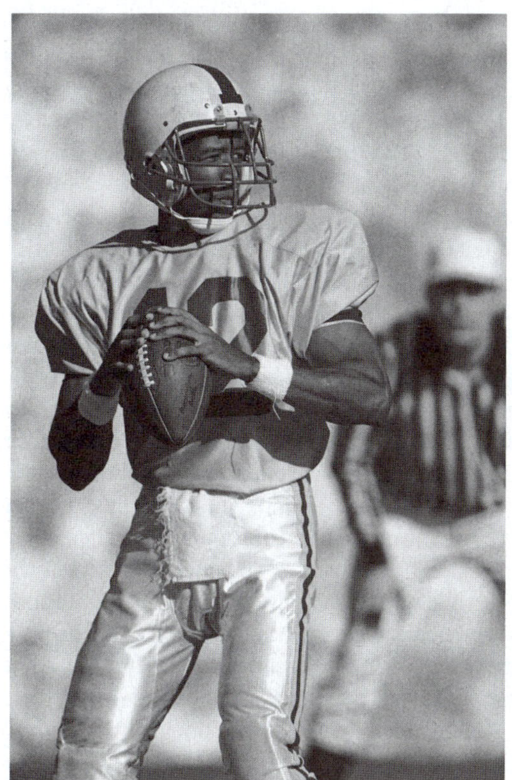

Black athletes are overrepresented in certain sports, such as football and basketball, and underrepresented in other sports, such as volleyball and ice hockey.

Comstock Images/Getty Images

serious disagreements about why stacking patterns exist. But even though a consensus is lacking about the causes of stacking, it is important to recognize that stacking perpetuates patterns of prejudice and discrimination in sport.

Native Americans have long participated in sports, often uniting physical activities with cultural rituals and ceremonies.[23] Although many Native Americans have achieved success in sport, little recognition has been given to their accomplishments. Public acclaim most often has focused on the few Native Americans, such as Jim Thorpe, who were outstanding athletes on segregated government-sponsored reservation school football and baseball teams. On the whole, participation by Native Americans in most sports has been and continues to be limited. Poverty, poor health, lack of equipment, and a dearth of programs are factors that often serve to limit Native American sport participation. Concern about loss of cultural identity, prejudice, lack of understanding, and insensitivity by others toward Native Americans act in concert with the other factors previously mentioned to curb sport involvement.

One example of this lack of sensitivity is the use of school names and mascots that perpetuate white stereotypes of Native Americans. Team names such as Indians or Redskins and a team mascot dressed up as a savage running around waving a tomahawk threatening to behead an opponent reflect distorted beliefs about Native Americans (*it is important to note that over the past couple of years, the Washington Redskins has changed to the Commanders and the Cleveland Indians has changed to the Guardians). Such inappropriate or distorted caricatures of Native Americans who, as school mascots, are painted on gymnasium walls and floors, do little to increase student and public awareness of the richness and diversity of Native American culture. It is even more ironic that this occurs in institutions that by definition exist to educate people about the different cultures within the world in which they live. These stereotypes are often accepted as valid depictions of native people and serve to demean the cultural heritage and history of Native Americans.

It is important to heighten public awareness of the racism experienced by Native Americans that has become an accepted aspect of sport in the United States (Figure 8-2). As Coakley writes:

> The use of the name Redskins cannot be justified under any conditions. To many Native Americans, redskin is as derogatory as "nigger" is for black Americans. It is symbolic of such racism that the capitol city of the government that once put bounties on the lives of native peoples has a football team named the Redskins. It symbolizes a continuing lack of understanding of the complex and diverse cultures and the heritage of native peoples and is offensive to anyone aware of the history of native peoples in North America.[3]

Figure 8-2 Should teams who use Native American names and imagery be required to change their name and mascot? Here a boy plays ball in the street wearing a Cleveland Indians hat and shirt.
Lars A. Niki

In 2001, the United States Commission on Civil Rights issued a statement on the use of Native American images and nicknames as sports symbols. The commission called for an end of the use of Native American images and team names by non-Native schools.[24] In 2005, the National Collegiate Athletic Association announced that they would not allow for championship games to be played at any schools that used Native American imagery as part of marketing for their sports teams; however, the NCAA did not take a stance to disbar any Native American imagery from member institutions using such imagery.[25] Legislators in a wide variety of states are attempting to pass legislation related to names, logos, and imagery of Native Americans.

Some institutions, such as Florida State University, home of the Seminoles, and the University of Utah, home of the Running Utes, appealed the ruling, citing in their cases that the local tribes supported their use of the nicknames, mascots, and imagery. After consideration, the NCAA exempted Florida and Utah from the ruling. However, the University of Illinois was not successful in its request for an exemption. The university wanted to retain its "Fighting Illini" and "Illini" nicknames. It also wanted to keep Chief Illiniwek, its mascot since 1920. Chief Illiniwek, dressed as an Indian brave in buckskin and a headdress, wearing "war" paint and carrying a feathered tomahawk, would mimic a war dance on the field and court to incite the crowds at university sport events. Unlike with Florida and Utah, the local Native American tribes did not support the retention of the chief. In response to the university's appeal, the NCAA allowed Illinois to keep its nicknames because they were deemed to reflect the origin of the name of the state. However, the appeal to retain Chief Illiniwek and associated imagery was denied.

For some, the NCAA's actions were controversial. The critics believed that the NCAA had exceeded its jurisdiction, making policy for institutions rather than limiting its efforts to intercollegiate athletics. Still others thought raising awareness of the issue was enough, and that institutions should be responsible for deciding whether to change their Native American mascots. Other critics were concerned that the NCAA in effect backed down from its ruling by allowing exemptions for Florida and Utah (there are currently five total exemptions).

Stereotypes are the foundation of prejudice and racism. Attitudes change slowly. This is particularly true concerning prejudicial beliefs about different racial and ethnic groups. As discussed in Chapter 3, equity, justice, and cultural humility are important in the disciplines of physical education, exercise science, and sport. Understanding and respecting cultures' worldviews is critical to addressing issues of opportunity and equity. In an era when our society is becoming increasingly multicultural and diverse, it is important that we, as physical education, exercise science, and sport professionals, step up and take a leadership role in this issue.

SPORT FOR CHILDREN AND YOUTH

For many Americans, participation in youth sport activities is an integral part of growing up. It is estimated that over 45.7 million young people participate each year in youth sport, that is, organized sport activities that take place outside the school setting.[26] Furthermore, it is estimated that over 3 million volunteer coaches are involved with these programs. Youth sport ventures are organized around such sports as football, basketball, baseball, softball, soccer, ice hockey, gymnastics, and swimming. An increasing number of opportunities for girls to participate in these programs at all levels are being offered, and it appears that many more children are beginning to compete in these programs at younger ages.

While participation in youth sport has grown tremendously over the past couple of decades, there is widespread concern about the nature and outcomes associated with these programs. Even though these programs are extremely popular, considerable criticism is voiced about the manner in which they are conducted. As you read about the benefits, harmful effects, and criticisms of youth sport programs, it may be helpful to keep in mind your own experiences and those of your friends in youth sport. Consider the following questions:

- What did you like most and least about your experiences?
- What did you learn from participating in youth sport?
- How did your parents/guardians/family influence your participation and what was the extent of their involvement with the program?
- How would you characterize the nature and effectiveness of the coaching you received or observed?
- How did you, your teammates, family, and coaches respond to your successes and failures?
- At what age did you discontinue your participation in youth sport and what were the reasons for stopping?
- What changes would you make in the organization of the program to make the experience a more positive one for all involved?

As with school sport, many benefits have been ascribed to participation in youth sport programs. Proponents of youth sport emphasize that it promotes physical fitness, emotional development, social adjustment, a competitive attitude, and self-confidence. In addition, youth sport programs provide opportunities for the development of physical skills, encourage the achievement of a greater level of skill, give youth additional opportunities to play, and offer a safer experience than participation in unsupervised programs.

As with school sport, one of the greatest criticisms of youth sport is its overemphasis on winning. Critics also voice concerns that children's bodies may be underdeveloped for such vigorous activities, that there is too great an emotional strain

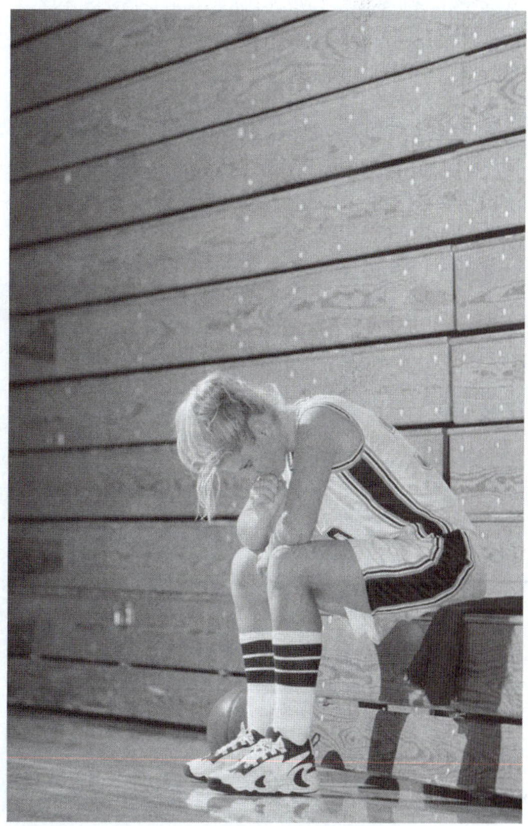

Too often, our attention is focused on the game or winning, leading us to overlook important messages from the athlete.

Lawrence M. Sawyer/J&L Images/Photodisc/Getty Images

and pressure on the participant, and that the players are too psychologically immature to compete in such a setting. Youth sport programs are cited as being too selective and excluding too many children who would like to participate, and as promoting specialization at too early an age. Additional criticisms are directed toward overenthusiastic coaches and parents who take winning too seriously, who pressure children to achieve, and who place their needs before the needs of the child.

Many professionals decry the overemphasis on winning. They believe that youth sport programs should be developmental in nature–that is, they should be organized and conducted in such a way as to enhance the physical, cognitive, social, and affective development of each child and youth participant. This development is particularly critical during the child's younger years. The fun of playing (rather than victory over an opponent) should be stressed, participation opportunities for many children of all identities should be provided, and the development of skills within the sport and in other sports should be stressed (rather than specialization).

Specialization is another frequently voiced concern. During their early years, children should be given an opportunity to develop proficiency in fundamental motor skills and be exposed to a variety of sports. Some children are guided at an early age into a specific sport, such as soccer, or into a specific position within a sport, such as a pitcher. This early specialization deprives children of an opportunity to develop an interest and skills in a variety of sports.

Concern about specialization has further increased within the last two decades. During this time, there has been a growth of private sport leagues and clubs that emphasize the development of skills in a particular sport. This often leads to beginning high-level sport instruction and competition at an early age; children may begin as early as 3 years of age in such sports as swimming, gymnastics, skating, and soccer. Training is serious and often occurs on a year-round basis. Physically, children may be at risk for the development of overuse injuries because they are often involved in practicing on a daily basis for several hours at a time.

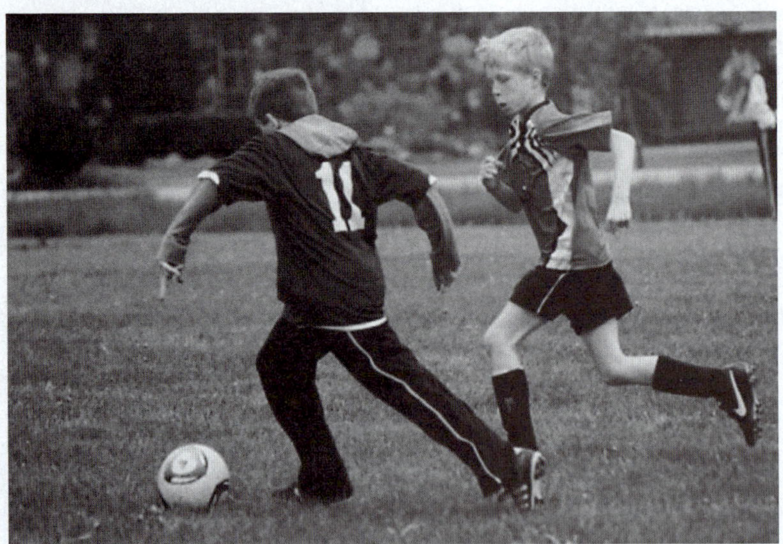

The quality of leadership exerts a significant influence on the outcomes experienced by youth sports participants.

Jennifer Walton-Fisette

Psychologically, these participants may experience burnout from doing the same thing year after year. They may drop out before reaching their optimal level of performance, even after many years of successful participation.

Many recommendations have been set forth by professionals to improve youth sport. Professionals suggest that programs be structured so that children can experience success and satisfaction while continuing to develop their abilities. This may mean modification of the rules, equipment, and playing area to promote success and participation rather than failure and elimination. For example, simplified and fewer rules, smaller balls, smaller fields, bigger goals, batting tees rather than pitchers, rule changes to facilitate scoring, and a requirement of equal playing time for all participants are some of the ways that youth sport programs can be changed to make the experiences more positive for all participants.

Programs should be structured to include elements that children find enjoyable within their own informal games. Plenty of action, opportunity for involvement, close scores to keep the game exciting and interesting, and friendship are important to children; these elements should be infused into youth sport programming. Children should also be given opportunities to be involved in decision making, such as deciding what strategies to use or planning a practice session. They can also be given the responsibility for self-enforcement of rules during the game.

As previously mentioned, the quality of leadership can exert a significant influence on the outcomes children derive from participating in youth sport. Coaches within youth sport programs are typically volunteers, often parents, who have received little if any training on how to coach children. Recognizing this, professionals within the field have directed increased attention toward the development of coaching education programs. These programs emphasize understanding the growth characteristics and developmental needs of children, modifying existing programs to meet these needs, incorporating proper training techniques into the design of the program, and supporting the efforts of children while providing developmentally appropriate opportunities to help them become better players. Enhancing children's self-esteem, recognizing their accomplishments, and praising their efforts are more appropriate than ridiculing, shaming, and belittling their achievements and attempts.

The key to successful youth sport programs is putting the needs of the child first. Programs should be designed to meet the children's needs, not those of adults. Youth sport programs should be organized on a developmental model, not a professional model. Programs should focus on fostering children's physical, cognitive, social, and affective development. The whole child as a moving, thinking, and feeling human being should be considered when designing and conducting youth sport programs.

VIOLENCE IN SPORT

Violence is one of the major problems facing sport today. It is particularly noticeable in professional contact sports such as football and hockey. Physical and psychological intimidation of one's opponent is considered an essential part of many sports. Yet do such forms of intimidation lead to violence? Have coaches gone too far in psyching up their teams to go out and "kill" their opponents? In some contact sports, such as hockey, some players are even designated as "enforcers"–charged with protecting their own players and aggressively intimidating their opponents. However, violence is not limited to contact sports; bench-clearing brawls occur with greater frequency in even noncontact sports such as baseball. Has violence gotten out of control?

The media has done much to bring incidences of sport violence to the public's attention. Television glamorizes such events, often replaying them in slow motion. Videos sent across social media and YouTube are being produced that show incident after incident of players and coaches using violence and force in pursuit of victory.

Some experts have expressed concern that the popularity and visibility of professional athletes lead athletes at lower levels of competition to imitate their actions, including their violent behavior. Other athletes, including those at the high school and even the youth sport level, may emulate the playing style of sport professionals. Thus, violence permeates other levels of sport and its impact on the nature of the game grows.

Spectator violence is also a concern, as media coverage of violent behavior at sport events throughout the world verifies. At some events, fans have stampeded the field and, in the process, trampled other fans to death. Outbreaks of fights among fans are reported. Experts have found that spectator violence is related to the actions of the players during the contests. In essence, player violence tends to increase the likelihood of violence by fans during and following the game. The media's promotion of games for their potential for violence tends to encourage spectator violence. The potential for violence also increases when fans believe that their team was robbed of a score or a victory by incompetent or unfair officiating. Crowd dynamics also influence the occurrence of spectator violence, including the amount of alcohol consumed, the importance of the contest, the demographics of the crowd, and seating arrangements.

Violence between players and spectators is also a concern and parental violence during youth sport events appears to be occurring with distressing frequency. Strong leadership is needed to eliminate parental violence in youth sports, and parents need to be held accountable for their actions. Policies must be established that will serve the best interests of the youth who are participating in these programs.

The question of how to deal with the problem of violence in sport has no single, simple solution. Experts are in agreement, however, that some type of control must be instituted, and it must start with people who love sport and want to protect it from intrusions that will lower its value. They point out that violence is to be abhorred, particularly because it interferes with proper play, detracts from excellent athlete performance, and is barbaric in nature. Most spectators, it is suggested, do not want to see players hurt or severely injured. They want to see clean, hard tackles and body checks. This is the essence of the game and sport itself.

It has been suggested that to reduce violence, stricter penalties should be imposed at all levels of sport. Indeed, athletes in some sports and at some levels of competition are being penalized more severely for violent acts. However, the real and best solution to the problem of violence is a change in attitude on the part of all people concerned. If subscribed to by professional and amateur players, coaches, spectators, sport entrepreneurs, and the public in general, the ideals of playing within the spirit and the letter of the rules, defeating one's opponent when at one's best, and having respect for other players will reduce the violence marring the playing fields and sport arenas today.

The potential for spectator violence can be reduced when some forethought is given to the factors that contribute to violence and thoughtful planning results in steps to minimize the occurrence of these factors. Reducing violence among contestants, decreasing the media hype that portrays the contest as a confrontation among hostile opponents, using competent officials to control the flow of the game, and taking preventive crowd control measures can decrease spectator violence. Violence can also be decreased by formulating better relations between the teams and the communities and by athletes' taking steps to become actively involved in the communities in which they play and live.

PERFORMANCE-ENHANCING SUBSTANCES IN SPORT

Citius, altius, fortius–the Olympic motto of "swifter, higher, stronger"–embodies the quest for excellence for many athletes. At the elite level, where races are won by a thousandth of a second, a gold medal by a tenth of a point, and fame by a fraction of a centimeter, athletes are constantly experimenting with new ways to enhance their performance. Today, being swifter, higher, and stronger than one's competitors may lead athletes to seek "better performance through chemistry" and use or abuse performance-enhancing substances. Unfortunately, the use and abuse of performance-enhancing substances is not only a problem at the elite level, but one that has filtered down to athletes at the collegiate and high school levels.

Professional leagues, sporting bodies, the International Olympic Committee, and the NCAA are among the organizations that have antidoping policies, with accompanying long lists of banned substances. Among those substances are anabolic steroids, human growth hormone, and amphetamines, as well as their derivatives. Athletes take these and other substances, often at many times the recommended doses, in an effort to gain strength, increase power, work harder during training, or enhance endurance. The ultimate goal is to improve one's performance.

Coakley defines sport ethic as a "set of norms accepted as the dominant criteria for defining what is required to be defined and accepted as an athlete in power and performance sports."[2] The three norms dedicated to "the game" are striving for distinction, taking risks and playing through the pain, and accepting no limits in pursuit of success.

When athletes embrace the sport ethic, they give sport priority over all aspects of their life. They pressure themselves to live up to their own expectations as well as those of their coaches and their teammates. They have the proper attitude and demonstrate their commitment to the game by meeting the expectations of other athletes, making sacrifices, and facing the demands of competition.[2] Athletes strive to achieve distinction, constantly seeking to improve and achieve at the highest level. Athletes take risks; they do not back down from a challenge. Courage enables them to overcome fear and accept risk of failure. It is courage that enables athletes to play in pain. Lastly, athletes pursue their dream with dedication, believing that success is possible for those willing to work hard to achieve it.

When athletes go to the extreme to conform to the sport ethic, this overconformity carries with it significant risks to their health and well-being. Examples of overconformity that present health risks to athletes include severely restricting food and prolonged exercising in rubber suits to make weight in wrestling, running an excessive number of miles in training for cross-country, and using huge doses of pain killers to play when injured. Why do athletes, often unquestioning, take such risks?

The use of banned performance-enhancing substances falls within the range of deviant overconformity to the sport ethic. It is not, as some would suggest, because athletes are not disciplined enough to achieve gains through hard work. Nor is it really a desire to cheat. Athletes view performance-enhancing substances as a means to gain an edge. Some see the use of such substances as the avenue to being able to play at the highest possible level, an opportunity to stay involved in a sport they love. Athletes who are deeply committed to their sport often will do whatever it takes to achieve distinction.

How widespread the use of banned performance-enhancing substances is among athletes is difficult to determine. One way the sport world has sought to cope with the use of illegal performance-enhancing substances is through drug testing. Two of the many drug testing agencies are the World Anti-Doping Agency and the United States Anti-Doping Agency. They conduct drug testing for athletes involved in Olympic sports.

Drug testing is controversial. Critics consider drug testing a violation of privacy rights, and in some societies, it violates cultural norms. Additionally, as rapidly as new tests are developed for banned substances, athletes switch to an undetectable drug or use masking drugs to obscure test results. Drug testing is also costly, and paying for testing draws on funds that could be used to provide health programs for athletes. Proponents of drug testing see it as necessary in order to protect the health of athletes. Testing is also necessary to guarantee a level playing field, where the winners are those who have toiled diligently to develop their skills rather than those athletes who have access to performance-enhancing substances.

Educational programs and treatment approaches have been used to try to stem the use of illegal performance-enhancing substances. Strong punishment for violators, such as a lifetime suspension or a 2-year ban from competition, stands

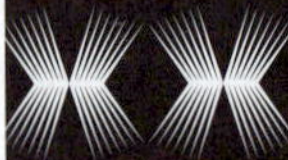

FOCUS ON CAREER: Sport Sociology

PROFESSIONAL ORGANIZATIONS	• International Sociology of Sport Association • North American Society for the Sociology of Sport
PROFESSIONAL JOURNALS	• *International Review for the Sociology of Sport* • *Journal of Sport and Social Issues* • *Quest* • *Research Quarterly for Exercise and Sport* • *Sociology of Sport Journal* • *Women in Sport and Physical Activity Journal*

as a powerful deterrent to the use of illegal performance-enhancing substances. Despite these and other approaches, news headlines continue to report stories of track stars, football players, baseball standouts, elite cyclists, and other athletes found to be using illegal drugs to gain a performance edge.

In order to transform sport and deal with current and future challenges, all those involved in sport should think critically about the meaning, purpose, and organization of sport and take an active role in addressing these challenges in order to maintain the integrity of sport performance.

CURRENT TRENDS: MOVING TOWARD THE FUTURE

- The names of team mascots will become more considerate and inclusive of all individuals and move away from the misrepresentation and racism that have been a part of team affiliation for many years.
- Sport will continue to be a big business deep into the twenty-first century. Athlete salaries will continue to rise. Ticket and clothing sales will be extensive for teams that are successful. Top collegiate athletes will face decisions on whether to take financial and gift offers or an opportunity to make millions of dollars before they complete their college education.
- Athletes involved in sport specialization and travel teams will become more prominent than multisport athletes, as early as the youth level.
- Performance-enhancing substances and other issues that question sport ethic will play a factor as to whether athletes are recruited into the big leagues or are selected into a sport hall of fame.

SUMMARY

Sport is an important part of American culture. As a social institution, sport influences and is influenced by other institutions in our society, such as politics, education, family, religion, and the media. Its pervasiveness has led to the study of sport from a sociological perspective.

Sport has a significant role in educational institutions. Almost 8 million youths play sports at the high school level. At the collegiate level, thousands of young adults compete. Sport can have both a positive and negative influence on the lives of its participants. Among the problems associated with sport in educational institutions are an overemphasis on winning, athletic goals overshadowing academic goals, soaring expenditures, continued growth of big-time sport, and inequities in opportunities for women and minorities.

Sport sociologists are interested in transforming sport, changing the nature of sport so that it is more equitable and beneficial for those involved. Racism, including the use of Native American imagery, is one of the topics studied by sport sociologists. Among other topics studied are gender issues, opportunities for girls and women in sports, sport for people with disabilities, violence in sport, and the use of performance-enhancing substances.

It is important for physical education, exercise science, and sport professionals to understand the significant role of sport as an institution in our society. In the future, it is hoped that as a professional in this field, you will take a more active role in creating greater opportunities for all people in sport.

DISCUSSION QUESTIONS

1. What is the role of sport in American culture and its impact on various institutions in society, such as economics, education, family, and the media?
2. How can social inequities in sport be addressed? Who can make such changes? How will this have an effect at the youth, interscholastic, intercollegiate, and professional levels?
3. Consider the information provided in this chapter on Title IX. Is your high school, college, or university meeting one or more prongs of the three-pronged test used to determine compliance? Describe how it is or is not in compliance. What implications could the results have on male and female sport participation?
4. What do you perceive will be the nature of the sport experience–for players, coaches, and spectators–over the next 10–20 years?

GET CONNECTED

University of Central Florida Institute for Diversity and Ethics in Sport–provides access to issues pertaining to race and gender within amateur, collegiate, and professional sports; current Race and Gender Report Cards for various sports; and information about the academic progress of collegiate athletes, including those who are participating in football bowl games or men's and women's NCAA Division I basketball championships.

https://www.tidesport.org/racial-gender-report-card

Institute for the Study of Youth Sports–offers information for parents, coaches, researchers, and youth on various aspects of youth sports, including the Bill of Rights for Young Athletes, coaching certification, and a coaches' code of conduct.

https://edwp.educ.msu.edu/isys/

National Alliance for Youth Sports–gives access to information about youth sports, links, and information for players, parents, coaches, and administrators.

https://www.nays.org

National Collegiate Athletic Association–provides information on many different aspects of collegiate sport, including current news. Click on Key Issues to access information on gender equity, participation rates, drug testing, and a multitude of other topics.

http://www.ncaa.org

Women's Sports Foundation–provides information on current issues, career opportunities, upcoming events, and links to research and topics of interest, including Title IX.

https://www.womenssportsfoundation.org/

SELF-ASSESSMENT ACTIVITIES

These activities are designed to help you determine if you have mastered the materials and competencies presented in this chapter.

1. Use the information provided in the Get Connected box to explore more deeply the extent of participation by girls and women in sport. What are the benefits of participation? How can participation be increased further, especially among underrepresented population groups such as racial minorities and girls and women from low socioeconomic backgrounds? What can be done to increase the number of women in coaching and athletic administration?
2. Using the information in the Get Connected box, access the University of Central Florida's Institute for Diversity and Ethics in Sport. Browse through the reports provided on gender equity, racial diversity, and academic progress of collegiate athletes. Select one report to read and summarize. Use a form of technology to make a presentation on your topic to your class or group. Be sure to include statistics to support your points.
3. Interview two college students who played high school sports, one of whom plays on an intercollegiate team, about their experiences as students and as athletes, and how their experiences of being athletes changed their experiences of being students. Using the information provided in the chapter, create specific questions in relation to race, gender, sexuality, opportunity, discrimination, GPA, standardized exams, and other topics you deem pertinent to the player's story. Write a reflective paper synthesizing the students' experiences and relate it back to the data in the chapter.
4. Native American imagery is used for sport team names and mascots at all sport levels: professional, intercollegiate, and interscholastic. Explore the sport teams, at all levels, in your area and evaluate their team names and mascots–do they use Native American imagery and if so, is it used appropriately? If not, write an argumentative letter to the organization as to why their team name and/or mascot is discriminatory and provide supportive reasons as to why they should change the name/mascot.

REFERENCES

1. Sporting News. (2022). Super bowl commercial cost in 2022: How much money is an ad for Super Bowl 56? https://www.sportingnews.com/us/nfl/news/super-bowl-commercials-cost-2022/v9ytfqzx74pjrcdvxyhevlzd.
2. Coakley, J. (2009). *Sport in society: Issues and controversies* (10th ed.). New York, NY: McGraw Hill.
3. Coakley, J. (1998). *Sport in society: Issues and controversies* (6th ed.). Dubuque, IA: WCB/McGraw Hill.
4. Coakley, J. (2015). *Sport in society: Issues and controversies* (11th ed.). New York, NY: McGraw Hill.
5. National Federation of State High School Associations. (2022). 2018–2019 high school athletics participation survey. http://www.nfhs.org/.
6. National Collegiate Athletic Association. (2022). *Membership. www.ncaa.org.*
7. Siedentop, D. (2009). *Introduction to physical education, fitness, and sport* (7th ed.). Mountain View, CA: Mayfield.
8. National Collegiate Athletic Association. (2006). 2006 fact sheet. Retrieved from https://www.ncaa.org.
9. National Collegiate Athletic Association. (2019). About us. Retrieved from https://www.ncaa.org/about.
10. National Collegiate Athletic Association. (2011). 2011 NCAA graduation rates report. Retrieved June 13, 2013, from http://www.ncaa.org.
11. National Collegiate Athletic Association. (2022). Academic Progress Rate. www.ncaa.org.
12. National Collegiate Athletic Association. (2009). History of academic reform. Retrieved May 26, 2010, from http://www.ncaa.org.
13. National Collegiate Athletic Association. (2022). Initial eligibility requirements for Division I student-athletes. www.ncaa.org.
14. National Collegiate Athletic Association. (2011). Remaining eligible. Retrieved June 14, 2013, from http://www.ncaa.org.

15. National Collegiate Athletic Association. (2010). NCAA signs new 14-year TV deal for DI men's basketball; CBS and Turner join forces to pay $10.8 billion for tournament rights fee. Retrieved from http://www.ncaa.org.
16. Knight Commission on Intercollegiate Athletics. (2022). www.knightcommission.org.
17. National Collegiate Athletic Association. (2022). Women's basketball attendance. https://www.ncaa.org/sports/2013/11/27/women-s-basketball-attendance.aspx.
18. Messner, M. A., & Cooky, C. (2010). *Gender in televised sports: News and highlights shows, 1989-2009*. California: Center for Feminist Research, University of Southern California.
19. Women's National Basketball Association. Retrieved from http://www.wnba.com.
20. FIFA. (2022). World ranking. https://www.fifa.com/fifa-world-ranking/.
21. Lapchick, R. E. (2022). 2021 racial and gender report card. Institute for Diversity and Ethics in sport. https://www.tidesport.org/college.
22. Lapchick, R.E. (2022). 2020 racial and gender report card. Institute for Diversity and Ethics in Sport, UCF College of Business Administration. https://www.tidesport.org/racial-gender-report-card.
23. Oxedine, J. B. (1995). *American Indian sports heritage* (2nd ed.). Champaign, IL: Human Kinetics.
24. United States Commission on Civil Rights. (2001). Commission statement on the use of Native American images and nicknames as sports symbols, Washington, DC: United States Commission on Civil Rights.
25. Staurowsky, E. J. (2013). U.S. Office for Civil Rights asked to ban American Indian mascots in Michigan public schools. Retrieved April 28, 2019, from http://www.huffingtonpost.com/ellen-j-staurowsky/us-office-for-civil-right_b_2665729.html.
26. Engaged Sport. (2016). Youth sport participation statistics and trends. Retrieved April 28, 2019, from http://www.engagesports.com/blog/post/1488/youth-sports-participation-statistics-and-trends.

Polka Dot Images/Getty Images

CHAPTER 9

SPORT AND PHYSICAL ACTIVITY PSYCHOLOGY

OBJECTIVES

After reading this chapter, students should be able to–

- Describe the psychological benefits of participation in physical activities.
- Comprehend the different theories of behavior and their potential application to physical activity behavior.
- Discuss the roles of anxiety and arousal in the performance of motor skills and the application of intervention strategies to enhance performance.
- Understand motivation, goal setting, self-talk, imagery, and how they can be effectively used in physical education, exercise, and sport.
- Articulate the importance of in addressing the mental health of athletes.

Sport and physical activity psychology has its legacy in psychology. In the 1970s, as the academic scope of physical education grew, sport psychology emerged as a subdiscipline. Initially, sport psychologists focused on competitive sport and the elite athlete. As sport psychology grew as an area of inquiry, sport psychologists became interested in studying participation in exercise and other facets of physical activity. Additionally, their focus broadened from working with elite competitors to include people of all ages and abilities. Today, the name of the discipline–sport and physical activity psychology–reflects its expanded focus and growth as an area of study in its own right.

This chapter provides a short introduction to sport and physical activity psychology. Selected topics within sport and physical activity psychology are briefly discussed; space limitations preclude the inclusion of more topics and limit the depth of discussion. Given that caveat, this chapter presents information on motivation, the psychological benefits of physical activity, exercise adherence, personality, anxiety and arousal, goal setting, self-talk, and various intervention strategies. It also includes an all too brief section on athletic participation and mental health. It is hoped that this brief glimpse will stimulate your interest in this area and encourage further study.

SOCIAL JUSTICE

Talking Points

- Professionals need to consider issues of privilege and oppression and how they might impact participants' motivation in physical activity, physical education, and sport.
- Culturally relevant strategies can play an important role in facilitating engagement in physical activity for people of all ages.
- Psychological skills training should be individualized, and professionals should strive to use culturally congruent approaches that are respectful of individual differences.
- Underrepresented populations need to be recruited and trained as sport psychologists.

SPORT AND PHYSICAL ACTIVITY PSYCHOLOGY

Sport and physical activity psychology continues to grow rapidly. Initially, sport psychology was closely aligned with motor learning; however, today it is a distinct field of study. The definition, scope, and areas of study within sport and physical activity psychology are described briefly in this section.

Definition and Scope

Sport and exercise or more broadly physical activity psychology is defined by Vealey as "the systematic scholarly study of the behavior, feelings, and thoughts of people engaged in sport, exercise, and physical activity."[1] According to the Association for Applied Sport Psychology (AASP), sport and exercise psychology focuses on the psychological and mental aspects of participation in sport and exercise, seeking to understand how psychological processes influence and are influenced by participation.[2] The International Society of Sport Psychology states that "this dynamic field can enhance the experience of men, women, and children of all ages who participate in physical activity, ranking from those who do so for personal enjoyment to those who pursue a specific activity at the elite level."[3]

The scope of sport and physical activity psychology is quite broad, encompassing both theoretical and applied approaches. The initial work in this area focused on sport and elite athletes.[4] Today, the focus has expanded and includes the psychological dimensions of competitive sport participation and engagement in fitness, exercise, and physical activity. Professionals seek to understand, influence, and improve the experiences of people of all ages and abilities, ranging from the youth sport participant to the elite Olympic performer and from the elderly individual engaging in a cardiac exercise rehabilitation program to the healthy adult who enjoys lifting weights on a regular basis.

Areas of Study

Sport and physical activity psychology includes many different areas of study. Professionals are interested in understanding factors that influence participation in sport and exercise. For example, why do some athletes "choke" under pressure? Why do some postcardiac patients fail to complete their rehabilitation program? Professionals also study the psychological outcomes derived from participation. For instance, does participation in an exercise program reduce stress and alleviate depression? Does participation in youth sport build character?

Sport and physical activity psychology can also help professionals make modifications to sport and exercise programs to enrich the experience for the participants involved. This could include helping athletes learn techniques to regulate their level of arousal to achieve optimal performance, teaching coaches how to promote self-confidence or to motivate their athletes, or building more social support into exercise programs to promote adherence and provide greater enjoyment for the participants.

Areas of study within sport and physical activity psychology include attentional focus, personality, aggression and violence, self-confidence and self-efficacy, self-talk, arousal, social reinforcement, adherence, team building, commitment, level of aspiration, and athlete mental health. Researchers design and assess the effectiveness of various interventions to enhance performance and participation, such as cognitive restructuring, mental rehearsal, and social support. Researchers are also interested in factors that cause people to become involved in sport and physical activity and those factors that lead to people dropping out or discontinuing participation.

The amount of research produced by scholars in sport and physical activity psychology has grown tremendously over the past decade. Examples of questions that may be investigated by researchers include:

- Is the personality profile of the outstanding or elite athlete different from that of the average athlete or nonathlete?
- How does participation in an exercise program influence one's body image? Or one's feelings of self-efficacy and control?
- What are the psychological benefits derived from participation in physical activity? How long and how intense (dose-response relationship) should physical activity be in order to yield psychological benefits?
- How can an athlete deal most effectively with the stress of competition?
- What factors influence an individual's adherence to an exercise or rehabilitation program?
- Does participation in sport empower athletes with disabilities?
- How can self-efficacy in adolescents be increased to promote the establishment of beneficial physical activity patterns?
- What early interventions are most effective in responding to athletes' mental health needs?

These are only a sample of the myriad of questions that may be addressed by researchers.

Sport psychologists today work with athletes to help them perform at their optimal level. They work with professional sport teams, national sport teams, and intercollegiate teams. Some professional athletes or elite athletes, such as figure skaters, may engage the services of a personal sport psychologist to help them achieve their goals.

Knowledge of sport psychology is important to coaches at all levels. It can help coaches more fully understand the psychological impact of their coaching behaviors and decisions on the athletes. Coaches can incorporate information from sport psychology into their preparation of athletes for competition and use information during competition to help their teams perform at their highest possible level. Additionally, coaches may find it beneficial to understand the factors that contribute to athletes' continuing commitment to a sport and the factors that predispose athletes to discontinue sport participation.

Specialists in physical activity psychology focus their efforts on individuals participating in exercise and rehabilitation programs. Researchers have sought to identify the psychological determinants of participation in physical activity and the factors that influence the completion of rehabilitation regimens. Given the documented evidence supporting the contribution of regular physical activity to health, understanding the psychological dimensions of participation is of critical importance to professionals working in these areas. Such an understanding can help practitioners design programs and structure experiences to enhance the probability that program participants will engage in physical activity to the extent necessary to realize health benefits and incorporate physical activity into their lifestyle.

Sport and physical activity psychologists can provide educational or clinical services, depending on their credentials. Clinical sport psychologists have extensive training in psychology and are licensed by state boards to treat people with psychopathology. Clinical sports psychologists may treat participants with personality disorders, eating disorders, or chemical dependency. They supplement their training in psychology with additional training in sport and exercise psychology. An increased awareness of the mental health needs of athletes highlights the importance of sport psychologists participating as a member of the athletes' care team, alongside team physicians and athletic trainers.

Educational sport and physical activity psychologists often have a background in physical education, exercise science, and sport, with extensive training in sport and exercise psychology. They are not licensed psychologists. The Association for the Advancement of Applied Sport Psychology (AASP) offers a certification program. The Certified Mental Performance Consultant (CMPC) for applied sport psychology recognizes attainment of professional knowledge in sport psychology, including health and exercise psychology, intervention and performance enhancement, and social psychology.[2]

Certified consultants engage in educational activities focused on "helping performers develop and strengthen their mental, self-regulatory, and life skills to optimize performance, enjoyment, and personal development."[2] Examples of these activities include educating individuals and groups about the role of psychological factors in exercise, physical activity, and sport and teaching participants' specific psychological skills such as goal-setting or coping skills that they can use to enhance their participation. Another activity is the education of organizations and groups in areas such as development of team cohesion, resolution of conflicts, strategies to promote exercise adherence, and modification of youth sport programs to enhance the experience for the young athletes.

Sport and physical activity psychology encompasses many areas of study. The next section will provide a brief overview of some topics within this discipline. First, the psychological benefits of physical activity are presented, followed by information on motivation and exercise adherence. Personality, anxiety and arousal, self-talk, and imagery are addressed. Athletes' mental health needs and a short discussion of various psychological intervention techniques concludes the chapter.

PSYCHOLOGICAL BENEFITS OF PHYSICAL ACTIVITY

The role of physical activity (PA) in enhancing well-being is receiving increased professional and public recognition. The physiological effects of engaging in PA on a regular basis are well documented. There is also a growing body of evidence supporting the psychological benefits of PA.[2,5,6] Psychological benefits have been noted for both aerobic and resistance exercise. It appears that moderate-intensity exercise is most effective in eliciting psychological benefits.

The psychological benefits of participating in PA include:

- improved health-related quality of life, by enhancing both psychological and physical well-being;
- improved mood. Mood states influence our outlook on life, emotions, thought processes, and behaviors;
- reduction of symptoms associated with mild depression. PA may be a valuable adjunct to therapy in cases of chronic, severe depression;
- reduced state anxiety–that is, feelings of tension, apprehension, and fear associated with various situations;
- effective stress management. PA can serve as a buffer against stress as well as provide a healthful means of stress reduction;
- contribution to the development of the self. PA enhances self-concept and improves self-esteem or feelings of worth. It can promote greater self-efficacy and self-confidence;
- recreation and a change of pace from long hours of work or study. Individuals return to their daily routine feeling refreshed, both mentally and physically;
- challenges that, when successfully met, provide a sense of achievement;
- aesthetic and creative experiences. Activities such as dance allow individuals to express their emotions in a nonverbal manner and provide opportunities for individual interpretation.

PSYCHOLOGICAL BENEFITS OF PHYSICAL ACTIVITY

- Improves health-related quality of life.
- Enhances mood.
- Alleviates symptoms of mild depression.
- Reduces state and trait anxiety.
- Serves as a buffer against stress and means of stress reduction.
- Enhances self-efficacy, self-confidence, and self-esteem.
- Offers a means of affiliation with others.
- Provides opportunities to refresh and reenergize.
- Presents challenges that can lead to sense of achievement.
- Gives means for nonverbal expression of emotion.
- Provides opportunities for creative and aesthetic expression.

The psychological benefits of PA are being increasingly understood and offer exciting possibilities for research.

The value of PA as a therapeutic modality is increasing, and new avenues are being explored. However, Fontaine points out that several important questions need to be addressed about the therapeutic value of PA. These questions include:

1. How and under what circumstances should PA be incorporated into therapy for patients with mental health disorders?
2. What are the long-term effects of PA on mental health disorders?
3. Does regular PA protect against developing mental health disorders?
4. What is the optimal PA prescription for various mental health disorders?[7]

Fontaine notes that despite these questions, it appears that PA can play an important role in the treatment of mental health disorders.[7]

Although the health benefits of exercise and its positive impact on psychological states are known, one of our challenges as professionals is to motivate people to initiate and maintain an exercise routine or engage in PA on a regular basis. For some individuals, getting started is an overwhelming task. While 30 minutes of moderate exercise a day is recommended (e.g., walking fast but still able to talk), this can be broken down into 10-minute sessions throughout the day. For some individuals, starting with just 5 minutes a day might be a good step forward. Additionally, encouraging individuals to exercise at an intensity that is comfortable for them may promote greater adherence to exercise. Pairing exercise with a pleasurable activity, such as listening to music, can also be helpful. Above all, individual differences should be respected while encouraging engagement in PA. Not everyone loves to jog; some may prefer swimming or biking or hiking. The key is to find what works for the individual.

MOTIVATION

Motivation is a critical factor in learning, performance, and participation in sport and physical activity. It influences the initiation, maintenance, and intensity of behavior. Motivation directs and energizes us; it determines whether or not we will practice with a high level of intensity or get up at 6 A.M. to work out before work. Motivation influences whether we will continue an activity or choose to discontinue participation. As previously discussed in Chapter 5, motivation can be influenced by internal and external factors.

Individuals are intrinsically motivated when the motive for starting or engaging in a behavior is derived from the individual's own desires, enjoyment, needs, and aspirations. For example, a soccer player who engages in the sport because of love and passion for the "beautiful game" or an adult who desires to be healthy and joins a water aerobics program are intrinsically motivated. Intrinsic motives drive a person who is quadriplegic to play quad rugby; the competition associated with the sport as well as the camaraderie gained from being part of a team are strong motives for participation.

On the other hand, individuals are extrinsically motivated when they engage in an activity in hopes of gaining external rewards. An employee who signs up for a worksite fitness program to gain the $1,000 bonus promised by the employer for participation is extrinsically motivated. A young gymnast who competes to gain trophies and parental approval is participating for the external rewards.

Intrinsic motivation is more conducive to long-term commitment and engagement in sport and physical activity. There are many theories explaining motivation. However, as Vealey points out, "the key to understanding motivation is realizing that all humans, regardless of their individual goals, are motivated to feel competent, worthy, and self-determining."[1] The question, then, for us as professionals is, what can we do to help individuals develop or increase their intrinsic motivation?[1] This answer is complex and reflects an intersection of a multitude of factors, but simply stated, we can create opportunities to help individuals develop competence and promote feelings of self-efficacy. We can promote feelings of personal accomplishment, recognize hard work, engender self-confidence, and offer support as individuals pursue their goals. It is important that we recognize that participants' motives for participation in our programs vary, and we need to respect their motives. However, if we want to sustain participation, we must focus on pro moting intrinsic motivation.

Professionals are increasingly concerned about amotivation. Amotivation is the lack of interest or desire to engage in a specific behavior, such as physical activity.[8] This may manifest itself in individuals lack of desire to be physically active, preferring to adopt a more sedentary lifestyle. One particular concern being voiced by physical educators is the presence of amotivated students in physical education classes. Amotivated students have low motivation, characterized by a lack of desire to engage in physical education activities.[8,9] As a result, they may not develop the skills, knowledge, or attitudes to participate in physical activity outside of the school setting or throughout life.

According to Perlman, these students are marginally involved and often perceive themselves as lacking ability.[8] They believe that the tasks are too difficult for them, even when tasks are modified to accommodate individual differences in skills. Another concern shared by amotivated students is the lack of social connection to their peers, in particular to those with high athletic ability or popularity.[9]

Researchers have found that physical educators who design learning experiences to promote perceived competence, address students' need for autonomy, and encourage relatedness can increase students' motivation.[8,9,10] Curriculum models, such as the sport education model, with its emphasis on game play, responsibility, and team affiliation, and teaching styles that promote autonomy can facilitate changes in amotivated students' behaviors (see Chapter 10).[8,11,12] The teaching of novel sport activities in physical education, such as disc golf, rather than more traditional activities, such as softball, and providing opportunities for students to select groups within to work can positively affect amotivated students.[9] As professionals concerned with the promotion of physical activity, both within and outside the school setting, we need to be aware of what motivates children and youth to be active, so we can develop effective programs to address their interests and needs. As Chen states, we need to figure out how to change children's motivation patterns from "What I have to do or need to do" to "what I want to do" if we aspire to address the growing sedentary behavior in our society.[10]

Motivation is critical to the initiation, persistence, or maintenance of the desired behavior, whether it is related to participation in competitive sport or engagement in physical activity for health, enjoyment, or recreation. What motivates an individual to begin a new sport or to start a fitness routine? Equally important, once the new behavior is initiated, what contributes to an individual's continuing the behavior? And what motivates an individual to work hard to achieve desired goals? Sustaining engagement in physical activity is important to the realization of the physiological and psychological benefits associated with participation in regular physical activity. Research on

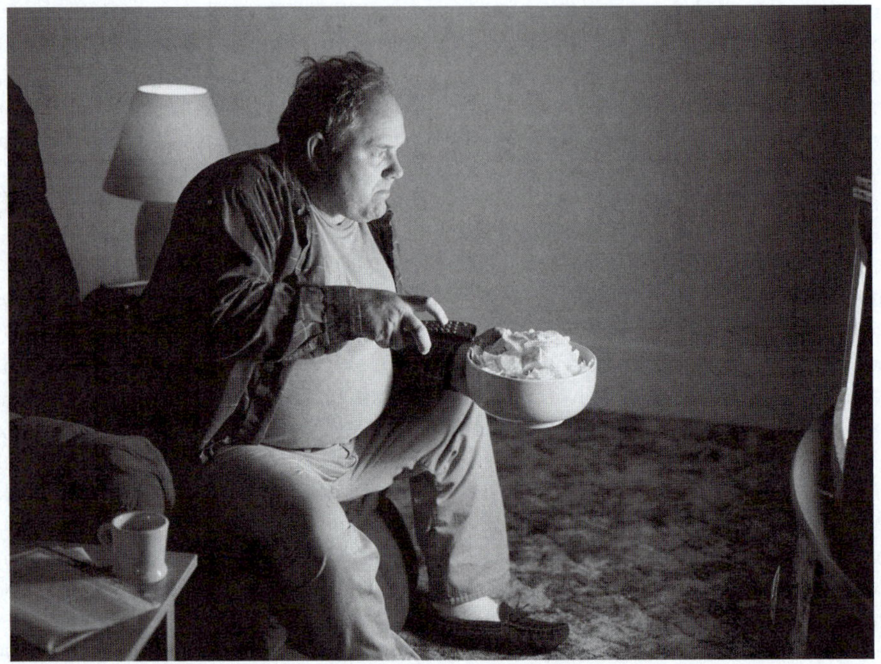

As professionals, we must develop effective behavioral strategies to help sedentary individuals adopt a healthy, active lifestyle.

Ryan McVay/Photodisc/Getty Images

exercise adherence has helped us determine factors that contribute to individuals' continuing to work out and incorporating physical activity into their lives.

EXERCISE ADHERENCE

An expanding area of research is investigation of exercise adherence. The past decade has brought greater recognition of the value of exercise as a therapeutic modality. Exercise is increasingly being prescribed as part of an overall treatment approach to several diseases, including cardiovascular diseases and diabetes. Unfortunately, adherence to supervised exercise programs is low, with about 50% of adults who start an exercise program dropping out within the first few months.[13] Other researchers report that only 30% of individuals who begin an exercise program will be exercising at the end of 3 years.[14] Dishman points out that much of our research efforts have focused on increasing adoption of physical activity.[13] Our efforts also have to focus on sustaining involvement in physical activity.

Understanding Behavior Change

How do you get people to begin to lead a more active lifestyle? How do you promote behavior change? Many theories and models of human behavior have been used to guide interventions to promote a more physically active lifestyle and encourage health-promoting behaviors. Among the models are the classic learning theories, the health belief model, social cognitive theory, theory of reasoned action and planned behavior, the transtheoretical model, and the ecological perspective.

The *classic learning theories* emphasizes that learning a new complex pattern of behavior, such as moving from a sedentary to an active lifestyle, is achieved by altering many of the small behaviors that comprise the overall behavior. This suggests that a targeted behavior, such as walking continuously for 30 minutes a day, is best learned by breaking down the behavior into smaller goals to be achieved, such as walking for 10 minutes daily. Incremental increases, such as adding 5 minutes to daily walking a week, are then made as the behavior is gradually shaped toward the targeted goal. Rewards and incentives, both immediate and long-range, serve as reinforcement and motivation for the individual to achieve and maintain the targeted behavior. Looking better, receiving a T-shirt for participation, and experiencing a feeling of accomplishment all strengthen and sustain the behavior change.

The *health belief model* emphasizes that the adoption of a health behavior depends on the person's perception of four factors: the severity of the potential illness, the person's susceptibility to that illness, the benefits of taking action, and the barriers to action. Incorporation of cues to action, such as listing walking on your daily to-do list, is important in eliciting and sustaining the desired behavior. *Self-efficacy*, a person's confidence in his or her capability to perform the desired behavior, is included as an important component of this model.

Social cognitive theory states that behavior change is influenced by environmental factors, personal factors, and attributes of the behavior itself. Self-efficacy is central to this model. A person must believe in one's ability to perform the behavior (self-efficacy) and must perceive an incentive for changing the behavior. The outcomes derived from the behavior must be valued by the person. These benefits can be immediate in nature, such as feelings of satisfaction or enjoyment from engaging in the behavior, or long-term, such as improved health from being physically active on a regular basis.

The *theory of reasoned action* is based on the idea that the most important determinant of an individual's behavior is the intention to perform that behavior. Intention is influenced by two factors: the individual's attitude toward the behavior and the influence of relevant others in the environment. The individual's attitude reflects beliefs about the outcomes of the behavior and the values gained from changing the behavior. If the individual sees the outcome of changing a behavior as positive, this increases the likelihood of change. If relevant, others support changing the behavior, and the individual is strongly motivated by the opinions of others, this also supports behavior change.

The *theory of planned action* incorporates the tenets of the theory of reasoned action and adds another concept–perceived control. *Perceived control* is similar to the concept of self-efficacy and reflects the individual's beliefs about one's ability to perform the behavior. Individuals who intend to become more active are more likely to do so if they see being active as having a positive benefit, receive support from others for being active, and perceive themselves as being successful in being physically active.

The *transtheoretical model* of health behavior uses the concept of stages of change to integrate the processes and principles of change relating to health behavior.[15] (See the Transtheoretical Model and Its Application to Promotion of Physical Activity box.) The transtheoretical model views behavioral change as a spiraling continuum that begins at a "firm conviction to maintain the status quo by never changing, and proceeds through the conditions of someday, soon, now, and forever."[16] The stages of change are:

- Precontemplation
- Contemplation
- Preparation
- Action
- Maintenance
- Termination[15,16]

In this approach, a relapse or discontinuation of the behavior, such as ceasing to exercise, is seen as a return from the action or maintenance stage to an earlier stage. Relapse should be dealt with in a positive way so that the person does not see it as a failure and become demoralized, but rather perceives it as a natural part of the process of change. Relapse presents individuals with an opportunity to learn which behavior strategies worked and which ones did not.[17]

SELECTED THEORIES AND MODELS OF HEALTH BEHAVIOR CHANGE

Theory/Model	Description
Classic learning theory	New behaviors are learned. • Achievement of smaller goals leads to attainment of overall goals. • Reinforcement and motivation are critical.
Health belief model	Adoption of a health behavior depends on the person's perception of four factors: • Severity of the potential illness. • Susceptibility to that illness. • Benefits of taking action. • Barriers to action. Self-efficacy plays an important role.
Social cognitive theory	Behavior change is influenced by environmental and personal factors and attributes of the behavior itself. • Self-efficacy is a critical component. • Requires a perceived incentive for changing behavior. • Outcomes must be valued by the person.
Theory of reasoned action and theory of planned behavior	Behavior change is strongly influenced by intention to change, which depends on: • Individual's attitude toward the behavior. • Opinions of relevant others regarding the change. • Perceived control over behavior.
Transtheoretical model	Behavior change proceeds through stages: • Precontemplation. • Contemplation. • Preparation. • Action. • Maintenance. • Termination. Decisional balance and self-efficacy play an important role in the adoption of new behaviors.
Ecological approach	Health behavior change is affected by: • Individual factors. • Sociocultural context. • Environmental influences.

Decisional balance and self-efficacy are important aspects of the transtheoretical model. *Decisional balance* involves weighing the relative pros and cons of the behavioral change–that is, perceived benefits, drawbacks, and barriers to change.[18] Self-efficacy is a person's confidence about their competence or abilities in a specific situation. In the context of behavioral change, self-efficacy is a person's belief that they can maintain a healthy behavior, such as exercising, or abstain from an unhealthy behavior, such as smoking.

TRANSTHEORETICAL MODEL AND ITS APPLICATION TO PROMOTION OF PHYSICAL ACTIVITY

Stage of Change	Behaviors	Suggested Approaches by Professional
Precontemplation	No intention to change behavior in next 6 months	Educate the individual and deliver a clear message about the importance of physical activity to health.
Contemplation	Awareness of the problem, the pros and cons of change; intention to take action within next 6 months	Highlight the benefits of change and try to shift the decisional balance.
Preparation	Taking small steps or developing a specific plan of action to begin physical activity program (e.g., checking out walking routes or joining a fitness club)	Help the individual identify the best time to walk and safe walking route; teach the individual warm-up and cooldown stretches; assist the individual in developing a progressive walking plan (20 minutes at a moderate pace three times a week progressing to 30 minutes of brisk walking most days of the week).
Action	Making modifications in lifestyle and engaging in physical activity (e.g., getting up an hour earlier to fit walking into day); commitment to exercise	Encourage and support the individual in becoming active; help the individual monitor physical activity; discuss modifications in program as situation changes.
Maintenance	Sustaining the change in behavior for at least 6 months; becoming increasingly confident in ability to sustain change (e.g., continuing to walk on daily basis); exercise becomes routine	Support the individual in remaining active; explore ideas with the individual for continuing to be active even when the schedule changes and the individual cannot walk at the usual time, etc.
Termination	Behavior is fully integrated into lifestyle (e.g., walking is planned for as part of the day's activities); exercise patterns are integral part of life	The individual walks as part of the daily routine; offer to be available as a resource.
Relapse	Move to previous stage	Remind the individual that relapse gives the opportunity to rethink physical activity strategy—what worked and what should be changed; encourage the individual to recommence physical activity at an appropriate level.

Source: Adapted from Duffy, F. D., and L. Schnirring. "How to Counsel Patients about Exercise: An Office-Friendly Approach." *The Physician and Sportsmedicine* 28, no. 10 (2000): 53–54.

The transtheoretical model has most frequently been applied to the cessation of unhealthy, addictive behaviors and more recently to the acquisition of healthy behaviors such as exercise. It offers professionals insight into the process of change and guidelines for developing intervention programs.

Another model that has increased in popularity in the last decade is the ecological approach. One criticism of many theories and models for changing health behavior is that they emphasize individual behavior change while paying little attention to the sociocultural and environmental

PROMOTING EXERCISE ADHERENCE

- Structure program to optimize social support to participants.
- Offer programs at convenient times and locations.
- Utilize goal setting, on both a short- and long-term basis.
- Provide frequent assessment of progress.
- Use qualified and enthusiastic leaders.
- Foster communication between leader and participants.
- Develop rapport among leader and participants.
- Involve a variety of enjoyable activities.
- Give participants a choice of activities.
- Tailor frequency, intensity, and duration of activities to individuals' needs.
- Incorporate reinforcement and rewards.
- Consider social and cultural factors in program design.

influences on behavior. The *ecological approach* emphasizes a comprehensive approach to health, including developing individual skills and creating supportive, health-promoting environments. Creating longer-lasting changes and maintaining health-promoting habits can be enhanced by addressing environmental and societal barriers to change, such as limitations imposed by poverty on access to services or the difficulty in jogging or walking if one lives in an unsafe neighborhood. These interventions can take place in the family, school, worksite, community, and health institutions. Societal and environmental influences on health behavior must be considered by physical education, exercise science, and sport professionals.

Promoting Adherence

What are factors that promote adherence, encourage persistence, and prevent dropping out? Researchers have identified several factors that predispose individuals to drop out of exercise programs. In general, the researchers found that low self-motivation, depression, and low self-efficacy were related to decisions to quit the program, as was denial of the seriousness of one's health condition.[19,20] Higher dropout rates were found among smokers; blue-collar workers; and individuals who either are obese, exhibit the type A behavior pattern, perceive that exercise has few health benefits, lead physically inactive lifestyles, or work in sedentary occupations. Lack of social support from significant others, family problems, and job-related responsibilities that interfered with the exercise program were also identified as factors associated with quitting.

Social support from other participants was important to individuals who continued in the program. Group exercise programs usually had lower dropout rates than individually designed programs. Programs that were inconvenient to attend and that involved high-intensity exercise were associated with higher dropout rates than programs that were conveniently located and offered exercise of a less-intense nature. One of the things that has become clearer is that a broader, ecological approach must be taken to understanding adherence. Environmental influences and factors that influence different types of physical activity with respect to different populations are increasingly important in understanding adherence. Factors such as access to facilities and neighborhood safety are an important consideration.[20]

Knowing the factors associated with exercise program dropout enables practitioners to target intervention strategies to those individuals at greatest risk of discontinuing their participation. Intervention strategies to improve adherence include educational approaches and behavioral approaches. Educational approaches provide participants with information to increase their knowledge and understanding. Behavioral approaches focus on increasing individual involvement in the program and creating more healthful behavior patterns. These methods use such strategies as reinforcement, contracting, self-monitoring, goal setting, tailoring programs to meet individuals' lifestyles, and enhancement of self-efficacy. Behavioral approaches have been found to be more effective than educational approaches in promoting adherence.

Exercise adherence can also be enhanced through careful program design. One approach is structuring the program to increase the social support available to participants. Successful strategies include forming exercise groups rather than having the individual exercise alone and involving significant others, such as family members or friends, in encouraging the participant to exercise. Offering programs at times and locations convenient to the participant is important in maintaining involvement. The use of goal setting combined with periodic assessment of progress, use of qualified and enthusiastic leaders, establishment of ongoing leader and participant communication and rapport, and inclusion of a variety of enjoyable activities to meet individual needs are some techniques that can promote exercise adherence and reduce dropout rates.

Technology has the potential to play an important role in promotion of physical activity. The use of smartphones by people of all ages is increasingly prevalent in our society. Users searching through iTunes (iOS) and Google Play (Android) find that there are thousands of apps that focus on health, fitness, and physical activity. Smart-phone apps offer many advantages to users: easy accessibility, adjustable to users' needs, and ability to provide timely individualized feedback to individuals about their efforts.[21] However, not all smart-phone apps are effective, well designed, or based on sound health behavior change theories. As the use of apps becomes increasingly prevalent, professionals need to be knowledgeable about apps and able to offer guidance to individuals seeking to take advantage of this technology.

The issue of adherence during sport injury rehabilitation is also a concern to sports medicine specialists. While the severity of the injury influences rehabilitation adherence, it is recognized that many of the psychosocial factors that contribute to exercise adherence also play a role in the success of sport injury rehabilitation. Sport medicine specialists' and athletic trainers' knowledge of injury mechanisms and treatment protocols is not enough to ensure successful completion of the rehabilitation program. Researchers have found that rehabilitation adherence can be enhanced through the use of such strategies as goal setting, establishing effective communication, active listening, tailoring the program to individual needs, monitoring progress, and building a collaborative relationship to achieve the goals of therapy.[22,23] Social support has also been linked to rehabilitation adherence.

Social support is a complex, multidimensional construct and has been found to be related in many ways to health outcomes. With respect to rehabilitation, social support has been found to relieve distress, enhance coping, and help an injured athlete remain motivated throughout the recovery.[24,25] It strengthens relationships between the injured athlete and team members, coaches, and providers of health care.[24] Understanding the significant role social support plays in exercise and rehabilitation adherence can assist professionals in developing psychosocial rehabilitation interventions.

Knowledge of sport and physical activity psychology is beneficial to professionals in the field. Understanding how to initiate and sustain involvement is important whether you are working with students in physical education, athletes engaged in rehabilitation, or adults participating in an exercise program. An individual's personality is another factor that needs to be considered in attaining desired program outcomes.

PERSONALITY

The role of personality in sport has long captured the interest of researchers. Some researchers sought to address the question of whether sport influences personality; other researchers investigated whether there were personality differences between athletes and nonathletes. Still other researchers undertook the task of identifying the psychological differences between elite athletes and athletes at different levels of sport. Others questioned whether it would be possible to predict the success of athletes based on their personality characteristics.

Nature of Personality

Personality has been defined in many different ways. For example, Vealey describes *personality* as "the unique blend of the psychological characteristics and behavioral tendencies that make individuals different from and similar to each other."[1] Weinberg and Gould define personality as "those characteristics or blend of characteristics–that make a person unique."[26] Anshel describes personality as traits possessed by an individual that are enduring and stable.[27] Because traits are enduring and stable, they predispose an individual to consistently act in certain ways in most, but not all, situations. For example, do you find yourself exhibiting more outgoing behavior in social situations, and less in classroom situations?

Personality and Sport

The early research focused on the relationship between personality traits and sport performance. Researchers addressed questions such as:

- Do athletes differ from nonathletes?
- Can athletes in certain sports be distinguished from athletes in other sports on the basis of their personality?
- Do individuals participate in certain sports because of their personality characteristics?
- Do highly skilled athletes have different personality profiles than less skilled athletes in the same sport?
- Are there certain personality traits that can predict an athlete's success in a sport?[28]

Researchers' findings have revealed contradictory answers to each of these questions. Cox, after an extensive review of the research on personality and sport, offers the following generalizations about athletes relative to the questions posed above:

- Athletes and nonathletes differ with respect to personality characteristics. Athletes tend to be more independent, objective, self-confident, competitive, and outgoing or extroverted, and less anxious than nonathletes.
- Sport participation has an effect on the personality development of young athletes during their formative years. Thus, youth sport experience can positively or negatively affect the development of personality.
- Athletes in one sport can be differentiated from athletes in another sport based on their personality characteristics. Individual sport athletes are less extroverted, more independent, and less anxious than team sport participants.
- World-class athletes can be correctly differentiated from less-skilled athletes by their psychological profile 70% of the time.[28]

While Cox has advanced some generalizations based on an overview of research in the area, it is important to remember that personality is complex

Marathoners use a variety of psychological strategies to help them go the distance.

David Madison/Photographer's Choice/Getty Images

and athletes' performance is influenced by a myriad of factors, both within and outside of the athletic arena. Anshel points out that while researchers have identified characteristics of elite athletes, the value of applying these characteristics as the basis for athletic selection, promotion, or elimination is questionable.[27]

The elite performer continues to remain of interest to sport psychology researchers who are exploring new concepts. Two concepts that have captured the interest of sport psychologists are psychological hardiness and mental toughness.

Hardiness has been linked with the ability to function at an optimal level in a variety of different environments and has been associated with persistence and resiliency. Hardiness consists of strategies, attitudes, beliefs, and behaviors that individuals use in coping with a multitude of stressors. According to Kobasa, hardiness consists of three components: commitment, control, and challenge; these traits are commonly referred to as the three Cs.[29] Hardy individuals are characterized by high involvement in life, a strong belief in their ability to take personal control over events, and enjoyment of challenges. Sheard and Golby studied more than 1,500 competitors at elite and subelite levels of performance and across different sports and genders. They found that elite, international competitors scored highest on overall hardiness and the components of commitment and control compared to other subelite performers.[30]

Gould, Dieffenbach, and Moffatt interviewed 10 US Olympic champions, winners of 32 Olympic medals, and their coaches as well as one of their parents, guardians, or significant others. The researchers found that these Olympians were characterized by "(a) the ability to cope with and control anxiety; (b) confidence; (c) mental toughness/resiliency; (d) sport intelligence; (e) the ability to focus and block out distractions; (f) competitiveness; (g) a hard-work ethic; (h) the ability to set and achieve goals; (i) coachability; (j) high levels of dispositional hope; (k) optimism; and (l) adaptive perfectionism."[31] Coaches and parents exerted an important influence on the athletes' psychological development, both directly by teaching psychological strategies or indirectly by modeling specific psychological strategies.

Mental toughness is another characteristic often associated with successful sport competitors. Many coaches believe that mental toughness is one of the most important psychological skills athletes can possess. Several researchers have investigated mental toughness and its role in athletic performance. Clough and his colleagues adapted the concept of psychological hardiness, adding a fourth C, confidence, to the three Cs.[32] Jones and his coresearchers defined mental toughness as a natural or developed cognitive advantage that enabled a performer to better cope with the demands of training and competing than an opponent.[33] They found that mentally tough athletes were "more consistent and better at remaining determined, focused, confident, and in control under pressure."[33]

In a later study, Jones and his fellow researchers sought to identify specific attributes of mental toughness possessed by elite athletes.[34] They interviewed eight elite athletes who were Olympic or world champions in their sport based on the premise that they would need to have a high level of mental toughness to be successful at this level. The researchers found that these athletes possessed a strong mindset, an unshakeable belief that they will achieve their goal in spite of obstacles and barriers confronting them, an inner arrogance, and an intense focus. They established short-term goals that served as stepping stones to the achievement of their long-term goal and developed planned strategies to achieve them. Achieving their goal was the number-one priority in their life. In training, they pushed themselves to the limit, challenging themselves and welcoming the hard work that would bring them closer to their goals. These champions loved the pressure of competition, were able to maintain a strong attentional focus during the event, and believed in their ability to cope with whatever situations came their way. When confronted with failure, they used it as an opportunity to learn from their mistakes and to motivate them to drive themselves harder toward their goal. As champions, they were able to handle success, taking some time to bask in its glory but knowing when to move on to focus on the next challenge.

Ultramarathon runners (ultras) engage in a sport that requires high levels of commitment and mental toughness to be successful. Ultra races are contested over long distances (e.g., 50 miles, 100 km) with performance defined by the time to cover the distance or over a period of time (e.g., 12 or 24 hours) with the objective to cover the most distance in that time. Ultras engaged in many hours of training each week and during the race often face unpredictable course conditions, encounters with wildlife, changes in altitude and climate, and the challenge of running many hours in darkness while seeking to push beyond their personal limits.[34] Jaeschke and her coresearchers studied 12 ultras' perceptions of mental toughness.[35] The y found that ultras were characterized by high levels of perseverance and persistence, the ability to push through and keep going, and commitment. Psychological skills such as positive self-talk, goal setting, and imagery were used to cope with the demands of racing. Additionally, the camaraderie found in the ultra community was an important source of support. One concern raised by the researchers with respect to mental toughness is that it can lead to negative effects, such as persevering through injuries or running in extreme heat with adverse health effects.

Can mental toughness be developed? Weinberg and his colleagues interviewed 15 sport psychologists to explore their perceptions of how coaches could build mental toughness in their athletes.[36] First, to build mental toughness coaches should behave mindfully; that is, they need to plan for its development in a systematic, thoughtful manner. Seeing athletes as individuals with a unique set of strengths, weaknesses, and responses to situations; being critical but encouraging of athletes' efforts; and fostering a sense of autonomy and control in athletes are some steps that contribute to the development of mental toughness. Next, coaches should structure their training and practices to create adversity, that is, situations that challenge athletes so that they can develop coping strategies to deal with difficult situations, similar to what they would encounter in competition. Athletes need to develop skills to deal with both success and failure, to put events into perspective, to see both successes and failures as learning opportunities, and to move forward to prepare for the next competition. Coaches who value mental toughness need to teach their athletes the mental skills that prepare them for difficult situations.

As interest in personality in sport grew, different approaches began to be utilized to study personality and psychological characteristics of athletes. The interactionist approach views behavior as being influenced by both the traits of the individual and situational and environmental factors. The study of personality states is another approach that has been undertaken by researchers to study athletes. Unlike traits, which are relatively stable, states fluctuate and are a manifestation of the individual's behaviors and feelings at a particular moment, reflecting the interaction of traits and situational factors. For example, anxiety has both a trait dimension (how you typically respond to situations) and a state dimension (how you feel at this moment, such as before the start of the competition, or in a particular situation, such as a state qualifying meet).

The emergence of cognitive psychology offers another perspective to understand the behaviors, feelings, and thoughts of athletes. According to this theory, individuals continuously process information from the environment, interpret the information, and then behave based on their appraisal of the situation. Cognitive psychology recognizes that individuals' thoughts about themselves and the situation influence their actions. Vealey reports that researchers using the cognitive approach were able to distinguish between successful and less-successful athletes.[1] Compared to less-successful athletes, successful athletes

- possess more self-confidence;
- employ more effective coping strategies to maintain their optimal competitive focus despite obstacles and distractions;
- more efficiently regulate their level of activation to be appropriate for the task at hand;
- tend to be more positively preoccupied with their sport;
- have a high level of determination and commitment to excellence.[1]

SIGNS OF ELEVATED AROUSAL AND HEIGHTENED ANXIETY

- Sweaty hands
- Frequent urge to urinate
- Increased respiration rate
- Elevated heart rate
- Deterioration in coordination
- Inappropriate narrowing of attention
- Distractibility
- Negative self-talk

The research on personality and psychological characteristics of athletes, while at times presenting conflicting results, does offer us some insights into the psychological characteristics and thoughts of athletes. Differences in traits, predispositions, and cognitions influence athletes' behaviors and experiences in sport. What can be said with some degree of assurance is that each athlete must be treated as an individual.

ANXIETY AND AROUSAL

The goal of coaches, teachers, and sport psychologists is to optimize an individual's performance. To achieve this goal, they must consider the effect of anxiety and arousal on performance.

Nature of Anxiety and Arousal

Arousal and anxiety are intimately related. According to Weinberg and Gould, arousal is a "general physiological and psychological activation, varying on a continuum from deep sleep to excitement."[26] Mediated by the nervous system, as arousal becomes heightened, it is accompanied by increases in muscle tension and respiration rate, elevated heart rate and blood pressure, greater mental alertness, and a host of other physiological and psychological responses. The intensity of arousal is influenced by a host of factors, including the individual, the environment, and the task and activities in hand. Arousal refers to a state of

Optimal arousal is important for superior performance. The level of optimal arousal varies according to the individual and the sport.

technotr/E+/Getty Images

activation and occurs in response to events, be they positive or negative in nature. On the other hand, anxiety is defined by Weinberg and Gould as a "negative emotional state in which feelings of nervousness, worry, and apprehension are associated with activation or arousal of the body."[26]

Arousal is a blend of physiological and psychological activity in a person, and it refers to the level of motivation, alertness, and excitement at a particular moment.[26] Athletes need to maintain optimal levels of arousal. The intensity of arousal falls along a continuum and is dependent on each individual and the activities in which they are participating.

Why Does Arousal Influence Performance?

You may be wondering how arousal specifically affects performance. Arousal increases muscle tension and affects coordination. Too much tension can create movement difficulties and negatively impact coordinated movement. Arousal also affects how athletes direct their attention. Attention can become too narrow with too much arousal and can make one pay attention to too much in their environment when there is too little arousal.

Anxiety is commonly classified in two ways. Trait anxiety is an integral part of an individual's personality. It refers to the individual's tendency to classify environmental events as either threatening or nonthreatening. State anxiety is an emotional

AROUSAL AND PERFORMANCE

Arousal levels too low:

- Low motivation
- Inattention
- Slow movement choices

Arousal levels too high:

- Deterioration in coordination
- Inappropriate narrowing of attention
- Distractibility
- Lack of response flexibility

Optimal state of arousal varies according to the individual and specific activity.

response to a specific situation that results in feelings of fear, tension, or apprehension (e.g., apprehension about an upcoming competition). The effects of both state and trait anxiety on motor performance have been studied by sport psychologists.

Anxiety, Arousal, and Performance

Coaches and teachers continually attempt to find the optimal level of arousal that allows individuals to perform their best. An arousal level that is too low or too high can have a negative impact on the performance. A low level of arousal in an individual is associated with such behaviors as low motivation, inattention, and inappropriate and slow movement choices. A high level of arousal in an individual can cause deterioration in coordination, inappropriate narrowing of attention, distractibility, and a lack of flexibility in movement responses. It is important individuals find their optimal level of arousal for a given activity. A variety of approaches have been employed by professionals in helping athletes reach an optimal level of arousal. These techniques include pep talks; motivational slogans and bulletin boards; self-talk strategies; relaxation training; imagery; and, in some cases, the professional services of a sport psychologist.

Sport psychologists and researchers have studied the relationships among anxiety, arousal, and sport performance. Cox, after a review of the research in this area, found the following:

- Athletes who feel threatened by fear of failure experience a high level of anxiety. Fear of failure can be reduced by defining success in individual terms and keeping winning in perspective.
- Athletes who possess high levels of trait anxiety tend to experience high levels of state anxiety when confronted with competition.
- Athletes' perceptions of a given situation influence their level of state anxiety. When placed in the same competitive situation, athletes experience different levels of anxiety.
- An optimal level of arousal is essential for peak performance. The individual characteristics of the athlete, the nature of the skill to be performed, and the competitive situation influence the level of arousal needed.[28]

Research in sport psychology suggests several ways that coaches can help their athletes achieve their optimal performance, whether that means decreasing their level of arousal and anxiety or increasing it. One way to determine whether an athlete is "feeling up" as opposed to "uptight" is to help athletes accurately identify their feelings, encourage them to monitor their feelings and arousal levels before, during, and after competition, and help them learn and use appropriate strategies to enable them to reach their optimal state.

Anshel identifies several different approaches that can serve to reduce anxiety and arousal. These approaches include:

- Use physical activity to release stress and anxiety. A warm-up can provide an effective means to reduce stress.
- Develop, teach, and practice a precompetition routine so that it is comfortable and familiar to the athletes.
- Simulate games in practice to allow athletes to rehearse skills and strategies until they are mastered.
- Focus on building self-confidence and high but realistic expectations. Highlighting the athletes' strengths, reviewing game strategies, and expressing confidence in the athletes' abilities

REDUCING ANXIETY AND AROUSAL TO ENHANCE PERFORMANCE

- Use appropriate physical activity, such as warm-ups.
- Develop and use a precompetition routine.
- Design practice situations to simulate competition.
- Tailor preparation to the individual.
- Build self-confidence and high, realistic expectations.
- Help athletes keep errors in perspective.
- Keep athletes' focus on the present event, not on past events.
- Promote the use of positive self-talk.
- Incorporate relaxation training as necessary.

help promote positive thoughts and decrease negative thinking.

- Assist athletes in coping with errors by keeping errors in perspective. Emphasize the opportunity to learn from mistakes, and help athletes avoid negative self-statements, which tend to exacerbate anxiety and disrupt performance.[27]

There are a host of additional strategies that coaches can use to help athletes manage their anxiety and arousal. Once again, coaches must be prepared to work with athletes as individuals and determine which approach best suits each athlete.

What can coaches do to "psych up" a team? Increasing the team's and athletes' levels of arousal is sometimes necessary. Anshel suggests that coaches take into account each athlete's ability level, age, psychological needs, and skills to be performed.[27] Remember that athletes respond differently to various techniques and need different levels of arousal to perform different tasks.[27] Coaches can also use a multitude of different strategies to increase arousal, including increasing the intensity of their voice, using loud and fast-paced music, setting specific performance goals, and using the warm-up to help athletes adjust their level of arousal. Some coaches show video of the opponents, whereas other coaches may show highlights of the athletes' successful performances.[27]

Managing anxiety and arousal is a challenging task. Coaches must recognize that athletes' perceptions of a situation influence their anxiety and arousal. Individual differences in athletes' physical

Psychological skills help athletes perform at their maximum level.
Purestock/SuperStock

and psychological states require that techniques to help athletes achieve their optimal performance must be individualized. Anxiety can affect other factors that influence an athlete's performance, such as attention.

GOAL SETTING

Goal setting is important in many of the different environments in which physical education, exercise scientists, and sport leaders work. Goal setting can be used to help students in school physical education, athletes on sports teams, clients rehabilitating an injury, or adults involved in fitness programs. Goal setting is important both as a motivational strategy and as a strategy to change behavior or enhance performance. It is also used as an intervention strategy to rectify problems or to redirect efforts.

Types of Goals

According to Weinberg, a *goal* is the task an individual tries to accomplish and reflects the desired outcome of an action.[37] Goal setting focuses on specifying a specific level of proficiency to be attained within a certain period of time. Goals can be categorized as outcome goals, performance goals, and process goals.

Outcome goals typically focus on interpersonal comparisons and the end result of an event. A 70-year-old athlete who aspires to win first place at the Senior Games track meet at the end of the season strives is expressing an outcome goal. Whether an outcome goal is achieved or is not influenced in part by the ability and play of the participants.

Performance goals refer to the individual's actual performance in relation to personal levels of achievement. Striving to increase ground balls won in lacrosse from 5 to 10, decreasing the time to walk a mile from 20 to 15 minutes, increasing the amount of weight that can be lifted following knee reconstruction, and improving one's free-throw percentage from 35% to 50% are examples of performance goals.

Lastly, *process goals* focus on how a particular skill is performed. For example, increasing axial rotation in swimming the backstroke and following through on the tennis backhand are two examples of process goals that focus on the improvement of technique. As technique improves, improvements in performance are likely to follow.

How Goal Setting Works

Goal setting leads to improved performance. Goal-setting influences performance because it focuses attention, mobilizes effort, nurtures persistence, and leads to the development of new learning strategies.[38,39]

Goal setting leads to the focusing of attention on the task at hand and on the achievement of the goal related to that task. When there are no specific goals, attention has a tendency to wander, drifting from one item to the next without any particular attention or intent. When specific goals are set, individuals can direct their attention to that task and its accomplishments. For example, a volleyball player sets the goal of getting 15 kills in a match. To achieve this, during practice, the player focuses on the specific elements of the skill that will help accomplish this goal.

Once a goal is determined, to achieve the goal, individuals must direct their efforts toward its attainment. This mobilization of effort, in and of itself, can lead to improved performance. Knowing what you want to accomplish and having specific strategies to achieve it influences motivation and increases effort.

Goal setting focuses one's attention and mobilizes one's efforts as well as encouraging persistence. Persistence is critical. Often, the attainment of goals involves a concentrated effort over an extended period of time. There may be periods of frustration and failure as individuals learn new strategies or challenge themselves to higher levels of achievement. Individuals need to persist in pursuit of their goals.

Development of relevant learning strategies is an essential aspect of goal setting. Strategies can include learning new techniques and changing the manner in which a skill is practiced. Strategies can also include developing a plan by which incremental changes in performance or behavior can be attained. For example, an individual desiring to lose 30 pounds through a combination of healthy dieting and increased physical activity may need to learn strategies to select healthier foods, to develop and modify a walking program, and to learn how to continue to maintain the weight loss once it is accomplished.

Properly implemented, goal setting can lead to improvements in performance and changes in behavior. Goals can be outcome-, process-, or performance-oriented. Goal setting improves performance by directing attention, mobilizing effort, encouraging persistence, and introducing new strategies. Goal setting requires careful planning if it is to be effective as a motivational strategy or intervention strategy.

Principles of Effective Goal Setting

Structuring and implementing the goal setting program correctly is important because a decrement in performance can actually occur from improper goal setting. To help you get started with goal setting, think "SMART." SMART is an acronym often used to help professionals and individuals remember the critical characteristics of effective goals. Goals should be specific, measurable, action-oriented, realistic, and timely.[26]

Specific goals have been linked to higher levels of performance than no goals or general do-your-best-type goals. While do-your-best goals may be motivating and encouraging, they do not have as powerful an impact on performance as having specific goals. Furthermore, general goals such as "I want to be a better swimmer" or "I want to be healthier" are not as effective as specific goals. It is hard to monitor general goals or to know what types of changes need to be made to achieve them. A specific goal, such as a swimmer stating, "I want to reduce my time in the 200 freestyle to 1 minute 56 seconds from 2 minutes 5 seconds by the championships," is more likely to result in improvements in performance.

SMART GOAL SETTING

- Specific–set specific versus general goals.
- Measurable–design measurable goals to facilitate monitoring of progress.
- Action-oriented–assess goal attainment by viewing person's actions.
- Realistic–make goals challenging but achievable with effort, persistence, and hard work.
- Timely–establish time frame for achievement.

Additionally, measurable goals allow progress to be more easily monitored. Measurable goals provide individuals with feedback, which helps motivate them and sustain involvement. An individual who sets a goal of walking 30 minutes a day for 5 days a week at a brisk pace of 12 minutes a mile or less can easily monitor whether progress is being made toward goal attainment. Action goals, also referred to as observable goals, are goals that can be assessed through observation of a person's actions. By viewing the person's actions, you can determine whether or not the individual is exhibiting the desired goal or behavior.

Identification of the time frame for achievement is a critical part of goal setting. Will the goal be accomplished by the end of the season? Or within 1 month? The time frame should be long enough so that it gives a reasonable time to accomplish the goal. If the time frame is too short, it appears unrealistic, which may cause the individual to give up prematurely. If the time frame is too long, there is a tendency to procrastinate.

Goals that individuals establish should be moderately difficult so that the individuals feel challenged and have to extend themselves to achieve the goals. Goals must be perceived by individuals to be realistic and achievable with effort, persistence, and hard work.

Sport psychologists suggest several other principles be incorporated into goal setting in addition to the SMART goal principles.[28,37] These include writing goals down, incorporating different types of goals into the program, setting short-term and long-term goals, providing individual goals within the group context, determining goals for both practice and competition, ensuring that goals are internalized by the individuals, regularly evaluating progress, and providing for individual differences.

Goals should be written down and monitored regularly to determine if progress is being made. Some swimmers religiously chart each practice, writing down times for each set of repeats in a swim diary. Other swimmers may only chart their meet performances. What is important is that individuals know their goals, write them down, and track their progress consistently. The use of smartphones and tablets, the availability of thousands of smart apps, and the growing popularity of wearable devices facilitate record keeping.

A variety of goals should be integrated into the goal setting plan. A combination of outcome, performance, and process goals is recommended. When individuals set goals based on their own performance, they feel more in control. Goals based on outcome measures, such as winning and losing, can lead to a loss of motivation and higher levels of anxiety.[28] The reason is that there are many aspects of an outcome goal that individuals cannot control, such as their opponents' ability. Furthermore, using a combination of different types of goals presents individuals with additional opportunities for success. For example, a swimmer can finish third and fail to achieve an outcome goal of finishing first in the event, but feel successful by posting a personal best time for the event, a performance goal.

Setting a long-term goal provides a direction for individuals' efforts. In addition to long-term goals, short-term goals should be established. Short-term goals serve as stepping stones to the long-term goal. Short-term goals provide individuals with benchmarks by which to judge their progress. This form of feedback serves to keep motivation and performance high. It allows individuals to focus on improvement in smaller increments and helps make the long-term goal task seem less overwhelming.

Goals should be set for different circumstances. Goals are important for both practice and competition. What happens in practice is reflected during performance in competition. Daily practices are a critical component of competitive success. If a tennis player wants to improve their

Setting goals helps motivate athletes and direct their efforts.
Christopher Purcell/Alamy Stock Photo

first-serve percentage during competition, they should practice with this goal in mind. Practices also provide the opportunity to work on other goals that contribute to team success, such as working hard or communicating more with teammates.

Goals can also be set for teams. Team goals provide a focus for practice goals. For example, if the lacrosse team's goal is to be ranked number 1 in the conference on winning ground balls, practice time should be allocated to the achievement of that goal. Additionally, individual performance goals that contribute to the achievement of the team goal, such as working on skills to increase the percentage of ground balls won, should receive attention.

Social support is acknowledged as an important factor in goal achievement. Social support has been found to be critical in achieving rehabilitation goals as well as health goals. For instance, in cardiac rehabilitation programs, where individuals set goals related to fitness and nutrition, eliciting the support of a spouse or significant other increases the likelihood that individuals will achieve their goals. Expressions of social support, such as genuine concern and encouragement, also help individuals remain motivated and committed when they are discouraged or frustrated or hit a performance plateau.

Acceptance and internalization of goals by the individual is one of the most critical aspects of goal setting. Individuals must commit to the goals and invest themselves in their attainment. Allowing individuals to set their own goals increases their commitment to their achievement. Individuals may experience a lack of ownership of goals set by others, such as a personal trainer or a coach. Ownership can be enhanced by using a collaborative approach to goal setting.

Provision for frequent evaluation needs to be incorporated into the goal setting plan. Evaluative feedback helps individuals assess the effectiveness of their goals and whether or not their goal achievement strategies are working. Additionally, goal setting is a dynamic process. Frequent evaluation allows both short- and long-term goals to be adjusted to reflect progress, the changing circumstances of the individuals, or the effectiveness of learning strategies.

Many professionals may find goal setting to be an integral part of their work. Goal setting can be used effectively in many different ways to help individuals improve their performance or change their behaviors relative to physical activity.

ENHANCING PERFORMANCE THROUGH SELF-TALK

What thoughts run through your head before an athletic performance? As you sit and wait to give a 10-minute speech in front of a class, what are you thinking? As you set out on your daily 3-mile jog, what conversations do you have with yourself in your head? What did you say to yourself as you took a test for this course? What is your inner dialog as your experience failure? Cognitive approaches in sport and physical activity psychology focus on understanding the relationship between individuals' thoughts, feelings, and behavior or performance.

Nature of Self-Talk

What individuals say to themselves during performance can be positive or negative. These thoughts and associated feelings can influence self-confidence, which, in turn, impacts performance. Who would you rather have take a penalty kick in soccer–a soccer player who steps up to take the shot and thinks, "I consistently make this shot in practice; I can do it" or a player who steps up to take the shot and thinks, "What if I miss?" Which player's self-talk is more conducive to successful performance? Understanding and modifying individuals' self-talk is one focus of cognitive sport and exercise psychology.

According to Williams and Leffingwell, "Self-talk occurs whenever an individual thinks, whether making statements internally or externally."[40] *Self-talk* is thoughts that occupy an individual's mind or spoken words, and they can be positive or negative in nature. Positive self-talk does not guarantee an outstanding performance, but it does enhance factors associated with better performance, such as self-confidence and a task-relevant focus of attention.[39] Sport and exercise psychologists use a variety

Self-talk can help individuals focus their attention and concentrate on relevant cues.
Tyler Stableford/Brand X Pictures/SuperStock

of strategies to promote positive self-talk and to counteract the effects of negative self-talk.

Types of Self-Talk

There are several different types of self-talk. Task-relevant statements reinforce technique. For example, volleyball setters may use the cue "diamond" to remind themselves of the correct hand position. Positive self-statements refer to talk that encourages effort or persistence or reinforces feelings of confidence. A cross-country runner, facing an uphill stretch during the last kilometer, may say to herself, "I can do it" as a way of encouraging herself to push through to the finish. A third form of self-talk is mood words–words designed to elicit an increase in intensity or arousal. "Turn it on," a swimmer says to himself as he completes the last 50 yards of a 1,500-yard freestyle race.

Application of Self-Talk

There are several uses of self-talk. Self-talk can be effective in enhancing skill acquisition, focusing attention, modifying activation, and promoting self-confidence.[40] Self-talk is not only for athletes, but can also be useful for individuals engaging in a variety of physical activities.

Self-talk can be useful when learning a new skill or modifying a previously learned skill or habit. Self-talk can range from rehearsing key words of the steps involved in a skill to the use of a cue word such as "step" to serve as a reminder of what to do. It is important that the self-talk focus on the desirable movement, versus what not to do. For example, if a tennis player wants to toss the ball higher in preparation for the serve, appropriate self-talk would be "High toss," not "Don't toss the ball so low."

Focusing attention is another effective use for self-talk. During practices or competition, athletes' attention may wander or be directed inappropriately. Cue words such as "focus" help athletes regain their concentration. Self-statements can also be used to help athletes focus on relevant task cues such as "mark up" or "adjust position relative to the ball."

The right intensity at the right time is critical in performance. Self-talk can be used by athletes to modify their intensity or arousal so that it is at an optimal level. Self-statements may be helpful in decreasing activation ("relax") or increasing it ("get psyched").

Promoting self-confidence is an effective use of self-talk. Self-confidence is influenced by a variety of factors, such as performance outcomes and skill ability. Self-confidence is also influenced by self-talk. Individuals' self-talk affects their self-confidence, either positively or negatively. Self-confidence is undermined with negative self-talk and feelings of doubt. Although self-criticism can provide an important source of feedback to improve later performances, it is important that it not be overgeneralized ("My shot went wide because of the direction of my follow-through" versus "I'm a terrible player"). Positive self-talk enhances feelings of competence. Self-statements prior to and during competition should be positive in nature and engender high levels of motivation and effort.

Self-compassion can play an important role our self-talk. Would you say that you are "your own worst critic?" When things do not go right, or you feel inadequate, do you engage in self-defeating self-talk, or harsh self-judgment? As you listen to your inner talk in these circumstances, ask yourself, "Would you say the same thing to a friend?" Or would you be more positive, encouraging, and compassionate? Neff argues that when things do not go right, we should treat ourselves with kindness and accept that we are not perfect.[41] We should acknowledge our feelings and recognize that things are difficult or did not go well as we had hoped. Self-compassion encourages us to take a more balanced approach to our negative emotions, seeing them in perspective, rather than exaggerating them or ignoring them or engaging in all or nothing thinking. Self-compassion helps individuals reflect on their behavior and helps them see what can be learned from their experiences.

Modifying Self-Talk

Some individuals may not even be aware of their self-talk or its potential to impact performance. Sport and physical activity psychologists work with individuals to help them use self-talk effectively. For individuals who have negative self-talk, steps can be taken to help them make changes. There are several approaches to modifying self-talk: thought stopping, changing negative thoughts to positive thoughts, countering, and reframing.[40]

Thought stopping uses a trigger or cue to immediately interrupt unwanted thoughts when they occur. An athlete who hears herself begin to say "I can't . . ." can interrupt this negative thought by saying to herself or out loud the word "Stop," or by visualizing a red traffic stop sign. Interrupting the negative thought before it leads to negative feelings and adversely influences behavior can have a beneficial effect on performance. With consistent use of thought stopping, the frequency of unwanted negative self-talk can be decreased.

Replacing negative thoughts with positive thoughts is another approach. With this approach, negative self-statements are immediately followed by positive self-statements. For example, a basketball player who misses a foul shot may make the negative statement "I never am good from the foul line." The player can replace that negative statement with "I made five of my eight shots tonight. With more practice, I can increase that percentage." Compared to thought stopping, this approach encourages individuals to replace a negative thought with a positive one, rather than simply stopping the negative thought.

Countering focuses on challenging individuals' beliefs that lead them to accept negative statements as being the truth. Countering uses facts, reason, and rational thinking to refute negative thoughts. Once these negative thoughts are refuted, individuals are more accepting of positive self-statements. For example, an athlete that perceives themselves as someone who chokes under pressure can counter that belief by examining their past performances in pressure situations. When the evidence is reviewed, it shows that the athlete actually performs well under pressure, especially in critical games. Now the athlete is encouraged to replace the negative thought with "I know I can come through under pressure."

The technique of *reframing* focuses on altering individuals' view of the world or changing their perspective. Through this approach, negative statements are changed to positive statements by interpreting the situation differently. Athletes who are nervous and perceive their pounding heart as reflecting and confirming their anxiety can reinterpret this as "I'm geared up and ready to go." Athletes fearful of competition and the associated stress of winning and losing can be helped to reinterpret competition as a challenge and an opportunity to test themselves while providing the additional benefit of identifying areas of improvement.

Changing the self-talk of individuals is a challenge. First, individuals may not be aware of their negative self-talk. Before modifying self-talk, sport and physical activity psychologists need to help individuals realize that self-talk can be self-defeating and adversely influence performance. Exploring the underlying beliefs that perpetuate negative self-talk, such as low self-esteem, is also an important part of the process. In some cases, dealing with the underlying cause of the negative self-talk will require additional interventions. Another challenge is that thought patterns are deeply ingrained and changing them, just like changing any other habit, requires motivation, new skills, practice, and patience.

For greatest effectiveness in modifying negative self-talk, Williams and Leffingwell suggest using a combination of thought stoppage, changing negative thoughts to positive thoughts, reframing, and countering.[40] Self-talk is only one cognitive approach that can be used to enhance the performance of individuals as well as their personal development.

The use of self-talk is not limited to the realm of athletics. Students in physical education classes can be taught to use cognitive strategies, such as self-talk, to enhance their feelings of competence as movers. When starting a new activity unit, some students might engage in self-talk such as "I'm no good at this." This negative statement and others like it result in loss of motivation and lack of effort. Instead, students can be helped to reframe their self-talk and to see that the new unit presents them with an opportunity to improve their skills or learn new ones.

Self-talk can play a critical role in the adoption of a physically active lifestyle. Middle-aged individuals just beginning an exercise program after two decades of inactivity may experience self-defeating thoughts that ultimately may lead to their discontinuing participation. "I can't do this–I was never athletic anyway" may precipitate participant dropout. Self-talk may also affect participation in rehabilitation programs. Athletes rehabbing an anterior cruciate ligament (ACL) injury may be beset with self-doubts about whether they will be able to return to competition and perform at a high level. Negative self-talk such as "This is a waste of time" may lead to less than full effort being expended during the performance of the rehabilitation exercises. As professionals, you need to recognize that such negative self-talk can have an adverse impact on achievements by participants in your programs. With training, professionals can learn how to effectively modify self-talk to enhance the experiences of participants in their programs.

MENTAL IMAGERY TO ENHANCE PERFORMANCE

Imagery is an important mental training tool found to be effective in improving the performance of athletes. Recreational marathoners, Olympic platform divers, and professional golfers are among the thousands of athletes who use imagery to improve their performance. Imagery develops a blueprint for performance, enabling athletes to improve their physical skills and psychological functioning during competition. Imagery can assist athletes in attaining their goals.

Vealey and Greenleaf define *imagery* as the "process of using all the senses to re-create or create an experience in the mind."[42] Anderson explains that "mental imagery occurs when a person images an experience. The person 'sees' the image, 'feels' the movements and/or the environment in which it takes place, and 'hears' the sounds of the movement–the crowd, the water, and the starting gun."[43] In contrast to daydreaming, imagery is a systematic process that is consciously controlled by the person, who takes an active role in creating and manipulating the images and structuring the experience. Imagery does not involve overt physical movements. Imagery in conjunction with physical practice can improve the performance.

Nature of Imagery

There are two types of imagery: external imagery and internal imagery. Athletes who engage in *external imagery* see themselves performing as if they were watching a video of their performance. For instance, when a golfer observes herself completing a putt for par on a sunny day or a quarterback watches himself successfully throw a pass through the hands of a defender to the outstretched hands of his receiver, they are using external imagery.

Internal imagery is when athletes construct the image of the performance from the perspective of their own eyes, as if they were inside their body when executing the skill. From this perspective, athletes' images are formed from what they would actually see, feel, and hear in the situation if they were actually there. Using internal imagery, a surfer would feel her muscles tense and relax as she balances and moves up and down the board, adjusting her body position to ride the wave; she would see the sun beating down on the ocean, the waves forming, and her feet's position on the board. She would notice the sparkling water droplets from the ocean on her body, and hear the sound of the surf. Athletes using internal imagery see the experience from within themselves.

Athletes who are skilled at the use of imagery can use both the internal and external perspectives effectively. Some sport psychologists suggest that internal imagery is most effective for rehearsing skills and refining performance, and external imagery may be most helpful in assisting athletes to correct critical aspects of their performance.[39]

Vividness is a critical feature of imagery. *Vividness* refers to the clarity and detail of the mental image constructed by the athletes. Vividness is enhanced through the use of color, incorporation of multiple senses, and integration of emotion within the imagery.[40] Imagery goes beyond just the visualization or seeing of an event. The incorporation of other senses–such as kinesthetic (sensations of the body as it moves into different positions), gustatory (taste), olfactory (smell), auditory (hearing), and tactile (touch) senses–adds much to the vividness of the image.

The use of multiple senses enriches the detail of the image. If you compare the two descriptions of the images that follow, it is easy to see how the use of multiple senses enhances the image. One swimmer uses only vision in constructing a visualization of his event–the 400-yard individual medley. The swimmer images swimming and seeing the wall coming closer and closer with each stroke as he approaches the turn. Another swimmer also visualizes the wall coming closer and closer with each stroke. But he adds information from his other senses to increase the richness of the image. The swimmer images feeling the undulations of his body in the butterfly stroke, smelling the familiar odor of the chlorine in the pool, maintaining the pressure on the palms of his hands and soles of his feet with each stroke, and hearing the roar of the crowd as he sprints home with his freestyle, closing in on a record time.

Adding emotions to imagery further enhances its vividness. The swimmer can enhance his image by adding the feelings associated with the anxiety he experiences as he walks out on deck to the event, waiting behind the starting block to be introduced. As he hears himself being introduced and the roar of the crowd, he can feel the excitement of the race and the challenge it presents, and replace anxiety with the confidence he has gained from months of hard work. As he completes the race and looks up to the scoreboard to see his time, he can image feeling jubilant and excited at achieving a personal best. In experiencing these emotions, athletes should tune into the associated physiological responses, such as their heart rate or sweaty palms, and recognize the positive and negative thoughts associated with the various emotions. Emotions coupled with multisensory input enhance the effectiveness of imagery.

Controllability is an essential feature of effective imagery. Vealey and Greenleaf define *controllability* as "the ability of athletes to imagine exactly what they intend to imagine, and also the ability to manipulate aspects of the images that they wish to change."[42] Athletes must be able to control their images so that they can manipulate the image in certain ways to focus on critical aspects of performance. The ability to control images allows athletes to recreate experiences and view them from different perspectives. It also allows athletes to place themselves in situations that have not occurred previously and rehearse different ways to effectively deal with these situations. If the situation occurs, athletes can respond to it competently and confidently because they have imagined their response. Being able to control the content and perspective of the image is critical to its effectiveness.

Uses of Imagery

Imagery is a versatile mental training technique and can be used in many different ways by athletes to enhance their performance. Vealey and Greenleaf identify seven uses for imagery: developing sport skills, correcting errors, rehearsing performance strategies, creating an optimal mental focus for competition, developing preperformance routines, learning and enhancing mental skills, and facilitating recovery from injuries and return to competition.[42]

Learning and practicing sport skills is one way that imagery can enhance athletes' performances. Athletes should select one or two skills to rehearse in their mind. They should rehearse these skills, focusing their imagery on executing the skill perfectly; this practice will help create a mental blueprint of the response. Athletes should incorporate as much relevant sensory information as they can. Athletes who are just beginning to learn a skill may benefit from viewing video of correctly performed skills. Coaches can also demonstrate the correct performance as well as provide verbal cues that will assist the athlete in correctly sequencing the skill's components or mastering its timing. Athletes can perform the imagery on their own or the coach can incorporate imagery into the regular practice.

IMAGERY USES

- Learn and practice sport skills.
- Correct errors.
- Rehearse performance strategies.
- Optimize mental focus.
- Enhance preperformance routines.
- Strengthen mental skills.
- Facilitate recovery from injury.

Error correction is another use for imagery. Athletes frequently receive feedback from their coaches suggesting corrections in skill execution or adjustments in execution of strategies. To enhance the effectiveness of this feedback, athletes can use imagery. After receiving feedback from the coach, athletes should image their performance with the corrections integrated into the image. Imagery allows athletes to experience how the skill or play looks and feels when performed correctly.

Learning and practicing performance strategies is another way that imagery can be used effectively by athletes. This allows athletes to rehearse what they would do in specific situations. For example, after a coach reviews set plays on a corner kick, soccer players can image themselves moving through the plays. This approach can also be used after the coach reviews a scouting report on an opponent. Using imagery, players can rehearse the strategies they will use against the opponent. For example, basketball players can rehearse the strategies they will use to counter the opponents' full-court press.

Imagery is a useful tool for athletes seeking to optimize their mental focus. They can rehearse creating and maintaining a strong mental focus during competition. Vealey and Greenleaf suggest that coaches can assist athletes with this aspect of imagery by posing and helping answer two questions: "What will it be like?" and "How will I respond?"[42] Helping athletes understand the distractions, crowd noise and booing, and challenges

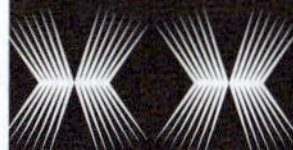

FOCUS ON CAREER: Exercise and Sport Psychology

PROFESSIONAL ORGANIZATIONS	• American Psychological Association–Division 47: Exercise and Sport Psychology • Association for Applied Sport Psychology • North American Society for the Psychology of Sport and Physical Activity
PROFESSIONAL JOURNALS	• *Journal of Applied Sport Psychology* • *Journal of Clinical Sport Psychology* • *Journal of Sport and Exercise Psychology* • *Sport, Exercise and Performance Psychology* • *Research Quarterly for Exercise and Sport* • *The Sport Psychologist*

in the competitive environment, such as poor officiating, allows them to imagine themselves effectively dealing with these situations. This advance preparation helps athletes to respond with greater confidence and composure, not react. Imagery allows athletes to gain experience in responding to a diversity of competitive challenges, whether expected or not.

Imagery is often incorporated into preperformance routines. Many athletes have a set routine they use prior to the performance of a skill, and imagery is a part of this routine. For example, a basketball player taking a free throw carefully positions her feet a certain way at the line, bounces the ball a set number of times, spins the ball in her hands, places her hands for the shot, and then takes a deep breath and exhales before shooting. Before releasing the ball, the player visualizes it leaving her hand, spinning, and entering the basket without touching the rim. Preperformance routines have beneficial effects on athletes' performance. These routines are practiced until they are automatic, essentially becoming part of the skill sequence.

Imagery can be used to strengthen a variety of mental skills critical to athletes' performance. It can enhance self-confidence and engender feelings of competence. This can be done by having athletes mentally re-create past successful performances, focusing on their accomplishments and the feelings associated with them. They can also rehearse via imagery coping confidently with performance errors, effectively managing their emotions in the heat of competition, and assertively meeting unexpected challenges during performance. The regulation of arousal is another way imagery can be used by athletes. Athletes can use imagery to psych up for a competition or to decrease their arousal if too high.

Imagery is an important mental skill. Even though imagery was discussed in relation to athletes, it can be used in a variety of performance situations, such as public speaking or taking the National Athletic Trainers' Association certification exam. Imagery, goal setting, and self-talk are important mental skills that can enhance the learning and performance of people in a variety of situations.

INTERVENTION STRATEGIES

In recent years, sport and physical activity psychologists as well as teachers and coaches have turned to a variety of intervention strategies to help athletes achieve their optimal performance. As discussed earlier, anxiety and arousal can have harmful effects on athletes' performance. Athletes' performance can also suffer due to lack of motivation, poor level of self-confidence, and, because of the intimate relationship between the mind and the body, negative thoughts and feelings about themselves and their capabilities. With the help of appropriate intervention techniques, athletes learn skills and strategies to regulate their physiological and psychological state to achieve optimum performance.

Sometimes, athletes experience excessive anxiety and arousal, which causes a deterioration in their performance. Intervention strategies focusing on reducing these levels would benefit these athletes. One way to deal with elevated levels of arousal is through the use of a variety of relaxation techniques. These techniques teach the individual to scan the body for tension (arousal is manifested in increased muscular tension) and, after identifying a higher-than-optimal level of tension, to reduce the tension to the appropriate level by relaxing. Once specific relaxation techniques are learned, this process should take only a few minutes. Types of relaxation training include progressive relaxation, autogenic training, meditation, and biofeedback. A note of caution is in order here, however. Athletes should be careful not to relax or reduce their level of arousal too much, because this will have a harmful influence on their performance.

The use of cognitive strategies to facilitate optimum performance is a popular intervention. Cognitive strategies teach athletes psychological skills that they can employ in their mental preparation for competition. In addition to focusing on alleviating the harmful effects of anxiety and arousal, these cognitive strategies can also be used to enhance motivation and self-confidence and to improve the performance consistency. These approaches include cognitive restructuring, thought stopping, self-talk, hypnosis and self-hypnosis, goal setting, and mental imagery.

Some cognitive intervention techniques focus on changing athletes' thoughts and perceptions. Self-talk, previously discussed, is an example of a cognitive intervention technique. Cognitive strategies can also be used to alter athletes' perceptions of events, thus reducing anxiety. Affirmation of athletes' ability to succeed in an upcoming competition is another cognitive strategy frequently used to promote optimal performance.

Imagery is the visualization of a situation. This technique has been used in a variety of ways to enhance the performance. It can be used to mentally practice skills or to review outstanding previous performances. By remembering the kinesthetic sensations associated with the ideal performance, the athlete hopes to replicate or improve performance. Imagery has also been used as an anxiety reduction technique. The athlete visualizes anxiety-producing situations and then sees himself or herself successfully coping with the experience, thus increasing confidence to perform successfully in similar situations.

Intervention strategies have proved useful in helping athletes maximize their performance. These strategies are not only for athletes but also have implications for all participants in physical activities and sport. For example, the beginning jogger may derive as much benefit from goal setting as the high-level performer. The practitioner using these strategies must be cognizant of individual differences; otherwise, performance may be affected adversely.

The growth of sport and physical activity psychology has provided professionals with a clearer understanding of various psychological factors that may affect an individual's performance. Sport and physical activity psychologists have been able to enhance individual performance through the use of a diversity of intervention strategies. Remember that these strategies are skills, and like any skill require regular practice to be able to perform them successfully. Although much of the work done in the area of sport psychology has been with athletes, many of the findings and techniques are applicable to participants in a variety of physical activity settings such as school, community, and workplace fitness and physical activity programs. As the field of sport and physical activity psychology continues to expand, practitioners will gain further insight into how to enhance the performance of all individuals.

MENTAL HEALTH OF ATHLETES

Athlete mental health is receiving increased attention in the sporting world as well as in the public arena. Elite, high-profile athletes–Michael Phelps,

Simone Biles, Kevin Love, Naomi Osaka, and Chloe Kim–have used their platforms as a vehicle to share their own struggles with their mental health. By doing so, these athletes demonstrated a commitment to prioritizing their own mental health above the demands of their sport and host of pressures confronting them to excel and win. Their actions helped shift the narrative about mental health in sport, opening the door for athletes, at all levels, to be more forthcoming about their own mental health needs.

There is increased recognition that while athletes experience comparable mental ill-health relative to their nonathlete peers, they also face sport-related risks that can contribute to their development or exacerbate existing mental health issues.[44,45] Expectations for perfection, heavy training demands both mentally and physically, constant drive for improvement, and enormous pressure to win are just a few of the added risks to athletes' mental health. Other risks include sport-related injuries that may limit participation or lead to retirement from sport, overtraining with its impact on physical and psychological health, and illness that may be compounded by the athletic environment, such as eating disorders. Some may suffer from an identity crisis–unable to clearly define who they are as a person as opposed to an athlete. Athletes also face risks when their cultural identities including gender, sexual orientation, race, ethnicity, nationality, education, and socioeconomic status are marginalized and/or their additional sources of stress not recognized. Social media's impact cannot be discounted; social media brings to the public's attention athletes' successes and failures, eliciting reactions and responses not always favorable to an athletes' mental well-being.

Depression and anxiety are increasingly prevalent in the general population, and likely in the athletic population as well, presenting additional threats to athletes' mental health.[44,45] Suicides are on the rise in the general population and presents a risk in the athletic population as well. Add to these risks additional pressures for student-athletes who are expected to excel both academically and athletically. Coaching styles and the coaching environment can also negatively impact athletes' health. Situate these risks within an athletic culture that often emphasizes "toughness" and "showing no weakness" increases the risks to athletes' mental health and can serve as a barrier to athletes seeking help.[44,45]

Removing Barriers, Facilitating Mental Well-being

The primary barrier to athletes seeking help is the strong stigma attached to mental illness both in the general population and in the sporting world.[44,45,46] While it appears that the stigma has, so some extent, lessened, it remains as an influential factor in determining whether athletes will seek help for their mental health symptoms and disorders. Other factors that influence one's beliefs about mental health are one's culture, race, familial values, religious beliefs, and strength of identification as a person outside of one's athletic identity.[44]

The pressure of maintaining the image of the strong, winning athlete and the fear of looking weak may limit health seeking behaviors. Other influential factors include fear of the consequences of seeking help such as loss of playing time or interruptions in training, poor mental health literacy, time constraints, negative past experiences with mental health treatment, and personal beliefs and attitudes regarding mental health. Some athletes might be concerned about the financial implications if others become aware of their mental health status. Concerns about how help-seeking might be perceived by coaches, peers, and significant others in their lives may also serve as a barrier to athletes seeking help.

What can be done to address the mental health of athletes? Seeking help for mental health issues can be facilitated by normalizing health-seeking behaviors of athletes, whether it be for physical or mental health concerns. Mental health must be on a parity with physical health. The same priority for optimizing athletes' physical health to enable them to perform at their best and achieve their potential should extend to mental health. The support and acknowledgment of coaches and athletic support staff can help create a nonstigmatized environment where mental health skills are nurtured, and help-seeking behavior normalized.

Supporting Athlete Mental Health

Mental health literacy is "knowledge about mental health disorders that is associated with their recognition, management, and prevention."[47] Mental health literacy programs are a key component of any effort supporting athlete mental health. Delivered by qualified professionals (e.g., sport psychologists, mental health professionals), these programs should improve understanding of mental health and strive to destigmatize mental health. The program should cover both general and athlete factors that increase athletes' susceptibility to mental disorders and illness. Athletes' awareness of how mental health and help-seeking is perceived in their own cultures is important in understanding why some athletes might be reluctant to seek help. Educating athletes about the signs and symptoms that indicate their mental health may warrant increased attention is critical. Mental performance training programs can also teach athletes self-management skills and coping strategies on how to optimize their mental health, while contributing to their ability to perform at their potential. Equally important, athletes need to know how to and where to go to seek help and believe that their help-seeking is supported.

Ideally, in the sporting environment, a system should be in place that encourages early detection of symptoms and referral to a health professional. Coaches, support staff, and teammates can play an important role in noticing early symptoms and referring athletes to care. Athletes might respond better to professional's care if the professional understands the unique demands associated with athletes and is familiar with the athletes' personal culture. The lack of diversity in mental health professionals is a concern as "cultural responsive" health care can make a difference in outcomes realized.[44,45]

Supporting athletes' mental health requires commitment beyond a one-time workshop on mental literacy. These topics should be consistently revisited and the conversation ongoing. Athletes, coaches, and the supporting staff all play a significant role in the well-being of athletes, both their physical and mental health. It is important that they are knowledgeable about the signs and symptoms of compromised mental health, aware of the presence of subclinical and clinical mental health conditions, promote help-seeking behaviors, and refer athletes for interventions. The key here is taking a proactive preventative approach rather than reacting to athletes in need. Coaches and programs need to be the ones to destigmatize mental health by offering mental health services to their players from the start–not just when it seems like they are in dire straits.

Your Role as a Professional

As a professional in this field, you are preparing to work with people of different ages, abilities, and backgrounds to promote their well-being through engagement in physical activity. You can educate people about the contribution of physical activity to their physical as well as their mental well-being. That is in the future. But there is something you can do right now to address the mental health needs of people in our society. Promote mental health literacy. Through your actions and words, seek to destigmatize mental health. Be supportive of a peer who seems to be struggling with mental health. Reach out–engage in a conversation with them and perhaps even suggest they get help. Be aware of your own mental health and seek help if you need it.

If you or someone you know is struggling and, in a crisis, take advantage of local resources or call the National Suicide Prevention Lifeline at 800-273-8255 or go online to suicidepreventionlifeline.org where you can speak to someone or engage in live chat. Consider putting this information in your phone so you have it readily available when needed. You can make a difference.

CURRENT TRENDS: MOVING TOWARD THE FUTURE

- More robust strategies to initiate exercise and enhance adherence will emerge, giving professionals more options to help individuals begin and remain engaged in physical activity.
- Technology will lead to more advances in the self-regulation of anxiety and arousal, potentially improving individual's performance in the athletic arena.
- Behavior change strategies will become increasingly refined, with greater consideration given to cultural and individual differences. The continued development of apps to support physical activity will help in this effort.
- Effective strategies to engage amotivated students in physical education will be identified, increasing the possibility that students will engage in physical activity both within and outside of the school setting.
- Greater attention will be given to the mental health of athletes and participants in our program. The psychological benefits of engaging in physical activity and great attention to promoting mental health literacy will benefit all populations.

SUMMARY

Sport and physical activity psychology is concerned with the application of psychological theories and concepts to sport and physical activity. Although the physiological benefits of physical activity are well documented, professionals also need to be familiar with the psychological benefits of engaging in physical activity on a regular basis. Unfortunately, too many adults are inactive, and many adults who start a physical activity program drop out. Motivation influences the initiation, maintenance, and intensity of behavior. Exercise adherence focuses on understanding the factors that influence initiation and continuation of physical activity programs. Several theories have been used in research on physical activity participation and health behavior change, including classic learning theories, the health belief model, the transtheoretical model, social cognitive theory, and the ecological perspective.

Sport psychologists have studied many different areas relative to athletic performance, including personality, anxiety, and arousal. Goal setting, imagery, and self-talk are three approaches used to help individuals improve their performance. To help athletes perform at their best, sport psychologists assist athletes in learning and using a variety of intervention strategies. Some of the findings, methodology, and intervention strategies of sport psychologists can also be used in other physical activity settings to help us better understand and enhance the experiences of participants in our physical activity programs.

The mental health of athletes is receiving increased attention. Actions by high profile athletes to prioritize their mental health have helped to shift the narrative about mental health in sport, encouraging more athletes to pay attention to their own mental health needs. Efforts to destigmatize mental health are critical, and efforts to seek help for mental health issues supported in the athletic environment should be supported. As a future professional, you can help promote the mental health of participants in your programs.

DISCUSSION QUESTIONS

1. Motivation affects our initiation, persistence, and intensity of behavior. Reflect back on your participation in athletics or consider your commitment to being physically active on a daily basis. What motivated you to begin participating in your sport or to start working out? What motivates you to continue your participation? If you ended your participation, what were the reasons for discontinuing? Were you more intrinsically or extrinsically motivated?

2. Many different models have been developed to provide a framework to understand and promote behavior change. Which model do you believe has the greatest potential to encourage adults to change from a sedentary lifestyle to a more active one? Explain your choice. What commonalities do you find between the models and how can you use this information to help participants engaged in physical activity programs?
3. Think carefully about your experiences in organized sport. What strategies did coaches use to motivate the team and psych them up for competition? Which strategies were the most effective and which were least effective? Why? How did coaches account for individual differences among athletes in their motivational strategies?
4. Self-talk can have an impact on performance, either facilitating or hindering achievement. Think back to a recent performance situation, in either sport or another aspect of your life, perhaps when you had to give a speech. What was your self-talk before, during, and after the event? Did it help, hurt, or not impact your performance?
5. As a future professional in the field, what can you do to promote mental health literacy?

GET CONNECTED

Association for Applied Sport Psychology (AASP)–contains information on sport psychology, certification information, code of ethics, and information about graduate programs in sport psychology. In the Resources section, there is a collection of articles on different sport psychology topics.

https://appliedsportpsych.org/

American Psychological Association Division of Exercise and Sport Psychology–information about career opportunities in sport and exercise psychology and provides a list of sport and exercise psychology links. Click on Resources on its website to access the newsletter.

https://www.apadivisions.org/division-47/

SELF-ASSESSMENT ACTIVITIES

These activities are designed to help you determine if you have mastered the materials and competencies presented in this chapter.

1. Using your library's databases, find an article to read on one topic in sport or exercise psychology. Then write one to two pages summarizing what you have learned and discussing how you can apply that information in your professional career.
2. Too many people are inactive on a regular basis. Furthermore, many people who begin an exercise program drop out. Using the information on exercise adherence, create a brochure, blog, or website that highlights both the physiological and psychological benefits of regular physical activity. Include information that would encourage people to begin and stay involved in a program. Be sure to include images and pictures highlighting physical activity and a catchy title.
3. As a practitioner, you are concerned with optimizing individuals' performance. Discuss how self-talk and goal-setting can be used to help participants in your program be successful.
4. Smart apps are popular. Search for three smart apps the focus on one topic in sport psychology (e.g., goal setting, relaxation training, imagery, enhancement of self-esteem). Compare each of the apps and evaluate their potential for use within the field.
5. As the incidences of depression, anxiety, and other mental illnesses rise in our society, there is a need to destigmatize mental health. What can professionals in the field do to promote mental health literacy?

REFERENCES

1. Vealey, R. S. (2009). Psychology of sport and exercise. In S. J. Hoffman & J. C. Harris (Eds.), *Introduction to kinesiology: Studying physical activity*. Champaign, IL: Human Kinetics.
2. Association for Applied Sport Psychology. Retrieved from https://appliedsportpsych.org/.
3. International Society of Sport Psychology. Retrieved from https://www.issponline.org/.
4. Gill, D. (1997). Sport and exercise psychology. In J. D. Massengale & R. A. Swanson (Eds.), *The history of exercise and sport science* (pp. 293–320). Champaign, IL: Human Kinetics.
5. Cooper, S.L. (2020). Promoting physical activity for mental well-being. *ACSM Health and Fitness Journal, 24*(3), 12–16.
6. U.S. Department of Health and Human Services. (2018). *Physical activity guidelines for Americans* (2nd ed). Washington, DC: U.S. Department of Health and Human Services.
7. Fontaine, K. R. (2000). Physical activity improves mental health. *The Physician and Sportsmedicine, 28*(10), 83–84.
8. Perlman, D. (2012). An examination of amotivated students within the Sport Education Model. *Asia-Pacific Journal of Health, Sport, and Physical Education, 3,* 141–155.
9. Hobin, T., Subramaniam, P. R., & Wuest, D. A. (2018). Impact of a novel sport activity on student motivation in high school physical education. *International Journal of Physical Education, 55*(1), 15–27.
10. Chen, A. (2013). Top 10 research questions related to children physical activity motivation. *Research Quarterly for Exercise and Sport, 84*, 441–447. doi: 10.1080/02701367.2013.844030.
11. DeMeyer, J., Soenens, B., Vansteenkiste, M., Aelterman, N., Van Petegem, S., & Haerens, L. (2016). Do students with different motives for physical education respond differently to autonomy-supportive and controlling teaching? *Psychology of Sport and Exercise, 22,* 72–82.
12. Hwang, Y., & Jin, J. (2016). How does student motivation affect different teaching styles and student engagement in physical education? *Journal of Physical Education, Recreation and Dance, 87*(7), 61.
13. Dishman, R. K. (2001). The problem of exercise adherence: Fighting sloth in nations with market economies. *Quest, 53,* 279–294.
14. Dishman, R. K., & Sallis, J. F. (1994). Determinants and interventions for physical activity and exercise. In C. Brochard, R. J. Shephard, & T. Stephens (Eds.), *Physical activity, fitness, and health: International proceedings and consensus statement*. Champaign, IL: Human Kinetics.
15. Prochaska, J. O., & Velicer, W. F. (1997). The transtheoretical model of health behavior change. *American Journal of Health Promotion, 12,* 38–48.
16. Samuelson, M. (1997). Commentary: Changing unhealthy lifestyle: Who's ready . . . who's not? An argument in support of the stages of change component of the transtheoretical model. *American Journal of Health Promotion, 12,* 13–14.
17. Duffy, F. D., & Schnirring, L. (2000). How to counsel patients about exercise: An office-friendly approach. *The Physician and Sportsmedicine, 28*(10), 53–54.
18. Herrick, A. B., Stone, W. J., & Mettler, M. M. (1997). Stages of change, decisional balance, and self-efficacy across four health behaviors in a worksite environment. *Journal of Health Promotion, 12,* 49–56.
19. Sallis, J. F., & Owen, N. (1998). *Physical activity and behavioral medicine*. Thousand Oaks, CA: Sage.
20. Trost, S. G., Owen, N., Bauman, A. E., Sallis, J. F., & Brown W. (2002). Correlates of adults' participation in physical activity: Review and update. *Medicine and Science in Sports and Exercise, 34,* 1996–2001.
21. Middelweerd, A., Mollee, J. S., van der Wal, C. N., Brug, J., & te Velde, S. (2014). Apps to promote physical activity among adults: A review and content analysis. *International Journal of Behavioral Nutrition and Physical Activity, 11,* 97–106.
22. Niven, A. (2007). Rehabilitation adherence in sport injury: Sport physiotherapists' perceptions. *Journal of Sport Rehabilitation, 16,* 93–110.
23. Christakou, A., & Lavallee, D. (2009). Rehabilitation from sports injuries: From theory to practice. *Perspectives in Public Health, 129*(3), 120–126.
24. Bianco, T., & Eklund, R. C. (2001). Conceptual considerations for social support research and exercise settings: The case of sport injury. *Journal of Sport and Exercise Psychology, 23,* 85–107.

25. Granquist, M. D., Podlog, L., Engel, J. R., & Newland, A. (2014). Certified athletic trainers' perspectives on rehabilitation adherence in collegiate athletic training settings. *Journal of Sport Rehabilitation, 23,* 123–133.
26. Weinberg, R. S., & Gould, D. (2007). *Foundations of sport and exercise psychology* (4th ed.). Champaign, IL: Human Kinetics.
27. Anshel, M. H. (2011). *Sport psychology from theory to practice*. Boston, MA: Benjamin Cummings.
28. Cox, R. H. (2012). *Sport psychology: Concepts and applications* (7th ed.). New York, NY: McGraw Hill.
29. Kobasa, S. C. (1979). Stressful life events, personality, and health–Inquiry into hardiness. *Journal of Personality and Social Psychology, 37,* 1–11.
30. Sheard, M., & Golby, J. (2010). Personality hardiness differentiates elite-level sport performers. *International Journal of Sport and Exercise Psychology, 8,* 160–169.
31. Gould, D., Dieffenbach, K., & Moffatt, A. (2002). Psychological characteristics and their development in Olympic champions. *Journal of Applied Sport Psychology, 14,* 174–204.
32. Clough, P., Earle, K., & Sewell, D. (2002). Mental toughness: The concept and its measurement. In I. Cockerill (Ed.), *Solutions in sport psychology*. London: Thomson.
33. Jones, G., Hanton, S., & Connaughton, D. (2002). What is this thing called mental toughness? An investigation of elite sport performers. *Journal of Applied Sport Psychology, 14,* 205–218. (http://dx.doi.org/10.1080/10413200290103509).
34. Jones, G., Hanton, S., & Connaughton, D. (2007). A framework of mental toughness in the world's best performers. *The Sport Psychologist, 21,* 243–263.
35. Jaeschke, A. C., Sachs, M. L., & Dieffenbach, K. D. (2016). Ultramarathon runners' perceptions of mental toughness: A qualitative inquiry. *The Sport Psychologist, 30,* 242–255.
36. Weinberg, R., Freysinger, V., Mellano, K., & Brookhouse, E. (2016). How can coaches build mental toughness? Views from sport psychologists. *The Sport Psychologist, 30,* 231–241. (http://dx.doi.org/10.1080/21520704.2016.1263981).
37. Weinberg, R. S. (2013). Goal setting in sport and exercise: Research and practical applications. *Revista da Educação Física/UEM, 24*(2), 171–179. (https://dx.doi.org/10.4025/reveducfis.v24.2.17524).
38. Locke, E. A., Shaw, K. N., Saari, L. M., & Latham, G. P. (1981). Goal setting and task performance. *Psychological Bulletin, 90,* 125–152.
39. Locke. E. A., & Latham, G. P. (2006). New directions in goalsetting theory. *Current Directions in Psychological Science, V5,* 265–268.
40. Williams, J. M., & Leffingwell, T. R. (2002). Cognitive strategies in sport and exercise psychology. In J. L. Van Raalte & B. W. Brewer (Eds.), *Exploring sport and exercise psychology* (2nd ed.). Washington, DC: American Psychological Association.
41. Neff, K. (2015). *Self-compassion: The proven power of being kind to yourself.* New York: Harper Collins.
42. Vealey, R. S., & Greenleaf, C. A. (2006). Seeing is believing: Understanding and using imagery in sport. In J. M. Williams (Ed.), *Applied sport psychology: Personal growth to peak performance* (5th ed.). New York, NY: McGraw Hill.
43. Anderson, A. (1997). Learning strategies in physical education: Self-talk, imagery, and goal-setting. *Journal of Physical Education, Recreation, and Dance, 68*(1), 30–35.
44. Chang, C. J., Putukian, M., Aerni, G., Diamond, A. B., Hong, E. S., Ingram, Y, M., Reardon, C. L, & Wolanin, A. T. (2020). Mental health issues and psychological factors in athletes: Detection, management, effect on performance, and prevention: American Medical Society for Sports Medicine Position Statement. Clinical *Journal of Sport Medicine, 30,* e61–e87.
45. Schinke, R. J., Stambulova, N. B., Si, G., & Moore, Z. (2018). International society of sport psychology position stand: Athletes' mental health, performance, and development. *International Journal of Sport and Exercise Psychology, 61,* 622–639. http://dx.doi.org/10.1080/1612197X.2017.129557.
46. Purcell, R., Gwther, K., & Rice, S. M. (2019). Mental health in elite athletes: Increased awareness requires an early intervention framework to respond to athlete needs. *Sports Medicine-Open, 5,* 1–8. https://doi.org/10.1186/240798-019-0220-1.
47. Furnham, A., & Swami, V. (2018). Mental health literacy: A review of what it is and why it matters. *International Perspectives in Psychology: Research, Practice, Consultation, 7*(4), 240–257. https://doi.org/10.1037/ipp0000094.

CHAPTER 10

PHYSICAL EDUCATION PEDAGOGY

Polka Dot Images/Getty Images

OBJECTIVES

After reading this chapter, students should be able to–

- Understand how the standards-based movement has influenced physical education programs in relation to curricular development, pedagogical practices, and assessment.
- Describe factors that influence curriculum development and know the goal, purpose, and characteristics of different pedagogical models implemented in physical education.
- Describe the role of assessment in physical education programs and apply different types of assessments within instruction.
- Discuss how to be an effective physical education teacher.
- Discuss how the social justice and equity issues influence students' experiences in physical education.

What can be done to increase quality physical education for all students in our schools? Physical education, exercise science, and sport professionals must take a leadership role in advocating for physical education. As advocates, we must be able to articulate the benefits of quality physical education and be knowledgeable about the role of physical activity in advancing the nation's health goals. As professionals, we must conduct quality programs, incorporate the physical education content standards, and assess student learning on a regular basis. Professionals must forge collaborative relationships with policy makers, community and school leaders, parents, and young people to increase physical education in the schools and expand opportunities for involvement in physical activity within the community. Although physical education pedagogy most closely aligns with physical education teachers, exercise scientists and sport leaders have an important role in promoting physical activity outside of the school setting. Conducting quality programs, advocating for increased opportunities for physical activity, including daily physical education, and becoming actively involved in working for change are just some

SOCIAL JUSTICE

Talking Points

- Teachers need to educate students about social justice and equity issues in physical education and create opportunities for students to collaboratively work with others who are different from them.
- Students with individualized education plans (IEPs) and 504 plans are increasing. Teachers need to be knowledgeable on how to adapt their lessons to meet the needs of all students, including those who are legally required to receive accommodations.
- Gender issues have been prevalent in physical education for decades. However, creating a comfortable and safe environment for transgender students was not part of the discourse. As more students identify as transgender and nonbinary, teachers need to ensure their safety both in the locker room and within the learning context.
- Appropriate language use is critical for teachers when working with students. Using terms such as "guys" and "sportsmanship" does not include girls or students who do not identify as a guy or man. Also, making statements such as, "you throw like a girl" or "out of the three passes, at least one has to be to a girl" sends implicit messages to girls that how they throw is less than or not good enough.

ways that professionals in physical education, exercise science, and sport can contribute to increasing physical activity opportunities for all people.

PHYSICAL EDUCATION PEDAGOGY: AN OVERVIEW

Physical education pedagogy continues to develop and evolve within the standards-based movement educational era. The emphasis on standards, assessment, and student learning has brought credibility and accountability to physical education. Although there is a dire need for students to be engaged in physical education and physical activity within and outside of school, physical education pedagogy continues to face challenges within educational institutions. The definition and scope and areas of study are discussed in this section.

Definition and Scope

Physical education pedagogy is concerned with the study of teaching and learning processes of human movement. Throughout the world, physical education pedagogy has also been referred to as sport pedagogy or pedagogy of physical activity. Regardless of the term used, each of these places an emphasis on curriculum and instruction (i.e., teaching) and teacher education.[1,2] Furthermore, physical education pedagogical work is primarily emphasized in PK-12 physical education and sport coaching. For the purpose of this chapter, physical education pedagogy will focus on physical education teaching in PK-12 schools.

Physical education is the subject matter taught in schools that provide PK-12 students with opportunities to learn and have meaningful content and appropriate instruction. Quality physical education programs focus on increasing physical competence, health-related fitness, personal and social responsibility, and enjoyment of physical activity for all students so that they can be physically active for a lifetime.[3] For this to occur, teachers should implement the Society of Health and Physical Educators (SHAPE) America physical education content standards that provide outcomes for elementary, middle, and high school students to achieve by the end of their grade.

Areas of Study

Research in physical education pedagogy has covered many topics of interest over the past 50 years. Researchers have investigated teacher characteristics,

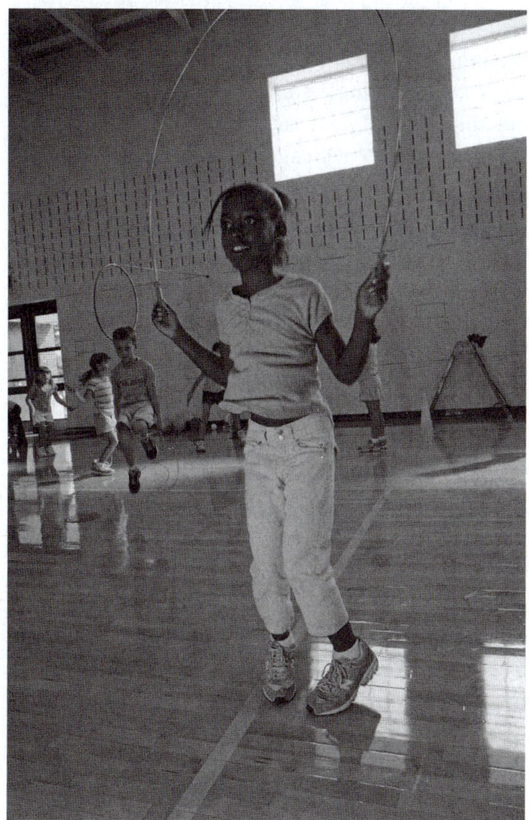

In physical education pedagogy, teachers educate students on the critical elements of skills and movements, such as jumping rope. Here, students are jumping rope in their personal space and at their own pace.

Lars A. Niki/McGraw Hill

different methods of instruction, teacher and student behaviors, the relationship between teacher behaviors and student achievement, student motivation, and curricular development. Furthermore, some scholars have studied social justice and equity issues within the context of physical education and how they influence student learning.

Physical education pedagogy research is conducted in PK–12 schools with physical education teachers and students. Researchers in physical education pedagogy may address questions such as:

- How does appropriate practice develop motor skills, improve performance, and enhance student learning?
- How do different pedagogical models enhance students' participation, enjoyment, and learning in physical education?
- How does personal and social responsibility influence students' comfort, sportspersonship, and engagement in physical education?
- To what extent does the social and public context of physical education impact students' experiences in physical education?
- How does motivation influence student engagement, performance, and level of participation?
- How do teachers and students navigate or address social justice and equity issues (e.g., (dis) ability, gender, race, socioeconomic status, sexuality) in the physical education setting?

These are only some of the questions that can be addressed in physical education pedagogy research. In answering these questions, researchers and teachers can learn the best practices and classroom environments that will best meet the needs of students and enhance learning opportunities. These questions also reflect an alignment with the SHAPE America physical education content standards and the learning domains as researchers and physical education teachers attempt to teach and learn about the whole student. The next sections in this chapter focus on the primary components needed to develop a quality physical education program.

STANDARDS-BASED EDUCATION

As a major institution of our society, education significantly influences the life of our nation. Today, at the beginning of the twenty-first century, we are entering an era in which technological advances, scientific progress, exponential knowledge growth, and greater diversity within our population will transform our society in many dramatic ways. It is within this context that America's educational institutions face the challenge of preparing today's students to live and work in tomorrow's world.

To successfully tackle these challenges, American education over the past 40 years has undergone significant reform as it entered into a standards-based education era. Prior to this movement, education throughout the country greatly varied from state to state and community to community. The national standards movement was not a quest to develop a national curriculum; rather, the charge was to formulate educational goals for the nation on "what a students should know and be able to do."[4,5] Another purpose of the national standards movement was to decrease the achievement gap between the economically advantaged and disadvantaged, whites and minority students, immigrant and US-born children, and students with or without disabilities.[4,6] In 2001, federal legislation proposed a new educational initiative, the No Child Left Behind Act (NCLB), to narrow the achievement gap.[7] NCLB mandated greater accountability for student learning. The goal of NCLB was to have every child attain proficiency in reading and mathematics.

NCLB did not identify physical education specifically as a subject in which children should become proficient. Most recently, in December 2015, NCLB was replaced with the Every Student Succeeds Act (ESSA). ESSA, which went into effect during the 2017–2018 academic year, has included physical education as a part of a students well-rounded education. Our continued hope is that the implementation of ESSA will not only provide more state and local control over student learning, but that we will gain support and recognition for the importance of health and physical education in every student's school experience.[8] As physical educators, we too must be committed to closing creating more equitable learning opportunities for all students.

Standards and assessment of learning are important in physical education, too, not just in math or reading. In 2014, SHAPE America released the third edition of *National Standards and Grade-Level Outcomes for K-12 Physical Education*[3] (see SHAPE America Standards and Outcomes box on page 284) and a task force is currently working on the fourth edition. These standards have been adopted by all states as their physical education content standards and have been used by teachers, school districts, and teacher educators to guide the development of program curricula, unit and lesson plans (i.e., instruction), and assessments.

For standards to have meaning, assessment must be conducted to measure student learning in relation to the performance outcomes. A plethora of scholars and physical education teachers have developed assessment tools over the past

SHAPE AMERICA'S NATIONAL STANDARDS AND GRADE-LEVEL OUTCOMES FOR K-12 PHYSICAL EDUCATION

Standard 1. The physically literate individual demonstrates competency in a variety of motor skills and movement patterns.

Standard 2. The physically literate individual applies knowledge of concepts, principles, strategies, and tactics related to movement and performance.

Standard 3. The physically literate individual demonstrates the knowledge and skills to achieve and maintain a health-enhancing level of physical activity and fitness.

Standard 4. The physically literate individual exhibits responsible personal and social behavior that respects self and others.

Standard 5. The physically literate individual recognizes the value of physical activity for health, enjoyment, challenge, self-expression, and/or social interaction.

Source: SHAPE America. *National Standards and Grade Level Outcomes for K-12 Physical Education.* Champaign, IL: Human Kinetics, 2014, http://www.shapeamerica.org/standards/pe/. Used with permission.

The standards-based movement has influenced physical education programs to focus on student learning within the psychomotor, cognitive, and affective/social domains. At the end of each class, it is important for physical education teachers to summarize the class or bring it to a close by asking students questions about the focus of the lesson content.

Lars A. Niki/McGraw Hill

20 years. However, until the development of Physical Education (PE) Metrics, physical education did not have assessment instruments to measure student achievement of the national content standards and grade-level outcomes.[9]

The standards-based assessment movement has advanced learning for many students throughout the country. Unfortunately, not all students are achieving–not because they are not capable, but because the standards do not focus on equity and justice for all. It is very important to have standards as a guide, but when they are not inclusive and do not overtly focus on equity and justice issues, some students are not going to "achieve" the stated outcomes. Furthermore, the standards focus on equally–all achieving the same versus equity where the learning is based on students' needs. We argue for the importance of critically examining and implementing the standards in your programs.

CURRICULUM DEVELOPMENT

The standards-based movement significantly changed physical education curricula (i.e., programs) throughout the nation. A physical education curriculum "includes all knowledge, skills, and learning experiences that are provided to students within the school program."[5] Prior to the development of the national standards, most physical education teachers based their programs on specific activities (e.g., basketball, volleyball, and flag football) they selected to teach, which were usually determined by their area of expertise and the number of students who could partake in an activity at one time. With the development of the national standards, the activity became the medium through which instruction was delivered for students to achieve performance outcomes. That is, the standards became the focal point rather than the activity. Figure 10-1 demonstrates how each component of a physical education program works or aligns with the rest.

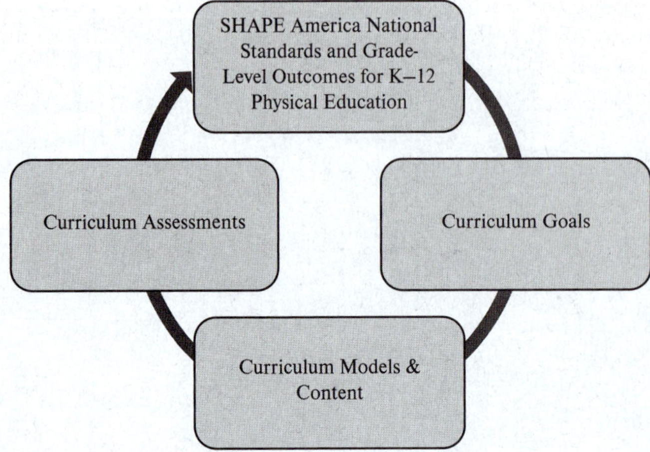

Figure 10-1 Curriculum alignment in physical education.

Source: Mitchell, S. A., and J. L. Walton-Fisette. *Essentials in Teaching Physical Education: Curriculum, Instruction and Assessment.* Champaign, IL: Human Kinetics, 2016.

For physical education teachers, unit and lesson planning is the primary focus of what occurs before teaching lessons to students. Although some teachers think well on their feet and can create activities and tasks on the spot, in a standards-based curriculum, it is very important that planning occurs in advance to ensure that the content taught is based on standards and objectives and ultimately has a purpose (see Figure 10-2 for instructional alignment). A *unit of instruction* incorporates all of the goals, objectives, content (i.e., tasks, activities, key terms, and concepts), instructional materials, and individual lessons. The *unit plan* allows teachers to make sure that the content and tasks taught

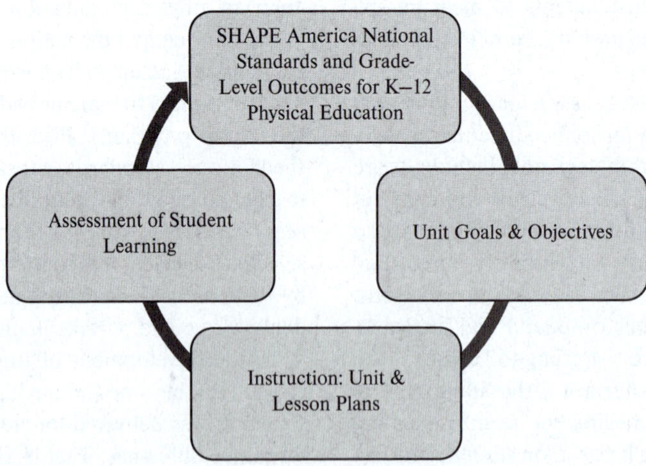

Figure 10-2 Instructional alignment in physical education.

Source: Mitchell, S. A., and J. L. Walton-Fisette. *Essentials in Teaching Physical Education: Curriculum, Instruction and Assessment.* Champaign, IL: Human Kinetics, 2016.

PHYSICAL EDUCATION PEDAGOGY

Unit Plan Outline

- Needs assessment
- National/state standards and outcomes
- Unit goals and objectives
- Assessment plan
- Management plan
- Content analysis/content map
- Block plan
- Instructional materials
- Resources

Lesson Plan Outline

- Lesson focus
- Learning objectives and standards
- Teacher goals
- Management plan
- Equipment needs
- Resources
- Instructional and activity tasks
- Modifications for differentiation
- Teaching cues and questioning
- Organization of tasks
- Closure
- Assessment

from lesson to lesson connect with one another and align with the standards and unit objectives. A *lesson plan* is a specific outline of all of the objectives, tasks, and assessments that will be included for one particular lesson. Most often, physical education teachers first develop the unit plan and work off of that plan as they make changes to their instruction from lesson to lesson. (See the Physical Education Pedagogy box on page 287 for components to consider when developing unit and lesson plans.)

Over the past 25 years, many teachers have been challenged to reorganize a program they have delivered for an extended period of time. Professional development opportunities have been provided by college and university faculty in physical education teacher education programs, by each state's association, and at state, district, and national conferences. Even with professional development opportunities and standards-based curricular texts, many physical education teachers have chosen not to restructure their program to be standards-based.

In addition to the education reform movement, other factors have contributed to the changes in physical education curriculum content. These factors include teachers' philosophies about physical education, geographic location, school and program context (e.g., facilities, equipment, and class size), and time.[5]

Teachers' beliefs and philosophies about physical education provide the lens through which a program is developed. For example, do teachers emphasize teacher- or student-centered instruction? Will the content focus be on sport-related games or will other content, such as dance, gymnastics, self-defense, swimming, and outdoor pursuits be included in the curriculum? Should the focus be on competency and proficiency in motor skills or student engagement in physical activity regardless of performance? These questions need to be discussed with physical education faculty, especially at the secondary level, before a program can be developed.

Geographic location can also be a contributing factor when designing a physical education program. Do you live in the north, where you can include winter activities such as snowshoeing and cross-country skiing? Do you live around lakes or rivers, so you can teach units on canoeing, kayaking, or fishing? Are there hiking and biking trails in the vicinity to offer outdoor pursuits such as hiking or cycling? Most often, there are activities formulated that are specific to an area (e.g., cornhole is very popular in Ohio), which may pique students' interest if offered in physical education. Understandably, some of the activities are costly, which can prohibit programs from offering such units; however, physical education programs can connect with the physical education teacher education or recreation programs at state colleges and universities or apply for grants that are available to pk–12 teachers. More than ever, it is important for physical educators to connect to physical activity options within the community as we encourage our students to be lifelong movers.

Physical educators are often challenged by the facilities in which physical education is taught, the equipment available for large or multiple classes, and large class sizes. Physical education classes are usually held in gymnasiums; however, elementary school teachers may have to teach in a gymnasium-cafeteria, may have a blacktop or outdoor grass space, and may at times have to teach in a hallway or classroom. Secondary school physical education teachers may have a gymnasium along with a wrestling room, auxiliary gym, weight room, fitness center, dance studio, or outdoor fields and tennis courts. The amount and type of equipment can vary from school to school and school district to school district. Funding is usually the primary factor in how much a physical education program will receive toward purchasing equipment. School systems with more funding, normally in higher socioeconomic communities, have more up-to-date equipment, compared to schools that receive less funding, which tend to be in lower socioeconomic communities. Lastly, class size significantly affects the curriculum, instruction, and form of assessment implemented in physical education. Physical education teachers need to know how many students are in each class and how many teachers are in each class period. School and program contexts such as facilities, equipment, and class size frequently influence one another.

Time is teachers' greatest challenge and barrier when developing a curriculum. Questions that need to be considered are how long are the class periods, how often do the students have physical education, and how long should each unit last? Most elementary school students receive 30–60 minutes of physical education once or twice a week; middle school physical education programs vary from every other day for a full year to every day for a quarter or semester; and high school students receive as little as one quarter or semester of physical education throughout their 4 years in high school. In 2015, 31 states allowed substitutions for physical

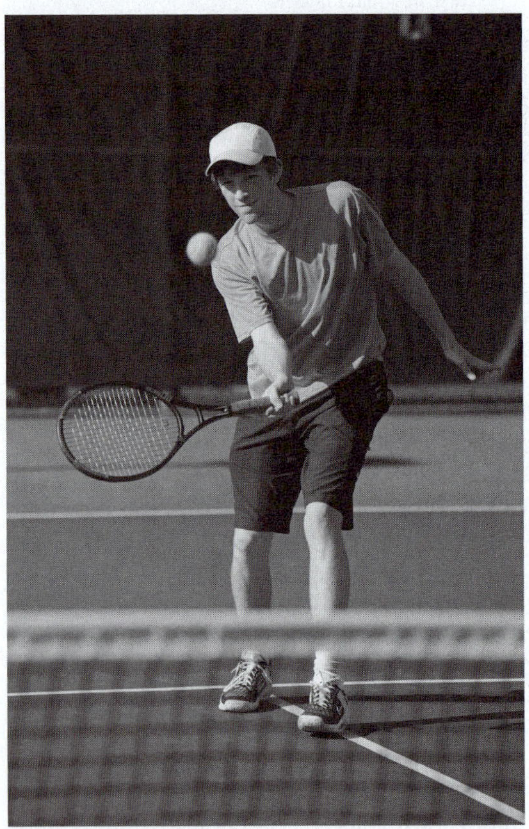

Geographic location, facilities, equipment, and time are some of the key factors that influence curricular development of physical education programs. Having access to facilities and equipment, such as tennis courts and racquets, creates valuable options to teach content that has potential to be a lifelong activity.

Wesley Hitt/Digital Vision/Getty Images

education (such as ROTC, band, and athletics) and 15 states allowed school district waivers in place of physical education requirements.[10]

PEDAGOGICAL MODELS

As physical education teachers develop their curriculum, a teacher's philosophy, along with program goals and objectives, influences the focus of instruction. Teachers need to ask themselves if they are more focused on skill and motor competence, cooperation and problem solving, social justice and equity issues, or development of a personal fitness plan. Many of these foci align with the national standards; however, how instruction is delivered to students may differ. Thus, pedagogical models have been developed by researchers, teacher educators, and physical education teachers over the past 25 years. These models have been labeled as curriculum or instructional models, and are currently most known as "models-based practice."[5] However, many educators with a critical perspective use pedagogical models, because it is vitally important to consider the contexts, needs, and experiences of students when implementing any "model." (See examples of Pedagogical Models in Physical Education box.)

Throughout this section, a brief introduction to the following pedagogical models will be provided: skill themes, personal and social responsibility, Teaching games for understanding (TGfU) and the tactical games model (TGM), sport education, fitness education, adventure education, outdoor education, activist approaches, and pedagogies of affect. Please know that this is not an exhaustive list. As you read about each of the models, it is important to remember that there is not a "one size fits all" model for all content taught in physical education. If teachers focus on sport-related games, the TGfU and the sport education models (SEMs) might be considered; whereas if the focus is on developing locomotor, nonlocomotor, and manipulative skills, the skill themes model should be the framework in which they base their planning. The key, across all of these models, is to engage in pedagogy that meets the needs of your students.

Skill Themes

The skill themes approach to games, sport, gymnastics, and dance, considered the "developmental model," is implemented in elementary school physical education.[11] Movement skills and concepts are the basis of this model. Basic skills focus on performance and concepts describe how the skill is going to be performed. There are four phases included in the skill themes approach:

1. Basic skill–mastery and achievement of the critical elements of the skill according to the age and developmental level of the students.
2. Combinations–addition of other skills and movement concepts once the basic skills and critical elements are mastered.
3. Skill in contexts–skills, movements, and combinations performed in a variety of contexts.
4. Culminating activity–application of the skill in different content areas within games, sport, gymnastics, and dance.[12]

The skill themes approach creates opportunities for all students to learn through developmentally appropriate skill theme progressions. Skill themes progress from simple to complex. All students may engage in the same skills and concepts; however, teachers will need to differentiate instruction according to students' skill development.

Personal and Social Responsibility

The personal and social responsibility model (PSRM) focuses on the development of the whole student, which includes how students think, feel, and interact with others. The model embraces students as individuals, provides them with a voice, allows them to make decisions on their own, and places less emphasis on skill development and academic achievement.[13] The goal of PSRM is for students to take more responsibility for their personal and social development in physical activity settings both in and outside of school.

Hellison's model is widely used in elementary school physical education programs, as elementary school students learn how to have respectful behavior and take responsibility for their actions;

PEDAGOGICAL MODELS IN PHYSICAL EDUCATION

Models	Purpose/Goal	Grade Level
Skill Themes	Develops competence in fundamental movement skills and concepts; locomotor, nonlocomotor, and manipulative skills are taught within games and sports, gymnastics, and dance.	Elementary
Personal and Social Responsibility	Assigns students more responsibility for their personal and social development in physical activity settings both in and outside of school.	Elementary Middle High
Teaching Games for Understanding/ Tactical Games Model	Improves students' game performance by combining tactical awareness with skill execution to increase interest and excitement about games and sports.	Elementary–second and higher Middle High
Sport Education	Educates and develops students to be competent, literate, and enthusiastic sportspersons through playing sports and undertaking various roles within the sport environment, such as coach, manager, official, and player.	Elementary–third and higher Middle High
Fitness Education	Uses many different approaches to incorporate fitness and wellness content into physical education programs by developing students' knowledge and skills to be physically active for a lifetime.	Elementary Middle High
Adventure-Based Learning	Involves activities that promote holistic student involvement (physical, cognitive, social, and emotional) in tasks that involve challenges and cooperation.	Elementary Middle High
Outdoor Education	Involves personal and group development, teamwork, trust, and taking on risks and challenges within a natural setting, typically in an outdoor environment.	Elementary Middle High
Activist Approaches	Codesign units of instruction with students rather than for or on them.	Elementary Middle High
Pedagogies of Affect • Meaningful physical education (PE) • Social & emotional learning • Trauma-informed practices • Pedagogies of love	Emphasizing the affective and social learning domains.	Elementary Middle High

Elementary school physical education teachers have the opportunity to utilize the skill themes and personal and social responsibility models as the framework for their units of instruction. These students are working in pairs on the skill development of the forearm pass. Working in pairs allows students to have sufficient repetitions and provides teachers time to observe students' performance and give feedback based on the critical elements of the skill.

Lars A. Niki/McGraw Hill

however, many secondary school programs integrate PSRM into their curriculum. Teachers and students can assess their personal and social responsibility based on five different levels:

- Level I–respecting the rights and feelings of others
- Level II–participation and effort
- Level III–self-direction
- Level IV–helping others and leadership
- Level V–outside of the gym[14]

Level I is the lowest and most basic (i.e., students having self-control), whereas Level V is the highest and most challenging (i.e., being a role model). Teachers can create laminated posters of the levels and place them on bulletin boards and gym walls, making them visible for students to see. As teachers provide instructional strategies that center on personal and social responsibility, students can self-assess which level they are at within each lesson.

Four primary themes of this model are that these levels should be *integrated* across all physical education content, not taught separately; personal and social responsibility behaviors should be *transferred* outside of the physical education and school settings; students should be *empowered*; and teachers and students should develop a *relationship*.[14] The key to the success of this model is for teachers to find a balance between instructional tasks that focus on responsibility and on physical education content. It is believed that the more responsibility and ownership (i.e., voice, choice, and empowerment) students have, the more open they will be to learning.

Teaching Games for Understanding/Tactical Games Model

TGfU/TGM is a problem-based approach to games teaching. When you played sports in physical education, did you ever ask your teacher, "When are we going to play a game?" Were you taught skill after skill long before you ever played a game? The goal of the model is to improve students' game performance by combining tactical awareness with skill execution and increase students' interest in and excitement about games.[15]

Because the focus of both models is on solving tactical problems in sport-related games, a games classification system was designed to group similar games together based on the problems that need to be solved, which include invasion (e.g., basketball, soccer), net/wall (e.g., volleyball, tennis), striking/fielding (e.g., softball, kickball), and target (e.g., golf, bowling). Here is an example of how games are similar within each classification: In a game of basketball, Team A is trying to invade Team B's territory in order to score, while Team B is trying to prevent Team A from scoring. The same is true in games such as soccer, hockey, and football, which is why they are all classified as invasion games. Although different movements and skills are needed on the offensive and defensive sides of the ball (or puck) in each of these games, the tactics to score and prevent scoring are similar.

The tactical approach to games teaching includes a game-practice-game instructional format. This format begins with a modified game (i.e., Game 1) to set up or expose the problem the teacher wants students to solve by setting game goals, conditions, and a scoring system. Then, the teacher brings the students together to ask them thought-provoking questions to guide them to solve the tactical problem. Once students have solved the tactical problem, the teacher designs a gamelike practice task that emphasizes the solutions to the tactical problem. After students have had sufficient opportunities to practice the task, they play another modified game (i.e., Game 2) to see whether their skills or movements improve during game play. Improved game understanding and game performance is a primary focus of the TGfU/TGM models.

Sport Education

The SEM was first developed by Daryl Siedentop in 1984 to create an authentic sport experience for students in physical education that is developmentally appropriate and to provide opportunities for boys and girls to participate equally. The SEM models genuine sport experiences enjoyed by athletes. The overall goal of the model is to educate and develop students to be competent, literate, and enthusiastic sportspersons.[16] SEM can be implemented as early as the third grade and at middle and high school levels.

The main features of the model include seasons, team affiliation, formal competition, record keeping, a culminating event, and festivity. *Seasons* include longer units, between 15 and 20 lessons, to provide students enough time for teams to practice together and compete against other teams in the class. *Team affiliation* can be developed since students are placed on the same team for the entire season (i.e., unit). This provides teams time to learn how to play and interact together as they work toward a common goal. *Formal competition* includes contests in formats such as preseason and regular-season play, tournaments, and leagues. All games are played according to a schedule designed by the physical education teacher. *Record keeping* primarily includes statistics taken by teachers or students during formal competitions. Records can include shot

In the teaching games for understanding, tactical games, and sport education models, students engage in sport-related games to improve their game performance and develop as competent, literate, and enthusiastic sportspersons. Small-sided games, as shown with these boys, provide increased opportunities for students to get involved in game play and enjoy their sporting experiences.
Jade/Blend Images LLC

attempts, batting averages, and points per game. These statistics can provide feedback for teams to help guide them in areas of the game in which they need to improve. Each season ends with a *culminating event* such as a championship in sport-related games or a final competition in gymnastics and dance. Normally, a winning team is declared in the culminating event. *Festivity* is included throughout the entire season as groups select their own team names and colors at the beginning of the season, take pictures or create posters that represent their teams, and perhaps even include an awards ceremony at the conclusion of the culminating event.

SEM is a student-centered, inclusive model that requires everyone to play and be involved with some aspect of the game in each lesson. At the start of the season, each student signs a team contract where they select a role and responsibility to perform throughout the season. In addition to being team players, students also have the opportunity to participate in the following roles: head and assistant coach, captain, trainer, statistician, referee, judge, equipment manager, publicist, and scorekeeper. Not all of these roles need to be filled for each unit. For example, in a floor hockey unit, a judge will not be required, whereas that would be an important role in a gymnastics or dance unit. Furthermore, teams might comprise only three to five students, which would not be enough to cover each role listed above. As in PSRM, the more responsibility and

In the fitness education model, it is important to apply the concepts discussed during classroom-based lessons in laboratory activities. These students may have learned about the muscular endurance component of health-related fitness, so are engaging in abdominal exercises with medicine balls to work on their abdominal endurance.

Claudia Gopperl/beyond fotomedia/Jupiterimages

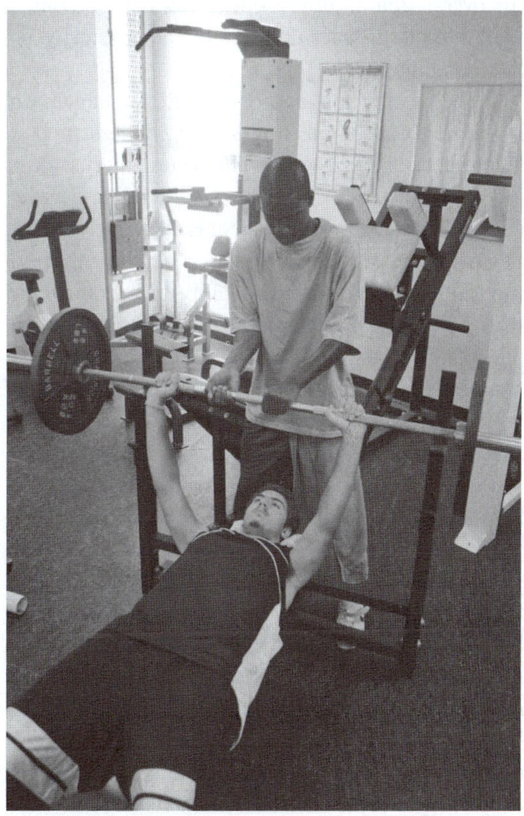

When engaging in fitness activities such as weight training, knowing how to spot is as important as understanding the training principles associated with quality form and performance of a particular exercise. These students are working together to ensure the safety of the student who is bench-pressing.

Gary He/McGraw Hill

ownership students have in physical education, the more opportunities they will have to learn.

Fitness Education

Fitness education is a broad and general term that encompasses the various ways physical educators can incorporate fitness and wellness content into physical education programs. Fitness education can include units on the health-related components of fitness, walking or hiking, or weight training. Teachers may choose to include fitness during class warm-ups, as fitness Fridays, or integrated throughout other games and activities. In all of these units, the overall goal in fitness education is for students to develop knowledge and skills to be physically active for a lifetime.

The most formal approach to fitness education is the concepts-based fitness and wellness model, where students engage in classroom discussions, laboratory activities, and physical activity experiences.[17] The goal of this model is the development of an understanding of physical activity–that is, that students learn how to develop and execute their own physical activity programs in which they can participate in and out of school. The health-related components of fitness, goal setting, nutrition, stress management, program development, and self-assessment are concepts taught at the secondary school level in the concepts-based fitness and wellness model. In physical education programs where students have physical education every day of the week, teachers will need to decide how to divide the classroom-focused and activity-based lessons. Laboratory experiences should involve the students in active learning and self-evaluation, whereas the classroom lessons should focus on cognitive learning and application.[17] Collectively, the laboratory experiences should integrate and reinforce the concepts taught in the classroom lessons. Whether fitness education is integrated with other curricular approaches and content or stands as the defining curriculum, fitness education is important.

As obesity rates continue to rise and physical activity levels decrease across the lifespan, it is important more than ever for students to learn fitness, physical activity, and wellness concepts and how to apply these principles in the development of their own physical activity and personal fitness programs. For students to be active outside of school, they need to be able to develop physical activity programs based on their own fitness levels and needs.

Adventure-Based Learning

Adventure-based learning (ABL) allows students to learn about themselves and their peers as they take on individual and group tasks and challenges. In ABL, physical education teachers act as facilitators, while students collaborate and problem-solve with one another to accomplish a task. Teachers support their students and ensure safety; however, students play a major role in their learning. A key component of ABL is self and group reflection to discuss how tasks were accomplished and, most importantly, how they felt throughout the different activities.

The most widely known student-centered ABL program integrated in physical education is Project Adventure.[18] Project Adventure is based on five philosophical concepts: challenge, cooperation, risk, trust, and problem solving. These concepts can guide students to develop personal goals in regard to achieving a particular task such as climbing a 25-foot climbing wall, walking across a high ropes course, or feeling safe during a trust fall.

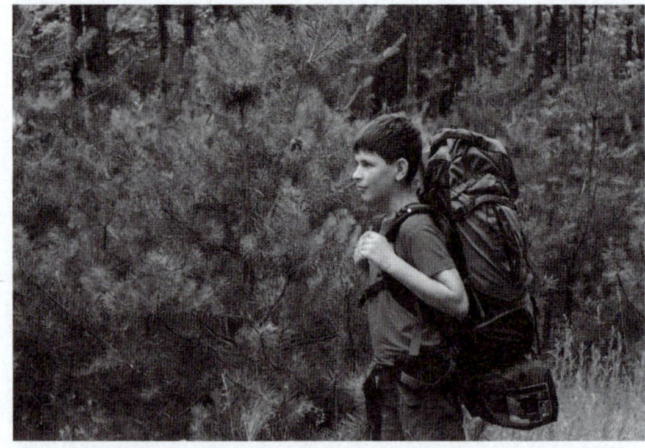

The adventure education and outdoor education models provide students with opportunities to engage in activities in the natural environment, take risks, face challenges, and problem-solve. This student has packed the necessary materials needed on a hike that includes appropriate clothing, food, water, and a first aid kit.
Sergiy Zavgorodny/iStock/Getty Images

Physical educators can base their instruction around the following three essential elements:

- *Experiential learning cycle*–The learning process begins with the learning experience, then proceeds to observations and reflections (what happened?) followed by abstract concepts and generalizations (so what?), and concludes with application and transference of the lessons learned to other adventure-based activities (now what?).
- *Full value contract*–Group members design and agree to a contract in regard to the behaviors they feel should be demonstrated among all group members throughout the task, activity, or unit.
- *Challenge by choice*–Students, within a lesson or activity, choose which task they want to perform and the level of physical or emotional risk they would like to take.

ABL provides students with a variety of opportunities to take on challenges, gain support, build trust, problem-solve, cooperate, reflect upon their experiences, and most importantly, learn through the experiences they undertake within an adventure-based unit.

Outdoor Education

When you think about outdoor activities, such as backpacking, orienteering, snowshoeing, and kayaking, do you consider them activities that can be implemented in physical education programs? Hopefully, your answer to this question is yes! Although some of these activities can be costly (e.g., kayaking) and will need additional funding from the school or grants awarded, others have minimal to no cost (e.g., hiking). Comparable to other pedagogical models, outdoor education can lead to increased physical activity for all students.

Outdoor education is similar to ABL, as they both focus on personal and group development, teamwork, trust, and taking on risks and challenges. The key difference between the two models is that outdoor education occurs in the natural setting, where teachers and students have little to no control over the environment and potential hazards that may arise.[19] Dealing with hazards such as severe and unexpected weather, variable terrain, and wildlife must be discussed, researched, and assessed before students embark on an outdoor excursion. Outdoor education places more emphasis on skill development than adventure education does; however, the premise of both models is the student-centered, experiential learning process. Outdoor pursuits have considerable potential to provide students with enjoyment and appreciation of the great outdoors.

Activist Approaches

An activist approach significantly differs from the models discussed previously in this section because this approach was initially developed as a "girl friendly" pedagogical model in physical education and youth sport.* An activist approach emphasizes how educators learn to listen and respond to the needs and interests of young people and attempt to challenge and change power relations in movement spaces.** Furthermore, an activist approach creates spaces for students to codesign units of instruction, so they have a voice in their learning opportunities. This is different from the other models where the educators identify the learning experiences. This sometimes can be difficult for teachers to engage in; however, students are more interested in the learning they need and desire versus what is put upon them. Below you will find two different four-step processes in the codesign process–both focus on listening and responding to students.

Four-Step Process #1

1. Student-centered pedagogy
2. Critical study of embodiment
3. Inquiry-based physical education centered in action
4. Listening and responding to girls (students) over time

---

*Oliver, K. & Kirk, D. (2015). *Girls, gender and physical education.* Routledge: London.

**Lynch, S., Walton-Fisette, J. L., & Luguetti, C. (2022). *Pedagogies of social justice in physical education and youth sport.* Routledge: London.

Four-Step Process #2

1. Building relationships with young people
2. Identifying barriers to sport in the community
3. Imagining alternative possibilities
4. Working collaboratively to create alternatives

Pedagogies of Affect

Pedagogies of affect focus on the affective and social learning domains that may include caring, love, joy, motivation, how one feels, interest, equity, justice, etc.* So, often in physical education, we emphasize the psychomotor domain; however, with the increased focus on mental and emotional health and social justice and equity issues, pedagogies of affect are becoming more prominent with educators and their pedagogical practices. We focus specifically on the following pedagogies of affect: meaningful physical education, social and emotional learning, trauma-informed practices, and pedagogies of love.

Meaningful Physical Education

- Designed to be used as a framework that can help guide teachers' pedagogical decision-making in order to prioritize meaningful experiences.
- A collection of ideas about the types of features that influence ways students experience meaningfulness and about how teachers might promote these.
- Designed to be integrated with local curricular and policy objectives and used in concert with other pedagogical models/approaches where appropriate.
- Designed to promote the types of experiences that will draw students back to movement both within and beyond PE.
- A way to involve students more in age-appropriate decision making to promote active learning.
- Built on the premise that meaningfulness is experienced in subjective ways in transaction with others in a social environment that necessitates regular reflection and adjustment.
- Democratic and reflective.**

Social and Emotional Learning

- The Collaborative for Academic, Social, and Emotional Learning (CASEL) defines social and emotional learning as "the process through which children and adults understand and manage emotions, set and achieve positive goals, feel and show empathy for others, establish and maintain positive relationships, and make responsible decisions."†
- The CASEL framework is based on five core competencies: self-awareness, self-management, social awareness, relationship skills, and responsible decision making.
- **Self-awareness** includes: identifying emotions, accurate self-perception, recognizing strengths, self-confidence, and self-efficacy.
- **Self-management** includes: impulse control, stress management, self-discipline, self-motivation, goal setting, and organizational skills.
- **Social awareness** includes: perspective-taking, empathy, appreciating diversity, and respect for others.
- **Relationship skills** includes: communication, social engagement, relationship building, and teamwork.
- **Responsible for decision making** includes: identifying problems, analyzing situations, solving problems, evaluating, reflections, and ethical responsibility.

Trauma-Informed Practices

- Being trauma-informed includes acquiring knowledge about childhood trauma and is versed in related strategies.
- Become self-aware of your social identities, biases, and systems of meaning through critical reflection.
- Engage in strategies that foster resilient learners:††

*Kirk, D. (2020). *Precarity, critical pedagogy, and physical education.* Routledge: London.

**Learning about meaningful physical education (LAMPE): https://meaningfulpe.wordpress.com/ Retrieved on April 21st, 2022.

†Collaborative for Academic, Social, and Emotional Learning (2017). CASEL's core competencies. https://casel.org/.

††Souers, K., & Hall, P. (2019). *Relationship, responsibility, and regulation: Trauma-invested practices for fostering resilient learners.* Alexandria, VA: ASCD.

Mitchell, S. A., & Walton-Fisette, J. L. (2022). *The essentials of teaching physical education: Curriculum, instruction, and assessment.* Champaign, IL: Human Kinetics.

- Create physically and emotionally safe spaces.
- Formulate positive and healthy relationships with students.
- Develop student responsibility.
- Guide students toward self-regulation.

Pedagogies of Love

- Critical educators emphasize choosing love and that emotions such as love should be viewed as complex and social, inseparable from actions and relations.
- Love goes beyond and "ethic of care"* as giving care does not equate to acting in a loving manner.
- Pedagogies of love are conceptualized as a practice that is both politically and socially constructed.
- Love cannot be present in a situation where one group or individual dominates over another, because without justice, there can be no love.
- Emphasize three core values:**
  - Love as dialog.
  - Love as solidarity.
  - Love as hope and imagination.

ASSESSMENT AND ACCOUNTABILITY

The standards-based movement has had significant influence on educational programs across all content areas, including physical education. As discussed previously, the physical education curriculum had to change from a "busy, happy, good" philosophy to programs that emphasized student learning.[20] Although making changes to goals, objectives, and instructional processes was critical, standards and instruction meant very little without knowing what students know and are able to do. Assessment is the salient component needed to measure whether students have learned and are achieving the national standards.[3] Furthermore, assessment holds physical education programs and teachers accountable for student achievement. Connecting the standards, instruction, and assessment components of physical education curricula and units of instruction is referred to as *instructional alignment.* With even just one of the components excluded in this alignment, physical education programs and lessons lack purpose and meaning.

Types of Assessment

Assessment can be implemented at the beginning of or during a unit of instruction (formative) or at the end of a unit (summative). Formative assessments are true to their name; they inform teachers whether students are learning and give them an indication of how to plan upcoming lessons for students to achieve the unit goals and objectives. Furthermore, teachers can notify students of their progress to give them a sense of where they are in the learning process. Formative assessments tend to be ongoing throughout the instructional process within a unit.[21] Summative assessments inform teachers and students about what students learned over the course of the unit and are usually associated with a grade.

Assessments used in physical education are performance-based and are used to measure higher levels of student learning–specifically students' understanding of concepts and ability to apply knowledge while engaging in a meaningful or worthwhile task.[21] Teachers do not have to conduct all assessments, as they can educate students on how to partake in peer and self-assessments. Performance-based assessments include observations, checklists, rubrics, journals, portfolios (print or electronic), essays, role-playing exercises, projects, and game performance. (See the Types of Assessment box on page 298.)

Teachers continuously observe students' performance and behaviors during physical education classes. Oftentimes, teachers provide students with feedback based on critical elements of skills or tactics and strategies that occur within game play. Teachers frequently make adjustments or think on their feet based on what they observe, deviating from the daily lesson plan. Without question, observation is important in physical education; however, it is even more critical that teachers document their observations in regard to student performance and learning. Checklists are an example of how teachers can document students' ability to perform the critical elements of specified skills. It allows

---

*Noddings, N. (1984). *Caring: A feminine approach to ethics and moral education*. Los Angeles: University of California Press.

**Lynch, S., Walton-Fisette, J. L., & Luguetti, C. (2022). *Pedagogies of social justice in physical education and youth sport*. London: Routledge.

Assessment is the key to determining whether students have learned throughout the course of a lesson or unit of instruction. There are many types of assessments. This physical education teacher is observing his students' performance during an activity, which will inform him what feedback or changes he needs to make in upcoming activities or lessons.

Richard Lewisohn/Digital Vision/Getty Images

TYPES OF ASSESSMENT

Formative Assessment

- Implemented at the beginning of or during a unit of instruction.
- Informs teachers and students whether students are learning.
- Suggests how to plan upcoming lessons for students to achieve the unit goals and objectives.

Summative Assessment

- Implemented at the end of a unit of instruction.
- Informs teachers and students about what students have learned over the course of the unit.
- Usually associated or equated with a grade.

Performance-Based Assessment

- Measures higher levels of student learning, specifically students' understanding of concepts and ability to apply knowledge.

Examples of Assessments

- Observations
- Checklists
- Rubrics
- Journals
- Portfolios (print or electronic)
- Essays
- Role plays
- Projects
- Game performance

teachers to assess performance systematically, which holds the teachers, along with the students, accountable for student learning. Students can also use checklists to conduct peer and self-assessments. Checklists can assess content taught within a variety of pedagogical models.

Rubrics are frequently used by teachers as criteria to assess students' knowledge and performance. Rubrics are based on descriptors of various levels, including "competent" (i.e., performing at the level teachers want all students to achieve), exceeding expectations (i.e., performing at a level higher than competency), and not meeting expectations or competency. Some teachers use "developing," "acceptable," and "target" as their different levels. Effective rubrics include detailed descriptors that make it clear how each level is differentiated from the next. For example, if a teacher is using a rubric to assess students' offensive skills in a game of basketball, and part of the criteria for competency is that students need to successfully complete two out of three passes, "exceeding" or "target" would be three out of three passes and "not meeting" or "developing" would be less than two out of three passes. If the criterion simply stated "successful passes," would one out of three be considered competent? The challenge for physical education teachers who develop their own rubrics is establishing the "competent" or "acceptable" level. This needs to be determined by the SHAPE America and state standards of performance outcomes for each grade band or level, as well as knowledge of their students' abilities. Rubrics can be used to assess student portfolios, projects, and role-playing exercises, along with other performance-based assessments not listed here. As with checklists, teachers can employ rubrics to assess content taught within a variety of curriculum models.

Journals are a great method of gathering information on students' thoughts, feelings, and cognitive knowledge about specific activities and experiences they have in physical education. Journals can be completed on a simple piece of paper, in a notebook or folder, electronically, through an app, or an audio recording. Journals are best used as a formative assessment, since it would be difficult to assign a grade to students' thoughts and feelings. Journals are particularly used to assess SHAPE America standards 4 and 5, which focus on students' personal and social responsibility and valuing physical activity.

Assessing game performance is imperative when teaching sport and game units, particularly at the middle and high school levels, because game play provides students the opportunity to apply the skills, knowledge, and tactics they have learned throughout the unit. Because game play is faster-paced than isolated skill practices, assessing students' offensive and defensive skills and movements or teamwork can be rather challenging. In units where teachers implement the sport education or TGfU/TGM curriculum models, the Game Performance Assessment Instrument can be used to assess students' base position, decision making, skill execution, support for teammates in possession of the ball, marking or guarding opponents, covering for teammates who are defending against opponents, and adjusting to the flow of the game.[15] Teachers can select several of the components out of the seven to assess students' game performance based on the unit of instruction. For example, skill execution and decision making can be assessed in all sports and games within the games classification system; however, support for teammates in possession of the ball is important in invasion games such as soccer or basketball, but not in golf or softball.

Over the years, teachers have struggled with implementing assessments within physical education lessons because it takes up too much instructional time, it is too complicated to develop their own assessment tools, or it is difficult to assess hundreds of students alone. We will not deny that conducting quality and authentic (i.e., realistic, gamelike) assessments is challenging; however, many resources have been developed (e.g., PE Metrics) to provide teachers with examples of assessments they can implement in their classes.

For teachers to be successful at implementing assessment within instruction, they should first determine which standards and learning domains they want to assess, and they take into consideration the number of students in each class, the frequency and duration of students' engagement in

Assessment can be conducted by teachers or students. This student is using a skills checklist to observe one of his classmates during physical education class.

Ken Karp/McGraw Hill

physical education, the aspects they want to assess within a single-class period or unit, and whether the assessment will be formative or summative.[22] Then we suggest that teachers select one class or grade level to conduct the assessment, so they can determine management procedures, instructional processes, and potential changes they would like to make to the assessment tool before assessing a larger number of students.

Our hope is that teachers become aware of how important it is to conduct assessments that measure student learning. As the standards-based movement continues to steer education in the twenty-first century, administrators, teachers, and students are being held accountable for academic achievement in relation to content standards. Assessment is the key that provides purpose and meaning to instruction and informs teachers, students, parents, and administrators of students' achievement of the national and state standards.

CHARACTERISTICS OF EFFECTIVE TEACHING

Teaching can be defined as those interactions of the teacher and the learner who make learning more successful.[23] Although it is possible for learning to occur without a teacher's involvement, it is generally accepted that teachers facilitate the acquisition of knowledge, skills, and attitudes. Effective teachers use a variety of pedagogical skills and strategies to ensure that their students are appropriately engaged in relevant activities a high percentage of the time, hold positive expectations for their students, and create and maintain a classroom climate that is warm and nurturing.[24]

Salient teacher behaviors can be divided into several broad areas: organization, communication, instruction, motivation, and human relations. (See the Salient Teacher Behaviors box.) These characteristics are common to effective teachers, regardless of the skill to be learned, the age of the students, or the setting in which the teaching occurs.

Organizational skills are very important for establishing the learning environment and facilitating student involvement in activities. To be effective, a teacher must ensure that the lesson to be presented relates to the stated objectives, meets the needs of the individual learners, and is sequenced in a logical manner. Through efficient and thorough planning, effective teachers minimize transition time (i.e., the time to move students from place to place) and management time (i.e., time used for tasks such as taking attendance). Lessons are planned to ensure that students receive maximum opportunities to practice relevant skills and experience success. Actively supervising and monitoring student performance and providing students with appropriate feedback are characteristics of successful teachers. Skilled teachers bring each lesson to an end by summarizing what has been accomplished and by providing students with an assessment of their progress toward the stated objectives.

SALIENT TEACHER BEHAVIORS

Organization

- Formulate plans with specific objectives and tasks that minimize transition and management time.
- Maximize opportunities for students to practice skills.
- Supervise and monitor student performance and provide feedback.
- Assess students' progress toward lesson plan objectives.

Communication

- Speak clearly and project your voice.
- Provide clear and precise directions, explanations, and instructions.
- Ask thought-provoking and critical-thinking questions to enhance students' involvement in the learning process.
- Use eye contact, smiles, and high fives.
- Articulate high expectations for all students.

Instruction

- Acquire expertise in instructional media, technology, and physical education content.
- Gather knowledge of students' needs and backgrounds.
- Sequence tasks progressively based on differing students' abilities and progress toward the lesson objectives.
- Modify lesson plans during instruction according to students' needs and abilities.

Motivation

- Learn students' interests and seek creative ways to involve students in the learning process.
- Use reinforcement techniques, such as checklists, contracts, and award systems.
- Give students a voice and provide them with choice and opportunities to be responsible.

Human Relations

- Listen to students and accept them for who they are.
- Provide students with opportunities to build their self-confidence and self-worth.
- Establish and maintain a rapport with all students.
- Have a sense of humor.

Communication skills needed by the teacher include verbal and nonverbal expressive skills, written competencies, and the ability to use various media. The ability to speak clearly and project one's voice in a pleasing manner is important. Other attributes of a successful teacher are the ability to give clear, precise directions and explanations and to use terminology and vocabulary that is appropriate to the activity and the level of the learners. The teacher's ability to use questions to elicit student input, to promote student involvement, and to clarify student understanding of the material being presented enhances the effectiveness of the learning process. Effective teachers are also aware of their nonverbal communication with students, such as use of eye contact, smiles, and high fives. Through their verbal and nonverbal behaviors, effective teachers model the kinds of behaviors they wish their students to exhibit, such as interest in and enjoyment of the activity and respect for other people's opinions and needs.

Written communication skills are also essential, especially in the planning and evaluation phases of teaching. Teachers who possess effective written communication skills are able to express themselves clearly. The ability to communicate

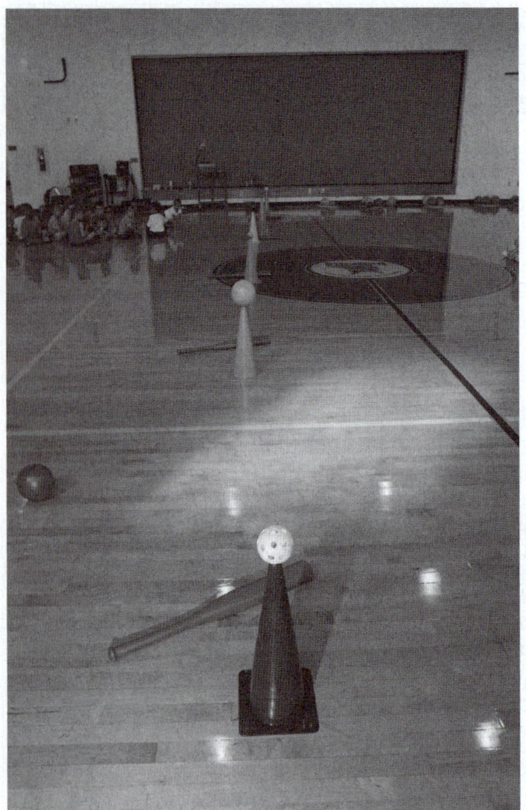

Planning and organization are key characteristics of effective teacher behaviors. Teachers who plan in advance of a lesson and are organized, such as having the equipment setup before the students come into the gymnasium, usually have lessons that provide students with more opportunities to learn and engage in more activity time.

Lars A. Niki/McGraw Hill

with supervisors, participants, parents, and community members will help to establish a more successful program.

Expertise in the use of various instructional media and technology contributes to a teacher's effectiveness. The use of computer programs, such as PowerPoint, Google Slides, Microsoft Word, and Excel, to present information to students is an important skill. Increasingly, technology is being incorporated into teaching. The Internet, handheld devices, fitness tools such as fitness watches with The Global Positioning System (GPS) and heart rate, pedometers, and smart-phone apps can enhance student learning. Incorporation of media and technology into student learning activities can contribute to the accomplishment of instructional goals and objectives.

Competency in a variety of *instructional skills* is essential for effective teaching. When planning lessons for students, effective teachers use their knowledge of the content to be taught, in conjunction with instructional objectives and students' needs, to provide appropriate experiences leading to the attainment of stated goals. Effective teaching requires the ability to sequence movement tasks by increasing difficulty and complexity as students progress, and by providing opportunities for students to develop and apply skills. Good teachers not only must be able to implement planned experiences effectively, but also must be flexible so that they can appropriately modify planned experiences to suit the needs of the students and the situations that arise within the learning environment.

Effective teachers are able to maintain an orderly, productive learning environment, handling discipline problems appropriately while encouraging and providing opportunities for students to learn responsibility and to be accountable for their actions. A wide variety of teaching methods and instructional strategies are judiciously employed to maximize students' active and successful engagement in relevant tasks. The ability to present clear expectations and offer accurate demonstrations contributes to learning. Effective teachers actively monitor their students' performances and are concerned about the quality of their efforts. Teachers are aware of, and capably respond to, the myriad of events that occur within the instructional environment; this quality, called "with-it-ness," is often described as "having eyes in the back of one's head." Evaluation skills are also important. Teachers must be able to observe and analyze student performance, focusing on the critical elements in relation to the goals, with feedback reinforcing or modifying responses as necessary.

The communication of high expectations for each student is also important. Teachers should hold high expectations for both student learning and behavior. Positive expectations, including the belief that all students are capable of learning, are important in establishing a warm, nurturing classroom climate and a productive learning environment.[24]

The *ability to motivate students* to perform to their potential is the goal of every teacher. Skillful teachers use a variety of teaching techniques to stimulate interest in participation and seek creative techniques to involve students in the learning process. They also use appropriate reinforcement techniques to maintain student involvement and promote a high level of student effort. These may include checklists, contracts, award systems, and verbal and nonverbal feedback. Praise is used thoughtfully; it is contingent on the correct performance, specific in its nature and intent, and sincere. Successful teachers continually update their lessons in an effort to meet students' needs and to make the material relevant and challenging to the students.

Effective teachers possess superior *human relations skills*. They listen to students and accept and treat them as individuals. They strive to instill in each student a sense of self-worth. Effective teachers show concern for the well-being of each student in their classes and endeavor to provide students with opportunities that will enhance their self-confidence. The ability to establish and maintain rapport with students and staff and a readiness to acknowledge their own mistakes are also characteristics that many successful teachers possess. A sense of humor is a welcome attribute as well.

In summary, effective teachers are able to successfully utilize a variety of skills pertaining to organization, communication, instruction, motivation, and human relations. However, effective teaching requires more than these skills; it requires the ability to accurately assess the needs of the moment and tailor the skills to the specific context and situation. Although many of these skills appear to be innate in certain individuals, all of them can be developed or improved by individuals who desire to become effective teachers.

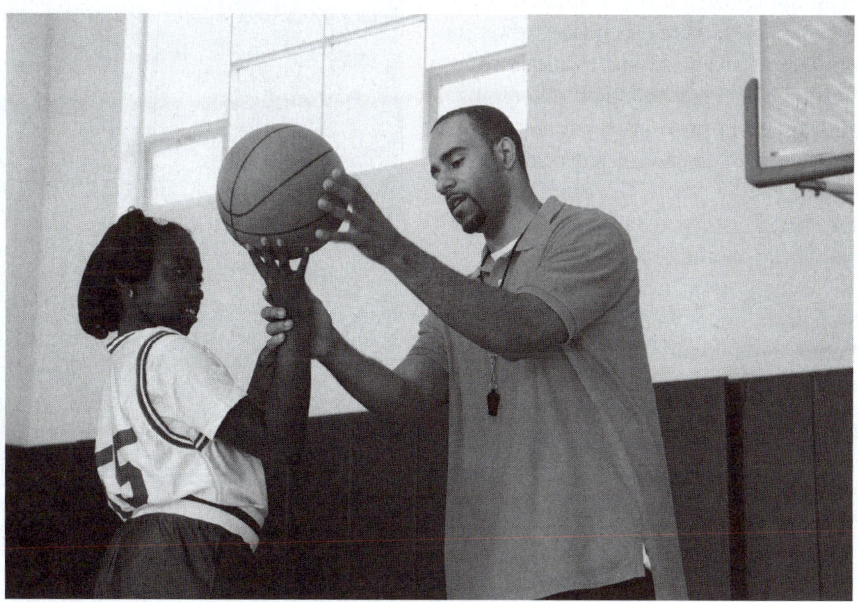

Teachers attempt to motivate their students by providing them with developmentally appropriate content and specific feedback based on their performance. This teacher is helping his student learn how to hold and shoot a basketball.

Colorblind/Fuse/Getty Images

ADDRESSING SOCIAL JUSTICE ISSUES IN PHYSICAL EDUCATION

As we begin this section on social justice issues in physical education, we would first like you to think back to your own PK-12 physical education experiences. As we argued for in the first chapter of this book, we hope you have most reflected upon your social identities, systems of meaning, and lived experiences in physical education when you were younger, which might have included what you enjoyed and did not enjoy, what you liked and disliked, and what role your teachers played in these experiences. Think back to those elementary, middle, and high school physical education classes and reflect upon the following questions: Were athletes and higher skilled students given special privileges? Did students with disabilities participate with the rest of the class or were they off to the side, away from the action? Were girls and boys treated the same? Were students treated differently or have differing expectations because of their race? It might take you some time to reflect upon these questions, and quite honestly, you might not remember the nuances that occurred in your physical education classes; however, the content of these questions is rarely discussed in physical education, which we find to be concerning.

As demonstrated in previous sections on curriculum, there is an abundance of physical education content that can be taught by teachers and a variety of ways teachers can deliver instruction to their students. The goals and objectives of each unit and lesson are usually stated by the teacher, so students are explicitly aware of what they are learning. However, there are times students learn additional lessons based on indirect messages teachers deliver. These messages are examples of what physical education teacher educators refer to as the *hidden curriculum*, which is based on unintended and implicit messages that are implied by teachers and learned by students.[25,26]

For years, social justice issues (e.g., gender, sexuality, (dis)ability, race, and class) have been vastly ignored by physical education teachers.[25] Most often, the lessons learned by students from the hidden curriculum are more powerful than the content being taught in physical education classes. Few physical education teachers explicitly educate their students about gender, sexuality, race, or class issues. Instead, dominance by white, male, heterosexual, high-skilled, thin and athletic, able-bodied teachers and students in physical education and sport continues to be the center of physical education curricula, which leave many students and teachers feeling isolated, oppressed, and marginalized.[25,27] Physical educators have the potential to introduce students to and educate them about the ideas of privilege, oppression, and power relations. A positive first step to empowering all teachers and students would be to explicitly address social justice and equity issues in physical education—at the curriculum, pedagogy and assessment levels. In this

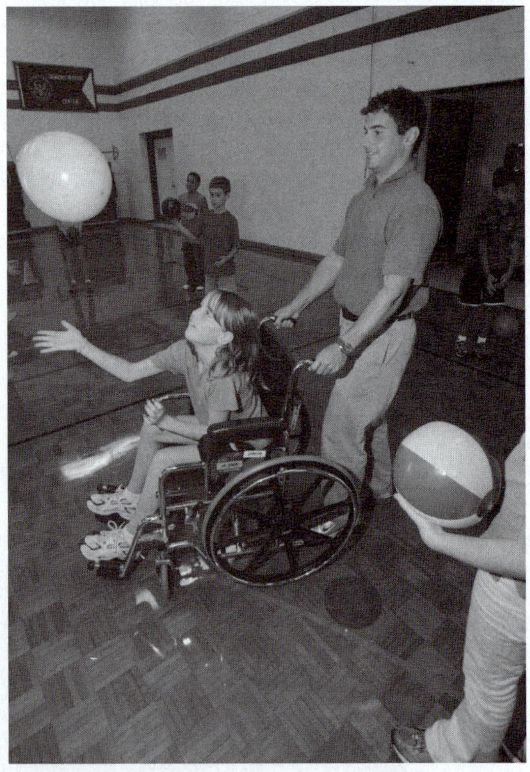

In physical education, it is important to include students with disabilities in the lesson. Here, students are using modified equipment to play volleyball with their classmate, who is in a wheelchair.

Lars A. Niki/McGraw Hill

Differences and diversity are present in physical education classes. Students will face and navigate different social issues, such as gender, (dis)ability, race, socioeconomic status, and body issues. It is important for the teacher to not only make students aware of these issues, but also educate them about the issues.

Ariel Skelley/Blend Images/Vetta/Getty Images

section, we will provide examples on how you, as a physical education teacher, can make equitable decisions and teach inclusively to all students.

(Dis)ability

On seeing the word *disability*, many may be quick to assume that it refers only to individuals with special needs, such as people who are in wheelchairs, are visually or hearing impaired, or have cerebral palsy. The reason "dis" is in parentheses is because students' ability, whether they are able-bodied or not, is observed, analyzed, and assessed by teachers and other students in the public arena of physical education.

We would be remiss to state that ability is not an important factor in physical education, since the psychomotor domain is the primary difference between physical education and other subject matter areas in schools. Students' experiences in physical education are often determined by their level of success in different sports and physical activities. Students who believe that they are lower skilled tend to take positions where they are least likely to be involved in the game (e.g., right field in softball), pace back and forth during a game of basketball to look like they are participating, and avoid opportunities to be embarrassed in front of their peers.[28] Over the years, lower-skilled students have had negative experiences in physical education due to lack of success, being ousted first in elimination games, and dominance by highly skilled students, particularly boys.*

Students with disabilities are even more marginalized than students who are lower skilled, as they are often left on the sidelines, placed in a corner, or completely ignored by teachers and students, despite federal laws (i.e., the Education of All Handicapped Children Act, the Individuals with Disabilities Education Act, and the Americans with Disabilities Act) that require the inclusion of students with disabilities

*Lynch, S., Walton-Fisette, J. L. & Luguetti, C. (2022). *Pedagogies of social justice in physical education and youth sport*. London: Routledge.

in physical education. By law, each identified student with a disability must have an individualized educational plan (IEP), which must include physical education. Students with disabilities include those with mental and emotional impairments, physical challenges such as cerebral palsy or amputation, vision and hearing problems, speech disorders, learning disabilities, and other health impairments such as asthma, heart problems, and cancer.

Physical education teachers often find it difficult to include students with disabilities and those who are lower skilled into daily instruction. It is much easier for teachers to focus on students who are able-bodied and higher skilled rather than students who are less skillful or have physical, mental, or emotional challenges. A sample of strategies that you can implement may include: Asking students who they want to be involved in the class is very important. Most activities can be adapted to include a wide variety of special learning needs. Getting the entire class to discuss the current unit of instruction and how it can be adapted/altered to involve all students in the class. Consider implementing disabled sports such as goal ball and seated volleyball should also be considered as long as it is not exploitive or employs tokenism.

Gender

Gender had limited consideration in educational policies and school reform in the United States until the enactment of Title IX in 1972. Title IX is the only federal policy that addresses gender in physical education.[29] Although physical education is not specifically mentioned within the law, requirements for physical education are provided in the Title IX regulations. Equal opportunities for boys and girls had to be established in activities, facilities, equipment, curriculum, testing and grading requirements, and behavior and dress codes.[29] These changes meant that a shift from same sex to coeducational physical education classes was needed to ensure that males and females were provided comparable educational opportunities.

Physical education teachers were not provided pedagogical strategies to teach students across genders. They had limited knowledge of and experience with the other gender's physical abilities, attitudes, and behaviors–or, most importantly, with the skills, activities, and sports that were geared toward the other gender. Whether because they lacked knowledge, felt comfortable with the same-sex curriculum, or were challenged by change, some teachers bypassed the law and still conducted same-sex classes, which continued to perpetuate the male and female ideologies and gender binaries.[30] For example, teachers would offer football and dance, with male teachers teaching all of the boys football, while female teachers would teach the girls dance. On the other hand, some teachers attempted coeducational classes, but the emphasis was placed on traditional male-dominated activities and sports (e.g., team sports).

Sadly, many of these gender binary stereotyped decisions continue 50 years later. Girls continue to feel that boys dominate game play, are excessively competitive, and tease, ridicule, and make fun of them, causing many girls to have negative experiences in physical education.[31] Girls' experiences are often made worse by teachers who make comments to boys such as "Don't throw like a girl" or rules such as "At least one girl must touch the ball before you shoot," along with boys' competitive and aggressive nature and dominating game play. The same is true for lower-skilled, noncompetitive, or nonsports-oriented boys who choose to not conform to the masculine stereotype. Oftentimes, these boys are bullied, teased, and laughed at by other boys. These problems tend to occur during the middle and high school years, but gender issues are becoming more and more prevalent in elementary school, even as early as first and second grades. There is significant concern with girls' and boys' negative experiences in physical education, since there is a likelihood that they will associate other physical activity with those negative experiences. From ages 9 to 15, when girls' physical activity significantly drops off, it is imperative that physical education teachers implement unit and lesson plans that are equitable and inclusive for all students. This is especially true for students who are gender nonbinary or transgender. These students face harassment and ridicule, especially in relation to which bathroom or locker room they use. A simple gesture to be inclusive is to share your gender pronouns when introducing yourself to the class. As a teacher, review the curriculum to identify if it is perpetuating gender stereotypes and reflect upon the language you use in your discussions with students and pedagogy. As more students in PK-12 feel comfortable and safe to share their true gender identity, physical education teachers need to embrace cultural humility and educate all students about being open, understanding, accepting, and inclusive of others.

Body Issues

In physical education, students' bodies are exposed and placed on display due to the public nature of the environment. Students, particularly girls, are concerned about other students observing their bodies in motion and feeling as if their bodies are objectified. During the adolescent years, when students' bodies are developing and changing, this public exposure creates a great challenge for students, which often supersedes their ability to focus on learning the physical education content.

In today's society, when bodies are socially constructed (i.e., influences within our society tell us what, who, and how we should be) and gender roles and expectations are formulated, students tend to compare their own bodies with those of their classmates and the idealized bodies they view in the media and consumer culture. The socially constructed, gendered ideal bodies are based on body size, shape, and appearance. The physical education context (i.e., same sex or coeducational) and the design of the physical education program influence students' feelings about their bodies, particularly in coeducational classes where the dominant male culture is promoted.

It is important that the body is discussed and addressed in physical education, particularly due to the public display of our content and the influence of media/social media. Gather an abundance of images/pictures and have the students review them and debrief about which images they believe include healthy, strong, and fit people. What are their reasons for this understanding? Furthermore, you may want to reconsider engaging in fitness testing and using fitness tracking devices as it encourage students to place emphasis on their bodies–why do they need to be measured and tracked for every moment they make? Who benefits from this and why? It is up to physical education teachers to break the silence and bring these important, yet uncomfortable and vulnerable issues to the forefront of physical education curricula. The hope is for physical education teachers to give students a voice and create a physical education context that challenges dominant and binary body ideals.

Race

Along with (dis)ability, gender, and body issues, race, class, and sexuality are also differences that teachers need to educate students about in physical education. As discussed in Chapter 8, students get assigned certain positions in sport based on their race. For example, white students tend to play positions that are considered more intellectual, such as quarterback or pitcher, whereas black students play running back, wide receiver, or forward in basketball, because those are positions that are considered more athletic. Teachers are predominantly white, yet the racial diversity of our country continues to increase, causing a gap across racial groups.[26] As previously suggested for gender, engaging in an equity audit of the curriculum to analyze how inclusive the units of instruction are across racial identities and not engaging in solely a white curriculum. At a pedagogical level, it is important for educators to teach young people language such as racism, racist, white supremacy–what they mean, how that impacts them in school and your class, and the inclusiveness expected in your class. Discuss a wide variety of sports and discuss who plays these sports and who does not and why.

Social Class

Social class also has an impact on physical education programs. In economically disadvantaged communities, particularly in urban and rural settings, many physical education teachers are limited in regard to facilities, equipment, and space. Within these same

Students are faced with many challenges in physical education, including the public nature of the environment. It is important for teachers to provide support to students of varying abilities.

Corbis/VCG/Getty Images

Students should be treated fairly, regardless of race, gender, or ability. Teachers need to have the same expectations for all students, regardless of their social identity.

Stockbyte/PunchStock

communities, students may not have the appropriate attire to participate in physical education. This is considered a major problem for physical education teachers who continue to grade students on dress and participation. If students do not have the appropriate clothes, they usually sit in the bleachers, waiting out the time on the sidelines or talking to classmates. To minimize the clothing issue, teachers can take clothing donations from others to provide to students when they do not have a change of clothes for physical education or simply do not require them to change at all. Social class also influences the out-of-school experiences that students have in sport and physical activity. Students who are from higher socioeconomic communities participate on traveling sport teams, attend specialized camps, and tend to have ample equipment at home to practice skills taught in physical education. On the contrary, students from lower socioeconomic communities cannot afford to play on traveling teams or go to camps and tend to live in neighborhoods that either are unsafe or do not have sidewalks and parks to engage in physical activity. As a class, discuss ways that access and opportunity can be provided to all students regardless of social class.

Sexuality

Sexuality closely intersects with gender. In the discussion on gender, we mentioned gender stereotypes that are socially constructed. An example of a stereotype is that girls are associated with the color pink, whereas boys are aligned with the color blue. In your everyday conversations with friends and family, what is said if a boy wears pink? What if girls want to play football or wrestle, or boys want to dance or be cheerleaders? Stereotypes are formulated because our society influences our knowledge and understanding of what is, yet few individuals ever ask the question, Why? When answering these questions, students may have labeled these boys and girls as gay, because society says that boys are supposed to play football and wrestle, not girls, and girls are supposed to dance and cheerlead. If individuals break the dominant belief–that is, what is considered to be normal–then their sexuality is immediately questioned. According to society, girls can be skillful in "female" sports such as soccer and volleyball, as long as they look feminine. Boys' sexuality is also questioned if they are uninterested in sport or do not have large, ripped muscles, regardless of their actual sexual orientation. How do students, especially at the secondary school level, navigate these socially constructed gender and sexuality stereotypes in physical education? If teachers allow students to choose between football and fitness, who tends to select football, and who fitness? Do some boys who would prefer to participate in fitness and girls who would like to play football break those gender barriers and select the activity of their interest, or is the social pressure too much or too great of a risk to challenge those norms? Physical education teachers need to be aware of gender and sexuality stereotypes and expectations and be cognizant of the language they use and the implicit messages they send to students. To minimize this, teaching students about what gender, sexuality, homosexuality, etc., mean is critical for students to start understanding and accepting differences of others. It is all too often that the saying "that's so gay" is used casually, but students do not realize the potential hurt and harm being caused to others when such a slur is used.

All of these social identities, along with ethnicity, religion, and language proficiency, are difficult to discuss in isolation; rather, identities tend to intersect with one another as demonstrated in the discussion on sexuality. It is imperative that physical education teachers, along with exercise scientists and sport leaders, have an awareness of the students, clients, and athletes with whom they work. To gain this awareness, it is important for professionals to learn how their students, clients, and athletes identify, where they come from, and who they are. Before doing this, however, it is important for all professionals to reflect upon their own identities and assess their biases and stereotypes about individuals with differences from themselves. We must minimize the unintended, implicit messages we deliver to students and create socially justice, equitable, and inclusive experiences in physical education for all students.

CURRENT TRENDS: MOVING TOWARD THE FUTURE

- The Every Student Succeeds Act will hopefully provide students with more time in physical education since physical education is considered a component of educating the whole child.
- The demographics of the PK-12 student body is changing calling for a great need for curriculum, pedagogy, and assessment in physical education to be more socially just, equitable, and inclusive.
- Models-based practice, particularly pedagogies of affect, will become more emphasized in physical education curricula.

SUMMARY

Physical education pedagogy is concerned with the study of teaching and learning processes of physical activity. The scope of physical education pedagogy is broad in nature, because it intersects with other disciplines due to the emphasis of teaching and learning in relation to human movement and physical activity. Physical education is the subject matter taught in schools that provide PK-12 students with opportunities to learn and have meaningful content and appropriate instruction. Quality physical education programs focus on increasing physical competence, health-related fitness, personal and social responsibility, and enjoyment of physical activity for all students so that they can be physically active for a lifetime.

Over the past 30 years, American education has undergone significant reform as it entered into a standards-based education era. The most recent SHAPE America standards (2014) attempt to provide physical educators a framework for student learning, specifically, "what a student should know and be able to do" as a result of a quality physical education program. These standards have been adopted by most states as their physical education content standards and have been used by teachers, school districts, and teacher educators to guide the development of program curricula, unit and lesson plans (i.e., instruction), and assessments. Assessment is the salient component needed to measure whether students have learned and are achieving the national standards. Furthermore, assessment holds physical education programs and teachers accountable for student achievement. Connecting the standards, instruction, and assessment components of physical education curricula and units of instruction is referred to as instructional alignment.

Pedagogical models have been developed by researchers, teacher educators, and physical education teachers over the past 30 years to provide teachers with different approaches to delivering instruction to students. These pedagogical models include skill themes, personal and social responsibility, teaching games for understanding and the tactical games model, sport education, fitness education, adventure-based learning, outdoor education, activist approach, and pedagogies of affect. Effective teachers use a variety of pedagogical skills and strategies to ensure that their students are appropriately engaged in relevant activities a high percentage of the time, hold positive expectations for their students, and create and maintain a classroom climate that is warm and nurturing. Salient teacher behaviors can be divided into several broad areas: organization, communication, instruction, motivation, and human relations.

In physical education, the goals and objectives of each unit and lesson are usually stated by the teacher, so students are explicitly aware of what they are learning. However, there are times students learn additional lessons based on indirect messages teachers deliver (i.e., the hidden curriculum). For years, social justice issues (e.g., gender, sexuality, (dis)ability, and race) have been vastly ignored by physical education teachers. Most often, the lessons learned by students from the hidden curriculum are more powerful than the content being taught in physical education classes. Physical educators have the potential to introduce students to and educate them about the ideas of privilege, oppression, and power relations. A positive first step to empowering all teachers and students would be to overtly address social justice and equity issues to create a more inclusive physical education curriculum.

DISCUSSION QUESTIONS

1. What is your philosophy on physical education at the elementary, middle, and high school levels? How would your philosophy impact your selection of curriculum content?
2. Describe instructional alignment. What components should be aligned with each other? Why is it important for these components to be aligned with one another?
3. Discuss why it is important for teachers to know who their students are and where they come from. What are three ways teachers can engage students in the decision making process within physical education and provide opportunities for student empowerment?
4. How would you consider social justice and equity issues in planning units of instruction in physical education?

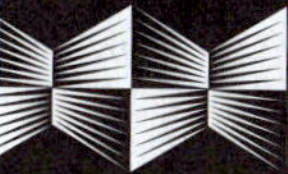

GET CONNECTED

PELinks4U–offers information on a variety of topics related to physical education, coaching, and adapted physical education, interdisciplinary efforts, and teaching in physical education.

http://www.pelinks4u.org/index.htm

SHAPE America–includes valuable information for physical educators to enhance their professional practice and their support for physical education, sport, and physical activity programs.

https://www.shapeamerica.org//

TPSR Alliance–provides information on teaching responsibility through physical activity, which includes news, events, current projects, and additional publications and links.

http://www.tpsr-alliance.org/

PE Central–offers information on how teachers can incorporate assessment into their programs, including the purpose and importance of assessment, examples and ideas, and additional resources.

https://www.pecentral.org/

SELF-ASSESSMENT ACTIVITIES

These activities are designed to help you determine if you have mastered the materials and competencies presented in this chapter.

1. Considering the Every Student Succeeds Act includes as one of its core areas to develop a "well-rounded" person, what arguments will you present to the principal to advocate for physical education? Write a letter to your principal that includes specific arguments why physical education should be an important component of the school curriculum.
2. Select two pedagogical models and describe the characteristics, components, and positive attributes of the model, and how you will assess student learning. Provide examples of how you will implement these models within a unit of instruction in your class.
3. Use the information provided in the Get Connected box to access the PE Central website. Review the information on assessment, particularly the assessment examples and ideas. What forms of assessment do they provide? How can these assessments be implemented into units of instruction? What steps would you take to construct your own assessment?

REFERENCES

1. Graber, K., & Templin, T. (2000). Pedagogy of physical activity. In S. J. Hoffman & J. C. Harris (Eds.), *Introduction to kinesiology: Studying physical activity.* Champaign, IL: Human Kinetics.
2. Tinning, R. (2008). Pedagogy, sport pedagogy, and the field of kinesiology. *Quest, 60,* 405–424.
3. SHAPE America. (2014). *National Standards and Grade-Level Outcomes for K-12 physical education.* Champaign, IL: Human Kinetics.
4. National Association for Sport and Physical Education. (2004). *Moving into the future: National standards for physical education* (2nd ed.). Reston, VA: AAHPERD.
5. Casey, A., & Kirk, D. (2021). *Models-based practice in physical education*. Routledge: London.
6. US Department of Education. (2001). *The condition of education 2000.* Washington, DC: NCES.
7. No Child Left Behind Act of 2001, P.L. 107-110, 20 U.S.C. § 6319 (2002).
8. SHAPE America. (2015, December 9). *SHAPE America applauds passage of the every student succeeds act* [Press release]. Retrieved April 5, 2019, from http://www.shapealaska.com/news/2015/12/9/shape-america-applauds-passage-of-the-every-student-succeeds-act.
9. SHAPE America. (2017). *PE metrics.* Champaign, IL: Human Kinetics.
10. SHAPE America. (2016). *2016 shape of the nation report: Status of physical education in the USA.* Retrieved April 7, 2019, from https://www.shapeamerica.org//advocacy/son/2016/upload/Shape-of-the-Nation-2016_web.pdf.
11. Graham, G., Holt/Hale, S., & Parker, M. (2013). *Children moving: A reflective approach to teaching physical education* (9th ed.). New York, NY: McGraw Hill.
12. Holt/Hale, S. (2014). The skill theme approach to physical education. In J. Lund & D. Tannehill (Eds.), *Standards-based physical education curriculum development* (3rd ed.). Sudbury, MA: Jones and Bartlett.
13. Parker, M. & Stiehl, J. (2014). Personal and social responsibility. In J. Lund & D. Tannehill (Eds.), *Standards-based physical education curriculum development* (3rd ed.). Sudbury, MA: Jones and Bartlett.
14. Hellison, D. (2010). *Teaching responsibility through physical activity* (3rd ed.). Champaign, IL: Human Kinetics.
15. Mitchell, S. A., Oslin, J. L., & Griffin, L. L. (2021). *Teaching sport concepts and skills: A tactical games approach for ages 7–18* (4th ed.). Champaign, IL: Human Kinetics.
16. Siedentop, D., Hastie, P., & van der Mars, H. (2019). *Complete guide to sport education* (3rd ed.). Champaign, IL: Human Kinetics.
17. McConnell, K. (2015). Fitness education. In J. Lund & D. Tannehill (Eds.), *Standards-based physical education curriculum development* (3rd ed.). Sudbury, MA: Jones and Bartlett.
18. Dyson, B. & Brown, M. (2015). Adventure education in your physical education program. In J. Lund & D. Tannehill (Eds.), *Standards-based physical education curriculum development* (3rd ed.). Sudbury, MA: Jones and Bartlett.
19. Stiehl, J., & Parker, M. (2015). Outdoor education. In J. Lund & D. Tannehill (Eds.), *Standards-based physical education curriculum development* (3rd ed.). Sudbury, MA: Jones and Bartlett.
20. Placek, J. H. (1983). Concepts of success in teaching: Busy, happy, and good? In T. Templin & J. Olsen (Eds.), *Teaching in physical education.* Champaign, IL: Human Kinetics.
21. Lund, J. & Tannehill, D. (2014). *Standards-based physical education curriculum development* (3rd ed.). Sudbury, MA: Jones and Bartlett.
22. Fisette, J. L., Placek, J. H., Avery, M., Dyson, B., Fox, C., Franck, M., . . ., Zhu, W. (2009). Instructional considerations for implementing student assessments. *Strategies, 22*(4), 33–34.
23. Wuest, D. A., & Lombardo, B. J. (1994). *Curriculum and instruction: The secondary school physical education experience.* St. Louis, MO: Mosby.
24. Siedentop, D., & Tannehill, D. (2000). *Developing teaching skills in physical education* (4th ed.). Mountain View, CA: Mayfield.
25. Bain, L. (1990). A critical analysis of the hidden curriculum in physical education. In D. Kirk & R. Tinning (Eds.), *Physical education, curriculum, and culture: Critical issues in the contemporary crisis.* London: Farmer Press.

26. Timken, G. L., & Watson, D. (2014). Teaching all kids: Valuing students through culturally responsive and inclusive practice. In J. Lund & D. Tannehill (Eds.), *Standards-based physical education curriculum development* (3rd ed.). Sudbury, MA: Jones and Bartlett.

27. Walton-Fisette, J. L., & Sutherland, S. (2018). Moving forward with social justice education in physical education teacher education. *Physical Education & Sport Pedagogy*, *23*(5), 461–468.

28. Fisette, J. L. (2010). Getting to know your students: The importance of learning students' thoughts and feelings in physical education. *Journal of Physical Education, Recreation, and Dance, 81*(7), 42–49.

29. Title IX, Education Amendments Act of 1972, 20 U.S.C. §§1681–1688 (1972).

30. Scranton, S. (2003). Equality, coeducation, and physical education in secondary schooling. In J. Evans (Ed.), *Equality, education and physical education.* London: Farmer Press.

31. Oliver, K. & Kirk, D. (2015). *Girls, gender, and physical education. An Activist approach.* London: Routledge.

ny Saint James/Photodisc/Getty Images

Anthony Saint James/Photodisc/Getty Images

Mitch Hrdlicka/Photodisc/Getty Images

III

Careers and Professional Considerations

In Part II, the historical and scientific foundations of physical education, exercise science, and sport were described. In recent years, the expansion of the knowledge base coupled with the tremendous growth of interest in physical activity, sport, and fitness in our society has resulted in the development of many career opportunities for qualified professionals.

In Part III, many career opportunities within physical education, exercise science, and sport are described. This section begins with a discussion of career preparation, professional responsibilities, and professionalism in Chapter 11. Chapter 12 discusses traditional career opportunities, such as teaching and coaching in the schools. The expansion of physical education, exercise science, and sport programs to nonschool settings and to people of all ages resulted in teaching and coaching opportunities outside of the school setting. The tremendous interest in physical fitness and health stimulated the growth of fitness-, health-, and therapy-related careers. Some students use their undergraduate background in physical activity and exercise science as a foundation for pursuing careers in allied health fields, such as chiropractic care. These careers are examined in Chapter 13. Chapter 14 describes career opportunities in media, management, performance, and other related areas. The pervasiveness of sport in our society, combined with the growth of the communications media, has encouraged careers in sport media, while the development of sport as big business has created a need for professionals trained in sport management. Opportunities for people interested in pursuing careers as performers have also increased during the last decade.

Polka Dot Images/Getty Images

C H A P T E R 11

Career and Professional Development

O B J E C T I V E S

After reading this chapter, students should be able to–

- Identify career opportunities in physical education, exercise science, and sport.
- Self-assess strengths, interests, goals, and career preferences.
- Understand their professional preparation curriculum and how to maximize educational opportunities.
- Discuss the role of practical experience in professional preparation.
- Describe strategies to enhance marketability.
- Understand the importance of professionalism in their career.
- Identify professional organizations within the field and understand the benefits of membership.

Career opportunities in physical education, exercise science, and sport have never been greater. Traditional careers of teaching and coaching have expanded from schools, colleges, and universities to nonschool settings such as community centers (e.g., YMCA) and commercial clubs (i.e., gymnastics or tennis). Many physical education, exercise science, and sport professionals are pursuing careers in the fitness field, working in health clubs or corporate fitness centers. Other professionals are employed in the areas of sport management, sports medicine, and sport media. The increased specialization within the field has created additional career opportunities. For example, biomechanists may work for sporting goods companies designing and testing sport equipment (e.g., running shoes) and performance apparel. Exercise physiologists may be employed in a corporate fitness center, a hospital cardiac rehabilitation program, or a sports medicine clinic. Professional preparation for a career in physical education, exercise science, and sport is discussed in this chapter.

SOCIAL JUSTICE

Talking Points

- Cultural competency suggests that there is a discrete endpoint to be achieved: mastery of a culture. However, cultural humility invites professionals to engage in critical self-reflection to understand their biases, prejudices, and own culture and how this might affect their interactions with others.
- Advocacy to promote access to quality physical activity programs is needed if we are to reduce disparities in physical activity seen in different population groups.
- Leaders must embrace differences in cultural perspectives to foster an inclusive environment.

CAREERS IN PHYSICAL EDUCATION, EXERCISE SCIENCE, AND SPORT

Career opportunities in physical education, exercise science, and sport have expanded tremendously during this decade. The expanded career opportunities are a result of several factors. First, millions of Americans from all segments of society engage in fitness activities on a regular basis. They participate in a variety of activities, including working out at health and fitness clubs and engaging in community and commercial fitness programs. This has led to a need for competent professionals to design, lead, and evaluate fitness programs. Additionally, people seeking to use their leisure time in an enjoyable manner have sought out physical activities and sports. Qualified individuals are needed to conduct recreational programs and to teach lifetime sport skills. Competent teachers and coaches are need to conduct high-quality programs in both school and nonschool settings.

The increased interest in competitive sports by all segments of the population has served as the impetus for the growth of competitive sport programs, sport clubs, and leagues, and the associated career opportunities in coaching, sport management, officiating, and athletic training. Finally, the increase in the depth and breadth of knowledge in the field has led to expanded career opportunities such as biomechanists, sport psychologists, exercise physiologists, and adapted physical activity specialists.

Career opportunities are limited only by one's imagination. Potential career opportunities are listed in the Physical Education, Exercise Science, and Sport Career Opportunities box on page 318. This list is by no means exhaustive but will help you realize the number and diversity of career opportunities available to you. These career options will be discussed further in other chapters. Careers involving the teaching and coaching of physical activity skills in a variety of settings are discussed in Chapter 12. Health- and fitness-related careers are described in Chapter 13. Career opportunities in sport management, sport media, and other areas are addressed in Chapter 14.

You can also use your imagination to create new job opportunities suited specifically to your abilities and interests. The growth of the knowledge base, combined with the expansion of our services to diverse populations, has created many new and exciting career opportunities. By combining your interests and abilities within an area with your desire to work with a specific population and age group and within a particular setting, you can create a career opportunity uniquely suited to you. The Creating Career Opportunities in Physical Education, Exercise Science, and Sport box will assist you in exploring these various career options.

The growth of career opportunities is an exciting development. Selecting a career from the many

PHYSICAL EDUCATION, EXERCISE SCIENCE, AND SPORT CAREER OPPORTUNITIES

Teaching Opportunities

School Setting

- Elementary School
- Secondary School
- Community College
- Adapted Physical Education
- International Schools
- College–Basic Instruction
- College–Professional Preparation
- College–Campus Recreation & Wellness
- Military Schools

Nonschool Setting

- Community Recreation
- Corporate Recreation
- Commercial Sport Clubs
- Correctional Institutions
- Geriatric Programs
- Youth-Serving Agencies
- Preschools
- Health Clubs
- Military Programs
- Resort Sport Programs

Coaching Opportunities

- Interscholastic Programs
- Intercollegiate Programs
- Commercial Sport Camps
- Commercial Sport Clubs
- Community Sport Programs
- Military Sport Programs

Fitness- and Health-Related Opportunities

- Cardiac Rehabilitation
- Athletic Training
- Health Clubs
- Community Fitness
- Worksite Programs
- Personal Training
- Space Fitness Programs
- Movement Therapy
- Medical Fitness
- Corporate Fitness Programs
- Sport Nutrition
- Health Spas
- Military Personnel Fitness
- Dance Therapy
- Physical Therapy
- Kinesiotherapy
- Recreation Therapy
- Chiropractic Care

Sport Management Opportunities

- Athletic Administration
- Facility Management
- Commercial Sport Club Management
- Community Recreation/Sport Management
- Campus Recreation
- Sport Organization Administration
- Health Club Management
- Sports Retailing
- Worksite Recreation Management
- Resort Sport Management

Sport Media Opportunities

- Sport Journalism
- Sport Photography
- Sport Writing
- Sport Art
- Sport Broadcasting
- Sports Information
- Web Design
- Social Media

Sport-Related Opportunities

- Sport Law
- Professional Athletics
- Entrepreneurship
- Research
- Sport & Physical Activity Psychology
- Sport Officiating
- Dance
- Sport Analytics
- Equipment/Clothing Design

Note: Some of these career opportunities require additional education beyond a bachelor's degree.

CREATING CAREER OPPORTUNITIES IN PHYSICAL EDUCATION, EXERCISE SCIENCE, AND SPORT

Explore career options by combining an area of study with a population group, an age group, and a setting or environment that matches your individual interests. Feel free to add additional items to each column as you think of them.

Area of Study	Population	Age	Setting
Adapted physical activity	Athletes	Adolescents	Athletic contests
Biomechanics	Cardiac risks	Adults	Clinic
Exercise physiology	Individuals with disabilities	Children	College/university
Motor development	Inmates	Youth	Community
Motor learning	Military personnel	Infants	Corporation
Sport history	Individuals who are obese	Elderly	Correctional institution
Sport management	Patients		Geriatric center
Sports medicine	Students		Health/fitness club
Sport nutrition	Healthy fit		Health spa/resort
Physical education pedagogy	Healthy unfit		Home
Sport philosophy	Chronically diseased		Hospital
Sport and exercise psychology			Media setting
Sport sociology			Park
Measurement and evaluation			Professional/sport organization
			Research laboratory
			Retail establishment
			School
			Space
			Sport facility

Create your own job title and define your responsibilities. In the first example below, exercise physiology is combined with an interest in working with adolescents with disabilities in the home setting to create a job as a personal fitness trainer to an adolescent with a disability, working in the youth's home.

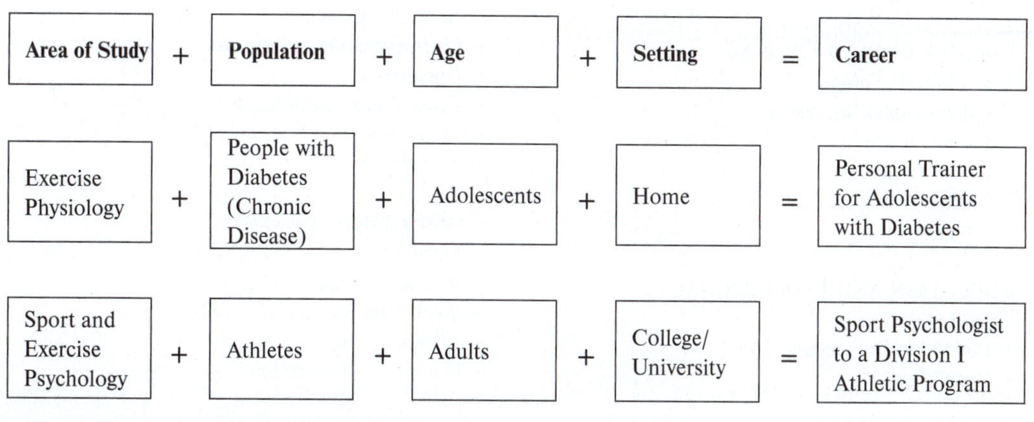

available options requires careful consideration of a number of factors.

Choosing a Career

Have you already chosen a career in the field? Did you decide to pursue a career in teaching, athletic training, or sport broadcasting? On the other hand, you may be like some students, undecided about a specific career and/or finding it hard to choose from the many of career opportunities within the field.

Making a career choice is a decision making process (see the Choosing a Career box). This typically involves gathering facts, evaluating information, and making a selection from the options available to you. The most important factor influencing your choice of a career is you! Take time to self-assess your values, strengths, abilities, interests, goals, personality traits, and preferences related to lifestyle and working environment. Take advantage of services offered through your institution's career center. They can administer online career assessment inventories that identify your characteristics and suggest possible career options. Use the results of your self-assessment to rule out careers that do not interest you and to identify possible career options to further explore. Try to winnow down your list to 5–10 careers; if you are stuck, try writing down the pros and cons for each career and using that list to help you eliminate some options.

Take time to explore various career options on your list. You can use the U.S. Bureau of Labor Statistics *Occupational Outlook Handbook*[1] to learn about each career option and the associated responsibilities, educational requirements, salaries, on-the-job training, opportunities for advancement, and future outlook for each career (e.g., projected growth rate). Finding out additional information may help you further reduce or expand your list of potential careers.

CHOOSING A CAREER

SELF-ASSESSMENT
- Values
- Skills
- Interests
- Personality
- Lifestyle Preferences
- Preferred Work Environment

EXPLORE CAREER OPTIONS
- Job Market Trends
- Informational Interviews
- Job Shadowing
- Career Center
- College Adviser
- Professors

EDUCATION AND PROFESSIONAL DEVELOPMENT
- Education Credentials
- Practicums
- Volunteer Activities
- Conferences
- Certifications
- Work Experiences
- Professional Organization

JOB SEARCH
- Networking
- Professional Organizations
- Openings
- Cover Letter and Resume
- Interviews
- Negotiations

CAREER DEVELOPMENT
- Mentoring
- Professional Development
- Work-Life Balance
- Advancement
- Ongoing Self-reflection

Learning firsthand about potential careers can be extremely helpful in your decision making process. Both informational interviews and job shadowing of professionals will provide you with a more in-depth understanding of each potential career. Faculty at your institution might be a good source of professional contacts, and your career center might be able to put you in touch with alumni employed in your prospective careers. You can also locate professionals by contacting professional organizations. Think about using the Internet to locate practitioners via LinkedIn, where you can search by interest area (e.g., sport psychologist). Another advantage is that you can learn about professionals' backgrounds through searching the Internet, reading their blogs, reviewing articles published, determining areas of interest, and/or following them on social media.

Informational interviews offer the opportunity to learn more about your career in-depth. Before the interview, take some time to prepare a list of questions. At the conclusion of the interview, be sure to thank interviewees for their time and follow up with a thank-you note. If some professionals work too far away from you, consider taking advantage of the Internet to interview them via Zoom or other communication programs, sending a request for an interview via e-mail and setting up a convenient time to speak.

Job shadowing a professional for a day or two helps you receive a more in-depth exposure to the workplace, day-to-day responsibilities, and some insight into the work culture. Your institution may already have a job shadowing program and/or an alumni network that you can tap into to locate professionals in your careers of interest. Your professors might also have some suggestions, and your own research might lead to some possibilities as well. Once you confirm a date for job shadowing, be sure to do your research beforehand, taking time to learn about the organization as well as developing a list of questions ahead of time. Dress professionally, be courteous, and show enthusiasm throughout your visit. At the end of the visit, extend your appreciation for the professional's time, and write a follow-up thank you. If your experience went well, consider asking the individual for a business card, adding that professional to your network.

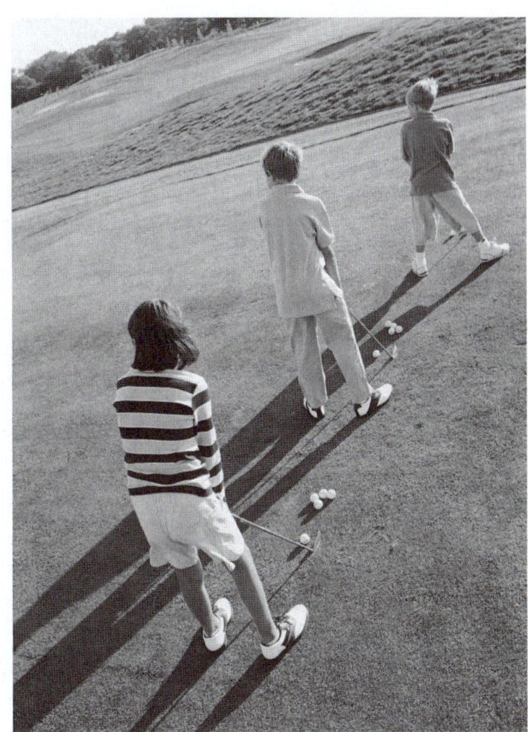

Many teaching opportunities are available outside of the school setting.

BananaStock/Alamy Stock Photo

Do not forget to take advantage of your college adviser's expertise and knowledge of the field as well as that of your course professors. And your institution's career center offers excellent resources, including self-assessment inventories, information about employment in specific careers, résumé building, job search advice, and information about alumni employed in your potential careers.

Lastly, do not overly stress or become anxious about your career decision. Many students change their mind about their major and/or career during the course of their education. Also realize that selecting a career is not a lifelong commitment. Changing careers has become increasingly common in today's world. Some people deliberately plan to pursue one career for a while to provide a foundation for a second career. For example, you might teach or coach for a few years before returning to school for training as a sport psychologist. Your practical experience gained from your first career provides a foundation for your new career as a sport psychologist with a professional team. Additionally, periodically evaluate your satisfaction from your chosen career to determine whether or not you might like to pursue other avenues within the field.

Maximizing Professional Preparation

The process of preparing for a career is referred to as *professional preparation.* Professional preparation involves the attainment of skills, knowledge, and dispositions required of professionals in our field. This includes a broad foundation in the liberal arts and focused professional course work. Professional preparation also includes maximizing strengths and developing abilities with reference to one's chosen career. In addition to providing the knowledge, skills, and dispositions necessary to be a successful practitioner, professional preparation may be thought of as the process of increasing personal competence, attaining the necessary credentials, and marketability. When viewed from this perspective, professional preparation includes not only one's course work and academics, but related career experiences as well (Table 11-1).

Education

Traditionally, professional preparation curriculums have been oriented toward preparing individuals for careers in teaching and coaching. The growth of the disciplines and the changing job market have stimulated the development of curriculums to prepare individuals for these expanded opportunities. Although professional preparation curriculums at different institutions vary, these curriculums share some commonalities.

Liberal Arts Professional preparation curriculums typically include liberal arts courses. Liberal arts courses provide the opportunity to obtain a broad base of knowledge. These courses are the sciences, math, languages, English, art, and music. All students must complete a certain number of liberal arts courses for their degree. Some courses are required, such as writing and speech. Other courses are elective, and students can select the courses they wish to take to fulfill their degree requirements. In some states, the state education department mandates that students take certain liberal arts courses, such as history and mathematics.

Professional Courses Building on this liberal arts foundation are the professional physical education, exercise science, and sport courses. The professional theory courses provide students with knowledge, skills, and dispositions relative to the discipline and are designed to prepare majors for their chosen career. Thus, students preparing for a career in teaching and coaching may take courses in physical education that include curriculum design, teaching methods, activity, performance analysis, and coaching; courses taken outside the area include education and psychology. Students preparing for a career in exercise science may take professional exercise science such as kinesiology, anatomy, and exercise physiology; outside courses might focus on science (e.g., chemistry), psychology, and nutrition. In addition to the required professional courses, students may take electives in this area.

Electives Most curriculums have electives, although the number of electives varies from program to program and from institution to institution. Electives may be used to pursue a special interest, to broaden your liberal arts background, and/or to enhance your marketability by complementing and strengthening your career preparation.

Choose your electives carefully to help you achieve your goals. If you anticipate attending graduate school, check to see if you have satisfied all the prerequisites for admission. Students who are planning or pursuing graduate study in another area to complement their degree may have to satisfy several prerequisite requirements. For example, someone majoring in athletic training who wishes to obtain a master's degree in physical therapy may have to take additional courses in biology, chemistry, and psychology. You can use your electives to take these courses.

Minors An increasing number of students are taking advantage of their electives to pursue minors or concentrations or areas of specialization. By doing so, they broaden their career options and increase their marketability. Sport management majors may be required to have a minor in business. Sport communication majors may have a minor in journalism, photography, or speech. Exercise science majors may choose a minor in biochemistry, nutrition, or health.

In some states, if physical education teaching majors take enough credits in a second academic area, they can become certified to teach in that area as well. Often, the number of credits required for certification is only a few more than the number required to complete a minor at your institution. Thus, physical education teacher majors could become certified to teach math, science, or health. Using credits judiciously can pay big dividends for all students, regardless of their course of study.

Practicums Provision for practical experience is a common feature of many professional preparation curriculums, regardless of the career being pursued. In teaching, this practical experience is referred to as student teaching. Student teaching typically takes place in the latter part of the student's junior year or during the senior year; this experience may last for a semester. In recent years, a concerted effort has been made by professionals to provide their prospective teachers with practical- or field-based experiences prior to their student teaching. This allows students to practice the teaching skills learned in their courses and can help them solidify their career decision.

Practical experiences associated with nonteaching programs are commonly referred to as fieldwork or internships. Fieldwork is typically shorter in duration than an internship. These courses focus on placing students in a practical setting on or off campus. Exercise science majors enrolled in fieldwork may work with clients in a commercial fitness center or health club. As interns, exercise science majors may spend a semester working in a hospital cardiac rehabilitation program or in a corporate fitness center. Sport management majors may intern with a professional athletic team, whereas sport media majors may gain practical experience with a radio or television station. Athletic trainers usually gain practical experience on campus, putting in hundreds of hours working in the training room and serving as the trainer for various athletic teams. Many professionals view the practical experience gained through fieldwork, internships, and student teaching as vital in career preparation.

Certifications You can enhance your professional credentials by taking advantage of various certification programs offered through your school or reputable outside agencies. For example, many students take a first aid or CPR course offered by the American Red Cross as part of their school's curriculum. You can enhance your credentials by taking the next step and becoming certified as a first aid or CPR instructor. The instructor certification allows you to teach CPR or first aid to others and certify them as qualified. If you were working as a fitness instructor in a corporate wellness program, you would be able to certify employees in first aid or CPR. A variety of certifications in first aid and water safety are offered by the American Red Cross and may be a wonderful addition to your professional skills.

Many professional organizations offer certifications, and you may find that certification is a necessary requirement for a job. The National Athletic Trainers' Association (NATA) offers certification for athletic trainers. Fitness certifications are offered by the American College of Sports Medicine (ACSM) and the National Strength and Conditioning Association (NSCA). The ACSM offers certifications in the areas of health fitness, clinical exercise, and several speciality areas. The NSCA offers certifications in the areas of strength and conditioning and personal training. More information about these certifications is found in Chapter 13.

Certifications can also be obtained in specific sport areas. For example, you can work toward becoming certified as a golf professional or a scuba instructor. Certification and training programs are offered by many professional organizations, such as

TABLE 11-1 Four-Year Timeline for Professional Preparation

Focus	First Year	Second Year
Academic	Learn about requirements of your major, including liberal arts and professional courses; determine how many electives you have to explore areas of interest or to use for a minor.	Begin working on requirements for a minor; carefully monitor your academic performance; remember that many graduate schools require a minimum GPA of 3.0 for admission.
Career Goals	Identify short- and long-term career goals.	Identify a unique skill and formulate a plan for its development.
Campus Activities	Become involved in some capacity in one sport or one fitness-related activity.	Continue involvement in sport and fitness activity; add involvement in another campus organization or other activities.
Professional Activities	Join your majors club; join a local affiliate of a professional organization (e.g., state athletic trainers organization).	Join a national professional organization; attend a professional conference and take advantage of special opportunities for students.
Volunteer Activities	Check out opportunities for volunteering in school and hometown communities.	Volunteer for a few hours a week in an organization of interest to you (e.g., Special Olympics, American Heart Association).
Related Work	Seek out related work experiences during the school term or summer.	Work in related area during the summer or the school year (e.g., aerobics instructor on campus, fitness trainer in a health club).
Practicums	Explore practicum opportunities, including both short- and long-term opportunities.	Participate in a short-term practicum, such as fieldwork.
Career Planning	Visit your career planning office; take advantage of self-assessment and guidance programs to clarify your interests, strengths, and areas needing improvement.	Write a draft of your resume and have it reviewed by a professional or career planning counselor.
Networking	Get to know faculty and students within your school; interview practitioners about their work.	Take advantage of local professional opportunities, such as conferences, to meet professionals in your field.
Certifications	Identify certifications that will enhance your professional skills and contribute to your marketability.	Begin to acquire certifications such as Cardiopulmonary Resuscitation (CPR), first aid, or water safety.
Application for Employment after Graduation	Become familiar with employment opportunities in the field.	Practice job search skills in securing summer employment, fieldwork, and internship experiences.
Application for Graduate School	Become familiar with areas of advanced study within the field.	Explore graduate school options and identify general program prerequisites; develop a plan to satisfy prerequisites.

Third Year	Fourth Year
Determine prerequisites for graduate school and plan how to satisfy them; check to make sure that you are on track to graduate; take advantage of opportunities to join academic honor societies.	Review carefully your requirements for graduation to make sure you have completed them.
Work on strengthening your transferable skills; reevaluate your short- and long-term career goals.	Solidify career goals for the next 1 year and for the next 5 years.
Undertake some leadership activity in a professional organization, such as chairing a committee or being an officer.	Advance in leadership responsibilities by taking on more challenging and responsible positions.
Attend a professional conference and become involved in the organization in a leadership capacity.	Attend a professional conference; take advantage of placement opportunities offered by professional organizations.
Increase volunteer hours or consider volunteering in a different area of interest.	Undertake some leadership responsibilities as a volunteer (e.g., volunteer recruitment).
Advance in responsibilities you undertake at work; consider a different job to broaden your expertise.	Continue to work and expand responsibilities undertaken; advance to a position of leadership or supervision.
Investigate internship opportunities in your major; continue to participate in practicum experiences.	Complete full-time internship or student teaching experience.
Take advantage of career planning seminars on interviewing, writing cover letters, and conducting effective job searches; update your resume.	Update your resume; attend on-campus job fairs; take advantage of alumni networks; use career planning, the Internet, and other resources to identify potential job openings.
Widen your professional contacts and expand your network.	Network with faculty, professionals, friends, and family to identify employment opportunities.
Add additional certifications as appropriate; find out the requirements to take major certification exams in your career field–athletic training, fitness, and teaching.	Take certification exams for athletic training, fitness, and teaching.
Establish a credential file; secure letters of recommendation for your file.	Apply for jobs.
Write for graduate school applications and determine entrance requirements; take examinations for entry.	Apply for graduate school and assistantships.

Practical experience and certifications, such as those offered by the American Red Cross in swimming, can be assets in preparing for a career.

FatCamera/E+/Getty Images

the Aerobics and Fitness Association of America. Officiating ratings in various sport areas can also be obtained from the specific sport officiating governing body.

Some of these certifications may be available through your institution. If not, you can obtain them on your own through appropriate agencies and professional organizations. Be sure to check to ensure that the certifying agency is reputable, and the certification is highly regarded by professionals in the field. It may be helpful to ask your instructors and practitioners in the field about the appropriate credentials and certifications.

Academic Performance A major determinant of your career opportunities and professional success is your academic performance. Potential employers view academic performance as a strong reflection of a prospective employee's abilities and often as an indicator of one's potential to succeed. Make a commitment to your academic performance at the start of your college years. Additionally, your academic performance may affect your ability to enroll in graduate school.

Some students enter graduate school immediately after completing their undergraduate degree. The increased specialization within the field has made graduate school a necessity for some students and an attractive option for those seeking to increase their knowledge in their area of interest. Attending graduate school for further work in exercise physiology, biomechanics, sport management, sport psychology, sports medicine, adapted physical education, and pedagogy is the choice of many undergraduates. However, this option may not be open to someone who has a poor academic record. Most graduate schools require a minimum grade point average (GPA) of 3.0 on a 4.0 scale. An even higher GPA may be required for you to get into the graduate school of your choice. Your undergraduate academic average may influence whether or not you are awarded a graduate assistantship to defray the expenses of graduate study. Graduate assistantships are also

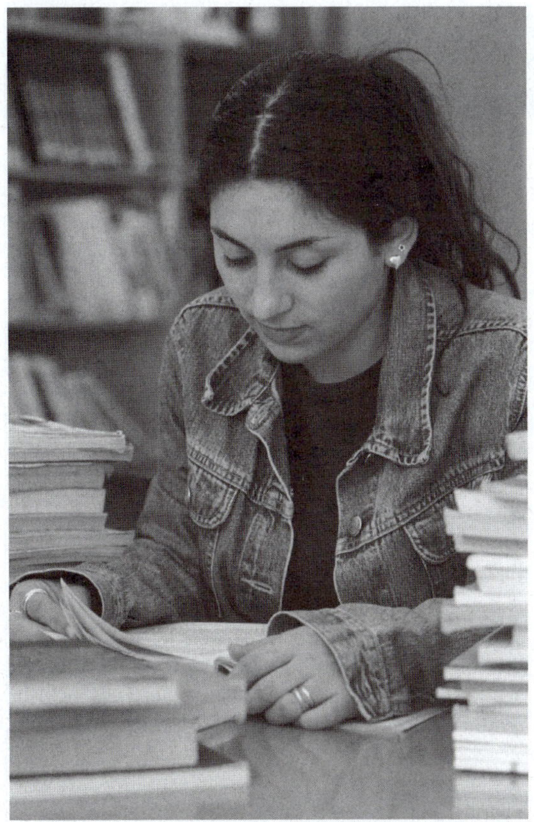

Your academic performance influences your opportunities for employment and advanced study.
Pixtal/age fotostock

highly prized because of the practical experience they afford the recipient.

Personal Development

Development of personal skills and abilities is an important part of the educational process. Your undergraduate preparation is also the time to develop professional dispositions–behaviors expected of professionals in the field. Dispositions vary widely but collaboration, critical reflection, commitment to professional growth, accountability, ethics, cultivating collaborative characteristics, creative flexibility, cultural humility, and responsibility are some examples of behaviors expected from professionals in the field.[2]

Additionally, you should carefully consider how you can develop transferable job skills, skills that can be used in many different positions. Communication, leadership, and human relations are applicable to working with people in many different settings. The Transferable Skills box on page 328 identifies these highly marketable job skills.

Effective physical education, exercise science, and sport professionals can educate and motivate others to adopt a healthy, active lifestyle. Are you a role model for a healthy lifestyle? Do you incorporate physical activity into your life on a daily basis? Eat a balanced diet? Deal with stress in a healthy manner? This is an important aspect of professional development to address and should be considered as part of your preparation for entering the field.

As a student, make an effort to become familiar with your curriculum so that you can take an active role in planning your education and strengthen your credentials for your chosen career. Most institutions assign professors to serve as academic advisors. Work closely with your advisor in planning your program of study. Take advantage of all your education has to offer to become an educated individual and a professional. Create options along your chosen career pathway through judicious selection of courses and commitment to your academics. Your activities and related experiences can also contribute to your professional development.

Related Experiences

Your activities and related experiences can significantly enhance your career preparation. Your extracurricular activities can help you develop skills that are relevant to your chosen career. Certainly, participation on an intercollegiate athletic team as a player, manager, or statistician can enhance your expertise in that sport. Your experience as a sport photographer, sport writer, or editor of the campus newspaper provides you with excellent training for your career in sport media. Being active in the physical education or exercise science majors club contributes to your professional growth. Serving as a member of the student government may develop leadership,

TRANSFERABLE SKILLS

Transferable skills are those skills that have application to many different careers. They can be developed through course work, related experiences, and personal activities. Examples of how these skills are important to professionals in different careers in physical education, exercise science, and sport are provided.

Speaking

Develop your skills as a public speaker through classwork and leadership experiences. Learn how to prepare remarks, effectively communicate ideas, and motivate people. (Applications: Appearing before the school board to justify your coaching budget; giving an update on local television about your sports program.)

Writing

Write often and learn how to write for different audiences. Shape your skills by writing letters to the editors of the college newspaper and publications that you read routinely. As a member, volunteer to write a newsletter for a club or organization. (Applications: Writing a brochure to promote your personal training business; publishing a newsletter for participants in a corporate fitness program.)

Teaching/Instructing

Refine your ability to explain things to people of different ages. Much of our work involves educating individuals with regard to skills, fitness, and healthy lifestyle. Develop your ability to share information and instruct. (Applications: Teaching students in the school setting; instructing an athlete how to rehabilitate an injured knee.)

Interviewing

Learn how to obtain information from people through direct questioning. Learn how to put a person at ease even when talking about difficult subjects. (Applications: Conducting intake interviews for fitness and rehabilitation programs; gathering information to resolve a problem under your athletic administration.)

Public Relations

Accept roles in which you must meet or relate to the public, such as greeting people, answering the phone and dealing with complaints, fund-raising, and making presentations to the public. (Applications: Engaging in athletic fund-raising at the professional organization where you are a staff administrator.)

Leadership

Assume responsibility for directing an event, supervising the work of others, initiating an activity, and directing it to completion. Learn how to advocate on behalf of yourself or others and promote change. (Applications: Advocating for additional community sports opportunities for people with disabilities; directing a corporate fitness program.)

Budget Management

Gain experience in working with a budget, even if it is small. Manage how the funds are dispersed, balance the books, and prepare reports. (Applications: Managing a facility; selling tickets, balancing the athletic training budget.)

Negotiating

Learn how to bring opposing sides together, help people discuss their differences, and resolve difficult situations; learn how to negotiate with those in power. (Applications: Resolving conflicts among employees of a fitness club; negotiating with the publisher of the local paper for more coverage of your events.)

Organizing

Take charge of an event. Manage projects and learn how to delegate and follow through. (Applications: Organizing a community health awareness fair; hosting a professional development conference for local teachers to share ideas and activities.)

Computer and Analytical Skills

Develop skills in word processing, spreadsheet, database, and presentation software; data analysis; and social media and web page construction. (Applications: Constructing a database to monitor the progress of your personal training clients; using social media to promote your program.)

Source: Adapted from Career Planning and Placement presentation and handout, *Career Planning*, Ithaca College, October 14, 2005, Ithaca, NY.

Participation in athletics can later prove valuable in securing employment as a coach.

U.S. Air Force photo by John Van Winkle

planning, and organizational skills applicable to a diversity of careers.

Your work experience can contribute to your professional development as well. Work experience gained through part-time and summer employment can give you valuable on-the-job experience. Although employment opportunities may be difficult to secure, try to find work that relates to your career goals. In the summer, gain experience teaching and organizing activities for people of all ages by working in a community recreational program. Or try to get a job working in a fitness or health club, teaching clients how to use the various pieces of exercise equipment, supervising their workouts, and teaching aerobic dance.

Another source of practical experience is on-campus jobs. Jobs may be available as an intramural assistant, researcher, tutor, lab assistant, or computer assistant. Of course, you must have the skills to perform the job or the willingness to learn if given the opportunity. Another campus employment opportunity open to qualified students is being a resident assistant in the dormitories. As a resident assistant, you will learn how to work closely with people and develop counseling and programming skills.

Volunteering is another means to gain practical experience. Although volunteering does not pay you any money, try to view it as an investment in your future. Perhaps, you would have liked to work for the summer at a corporate fitness center, but have found that the center cannot hire you due to budgetary constraints. Ask if the center would be willing to accept your services as a volunteer. This means that if you need money for tuition and related costs, you may have to work nights and weekends to secure the necessary funds for school. However, volunteering may pay big dividends when it comes to your career. One word of advice: Even if you are a volunteer, devote as much time and energy to the job as if you were a paid employee. You are being viewed by the management as a potential employee. Perhaps, if you do a good job this summer, you may be hired on a regular basis for the next summer or after graduation.

Volunteering is a good way to gain entry into your career field. Considering a career in sport broadcasting? Volunteer to be a gofer at a local television station to gain exposure to life behind the scenes. Perhaps, this will put you in the right place at the right time to take advantage of any opportunities that may come your way. Volunteering will also allow you to make professional contacts for the future and enlarge your professional network.

Consider volunteering to work with one of your professors on a research project he or she is conducting in your area of interest. If you are attending an institution with a master's or doctorate program in physical education, exercise science, and sport, volunteer to help one of the graduate students collect data for a research project. This research experience can be helpful when you are involved in your own graduate education. Again, a reminder: Make a commitment to the research project and let the researcher know you can be counted on to fulfill your responsibilities.

Extracurricular activities, work experiences, and volunteer activities can contribute to your professional development. These practical experiences provide you with the opportunity to work in your chosen career, learn necessary skills, and develop professional contacts. Even though you are just starting your preparation for your career, it is not too early to start thinking about being a professional and planning for the future.

Professional Involvement

Start early to become a professional. Professional activities are a source of knowledge and growth. One way to start is by becoming active in the majors club at your institution. If there is not a professional club, try to start one with the help of fellow students and interested faculty.

Join the national association affiliated with your career interest (e.g., SHAPE America, ACSM, or NATA). Many professional organizations offer student memberships at reduced rates. If you can, attend the national conventions, where you will have the opportunity to meet professionals, make personal contacts, and attend meetings and workshops on research findings and new techniques. In addition to national meetings, many organizations have state or regional associations that hold their own conventions. These may be more convenient to attend and allow you to meet professionals within the same geographical area. Association members, as part of their membership fee, receive professional periodicals. For example, NATA members receive the *Journal of Athletic Training* and NATA news as well as access to a host of other professional publications.

Attaining a Professional Position

Whether you are seeking full-time employment following graduation, part-time or summer employment, an internship, a graduate assistantship, or a position as a volunteer, obtaining the desired position requires a well-planned effort. Highly desirable positions attract numerous applicants, and competition is strong. Therefore, it is important to market yourself effectively and prepare thoroughly for this effort.

Preparing yourself to attain a professional position can be viewed as a 4-year ongoing effort. Each year can be viewed as a stepping stone toward achieving your long-term goal of employment as a professional or entry into graduate school. Again, review the 4-year timeline for achieving your goal presented earlier in Table 11-1. If you proceed in a systematic manner, you will maximize your professional preparation and enhance your marketability.

Resume Building

Early in your educational career you should begin the process of developing a resume. A resume is a summary of your qualifications and relevant experiences. While there are many different formats for writing a resume, typically they include sections listing a career objective, education, relevant employment and experiences, contact information, and where to obtain references. Some additional sections are honors and awards, volunteer activities, campus activities, certifications, professional memberships, and skills (e.g., fluency in a language or expertise in social media). A sample resume is shown in Figure 11-1.

Make sure that the information you collect is accurate and complete. For student teaching, internships, work, and related experiences, be sure that you have the correct title, the correct spelling of the organization, the address, the name and the title of the person who supervised you, and the correct contact information. Carefully and accurately portray the responsibilities you performed and give the relevant dates.

Customize your resume for the particular position that you are pursuing. This may involve developing several different resumes, tailoring your background, strengths, and experience to fit the position being sought. You should select information and activities to present the best picture of yourself to the potential employer and enable you to include all relevant information on the resume.

Resumes should be prepared meticulously and proofread several times to ensure that there are no errors. The resume serves as a writing sample and reflects how well you can communicate. It also demonstrates your neatness and attention to detail. Organize the resume so that the reader's attention is easily drawn to the most important information.

ROBYN LEE WEST

School Address	Permanent Address
221 Eastview Road, Apt. 1	312 Cherry Lane
Ithaca, NY 14856	Floral Estates, NY 11003
Phone: 607-111-5555	Phone: 516-222-5555
	robynleewest2021@IC.edu
	www.linkedin.com/in/robynleewest2021

CAREER OBJECTIVE	To contribute to the well-being of all young children by conducting a high-quality physical education program, work with children with disabilities to improve their motor performance and movement confidence, and coach soccer and track.
EDUCATION	Ithaca College, Ithaca, NY, May 2022 Bachelor of Science in Physical Education Provisional certification K-12 Minor in Health Concentration in Adapted Physical Education
PROFESSIONAL EXPERIENCE	Student teacher, Pine Elementary School (1/3-3/7 2021) Student teacher, Cayuga High School (3/10-5/14 2021) Fieldwork in adapted physical education, United Children's Center (1/4-5/2 2021) Youth Bureau volunteer soccer coach (Fall 2020, 2021) Counselor for children with special needs, Floral Estates Youth Summer Camp (Summers 2013-2019)
HONORS AND AWARDS	Dean's List (Fall 2018, 2019, Spring 2020) Who's Who in American Colleges and Universities Ithaca College HPER Professional Achievement Award
COLLEGE ACTIVITIES	Physical Education Majors' Club (2019-2021; Vice-President 2020-2021) Intercollegiate Soccer Team (2018-2021; Captain 2021) Intercollegiate Track and Field Team (2018-2019) Peer counselor, Health Center (2018-2020) President's Host Committee for Admissions (2019-2022)
CERTIFICATIONS	American Red Cross Community First Aid Instructor American Red Cross Water Safety Instructor American Red Cross Adapted Aquatics Instructor American College of Sports Medicine Health Fitness Instructor Rated official in volleyball and basketball
PROFESSIONAL AFFILIATIONS	New York State Association for Health, Physical Education, Recreation, and Dance American College of Sports Medicine
REFERENCES	Available from the Placement Office, School of Health Sciences and Human Performance, Ithaca College

Figure 11-1 Sample resume.

Resumes typically are printed on high-quality paper and mailed to prospective employers. Some students bring their resume to conferences to distribute when appropriate to professionals in attendance. More and more students are also posting their resumes online, using major sites like LinkedIn, and then including the link in a letter of inquiry and/or on their business cards.

Portfolios

Portfolios are used by some students to showcase their work and document their attainment of stated standards for the field. Although primarily used in teaching, other professionals, such as those entering the field of sport media, may find portfolios useful to highlight their qualifications for a job and document their professional competence and achievements.

To create a portfolio, samples of your work–artifacts–are collected over the 4-year professional preparation program. Artifacts can include a wide variety of objects, such as essays (e.g., professional philosophy), samples of work (e.g., case study or unit plan), videos (e.g., instructional video of you leading an exercise class or teaching a class in a public school), photographs (e.g., programs in action or a bulletin board you designed), links to a blog or website you created, and published works (e.g., journal article or news article you authored). Additionally, your resume, a statement of professional philosophy, and copies of relevant certifications (e.g., teaching license or ACSM certification) are included. Your artifacts should represent a sample of your abilities, strengths, quality of work, and attainment of specific competencies for the field.

Each artifact should be accompanied by an explanation of what the artifact is (e.g., personalized training program for a child newly diagnosed with Type II diabetes) and, if appropriate, the course for which it was created and the assignment. Additionally, include a reflective statement on what you learned and how it ties into competencies required in your field. This helps the reader–the potential employer–to understand the material presented. The portfolio used for employment should be neat, free from grammatical and spelling errors, and easy for the employer to use. Not all artifacts are used in construction of a portfolio for employment, only those relevant to the specific situation.

Electronic portfolios or e-portfolios are popular today. E-portfolios are displayed via the web or on mobile devices, such as tablets and smartphones. They are easy to update and modify according to the position being sought for employment. In setting up your e-portfolio, make sure that it is easy to navigate and that the menu reflects the organization of your portfolio. When possible, convert your documents to PDF files so that they can be easily read, even by those who do not have the software you used to create your work. One advantage of the electronic format is the ability to present videos demonstrating specific skills or a presentation you made about your professional philosophy. Make sure that all links function. Students can include the web address in their cover letter, enabling a potential employer to easily review their portfolio. Some prospective employers now require all job credentials to be submitted via the web, and ask students to provide samples of their work. Having a well-designed e-portfolio that highlights your accomplishments and showcases your competencies is a valuable employment tool.

Placement File

As a senior, open up a placement file at your institution's career office. Placement files generally contain demographic information, a resume, and letters of recommendation. Letters of recommendation should be solicited from people who are well acquainted with your abilities. Professors familiar with your work, student teaching or internship supervisors, and individuals for whom you worked or volunteered may be able to accurately assess your abilities and qualifications for employment or further study.

Searching for a Job

Many sources will assist you in locating job openings. Your institution's career office maintains job listings and updates them on a regular basis. Some professional organizations offer placement services to their members and periodically disseminate

YOUR ONLINE PRESENCE AND YOUR PROFESSIONAL PROFILE

How much thought have you given to your online presence? If prospective employers or graduate admission officers Googled your name, what would they find? This is an important question as more and more employers and admission officers are using the web to find out information about you.

Before your internship or student teaching, take the time to scrutinize your online presence. Given the proliferation of social media sites like Facebook, LinkedIn, and others; opportunities to share your thoughts with the world via blogs and websites; and letting others see how you spend your time via photo and video sharing, it is important to manage your online presence so it presents a positive, professional image. Some colleges and universities consider this so important to their students' future opportunities that they are providing their graduating students with free "apps" to help them create a more positive professional image. These apps help students achieve more favorable search results, typically pushing their more recent and professional profiles to the first few pages and helping place older and less favorable profiles to more distant pages.

Here are some suggestions to help you:

- Google your name and all its variations (nicknames, with and without middle initials, etc.) to see what is out there about you.
- Check all your privacy settings on all your accounts to make sure that they are, indeed, private and available to only those you choose.
- Remove less favorable images that come up in a search if you can by "de-tagging" yourself or asking those who have posted these images to remove them.
- Remove or hide tweets, blogs, and web pages that convey less than a positive impression of you.

Use your online presence and social media to maximize your professional opportunities and to network. Here are some suggestions:

- Use the same professional profile photo in all your professional social media sites. This helps professionals become familiar with who you are.
- Use LinkedIn or other job and resume sites to showcase your professional qualifications. Be sure that you are consistent in your information on your resume and what you have posted online.
- Take advantage of the social media to interact with other professionals. Take part in a discussion, ask for advice, and/or volunteer to assist with special projects. For example, go beyond just "Liking" a Facebook page or joining a group; contribute and interact, taking advantage of these online networking opportunities.
- Lastly, get a professional e-mail address. While "born2partee" may be a great user name, it falls short in terms of creating a professional impression. Use your name or some variation in creating your professional e-mail account.

information about job openings. Newspapers, state employment offices, and some state education departments have lists of job openings. Job listings are also posted on the World Wide Web.

Networking

Networking is a critical part of today's job search. Kish writes, "It's not who you know . . . but who knows YOU!"[3] Contact faculty members, friends, relatives, former employers, and practicum supervisors to see if they know of any job openings. It is through personal contacts that people learn about jobs before they are even advertised. Attending conferences or participating in professional organizations is a great way to build contacts and. expand your network. Be sure to follow up on all leads in a timely manner.

Use social media to connect with other professionals in the field. Web sites like LinkedIn help make your resume available to a wide audience and facilitate connecting with professionals in the field.

Applying for a Job

Once you are aware of possible vacancies, send a copy of your resume along with a cover letter requesting an interview or application. The cover letter's purpose is to interest an employer in hiring you. When possible, address the letter to a specific person. It should set forth the purpose of the letter, refer the reader to the resume to note certain qualifications particularly relevant to the position, and relate why you are interested in the position, emphasizing your career goals and potential contributions to the organization. The letter should close with a request for action, either an interview or an application, and should thank the reader for his or her time.

Interviewing

If you are invited for an interview, prepare carefully—in other words, do your homework. Find out as much as possible about the organization, the job responsibilities, and other relevant information. Before the interview, take some time to formulate answers to commonly asked interview questions. The following list contains some common questions.

- What are your career plans and goals?
- How has your education prepared you for this job?
- What are your greatest strengths? What are your major weaknesses?
- What is your professional philosophy? Can you give an example of how your philosophy has guided your actions?
- What jobs have you held? How did you obtain them, and why did you leave? What would your former supervisors tell us about your job performance?
- What have you done that shows leadership, initiative, and a willingness to work?
- Why should I select you above all other candidates for this position?
- What questions do you have about our organization?

As part of the preparation process, you also should prepare a list of questions to ask the interviewer. Some possible questions are:

- What are the opportunities for personal growth?
- What are the training programs or educational opportunities offered to employees?
- What are the challenging aspects of this position?
- What are the organization's plans for the future?
- What qualities are you looking for in new employees?

Develop additional questions appropriate to the specific job for which you are interviewing.

First impressions are critical. One of the first things a prospective employer may do is search the web for information about you. Take the time to clean up your online presence and make sure that your privacy settings for sites such as Facebook are set to limit viewing. When interviewing, create a positive first impression through your professional appearance, attitude, and personality. Dress appropriately for the interview. To be sure to be on time, plan on arriving ahead of the scheduled appointment time. Greet the interviewer with a firm handshake and be courteous, poised, interested, responsive, and enthusiastic. Be prepared to discuss your accomplishments, skills, interests, personal qualities, and work values in an honest, self-confident manner. Listen to each question carefully and take some time to formulate a thoughtful, concise answer. Remember that you are being evaluated not only on your achievements, but also on your ability to think and communicate. At the close of the interview, thank the interviewer for his or her time.

Follow-Up

Follow each interview with a thank-you letter. The letter should stress your interest in the position and highlight important topics that you believe went particularly well in the interview. Be sure to thank the interviewer for his or her time and consideration. If you decide after the interview that the position is not for you, thank the interviewer for his or her time and say politely that you are not interested in the position.

Accepting a Position

When offered a position, again carefully weigh the characteristics of the job with the results of your self-assessment pertaining to your skills, interests, personal and work values, and career goals. If you accept the position, your letter should confirm previously agreed-on terms of employment and reflect your excitement at meeting the challenges of the position. If you decide to decline the offer of employment, the letter of rejection should express your regrets as well as your appreciation to the employer for his or her time, effort, and consideration.

Attaining a desired position requires a commitment to marketing yourself effectively. Actively seeking information about position vacancies and diligently pursuing all leads are important for conducting a successful job search. Your resume should truthfully portray your abilities and accomplishments and be tailored to fit the position. Prepare thoroughly for each interview and present yourself as a professional. Make your final decision thoughtfully and communicate this decision to your potential employer in a professional, timely manner.

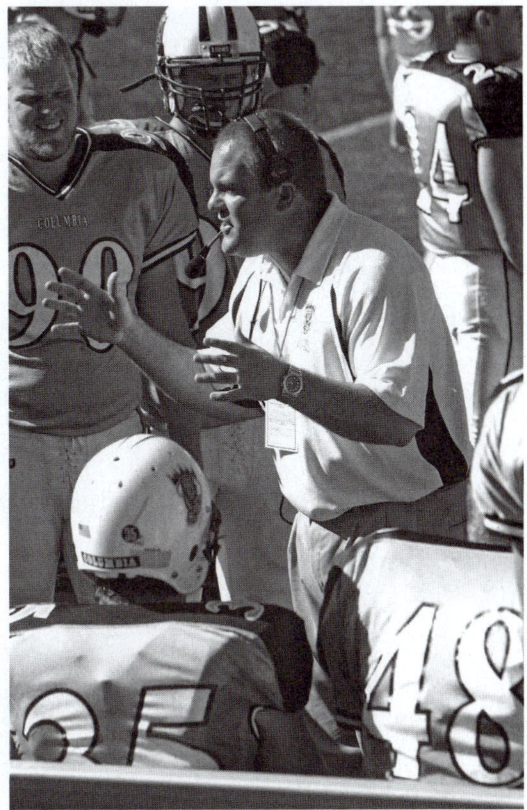

Leaders have a vision, a strong belief in the value of their endeavors, and a commitment to their profession.

Lars A. Niki

PROFESSIONALISM

Professionalism is one hallmark of those actively engaged in our field. Graduating with a degree provides you with the necessary credentials and competencies required of beginning professionals entering the field. In addition, you will also need to learn, either formally (e.g., course work) or informally (e.g., observing professionals), the behaviors and dispositions expected of people working in the field. Professionalism is a difficult concept to define, and perhaps the easiest to explain by highlighting key behaviors associated with professionalism. Professionalism encompasses competency, credibility, accountability, and advocacy. Professionals embrace and practice cultural humility. They adhere to the highest ethical standards, are involved in the field, and demonstrate a commitment to service.

Leadership

Effective leadership is essential to the success of our programs. As professionals, we must be leaders in developing and advocating for quality programs. Moreover, as leaders within our programs, we play an important role in influencing the experience of program participants, addressing their needs, and supporting their efforts to achieve their goals. Leadership is the art and process of influencing individuals and groups to achieve agreed-upon goals.[4] Leaders have passion, vision, and commitment. They inspire and motivate others to achieve their goals and strive to reach their potential.

Effective leaders possess integrity and emphasize ethical behavior.[5] By their actions, leaders earn trust and respect. Competence and credibility are other qualities often cited when discussing leadership. Leaders lead by example; they are role models and "practice what they preach." Strong communication skills, both verbal and nonverbal, are an asset. Leaders embrace differences, exhibit

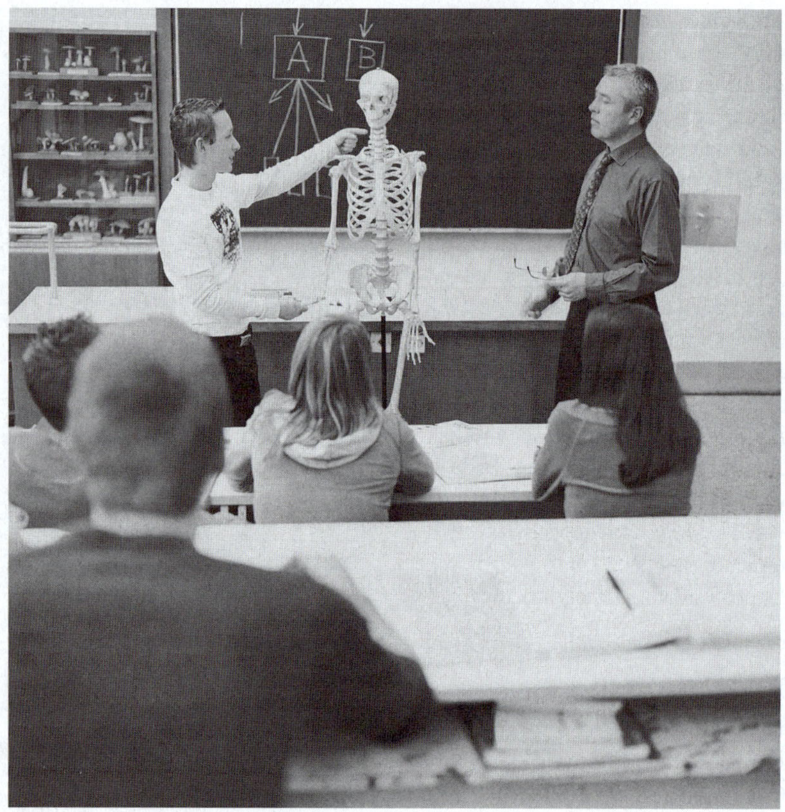

Professionals should understand the scientific and theoretical foundations of their field.
Matthias Tunger/Rayman/Digital Vision/Getty Images

fairness, and are inclusive, qualities important in our increasingly diverse society.

Advocacy

As a professional, it is incumbent upon you to advocate for your programs. Daily physical education in the nation's schools is far from being a reality, limiting the opportunities of children and youth to learn the skills, knowledge, and attitudes that form the foundation for a physically active lifetime. While sport programs have grown dramatically, they have become increasingly privatized, decreasing opportunities for individuals with limited economic resources to participate. Access for adults to health promotion programs at the workplace or cardiac rehabilitation programs in clinics might be limited to those with insurance and/or those with the ability to pay. As advocates, we must take an active role in promoting the value and growth of our programs. We must seek to influence public policy to strengthen our programs and work to ensure that they are not reduced or cut because of a lack of resources. Furthermore, we need to take steps to ensure that social determinants, such as economic status, do not restrict access to our programs.

One critical undertaking is working to address inequities of opportunities present in our society with respect to physical activity. Race, ethnicity, gender, age, education, sexual orientation, ability, and income impact individuals' opportunities to be active. As professionals, we must step forward and embrace a greater role working as agents for social change and social justice. This requires we take a more active leadership role if we are to attain our goal of lifetime physical activity for all people.

Accountability

Professionals exhibit accountability. They fulfill their many professional obligations in an exemplary fashion. Programs are planned and have established goals. They are implemented according to current standards of professional practice and conducted in the best interests of the participants. Additionally, programs are monitored for quality on a continuous basis and evaluated periodically using accepted assessment techniques. Equally important, the public statements and claims that professionals make about their credentials, programs, and outcomes are accurate and truthful.

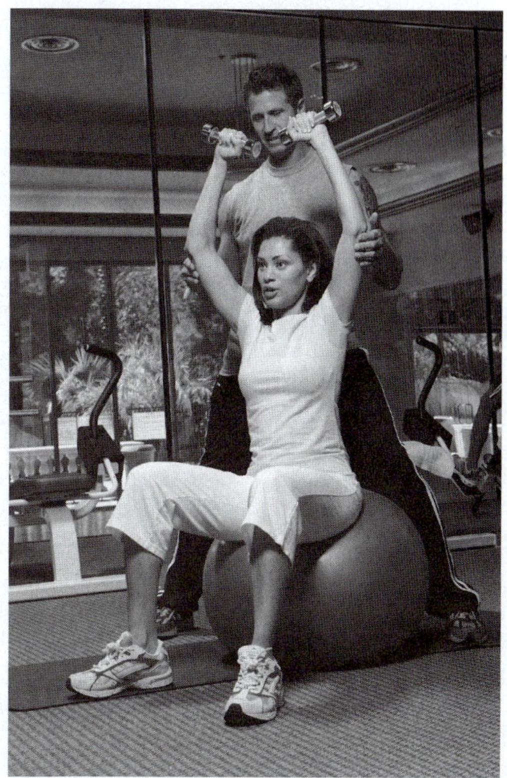

Personal trainers and other physical activity professionals should engage in regular physical activity at a sufficient level to promote health fitness. Practicing what we preach enhances our credibility as professionals.

Chris Clinton/Digital Vision/Getty Images

Cultural Humility

Our society is becoming increasingly diverse. To effectively provide services in this dynamic, multicultural environment, professionals need to develop skills relating to cultural competency (see Chapter 3). However, the dynamic, fluid nature of culture and the intersectionality of cultural influences such as race, ethnicity, gender, class, education, religion, sexual orientation, and geographic origin on individual's well-being, including beliefs regarding the body and physical activity, make achieving cultural competency a challenge.

Tervalon and Murray-Garcia suggested that, in practice, cultural competency is not a discrete endpoint to be achieved but a process they termed *cultural humility*.[6] Cultural humility is an ongoing process of self-reflection and self-critique that one engages in as part of their commitment to lifelong learning and professional growth.[6] As part of this process, we are each asked to examine our own biases, prejudices, values, and stereotypes and understand how they influence our interactions with participants in our programs. Cultural humility is an acknowledgment of how our own perspectives may limit our understanding of others' culture and their worldview. It requires us to develop an understanding of traditional power imbalances within our society and those that might be present in our interactions with our program participants and how they might be addressed. Additionally, cultural humility asks us to be advocates for change, to develop respectful partnerships with individuals and communities to address inequities. The increasing diversity of the United States requires that professionals who work in physical activity settings take steps to increase their cultural competence and develop cultural humility.[7]

Ethics

Professionals adhere to ethical standards of conduct in their interactions with participants in their programs. These ethical standards serve as guidelines for actions and aid in decision making. Interactions with participants in programs should be appropriate. For example, many codes of conduct and common professional consensus prohibit inappropriate personal relationships between coaches and their athletes, disclosure of confidential information about an employee by a worksite health professional, or discrimination by athletic trainers in their treatment of starting and nonstarting athletes (see Table 11-2). Actions toward program participants and other professionals in the field reflect honesty, respect, and fairness.[8]

Table 11-2 Examples of Codes of Ethics and Conduct for Physical Education, Exercise Science, and Sport Professionals

SHAPE America National Standards for Initial Physical Education Teacher Education[9*]	• "Physical education candidates demonstrate behaviors essential to becoming effective professionals. They exhibit professional ethics and culturally competent practices; seek opportunities for continued professional development; and demonstrate knowledge of promotion/advocacy strategies for physical education and expanded physical activity opportunities that support the development of physically literate individuals."
SHAPE America National Standards for Sport Coaches[10*]	• "Develop and enact an athlete-centered coaching philosophy. Focusing on the development of the whole athlete, sport coaches prioritize opportunities for development over winning at all costs. Sport coaches provide opportunities for athletes to reach their full potential within the sport."
Association for Applied Sport Psychology (AASP) Code of Ethics[11]	• "AASP members recognize that differences of age, gender, race, ethnicity, national origin, religion, sexual orientation, disability, language, or socioeconomic status can significantly affect their work. AASP members working with specific populations have the responsibility to develop the necessary skills to be competent with these populations, or they make the appropriate referrals."
North American Society for Sport Management (NASSM) Canons or Principles[12]	• "That professionals shall (a) hold as primary their obligations and responsibilities to students/clients; be a faithful agent or trustee when acting in a professional matter; (b) make every effort to foster maximum self-determination on the part of students/clients; (c) respect the privacy of students/clients and hold in confidence all information obtained in the course of professional service; and, (d) ensure that private or commercial service fees are fair, reasonable, considerate, and commensurate with the service performed and with due respect to the students/clients to pay."
National Athletic Trainers' Association (NATA) Code of Ethics[13]	• "Members shall accept responsibility for the exercise of sound judgment. Members shall not misrepresent in any manner, either directly or indirectly, their skills, training, professional credentials, identity or services." • "Members shall maintain and promote high standards in the provision of services."
American College of Sports Medicine (ACSM) Code of Ethics[14]	• "Members should continuously strive to improve knowledge and skill and make available to their colleagues and the public the benefits of their professional attainment."
National Strength and Conditioning Association (NSCA) Code of Ethics[15]	• "Members shall respect the rights, welfare and dignity of all individuals. . . . Members shall maintain and promote high standards . . . [and] shall not misrepresent, either directly or indirectly, their skills, training, professional credentials, identity or services."

*NASPE was an association of AAHPERD. AAHPERD is now SHAPE America.

Role Modeling

Remember that they are in a position of influence and serve as role models for participants in their programs. Initially, young professionals may want to discount the idea that appearance is important and believe that competence is what matters the most. Yet, first impressions and appearances do influence people's perceptions and beliefs. What impression do sloppily dressed, overweight, out-of-shape, smoking, inarticulate professionals make on participants in their program? Compare that impression to the one made by professionals who are nicely groomed, well-spoken, fit, dynamic, and enthusiastic and possess good health habits. Which professionals have more credibility? Effective professionals are exemplary role models; they practice what they preach.

Modeling is an important factor in changing the behaviors and attitudes of others. Modeling influences health practice, motor skill acquisition, and adoption of a physically active lifestyle.[16] Physical activity professionals are important models for the individuals with whom they work. Additionally, they will enjoy greater credibility and exemplify the value of a physically activity lifestyle.

Involvement and Continued Professional Development

Our field is growing rapidly. Professionals are committed to staying up-to-date with new research findings and changing techniques. They are interested in learning and take advantage of continuing education courses, workshops, webinars, conferences, and professional journals to stay abreast of the latest changes. Professionals take an active role in advancing the field through conducting and sharing research, exploring new ideas, and undertaking leadership responsibilities at various levels (e.g., local to regional to national levels). Through networking, professionals exchange ideas and support each other's efforts.

Service

Professionalism includes service not only to the profession but also to society. Professionals recognize their responsibility to be involved in community service, not only to offer leadership in their area of expertise, but also to participate in activities that enrich the community as a whole. Professionals advocate for increased opportunities in physical activity and sport for those who have been denied or have limited access to services.

Bradley Cardinal emphasizes the importance of professionals having a "service" mindset, where professionals participate in activities with the authentic goal the betterment of others and the field.[17] He raises concern about professionals who have a "serve-us" mindset, where they only participate in activities that have a direct benefit to themselves. He recognizes that professionals have a multitude of demands placed on them, but writes "Learning how to balance service work among other commitments, duties, obligations, and responsibilities reflects personal and professional maturity" (p. 5).

Noted adapted physical activity specialist Claudine Sherrill views service as the most critical aspect of professionalism. Sherrill states that professionalism "is manifested in SERVICE to one's place of employment, SERVICE to the community, SERVICE to one's professional organizations, and SERVICE to one's discipline or body of knowledge (generating, using, and disseminating research) justifying and strengthening the existence of the profession."[18] According to Sherrill, "SERVICE is the closest synonym to professionalism."[18]

Professionalism is a concept with many different meanings. It reflects commitment to the field and people whom we serve, respect and consideration for others, and responsibility to oneself, others, and society.

PROFESSIONAL ORGANIZATIONS IN PHYSICAL EDUCATION, EXERCISE SCIENCE, AND SPORT

Professional organizations play an important role in the growth and development of our field. Many of the greatest changes in physical education, exercise science, and sport have their beginnings in organizational meetings and conferences. Scholarly research, curricular development, certification requirements, and hundreds of other topics are discussed and implemented at conferences and other activities associated with professional organizations.

All physical education, exercise science, and sport professionals should belong to the national and state associations in their areas of interest. If all professionals belonged to and worked for their professional organizations, the concerted effort of such large professional groups would result in greater benefits for the membership and participants in our programs.

Besides the many national organizations, there are a myriad of international organizations for professionals in the field. Through their involvement in international organizations, professionals can work with people from other countries to promote physically active lifestyles for all people on a global scale.[19]

Why Belong to a Professional Organization?

Belonging to a professional association has many advantages:

1. *Membership provides opportunities for service.* Associations have many offices to fill, committee responsibilities to fulfill, and programming needs. As a member of an association, your involvement in these efforts helps advance the field. Being involved helps you develop your leadership skills, a valuable asset as a professional.
2. *Engagement offers opportunities to shape the future of the profession.* Members can work actively to influence the direction of the field. This can be accomplished through involvement in committees, task forces, and governance. As advocates, members can work to influence legislation that will benefit the profession. For example, the National Athletic Training Association (NATA) lobbies legislatures on behalf of their members to pass laws supporting athletic training and athlete safety.
3. *Associations offer multiple avenues for professional development.* As a professional, it is your responsibility to stay abreast of the latest developments in the field. Through conferences, workshops, publications, webinars, and affiliated social media, organizations help professionals learn the latest techniques, gain additional knowledge, and become aware of the many trends that emerge continually in a growing field. Continuing education offerings, conference workshops, online courses, and webinars are just some of the ways organizations help professionals continue to learn and grow as members of the field.
4. *Members can benefit from assistance in solving professional problems.* Often, professionals encounter problems or face challenges in their work. Professional organizations can offer guidance on solving these problems and meeting these challenges. For example, a professional implementing an adapted physical activity program can use guidelines developed by the organization to delineate content, implement the program, and assess outcomes.
5. *Networking with other professionals in a benefit of membership.* Through conferences and meetings, you get to know other professionals in the field. Interacting with others during formal meetings and/or conference social activities broadens your professional network. Social media makes it possible for professionals to connect and exchange ideas with other professionals across the globe.

BENEFITS OF PROFESSIONAL ORGANIZATIONS

- Opportunities for service
- Leadership development
- Impact future of profession
- Professional development
- Professional assistance
- Networking
- Forum for research
- Career advancement
- Professional identity
- Financial benefits

6. *Associations offer forum for research.* Professionals conduct research on a multitude of topics within the field. Professional organizations aid in the dissemination of research findings through conferences, workshops, newsletters, publications, and websites. They also support research efforts by promoting collaborative projects or by offering grants to help defray costs.
7. *Participation strengthens your professional identity.* Membership can help strengthen your sense of belonging and being a part of the profession. Engagement in association activities contributes to your sense of pride in engaging in service to the profession and opportunities for recognition.[20]
8. *Employment assistance is a valuable benefit.* Many professional associations offer placement services for their members. Members receive updates of job openings and often placement services at their conventions. Participation in associations helps you develop professional contacts that may prove useful in gaining employment. Through such contacts, professionals can learn of prospective employment opportunities or obtain a letter of recommendation for a desired position.
9. *Members can advantage of some financial benefits.* Some organizations offer liability insurance, conference registration, and certification opportunities at reduced costs to their members.

Numerous professional associations within the realm of physical education, exercise science, and sport help meet the diverse interests and needs of professionals. From the many associations available, you should select carefully those that best meet your needs and interests. Become involved. Be a committed, active professional willing to work hard to shape the direction and future of this dynamic field.

Professional Organizations

It would be difficult to discuss all the organizations associated with physical education, exercise science, and sport. The growth of the field has led to the formation of numerous organizations; it seems that for every specialized area of study, as well as for each sport, there are organizations for interested professionals.

You can find out about organizations in your areas of interest in several ways. First, talk to other professionals, such as faculty at your undergraduate institution, who may share the same interests. Second, talk with practitioners in your prospective field of employment and find out the organizations in which they hold membership. Third, you can search the World Wide Web for organizations in your area of interest.

The Society of Health and Physical Educators or SHAPE America, the American College of Sports Medicine (ACSM), and the National Athletic Trainers' Association (NATA) will be described here. Examples of associations for individuals interested in sport and exercise psychology, sport sociology, sport philosophy, sport history, and collegiate recreation and wellness are mentioned. Finally, examples for professionals interested in specific sport areas are provided. Because many professional organizations now have websites, it is easy to obtain information about professional organizations.

American College of Sports Medicine

ACSM, founded in 1954, is the largest sports medicine and exercise science organization in the world. The purpose of ACSM is to promote and integrate "scientific research, education, and practical applications of sports medicine and exercise science to maintain and enhance physical performance, fitness, health, and quality of life."[21] From astronauts to athletes to those people chronically diseased or physically challenged, ACSM seeks to find methods that enable people to live longer, work more productively, and enjoy a better quality of life.

Nationally, ACSM is divided into several regional chapters, such as the Mid-Atlantic chapter. Many states have their own chapters as well. More than 50,000 members of ACSM include physicians, fitness professionals, cardiac rehabilitation specialists, sports medicine practitioners and athletic trainers, physical education teachers, and coaches.

ACSM supports many different activities related to health, fitness, exercise, and sports medicine. These activities include:

- Promoting public awareness and education about the benefits of physical activity and exercise for people of all ages and abilities.
- Sponsoring certification programs for professionals interested in preventative and rehabilitative exercise.
- Holding conferences and workshops throughout the year for professionals in the field.
- Publishing journals, including *Medicine and Science in Sports and Exercise, Exercise and Sport Sciences Reviews,* and *Current Sports Medicine Reports*.
- Supporting scientific studies and encouraging research efforts to advance the field.
- Cooperating with other organizations concerning sports medicine and related areas.

Additional information about ACSM can be found at https://www.acsm.org.

National Athletic Trainers' Association

The mission of NATA, founded in 1950, is to "enhance the quality of health care for athletes and those engaged in physical activity and to advance the profession of athletic training through education and research in the prevention, evaluation, management, and rehabilitation of injuries."[22] There are more than 45,000 members nationwide. NATA establishes the standards for athletic trainers through its education programs. Nationwide, over 300 colleges and universities offer NATA-approved curricula. Each year, about 3,000 individuals earn certification through its program.

NATA provides a variety of services to its members, including:

- establishment of professional standards and a code of ethics for athletic trainers;
- administration of the certification program;
- continuing education opportunities through conventions and workshops;
- annual conventions for the benefit of its members;
- advocacy efforts to influence legislation beneficial to the field;
- promotion of athletic training through public relations efforts;
- job placement services for its membership;
- publication of journals and newsletters, including the *Journal of Athletic Training,* a quarterly scientific journal, and *NATA News,* a monthly membership magazine.

For further information, visit the NATA website at https://www.nata.org.

SHAPE America–Society of Health and Physical Educators

The forerunner to SHAPE America is the American Alliance for Health, Physical Education, Recreation, and Dance or AAHPERD, which traces its roots back to 1885 and its founding as the Association for the Advancement of Physical Education.[23] SHAPE America serves pre-K to 12 health educators and physical educators; community physical activity specialists; college faculty in kinesiology, exercise science, and pedagogy; and college faculty in teacher preparation programs in health education, physical education, dance, and sport.[23]

SHAPE America focuses on promoting lifelong habits that contribute to individuals' health and physical activity.[23] Establishing standards of excellence for school health education and physical education programs is part of SHAPE America's goal. The organization also advocates and seeks to influence policy related to school health education and physical education.[23]

At the state level, former AAHPERD state organizations have the option of retaining the Association of Health, Physical Education, Recreation and Dance name for their organization or changing their name to the new name, so the name of your state organization affiliated with SHAPE America will vary. State associations provide services to professionals within the state, typically hold conferences, and offer young practitioners the opportunity to attend workshops, network with other professionals in the state, and become involved in their profession.

Professional Organizations within the Field

Within the field, there are many specialized organizations. These continue to grow as professionals

SELECTED INTERNATIONAL AND NATIONAL PROFESSIONAL ORGANIZATIONS

NASPSPA — **North American Society for the Psychology of Sport and Physical Activity** (https://www.naspspa.com) focuses on the "scientific study of human behavior when individuals are engaged in sport and physical activity."[24] Members are interested in the areas of motor behavior, motor development, motor learning, motor control, and the psychology of sport and exercise. Journals include *Motor Control* and the *Journal of Sport and Exercise Psychology.*

IAPS — **International Association for the Philosophy of Sport** (https://www.iaps.net) strives to "foster philosophic interchange among scholars interested in better understanding sport."[25] IAPS publishes the *Journal of the Philosophy of Sport.*

NASSH — **North American Society for Sport History** (https://www.nassh.org) strives "to promote, stimulate, and encourage study and research and writing of the history of sport"[26] and physical activity across different time spans and within diverse historical contexts. NASSH publishes the *Journal of Sport History.*

NASSS — **North American Society for the Sociology of Sport** (https://nasss.org) seeks to "promote, stimulate, and encourage the sociological study of play, games, and sport . . . and shall recognize and represent all sociological paradigms for the study of play, games, and sport."[27] The *Sociology of Sport Journal* is a publication of NASSS.

NASSM — **North American Society for Sport Management** (http://www.nassm.org) endeavors to "promote, stimulate, and encourage study, research, scholarly writing, and professional development in the area of sport management (broadly interpreted)."[28] The society focuses on both the theoretical and applied aspects of sport management as related to sport, exercise, dance, and play as these activities are engaged in by diverse populations. Its official publication is the *Journal of Sport Management.*

NIRSA — **NIRSA: Leaders in Collegiate Recreation (http://nirsa.net)** is a "leader in higher education and the advocate for the advancement of recreation, sport, and wellness by providing educational and developmental opportunities, generating and sharing knowledge, and promoting networking and growth for our members."[29]

within the field come together to start new organizations in their areas of expertise. A few of these organizations are shown in the Selected International and National Professional Organizations box.

Sport Organizations for Coaches and Interested Professionals

Numerous organizations are affiliated with specific sport areas. Many of these organizations sponsor annual conferences and clinics for interested professionals, conduct certification programs, and publish newsletters and journals related to the sport. They provide a wonderful means to network with other professionals, learn new skills and techniques, and stay up-to-date with new advances in the sport. Professionals who are coaching or teaching in the specific sport are good sources of information about these sport associations.

CURRENT TRENDS: MOVING TOWARD THE FUTURE

- The disciplines within the field of kinesiology will continue to grow and become interdisciplinary in nature, offering new career opportunities.
- Millennials will change jobs more often than their grandparents, who typically worked in one job for their entire career.
- Technological skills will be increasingly required of professionals as these play a great role in many careers.

OCCUPATIONAL SOCIALIZATION AND SELF-CARE

Completion of your professional preparation program is just the start of your professional journey. As you pursue your career in the workplace,you will encounter many challenges, issues, and opportunities that will contribute to your growth, both professionally and personally. Engaging in self-care is important as you navigate the demands of your career and seek to balance your personal and professional lives.

Occupational socialization is the process of becoming a part of an organization, moving from your role as an "outside" to an "insider."[30] This process involves "learning how things are done here"–that is, learning the attitudes, skills, and behaviors expected from people within the organization. Learning the norms, expectations, and values within the culture of the organization is a critical part of the socialization process. Organizations recognize that the support given to "newcomers" and the "on-boarding" process can exert a significant influence on people's satisfaction, productivity, and longevity in their workplace.[30] Socialization can take place through many different avenues, including formal and informal training, mentorship, and peer-group relationships.

As a newcomer, you are challenged to understand the requirements of your role–the job tasks to be performed, identification of priorities, and delineation of your responsibilities. It is important to know by whom and how you will be evaluated and how often this evaluation will take place. Acceptance by peers and the growth of a support network within the workplace aids in the transition and will help you navigate the organization's culture and the stressors you will encounter.

Occupational demands and the workplace environment can lead to stress. Workload, job insecurity, role conflict, role ambiguity, personality conflicts, and leadership style are just some of the many stressors you may encounter.[31] Discrimination, prejudice, bias, sexual harassment, and bullying also contribute to a stressful work environment. It is important to realize that these and other workplace demands interact with our personal lives and may make it difficult to maintain a work-life balance.

The stressors we encounter can challenge us to grow to meet the demands. They can also negatively impact our well-being. Unchecked, occupational stress can lead to burnout–feelings of depersonalization, lack of job satisfaction, emotional exhaustion that negatively impacts job performance and can result in leaving the profession. Individual differences in the perception of stress, personality, and life experiences are just a few factors that influence our response to the stressors we encounter.

Resilience and adaptability are two qualities that can help you deal with occupational stressors.[32] Resilience is the ability to adapt well, cope, and rebound in the face of challenges. Adaptability is the ability to be flexible and to strategically explore different options to achieve desired goals. Both qualities can be developed and strengthened and serve as a protective factor to stress. However, it is essential that you understand the complexity of societal and environmental factors that contribute to stress and your ability to cope and manage it.

Self-care is critical to your well-being and enhances your ability to navigate the professional demands of your job and cultivate a work-life balance.[33] Take steps to prioritize your own well-being and realize its okay to put yourself first. As professionals, as cliché as it sounds, it is important to "practice what we preach." Being physically active, eating healthy, and getting enough sleep are important aspects of a self-care routine.

Nurturing your mental health is important. Set aside time to reflect on what is going well and what changes might be beneficial. Explore and learn cognitive strategies that allow you to see things from different perspectives. Try to adopt a more realistic, positive outlook. Take time to reflect and identify what you can control and change and what you cannot. Be proactive in using professional resources, such as seeking out a therapist or taking advantage of the human resource programs at your workplace.

Think about engaging in preventive stress management. There are a host of stress management strategies, and it is important to find one or two that work best for you. While some people might find yoga relaxing, others might find the solitude of a long run or engaging with nature to be just the thing to relax and recharge them. Being assertive and learning to say "no" are two strategies that can help you manage your time.

Social support is a critical factor in our well-being. As you move from college to your new job, you will need to adjust your social support network. Finding people in the workplace you can trust is important and they can help you navigate being a newcomer, giving you insight, different perspectives, assistance, and encouragement. Friends and family may offer us emotional support, acceptance, and comfort. Connecting with others can help us navigate tough times and help us see solutions when we are feeling overwhelmed.

Remember to adopt a growth mindset and practice self-compassion. The experiences and challenges you encounter are opportunities to learn and grow. We can learn from our successes and failures. Be open to the feedback you receive and consider how it can help you enhance your professional competencies. Not all you do will be successful. Acknowledge that things did not go the way you had planned and hoped, but also reflect and see what lesson can be learned. Think about whether you should retry the same approach and perhaps tweak it a bit, employ a different strategy, or redefine your goal and desired outcome.

Self-compassion invites you to treat yourself with the same kindness as you would treat others.[34] Many of us would say that we are our harshest critic. When things do not go well, take a moment to listen to your self-talk. Are you berating yourself for failure or being inadequate? Would you say the same thing to a friend? Mostly likely, you would be more positive and encouraging. Now, change your self-talk to be kinder and more compassionate to yourself.

Lastly, recognize the transition from your being a student in your professional preparation program to being a professional in the field is a challenging one. Realize that socialization into the field will take time. Additionally, there are a multitude of occupational stressors you will need to manage. Make practicing self-care a priority, engage in preventive stress management, and strive to find a work-life balance that works for you.

SUMMARY

Many exciting opportunities await individuals interested in pursuing a career in this field. Teaching and coaching in schools at all levels remains a popular career choice. Teaching and coaching opportunities have also expanded to nonschool settings. With the growth of the field, career opportunities are available for qualified individuals in fitness, health promotion, cardiac rehabilitation, athletic training, sport management, and sport media, to name a few of the many career choices available.

Selecting a career pathway from the many available options requires careful consideration of many factors. To make an informed decision, you must gather information from the appropriate sources and evaluate it. Your values, personal strengths, interests, goals, and preferences are the most important considerations in choosing a career. In selecting a career, you must also consider information about the career itself. This information may be gathered through research and by talking to practitioners in your prospective career.

Professional preparation for a career involves academic studies, related experiences, and professional activities. Planning for a career demands understanding the nature of the work to be performed and the requirements of the job. Professionalism embodies competence, credibility, accountability, and cultural humility. Critical aspects of professionalism are ethical behavior, role modeling, active involvement, and service.

There are many advantages to belonging to a professional organization. Professional organizations provide opportunities for service, facilitate communication, and serve as an avenue to disseminate research findings and other information to professionals. Membership in a professional organization provides opportunities for networking, professional assistance in meeting challenges, and strengthens one's professional identity. It may enhance one's employment opportunities.

Occupational socialization is the process of learning to be a part of an organization, learning its culture and "how things are done". Occupational stressors can challenge us to learn and grow, but they could also have adverse consequences on one's health and well-being. Preventive stress management and engaging in self-care can help mitigate some of the occupational demands and help individuals achieve a desirable work-life balance.

DISCUSSION QUESTIONS

1. What were the most significant factors influencing your choice of a career in the area of physical education, exercise science, and sport?
2. As a professional, do you believe that it is important to be a role model? Why or why not? Do you have a professional role model? What qualities does that individual exhibit?
3. Reflect on your cultural heritage. Think about the different cultures to which you belong and your identity (e.g., gender, geographic location, language, and education) and how they intersect with each other. What are some beliefs within your culture about physical activity, body image, health, and illness? How do these beliefs influence your actions?

GET CONNECTED

Occupational Outlook Handbook–provides career information, including job responsibilities, working conditions, education needed, earnings, and future outlook in many occupations.

https://www.bls.gov/ooh/

Professional Organizations–these websites give information about the mission of the organization, services, membership, publications, limited access to resources, and educational opportunities.

AAASP	https://appliedsportpsych.org/	**Association for Applied Sport Psychology**
ACSM	https://www.acsm.org/	**American College of Sports Medicine**
IAPS	https://iaps.net/	**The International Association for the Philosophy of Sport**
NASSH	https://www.nassh.org/	**North American Society for Sport History**
NASSM	https://www.nassm.com/	**North American Society for Sport Management**
NASPSPA	https://www.naspspa.com/	**North American Society for the Psychology of Sport and Physical Activity**
NASSS	https://nasss.org/	**North American Society for the Sociology of Sport**
NATA	https://www.nata.org	**National Athletic Trainers' Association**
SHAPE America	https://www.shapeamerica.org/	**Society of Health and Physical Educators/SHAPE America**
NIRSA	https://nirsa.net/nirsa/	**NIRSA: Leaders in Collegiate Recreation**

Self-Assessment Activities

These activities are designed to help you determine if you have mastered the materials and competencies presented in this chapter.

1. Identify five career opportunities that interest you. Using the information provided in the Get Connected box, access the *Occupational Outlook Handbook* site and search for information about each career. Find out the skills required, potential employers, future outlook, and salary associated with each career.
2. Using the information provided in the chapter, access the website of one of the professional organizations in your area of interest. Find out the fees for membership, membership benefits, and publications at both the national and state levels. Be sure to check to see if the organization offers special rates and benefits for students.
3. Develop a multiyear plan to enhance your credentials. Specifically, in addition to the requirements of your professional preparation program, what other opportunities will you pursue (e.g., certifications, extracurricular activities, employment, volunteering) to enhance your professional qualifications?
4. Carefully read the statements in Table 11-2 regarding codes of ethics and conduct for professionals. Working as a group, select one career area and develop a five-point code of conduct for that career.
5. Work with a partner. Google your name and evaluate the information that comes up on the first two pages of results. With your partner, review your results and decide what actions you can take to upgrade your professional web profile. Be specific.

References

1. US Department of Labor. (2019). *Occupational outlook handbook*. Washington, DC: Department of Labor. Retrieved from https://www.bls.gov/ooh/.
2. Henninger, M. L., & Ensign, J. (2020). Transitioning from students of teaching to teachers of students: Developing professional dispositions (Part 1). *JOPERD, 91*(1) 33–37.
3. Kish K. (2012). Networking for the young professional. *Parks and Recreation, 47*(2), 45–47.
4. Northhouse, P. G. (2016). *Leadership theory and practice* (7th ed.). Thousand Oaks, CA: Sage.
5. Armstrong, S. (2001). Are you a "transformational" coach? *Journal of Physical Education Recreation & Dance, 72*(3), 44–47.
6. Tervalon, M., & Murray-Garcia, J. (1998). Cultural humility versus cultural competence: A critical distinction in defining physician training outcomes in multicultural education. *Journal of Health Care for the Poor and Underserved,* 9, 117–125.
7. Tritschler, K. (1998). Cultural competence: A 21st century leadership skill. *Journal of Physical Education, Recreation & Dance, 79*(1), 7–9.
8. Stoll, S. K., & Beller, J. M. (1995). Professional responsibility–A lost art. *Strategies, 9*(2), 17–19.
9. SHAPE America. (2017). *Initial physical education teacher education standards*. Reston, VA: SHAPE America.
10. SHAPE America. (n.d.). *National standards for sport coaches*. Reston, VA: SHAPE America.
11. Association for the Advancement of Applied Sport Psychology. (2011). *Ethical principles and standards of the Association for the Advancement of Applied Sport Psychology*. Retrieved from https://www.aaasponline.org.
12. North American Society for Sport Management. *Position statement*. Retrieved from https://www.nassm.com.
13. National Athletic Trainers' Association. (2018). *NATA code of ethics*. Retrieved from https://www.nata.org.
14. American College of Sports Medicine. (2019). *Code of ethics*. Retrieved from https://www.acsm.org.
15. National Strength and Conditioning Association. (2019). *Code of conduct*. Retrieved from https://www.nsca.com/.
16. National Association for Sport and Physical Education. (2002). *Physical activity and fitness recommendations for physical activity professionals* [Position paper]. Reston, VA: NASPE.

17. Cardinal, B. J. (2013). Service vs. serve-US: What will your legacy be? *Journal of Physical Education, Recreation & Dance, 84*(5), 6.
18. Sherrill, C. L. (2006). Giants, role models, and self-identity: Issues in professionalism. *Palaestra, 22*(3), 56–58.
19. Kluka, D. A. (2003). Finding our rightful place in the world. *Journal of Physical Education, Recreation & Dance, 74*(6), 6.
20. Seymour, C. M. (2020). A professional legacy is a journey: What path will you travel? *JOPERD, 91*(3), 3–4.
21. American College of Sports Medicine. (2019). Retrieved from https://www.acsm.org.
22. National Athletic Trainers' Association. (2019). Retrieved from https://www.nata.org.
23. SHAPE America: Society of Health and Physical Educators. (n.d.). Retrieved from https://www.shapeamerica.org.
24. North American Society for the Psychology of Sport and Physical Activity. (2016). Retrieved from https://www.naspspa.com.
25. International Association for the Philosophy of Sport. (n.d.). Retrieved from https://iaps.net.
26. North American Society for Sport History. (n.d.). Retrieved from https://www.nassh.org.
27. North American Society for the Sociology of Sport. (n.d.). Retrieved from https://nasss.org.
28. North American Society for Sport Management. (n.d.). Retrieved from https://www.nassm.com.
29. NIRSA: Leaders in Collegiate Recreation. (.n.d.). Retrieved from https://nirsa.net.
30. Bauer, T. N., Bodner, T., Erdogan, B., Truxillo, D. M., & Tucker, J. S. (2007). Newcomer adjustment during organizational socialization: A meta-analytic review of antecedents, outcomes, and methods. *Journal of Applied Psychology, 92*, 707–721. DOI: 10.1037/0021-9010.92.3.707.
31. Quick, J. C., & Hendeson, D. F. (2016). Occupational stress: Preventing suffering, enhancing wellbeing. *International Journal of Environmental Research and Public Health, 13*, 459; doi:10.3390/ijerph13050459.
32. B owles, T., & Arnup, J. L. (2016). Early career teachers' resilience and positive adaptive change capabilities. *Australian Educational Research, 43*, 147–164. DOI 10.1007/s13384-015-0192-1.
33. Wuest, D. A., & Subramaniam, P.R. (2021). Building teacher resilience during a pandemic and beyond. *Strategies, 34*, 4, 8–12.
34. Neff, K. (2022, March 20). Self-compassion. https://self-compasion.org.

CHAPTER 12

TEACHING AND COACHING CAREERS

Polka Dot Images/Getty Images

OBJECTIVES

After reading this chapter, students should be able to–

- Describe the rewards, benefits, and challenges of pursuing a teaching and/or coaching career in a school or nonschool setting.
- Describe the similarities and differences between teaching and coaching.
- Discuss the importance of self-care for teachers and coaches.
- Identify strategies to maximize opportunities for employment in a teaching or coaching position.

Note that this chapter contains information on trauma. Please take a moment to consider if this information might be stressful for you. If so, you might want to speak to your instructor and/or reach out for support.

Teaching and coaching opportunities for physical education, exercise science, and sport professionals have expanded from the school to the nonschool setting and from school-aged populations to people of all ages, ranging from preschoolers to senior citizens. Although traditional opportunities in the public schools are available, some professionals are seeking other avenues for teaching and coaching careers. The national interest in fitness and sport has contributed to the growth of these alternative areas of employment. Moreover, the continued emphasis on fitness, physical activities, and sport opportunities for all age groups presents an encouraging employment picture to potential physical education teachers and coaches.

Cultural competency and cultural humility are important for both teachers and coaches (see Chapter 3). In our increasingly cultural diverse society, both teachers and coaches must be committed to conducting culturally responsive programs that are sensitive to the needs of students and athletes from different cultural backgrounds. This includes being committed to the equitable treatment of all people participating in our programs.

Teaching and Coaching in Today's World

As the twenty-first century continues to fold, we are impacted by societal forces that have and will continue to exert a significant influence on education and schooling at all levels, impacting the circumstances you will encounter as teachers and coaches in the schools and the lives of the students in your classes and participants on your teams.[1] The pervasiveness of trauma in the PK-12 population and the growing diversity of our population requires teachers and coaches use strategies that are trauma-informed and culturally sensitive.

Three of the many forces that will continue to influence education are the multiyear COVID-19 pandemic, the growing focus on civil rights and activism, and digital technologies that have changed the many facets of education.[1] The pandemic created hardships for people all over the global, with over 6 million deaths and over 500 million cases worldwide, and in the United States, nearly 1 million deaths and over 81 million cases. Pandemic restrictions led to an increased reliance on digital technologies, altering conventional models and strategies of education and schooling.[1] Among the changes were the institution of virtual and hybrid models of instruction. Teachers were frequently requested to "pivot" from one approach to another while continuing to learn how to incorporate technology into their approaches and promote engagement in physical activity. Educators were challenged to ensure they provide accessible and equitable access to online learning. The coverage of COVID-19 by the media brought increased attention to inequities in our society, highlighting the prevalence of poverty, disparities in health and access to health care, growth of mental health issues, and differences in the quality of education, including differential access to technologies that were increasingly essential to learning.

We can no longer ignore the prevalence of systemic and institutional racism in our society nor inequities all too present in our educational institutions. Educational institutions need to take a hard look at their policies, procedures, and practices and address those that are social unjust.[2] When you reflect back on your PK-12 educational experiences, can you identify inequitable practices? For example, did you notice that marginalized students–students who are nonwhite, economically disadvantaged, English language learners, special needs, LGBTQ+–were disciplined more frequently and more severely that nonmarginalized students? As you continue your professional journey, it is important you think about your own educational experiences, become more aware of inequities you see as well as reflect on your personal identity and its influence your interactions with others, be it in your future professional setting or your personal life. We hope that you will make a commitment to equitable and social justice practices in your career and be an advocate for change.

As a future professional, it is important you are informed about trauma, its impact, how to respond, and the implications for teaching and coaching. Trauma among children and youth is more common than you can imagine. Trauma is a response to one or more overwhelming stressful events or circumstances that exceeds one's ability to cope.[3] It is not the event or circumstances but the individual's response to them. An individual's experience of the event or circumstances determines whether it is traumatic. Abuse, witnessing domestic violence, parental divorce, neglect, homelessness, community violence, racism, and poverty are a few examples of the trauma facing children and youth today.

Trauma can have adverse effects on individuals' functioning and well-being. The effects of trauma often leave individuals in a state of toxic stress. It impacts individuals' ability to succeed in school often leading to problems in academic performance, inappropriate behavior, and difficulty in forming meaningful relationships with teachers and peers. Additionally, distrust and fears about personal safety, sensitivity to noise, and dislike of being touched are some effects that might influence learning in physical education or coaching.

As a teacher, it is critical that you are sensitive to trauma and informed about its causes, manifestations, and strategies that are helpful in working with those affected by trauma. The Substance Abuse and Mental Health Services Administration (SAMHSA) offers an approach that would be helpful to you in working with individuals who have experienced trauma.[3] The approach is often referred to as the four Rs. First, it is important to realize the widespread prevalence of trauma and understand what actions might contribute to healing. Second, recognize the signs and symptoms of trauma. Third, respond to the presence of trauma by integrating policies, procedures, and practices that support students with trauma and are socially just. Lastly, take care to nurture students' well-being and take steps to ensure that students would not be retraumatized. One of the key things is to help students feel physically, socially, and emotionally safe within the school environment–whether it be in the classroom, hallway, cafeteria, gym, or locker room. Be aware of situations and encounters that could be a potential trigger and elicit a trauma-mediated response.

One way you can support children and youth experiencing trauma is to create an environment and make intentional decisions that foster resiliency in our students. Resiliency is considered a protective factor that can help children and youth deal with the pervasive impact of trauma. Walton-Fisette identifies four ways that we can accomplish this goal: create physically and emotionally safe spaces, cultivate positive and healthy relationships with students, promote student responsibility, and help students move toward self-regulation.[4] For many children and youth, having one person in their life, be it a teacher or a coach, that consistently demonstrates that they care can make an important difference to them, a difference that often extends beyond the educational environment.

Today, diversity is the norm. The US population continues to grow in diversity. We are challenged to teach students who are significantly diverse in their backgrounds–socioeconomic status, race, ethnicity, family structure, religion, gender, sexuality, and immigrant status–residing in communities that exert a considerable influence on their opportunities. Our social identities reflect our uniqueness, beliefs, and values. We also know that the context of the school–its leadership, policies, procedures, practices, standards, and staff–and the community and state in which it resides exerts a powerful influence on the educational experience of students and educational outcomes. We cannot discount this uniqueness. Quite simply, a one size fits all approach to education does not fit everyone. Variability, adaptability, and flexibility are the keys to creating educational experiences that fit the needs of twenty-first century students in significant, meaningful, socially just ways.

SOCIAL JUSTICE

Talking Points

- Physical activity opportunities must be provided to low-income communities to ensure equitable access to these opportunities for all people.
- Physical educators must strive to help all students achieve physical literacy, not just the highly skilled.
- Authentic assessments that offer students multiple ways of demonstrating learning, differentiated instruction to address diverse needs, and embracing cultural humility and sensitivity are some ways that teachers can address social inequities.
- As technology becomes more present in physical education and coaching, we must make provisions to ensure that all students and athletes have access to it.
- Coaches have an ethical obligation not to exploit their athletes, yet this happens too often as winning is prioritized over athletes' well-being.
- Access to sports and opportunities to train at a high level are limited by money. Addressing this issue will allow those talented individuals who aspire to compete at the highest levels the opportunity to pursue their goals.

THE TEACHING PROFESSION

Teaching has been the traditional focus of the field of physical education. Even though many types of jobs are now available in the field, many people still choose to teach and to coach. The school setting remains the most popular setting for teaching, and job opportunities look promising. Employment of teachers is projected to grow through 2030.[5]

Teaching in school and nonschool settings has many benefits, rewards, and challenges. Regardless of the setting, effective teachers hold high expectations for their students, keep them involved in relevant learning activities, and create an inclusive environment that promotes learning for all students. Beginning teachers possess competencies in many different areas that enable them to enhance student learning. The use of developmentally appropriate teaching practices helps teachers more effectively address the needs of their learners.

Why Teach?

Why choose a career in teaching? Many prospective physical educators desire to teach to help children and youth learn the skills, acquire the knowledge, and gain the confidence to participate in a variety of physical activities. Some are drawn to teaching physical education because of the opportunity to be active all day, to teach a variety of activities, and to build meaningful relationships with their students. Still others are attracted to the field because of their passion for and/or expertise in sport, and the desire to share this with others. Individuals who aspire to coach may find schools require that they possess a teacher certification and/or that they be employed by the school district. Teaching physical education may be seen by some individuals as a stepping stone to a career as an athletic administrator. What is your reason?

Many professionals who teach physical activities in a nonschool setting offer similar reasons for pursuing teaching as a career as those teaching in a school setting. The opportunity to capitalize on one's proficiency in a sport, the desire to share the benefits of participation with others, and the love of working with people to help them achieve their goals may motivate physical educators to seek out a teaching position in community programs, recreation agencies, or sport clubs.

Rewards, Benefits, and Challenges of Teaching

The rewards, benefits, and challenges of teaching vary greatly, influenced by many factors, including the societal forces impinging on us. Your social identity, your professional philosophy, the quality of your professional preparation, and the school in which you find yourself teaching are just a few factors that influence your teaching. We would be remiss if we did not address some of the realities of teaching experienced by those who work in public schools today. Today, high-stakes testing, increased teacher accountability for students' learning, and the growing amount of required paperwork and meetings place increased demands on teachers, expanding their workload tremendously.[6] The greater diversity of the student population and the commitment to achievement for all students present great challenges to teachers as they strive to meet students' needs and achieve program goals.

The culture of the school, the politics, and bureaucracies can affect your teaching experience. In some schools, there is strong administrative support for teachers, high morale, mentoring, and professional development. In other schools, administrative support is lacking, morale is low, and opportunities for professional development are noticeably absent. Student discipline issues, school violence, and lack of parental support influence teachers' effectiveness. Increasingly, insufficient budgets and, in some cases, inadequate facilities pose additional challenges. Teacher preparation programs can help teachers meet these challenges by orienting them to the realities of teaching and providing their teacher education candidates with the skills to address these issues.[6]

Physical educators may find they have some additional challenges confronting them.[7] In some schools, physical education is marginalized and not considered a core subject. The contributions of physical education to the education of students are minimized. This lack of respect for physical education as a subject might be reflected in class sizes that are larger than in other subject areas or requests that students be excused from physical education to make up work. For some physical educators, the expectations that they assume additional responsibilities, such as coaching or coordinating the staff wellness program, greatly add to their workload. On the other hand, beginning physical educators may find themselves in a school setting that values physical education and recognizes its contribution to students' education. Being aware of these realities can help you prepare to navigate them as you begin your teaching career.

For those who choose to teach, the intrinsic rewards are great. The opportunity to make a difference in the lives of their students is rewarding in and of itself. Seeing students enjoy being physically active is one of the joys of teaching physical education, as is helping students acquire skills, knowledge, and confidence to be lifelong participants in physical activity. Some physical educators find the chance to teach a variety of activities or to share their love of a sport rewarding. For many pursuing a career in physical education, the opportunity to coach is also a benefit.

There are some tangible benefits to choosing to teach in the public schools that make teaching an attractive opportunity for many. In the school setting, the long vacations, the informality of teaching in the gymnasium rather than the classroom, and the job security offered by tenure make teaching an attractive career choice. Though teaching salaries vary widely from district to district and state to state, remember that teachers typically work only 9 months or about 180 days per year. Many teachers receive additional compensation for coaching or supervising extracurricular activities, such as the student yearbook staff. The long vacation periods provide opportunities to earn additional money, pursue other interests, travel, and/or continue one's education.

Meaningful rewards and several benefits are associated with teaching in the nonschool setting. Examples of teaching opportunities in the nonschool setting include working as a tennis or

Elementary schoolchildren practice their ball handling skills.

Lars A. Niki/McGraw Hill

golf professional and teaching in a community recreation program, YMCA/YWCA, or commercial sport club, such as a gymnastics club, swim club, or racquetball club. Similar to teaching in the school setting, the opportunity to help people achieve their goals is a major reward. One benefit is that as participation in these programs is voluntary, the teacher generally works with individuals and students who are highly motivated and eager to be involved in the activity. Another benefit of teaching in the nonschool setting is the opportunity to specialize; many physical educators like the idea of teaching just one activity, such as golf, tennis, or swimming. However, many nonschool settings such as YMCA/YWCA and community recreation programs require the ability to teach a variety of activities.

There are some challenges to teaching in the nonschool setting. Unlike teaching in the schools, there is a lack of job security. The number of participants enrolled in a program may determine whether it continues to be offered and may also determine your salary. Salaries vary widely as well. In contrast to school, where the working hours are confined to weekdays (unless one is coaching), working hours at a nonschool setting may be late afternoons and evenings and often weekends. Working hours need to be responsive to the hours the clients have available for leisure-time pursuits. Work may also be seasonal, but this depends on the nature of the activity and the location. For example, golf professionals in the Northeast may find work only from April to September, but those pursuing this profession in the South may be able to work year-round.

Prospective teachers should reflect upon their reasons for entering the teaching profession as part of their career self-assessment. There are many rewards, benefits, and challenges associated with teaching in both the school and nonschool settings. These must be considered in making a career choice.

Competencies for Teachers

What should teachers know? What should they be able to do? What competencies do teachers need to help ensure every K-12 student learns? The Council of Chief State School Officers Interstate Teacher Assessment and Support Consortium (InTASC) developed a set of teaching standards that transcends different disciplines and grade levels and focuses on knowledge and skills necessary to promote engagement and achievement for all students.

InTASC Standards

The 10 InTASC Standards are organized into four themes: the learner and learning, content, instructional practice, and professional responsibility.[8] Within each standard, specific performance expectations are described, essential knowledge listed, and critical dispositions identified. Equally important, these standards stress that professional development and institutional support is necessary to help teachers achieve these standards. Many professional preparation programs reflect these standards in their curriculum, and these standards are aligned with accreditation requirements.

The InSTAC standards offer guidelines to professionals entering the field as beginning teachers and to veteran teachers. At a time when teachers are held increasingly accountable for student achievement, these evidence-based standards describe effective teaching that is associated with student learning. While these standards are relevant across all disciplines and grade levels, it may be helpful to you to learn about SHAPE America's standards for physical education teachers graduating from a professional preparation program.

Competencies for Physical Education Teachers

What competencies should physical educators possess as they graduate from their professional preparation program? SHAPE America's initial physical education teacher education standards identify six standards to be achieved (see 2017 National Standards for Initial Physical Education Teacher Education box).[9]

As you prepare to enter the field, you should know disciplinary content and be able to apply this

2017 NATIONAL STANDARDS FOR INITIAL PHYSICAL EDUCATION TEACHER EDUCATION

Standard 1. Content and Foundational Knowledge
Standard 2. Skillfulness and Health-Related Fitness
Standard 3. Planning and Implementation
Standard 4. Instructional Delivery and Management
Standard 5. Assessment of Student Learning
Standard 6. Professional Responsibility

SHAPE America-Society of Health and Physical Educators. (2017). *2017 National Standards for Initial Physical Education Teacher Education*. Reston, VA: SHAPE America. Used with permission.

content to meeting the needs of the students. It is expected that physical educators demonstrate competence in skill performance and possess health-enhancing levels of fitness.

As a teacher, you are tasked with planning and implementing developmentally appropriate learning experiences that are aligned with standards, while considering the individual differences and addressing the diverse needs of all students. The use of effective pedagogical skills and strategies to enhance student learning, such as demonstrations, explanations, management, and provision of feedback, to create a safe, productive learning environment are emphasized. Self-reflection and the ability to make adjustments to instructional tasks and the learning environment as students engage in learning are important. Having the ability to use a wide variety of assessment strategies to monitor students' progress as well as to make adjustments in your teaching contributes to student learning.

As a professional, you are expected to demonstrate ethical behavior and engage in culturally-sensitive, socially just practices. Professional development opportunities enable you to continue to grow as a teacher. Your professional responsibilities also include knowing advocacy strategies that promote and expand opportunities for physical activity for all people.

Realistically, although these national standards serve as guidelines for professional preparation programs, these programs cannot prepare beginning teachers for all the challenges they face in their first year and within their job.[7] Many beginning physical educators feel well prepared to teach their content, align their objectives to state standards, differentiate instruction to meet the needs of diverse learners, and employ a variety of instructional strategies and methods. However, many beginning teachers report that they struggle with classroom management, using assessment data to support student learning, and incorporating technology in meaningful ways.[10,11] As professionals, teachers need to seek out professional development opportunities to enhance their teaching skills and help them address these challenges. Professional development opportunities are available through school district programs, attending conferences, taking advantage of mentoring, and creating a personalized learning network.[10,11] By actively seeking professional development opportunities, teachers can enhance their skills and positively affect student learning.

PHYSICAL EDUCATION AND PHYSICAL ACTIVITY INITIATIVES

Quality Physical Education

An effective, quality physical education program is committed to the goal of physical education—achievement of physical literacy by all students. According to SHAPE America, physically literate individuals have the "knowledge, skills, and confidence to enjoy a lifetime of healthful physical activity" (p. 4).[12] Quality physical education programs are aligned with the national standards for K-12 physical education. These five standards reflect the outcomes that should be achieved in physical education (see the SHAPE America's National Standards and Grade-Level Outcomes for K-12 Physical Education box).

SHAPE AMERICA'S NATIONAL STANDARDS AND GRADE-LEVEL OUTCOMES FOR K-12 PHYSICAL EDUCATION

Standard 1. The physically literate individual demonstrates competency in a variety of motor skills and movement patterns.

Standard 2. The physically literate individual applies knowledge of concepts, principles, strategies, and tactics related to movement and performance.

Standard 3. The physically literate individual demonstrates the knowledge and skills to achieve and maintain a health-enhancing level of physical activity and fitness.

Standard 4. The physically literate individual exhibits responsible personal and social behavior that respects self and others.

Standard 5. The physically literate individual recognizes the value of physical activity for health, enjoyment, challenge, self-expression, and/or social interaction.

Source: SHAPE America. *National Standards and Grade Level Outcomes for K-12 Physical Education.* Champaign, IL: Human Kinetics, 2014, http://www.shapeamerica.org/standards/pe/. Used with permission.

Quality physical education programs are structured around four essential components: policy and environment, curriculum, appropriate instruction, and student assessment (see the Essential Components of Physical Education box).[13] Policy has a profound influence on physical education programs. Local school's policies regarding physical education influence the amount of time physical education is offered to students. Ideally, it is recommended that school policies require physical education in grades K-12, with class periods totaling 150 minutes per week for elementary students and 225 minutes per week for upper-level students. Often, this is not the case as waivers from state requirements, exemptions to allow students to take another class, and substitutions of other experiences, such as interscholastic athletics for physical education, serve to reduce time for physical education.

ESSENTIAL COMPONENTS OF PHYSICAL EDUCATION

- Policies and environment
- Curriculum
- Appropriate instruction
- Student assessment

Source: SHAPE America. *The Essential Components of Physical Education.* Reston, VA: Author, 2015.

Other policies that impact the quality of physical education relate to such issues as class size and grading practices. Utilizing different teacher/student class ratios and grading practices for physical education than for other classes, like math, reflect policies that are not supportive of physical education (nor conducive to achievement of its goal). In reflecting on your own experiences in physical education, did you have policies that supported physical education or those that did not?

The second essential component is curriculum. School districts should have a written curriculum that is aligned with national and state standards. The curriculum should be comprehensive in its scope and sequenced to ensure that students learn the basic skills before being taught more complex, advanced skills. Specific objectives for students to attain, units and lessons to be implemented, and provision to assess outcomes are found in a well-developed curriculum. Different curricular models are described in Chapter 10.

The growing number of students who are overweight challenges physical educators to provide activities in which all students can participate.

Corbis/Image Source/Getty Images

Appropriate instruction is the third component. When you look at students in physical education class, you will see some evident differences (e.g., skill ability) between students but also some that are not quite as evident (e.g., social development). Quality physical education addresses the diverse needs of students through the use of differentiated instruction and using a variety of instructional practices that include all students. Instructional practices that maximize opportunities to practice, the use of feedback to reinforce learning and encourage efforts, and the incorporation of chances for students to self-assess their learning are hallmarks of quality physical education. Well-designed lessons aligned to curricular objectives and that engage students in moderate to vigorous physical activity for at least 50% of the class time are characteristic of quality physical education.

Assessment is the fourth component that is an integral part of quality physical education. Assessments aligned with standards and student objectives and administered following a consistent protocol promote accountability. Regular student assessments help teachers track student achievement. Assessments also provide teachers with evidence to reflect on the effectiveness of their efforts and to determine whether changes in their instructional practices and/or the curriculum are warranted. Many different assessment approaches can be used to provide evidence of student learning. You might remember your physical education teacher evaluating your skill performance using a checklist or giving a written test in physical education to assess your learning. Opportunities for students to self-assess their learning and self-monitor their progress are important aspects of a quality physical education program.

Communication of assessment results on a regular basis to students and parents is seen in quality physical education programs. Grades should be in line with other subjects in the curriculum; for example, if a letter grade is issued in biology, a letter grade, not a pass/fail grade, should be used in physical education to reflect student achievement. How was your grade determined in physical education? Was it based on skill performance? Fitness test results? Attendance? Dressing out? Behavior? In a quality program, grading practices are directly related to the learning objectives and specific elements comprising the grade clearly stated and communicated to students and their guardians.

Quality physical education is goal centered, instructional in nature, and teaches students the skills, knowledge, and confidence to achieve and maintain physical literacy throughout their lifetime. Policies and an environment that support physical education, a sequenced curriculum aligned with the national and local standards, appropriate instructional strategies, and assessments that provide evidence of student learning are components of quality physical education programs.

Connecting School and Community for the Well-Being of Students

Schools play a vital role in the development of student well-being. Student well-being is central to learning and impacts academic achievement. Today too many students come to school hungry, homeless, feeling unsafe, and facing discrimination. They struggle with their mental health, deal with physical illness, and face challenges associated with their disability. These and a host of unmet needs can interfere with learning and their success.

Schools provide a venue to reach more than 56 million students and can address some of these needs. However, the reality is that schools cannot meet all the students' needs; limited time, resources, expertise, and staffing are just a few of the factors that limit schools' efforts. These limitations and others can be addressed through collaboration between the education and community public health sectors. Physical educators can play a significant role in these collaborative endeavors. There are two models that offer physical educators a framework for promoting student physical activity and enhancing their well-being.

Whole School, Whole Community, Whole Child Model

The Whole School, Whole Community, Whole Child (WSCC) model offers a framework for collaboration between the schools and communities to address students' needs and foster each student's development, both within and outside of school in each community.[14] The WSCC model offers guidance for schools and communities on ways to connect, coordinate, and integrate their policies, practices, and resources to promote the well-being of each person and improve learning.

The WSCC model features 10 components: health education; physical education and physical activity; nutrition environment and services; health services; counseling, psychological, and social services; social and emotional climate; physical environment; employee wellness; family engagement; and community involvement.

The WSCC model places at its center the health and well-being of each student. Each student is challenged academically in a learning environment that prepares the student for success in a career or future study. The learning environment is physically and emotionally safe and each student is supported by qualified, caring adults.

The WSCC model provides opportunities for physical educators to be engaged in many different ways in promoting healthy lifestyles and highlighting the role of physical activity in health. Teaching skills, knowledge, and dispositions to foster engagement in physical activity across the lifespan is an important contribution of physical education to the health and well-being of students.

Comprehensive School and Physical Activity Program Model

Schools can play a critical role in helping children and youth accumulate the recommended 60 minutes of physical activity each day. The WSCC

Whole School, Whole Community, Whole Child (WSCC) Model

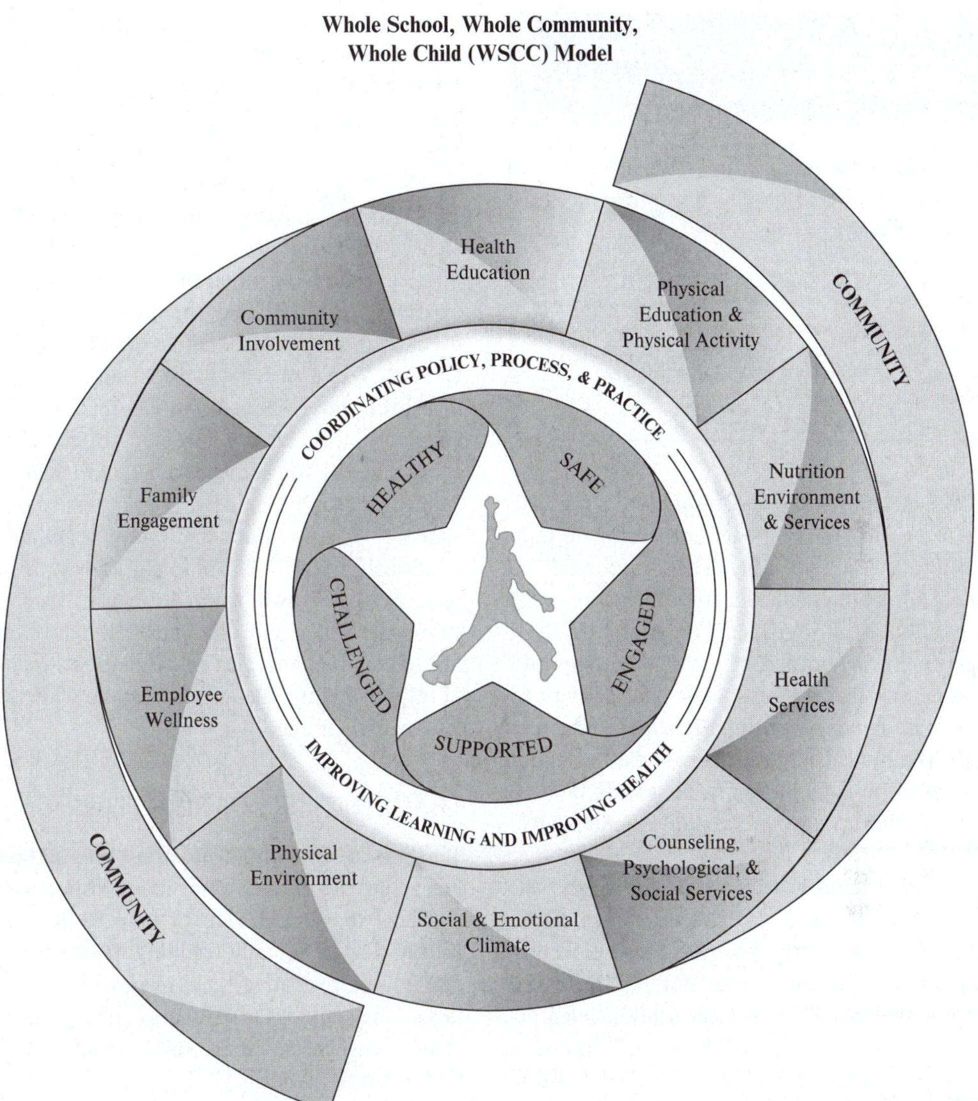

Source: U.S. Department of Health and Human Services

model includes physical education and physical activity as one component. Physical educators can use the Comprehensive School and Physical Activity Program model (CSPAP) to plan and organize activities that will help students meet the recommended 60 minutes of daily physical activity.

The CSPAP consists of five components: quality physical education, physical activity during the day, physical activity before and after school, staff involvement and engagement, and family and community engagement (see the Comprehensive School Physical Activity Program box).[15] A quality physical education program is central to the CSPAP and is instructional in nature, helping students learn the skills, knowledge, and values for participation in physical activity. These other components complement the physical education program; they do not replace it.

COMPREHENSIVE SCHOOL PHYSICAL ACTIVITY PROGRAM

- Physical education
- Physical activity before and after school
- Physical activity during school
- Staff involvement
- Family and community engagement

Source: Centers for Disease Control and Prevention. *National Framework for Physical Activity and Physical Education*. Atlanta, GA: U.S. Department of Health and Human Services, 2013.

Physical activity opportunities during the school day contribute to students accruing 60 minutes of physical activity daily. These opportunities occur outside of physical education through recess, drop-in activities during lunch or open gym, and through the incorporation of physical activity into classroom lessons (e.g., using physical activity to explore math concepts or to understand principles in physics). Physical activity before and after school can range from clubs (e.g., morning walk club or badminton club), intramurals, and interscholastic sports.

Staff engagement in physical activities and the promotion of physical activity are part of the CSPAP. Much like worksite health promotion programs, schools can offer their staff wellness and physical activities before or after school. Such activities as nutritional counseling, fitness classes, or yoga instruction help promote staff wellness. Additionally, staff engaging in physical activities provide important role models for their students.

The last component, family and community engagement, focuses on taking advantage of school as a venue for physical activity. In some areas, such as in rural communities or urban neighborhoods, the school is the sole venue where families can engage in a variety of physical activities. Opening the weight room or gym on the weekends, providing instruction in activities at night, and offering recreational programs for adults and youth take advantage of the school's physical activity resources. Facilitating collaborative relationships between schools and community resources, such as the YMCA, to use the community facilities during certain times expands opportunities for youth and adults to be active.

What is your role as a physical educator in the WSCC model and implementing the CSPAP? Most clearly, your primary role is to conduct a quality physical education program. However, given your expertise, you are also the most logical person to champion physical activity and promote the CSPAP. While this might seem an overwhelming task given your responsibilities for teaching physical education, this leadership role might be better conceptualized as you acting as a facilitator. This might lead to you recruiting help from others to organize staff wellness programs or develop a collaborative relationship with local physical activity providers (e.g., YMCA, Town Youth Bureau). Developing a step-by-step plan and timeline for the development of each component, plus enlisting the collaboration of others, might make promoting the CSPAP seem less overwhelming.

TEACHING RESPONSIBILITIES

Teachers in both school and nonschool settings perform a myriad of tasks every day. Prospective teachers need to be cognizant of their responsibilities. In addition to actually teaching, teachers perform many administrative and professionally related tasks. The activities of teachers can be grouped into three areas: instructional tasks, managerial tasks, and institutional tasks.[16]

Instructional tasks are responsibilities and activities that relate directly to teaching. These tasks include explaining and demonstrating how to perform a skill, describing how to execute a particular strategy in a game, assessing individuals' performance, and motivating individuals through the use of various techniques. Planning is an often overlooked instructional task.

Managerial tasks are activities related to the administration of the class. In the school setting, these activities may include taking attendance, dealing with discipline problems, and supervising the locker room. In a nonschool setting such as a commercial health or sports club, managerial responsibilities may include setting up and dismantling equipment, repairing equipment, handing out towels, distributing workout record sheets, and recording individuals' progress.

Institutional tasks are activities related to the organization in which the teacher works, be it the school or nonschool organization such as a YMCA. In the school setting, teachers may be expected to assume hall duty or lunchroom supervision, attend curriculum or departmental meetings, and conduct parent–teacher conferences. In the nonschool setting, teachers may also perform institutional duties such as checking membership cards at the front desk, mailing promotional brochures to attract new members, and filling out a variety of reports. In some situations, managerial and institutional responsibilities occupy more of a teacher's time than actual instructional tasks.

Teachers have numerous professional responsibilities in addition to the responsibilities previously described. They are advocates for their programs, and need to convey to all stakeholders the worth and value of physical education and physical activity. This is especially critical now as programs are facing budget cuts and reductions in time for physical education in the schools.

TEACHING CAREERS

Traditionally, physical education teachers have worked in the school setting with children and youths. Today, however, there are teaching opportunities available in many settings outside of school, giving teachers the wonderful opportunity to work with people of all ages.

Teaching in the School Setting

Teaching positions in the school setting are available in public and private school systems, higher education, and specialized schools. Public and private schools are organized according to various administrative patterns. Today the most typical pattern is the elementary school (grades PK–5), middle school (grades 6–8), and high school (grades 9–12) configuration. The growth of preschool programs has created additional opportunities for physical educators to work with young children to develop motor skills and promote the development of a healthy lifestyle.

In higher education, professional opportunities include teaching in 2-year junior or community colleges and 4-year colleges or universities. There are also teaching positions for those professionals who want to work with people with disabilities and for those who aspire to instruct in a professional preparation program. Teaching opportunities also exist in specialized schools, such as vocational and technical schools, as well as in developmental centers.

Teaching Elementary School Physical Education

Providing a quality physical education program for these young students is critical, for it represents their first steps toward becoming physically literate and having a lifetime of physical activity. Students' first experiences with physical education could influence whether they see physical education as an enjoyable, positive experience or as a negative one. These attitudes can influence their participation in physical education programs throughout their school years.

At this level, children should learn fundamental motor skills because these skills serve as the foundation for more advanced specialized sport and physical activity skills. Locomotor skills, such as running and jumping, nonlocomotor skills such as balance and twisting, and manipulative skills such as throwing and catching are emphasized (see Chapter 5 for more information on fundamental motor skills).[17] Engaging children in creative and problem-solving activities helps them learn movement concepts such as body and spatial awareness or moving through different pathways. Perceptual-motor activities help children develop skills in eye–hand and eye–foot coordination or tracking an object. One of the challenges is making sure to accommodate different levels of ability, different rates of learning, and different

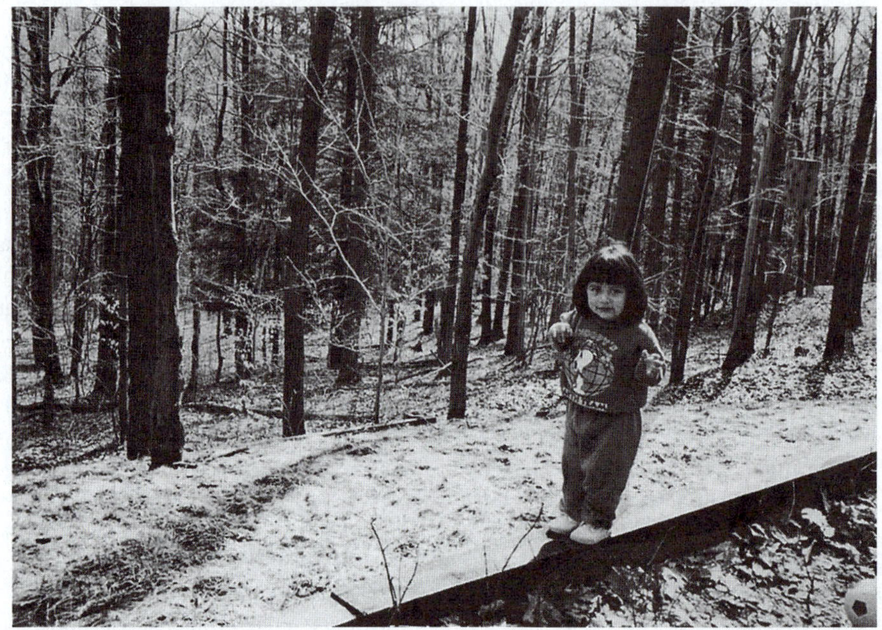

Young children like to test their abilities, such as balance, in a variety of environments.
Deborah Wuest

development levels in each domain by using differentiated instruction. Appropriate game play gives children the opportunity to apply some of these skills and use basic strategies as they interact with their peers.

Activities that capitalize on the energy and enthusiasm typical of this age group contribute to their overall fitness. Basic fitness concepts, such as your heart beating faster when you work harder, can be introduced at the primary level and progressively refined in the upper levels to include basic information about the different fitness components and their development.

Attention should also be given to helping students learn personal responsibility for their behavior. Rules, routines, and clear expectations offer students some guidance as they learn how to manage their own behavior in physical education.[17] Being respectful of others, appreciating differences, accepting feedback, working independently, collaborating with peers, and working safely are some objectives that begin to be developed at this level. One of the most important outcomes is helping children develop a positive self-image of themselves as a mover and confidence in their abilities. Appropriate challenges, self-expression, and enjoyment help children value physical activity and contribute to children's confidence and enjoyment of physical activity.

Teachers vary in why they prefer to teach certain grade levels. Many physical educators are drawn to the elementary level because of the enthusiasm, energy, and enjoyment of physical activity many children show at this level. Helping children develop the skills, knowledge, and values that will hopefully lead to them continuing to engage in physical activity later on in life is rewarding. Teaching at the elementary level also presents some challenges. The class periods are shorter than those at the middle and high school levels, often 30 minutes in length, and you will see many classes during the course of your day. Typically, there are no breaks between classes. It is not unusual for teachers to line students up to leave at the end of the period and then open the door to find another class waiting to come in. As you continue your preparation for teaching and complete your student teaching, you will have a better idea of whether teaching at the elementary level is the best choice for you.

Teaching Middle School Physical Education

At the middle school level, physical education should build upon and provide for the application of motor skills, knowledge, and values learned at the elementary level. Skills and concepts learned previously are combined (e.g., using dribbling, passing, and shooting in soccer as well as concepts related to spatial awareness) and incorporated into sports and games.[17] In providing for skill development and game play, keep in mind that you will need to modify adult versions of activities to be appropriate for middle school students.[17] Rather than play 11 versus 11, where opportunities to touch the ball are limited, create multiple simultaneous 3 versus 3 games that provide more opportunities for practice. A variety of games and sports, outdoor pursuits, individual-performance activities (e.g., dance) can be offered at this level. Curriculum models such as sport education and tactical approach can be used with success. These activities provide opportunities for students to apply concepts to their performance, such as the use of offensive and defensive strategies necessary in many sports. Given the myriad of stressors associated with puberty, middle school years are a good time to offer some approaches to stress management, such as deep breathing, tai-chi, and simply taking an "activity" break.

At this level, students expand their knowledge of fitness, gaining a greater understanding of fitness principles (e.g., frequency, intensity, specificity) and how to incorporate them into physical activities to gain health benefits. As teachers, you should encourage students to be physically active outside of school, but also take time to discuss some of the barriers that might limit their physical activity (e.g., too much homework or responsibilities at home) and some strategies to address them (e.g., take advantage of before- or after-school programs offered as part of the CSPAP).

The development of personal and social responsibility should continue, and students should exhibit these behaviors more consistently. Greater understanding of rules governing game play and etiquette should be expected, while the emphasis on safety remains paramount. Given the social development associated with adolescents, the importance of peers, threats of exclusion from groups, increased bullying, and the negative focus on differences, now is the time for teachers to heighten their emphasis on respect for others and acceptance of, if not appreciation for, individual differences.

Why choose to teach middle school physical education? Middle schoolers are a challenging age group. As they enter adolescence, students experience a myriad of development changes, puberty, that impact all aspects of their lives. Different rates of growth leave some middle schoolers much taller than their peers, an embarrassment to some who have grown and a concern to those who still have not experienced their growth spurt. Development of secondary sex characteristics may make students self-conscious; they dread using the locker room and changing in front of their peers. Social pressures abound; peer pressure grows in influence. What students need at this time in their life are teachers who are sensitive to their needs and who recognize the changes and difficulties they are experiencing and help them deal with some of them. This is an age group where you truly can make a difference.

Teaching High School Physical Education

The primary goal for teachers of high school physical education should be ensuring that all students graduate as physically literate adults. High school physical education should prepare students to assume responsibility for meeting their physical activity needs as adults. Lifetime activities such as outdoor pursuits (e.g., geocaching, canoeing), aquatics, and individual-performance activities (e.g., pickleball) should have a prominent place in the curriculum.[17] There are opportunities for adults to participate in competitive team sport leagues (e.g., Slo-pitch softball, adult volleyball), and many adults enjoy pickup games (e.g., basketball or soccer). However, many more adults are likely to participate in individual sports, either as an individual or with a partner (e.g., badminton singles, tennis doubles), which supports the emphasis on these types of activities within the curriculum.[17]

Health-fitness activities are also important at this level, with an emphasis on different types of activities that address different fitness components and how to perform them correctly and effectively. Activities like resistance training for muscle strength and endurance, biking for aerobic endurance, or tai-chi for flexibility may also be taught. Additionally, teachers should encourage students to participate in physical activities outside of the school setting, either independently or with a community-based group.

Emphasis on personal and social responsibility, exhibiting ethical behavior in physical activity settings, and showing respect for others should be an integral part of the high school program. At this point, students should show increased personal responsibility for their health. They should be able to design a fitness program based on their current level of fitness, develop a sound nutritional plan, and be able to identify stress management strategies that work well for them. Additionally, students should be able to choose physical activities that provide appropriate challenges for themselves, as well as opportunities for enjoyment, self-expression, and social interaction.[17]

Teachers will find that high schools vary in implementing their physical education programs. In some schools, physical education is required in grades 9 and 10 and are optional in grades 11 and 12. Some schools offer an elective program for all grades; students get to select the physical activities in which to receive instruction. Some schools have expanded their curriculum offerings by using off-campus community facilities such as a golf course, an ice rink, an aquatics center, or a ski slope. Using community-based facilities and programs is important in helping students transition from physical education in the high school setting to choosing to take advantage of opportunities for physical activity within their community.

Why teach high school students? Some physical educators choose to teach at this level because they enjoy working with this older age group. However, at this level, the students might be just a bit younger than you as you start your teaching career, so earning their respect for you as a teacher is a challenge. Because many curriculums at this level are more aligned with sports, some physical educators choose to teach high school because they want to teach more sport-related activities than the content typically included within the elementary education curriculum. As students move through the school years, some may become less motivated to put forth effort in physical education. As a teacher, you have the challenge of reaching these students and getting them to reengage in physical education. Focusing on individual effort, providing multiple levels of difficulty for tasks, and introducing new activities may help these students regain interest in physical education. Lastly, one of the great responsibilities at this level, and one of the most rewarding, is preparing your students with the skills, knowledge, and confidence to be physically active as adults.

Teaching Physical Education in Higher Education

Prospective physical education teachers may also take advantage of opportunities to teach in higher education. Opportunities may be found to teach at 2-year community colleges or at 4-year colleges or universities. Usually, a master's degree in an area of physical education is a prerequisite to obtaining a job at this level. In some institutions, coaching responsibilities may be associated with teaching positions, whereas in other institutions, coaches carry no teaching responsibilities.

Physical education at this level is usually voluntary, thus placing responsibility on the physical education department to offer courses that are appealing to students. Because of this need, curriculums at this level tend to be more flexible and to change more often in response to students' interests and needs.

Lifetime sports and recreational activities are emphasized at this level, including such activities as tennis, golf, self-defense, dance, and personal fitness; outdoor pursuits such as canoeing, camping, and rock climbing; and aquatic activities. Students may have the opportunity to enroll in theory courses. Class topics may include health concepts, cardiovascular fitness, principles of exercise, and development of personalized fitness programs. Some colleges offer courses called Wellness for Life or Fitness for Life. These courses combine theoretical information with laboratory experiences designed to help students acquire the knowledge and skills necessary to lead a healthy lifestyle.

Sport clubs provide interested participants an opportunity for social group experiences and enjoyment of a particular sport activity. Intramurals and intercollegiate sports play an important part in college and university physical education programs. They offer students additional opportunities for participation according to their abilities, needs, and interests.

Teaching Physical Education in Professional Preparation Programs

Professional preparation programs at colleges and universities educate students for careers in physical education, exercise science, and sport. Professionals who teach in these programs typically possess advanced degrees, a strong academic record, and, many times, previous experience in their area of interest. For example, a physical educator desiring to teach in a professional preparation program to prepare future teachers may find it advantageous to have at least 3 years of teaching experience in the public schools at the elementary, middle, or secondary school level. Similarly, a professional desiring to teach in an exercise science professional preparation program may find it helpful to have several years of practical experience, such as working in a fitness center, worksite wellness program, or cardiac rehabilitation program.

A professor in a professional preparation program may teach theory courses in the disciplines and related areas such as history and philosophy of physical education, biomechanics, exercise physiology, curriculum and methods, sociology of sport, sport psychology, and adapted physical activity. These individuals typically possess doctorate degrees in their areas of expertise. Individuals who aspire to teach in professional preparation programs may also teach professional activity and skills courses, as well as courses in coaching methods. These individuals usually possess a high degree of skill in their areas of expertise. Professionals teaching activity and skills courses typically possess master's degrees, and some individuals may have earned doctorate degrees.

In addition to their teaching responsibilities, teachers are expected to conduct research, participate on department and college or university committees, and advise students. They are expected to write for professional publications, perform community service, and participate in the work of professional organizations.

Teaching Adapted Physical Activity

Teaching physical education to students with disabilities is another career opportunity. About 14% of the school population, or more than 7.3 million students, have a disability.[18] These students include those with physical challenges such as cerebral palsy or mental or emotional impairments, hearing and visual impairments, learning disabilities, and other health impairments such as asthma or heart problems.

Adapted physical activity focuses on adapting or modifying physical activity to meet the needs of students. Good physical education is adapted physical education, for the heart of quality physical education and adapted physical activity is education that is developmentally appropriate for the needs of the individual student. By law, each student identified with a disability must have an individualized education plan (IEP). Physical education is mandated by law to be included in each student's educational program.

There are several approaches to the inclusion of children with disabilities into the educational setting, including physical education. The least restrictive environment approach places students with disabilities in an educational setting that matches the students' abilities and provides as much freedom as possible. For some students, this may be a placement, with or without an aide, in a "regular" physical education class with peers who are not disabled, or it may be placement into a special class or adapted physical education. These classes are generally smaller and contain only students with special needs. The placement of students with disabilities into the regular class is referred to as *mainstreaming*.

Physical education teachers provide many different services to individuals with disabilities. Some schools or school districts have an adapted physical education specialist who provides direct services to individuals with disabilities. In other settings, the adapted physical educator serves as a consultant to help other teachers provide needed services.

All physical education teachers should be prepared to work with students with disabilities. Physical educators will be involved in the writing of IEPs. These plans may focus on helping the student to correct physical conditions that can be improved with exercise, assisting each student in achieving the highest level of physical fitness within his or her capabilities, aiding the student in identifying physical activities and sports suited to his or her abilities and interests, and providing each student with positive experiences conducive to the development of a healthy self-concept.

If you are interested in working with individuals with disabilities, you can prepare for this opportunity by taking additional course work in the area of adapted physical activity and special education. Try to obtain practical experience working with individuals with disabilities as part of your preparation for a physical education career.

Physical education teachers can also become certified as adapted physical educators. The Adapted Physical Education National Standards project was designed to ensure that physical education for students with disabilities is provided by qualified physical educators. As part of this project, national standards were developed and a certification examination was designed to measure knowledge of these standards.[19] (See the Adapted Physical Education National Standards box on page 367.)

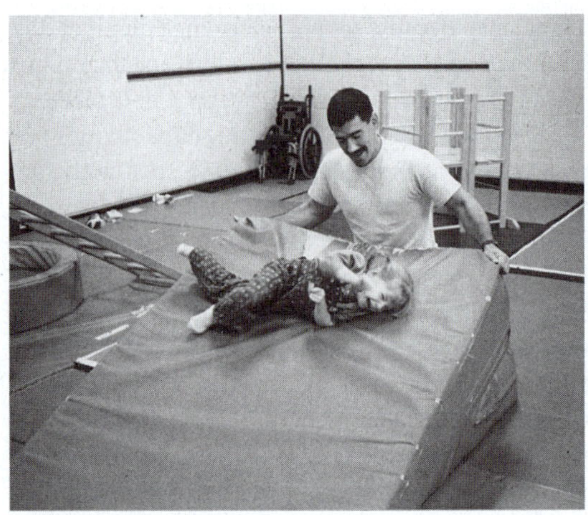

Adapted physical education focuses on modifying activities to meet students' needs.
Sarah Rich

Physical educators interested in taking the certification examination must demonstrate that they have a bachelor's degree in physical education, 200 hours of documented practicum experience in teaching physical education to individuals with disabilities, and additional course work focusing on adapted physical education and meeting the needs of individuals with disabilities. Teachers who pass the exam are certified for 7 years and can use the acronym Certified Adapted Physical Educator (CAPE) after their name. They are listed in the National Registry of Certified Adapted Physical Educators that is distributed to each state education department.

A diversity of opportunities exists for individuals interested in teaching in the school setting. Many opportunities can also be found for the physical educator who is interested in working in countries outside of the United States. International schools and the Peace Corps offer the opportunity

ADAPTED PHYSICAL EDUCATION NATIONAL STANDARDS

Human Development
Motor Behavior
Exercise Science
Measurement and Evaluation
History and Philosophy
Unique Attributes of Learners
Curriculum Theory and Development
Assessment
Instructional Design and Planning
Teaching
Consultation and Staff Development
Student and Program Evaluation
Continuing Education
Ethics
Communication

Source: National Consortium for Physical Education and Recreation for Individuals with Disabilities. In *Adapted Physical Education National Standards, 3rd ed*, edited by L. Kelly. Champaign, IL: Human Kinetics, 2020. For a complete description of each standard, visit the website at https://www.ncpeid.org/apens.

to teach in elementary and secondary schools, as well as colleges and universities, in other countries.

Teaching in Nonschool Settings

Obtaining a teacher certification in physical education opens up many doors for you. Opportunities to teach physical education outside of the school setting continue to increase. The growth of interest in physical activities and sport by people of all ages has stimulated the development of these additional teaching avenues. Teaching opportunities may be found today in commercial sport clubs, community recreational and sport programs, resorts, the armed forces, as well as in senior citizen and retirement centers.

The requirements for employment in these positions, working conditions, and salaries and other benefits vary widely. Some of these teaching positions require a high level of expertise in a particular sport, whereas others require individuals to teach a variety of activities. Working hours vary a great deal as well. For some positions, hours are often dictated by the times clients or students are available. If one is working with youths, hours are likely to be after school and on the weekends. If one is working with adults, hours tend to be in the evenings and on weekends. Daytime work is also available, however. These positions may pay on an hourly basis, have a set salary, or pay based on the number of students taught. Benefits may vary from none to complete medical, dental, and life insurance plans.

Some teaching positions in nonschool settings require that individuals assume other responsibilities as well. These may include being responsible for the organization's social media, soliciting memberships, record keeping, and equipment and facility maintenance.

Some work may be seasonal in nature, depending on the climate or type of facility. For example, if you were a teacher or director of aquatics at an outdoor facility in the northeastern United States, your employment would probably last from June to September; working at an indoor facility in the Northeast would likely result in a year-round position. In the Southwest, the same job might be year-round regardless of the type of facility.

Because these jobs, in essence, require teaching skills, many physical educators who desire to teach in the nonschool setting also complete the requirements for teaching certification. By doing so, they increase their range of job opportunities.

Physical educators may find teaching and coaching opportunities outside the school setting in sport clubs or recreational programs.

(left): Brian McEntire/iStock/Getty Images; (right): Olga Yastremska/belchonock/123RF

Other physical educators, having prepared for teaching in the schools, look to these other avenues of employment when they are unable to find a teaching position suited to their needs and interests or as a means of part-time and summer employment. Many employers hiring physical educators to fill these positions also view favorably the credentials of those applicants able to list a teaching certificate on their resume. For some positions, special certificates may be required, such as certification by the Professional Golfers' Association (PGA) or Ladies Professional Golf Association (LPGA) as a golf professional.

Understanding some of the reasons adults and youth enroll in physical activity instructional programs is important. So, be sure to take the time to get to know the program participants and understand why they are choosing to learn and engage. Adults seek instruction for many reasons. First, they may not have had instruction in the activity during their youth in their physical education classes. Second, they may seek instruction for their own personal growth and pleasure. Instruction may be sought for social reasons, such as the desire to be able to participate in specific activities with friends and family. For example, some adults may seek instruction in golf to be able to successfully participate with business associates in this accepted social activity. The desire to improve and refine one's performance by seeking instruction from a professional is often cited as the reason for enrolling in instructional classes.

Youths enroll in these organizational programs and classes for many of the same reasons as adults. Additionally, youths may enroll in certain activity classes because instruction or interscholastic competition in that activity is not offered in their school. Youths desiring to develop more advanced skills, such as in gymnastics, or to compete in certain sport activities such as swimming may find that these organizations offer experiences that meet their needs. Youths and their parents may seek expert instruction because of aspirations to be a professional player, such as in tennis or because of the desire to successfully compete for a college scholarship in certain sport areas; they may find nonschool instructional opportunities essential to the realization of these goals.

Teaching in Commercial Sport Clubs

In recent years, the number of commercial sport clubs and facilities has grown tremendously. Tennis and racquetball clubs, gymnastics clubs, swimming clubs, country clubs offering golf and tennis, karate and judo schools, and bowling establishments are examples of commercial sport enterprises.

Because commercial sport clubs usually focus on a particular sport, physical educators desiring to teach in such an organization should possess a high level of expertise in that sport. Teaching responsibilities may include private lessons as well as group lessons. There may be the opportunity to coach high-level performers. Additional responsibilities may include setting up tournaments, such as in a tennis and racquetball club, selling sport equipment and apparel, such as in a golf pro shop at a country club, or transporting individuals to competitions, such as in a swimming club or a gymnastics club. Many commercial clubs also expect the teachers to assume managerial responsibilities at times.

Employers, in addition to requiring a high level of expertise as a condition of employment, may also require certification. In the aquatics area, certification as a water safety instructor and lifeguard instructor and in pool management may be required. Certification as a golf professional such as through the Professional Golfers' Association (PGA) or Ladies Professional Golf Association (LPGA) may be necessary. Where not required, certificates may enhance one's employment opportunities.

Teaching in Youth and Community Organizations

The YMCA and similar organizations serve both the youth and adult populations in the community. Sport and fitness are an integral part of their programs. Included in the programs are classes in various physical activities; athletic leagues for corporate employees, youth, and adults; and youth groups. The cost of financing such organizations is usually met through membership dues, community and business contributions, and private contributions.

These organizations often employ physical educators and recreation specialists to teach a wide variety of activities. In many communities, events are scheduled from early morning to late at night—early-bird swim at 6 A.M. and late-hour pickleball games. Besides instructing clients in sport activities, physical educators may have the opportunity to serve as a coach of a team. Many youth clubs offer young people and adults the opportunity to compete on athletic teams at the local, state, regional, and national levels. Additional responsibilities include developing health and fitness programs, managing facility and budget, and supervising personnel. Many centers, in addition to physical activities, offer programs in exercise and fitness evaluation, cardiac rehabilitation, and health counseling. A background in these areas as well as in teaching would be helpful in seeking employment.

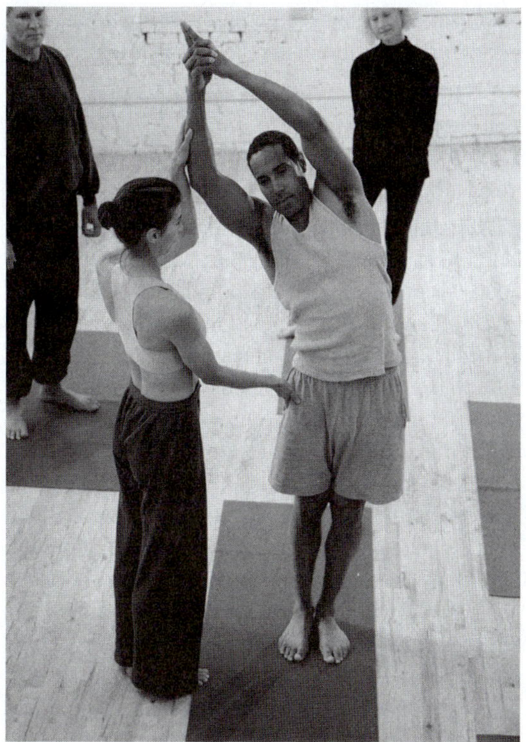

Teaching opportunities outside of the school setting include working with adults providing specialized instruction in many different activities. This yoga instructor assists a student in attaining the correct posture.

Ryan McVay/Photodisc/Getty Images

Physical educators may also find positions working for town and city recreation departments, community centers, youth centers, and playgrounds. Some of these opportunities may be seasonal, generally available in the summer, but the trend is for more and more programs to operate year-round. These programs provide instruction in physical activities for people of all ages, recreational sport leagues, and recreational activities. In addition to jobs teaching and coaching for these organizations, other job possibilities include the supervision of personnel and program development.

Teaching Older Adults

The population of older Americans is growing. In 2019, there were more than 54.1 million adults 65 years and older, representing 16% of the population, that is, one in every seven Americans.[20] By 2060, it is estimated that this population will increase to 98 million.[20] The population of adults 85 years and older is estimated to increase from 6.4 million in 2016 to over 14.6 million in 2060.[20] As you can see, there is a growing need to provide physical activity services for this population group. In recent years, programs for older adults offered by recreational agencies, retirement centers, and health care facilities have expanded in the number and types of offerings.

Many of these programs offer instruction in physical activities suited to the abilities and interests of the participants. Exercise is frequently included in these programs. In addition to the physical benefits, these programs provide the opportunity for socialization. Physical educators interested in working in such programs may benefit from classes in adapted physical education, sociology, psychology, and gerontology.

Teaching in Resorts

The increase in leisure time has stimulated an increase in the travel and tourism industry. The number of resorts has grown, and many resorts offer instruction in various physical activities as part of their programs. Activities offered may include sailing, scuba, tennis, golf, swimming, waterskiing, and snow skiing. Expertise in specific sport areas is required for employment in these resorts. Instruction is usually done in small groups or in private lessons. Additionally, responsibilities may include managerial activities and directing social activities. Pay varies, and depending on the location of the resort, work may be seasonal, although many resorts operate year-round. Working in a resort offers many desirable side benefits, such as working in an attractive location, and the opportunity to work with changing clientele.

Teaching in the Military

The Army, Navy, Marines, Air Force, Coast Guard, and National Guard have extensive physical activity programs that aid in keeping service personnel in good physical and mental condition. In addition to the personnel used to direct the fitness and physical training programs of these organizations, physical educators are needed to instruct service personnel and their dependents in physical activities and sport and direct extensive recreational programs on its bases. Coaches are also needed to assist military athletes in their training for competitions throughout the world. The military also sponsors schools for children of military personnel. Physical educators who desire to teach in a country other than the United States may wish to consider employment in these schools. For many of these positions, physical educators do not have to belong to the military. Physical educators interested in further information about these opportunities should investigate opportunities on the Department of Defense website.

TEACHING CERTIFICATION

Each state has established minimum requirements that prospective teachers must meet before they become legally certified to teach. The certification of teachers protects schoolchildren by ensuring a high level of teaching competency and the employment of qualified personnel.

Because certification procedures and requirements vary from state to state, prospective teachers should obtain the specific requirements from their college or university or by directly contacting the state education department. Due to variations in state requirements, a certificate to teach in one state is not necessarily valid in another state. However, reciprocity among states in a region is increasingly common. Sometimes, where there is not reciprocity, prospective teachers can become certified in another state by merely taking a few additional required courses.

Teaching certificates are required to teach in the public schools. Some private schools may not require their teachers to possess a certificate. Teaching certificates are also an asset to individuals desiring to teach in nonschool settings. Prospective employers may be impressed by candidates who have fulfilled the necessary requirements for certification.

COACHING CAREERS

Many physical educators aspire to a career as a coach. Because a teaching certificate is required by many states to coach, many prospective coaches pursue a degree in physical education. Some of these prospective coaches seek a dual career as a teacher and a coach, whereas others desire solely to coach and view a teaching career as a means to attain their ultimate ambition.

As with teaching, coaching opportunities today exist in both the school and nonschool settings.

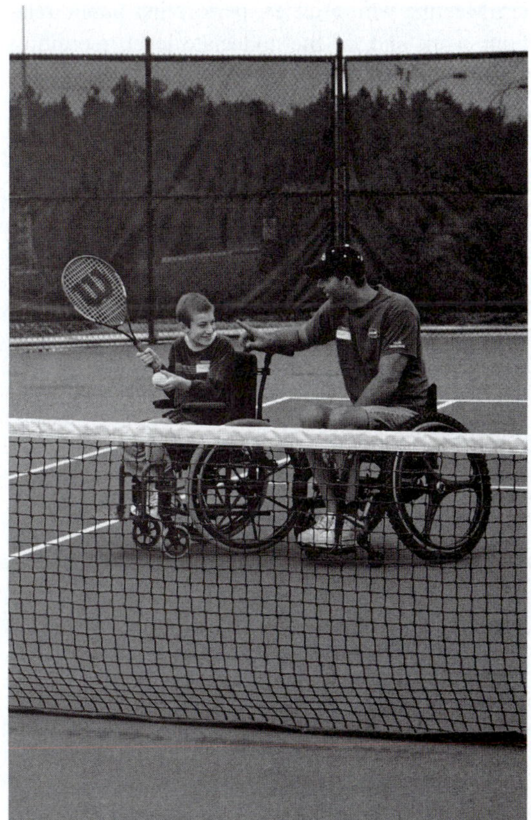

More and more people with disabilities are participating in sports and taking an active role in coaching.
Realistic Reflections

In the school setting at the interscholastic level, coaches work with middle school and high school athletes. Intercollegiate coaching opportunities are found in 2-year community colleges as well as 4-year colleges and universities.

Many different coaching opportunities are available outside of the school setting. Some young people aspire to coach at the professional level. An increasing number of coaching opportunities are available in commercial or private clubs, such as coaching elite gymnasts or promising young tennis professionals. Community-based programs offer a multitude of coaching opportunities as well.

In the past two decades, participation in sport by older adults and people with disabilities has increased. For example, in 2019, nearly 14,000 athletes age 50 and over participated in the biennial US Summer National Senior Games–the Senior Olympics.[21] There were over 800 events in 19 sports.[21] The Special Olympics, the Paralympics, and the Games for the Deaf are attracting record numbers of participants. Coaching opportunities within these populations are increasing as participation grows.

Teaching responsibilities may be associated with coaching. At the interscholastic level, it is expected that coaches will teach classes in the school; often, coaches teach physical education. At the collegiate level, some coaches are hired solely to coach and have no teaching responsibilities. At other higher education institutions, coaches may have teaching responsibilities in the general physical education program or in the professional preparation program. Administrative responsibilities may also be associated with coaching.

Why Coach?

Passionate about a sport? Want to make a difference in the lives of others? Coaching is a great way to be actively involved in a sport and have a positive influence on people's lives, both during their playing years and beyond. For many, coaching is a way for former athletes to stay involved and for some to "pay it forward" in appreciation for the contributions their coaches and playing a sport has made to their own lives. Others choose to coach because they want the opportunity to work with children and youth to help them develop and grow while teaching them skills and strategies as well as developing attitudes to successfully participate in a sport. Some individuals are drawn to coaching for the enjoyment of competition and/or the camaraderie and genuine relationships they build between themselves and the team members. Yet, still others realize that there is a need for a coach and step forward and volunteer. There are many reasons for choosing to coach, and they may evolve over time, but it is important that you give some thought to why you are entering the coaching profession.

Millions of people, ranging from young children to adults, participate in sports, their skill levels varying from the beginning athlete to the elite performer. Opportunities to coach exist at many levels, ranging from community programs for all ages to interscholastic sports and intercollegiate sports. Professional sports and private sport clubs offer other venues to those desiring to coach. Oftentimes, your previous coaching experience impacts your opportunities, and you may have to "pay your dues" so to speak, as you seek to advance up the coaching ranks. You might start out coaching a modified team, advance to coaching the junior varsity team, and then move on from there to coach the varsity team. Or, you may start out as an assistant coach before having the chance to be a head coach.

Many choose to coach because of the opportunity to work with highly skilled and motivated individuals. Some coaches enter the profession because of their belief that participation in athletics can be a positive experience; they are committed to providing opportunities by which young people can develop to their fullest potential, both as athletes and as individuals.

Coaching is a highly visible occupation. Coaches may have a great deal of influence and power within both the institution and the community. The excitement, attention, influence, and recognition associated with coaching make it an attractive career choice.

Rewards, Benefits, and Challenges of Coaching

Like teaching, coaching offers rewards, benefits, and challenges to those pursuing this career. Many intrinsic rewards are associated with coaching. The opportunity to work with athletes to achieve their fullest potential, the excitement of winning, the satisfaction associated with giving the best of oneself, and the respect accorded to a coach are some of the intrinsic benefits of coaching.

Several challenges are associated with coaching. The hours are often long and arduous. The practice hours and the hours spent coaching during a competition are the most visible indications of the amount of time involved in coaching. Untold hours may be spent in preparing practices, reviewing the results of games and planning for the next encounter. Meeting with athletes, performing public relations work and, at the collegiate level, recruiting place additional demands on coaches' time.

Salaries vary greatly depending on the level coached, the sport coached, and the coach's position as head or assistant coach. Salaries at the high school level can range from a small stipend to several thousand dollars, whereas coaches at the collegiate and professional levels may have contracts worth hundreds of thousands or even millions of dollars.

A high turnover rate is associated with coaching. Coaches are often placed under tremendous pressure to achieve–to have a winning season. Many coaches are fired because of a lackluster win-loss record or for having a poor working relationship with the administration or alumni. Other coaches choose to leave the profession voluntarily, overwhelmed by the pressures and exhausted by the demands, suffering from burnout, disenchanted with the profession, or desirous of a career change.

Role conflict is one problem some teachers and coaches struggle with in an effort to balance their jobs as a teacher and a coach. Individuals occupy many different roles in our society, both personally and professionally. Both positions or roles–teaching and coaching–carry with them responsibilities and associated expectations for performance. Both roles carry a multitude of responsibilities that often

Coaches fulfill many different responsibilities, including helping athletes put winning and losing in perspective.

IPGGutenbergUKLtd/iStock/Getty Images

consume many hours–preparing lessons, formalizing practice plans, teaching classes, conducting practices, and a host of other demands.

Personal and external expectations relative to performance induce additional pressure. Teachers are expected to teach challenging lessons to all students, maintain discipline, assess students' learning, participate on school committees, and fulfill many other functions. Coaches are expected to conduct practices, coach games, motivate athletes to achieve, interact with the public and press, and many times go on the road to scout the opponent. These and many more demands are coupled with the pressure to win.

Sometimes, the pressure to do it all and do it well can be overwhelming. Role conflict occurs when teacher-coaches, in an effort to fulfill the demands associated with these two roles, have to make choices about how to apportion their time and effort in order to juggle those demands. The perceived value of each of the roles affects how teacher-coaches choose to balance their demands. Teachers hired to instruct physical education and committed to delivering a quality physical education try to maintain that goal in the face of pressures to produce a winning team as a coach. To resolve this conflict, some teachers choose to spend less time on their teaching, perhaps to the extent that they offer a "roll out the ball" physical education program. This compromise in use of time and values allows teachers to spend more time on their coaching, a role for which there is often more public recognition and reward. Trying to resolve this conflict between multiple roles can be stressful and can result in a decrease in the quality of performance. Yet, many teachers and coaches successfully balance the demands and conduct high-quality physical education programs while helping students to achieve in the athletic arena.

Teaching and Coaching

Because coaching is, in essence, teaching, the qualities that exemplify good teachers–organizational, communication, human relations, instructional, and motivational skills–may also be characteristics of effective coaches. Coaches must be able to organize their practices to provide maximum opportunities for all players to learn the skills and strategies essential for play. They must be actively engaged in monitoring the efforts of their athletes. They must be able to communicate what is to be learned in a clear manner and provide athletes with appropriate feedback to improve their performances. Coaches must instill in each athlete a feeling of self-worth and self-confidence and be able to motivate all players to put forth their utmost effort to achieve their goals.

Although coaching is similar in nature to teaching, there are some dissimilarities. Both teachers and coaches are engaged in instructional activities and both must provide opportunities for the learners–students and athletes–to attain the skills and knowledge presented. However, coaches must have the expertise to teach their athletes more advanced skills and are often held more accountable for their athletes' learning than teachers are for their students'. The caliber of a coach's instruction is scrutinized by both the administration and the public. If a coach has failed to prepare the athletes for competition or their learning appears inadequate (by the often-used standard of the win-loss record), the coach may be dismissed. Teachers, on the other hand, while increasingly held accountable for their students' learning, are less likely to be dismissed for low levels of student achievement. The coach must work in a pressure-filled arena, whereas the teacher works in a less stressful environment.

Teachers must work with a diversity of skill levels and interests within their classes. Students may be mandated to take "gym" class and may be difficult to motivate. In contrast, coaches work with highly skilled athletes who often possess a high level of commitment to their sport. Their decision to participate is voluntary, and they may be united in their effort toward a common goal. Thus, although there are some similarities between teaching and coaching, there are some striking differences.

Coaching Responsibilities

Many responsibilities are associated with coaching. As in teaching, these responsibilities may be classified as instructional, managerial, and institutional in nature.

The coach's instructional responsibilities include conducting practice and coaching during the game. Although the coach is working with highly skilled athletes, the coach must be a good teacher to instruct the athletes in the more advanced skills and strategies necessary to perform at this level. During practices and games, the coach must motivate the athletes to put forth their best effort so that their optimal level of performance can be achieved. In many cases, these instructional responsibilities may be the least time-consuming of all the coach's responsibilities.

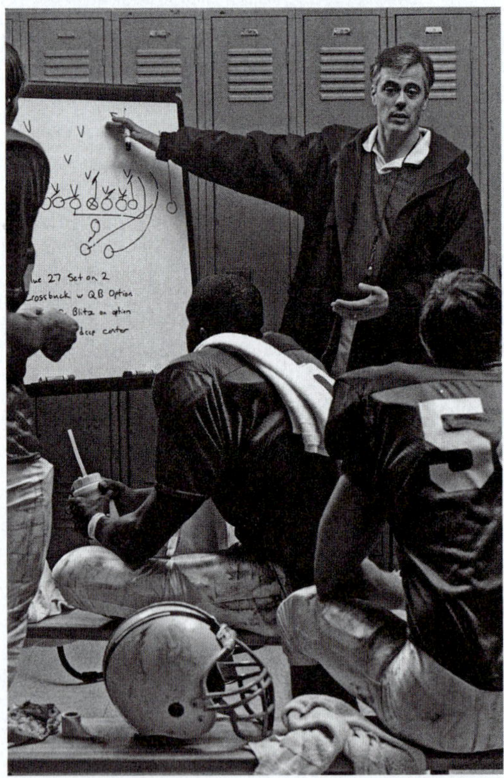

Coaches must be able to clearly explain strategies and teach their players skills.

Comstock Images/Getty Images

Many coaches spend untold hours evaluating practices and the results of competitions and then using this information to plan for forthcoming practices and upcoming competitions. For those coaches fortunate enough to have assistant coaches, time must be spent with them reviewing this information and delegating responsibilities for future practices and games. Team managers may relieve the coach of many of the necessary but time-consuming managerial tasks such as dealing with equipment or recording statistics. Additionally, the coach must take care of the necessary public relations functions, such as calling in contest results, giving interviews, and speaking in front of groups. Where allowed, recruiting occupies a tremendous amount of time. Phoning prospective athletes, arranging for campus meetings, talking with parents, and scouting contests for potential athletes add many hours to the day.

The institutional responsibilities are many as well. Interscholastic coaches are expected to take part in many school activities in addition to their teaching responsibilities. Intercollegiate coaches may be expected to attend athletic department meetings or represent the institution on a community committee.

Many other responsibilities and expectations are associated with coaching. Coaches occupy highly visible positions in their institution. In institutions of higher education, it is not uncommon for more students to recognize the face of the football or basketball coach than the face of the college president. The coach is expected to reflect a positive image and the values associated with sport. The actions of the coach as the team wins or loses will influence the public's opinion of the sport program. Establishing and maintaining positive relationships with the community, alumni, and parents is often seen as vital to a coach's success in generating support for the athletic program. Because of their influence and visibility, coaches may be sought after to take an active part in community and civic affairs. They may be called on to train volunteer coaches for community recreational and sport programs or to spearhead a fund-raising drive for United Way.

Many other duties are incumbent on coaches by virtue of their position. Coaches, because of the close relationship that develops from the many hours of working with their athletes, are often sought out by their athletes for advice. Athletes may talk with their coach about their athletic performance or financial, academic, or personal concerns. Because of their positions as leaders, coaches are viewed as role models. They are expected to exemplify the highest standards of conduct and are under pressure to live up to these expectations.

Coaches have many professional responsibilities. They must attend sport and rules clinics so that they are aware of the current trends and latest rule changes in the sport. They are often active in professional organizations related to the sport they coach such as the National Soccer Coaches Association of America. They may be called on to serve as clinicians at some of these associations' meetings, asked to write an article for a professional journal, or host a podcast.

The responsibilities and expectations associated with coaching are many. Instructional, managerial, institutional, community, and professional responsibilities compose the work of the coach.

Securing a Coaching Position

Depending on the level at which you wish to coach, you can take several steps to enhance your chances of securing the coaching position you desire. First, coaching requires a great deal of expertise. Playing experience in the sport you wish to coach may be helpful in this respect. Attending clinics and workshops on advanced techniques and rules may add to your knowledge. Consider becoming a rated official in your sport. Take advantage of coaching certification and licensing programs, such as the one offered for soccer by the United States Soccer Federation. Second, particularly for coaching at the interscholastic level, a teaching certificate may be required. However, this depends on the state in which you wish to coach. Coaching at the intercollegiate level often requires a master's degree.

Prospective coaches should consider developing expertise in a second sport, preferably one that is not in season at the same time as your other sport. For example, if you want to coach soccer, a fall sport, develop expertise in a spring sport such as lacrosse, baseball, or softball. In many institutions, at both the interscholastic and intercollegiate levels, coaches may be required to coach two sport activities or sometimes be the head coach in one sport and serve as an assistant coach in a second sport. At other institutions, a coach may be involved in one sport throughout the year because of the length of the season and/or its high profile.

Practical experience is helpful as well. Volunteering to serve as an assistant coach or working with a youth sport program as a coach during your undergraduate preparation is a step in the right direction and an invaluable experience. It is important that prospective coaches realize that oftentimes, one must be willing to work in other positions in the coaching organization before achieving the head coaching position desired. Serving as a junior varsity coach, working as a graduate assistant coach, or accepting a position as an assistant coach can be helpful in attaining a head coaching position at the desired level.

Coaching Education and Certification

Participation in sports at all levels involves millions of children, youth, and young adults. Nonschool sports ranging from community recreational programs to elite clubs attract more than 60 million children and youth.[22] Interscholastic sports draw nearly 7.9 million students, with programs typically organized into modified, junior varsity, and varsity teams.[23] At the collegiate level, including community colleges, more than half a million students participate in sports.[24] Untold numbers of coaches, whether compensated or volunteers (common at the youth sports level), work with these participants, playing a significant role in the quality of the participants' sport experience.

Coaches' impact on the experience of their athletes varies considerably. Some coaches do an outstanding job of keeping winning in perspective, developing their athletes' skills and understanding of the game and its strategies, and acting to ensure their athletes' safety during games, practices, and conditioning. Many coaches recognize that sport experiences provide opportunities for social and emotional development and are sensitive to their athletes' needs in this area. On the other hand, some coaches lack preparation in skill development, conditioning, safety, and understanding how their actions could negatively impact their athletes' social and emotional development. Given the impact of coaches on athletes' experiences and development, preparing coaches to assume these important responsibilities is critical. Coaching standards and coaching certifications can help those involved in coaching prepare to be more effective coaches.

SHAPE America's *National Standards for Sport Coaches* provides a framework for organizations and agencies offering coaching education. The standards also set forth expectations for coaches.[25] Knowledge, skills, and values associated with effective and appropriate coaching of athletes are organized into 42 standards highlighting coaches' responsibilities and are grouped into seven domains (see the National Standards for Sport Coaches box).

The seven domains of coaching competency are:

- Vision, goals, and standards.
- Ethical practices.
- Relationships.
- Safe sport environment.
- Positive and inclusive sport environment.
- Conduct practices and prepare for competition.
- Continuous improvement.[25]

NATIONAL STANDARDS FOR SPORT COACHES

Set Vision, Goals, and Standards for Sport Program
Engage in and Support Ethical Practices
Build Relationships
Develop a Safe Sport Environment
Create a Positive and Inclusive Sport Environment
Conduct Practices and Prepare for Competition
Strive for Continuous Improvement

SHAPE America. *National Standards for Sport Coaches*, 2021. https://shapeamerica.org/coaching. Used with permission.

These standards emphasize the importance of coaches having an athlete-centered philosophy, giving priority to the long-term development of the athlete over winning at all costs. Coaches are expected to model ethical behavior while teaching and reinforcing ethical behavior in their athletes. Effective interpersonal and communication skills are used to build positive relationships with stakeholders involved in sport program, be they athletes, referees, parents, or sports medicine professionals. Cultural competency, professionalism, and leadership are evident in coaches' interactions and contribute to creating a positive, inclusive sport environment. Safety is paramount, and the sport environment should be one that is free from abuse and harassment and supports the health and welfare of the athletes. This includes reducing risks, using proper training procedures, promoting sound nutritional practices, and maintaining a drug-free environment.

Practices are planned to prepare athletes for competition and incorporate current scientific principles and sport-specific techniques and strategies in a progressive fashion. Attention is given to preparing athletes both physically and mentally. Sound teaching and learning principles contribute to athletes' development and competitive performance. Coaches help athletes learn the skills to self-assess their performance, take responsibility for their own development, and acquire life skills. Coaches are also responsible for adapting practices and competition plans, and using decision making skills to make strategic adjustments during competition.

Coaches are expected to take responsibility for continuous improvement. Self-reflection, mentoring, and professional development contribute to coach learning and growth. Equally important, coaches need to strive to maintain a work–life balance that helps minimize stress and reduce the chances of burnout.

There are several coaching certification programs available for those working in the sports field. Two available programs are the National Alliance for Youth Sports coaching training program[26] and the National Federation of State High School Associations certification program.[27] Additional coaching certification programs might be offered by sport federations and organizations, such as the ones offered by the USA Track and Field, USA Football, United States Soccer Federation, and Special Olympics.

If you think that coaching is an opportunity you would like to pursue, take advantage of your professional preparation courses to learn the skills, knowledge, and behaviors needed to coach safely and effectively and ensure positive experiences for your athletes. Think about becoming certified through one of the many coaching education programs. If you anticipate coaching at the interscholastic level, be aware of your state's coaching certification requirements that you must meet before beginning to coach. As you know, coaches have a tremendous impact on the experiences of athletes and their well-being, both in the immediate and long term, so commit yourself to making the athletic experience a positive one.

BURNOUT AND SELF-CARE

Burnout is a problem among teachers and coaches. Noted researcher Christina Maslach defines job *burnout* as "a psychological syndrome in response to chronic interpersonal stressors on the job. The three key dimensions of this response are an overwhelming exhaustion, feelings of cynicism and detachment from the job, and a sense of ineffectiveness and lack of accomplishment."[28] Because burnout can have a devastating effect on dedicated individuals, young professionals need to be aware of the causes and consequences of burnout and strategies they can use to prevent its occurrence.

There are many causes of teacher burnout: lack of administrative support, lack of input into the curriculum process, and public criticism and the accompanying lack of community support. Inadequate salaries, discipline problems, too little time to do the ever-growing amount of work, large classes, and heavier teaching loads may also contribute to this problem. The lack of challenge, inadequate supervisory feedback, and the absence of opportunities for personal and professional growth also may lead to burnout.

In the coaching realm, burnout may be caused by seasons that go on without end; preseason, in-season, and postseason obligations result in only a short break for coaches, giving them little time to rest or recharge. Extended time spent in preparation and planning, excessive paperwork, and a myriad of administrative tasks that consume coaches' time are contributing factors. The lack of administrative support coupled with administrative demands and pressure take their toll. Traveling for games; scouting your opponents; and, in some cases, recruiting trips all occupy coaches' time. Conflict with athletes, pressures from parents, and community and institutional expectations add to coaches' stress. Teacher-coach role conflict may also contribute to burnout.

In both the teaching and coaching realms, personal problems may interact with professional problems to exacerbate burnout. Personal problems such as family conflicts, money difficulties, or perhaps even divorce or problems with relationships may cause additional stress for the individual. These stresses coupled with professional problems may hasten the onset of burnout.

The consequences of burnout are many and are often quite severe, affecting teachers and coaches as well as their students and athletes. Burnout is associated with absenteeism, intent to leave the job, and actual job turnover.[28] For people who continue to work, burnout leads to lower productivity and effectiveness.[28] Teachers'/coaches' interactions with their students/athletes may also suffer. Burned-out teachers/coaches may treat their students/athletes in a depersonalized manner, providing them with little encouragement, feedback, and reinforcement of their efforts, and many have lower expectations for their performance.

Professionals who are burned out may feel dissatisfied with their accomplishments and believe that they are wasting the best years of their lives. Burnout can result in deterioration of health. Insomnia, hypertension, ulcers, and other stress-related symptoms may manifest themselves in burned-out teachers.

What can be done to cope with burnout? The varied causes and consequences of burnout require a diversity of solutions. Supervisors such as principals and athletic directors can play a crucial role in the prevention and remediation of burnout. Supervisors can provide teachers and coaches with meaningful in-service programs, focusing on developing a variety of teaching and coaching techniques, learning efficient time management, and acquiring effective communication skills. They can also provide teachers and coaches with more feedback about their performance, which can serve as a stimulus for growth. Teachers and coaches can seek out new ideas, professional contacts, and opportunities through participation in professional organizations and conferences.

You can reduce the potential and/or impact of burnout by developing a thoughtful self-care plan and actually implementing it. Having a plan can strengthen your resilience and enhance your ability to deal with stress.[29] Your self-care plan should start with investing in your own health and wellness. First, we should practice what we preach—take time to engage in enjoyable physical activity, eat healthy, and get enough sleep.

Nurture your mental health by using cognitive strategies such as positive affirmations that empower you. Take some time to frame your experiences and examine issues and challenges from different perspectives. Rather than engage in all-or-nothing thinking, arrive at a more realistic perspective. Did you have a "bad" day or did one or two things not go as planned and the rest of the day went well? Take time to reflect on your social identity and how it influences your professional practices. Try to identify things that can be controlled and changed and use that information to guide where to focus your actions and efforts. For some individuals, their religion or spiritual beliefs play an instrumental role in managing stress.

Try not to be your harshest critic! Adopt a growth mindset when you analyze your experiences, whether successes or failures, to see what lessons can be learned. Most of us feel compassion for others when they are struggling. Recognize that you would benefit from the same compassion that you extend to others. Practice self-compassion by speaking to yourself in encouraging and positive ways, much like you would say to a friend who is experiencing the same issues.

Time management plays an important role in managing stress. Learn to prioritize items on your "to-do" list and give yourself permission to move today's items to tomorrow's list or cross them off all together. One of the best time management strategies, and often hard to do, is learning to say "no" to new commitments and choosing to say "yes" to your own health.

There are many different ways to relax and unwind, so take time to find out which one or two work for you. While some people might find practicing yoga to be relaxing or engaging in mindfulness to be beneficial, others might find the same benefits from taking their dog for a long walk or engaging in their favorite hobby. Relaxation is personal! Taking some time off to revitalize yourself during the summer.

Connecting in meaningful ways with others can play an important role in managing stress. Your support network can offer comfort, acceptance, and encouragement. If you feel overwhelmed or alone in your struggles, reaching out and connecting with others can be helpful in navigating tough times. Your professional support network can offer encouragement, opportunities to discuss challenging situations, and exchange of ideas and other forms of assistance. The growth of social media makes connecting with other professionals around the globe easy and offers numerous opportunities for professional development.

If you are overwhelmed, anxious, or depressed, consider speaking to a mental health professional. Remember that working with students who have experienced trauma may lead to personal retraumatization based on your past experiences or secondary trauma arising from being a caring adult and working with students in need. While you might be reluctant to do so, mental health professionals are a valuable resource in dealing some of the stress associated with burnout. Would you recommend that option to others who are feeling similar to what you are experiencing? Consider taking your own advice and trying this avenue. Along the same lines, do not hesitate to see a physician if you are experiencing illness.

Some teachers and coaches seek to cope with the consequences of burnout by adopting inappropriate solutions such as excessive use of alcohol or drugs. While this might alleviate the stress and pain in the short term, use of these substances in the long run may lead to serious health consequences, without alleviating the issues associated with burnout.

The pervasiveness of burnout and the serious consequences for teachers, coaches, students, and athletes should make dealing with burnout an important professional concern. Remember make caring for yourself a priority. Caring for yourself enables you to better care for others. Working in a field that promotes health and well-being, it is important not to sacrifice your own well-being for the sake of your career.

INCREASING YOUR PROFESSIONAL MARKETABILITY

If you are interested in a teaching career, whether it be in the school or nonschool setting, you can often enhance both your marketability and your ability to teach by building on your assets and interests. Through careful planning of your study program and wise use of your electives and practicum experiences, you can improve your chances of gaining the professional position you desire. Many of the same strategies are applicable to coaching as well.

You can enhance your opportunities to teach in the school setting in several ways. One way is to build on talents or skills you already possess. For example, the need is great for bilingual educators. Perhaps, you have gained proficiency in a second language because of your family background, the location in which you grew up, or the foreign language you studied in secondary school. These language skills can be built on with further course work at the college or university level.

Second, additional course work can be beneficial in broadening the abilities of the prospective teacher. Courses in the area of adapted physical education are an asset whether or not one is interested in specializing in adapted physical education. Because adapted physical education emphasizes individualized instruction, the knowledge gained from its study can be applied to all children, including those with special needs mainstreamed into or included in regular physical education classes. Additional courses in health may be helpful because physical educators often find themselves teaching one or two health classes in addition to their physical education courses. The close relationship between wellness and fitness makes knowledge of health important to the practitioner.

Another possibility, depending on the state in which you plan to teach, is to gain certification to teach in a second academic area. If you enjoy other areas such as math, science, or health, dual certification would enable you to qualify for additional jobs such as a teaching position that has a teaching load of one-third math and two-thirds physical education or one-third health and two-thirds physical education. Certification in driver education is also a popular choice that enhances one's credentials. To gain dual certification, you typically take several courses in your secondary area of study. The education department in the state in which you plan to teach can provide you with additional information about the requirements for certification.

Individuals interested in teaching in a nonschool setting can enhance their marketability in a similar way as individuals preparing for a teaching position in the public schools. Depending on where you seek employment, having a bilingual background might be an asset. Experience in adapted physical education will be useful in working with individuals of different abilities and ages. Courses in math and business may be helpful if you are employed by a commercial sport club or fitness center or community sport program, where the position often involves managerial duties. Because many of these organizations offer some type of health counseling and because of the interest of many of the clientele in health, courses in health will be an asset as well. Expertise in one or several sport areas may also be a plus, as is possession of specialized certifications.

In the coaching realm, one's previous experience as an athlete in the sport is an asset. Many former athletes have capitalized on their experience to secure coaching positions. Previous work as an assistant or head coach enhances your credentials. Professional contacts, official ratings in a sport, and membership in a professional organization are helpful in getting hired or advancing. Many states require that coaches hold teaching certification; holding such certification gives one more flexibility in selecting from job opportunities.

Finally, you can enhance your credentials by gaining as much practical experience as possible, working with people of all ages and abilities. This holds true whether you are seeking work in a school

FOCUS ON CAREER: Teaching and Coaching

PROFESSIONAL ORGANIZATIONS	• SHAPE America: Society of Health and Physical Educators • National Education Association
PROFESSIONAL JOURNALS	• *Adapted Physical Activity Quarterly* • *JOPERD* • *Journal of Teaching in Physical Education* • *Palestra* • *Research Quarterly for Exercise and Sport* • *Sports and Spokes* • *Strategies*

or nonschool setting or in coaching. This experience can be gained through volunteer work, part-time employment, summer employment, or supervised field experiences sponsored by your college or university. Being able to cite such practical experiences on your resume may prove invaluable when you are seeking to gain employment. Membership in professional organizations and growing your professional network may also be helpful in securing employment.

Teachers and coaches can improve their marketability by acquiring skills in the use of technology. Technology can help teachers and coaches enhance their instructional effectiveness and manage their time more efficiently. Many teachers are now using heart rate monitors in their classes. These monitors, which attach to the student's wrist, provide immediate and ongoing feedback to students about their heart rate. Many heart rate monitors store the information so that it can be downloaded to a computer and later analyzed by the teacher. Some monitors include accelerometers that allow for monitoring the amount of movement. Newer wearable technology uses Global Positioning System (GPS) and radiofrequency identification (RFID) to actually track the movements of participants, monitoring such information as miles covered, speed of movement, and other parameters. This technology is expensive at this time and more often used by intercollegiate and professional sports teams. However, as it becomes cheaper, this technology may become more readily available to coaches and teachers.

Many teachers and coaches use mobile devices, such as tablets and smartphones, in their work. There are many applications available for these devices. These apps help professionals perform managerial tasks, such as taking attendance, keeping track of equipment, budgeting, and scheduling. Using these mobile devices lets professionals easily show videos of expert performance, as well as capture the performance of their students or athletes, and then analyze their performance and provide annotated video feedback. Apps are available to help with grading and assessment of performance as well.

The use of the web as a resource for teachers and coaches is growing. There are many websites for physical education teachers to use as resources and a means to communicate with other teachers throughout the country. Professional development and learning communities facilitate the exchange of ideas and contribute to professional growth. PE Central (Figure 12-1) is one of the premier websites for physical educators. It offers teachers access to lesson plans, instructional resources, assessment ideas, professional information on conferences and

Figure 12-1 PE Central is a popular website for physical educators.

Used by permission of PE Central (pecentral.org), the premier website for physical education teachers.

workshops, job openings, equipment purchasing, and related websites. Physical education teachers can share information and engage in problem solving with other teachers throughout the nation.

Coaches find that the web offers them the opportunity to share information with other coaches throughout the world. A coach may find posted on the web information about drills, training techniques, and upcoming conferences and clinics. Through several different sites on the web, college coaches can contact and recruit prospective athletes. Through various sport-specific e-mailing lists, coaches can communicate with colleagues worldwide.

Prospective teachers and coaches can enhance their marketability. Building on your skills, taking additional courses, and gaining as much practical experience as possible will increase your options and enhance your opportunities for employment.

CURRENT TRENDS: MOVING TOWARD THE FUTURE

- Technology will play a role in helping students become more self-directed learners, and teachers will assume a greater role as instructional facilitators.
- Increased use of social media by teachers and coaches, coupled with growing online resources, encourages the sharing of best practices, facilitates collaboration, and enriches social support.
- The use of wearable technology by athletes during practices and games will provide coaches with faster and more detailed information about athletes' performance.
- As the cost of wearable technology decreases, these devices will become available for use in physical education. GPS and RFID devices will allow teachers to more accurately monitor their students' activity during class. Drones used by teachers and coaches to video game play make it easier to assess the movements of students and athletes, for example, in volleyball looking at movements on and off the ball.
- Individuals will increasingly use smartphone apps to monitor their performance and personalize their training.

SUMMARY

Teaching and coaching in the twenty-first century is impacted by a host of events that have impacted our society: the COVID-19 pandemic, activism and emphasis on social justice, advances in digital technologies, and increased diversity. Teaching and coaching opportunities have broadened from the traditional school setting to the nonschool setting and from school-aged populations to people of all ages, ranging from preschoolers to senior citizens. Teaching opportunities in the school setting are available at the elementary level, secondary level, and in higher education. New initiatives, such as the focus on physical literacy; the Whole School, Whole Community, Whole Child model; and the Comprehensive School Physical Activity Program, have the potential to positively impact physical education. Prospective teachers may also teach physical education in adapted physical education programs and in professional preparation programs. In the nonschool setting, opportunities exist in commercial sport clubs, community and youth agencies, resorts, corporate fitness programs, the armed forces, and preschool and day-care motor development programs. Many individuals choose a teaching career because of their strong desire to work with people, because of personal interests, and because of the nature of the job. Individuals desiring to pursue a teaching career, regardless of setting, should be cognizant of the numerous rewards, benefits, and challenges associated with this career.

Many prospective physical educators aspire to a career as a coach. Some seek a dual career as a teacher and a coach, whereas others desire solely to coach and view a teaching career as a means to attain their ultimate ambition. The prospective coach should be knowledgeable of the rewards, benefits, and challenges of the career.

Teachers have a myriad of responsibilities; those responsibilities may be classified as instructional, managerial, and institutional in nature. Coaching is similar in many respects to teaching. Effective coaches possess many of the characteristics of effective teachers and must assume many of the same responsibilities as well. Coaching certification programs offer coaches training and standards to guide their interactions with their athletes.

One problem that has become increasingly prevalent among teachers and coaches is burnout. Burnout is physical, mental, and attitudinal exhaustion. The causes of burnout are many, and personal problems may interact with professional problems to exacerbate burnout. Self-care and a variety of strategies can help alleviate this problem.

Many strategies can be used by prospective teachers and coaches to enhance their marketability. They can build on their talents and interests, take additional course work in a supporting area, and gain as much practical experience as possible.

Discussion Questions

1. Reflect on your physical education experiences at the elementary, middle school, and high school levels. What are your memories of physical education classes? Your physical education teacher? Does your physical education experiences reflect the essential components of physical education: policies and environment, curriculum, appropriate instruction, and student assessment?
2. Did you play dodgeball in your physical education classes? Whether dodgeball should be played or banned in physical education classes is a controversial subject. What is your position? How does dodgeball fit into the curriculum? You may want to search the web to find more information about dodgeball and its inclusion in physical education.
3. How are teaching and coaching different? How are they similar? Within the public school setting, should all coaches be required to be certified teachers? Certified physical education teachers?
4. Many societal changes and forces impact education and by extension physical education. What two forces do you think will have the greatest impact on your teaching?

GET CONNECTED

SHAPE America–offers access to position papers, standards for teachers and coaches, and careers in the field.

https://www.shapeamerica.org

PE Central–serves as a major resource for physical educators of all levels, offering access to lesson plans for all levels of physical education and adapted physical education, information on assessment, positive learning environment, professional links, jobs, and resources.

https://www.pecentral.org

PHEAmerica–Physical and Health Education America–offers information, lesson ideas, and tips for teachers and coaches of all levels as well as current news in the field of physical education, health education, and sport. Areas include technology, interdisciplinary learning, coaching, teaching, and current events.

http://www.pheamerica.org/

National Consortium for Physical Education and Recreation for Individuals with Disabilities–presents information about the Adapted Physical Education National Standards project and links to resources.

https://www.ncpeid.org

National Federation of State High School Associations–information about participation in high school athletics. Access the learning center for information about coaching requirements in each state and coaching certification courses.

http://www.nfhs.org/

SELF-ASSESSMENT ACTIVITIES

These activities are designed to help you determine if you have mastered the materials and the competencies presented in this chapter.

1. What is physical literacy? What can we do as professionals to help the general public understand the importance of physical literacy as a goal of physical education?
2. Discuss the advantages and disadvantages of pursuing a teaching or coaching career in a school and a nonschool setting. If possible, try to interview a physical educator or coach presently working in each setting.
3. Using the information provided in the Get Connected box, access the PE Central website. Explore the information contained within the site. Write a one- to two-page paper on the usefulness of the web to teachers and coaches.
4. Using the information provided in the Get Connected box, access the SHAPE America website and then search for and read the *National Standards for Sport Coaches*. Carefully review your own athletic experiences and compare the actions and behaviors of your coaches to the standards. Did your coaches meet these standards? Where did they fall short? Discuss the importance of standards for coaches, especially at the youth sport level.
5. Access the SHAPE America website and browse through the resources offered for professional development as well as standards and guidelines. Select one resource to read and summarize. List three things you have learned as a result of browsing the site.
6. Research the teacher certification and coach certification requirements for your state. Write a short paper summarizing these requirements and providing links to the specific regulations.
7. Burnout can be a problem for teachers and coaches. One thing that can help prevent burnout is having a self-care plan. Create a short self-care plan for yourself that would reduce stress you might experience as a teacher or coach in the future. Do you have a self-care plan for yourself as a student?

REFERENCES

1. Ward, P., Larsen, H. A., van der Mars, H., & Mitchell, M. F. (2021). Chapter 1: 21st century physical education in the United States: Introduction to the special issue. *Journal of Teaching in Physical Education, 40*, 345–352. https://doi.org/10.1123/jtpe.2020-0239.
2. Walton-Fisette, J. L. (2020). Preparing health and physical education teachers to become trauma invested: Introduction to feature series. *JOPERD, 91*(9), 6–7.
3. Substance Abuse and Mental Health Services Administration. (2014). SAMHSA's Concept of Trauma and Guidance for a Trauma-Informed Approach. HHS Publication No. (SMA) 14-4884. Rockville, MD: Substance Abuse and Mental Health Services Administration.
4. Walton-Fisette, J. L. (2020). Fostering resilient learners by implementing trauma-informed and socially just practices. *JOPERD, 91*(9), 8–15.
5. Bureau of Labor Statistics, US Department of Labor. (2021). Education, training, and library occupations. https://www.bls.gov/ooh/education-training-and-library/home.htm.
6. Richards, K. A. R., Gaudreault, K. L., & Templin, T. J. (2014). Understanding the realities of teaching: A seminar series focused on induction. *Journal of Physical Education, Recreation & Dance, 85*(2), 28–35. (doi: 10.1080/07303084.2014.958251).
7. Ward, P., van der mars, H., Mitchell, M. F., & Lawson, H. A. (2021). Chapter 3: PK-12 school physical education: Conditions, lessons learned, and future directions. *Journal of Teaching in Physical Education, 40*, 363-371. https://doi.org/10.1123/jtpe.2020-0241.
8. Council of Chief State School Officers. (2011). *Interstate teacher assessment and support consortium (InTASC) model core teaching standards: A resource for state dialogue.* Washington, DC: Author.
9. SHAPE America. (2017). *2017 national standards for initial physical education teacher education.* Reston, VA: Author.

10. Cardina, C. E., & James, A. R. (2018). Targeting professional development for beginning physical education teachers. *Journal of Physical Education, Recreation & Dance, 89*(7), 41-47.

11. Cardina, C. E., & DeNysschen, C. A. (2018). Professional development activities and support among physical education teachers in the United States. *Physical Educator, 75*, 136-157.

12. SHAPE America. (2014). *National standards and grade level outcomes for K-12 physical education*. Champaign, IL: Human Kinetics.

13. SHAPE America. (2015). *The essential components of physical education*. Reston, VA: Author.

14. Centers for Disease Control and Prevention. (n.d.). Whole School, Whole Community, Whole Child (WSCC). Retrieved from https://www.cdc.gov/healthyyouth/wscc/model.htm.

15. Centers for Disease Control and Prevention. National Framework for Physical Activity and Physical Education. Atlanta, GA: U.S. Department of Health and Human Services, 2013.

16. Gensemer, R. E. (1985). *Physical education: Perspectives, inquiry, and application*. Philadelphia, PA: W.B. Saunders.

17. Mitchell, S. A., & Walton-Fisette, J. L. (2016). *The essentials of teaching physical education*. Champaign, IL: Human Kinetics.

18. National Center for Educational Statistics. (2019-2020). *Children and youth with disabilities*. Retrieved from http://nces.ed.gov/.

19. National Consortium for Physical Education and Recreation for Individuals with Disabilities & Kelly, L. E. (Ed.). (2020). *Adapted physical education national standards* (3rd ed.). Champaign, IL: Human Kinetics. Retrieved from https://www.ncpeid.org/apens.

20. Administration on Aging. (2020). *A profile of older Americans*. Retrieved from https://www.acl.gov/aging-and-disability-in-america/data-and-research/profile-older-americans.

21. 2019 National Senior Games Presented by Humana Smashes Athlete Participation Record. Retrieved from https://nsga.com/2019-national-senior-games-presented-by-humana-smashes-athlete-participation-record/.

22. National Council of Youth Sports. (n.d.). Enhancing the youth sports experience. Retrieved from http://www.ncys.org/about/about.php.

23. National Federation of High School Associations. (2019). High school sports participation registers first decline in 30 years. Retrieved from https://www.nfhs.org/articles/participation-in-high-school-sports-registers-first-decline-in-30-years/.

24. NCAA. (2021) Number of student athletes in the United States in 2020, by gender. NCAA.

25. Gano-Overway, L., Thompson, M., & Van Mullum, P. (2021). *National Standards for Sport Coaches: Quality Coaches, Quality Sports* (3rd ed.). SHAPE America. https://www.shapeamerica.org/standards/coaching.

26. National Alliance for Youth Sports. (2019). National Youth Sports Coaching Association: Overview. Retrieved from https://www.nays.org/coaches/.

27. National Federation of State High Schools Associations. Retrieved from https://nfhslearn.com/home/coaches.

28. Maslach, C., Schaufeli, W. B., & Leiter, M. P. (2001). Job burnout. *Annual Review of Psychology, 52*, 397-422.

29. Wuest, D. A., & Subramaniam, P. R. (2020). Building teacher resilience during the pandemic and beyond. *Strategies, 34*, November-December, 8-12.

Polka Dot Images/Getty Images

CHAPTER 13

FITNESS- AND HEALTH-RELATED CAREERS

OBJECTIVES

After reading this chapter, students should be able to–

- Discuss the responsibilities, opportunities, and preparation for professionals interested in working in fitness- or health-related careers.
- Describe the opportunities available and preparation needed by professionals desiring to pursue a therapy-related career.
- Discuss the various strategies that can be used to enhance one's professional marketability.

Today there is great interest in preventative medicine and a wider public awareness of the values of physical activity. The increased awareness stimulated the growth of community, commercial, medical fitness, and work-site wellness and fitness programs. As a result, employment opportunities for professionals with preparation as exercise and fitness specialists grew tremendously prior to the COVID-19 pandemic. The pandemic led to the temporary and, in some cases, permanent closure of many health and fitness facilities, and thousands of fitness professionals lost their jobs. Although many health and fitness clubs have reopened, the industry has not returned to pre-COVID conditions. However, increased opportunities have emerged for professionals qualified to provide on-demand virtual training and personal training.[1]

Another field that has experienced growth is athletic training. Although athletic trainers have typically been employed by professional and college athletic teams, their employment at the secondary school level continues to rise. Furthermore, the public's increased participation in a variety of sport activities and the medical profession's interest in sport have led to increased employment opportunities for qualified athletic trainers in commercial sports medicine clinics, physical therapy clinics, hospitals, and even corporate workplace wellness programs.

Many employment opportunities are available for qualified professionals in fitness centers and health clubs. They may be employed as dance exercise

SOCIAL JUSTICE

Talking Points

- Access to opportunities to work out at one's workplace, in a health and fitness club, or to engage a personal trainer is influenced by one's socioeconomic status. For example, the majority of gym members come from a household with an income of $75,000 or above. These opportunities may be too expensive for some people to afford.[1]
- Minorities are underrepresented in our professional fields. For example, minorities comprise less than 20% of certified athletic trainers.[2] Greater efforts must be made to recruit minorities into higher education and into our professional fields.
- Health and fitness clubs need to be more inclusive, providing opportunities for diverse populations.

specialists, exercise leaders, exercise test technologists, health and wellness coaches, and nutrition consultants.

An increasing number of medical and health care professionals, as well as members of the general public, realize the significant physical and psychological benefits gained by individuals who participate in regular, appropriate physical activity. There is greater recognition of the therapeutic values of movement in helping individuals attain an optimal state of well-being, as well as recover from illness. Careers in therapeutic recreation and dance therapy are available to professionals who desire to work in a therapeutic setting. Some students build on their undergraduate degree in physical education, exercise science, or sport and pursue advanced study in health-related fields. These students enroll in programs leading to careers as kinesiotherapists, physical therapists, and chiropractors.

FITNESS- AND EXERCISE-RELATED CAREERS

Preventative and rehabilitative exercise programs differ in their focus and in the nature of their participants; the setting in which these programs are conducted often is different as well. Preventative exercise program specialists work with healthy individuals to increase their level of fitness and realize concomitant gains in health. Rehabilitative exercise program specialists work primarily with individuals who exhibit the effects of coronary heart disease; they focus on helping these individuals attain a functional state of living and an enhanced quality of life. Preventative exercise programs are commonly found in workplace fitness centers, commercial fitness centers, and community agencies such as the YMCA. An increasing number of hospitals are now offering wellness programs. Rehabilitative exercise programs are most often found in hospitals, although some may be found in medical clinics or community agencies or be affiliated with worksite fitness centers.

Preventative and rehabilitative programs often vary in their scope and comprehensiveness. However, some commonalities may be discerned. Although these programs typically focus on improvement of fitness, they may include other components such as educational programs, health promotion programs, and lifestyle modification.

Comprehensive wellness programs are growing in popularity. The fitness component of these programs typically includes some assessment of the individual's current level of fitness, prescription of a program of exercise and activity, opportunities to engage in exercise and activities, and periodic reevaluation of the individual's level of fitness.

Educational efforts often focus on instructing individuals on the principles underlying the performance of exercises and physical activity so that individuals can learn to properly plan their own exercise and activity programs. Health promotion efforts may include health education, such as providing participants with nutritional information, as well as measures focusing on the early detection of diseases, such as hypertension screening and cancer detection. Lifestyle modification may include counseling individuals regarding stress management, weight control, tobacco cessation, and alcohol and drug abuse. Some programs offer health and wellness coaching to help individuals achieve their goals and sustain changes in their behaviors (e.g., being more active). In addition to these program components, recreational sport opportunities may be offered.

Professionals working in these programs must be able to perform a wide variety of tasks and be capable of assuming responsibility for numerous aspects of the program. The responsibilities of an exercise program specialist as:

- Directing the exercise program, which may be oriented to prevention or rehabilitation.
- Training and supervising staff.
- Developing and managing the program budget.
- Designing and managing the exercise facility and laboratories.
- Recruiting and retaining members
- Marketing the exercise program.
- Evaluating–sometimes in conjunction with a physician–each participant's medical and activity history, administering a graded exercise test, pulmonary function tests, and assorted fitness tests.
- Developing individual exercise prescriptions for participants.
- Researching, analyzing and incorporating evidence-based practices.
- Evaluating or counseling participants, on request, about nutrition, smoking cessation, weight control, and stress.
- Accumulating program data for statistical analysis and research.
- Maintaining professional affiliations.
- Securing advanced certifications.
- Engaging in continuing education.[3,4]

The responsibilities that each professional in the program will be asked to assume depend on several factors, including the scope and comprehensiveness of the program, the number of participants, the size of the staff, and qualifications of other staff members.

Spinning is a popular activity, offered in person at clubs and through virtual programs.
Kzenon/Shutterstock

Opportunities for qualified individuals may be found in a diversity of preventative and rehabilitative exercise programs offered in a variety of settings. These include workplace wellness programs, commercial and community wellness programs, and rehabilitation programs. Some individuals are finding employment as personal fitness trainers, strength and conditioning coaches, and health and wellness coaches. Salaries vary widely, depending on the qualifications of the individual, years of experience, responsibilities assigned, location of the facility, and nature of the job.

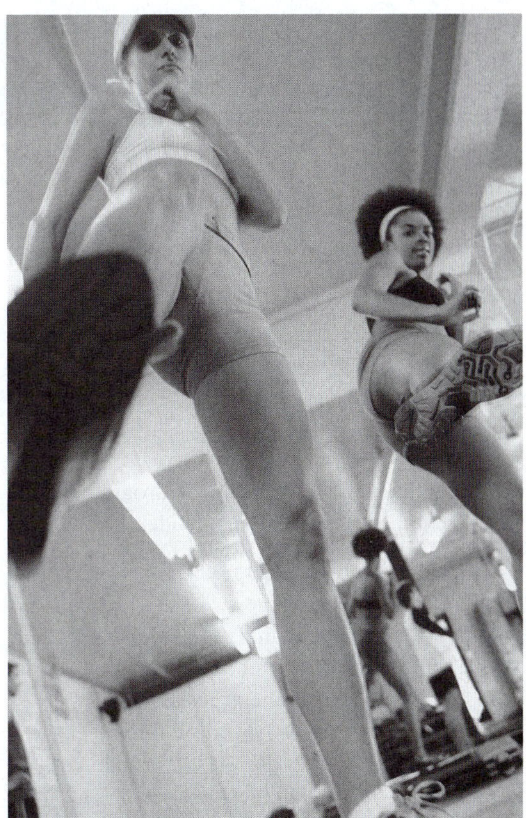

Aerobics are a popular offering in wellness programs and fitness clubs.

Comstock Images/Getty Images

Workplace Wellness Programs

Workplace wellness programs have grown dramatically over the past decade. The Affordable Care Act created new incentives for employers to invest in workplace wellness programs.[5] Workplace wellness programs are a critical component of the national health promotion and disease prevention effort because they have the potential to reach a large percentage of the population. The workplace offers an effective way to reach these adults and to provide them with education and access to the means to adopt and maintain a healthy lifestyle. Onsite programs are convenient for employees and offer the peer social support so important for continued participation.

Corporations invest in workplace wellness programs for many reasons.[6,7] Quality worksite wellness programs contribute to high productivity. Improvements in job performance, increases in productivity, and reduced absenteeism are some of the benefits for companies that choose to invest in worksite wellness programs. Corporations also sponsor wellness programs as a cost containment measure. Health care costs are spiraling, and health insurance premiums continue to rise astronomically. Workplace programs have been associated with reduced injury rates, lower worker's compensation costs, and reduced health care costs. Corporations may also invest in workplace wellness programs because of the benefits in terms of human relations and enhancement of morale. Workplace wellness programs can play an important in recruiting and retaining employees.

Workplace wellness programs vary widely in comprehensiveness–that is, the number and nature of activities offered. According to health promotion expert Larry Chapman, virtually all worksite wellness programs should address 12 "core" topics. (See the Twelve Core Components of Worksite Wellness Programs box.) These topics address a myriad of wellness concerns and health risk factors. Chapman points out that these topics have a "great deal of inherent synergy."[8] He explains, "For example physical activity programming has been shown to have collateral benefits effects on weight management, tobacco use, nutritional practices, back pain, stress management and blood pressure. Any program that offers a mix of interventions in these areas will naturally benefit from their natural synergy."[8]

TWELVE CORE COMPONENTS OF WORKSITE WELLNESS PROGRAMS

Back Care and Injury Prevention	Medical Self-Care
Exercise/Physical Fitness	Consumer Health Education
Stress Management	Cholesterol Reduction
Smoking Control	Nutritional Intervention
Substance Abuse	Select Biometrics Screenings
Weight Management	Hypertension Management

Source: Chapman, L. S. "Fundamentals of Wellness." *Absolute Advantage*, Winter 2006 (www.welcoa.org).

Effective workplace wellness programs share several characteristics. These include:

- Incorporation of a culture of well-being into the organization's core values.
- Support from the organization's leaders at all levels and who often lead by example, engaging in program offerings themselves.
- Offerings and approaches tailored to meet the needs of the organization and its employees, rather than relying on the "on e size fits all" approach.
- Incentives are used judiciously, with both external rewards (e.g., reduction in cost for insurance premiums) and intrinsic rewards (e.g., feeling healthier or a sense of accomplishment) used carefully to initiate and sustain participation and behavior change.
- Multiple opportunities and varied activities for employees to engage in health promotion activities, ranging from offering group exercise classes to 10-minute stretch breaks to placing signs by stairways encouraging employees to take the stairs rather than ride the elevator.
- Persistent and ongoing communication promoting health and well-being, ranging from posters to social media to mobile apps to mailed newsletters.
- Measurable outcomes not only in terms of dollars, but also in terms of increased productivity, low turnover rates, and enhanced quality of employees' lives.
- Long-term commitment to wellness programs by the organization, solicitation of feedback from employees, and ongoing assessment that helps programs continue to grow and evolve.[6,7]

These best practices highlight features of effective workplace wellness programs.

Workplace wellness programs, especially for physical fitness and activity, are most effective when they can attract at-risk employees, that is, those employees who will benefit the most from the program. At-risk employees are those members of the workforce who are sedentary or obese, possess high cholesterol levels, are hypertensive, experience high levels of stress, and smoke.[9] It has been found, however, that participants in the fitness program tend to already be healthier than nonparticipants.[9,10] Therefore, sustained targeted efforts and a variety of approaches need to be directed toward encouraging at-risk individuals to enroll in the program and, one enrolled, continue their participation.

Professionals must realize that part of their job responsibilities will be the active and ongoing recruitment of employees to participate in the program. Employee recruitment is one of the key factors in program success. Once employees have begun a program, efforts need to be directed at maintaining involvement so that desirable health benefits can be achieved.

Workplace facilities vary greatly. Some corporations have invested in multimillion-dollar facilities–gymnasium, pool, indoor track, aerobics studio, racquetball courts, weight rooms, and playing fields–for sport activities. Facilities at other workplaces might be more modest, perhaps only a weight room and a multipurpose gymnasium or walking trails.

School wellness programs for faculty and staff have received increased emphasis during the last decade. These programs vary in nature and scope. Like those found in corporate settings, school programs focus on protecting and improving employees' health status. These worksite programs are seen by professionals as an integral part of school's comprehensive wellness program.

Colleges and universities also are offering programs for their employees. These programs typically emphasize prevention and improvement of health through appropriate lifestyle management. Some institutions offer wellness and fitness programs to their students, on either a credit or noncredit basis. The emphasis is on learning skills and acquiring knowledge to lead a healthy, active life.

Opportunities for employment in workplace programs are increasing for qualified professionals. A professional may work as a group exercise instructor, personal trainer, or wellness coach. As a professional, you may work with people of all fitness levels and all ages, or you may offer specialized classes for women who are pregnant or for people with lower back pain. Class offerings vary widely, ranging from low-impact aerobics to high-intensity cardiovascular workouts and from water-based resistance programs to cycling. Classes may also focus on ergonomics, such as proper posture for performing some tasks, such as lifting heavy objects.

Another opportunity is working as the director of the employee fitness or wellness program. In this capacity, you may lead a variety of wellness and fitness classes, train and supervise other instructors in the program, and educate employees on a variety of topics, such as worker safety or stress management.

Workplace wellness programs may also employ exercise physiologists. Exercise physiologists administer and evaluate exercise tests and supervise exercise sessions. Exercise physiologists work with both healthy individuals and those with special medical concerns. Depending on the scope of the worksite health promotion program, exercise physiologists may direct a cardiac rehabilitation program.

Commercial and Community Fitness Programs

The number of health clubs and fitness centers have grown dramatically within the past decade. This growth was impacted by the COVID-19 pandemic. According to IHRSA, the Global Health and Fitness Association, prior to the pandemic, in 2019, fitness revenues for the US market topped $35 billion. The more than 100,000 clubs served 64 million members. COVID-19 resulted in the loss of $13.9 billion in revenue, the permanent closure of 15% of health clubs and fitness centers, substantial decrease in club memberships, and the loss of thousands of fitness jobs.[1]

While it remains uncertain if revenues, membership and employment will return to pre-pandemic conditions, opportunities for virtual training and at-home workouts continue to grow.[1] Advances in technology facilitated the delivery of both live streaming and on-demand virtual programs. Purchases of in-home exercise equipment increased, providing opportunities to capitalize on this trend. Wearable technologies and mobile apps allowed for the tracking of participants' progress. These changes require fitness professionals to develop new skills required to deliver these programs.

While the cost of membership and services varies considerably, it is important to realize that membership can be costly and economically out of reach for many individuals. Economics also influences member retention, with many former members reporting they quit because it was too expensive to train at health clubs. Convenience is also a major factor influencing membership and usage, with location and hours a major consideration in deciding to join a club and frequency of participation.

The types of programs offered at clubs and fitness centers vary greatly. Graded exercise tests, individualized fitness evaluation and prescription, educational programs, and lifestyle modification are some services offered by more comprehensive programs. Group exercise programs of all sorts, ranging from aerobic dance class to yoga instruction to cardiac rehabilitation to sport-specific training, are offered to members. Strength training, body weight resistance training, high-intensity interval training (HIIT), and functional training are popular offerings in some clubs. The top fitness trends for 2022 offer the health and fitness industry some direction to guide their decisions regarding programming and offerings. (see the Health and Fitness Trends box).

More and more services are being offered to club members. Wellness and health coaching is growing in popularity, and nutritional counseling is a natural complement to fitness training. Many clubs are offering more age- and population-specific programming. Programming for older adults, youths who are overweight and obese, sport-specific training for adolescents, and rehabilitation training are seeing a rise in popularity. An increasing number of programs are available to address the fitness needs of individuals with disabilities. These programs tend to focus on improvement of fitness and functional independence. Improvement of functional independence allows participants in the program to assume a greater responsibility for their personal care and other activities of daily living. For individuals with severe limiting conditions, such as quadriplegia or multiple sclerosis, increasing their basic muscular strength, endurance, and balance allows them more independence and greatly enhances the overall quality of their lives.

HEALTH AND FITNESS TRENDS

- Wearable technology–fitness trackers, Global Positioning System trackers, and apps
- Live stream and on-demand virtual training
- Home exercise gyms
- Outdoor activities
- Strength training with free weights
- Exercise for weight loss
- Personal training
- Body weight training
- Health and wellness coaching

Source: American College of Sports Medicine. Worldwide Survey of Fitness Trends for 2020.

A growing site for community fitness and wellness programming is medical fitness centers. These centers focus on providing services to individuals with chronic diseases and multiple risk factors. They are also open to healthy individuals and focus on disease prevention and health promotion. These medical fitness centers strive to offer a continuum of care for people within their community, ranging from rehabilitation to prevention, with the goal of improving the health status of the entire community.[11] Medical fitness centers may be incorporated within a hospital or, most commonly, as a standalone center, often in partnership with a local community fitness or wellness center.

These medical fitness centers offer an array of clinical services. These services focus on meeting the needs of special populations such as patients with cardiovascular disease, arthritis, diabetes, and cancer. Services range from cardiac and pulmonary rehabilitation, weight management, and physical therapy to sports and occupational medicine. Like many health clubs, these fitness centers make available cardiovascular and weight training equipment, group exercise programs, and personal training. Some have swimming pools and indoor running tracks.[11] Medical fitness centers also focus on meeting the needs of healthy community members, and offer an array of services such as health screenings for cholesterol and health education seminars on nutrition, smoking cessation, and stress management.

Medical fitness centers involve physicians as directors or part of a medical advisory board.[11] The staff typically have degrees in exercise physiology and certifications that reflect their ability to meet the needs of individuals with specific medical conditions. The global initiative, Exercise is Medicine, managed by the American College of Sports Medicine (ACSM) encourages physicians and fitness professionals to work together to incorporate exercise into a prevention or treatment plan for their patients.[12] Qualified exercise professionals can earn the ACSM Exercise is Medicine Credential, indicating they have the skills and knowledge to plan and implement fitness programming.

One factor that may counter the growth of employment opportunities is the tremendous increase in the sales of home exercise equipment. Many adults who in the past would have paid a membership fee to participate in these programs have chosen to invest the money in home exercise equipment, such as home gyms, bicycle ergometers, treadmills, and rowing machines. Free weights are a popular purchase. These individuals prefer the convenience of being able to exercise at home. Some professionals have capitalized on this trend by working as personal trainers, offering one-on-one fitness instruction in the home. Another trend in working out at home is the growth of live stream or on-demand virtual training. This offers people the ability to work out at a convenient time as well as the opportunity to take advantage of professional instruction.

Personal Trainers

A number of physical education, exercise science, and sport professionals have pursued careers as personal fitness trainers. They meet with clients individually or in small groups in their homes or fitness center on a regular basis, sometimes as often as 5 or 6 days per week. For each client, the personal trainer conducts a fitness assessment, develops specific goals and designs a program leading to their attainment, coaches the individual through the workout, and monitors progress. Additional services often include nutritional counseling. Personal trainers' salary and hourly rates vary by experience, level of education of the trainer, location, and clientele.

Some fitness programs and health clubs also offer members the services of a personal trainer at

Many people prefer to exercise at home. The COVID-19 pandemic promoted the use of on-demand virtual training.

Prostock-Studio/iStock/Getty Images

an additional cost. Members like the one-on-one attention offered by a personal trainer, believing that it enhances their motivation and their effort in performing their program. A growing trend is small-group, fee-based personal trainers, where trainers work with usually fewer than six persons in a group setting.

Some personal trainers work for a health club or fitness center. Members have the option of paying an additional fee to utilize the services of the personal trainer. In these circumstances, trainers may be required to give the club a percentage of their earnings. Other professionals run their own personal training business; they may be the sole provider of care or have other professionals who work for them.

One new trend is the growth of online virtual training. Clients sign up with a personal trainer online. Via e-mail, Zoom, video chat, or phone, the personal trainer and the client establish fitness goals, and then the trainer prescribes a fitness regimen tailored for the needs of the client. The increased use of wearable fitness technology and a growing number of apps make it easier for clients to track their performance and exchange information with their personal trainers. Some personal trainers make videos that clients can download or stream, making it easy for clients to work out at their convenience.

Personal trainers typically possess a fitness certification from a recognized accredited organization. In addition to their expertise and commitment to staying up-to-date, there are several characteristics that good personal trainers possess.[13] They tailor their training to the needs, motivations, and goals of their individual client, rather than embracing a "one size fits all" philosophy. They are a good teacher–they educate their clients, provide feedback, and communicate effectively. They "walk the talk," being a role model for what they preach. Compassion, patience, and positive nature are some additional characteristics that can contribute to the personal trainer's success.

Health and Wellness Coaches

Personal trainers, professionals working in worksite promotion and medical fitness programs, and those employed in commercial and community fitness programs might find health and wellness coaching to be a complement to their professional credentials.[14] Coaches help their clients make lasting changes that enhance their health and well-being. They may work with clients who are healthy and want to enhance their level of health, whether overall or in a specific aspect of wellness such as physical fitness or nutrition. Coaches also work with clients who desire to decrease their risk of disease or those who want to better manage an existing health condition. Coaches may work with their clients to address issues such as weight management, leading a more physically active lifestyle, eating healthier, reducing stress, gaining skills to help manage type 2 diabetes, or tobacco cessation.

Health and wellness coaching draws on theories and skills from positive psychology, health, and behavior change to help their clients reach self-determined goals. Clients are encouraged to build on their strengths, learn strategies to adapt to setbacks, and understand how to sustain change. Coaches work with clients to teach them important skills such as effective goal setting, and they promote self-efficacy as a means to empower clients take charge of their own health.

Health and wellness coaches work with their clients either on a one-on-one basis or in small groups. They coach their clients through face-to-face meetings, via the telephone, or using video-chat. Coaching may last for weeks or months as the coach facilitates client change. Coaches may work privately, find employment in fitness centers, or serve as part of the worksite health promotion or medical fitness center staff. Costs to the client vary greatly, and some costs may be covered by insurance or as part of employee benefits.

While you may already possess the skills needed for health and wellness coaching, certification programs are available. Like other certification programs, it is important to make sure that the certification is respected and recognized in the field. One popular certification program is Well-coaches Certified Health and Wellness Coach, which is offered in partnership with the American College of Sports Medicine and the American College of

Lifestyle Medicine.[15] Health and wellness coaching offers professionals in our field the opportunity to help people make sustained lifestyle changes and optimize their health and well-being.

Strength and Conditioning Professionals

According to the National Strength and Conditioning Association (NSCA), strength and conditioning professionals "assess, motivate, educate, and train athletes for the primary goal of improving sport performance."[16] Strength and conditioning professionals work with interscholastic, intercollegiate, amateur, and professional athletes. They are employed in colleges and universities, high schools, sports medicine and physical therapy clinics, and health and fitness clubs.

Strength and conditioning professionals have a rather varied job description. They assess athletes' health status and fitness levels by conducting a multitude of tests, including evaluation of sport-specific abilities. Based on the results of the assessment, they design and implement safe and effective training programs to maximize performance and help athletes achieve their goals. Additionally, they provide guidance to athletes, as well as their coaches, in areas such as injury prevention and nutrition.[16] They work closely with coaches, athletic trainers, medical staff, and nutrition specialists to ensure the health and well-being of athletes. Record keeping, management of the fitness facility, and administration of the program often are part of the strength and conditioning professionals' responsibilities.

Many strength and conditioning professionals work with collegiate athletes, although an increasing number of professionals work in scholastic settings. Recognizing the critical role that fitness and sport-specific conditioning can play in enhancing performance and helping athletes remain healthy and injury-free, many colleges and university athletic departments hire strength and conditioning specialists.

The NSCA identifies several competencies needed by strength and conditioning coaches. Strength and conditioning professionals need competency in the scientific foundations of sport and exercise science and nutrition. Competency is also needed in the practical and applied areas of the field, such as exercise leadership and program design. Sport and exercise science competencies include an understanding of human physiology, exercise physiology, motor learning, physical education pedagogy, and biomechanics, and the ability to utilize these understandings in the design and implementation of muscular strength and endurance training programs, as well as aerobic and anaerobic fitness programs. Sport and conditioning professionals must be able to utilize techniques from sport psychology to maximize the training and performance of athletes. Professionals

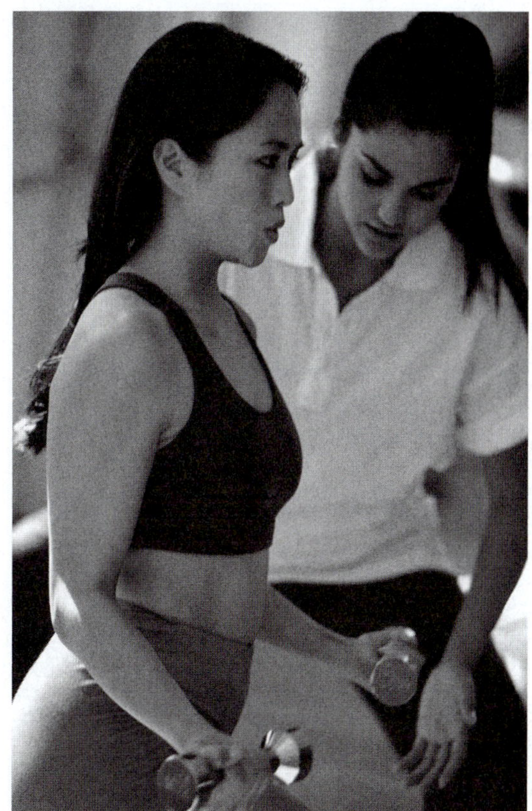

Personal trainers work with individuals typically in the home or club setting. Personal trainers tailor the fitness program to meet the client's needs.

Photodisc Collection/Stockbyte/EyeWire/Getty Images

must also be cognizant of risks and the effects of performance-enhancing substances. In terms of nutrition, strength and conditioning professionals should be knowledgeable of how nutrition affects health and performance.[16]

Within the applied realm, strength and conditioning coaches need to be able to design training programs that take into account an individual's health status, current fitness level, and training and performance goals. They need to be knowledgeable about many different forms of exercise, including flexibility, plyometrics, strength training, and conditioning, and be able to instruct athletes in these exercise techniques, including spotting when appropriate.[16] Competencies also include assessment and evaluation, as well as administration and record keeping.[16]

Physical education teachers, coaches, exercise and fitness specialists, physical therapists, and athletic trainers pursue opportunities as strength and conditioning professionals. Certification as a strength and conditioning specialist is often required for many of these job opportunities.

Rehabilitation Programs

As the role of exercise in the rehabilitation of individuals with illness, particularly cardiovascular diseases, has become increasingly well documented, the number of rehabilitation programs has grown. Typically, rehabilitation programs are offered at hospitals and clinics, although some programs may be offered through community agencies such as the YMCA. Besides the development of fitness, health promotion and lifestyle modification are integral parts of these programs.

Clinical exercise physiologists work in rehabilitation settings. The scope and responsibilities of clinical exercise physiologists are quite broad. They work with clients with a host of conditions, such as cardiovascular and pulmonary disease, as well as those who may have orthopedic or musculoskeletal problems; these clients are referred by a physician. Their responsibilities include exercise evaluation, exercise prescription, exercise supervision, exercise education, and assessment of exercise outcomes.

Clinical exercise physiologists work closely with physicians and medical personnel to meet the needs of their diverse clientele. To plan rehabilitation programs, clinical exercise physiologists must be familiar with the medical aspects of their clients' diseases or conditions, cognizant of the limitations faced by clients, and aware of drugs commonly used to treat the diseases or conditions and their effects. Clinical exercise physiologists must be prepared to help their clients deal with some of the psychological aspects associated with participation in an exercise program, such as the often-expressed fear that exercise will lead to another heart attack.

Career Preparation

Preparation for a career in this area requires a strong background in the exercise sciences and fitness as well as practical experience. Students will also benefit from obtaining certification from a recognized organization and becoming involved in professional organizations.

Preparation

Today, many colleges and universities offer undergraduate and graduate degrees in areas related to health promotion, fitness, or exercise. Undergraduate degree programs are available in exercise science, fitness and cardiac rehabilitation, clinical exercise science, adult fitness, corporate fitness, and fitness programming. Although the requirements for the degree vary by institution, in the typical program, the student takes core courses such as foundations of exercise science, anatomy and physiology, kinesiology, biomechanics, exercise physiology, injury prevention and care, sport and exercise psychology, sport sociology, and assessment.

In addition to these core courses, more in-depth instruction is provided in exercise science, focusing on assessment of cardiopulmonary function and health status, exercise prescription, exercise leadership, and fitness programming. Certification in cardiopulmonary resuscitation (CPR) and the use of automated external defibrillators (AEDs) is commonly required. Because of the strong relationship of this field to health promotion, students may take courses in nutrition, drug education, pharmacology, and stress management. In completing their preparation, students may find it helpful to take several psychology courses, such as motivation, behavior modification, and individual and group counseling. Computer science courses, statistics, and research methodology are helpful to students in preparing for the administrative and evaluative responsibilities associated with a position in this field. Finally, business courses assist students in dealing with the myriad responsibilities associated with these programs, such as budgeting, marketing, and personnel supervision.

To provide students a supervised practical experience in which they have the opportunity to apply and further develop their competencies, most programs require an internship. This internship can take place in a diversity of settings, such as a hospital, corporate fitness center, campus fitness program, or commercial enterprise. The internship typically occurs near the end of the program and serves as a capstone experience.

Also, many programs across the country offer a graduate degree in this area. These programs provide advanced training and an opportunity to specialize. Programs are offered in exercise physiology, fitness programming, cardiac rehabilitation, strength development and conditioning, fitness management, corporate fitness, health fitness, and health promotion.

Certification

Certification programs offered by professional organizations continue to grow in order to meet new needs and demands. As you look at the many certifications available, be sure to take the time to determine if the certifying organization is reputable and accredited. The National Commission for

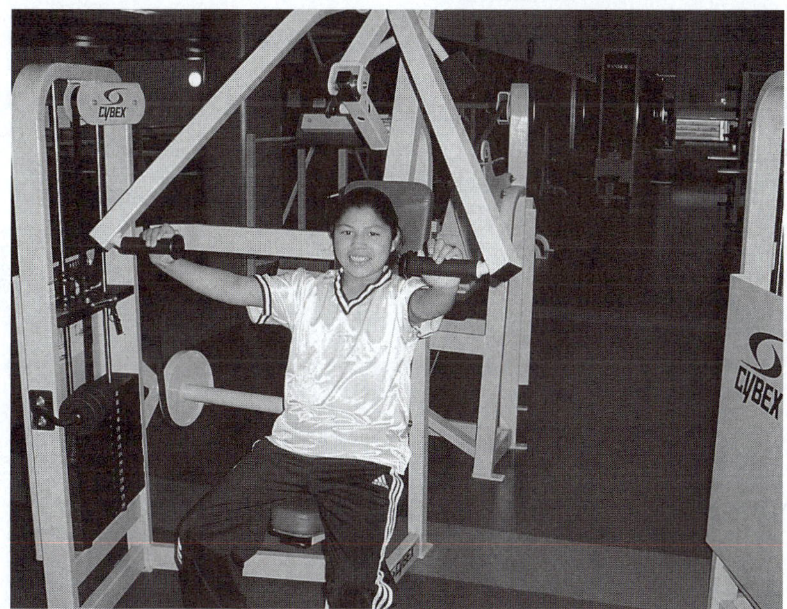

Weight training for children is becoming popular. Professionals working with young children and adolescents must be aware of their special needs.

Deborah Wuest

Certifying Agencies (NCCA) is considered to be the "gold standard" for accreditation in this field.[17] Certifications reflect attainment of a prescribed level of competence, knowledge, skills, and abilities. Certifications vary by prerequisites, requirements, and price. Some certifications require at least an associate degree in a health-related or exercise science–related field; others require a bachelor's degree before taking the certification exam. Certification exams vary as well. Some certification programs require a written and a practical exam; others only a written one. For some certifications, candidates must accumulate a certain number of hours of experience prior to sitting for the exam. Continuing education requirements vary by program. Given so many certifications available, it is important that you check with your professors and respected professionals in the field to make sure that the certification is rigorous and well respected within the field. Selected certification programs generally recognized within the field are shown in Table 13-1.

Professional Organizations

Membership in organizations and establishment of affiliations are important for young professionals. Membership will facilitate the development of professional contacts. It provides the opportunity to update one's skills and knowledge through continuing education programs, workshops, and conventions. Students preparing for a career in this area may find membership in SHAPE America, ACSM, and NSCA to be a valuable professional asset.

TABLE 13-1 Fitness Certifications

Organization	Certifications
American College of Sports Medicine (ACSM)[18]	• ACSM-CPT Certified Personal Trainer • ACSM-GEI Certified Group Exercise Instructor • ACSM-EP Certified Exercise Physiologist • ACSM-CEP Certified Clinical Exercise Physiologist • ACSM Exercise Is Medicine Credential • ACSM/ACS Certified Cancer Exercise Trainer • ACSM/NCHPAD Certified Inclusive Fitness Trainer • ACSM/NPAS Certified Physical Activity in Public Health Specialist
American Council on Exercise (ACE)[19]	• Personal Trainer • Group Fitness Instructor • Health Coach • Medical Exercise Specialist
Athletics and Fitness Association of American (AFAA)[20]	• Personal Fitness Trainer • Group Exercise Instructor
National Strength and Conditioning Association (NSCA)[21]	• Certified Strength and Conditioning Specialist (CSCS) • NSCA-Certified Personal Trainer (NSCA-CPT) • Certified Special Population Specialist (CSPS) • Tactical Strength and Conditioning Facilitator (TSAC-F) • Certified Performance and Sport Scientist (CPSS)

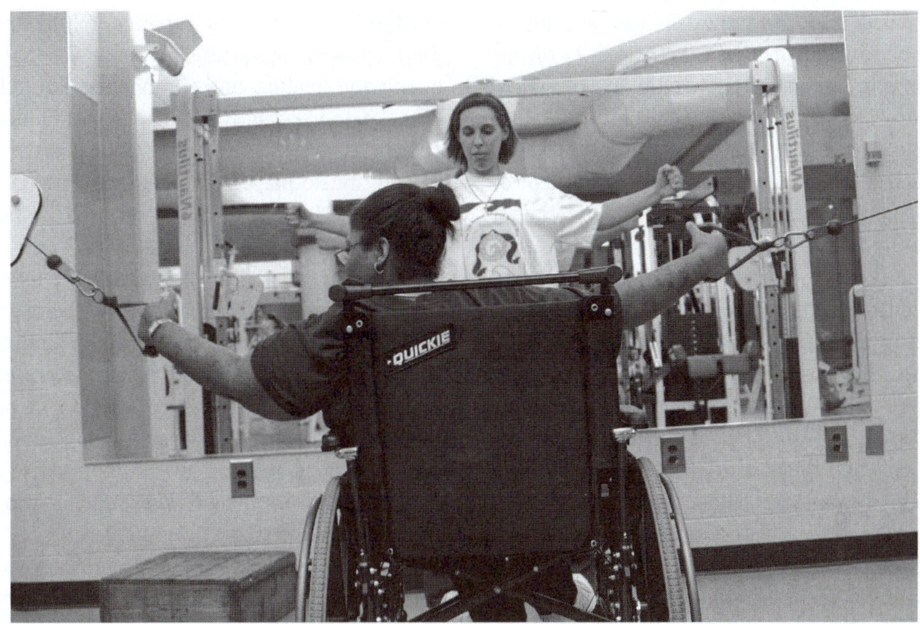

Fitness programs for individuals with disabilities continue to grow. The American College of Sports Medicine in collaboration with the National Center of Health, Physical Activity, and Disability offers a specialty certification, Certified Inclusive Fitness Trainer, for fitness professionals interested in working with individuals with disabilities.

Realistic Reflections

HEALTH-RELATED CAREERS

Health-related career opportunities in the realm of physical education, exercise science, and sport have expanded. Careers in athletic training have become increasingly available. Career opportunities also exist for physical educators, exercise scientists, and sport leaders in health clubs and spas.

Athletic Training

According to the National Athletic Trainers' Association,

> Athletic Trainers (ATs) are health care professionals who collaborate with physicians. The services provided by ATs comprise prevention, emergency care, clinical diagnosis, therapeutic intervention, and rehabilitation of injuries and medical conditions. Athletic training is recognized by the American Medical Association (AMA) as a health care profession.[22]

In recent years, employment opportunities have increased for professionals with expertise in athletic training. Traditional employment opportunities can be found at the college and professional levels. Employment opportunities at the secondary school level are growing. New avenues of practice include working with performing artists, such as dancers.

Another avenue of employment that is available to athletic trainers is in sports medicine clinics. These clinics can be commercial enterprises, affiliated with hospitals, or associated with physical therapy practices. An increasing number of athletic trainers are employed in worksite settings. As part of the wellness programs, athletic trainers can use their knowledge as allied health professionals to provide health education on a diversity of topics and educate employees about the prevention of injury.[23] They may also work in onsite rehabilitation programs.

An athletic trainer's responsibilities are numerous and varied in nature, focusing primarily on the prevention of injury and the rehabilitation of injured athletes. In terms of injury prevention and safety, the athletic trainer performs such preventative measures as taping the ankles and knees of athletes prior to practices and competitions. The athletic trainer works closely with coaches in designing and supervising conditioning programs. Advising coaches and athletes regarding the prevention of injuries is an important responsibility of the athletic trainer. Athletic trainers may also assist in preseason physicals. Checking equipment and checking facilities for safety are tasks often performed by the athletic trainer.

The athletic trainer is often the first person to reach an injured athlete. Thus, the athletic trainer must be prepared to deal with a variety of emergencies. The athletic trainer diagnoses injuries and refers athletes to the appropriate medical personnel for treatment. Working closely with the physician, the athletic trainer implements the prescribed rehabilitation program and administers the appropriate therapeutic treatments. The athletic trainer closely monitors the athlete's efforts and progress during the rehabilitation program. Rehabilitation may be a long and arduous process, and the athletic trainer may need to motivate and encourage the athlete during this trying period to put forth the necessary effort to attain complete recovery. Keeping accurate records of athletes' injuries, the treatment program prescribed, and each athlete's progress during the rehabilitation program is part of the athletic trainer's job.

In addition to competencies pertaining to training, an athletic trainer must possess excellent interpersonal skills. The athletic trainer must work closely with the coaches and the team physician. Establishing and maintaining good rapport with these individuals contributes to a harmonious working relationship. Often, the athletic trainer is placed in a position of telling a coach that an athlete cannot practice, play in an upcoming game, or return to the competition after an injury. Professional competency and a good rapport help make these difficult tasks a bit easier.

Cultural humility is important for athletic trainers. As allied health professionals, athletic trainers need to be aware of how athletes' cultures influence their choices, behavioral decisions, beliefs about health and healing, and compliance with rehabilitation.[24] The training room or clinic should reflect a culturally sensitive environment, be it in the pictures posted, music played or use of educational materials. Culturally sensitive care can help promote optimal outcomes.[24]

The hours worked by trainers are long. In addition to being in the training room before practice and on the sidelines during practice and competition, the trainer must often spend several hours in the training room at the conclusion of practices and competitions, dealing with any injuries that may have occurred and giving treatments. Trainers may have to come in on weekends for practice or contests and to give athletes treatments.

During the season, the athletic trainer travels with the team, and this travel can be quite extensive. Because athletic trainers frequently work several sport activities during the year, the season can go on without end. Less visible responsibilities also consume quite a bit of the athletic trainer's time. Cleaning up the training room, rerolling bandages, sterilizing the whirlpool, and ordering supplies are some of the other responsibilities of the athletic trainer. The long and demanding hours and lack of days off have resulted in some athletic trainers experiencing burnout, just as teachers and coaches do. (See Chapter 12 for a further discussion of burnout and its solutions.)

At the professional level, the athletic trainer's responsibilities include injury prevention and the care and rehabilitation of injured athletes.[25] (See the Athletic Training Practice Domains box.) At the collegiate level, the athletic trainer's responsibilities may be expanded to include teaching courses in the physical education or health program. In an institution that offers an approved athletic training curriculum, athletic trainers can teach courses within the curriculum as well as supervise student athletic trainers.

At the secondary level, an athletic trainer may be employed in several different capacities. A school may employ a full-time athletic trainer, or the district may employ a full-time athletic trainer to serve all of the schools within the district. An individual may

ATHLETIC TRAINING PRACTICE DOMAINS

- Injury and Illness prevention and wellness promotion
- Examination, assessment, and diagnosis
- Immediate and emergency care
- Therapeutic intervention
- Health care administration and professional responsibility

Source: NATA.org.

also be hired as a teacher and athletic trainer. Therefore, athletic trainers may find it advantageous to possess a teaching certificate in physical education, health education, or another academic area. Some schools may contract with a sports medicine center for an athletic trainer and for related services.

Athletic trainers affiliated with clinics generally work fewer hours than individuals in a school or professional setting, and their work schedule is often more regular. Trainers who work in these settings typically work on a one-on-one basis with the athlete. However, an increasing number of schools and community sport programs are contracting with these clinics for services. Therefore, hours worked and working schedules may be similar to those of athletic trainers employed in a school setting.

Salaries for athletic trainers vary widely. The work setting, responsibilities, and amount of experience possessed by the individual influence the salary. In 2020, the median pay was nearly $50,00 a year.[26]

Nearly all states require athletic trainers to be certified and licensed to practice. In order to obtain certification, an individual must be a graduate of an approved athletic training curriculum. Certification requires membership in NATA and passing a written and a practical exam. Information regarding certification procedures can be obtained from NATA's website (www.nata.org).

Wellness, Health Clubs, and Spas

The number of clubs and spas focusing on well-being has increased greatly during the last decade. This industry provides a host of professional services, focusing on enhancement of well-being. The wellness clubs and spas are a global, trillion-dollar industry. For example, pre-COVID, in 2019, the global wellness economy was valued at $4.9 trillion and fell to $4.4 trillion due to the impact of pandemic. As we emerge from the pandemic, the industry is expected to grow and exceed 2019 level.[27] There are multiple sectors to this economy, including healthy eating, nutrition, and weight loss ($946 billion); physical activity ($738 billion); workplace wellness ($49 billion); and spas($68 billion).[27]

LIFESPAN AND CULTURAL PERSPECTIVES: FITNESS, EXERCISE, AND HEALTH

- How can access to health and fitness facilities be improved for underserved populations?
- What modifications to adult exercise tests (e.g., treadmill tests) need to be made to safely and accurately assess fitness in children and adolescents?
- What factors influence employees' use of corporate wellness programs? What can be done to increase usage by all segments?
- How does one's body image influence enrollment and continued participation in a health club?
- What are the effects of long-term resistance training on fitness levels, body image, and self-concepts of adolescents? On adults over 55?

The activities and services offered vary widely. Fitness activities are an integral part of many programs, whether offered on a group or individual basis. Yoga and meditation are popular offerings. Health promotion activities such as healthy eating, nutritional counseling, stress management, and massage are often offered to the clients.

The growth of the wellness industry has led to a variety of employment opportunities for professionals interested in working in these health-related careers. Responsibilities associated with these positions vary widely. Professionals may gain employment in these commercial enterprises as activity instructors or as exercise leaders. They may be responsible for leading an aerobic dance class or for setting up a weight training program for clients and monitoring their performance. In large clubs, professionals may be responsible for training the club's instructors in various exercise techniques and supervising their work with the club's clients. Where weight management and nutritional counseling are primary concerns, professionals may evaluate the clients' dietary habits, design a diet to help them reach their goal, plan individual exercise programs to be followed in conjunction with the diet, and offer nutritional counseling.

Professionals may also be employed to manage these facilities. Even if professionals are employed as fitness instructors, they have many other responsibilities that are managerial in nature. These responsibilities may include record keeping, training and supervising employees, developing and implementing social programs, and soliciting memberships. The varied responsibilities associated with these jobs suggest that in addition to courses in fitness, students should take courses in health, business, psychology, and recreation. As the interest in being fit and healthy in our society grows, opportunities for employment in these settings appear to be excellent.

THERAPY-RELATED CAREERS

There are several therapy- and health-related careers where physical activity plays an important role in working with clients. Dance therapy and

Yoga and meditation are popular offerings at health clubs and spas.

Ryan McVay/Photodisc/Getty Images

therapeutic recreation are two careers in which professionals use physical activity to help their clients improve their well-being. Kinesiotherapists, physical therapists, and chiropractors also use physical activity in working to help their clients achieve their goals.

Dance/Movement Therapy

According to the American Dance Therapy Association (ADTA), dance/movement therapy is the "psychotherapeutic use of movement to promote emotional, social, cognitive, and physical integration of the individual."[28] In dance/movement therapy, a therapeutic relationship is forged between dance/movement therapists and their clients. As an intervention, dance/movement therapy focuses on the needs, interests, and abilities of the individuals and may be an appropriate treatment for individuals with a wide range of developmental, medical, social, physical, and psychological needs. In a manner similar to other therapeutic interventions, dance/movement therapists develop treatment plans and goals, document their sessions, assess participants' progress, and often work as part of an interdisciplinary treatment team.

Dance/movement therapists help individuals develop and expand their movement and dance repertoire, expanding the tools they have to communicate their feelings and ideas to others and perhaps portray emotions they cannot verbally express. Dance/movement therapy can help individuals identify patterns of behavior, improve their self-esteem, and gain confidence. Dance/movement therapy is used in rehabilitation centers, psychiatric centers, geriatric programs, hospitals, and programs for people with disabilities. This therapeutic approach can be used with all segments of the population, from very young to very old people. Opportunities are predicted to increase with the needs of the aging population and expansion of services to people with disabilities driving this growth. Certification standards for dance therapists have been established by the ADTA (www.adta.org).

Therapeutic Recreation/Recreation Therapy

The American Therapeutic Recreation Association defines recreational therapy, sometimes referred to as therapeutic recreation, as a "systematic process that utilizes recreation and other activity-based interventions to address the assessed needs of individuals with illnesses and/or disabling conditions, as a means to psychological and physical health, recovery and well-being."[29] As part of this process, recreational therapists plan, lead, and coordinate programs to address the needs of people with disabilities, injuries, or illnesses. They use a variety of activities, including games, sports, arts and crafts, dance, and music to help individuals improve their well-being. These activities can be individually or group based, address limitations and barriers to participation in recreation, and are selected to help individuals gain the skills and independence to enjoy recreational pursuits related to their interests.

Both undergraduate and graduate degree programs in therapeutic recreation are available. If you have a degree in physical education and/or a foundation in adapted physical education, you may find the field of therapeutic recreation to be of interest to you. More information about therapeutic recreation and certification is available from the American Therapeutic Recreation Association (www.atra-online.com).

Physical Therapy

Physical therapists provide services directed at the restoration, maintenance, and promotion of overall health. Physical therapists work with individuals of all ages to prevent or limit physical disabilities of patients who are injured or who are suffering from disease.[30] Physical therapists work with their patients to restore function, improve mobility, and limit pain.[30]

After reviewing patients' medical histories, physical therapists assess the patients' abilities, including strength, range of motion, balance, coordination, posture, and motor function. A treatment plan is developed and implemented. Treatments might include exercises to help patients who have been immobilized regain their strength, flexibility,

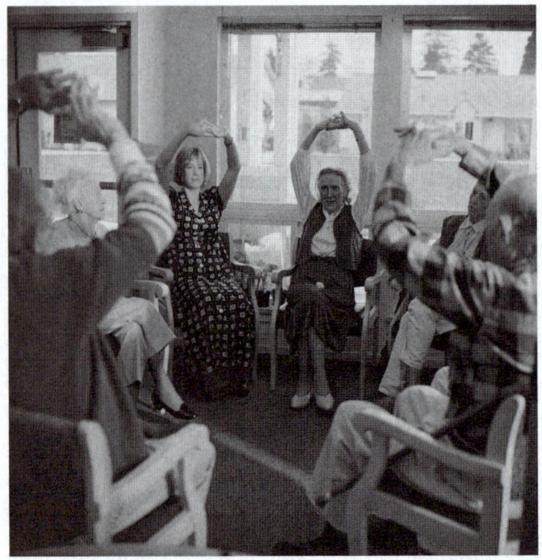

Exercise is important for people of all ages. Flexibility exercises help the elderly retain their range of motion, allowing them to be more independent.

Keith Brofsky/Photodisc/Getty Images

and endurance. To help patients improve their ability to function, physical therapists use many techniques, such as electrical stimulation, hot packs, cold compresses, ultrasound, traction, and massage.[30] They may teach patients how to effectively and efficiently use adaptive and assistive devices, such as crutches and prostheses.[30] Physical therapists also teach patients exercises to do at home.

Physical therapists often practice as part of a health care team that includes physicians, therapists, educators, occupational therapists, and speech-language pathologists. Some physical therapists are generalists who treat a wide range of patients and needs. Others are specialists, focusing on pediatrics, geriatrics, orthopedics, sports medicine, and cardiopulmonary physical therapy. Physical therapists are employed in many different settings, most often in hospitals, clinics, and private offices. Some physical therapists work with their clients in their homes.

Some physical education, exercise science, and sport professionals decide to build upon their education and obtain a doctorate degree in physical therapy. For those who aspire to continue their education in this area, it is important to note that physical therapy programs have strict admission requirements. Biology, chemistry, and physics are just some of the many requirements that must be satisfied. Additionally, most programs require prospective students to work as volunteers in a physical therapy setting for a specified number of hours. For more information about physical therapy, contact the American Physical Therapy Association (www.apta.org).

Chiropractic Care

Chiropractors treat individuals who experience problems with their neuromusculosketal system, such as neck and back pain, to help them regain their health and improve their functional abilities. Chiropractors believe that misalignment of the spinal column impacts the overall health of the individual and, in some cases, lowers resistance to disease. They use a variety of tests to assess individual's status, and then based on the results design a treatment plan.

A variety of treatment approaches are used by chiropractors. Typically, when the individual's problem involves the musculoskeletal system, chiropractors manually adjust the spinal column and, if necessary, other joints using a variety of techniques. Other treatment approaches involve massage, ultrasound, acupuncture, electrical stimulation, and heat therapy. Chiropractors also embrace a holistic approach to health, often counseling their patients on different facets of wellness including nutrition, physical activity, stress management, and lifestyle changes. They do not prescribe drugs or perform surgery.

To become a chiropractor, you must complete a 4-year Doctor of Chiropractic program, which usually requires at least 3 years of undergraduate study to be considered for admission. In order to practice, you must pass the state licensing exam and the National Board of Chiropractic Examiners test. Most chiropractors are self-employed or work as part of a group practice. Some chiropractors may choose to focus their practice on specific

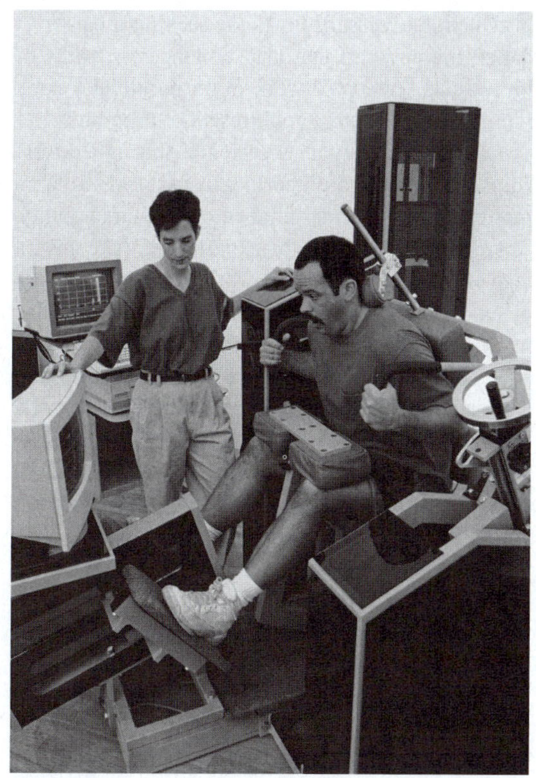

Some physical education, exercise science, and sport professionals build on their undergraduate preparation and obtain a degree in physical therapy.

Keith Brofsky/Photodisc/Getty Images

areas, such as sports or orthopedics. Physical education, exercise science, and sport professionals may find that their studies in anatomy, physiology, natural sciences, physical activity, and health give them a strong background to pursue a career in this area and are an asset in discussing the different facets of wellness with their clients. For more information about pursuing a chiropractic career, contact the Council on Chiropractic Education (www.cce-usa.org).

• • •

Individuals interested in pursuing careers in dance/movement therapy and therapeutic recreation may benefit from courses in adapted physical education, psychology, health, recreation, and counseling. Some professionals build on their background in physical education, athletic training, or exercise science at the undergraduate level to pursue advanced degrees in physical therapy or become a doctor of chiropractic. Professionals aspiring to continue their studies and pursue careers in these areas should, early in their professional preparation, identify courses that are needed as prerequisites for entry into graduate programs in these areas. Students may then use these prerequisite courses as electives in their undergraduate curriculum.

As recognition of the therapeutic, recreational, and social benefits of movement increases, employment opportunities for physical education, exercise science, and sport professionals in these areas will expand.

INCREASING YOUR PROFESSIONAL MARKETABILITY

Students who are interested in fitness-, health-, or therapy-related careers can do much to increase their professional marketability. Taking additional course work, pursuing certification, building on their talents and interests, and gaining practical experience will enhance the credentials of individuals seeking a position in these areas.

Additional courses in health will increase one's marketability. Conducting health promotion programs—nutritional counseling, weight management, substance abuse, smoking cessation, and stress management—is often a responsibility associated with positions in this career area. Thus, courses in nutrition, stress management, pharmacology, and drug education are helpful to students preparing for careers in these areas. Courses in counseling, psychology, and sociology will be helpful as well. Prospective professionals need to develop the skills necessary to help individuals change their fitness and health habits. By understanding various decision making approaches, motivational techniques, and behavior modification strategies, physical education, exercise science, and sport professionals can help clients achieve their goals, whether those goals are increased fitness, weight loss, or learning to manage stress. Because many fitness- and health-related careers include responsibilities such as budgeting, program promotion, membership solicitation, and bookkeeping, courses in business and computer science help professionals perform these aspects of the job.

Obtaining certification may also increase one's marketability. In many exercise specialist and fitness-related jobs, certification is becoming an increasingly common requirement. Even if such certification is not required for employment, certification as a Health Fitness Instructor, for example, may be viewed positively by a prospective employer. Professionals interested in working as exercise specialists or athletic trainers may wish to become certified as Emergency Medical Technicians (EMTs). This will provide additional expertise in the area of emergency care. Belonging to professional organizations such as SHAPE America, ACSM, NSCA, or NATA will also allow one to take advantage of workshops and clinics in one's area of interest.

Building on one's interests and strengths through extracurricular and outside experiences can contribute to one's professional expertise. If you are interested in weight training, for example, and work out frequently, take the time to learn about the different approaches to weight training. Expertise in dance is necessary for those seeking a career in dance therapy and can also enhance the skills of individuals seeking to work in corporate and community fitness centers and preschool programs.

Gaining practical experience through internships, fieldwork, volunteering, or part-time or summer employment can enhance one's marketability. There is no substitute for experience. Take advantage of the opportunities to work in potential places of employment to gain insight into the day-to-day work. Working as an assistant to a recreational therapist or physical therapist in a hospital, assisting in a sports medicine clinic, supervising clients working out in a health spa, and interning in a corporate fitness center provide practical experience and the opportunity to put theoretical knowledge gained in your undergraduate preparation into practice, as well as teach you the skills necessary for employment in these positions. Through various practical experiences, professional contacts can be developed as well.

Professionals can increase their opportunities for employment in fitness-, health-, and therapy-related careers by several means. Taking additional course work, building on one's interests and strengths, obtaining relevant certifications, and gaining practical experience are strategies that will enhance your marketability.

FOCUS ON CAREER: Health, Fitness, and Sports Medicine

PROFESSIONAL ORGANIZATIONS

- American College of Sports Medicine
- National Athletic Trainers' Association
- National Strength and Conditioning Association

PROFESSIONAL JOURNALS

- *Clinical Exercise Physiology*
- *Journal of Athletic Training*
- *Journal of Sport Rehabilitation*
- *Journal of Strength and Conditioning Research*
- *Medicine and Science in Sports and Exercise*
- *The Physician and Sportsmedicine*
- *Strength and Conditioning Journal*

CURRENT TRENDS: MOVING TOWARD THE FUTURE

- The emphasis on prevention and a greater interest by the public in their help will help stimulate the growth of fitness and wellness programs and employment opportunities.
- Medical fitness programs offering a continuum of care will play a greater role in helping individuals of all ages prevent disease, while offering opportunities for rehabilitation for those individuals with various conditions, such as diabetes, cardiovascular disease, and stroke.
- Technology will play an increasing role in helping fitness professionals more closely monitor program participants' progress and assist them in achieving their goals.
- Live streaming and virtual on-demand personal and group training offers convenience to individuals striving to fit a workout into their day.
- Health and wellness coaching will grow in popularity as people seek ways to change their lifestyle and sustain the changes they have made.

SUMMARY

Within the past decade, the contribution of physical activity to health has gained increased recognition. The opportunities for individuals desiring to pursue a career as a fitness or exercise specialist have increased tremendously. Career opportunities exist in preventative and rehabilitative exercise programs. Preventative exercise programs are conducted by corporations, community agencies, and commercial fitness clubs. Rehabilitative exercise programs are typically conducted in a hospital setting, but may be affiliated with corporate fitness programs or community agency programs.

Opportunities for professionals to pursue health-related careers have also grown rapidly. Professionals possessing qualifications in athletic training may find employment working with athletic programs at the professional, collegiate, and, increasingly, secondary level. Employment opportunities also are available in sports medicine clinics, physical therapy clinics, and hospitals. Health clubs and spas provide additional opportunities for employment for qualified professionals.

The recognition that participation in movement and physical activities has therapeutic and psychological benefits as well as physical benefits has stimulated the growth of therapy-related careers. These include careers as dance therapists, recreational therapists, physical therapists, and chiropractors. These careers typically required additional advanced study.

If you are seeking employment in fitness- and health-related careers, you can increase your marketability by becoming certified and taking additional course work in health, business, and psychology. Gaining as much practical experience as possible will also be an asset in securing employment.

It appears that opportunities for qualified individuals in fitness- and health-related careers will continue to increase in the future.

DISCUSSION QUESTIONS

1. Fitness and health clubs have gained in popularity. However, the majority of gym goers have an income of $75000 or above. What can professionals do to reach more individuals whose income is below that figure and provide opportunities for them to be physically active?
2. Should health clubs be mandated to hire only certified fitness professionals? Explain your reasoning. If you believe that health clubs should hire only certified fitness professionals, from what organizations would you accept certifications and why?
3. Worksite wellness programs continue to grow, stimulated in part by the Affordable Care Act. Should employees be mandated to participate in these programs to reduce the burden of health care costs? Why or why not?

GET CONNECTED

American College of Sports Medicine–gives information about the organization, membership, certification, research reports, publications, and official position papers on a variety of topics.

https://www.acsm.org/

American Council on Exercise–contains information on certification, fitness news and facts, and trends. Access the press releases to read information about research projects, such as the most effective exercises or tests of claims made for different fitness products.

https://www.acefitness.org/

National Athletic Trainers' Association–provides information on NATA, membership, certification, position papers, and listing of undergraduate and graduate schools offering an approved NATA curriculum.

https://www.nata.org/

National Strength and Conditioning Association–presents information on membership, certification, and research abstracts.

https://www.nsca.com/

Wellness Council of America–offers an array of resources, many of them free, for professionals employed in corporate wellness programs. Free presentations, publications, and a newsletter help professionals stay abreast of developments in the field.

https://www.welcoa.org/

SELF-ASSESSMENT ACTIVITIES

These activities are designed to help you determine if you have mastered materials and competencies presented in this chapter.

1. Describe the responsibilities of a fitness or exercise specialist. If possible, interview a professional in this career regarding their responsibilities and qualifications.
2. Describe the various employment opportunities for a fitness or exercise professional. Search for jobs online; describe the positions that you found available and qualifications required for employment.
3. Using the information provided in the Get Connected box, read about one of the certification programs available through the American College of Sports Medicine, American Council on Exercise, National Athletic Trainers' Association, or the National Strength and Conditioning Association. For the association you selected, investigate the certification programs, benefits offered to members, costs for certification and membership, and opportunities for continuing education. How could this certification be beneficial to you in your chosen career?
4. Using the information provided in the Get Connected box, locate new research, industry news, and position papers pertaining to health and fitness. Summarize your findings in a brief report.

REFERENCES

1. IHRSA. (2022). The 2021 IHRSA Global Report. Retrieved from ihrsa.org.
2. National Athletic Trainers' Association. Diversity Resources. Retrieved from nata.org/diversity-resources.
3. Sol, N. (1981). Graduation preparation for exercise program professionals. *Journal of Physical Education and Recreation, 52*(7), 76–77.
4. Chittenden. K. (2019). How to be an evidence-based professional. *Personal Training Quarterly*, *6*(1).

5. U.S. Department of Labor. (2004, October 17). *Fact sheet. The affordable care act and wellness programs.* Washington, DC: Author.
6. Johns Hopkins Bloomberg School of Public Health, Institute for Health and Productivity Studies. (2015, February 11). Making workplace health promotion (wellness) programs "work."
7. Goetzel, R. Z., Henke, R. M., Tabrizi, M., Pelletier, K.R., Loeppke, R., Ballard, D. W., Grossmeier, J., Anderson, D. R., Yach, D., Kelly, R. K., McCalster, R., Serxner, S., Selecky, C., Shallengerger, L. G., Fries, J. F., Baase, C., Isaac, F., Crighton, K. A., Wald, P., Exum, E., Shurney, D., & Metz, R. D. (2014). *Do Workplace Health Promotion (Wellness) Programs Work? Journal of Occupational and Environmental Medicine, 56*, 927–934.
8. Chapman, L. S. (2006). Planning wellness: Getting off to a good start, Part 1. *Absolute Advantage, 5*(4).
9. Lewis, R. J., Huebner, W. W., & Yarborough, C. M., III. (1996). Characteristics of participants and nonparticipants in worksite health promotion. *American Journal of Health Promotion, 11*(2), 99–106.
10. Hall, J. L., Kelly, K.M., Burnmeister, L.G., & Merchant, J. A. (2017). Workforce characteristics and attitudes regarding participation in worksite wellness programs. *American Journal of Health Promotion, 31*(5), 391–400. doi: 10.4278/ajhp.
11. Attwood, E. (2015). Prescriptions for fitness. *Athletic Business,* November/December, 86–88.
12. American College of Sports Medicine. (2019). Exercise is medicine: A global initiative. Retrieved from https://www.acsm.org/get-stay-certified/get-certified/specialization/eim-credential.
13. amStatz. (2015). What makes a good personal trainer? These 7 characteristics. Retrieved from acefitness.org/education-and-resources/professional/author/69/amstatz.
14. Pettitt, C. (2013). Wellness coaching certifications: A new career for personal trainers in health care. *Strength and Conditioning Journal, 35*(5), 63–67.
15. Wellcoaches. (2022). Coach certification process. Retrieved from http://wellcoaches.com.
16. National Strength and Conditioning Association. (n.d.). Retrieved from http://www.nsca.org.
17. Collora, C. (n.d.). Choosing the best type of fitness certification. ExerciseScienceGuide. Retrieved from exercise-science-guide.com/.
18. ACSM Certifications. (2019). Retrieved from http://www.acsm.org.
19. American Council on Exercise. (n.d.). Certifications. Retrieved from http://www.acefitness.org.
20. Athletics and Fitness Association of America. (2022). Certifications. Retrieved from http://www.afaa.com.
21. National Strength and Conditioning Association. (202). Certification overview. Retrieved from https://www.nsca.com/certification/certification-overview/.
22. National Athletic Trainers' Association. (2016). Retrieved from http://www.nata.org.
23. Kaiser, D. A. (2006). Location, location: Where are athletic trainers employed? *Athletic Therapy Today, 11*(6), 6–11.
24. Ford, M. G. (2003). Working toward cultural competence in athletic training. *Athletic Therapy Today, 8*(3), 60–66.
25. Board of Certification for the Athletic Trainer. (2017). *Athletic training practice domains 2017.* Retrieved from https://www.bocatc.org/.
26. Bureau of Labor Statistics, U.S. Department of Labor. (2018). Occupational outlook handbook, athletic trainers. Retrieved from http://www.bls.gov/ooh/healthcare/recreational-therapists.htm.
27. Global Wellness Institute. (n.d.) Retrieved from globalwellnessinstitute.org.
28. American Dance Therapy Association. (2016, September 3). Informational brochure. Retrieved from http://adta.org.
29. American Therapeutic Recreation Association. (2019). RT/TR: Restoring function and recreating lives. Retrieved from https://www.atra-online.com/.
30. Bureau of Labor Statistics, U.S. Department of Labor. (2018). Occupational outlook handbook, physical therapists. Retrieved March 15, 2019, from http://www.bls.gov/ooh/healthcare/physical-therapists.htm.

Polka Dot Images/Getty Images

CHAPTER 14

SPORT MANAGEMENT, MEDIA, AND SPORT-RELATED CAREERS

OBJECTIVES

After reading this chapter, students should be able to–

- Identify opportunities for professionals in sport management and entry-level positions in these careers.
- Describe expanding career opportunities in sport media.
- Describe career opportunities in performance and other sport-related careers.
- Discuss how professionals can increase their marketability.

Sport is big business! Although you might think that this is not a very "academic" statement to make, it is probably the best way to sum up the magnitude of the sport industry, both in the United States and globally. Worldwide, millions of people play sport, and billions of people consume it, attending contests in person or taking advantage of the many media outlets to follow events.

Prior to the COVID-19 pandemic, the sport industry had risen to an unprecedented level. In 2019, the global sports market reached an estimated value of $458.8 billion. Participation was on the upswing, sporting good sales reached an all-time high, and fan interest in college and professional teams continued to rise. Media coverage was growing, with broadcast rights sell for billions of dollars, and sport events attract millions of viewers. Digital technologies offered new avenues for promotion of sport and engagement of participants. The continued growth of eSports and fantasy sport captured the interest of millions.

Like businesses across the globe, the sport industry was greatly impacted by the COVID-19 pandemic. Closures of venues, cancellations of live sports, absence or limited spectators, postponements of events, decreases in participation, downturns in sporting goods sales, limited broadcasts, and unemployment of professionals are just a few of the many challenges that confronted the industry.

SOCIAL JUSTICE

Talking Points

- Minorities and women are underrepresented in the sport industry, particularly at upper-level positions. Efforts to enhance diversity in the field need to increase.
- Many stadium and arenas are publicly financed, with owners receiving a host of incentives and tax breaks. Yet, the rising price of tickets stratifies fans across socioeconomic lines, making attending events out of reach for many members of the public.
- The fact that salaries of intercollegiate athletic directors and coaches sometimes exceed that of the college president and that multimillion dollar income is derived from high-profile programs brings into question the place of sport on collegiate campuses and the issue of compensation for student athletes.

Impacted by COVID-19 and measures to contain it, the value of the sport industry declined from $458.8 billion in 2019 to $388.3 billion in 2020. In 2022, we saw the sport industry slowly rebound, recovering from its losses, and taking advantage of new opportunities. As we move forward, the global sports market is expected to reach $599.9 billion by 2025, with a projected growth to $828 billion by 2030.[1]

As you can see, sport is a multibillion dollar business. And, as a big business, with many different sectors–such as sport participation, spectatorship, promotion, administration, sporting goods manufacturing, marketing, and media–it provides a multitude of career opportunities for those who want to work in this field.

However, you should be aware that many of the managerial as well as coaching positions in sport are occupied by white males. The Institute for Diversity and Ethics in Sport (TIDES) assesses the hiring practices of professional and amateur sport organizations in the United States, including such organizations as the National Basketball Association and Division I athletic departments. Based on their research, they issue Racial and Gender Report Cards highlighting diversity among coaches, front office staff, administration, and other key employees.[2] The most recent report cards indicate that while hiring practices have improved, there are still significant gender and racial disparities within sport organizations.

SPORT MANAGEMENT

Sport management is a rapidly growing area of study. Sport management can be defined in many different ways. According to DeSensi, Kelley, Blanton, and Beitel, sport management is "any combination of skills related to planning, organizing, directing, controlling, budgeting, leading and evaluating within the context of an organization or department whose primary product or service is related to sport and/or physical activity."[3] Opportunities within this broad field are many and continue to grow, both within the public and private sectors.

Parkhouse and Pitts define sport management as:

> the study and practice involved in relation to all people, activities, organizations, and businesses involved in producing, facilitating, promoting, or organizing any product that is sport-, fitness-, and recreation-related; and, sport products can be goods, services, people, places, or ideas.[4]

As you can see, sport encompasses a wide range of activities, thereby offering a multitude of career opportunities. Career opportunities can be found in many different areas of sport, including administration, communications/media, facilities and events, finance, law, marketing, personnel, public relations, sponsorship, and tourism.

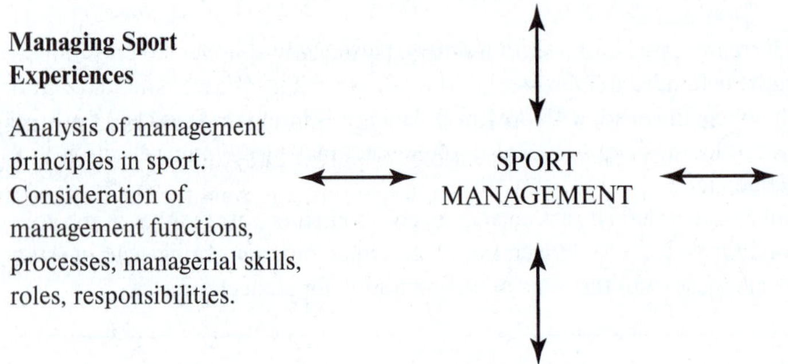
The Sport World
Analysis of the sport environment. Consideration of sport experiences, types of clients, types of activities.
Managing Sport Experiences
Analysis of management principles in sport. Consideration of management functions, processes; managerial skills, roles, responsibilities.
SPORT MANAGEMENT
Organized Sport
Analysis of cultural-philosophical, institutional-organizational aspects of sport. Consideration of sport roles, functions, expectations.
The Sport Enterprise
Analysis of the sport domains. Consideration of purposes, objective, goals, clients of sport organizations, broad career paths, specific career opportunities.

Figure 14-1 Four-factor analysis of sport management.

A conceptual analysis of the dimensions of sport management developed by Blann is shown in Figure 14-1.[5] Sport management is conceptualized as encompassing the sport world, organized sport, management of sport experiences, and the sport enterprise.

With the growth of the sport industry and career opportunities, academic programs in sport management were established. For those aspiring to pursue a career in sport management, there are more than 400 undergraduate and 200 graduate programs in the United States offering a degree in this area. Typically degree programs focus on helping students develop knowledge and skills while integrating sport, business, and management principles and practices needed in the sport industry. Some programs offer students the opportunity to specialize in certain areas, such as sport marketing, athletic administration, or sport media.

To ensure that undergraduate majors in sport management acquire needed competencies, in 2000, the North American Society for Sport Management (NASSM) and the National Association for Physical Education and Sport (NASPE) Taskforce were formed to identify competencies that should be included within an undergraduate professional preparation curriculum. The undergraduate content areas include:

- Sociocultural dimensions
- Management and leadership in sport
- Ethics in sport management
- Marketing in sport
- Communication in sport
- Budget and finance in sport
- Legal aspects of sport
- Economics in sport
- Governance in sport
- Field experience in sport management[6]

The field experience is considered a critical aspect of preparation for a career in sport management. Students usually intern in a sport management setting for a semester or summer, working at least 40 hours a week and accumulating at least 400 hours. This experience is supervised by a faculty member from the undergraduate institution, as well as by a professional at the internship site. Additional practical experience can be gained by volunteering or working in a sport management position during the summer or on a part-time basis during the school year. Practical experiences are also a good way to investigate the growing number of career opportunities in this rapidly expanding field and to begin to network with professionals in the field.

In 2008, the Commission on Sport Management Accreditation (COSMA) was established by NASPE and NASSM.[7] This accrediting body strives to promote and recognize excellence in sport management education, at both the undergraduate and graduate levels. Programs that meet the standards are accredited for a period of 7 years.

While the sport industry is a broad field, there appear to be some common functions associated with its practices. These are typically grouped into planning, organizing, leading, and evaluating.[8] Being able to establish both short- and long-term goals, and set forth a strategic plan to attain them, is one function of sport managers. Organizing people and a multitude of resources to be in line with your goals is critical. This aspect includes identifying tasks to be performed, responsibilities that need to be fulfilled, and hiring and ongoing training of employees. Leading involves delegating tasks and responsibilities to specific people, motivating employees to achieve specific goals, and managing change. Evaluating encompasses assessing progress toward attaining short- and long-term goals, reviewing job performance by employees, and incorporating this information into the planning process.

Sport managers need many different skill sets, but among the most important are people skills.[9] The ability to work with people, to communicate effectively, to motivate people to achieve, to acknowledge their contributions, to foster collaboration, and to interact in ways that respect people's dignity are important skills. In today's multicultural society and with the increasing globalization of sport, the ability to work effectively and respectfully with diverse populations is important.[9] Other skills that are important are those related to technology, an increasing necessity for many sport management positions.

The increased growth of athletics, sport participation by all segments of our society, and sport-related businesses has created a need for individuals trained in sport management. There are many different career paths that students with an interest in sport management can pursue. The dynamic nature and growth of the field lead to new and plentiful career opportunities for students well prepared in this area. Figure 14-2, developed by Blann, shows some of the sport management career paths.[10] Employment opportunities include sport administration, management of sport clubs and facilities, administration of sport and leisure social services, sport marketing, and sport communication.

Individuals interested in pursuing a career in sport management need to realize that they will likely begin their career working in an entry-level position, often with limited responsibilities. From this position, competent individuals can work their way up the career ladder to middle and top management positions. Each step-up the ladder typically requires assuming increased, and often broader, responsibilities. Salaries in this field vary widely, commensurate with the position and responsibilities.

CAREERS IN SPORT MANAGEMENT

Athletic administration, collegiate and workplace recreation management, sport facilities management, sport retailing, and sport marketing opportunities are described in the next section. Additionally, a myriad of opportunities exist for qualified individuals in professional organizations, conferences, and leagues.

Athletic Administration

There are many job opportunities in the field of athletic administration, both at the high school and collegiate levels. Opportunities available at each level are influenced by many factors, such as the size of

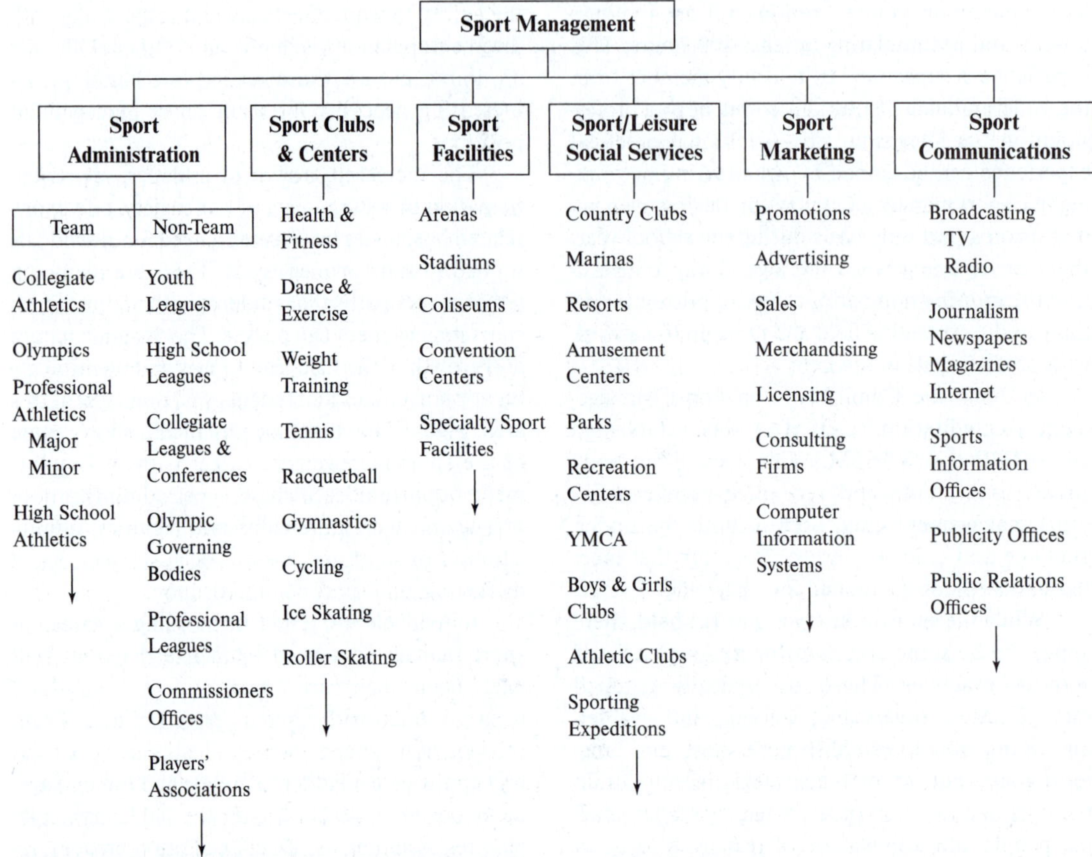

Figure 14-2 Sport management career paths.

the program, level of competition, budget, and support from institutional administrators, such as the superintendent of schools or the president of the college/university.

At the high school level, athletic directors' responsibilities and support staff vary, based on the size of the school and athletic programs. Some athletic directors may have as their sole responsibility the overseeing all aspects of the athletic programs. This is often the case at very large schools, with extensive athletic programs at the modified, junior varsity, and varsity levels. In smaller schools, athletic directors may teach, coach, and even serve as the director of physical education. At the college level, the athletic director, as an administrator, may delegate some of these responsibilities but maintains the responsibility for overseeing all aspects of the program.

At the collegiate level, many administrative opportunities exist, with the number of administrative positions and associated responsibilities depending on the nature and size of the athletic program. While athletic directors are responsible for overseeing the program, they typically have other administrators reporting to them such as associate and/or assistant athletic directors. Other administrative positions that might be found in collegiate athletic programs include director of fund-raising, marketing director, recruiting coordinator, compliance coordinator, director of ticket sales, director of facilities, and student academic advancement coordinator. Not all colleges and universities have these positions; oftentimes, in smaller programs, athletic directors and their assistants may fulfill the responsibilities associated with these positions.

At all levels, athletic directors are responsible for the administration of all facets of the men's and women's athletics. First and foremost, this includes ensuring the well-being of student athletes. Responsibilities include both the hiring and ongoing supervision of coaches and assistant coaches as well as their staff. Athletic directors must be knowledgeable regarding the rules and regulations governing athletic competition, including rules pertaining to the recruitment and eligibility of athletes. Other tasks are scheduling athletic contests; arranging for officials; and, for competitions involving travel, planning for transportation, lodging, and meals.

Athletic directors are also responsible for the safety of the coaches, athletes, and spectators at home contests. This involves working closely with security personnel and making careful provisions for crowd control. Athletic directors work closely with other personnel involved in athletics such as the athletic trainers and sport information directors. Establishing a good working relationship with the facilities manager and maintenance staff is important as well.

Development and management of the athletic budget is an important function. In some institutions, athletic directors engage in extensive fundraising activities. Establishing and maintaining good relationships with the community, local support groups such as booster clubs, and alumni are vital to the success of the athletic program. Athletic directors must also attend professional meetings to keep abreast of changes in rules and governance.

Many institutions have academic support programs for their student athletes. Through these programs, student athletes have access to tutoring, supervised study tables, and courses in life skills. The academic coordinator works with faculty and other academic resources across campus to help student athletes fulfill their academic obligations. At the collegiate level, tutors may travel with the team, providing student athletes with academic support when they are on the road for an extended period of time.

Salaries associated with the various jobs in athletic administration vary widely, depending on the extent of the responsibilities and the size of the program. Salaries at the high school level can range from a stipend added to their teaching salary or an administrative salary. At the collegiate level, salaries depend on the level of responsibility and the profile of the athletic programs. Athletic directors at NCAA Division I schools in major conferences, such as the SEC or Big Ten, can make millions of dollars.

Students interested in pursuing a career in athletic administration may find it helpful to know that at the high school level, directors of athletics typically have a degree in physical education and coaching experience. They might have teaching responsibilities in addition to their administrative responsibilities.

At the high school level, most athletic directors have a physical education degree, some teaching experience, and often an advanced degree in athletic administration. Collegiate athletic directors may have a physical education degree, a sport management degree, or a business degree. Additionally, oftentimes, an advanced degree, either a master's or doctoral degree, is required. Students aspiring to a career in athletic administration may want to take advantage of opportunities to intern or volunteer at their college or a high school athletic department. Additionally, the NCAA offers scholarships for postgraduate internships in athletic administration.

Collegiate Recreation and Wellness

In the past decade, college and university recreation programs have grown tremendously. According to NIRSA: Leaders in Collegiate Recreation, collegiate recreation encompasses services and programs that provide recreation opportunities for the entire campus community. These include both formal and informal recreational activities, encompassing intramural sport, fitness and wellness programs, sport clubs, collegiate competition, outdoor recreation, and aquatic programs and are available to students, faculty, and staff.[11] The development of multimillion-dollar facilities, the increasing comprehensiveness of campus recreational programs, and the growing interest in fitness and wellness have created an array of job opportunities for competent professionals.

Many titles have been used to describe the individual charged with the administration of these programs. These titles include director of campus recreation and wellness, director of recreational sports, and director of intramurals. Depending on the institution, the intramural and campus recreation programs may be administered through student services, the physical education department, or the athletic department.

Responsibilities associated with this position are wide-ranging. One of the primary responsibilities is promoting participation. This requires scheduling activities and tournaments that are of interest to students, publicizing programs, and working closely with campus groups such as residential life and student government to promote these programs. Training and supervision of officials are essential if programs are to run smoothly and safely. The director may also be responsible for instructional programs and the supervision of sport and recreation clubs. Often, the director is assigned to supervise physical education and athletic facilities and open recreation programs such as recreational swimming. This may entail the training and supervision of numerous students to serve as lifeguards, gymnasium supervisors, or building security guards.

Teaching responsibilities may or may not have teaching responsibilities, depending on the size of the program. Programs are usually offered from late afternoon to late at night; frequently in schools with limited facilities, intramurals cannot start until the athletic teams have finished their practices. Programs may also be offered on weekends. Professionals who are interested in promoting educational values through activities and in providing opportunities for others to experience the satisfaction derived from participation will find working in intramural and campus recreation programs an enjoyable career.

As a student, you can gain experience in this area by participating in some of these activities yourself. In addition to playing in the intramural program, you can take advantage of opportunities to advance by accepting positions as a building supervisor, working as an official, and instructing classes, such as rock climbing. You can also seek out opportunities dealing with program administration, such as promoting the program through social media, holding precompetition orientations for teams, or working with the leader of sport clubs. Additional information on career opportunities and programming is available on the NIRSA website.

Workplace Recreation

More and more companies are providing recreational and sport opportunities for their employees. As the number of programs has increased, so has the need for qualified professionals to direct these activities. The responsibilities associated with this position are similar to those associated with the director of intramurals or collegiate recreation. These responsibilities include establishing a program of activities, setting up athletic teams, scheduling contests, providing for instruction, and supervising personnel. Professionals may also direct wellness and fitness activities, offer team-building activities, and conduct adventure programs, such as high and low ropes courses. As workplace recreation programs continue to grow, so will opportunities for qualified professionals.

Sport Facilities Management

Facilities managers are needed to manage community, municipal, and commercial facilities such as aquatic centers, ice arenas, domed stadiums, sport complexes, and golf courses, just to name a few sites. College and university facilities, fitness centers and health clubs offer opportunities for employment.

Of primary concern to the sport facilities manager is the safety of individuals using the facility. This involves making sure that the facility and equipment are maintained according to accepted industry standards. Knowledge of building codes, health and sanitation requirements, and regulations governing operations are necessary in this position. In facilities that are used for competitions, such as stadiums, the facilities manager must make

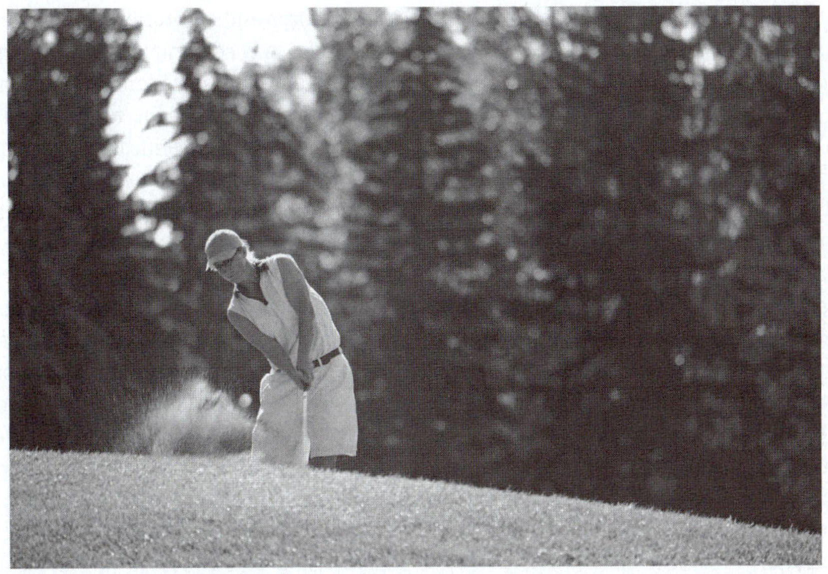

Maintenance of facilities, such as golf courses, often require specialized training.
Don Hammond/Design Pics

Job opportunities in collegiate and professional athletics have increased during the last decade.
U.S. Air Force photo by Staff Sgt Alan Garrison

provisions to ensure the safety and well-being of spectators as well as participants. The manager must be concerned with crowd control and is responsible for security personnel.

The facilities manager also is concerned about the business aspects of managing the facility, and can impact the financial success of the operation. The facility must be scheduled for maximum use to ensure a profitable financial status. The manager may also supervise other financial aspects of the facility, such as ticket sales, concessions, and parking. The last decade has seen an increased focus on sustainability in the building and the management of facilities; overseeing sustainability and environmental efforts might fall within the scope of the facility manager. As the number of facilities continues to grow, opportunities in this area for qualified personnel will expand.

Sport Retailing

Sales of sporting goods–equipment, apparel, and shoes–were at an all time high prior to COVID-19 pandemic. Sales are rebounding and are predicted to continue to grow and surpass previous levels. Exercise equipment and golf equipment top sporting goods sales. Sales of sport apparel, sport activewear, athletic footwear, and licensed sports products are in the billions of dollars. Sport retailing is a booming business. The public's growing interest in sport, fitness, and physical activity has stimulated sales, and the traditional markets such as schools, colleges, universities, and professional teams have remained strong. Consequently, job opportunities in sport retailing, in both management and sales, have increased and will continue to grow.

Job opportunities are available as manufacturers' representatives. An individual employed in this capacity, perhaps as a representative for Nike, may sell to buyers for sporting goods stores and to athletic teams in a certain region. Manufacturers' representatives are committed to increasing their company's share of the market. A manufacturer's representative success depends to a great extent on the quality and reputation of the product and the establishment of personal contacts with buyers for these stores and institutions. Manufacturers' representatives may often submit bids for equipment and goods wanted by stores and institutions. Successful bidding requires that the representative be able to meet the buyer's specifications for the equipment and goods at the lowest cost. Other opportunities in sport retailing include positions as a manager or owner of a company.

Sporting goods stores, like Dick's Sporting Goods, retail a variety of sporting goods, ranging from bicycles, camping equipment, fitness equipment, apparel, footwear, and a host of other products. These products, sourced from manufacturers and wholesalers, are then sold to the consumer. These purchases take place in the store or increasingly via online ordering or e-commerce. As a store manager, you are responsible for hiring, training, and supervising employees as well as scheduling their work hours to ensure store coverage. Your responsibilities might encompass budgeting, payroll, ordering, promotions and a host of other tasks designed to contribute to the overall profitability of the store.

Jobs are available as salespeople selling directly to the consumer in sporting goods stores. Working

Job opportunities in sport retailing may involve direct sales, retail management, or serving as a manufacturer's representative.

Richard Ransier/Corbis/VCG/Digital Stock/Getty Images

in sales requires you to be extremely knowledgeable about the products you are selling. The consumer typically expects the salesperson to be an expert on all types of equipment and products. This position requires strong interpersonal skills as well as the ability to identify individuals' needs and to sell them a product that meets those needs. These sales positions provide experience in the retail environment and down the road could lead to a position as an assistant store manager or manager.

Sport Marketing

Sport marketing is a growing, dynamic field, with new technologies creating a myriad of career opportunities for those interested in this area. Sport marketing typically involves the marketing of sports events, teams, and athletes as well as the use of sports to market products to target audiences, be they fans or a specific population of consumers (e.g., adults age 20–30 years with an income of $75,000 or more). Today, sport marketers actively pursue new and varied revenue streams, strive to find ways to forge deeper fan connections, and use digital media and immersive technologies to expand their marketing efforts.

Negotiating then nurturing sponsorship deals is one career option. Sport organizations at all levels have turned to sponsorships as a means to earn revenue, and sponsors are turning to sports as a means to promote visibility and sales. The National Football Leagues (NFL) sponsorship revenue was $1.8 billion U.S. dollars in 2021, technology businesses, lottery and gambling companies, and alcohol accounting for a significant portion of the revenue.[12] In the National Basketball Association (NBA), sponsorship revenue reached $1.46 billion in 2020–2021 season. In addition, some teams earn more than $15 million a year from sponsors who paid to have their 2-inch branded patch appear on team jerseys.[13] Naming rights to stadiums are offer tremendous visibility to the company's brand, serving as a long-term advertisement. In late 2021, Staples Center, home of many professional Los Angles teams, changed its name to Crypto.com Arena in a $700 million, 20-year deal. Some teams, such as the MLS Red Bulls, are sponsored by corporations. Sponsorships for major sports events, such the FIFA World Cup, easily reach over $100 million.[14] During the last World Cup, Adidas and Nike both spent millions sponsoring teams, knowing that as teams advanced in the tournament, their sale of products, such as jerseys, would increase, yielding a strong return on their investment.[14]

Team endorsements of specific products capitalize on fans' loyalty to the team. Athletes capitalize on their celebrity, earning millions, to endorse specific products. Recent NCAA changes allow intercollegiate athletes to monetize their fame, capitalizing on their name, image, and likeness (NIL). This allows collegiate athletes to take advantage of sponsorship opportunities. These opportunities for personal branding open up additional employment possibilities for those interested in this field.

Sports marketers use research to ensure that their product and advertising is reaching the right target audience. Careers in designing advertising, negotiating sponsorships and endorsements, and analyzing the effectiveness of various marketing campaigns are just some of the opportunities associated with sport marketing.

Some jobs focus on promoting attendance at sports events as well as enhancing the sport experience for the consumer–the fans. This focus on customer relationship management encompasses a myriad of opportunities for individuals interested in this aspect of sport marketing. Ticketing strategies and the use of video and digital technologies to enrich the in-person experience for fans attending the event are an important part of this endeavor. Other jobs focus on the development of attractive immersive programs to engage fans off-site.

The tremendous growth of eSports presents other opportunities for sports marketers. eSports feature players or teams competing in video game competitions, with an increasing number of tournaments, such as the Dota 2 or League of Legends, broadcasting live through online streaming services.[15] In some tournaments, gamers compete for millions of dollars in prize money. More professional sport organizations, such as the NBA and FIFA, are sponsoring their own eSport

The growth of eSports presents many opportunities for sports marketers.
Gorodenkoff/Shutterstock

competitions. It is estimated that more than 59 million players engage in eSports, with a viewership approaching 500 million worldwide.[15] With market revenues projected to grow to as much as $1.62 billion in 2024, opportunities for management and marketing in this growing enterprise continue to grow.[16]

Career Opportunities in Professional and Sport Organizations

Qualified physical education, exercise science, and sport professionals may find employment in one of the many professional or specific sport organizations such as SHAPE America, NCAA, NFHS, Ladies Professional Golf Association (LPGA), the NHL, or the United States Tennis Association (USTA). The globalization of sport creates more opportunities for employment in countries outside of the United States. For example, the National Basketball Association (NBA) has international offices in South Africa, London, China, Mexico, and Canada, to name a few. The National Football League (NFL), in an effort to expand their global reach, has offices in the United Kingdom, China, Mexico, and Canada. Sports leagues in other countries, such as the renown English Premier League [i.e., football (soccer)] or Australian cricket, offer opportunities for employment as well. Other jobs are available in athletic conferences, such as in the offices of the Big Ten or the Big East or in foundations, such as the Women's Sports Foundation.

The jobs available in professional organizations vary, depending on the nature of the organization and its size. Entry-level managerial positions may be available dealing with the day-to-day operations of the organization. Other positions may entail fund-raising, handling public relations, conducting membership drives, and directing special projects. Writing for the organization's newsletter, editing its periodicals, and directing its social media effort are among the jobs performed by employees working for professional organizations. Professionals are also needed to serve as liaisons with the various committees of the organization. Still other positions in the organization may involve conducting special research projects, gathering data, and performing statistical analyses. Many of the responsibilities associated in working in a professional sport organization, such as the NFL or the Big Ten, entail responsibilities similar to those found in collegiate athletic administration. Compliance with rules, administration of the budget, scheduling, and social media outreach are just a few of the many responsibilities typically found in these organizations.

Individuals interested in this kind of career can obtain further information by contacting professional organizations in their area of interest or speaking to knowledgeable faculty. Some organizations may offer internships to students. Students interested in internships should write to the organization requesting information on these opportunities or check on the Web.

Sport Analytics

Sport analytics is a growing career. More sport organizations and teams at all levels are incorporating sport analytics to help them make a multitude of decisions related to such areas as player talent, injury prevention, coaching strategy, and profitability.

The performance of players during competition and training and analysis of teams' strategies are one of the biggest areas of sport analytics. Today's technologies generate a huge amount of data; the ability to analyze this data and use it to make decisions to improve performance and gain an edge on the competition is one of the key goals of sport analytics.[17]

Wearable technology provides information about players' performance, including key physiological parameters such as heart rate or respiration.[18] Tracking technology using RFID tags attached to players allows the monitoring of players' movements, providing such information as mileage covered, speed, acceleration, and movement patterns.[18] The generation of real-time data during games and practices can help the coaching staff to adjust their plans to optimize players' and teams' performance.

Organizations use marketing analytics to improve their business operations, incorporating the marketing research data into their decision making as they strive to improve their profit. The use of analytics in customer relationship management is a critical aspect of many organizations. Analytics help organizations grow their fan base, and engage with them effectively. Analysis of data gathered from ticketing programs, point-of-sale terminals at concessions and stadium stores, and staffing programs allow organizations to sell more tickets, retail more merchandise, and staff events properly–all important considerations relative to the bottom line.

Computer technology, applied mathematics, statistical analysis, predictive modeling, database management, and sport economics are just some of the skills needed in the area of sport analytics. However, the ability to "crunch" all this data is not enough. You have to be able to translate all the data into "actionable insights" and communicate this information to players, coaches, and managers in an easily understandable way so that they can consider the information as they make their decisions.[19] If you have a passion for sports and a love for analysis, sport analytics might be a good career for you.

CAREERS IN SPORT MEDIA

The pervasiveness of interest in sport in our society has contributed to the growth of career opportunities in sport communication. The last decade has also seen an increase in sport coverage by the media. For example, the number of sport periodicals–both print and digital–has grown, including the number of periodicals dealing with specific sport areas such as running, body building, skiing, swimming, and bowling. Cable television channels such as ESPN and FS1 provide round-the-clock coverage of sport. The growth of the Internet and digital media have created a whole new host of media opportunities and related occupations.

If you are interested in a career in sport media, many different opportunities are available. These careers include sport broadcasting, sportswriting, sport journalism, sport photography, and sports information. Jobs in web development are available and there is a growing market for professionals with expertise in social media.

Sport Broadcasting

Sport broadcasting is a career field that offers many different opportunities for those individuals with a passion for sharing their love of sport with others.

Radio, television, and digital media platforms enable broadcasts of news, programming, and stories to reach local, regional, national, and international audiences. The growth of live streaming of events, on-demand replay, satellite radio, and mobile apps provides greater access for fans while increasing opportunities for those who want to work in this field.

Career opportunities in this field tend to focus on three areas: on the air, content production, and technical production.[20] On-the-air positions are the most visible careers. In these positions, sportscasters work as play-by-play announcers, color commentators, and/or sideline reporters. Sportscasters might host a program from a studio or onsite at live events. This position requires the ability to work well under pressure, communicate clearly and articulately to the audience, and write effectively. In addition, an encyclopedic knowledge of sports is needed. Sportscasters need to be knowledgeable about the skills, strategies, tactics, and rules used in sport, including the techniques of officiating. The audience looks to sportscasters to provide expert insight into what the athletes are experiencing, discuss the significance of the competition in relation to the season, and comment on coaching decisions. Sportscasters may focus on an array of different sports or specialize in one particular sport, such as ice hockey or curling.

Content production is another facet of broadcasting operations.[20] While on-the-air talent might do some of these responsibilities, in larger organizations, professionals specialize in these behind-the-scene tasks. Writing and editing copy for the on-the-air talent, preparation of video clips for broadcasting, and creating graphic packages are a part of content production. Another aspect of content production is operating the camera. Camera operators work either in a studio or film live events. Working in a studio is easier than filming live events as the camera operator responds to cues from the director and keeps the camera focused on the on-the-air talent. Working live events is a bit more challenging; often, camera operators have specific responsibilities at these events whether it is to focus on the end zone or provide a wide angle view of the players on the pitch. Producers are in charge of the sportscast. They organize the content, deciding the time allotted to each story or segment, and the order in which content is aired.

Technical production focuses on different aspects of getting the sportscast on the air, controlling the audio and visual aspects of sportscasts.[20] Audio engineers deal with complex equipment and all aspects of production of audio for the sportscasts. Some engineers work with satellite feeds, making sure to upload content in the most efficient way possible while troubleshooting any issues that might occur. Graphic operators are responsible for putting graphics dealing with scores, players' stats, and a host of other information upon the screen to support the video and sportscasters' comments. Directors are in charge of the entire operation and work in the control room to orchestrate the production.

Preparation for careers in this industry varies according to the position being sought, and sport media programs vary from institution to institution. As you can see, some positions require a great deal of technical knowledge and skills (e.g., audio engineer), while others emphasize more the ability to communicate and knowledge of sports (e.g., on-the-air sportscaster). However, gaining practical experience can enhance your chances of gaining an entry-level position in this career field. You can gain experience by volunteering to announce and provide live commentary at college or university sporting events or events at the local high school. Try to gain employment or even serve as a volunteer at a local television or radio station for the summer or on a part-time basis throughout the year. Prospective sportscasters should also collect samples of their work to share with future employers. Audio and video recordings of one's performance as a broadcaster and copies of any reviews received can be an asset in gaining employment in this field.

Sportwriting and Journalism

Individuals with a talent for writing may decide to pursue a career as a sport journalist or a sportswriter. Writing for online sports sites is another popular career. The sport journalist may find opportunities for work with newspapers and in sport magazines, the number of which is increasing all the time. Sport magazines, such as *Sports Illustrated*, may provide coverage of several areas or, like *Runner's World*, provide coverage of one specific sport.

Sportswriters and journalists may cover events live or write in-depth or feature articles about athletes or various topics in the sport world. As in sport broadcasting, covering the athletic event and reporting, it is the most visible part of this occupation. Researching stories, compiling statistics, and interviewing athletes and coaches are all functions of the sportswriter and journalist. The ability to meet deadlines and to write stories under time pressures is required. The work hours, opportunities to travel, and the rewards associated with this profession are similar to those associated with sport broadcasting.

A background in physical education, exercise science, and sport can be helpful to the sportswriter and journalist. It provides the writer and journalist with a broader understanding of the demands and nature of sport. For example, a sport journalist with course work in sport psychology may be better able to explain to the public why some athletes fail to perform under pressure, or "choke," whereas other athletes appear to rise to the occasion. A sportswriter with an understanding of exercise physiology may be better able to explain what happens physiologically to athletes as they endeavor to complete the rigorous marathon.

Today, with the increase in the digital media, experience with technology and social media is an asset. Practical experience, as in all careers, is a plus in gaining employment. Many sportswriters and journalists have gotten their start covering sports for their high school papers and have continued this work for their collegiate newspaper. Experience working as an editor of the high school or college paper is an asset as well. These experiences can help prospective sportswriters and journalists gain internships or employment with local newspapers and sport publications. To assist in gaining employment in this field, individuals should keep a well-organized portfolio of their work.

Interest in sports for athletes with disabilities continues to grow. Here, a local news station interviews a basketball player who has a double amputation.

Realistic Reflections

Sport Photography

A career as a sport photographer may be attractive to individuals who have a strong interest in photography and the desire to communicate to others the essence and meaning of sport through this medium. Opportunities for sport photographers exist with newspapers and sport publications, be it in the print or digital medium. Additionally, many sport photographers pursue their careers independently as freelance photographers, taking advantage of the web to showcase their work to a wide audience.

Your sports background can enhance your career as a sport photographer. Knowing the essentials of sport skills from work completed in biomechanics can help you understand the critical aspects of the skill performance and where to position yourself to get the best angle for the photograph. Knowledge gained from exercise physiology of the stress endured by athletes working at their utmost level of effort, understanding gained from the sociology of sport of the significance of sport in our society, and appreciation gained from sport philosophy of the personal meaning that sport holds for its participants can help the sport photographer better capture the true nature and meaning of sport in pictures.

Courses in photography, graphics, and art will be of assistance to the potential sport photographer. Take advantage of opportunities to gain practical experience. Covering sporting events for the campus or local newspapers, taking sport photographs for the yearbook, and contributing photographs to the sports information office to be used in promotional efforts are several ways to gain practical experience and exposure. Sport photographers should maintain a portfolio of their work so that potential employers may readily discern their talent.

Sports Information

The sports information director's primary function is to promote athletic events through the various media. Opportunities for employment as a sports information director are found mainly at colleges and universities. At the professional level, many of the same responsibilities performed by the sports information director are handled by the director of public relations.

Among many responsibilities, sports information directors must maintain records and compile statistical information on all teams. They design and prepare promotional brochures for each sport; this involves writing the copy for the text, obtaining photographs of the athletes, preparing the layout, and making arrangements for printing. Preparation of programs for various contests, including obtaining advertisements for the programs, is another professional task. Responsibilities may encompass preparing material and/or designing the institution's athletic website. The management of social media may also fall under the director's responsibilities.

The sports information director provides assistance to the media covering home contests, phones in contest results to various media, writes press and television releases, writes commercials, and arranges press conferences and interviews for the media with coaches and athletes. Organization of special promotional events is also the responsibility of the sports information director. In a small school, the sports information director may handle all these responsibilities personally, whereas in a larger school, the sports information director may have several assistants. The hours are long, because the sports information director may be expected to personally cover many of the athletic events, and quite a bit of travel may be required.

Being a sports information director requires the ability to work closely with the members of the college and university administration, as well as the athletic administration, coaches and athletes, and members of the various media. Excellent communication skills–writing, speaking, and interpersonal skills–are essential to this profession. In addition to a background in sport, courses in public relations, advertising, writing, speech, and web development are helpful. Experience gained in covering high school or college sport as a sportswriter or journalist or as a sport broadcaster is valuable. Faced with numerous responsibilities and demands, many college sports information directors would welcome volunteers interested in

Marketing of events is one career option within this field.
U.S. Air Force photo by Master Sgt Michael A. Kaplan

working in this career field. Volunteers may be assigned to work on promotional brochures, travel with teams to cover the competition, or work with the media covering home events. Volunteers should keep a file of their work. Prospective sports information directors may wish to obtain additional information from the College Sports Information Directors of America (COSIDA) (https://cosida.com/).

Web Development and Social Media

The growth of the Internet and the web expanded opportunities for individuals interested in sport communication. The online sport industry is rapidly expanding, and there is a need for individuals who have the technological qualifications and sport expertise to work in this area. Web developers design, create, and update sports sites for athletic departments, professional teams, sport organizations, newspapers, and television networks. They write the material, create the layout, incorporate graphics and other electronic media into the site, and upload the site to the organization's server. They update the site and continually strive to promote the organization's presence on the web.

The omnipresence of social media and the proliferation of digital technologies has created numerous employment opportunities in this area. The social-media marketing director assumes responsibility for promoting the sports program through the use of social media. Social media is typically part of an integrated marketing program that allows organizations to communicate, share information, and connect with their target audiences. Organizations can use social media to readily implement marketing campaigns, not only focusing on reaching their target audiences but receiving communication from them as well. Opportunities for individuals skilled in the use of social media continue to increase as many elements of their sport industry see this as a valuable addition to their organizations.

PERFORMANCE AND OTHER SPORT CAREERS

Dance

Individuals talented in the various forms of dance may aspire to careers as professional dancers. Although college and university programs offer a major or a minor in dance performance, most college-age dancers have developed their talents through many years of private lessons, often beginning at an early age. Opportunities for professional dancers may be found with dance companies, theater companies, and television shows. Resorts, cruise ships, and clubs where nightly entertainment is offered to guests are other settings for employment.

Individuals who enjoy dance but do not aspire to careers as professional dancers may decide to transmit their love for dance to others through teaching. Opportunities for dance teachers may be found at schools, colleges, and universities. Many individuals choose to teach dance at private studios; some start their own studios as well. Working as a dance therapist (Chapter 13) is also a viable career choice.

Opportunities for individuals interested in a dance-related career can be found in dance administration. Lee states that

> dancers should capitalize on their professional strengths of fund raising, promotion, management, and administrative skills while integrating their knowledge of dance in such careers in dance company management as artistic director, managing director, development officer, public relations officer, and booking agent.[21]

Dance administration offers many exciting careers for those who have a passion for dance.

Professional Athletics

Highly skilled athletes may desire to pursue a career in professional athletics. Although many aspire to a career as a professional athlete, few individuals actually attain this goal. The number of positions for individuals in professional sports is very limited. The NCAA estimates that only 1.2% of NCAA men's basketball players enter the professional ranks, and about 1% of women basketball players.[22] The NCAA estimates that the percent of NCAA football players who enter the professional ranks is 1.6%; baseball players have the greatest percentage entering the professional league–9.5%.[22] There are professional opportunities in other sports as well such as motor cross, soccer, volleyball, golf, or track and field, just to name a few.

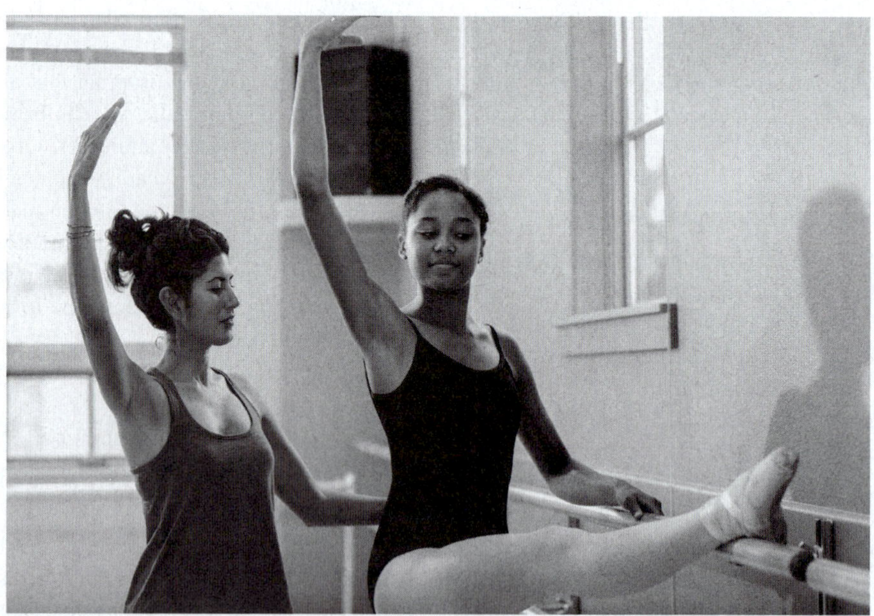

Professional dance requires a great deal of preparation and a high level of skill.
Marc Romanelli/Blend Images LLC

Opportunities to participate in sports after high school and college are limited. However, sport participation is an asset to physical educators who aspire to teach and coach.
moodboard/SuperStock

The salaries paid to top professional athletes are astronomical and range from hundreds of thousands to millions of dollars. Well-known athletes earn even millions of dollars more in commercial endorsements. Other professionals may not fare as well. Baseball players may spend years in the minor leagues before being sent to the majors, and golfers may spend years on the professional tour, struggling to make ends meet, before attracting a sponsor or winning enough money to break even.

Because of the limited opportunities in professional sports, and because many professional careers can be short-lived, individuals who desire to pursue this career should make every effort to ensure that they have the skills to earn a living should they fail to attain the professional ranks, or have to leave the professional arena after a few years. Sometimes, collegiate athletes leave college to pursue a professional career without completing their degree. An increasing number of colleges and universities provide academic and tuition to their former student athletes, enabling them to complete their undergraduate coursework and graduate.

Officiating

Sport officiating usually starts out as a part-time job, but after gaining experience some individuals pursue it on a full-time basis. The growth of competitive athletics at the high school and collegiate levels as well as the rise of competitive club teams has created a need for qualified officials for all

Officiating is a challenging career option that can be pursued on a full- or part-time basis.
U.S. Air Force photo by John Van Winkle

sports. Opportunities are also available at the professional level and at the recreational level to officiate for adult and youth leagues.

Part-time officials can increase their chances for year-round work by becoming certified or rated in two or more sports, each with a different season. Attaining a rating typically requires passing a written exam as well as a practical exam. In some sports, beginning officials must spend a certain period of time or probationary period working with experienced officials before being able to officiate alone. Individuals interested in information about becoming a rated official should ask an official in the sport, coach, faculty member, or director of recreational sports. You can also contact the local officials association.

In officiating, one must not only know the rules but possess good officiating mechanics. For example, being able to place oneself in the right position at the right time requires an understanding of the flow of the game. In addition, officials must be able to work under pressure. Officiating also requires good interpersonal skills and communication skills to work with coaches and athletes in highly competitive and stressful situations.

Officials usually work on afternoons, nights, and weekends because this is when most athletic contests are conducted. Some travel is involved. Salaries have improved considerably during the last few years, and officials are often reimbursed for their travel costs. Officiating can be a challenging career on a part-time or full-time basis.

Sport Law and Agency

One career that has attracted the interest of some professionals is sport law.

A career in sport law requires study beyond your bachelor's degree. The practice of sport law requires the completion of law school, which typically involves a 3-year program of study. Admission to law school is very competitive. It requires an excellent GPA, and many law schools also have prerequisites or prefer the candidate to have certain areas of undergraduate study. For practitioners with experience seeking to change their career focus, however, sport law may be an attractive area of study. The growth of sport management academic programs has also created a need for individuals with preparation in sport law to teach courses in sport law and liability.

A career in sport law presents an array of options for qualified individuals. Some opportunities include working as an agent, involvement in contract negotiations, litigation, and teaching.

Keith Brofsky/Photodisc/Getty Images

Another career opportunity for individuals with expertise in sport law is working with professional athletes, serving as their agents in contract negotiations. They may also serve as financial consultants–managing athletes' finances, investing their income, and structuring their financial portfolio for retirement. Some sport agents manage athletes' endorsements; they negotiate the endorsement contract and arrange promotional opportunities. Some sport agents perform a myriad of services, while others prefer to specialize in one area, such as contract negotiations. While you do not have to have a law degree to be a sport agent, knowledge of the law, as well as a background in business, is helpful.

Entrepreneurship

Some professionals are using their skills and competencies to become entrepreneurs. They develop services and products to meet the public's needs and interests. The broad area of physical education, exercise science, and sport offers many entrepreneurial opportunities to motivated professionals. You may choose to pursue these opportunities on a full- or part-time basis.

Perhaps, the most visible of all entrepreneurs in the profession are personal trainers. As discussed in Chapter 13, these professionals work one-on-one with the client, designing and implementing fitness programs tailored specifically to the client's needs. Personal trainers may work with clients in their homes or provide one-to-one or small group instruction at a fitness center.

Some professionals with a strong background in exercise science and administration use their skills to serve as consultants. They visit various fitness sites, such as a health club, assess the current program, make recommendations for improvement, train employees, and organize a system for ongoing program and employee evaluation.

Personal coaching is a viable business opportunity for individuals with expertise in a specific sport and the ability to coach individuals to achieve a high level of performance. Parents may be interested in obtaining private coaching to help their children further develop sport skills. Many amateur and professional athletes use the services of a personal coach on a regular basis. Opportunities for personal coaching are most commonly found in individual sports such as swimming, diving, golf, tennis, track and field, and ice skating, although participants in team sports (e.g., basketball) may use a personal coach to refine selected aspects of their performance.

Professionals can offer computerized skill analysis services to athletes, as well as to coaches interested in furthering their team's performance. The athlete is recorded on video and the performance is computer-analyzed. The analysis is reviewed with the athlete and suggestions for improvement are given. While very sophisticated technology can be used, mobile apps are also available to provide quick analysis and feedback to the performer. Instructional videos can be offered to complement this service. Sites for this service typically include golf courses, tennis clubs, sporting goods stores, and various other sport facilities. The professional can also contract for this service with interested individuals, such as coaches desiring an analysis of individual team members' skills or parents wishing a more detailed assessment of their children's skill performance.

Throughout the United States, sport and fitness camps for individuals of all ages are proliferating. Instructional camps are available for virtually every sport, although the most popular sports tend to be soccer, baseball, softball, tennis, golf, and volleyball. The number of instructional sport camps for youths with disabilities also is growing. There are also camp programs that focus on increasing fitness and reducing weight. Although camp programs traditionally have focused on children and youth, a growing number of programs target the adult population in the areas of both sport and fitness. Directing sport and fitness camps offers many fine entrepreneurial opportunities. Because many of these programs are offered during the summer months or school vacations, teaching and coaching professionals often find employment in such programs and welcome the opportunity to supplement their salary.

There are numerous entrepreneurial opportunities for motivated physical education, exercise science, and sport professionals. Individuals aspiring to such a career must ask themselves two critical questions: (1) Do I have a viable, marketable service or product? and (2) Is there a consumer desire for the service or product? Perhaps, you have some ideas for a service or product that might inspire you to become an entrepreneur. Kevin Plank, a 1996 football player for the University of Maryland, was tired of sweating through his t-shirts at practice. To solve this problem, he created moisture wicking sports apparel designed to keep athletes cool and dry while they exercised. Today, Under Armour is a highly successful sports business, and Plank is a billionaire.

Having a great idea is not enough. You need dedication, enthusiasm, initiative, and self-confidence to pursue this career successfully. The amount of financial resources needed to start

FOCUS ON CAREER: Sport Management, Media, and Performance

PROFESSIONAL ORGANIZATIONS

- College Sports Information Directors of America
- National Association of Collegiate Directors of Athletics
- National Association of Collegiate Women Athletic Administrators
- North American Society for Sport Management
- NIRSA: Leaders in Collegiate Recreation
- National Interscholastic Athletic Administrators Association
- Sport Marketing Association

PROFESSIONAL JOURNALS

- *Journal of Sport Management*
- *Journal of Legal Aspects of Sport*
- *Recreational Sports Journal*
- *Sport Marketing Quarterly*
- *International Journal of Sport Communication*
- *Journal of Intercollegiate Sport*
- *Sports Business Journal*

and sustain a business varies. Starting a personal-training business may require little capital, but opening a year-round facility to coach and train youth basketball players may require a greater investment. Young professionals who are innovative and aspire to be their own bosses will find a host of entrepreneurial opportunities available to them in the twenty-first century.

INCREASING YOUR PROFESSIONAL MARKETABILITY

If you are interested in pursuing a career in the sport industry, there are several things you can do to increase your marketability. Taking extra course work and minors in appropriate areas can enhance your marketability. Those who are interested in sport management careers can benefit from courses in business, management, law, communication, and data analytics. For individuals interested in sport media careers, courses or a minor in speech, photography, journalism, and broadcasting is an asset. Today there is a high demand for individuals with expertise in social media and digital technologies.

Individuals interested in pursuing sport-related careers need to be cognizant that the positions described in this section are often top-level positions. Professionals typically gain access to these positions through entry-level positions and then work their way up the ladder. For example, if your aspiration is to be an athletic director, you may first have to work as an assistant athletic director to gain the necessary experience and skills.

Practical experience is necessary to employment and moving up the career ladder. It can be gained from volunteering one's services, summer employment, and collegiate fieldwork and internship opportunities. Practical experience enables you to gain and refine the necessary skills but also importantly allows you to develop professional contacts and exposure. These skills and professional contacts will help you gain a job and advance up the career ladder.

Another way you can increase your marketability is by joining and becoming actively involved in professional organizations. As a member, you will have the chance to learn about new developments and have the opportunity to network with professionals in the business. The North American

Society for Sport Management (NASSM) promotes and encourages research, scholarly writing, and professional development in sport, leisure, and recreation. Their conferences are held each year and offer the opportunities to interact and learn from professionals. There is a special student rate for membership and a student section, so you would get to meet other students from colleges and universities.

While the membership of the NASSM includes professionals in many different areas of sport management, there are also organizations that have a more specific focus. For example, the Sport and Recreation Law Association focuses on the legal aspects of the law. The Sport Marketing Association provides professionals the opportunity to interact with other professionals who share a similar interest in sport marketing. NIRSA: College Leaders in Collegiate Recreation brings together professionals working in the area of campus recreation, including intramurals and sport clubs. There are professional organizations for many of the different areas of sport management. Joining an organization as a student will allow you to take advantage of student membership rates. You can further develop your skills through attending workshops and conferences and there are tremendous opportunities to network.

CURRENT TRENDS: MOVING TOWARD THE FUTURE

- Technological advances will play a significant role in the experience of fans at events, offering Wi-Fi connectivity for smartphones and tablets, massive video boards, sophisticated player tracking systems, and greater fan interactivity. In the future, there will be greater use of virtual reality to enrich the fan experience.
- Globalization of sport offers enormous potential to bring people together across the world through a common shared interest in sport. Sport has the ability to cross-cultural boundaries (e.g., football/soccer).
- Greater emphasis on social responsibility will be seen, with the sport industry demonstrating greater sensitivity to environmental sustainability, addressing socioeconomic disparities in access, addressing societal inequities, and increasing commitment to diversity in the sport management field.

SUMMARY

Sport has developed into a big business, creating a myriad of career opportunities for qualified individuals. Individuals interested in sport management may pursue careers as athletic administrators, leaders of campus recreation, directors of workplace recreation, and sport facilities managers. Sport retailing and sport marketing may be attractive careers to some individuals. Managerial opportunities are also available in professional organizations.

The intensity of interest in sport in our society, coupled with the growth of the communication media, has resulted in the expansion of career opportunities in the field of sport media. Individuals interested in this area can pursue careers in sport broadcasting, sport writing, sport journalism, sport photography, sports information, web development, and social media.

Talented individuals may elect to pursue careers as performers. Other sport-related careers that may be attractive to qualified individuals are sport officiating and sport law. Sport analytics is a growing career. Some professionals use their skills to become entrepreneurs.

Individuals interested in these careers can use many strategies to enhance their professional marketability. Taking course work in supporting areas, gaining practical experience, and networking help individuals attain the position that they desire after graduation.

Discussion Questions

1. How have new technologies contributed to the development of sport and opportunities for viewing and promoting sport events?
2. Discuss the administration of athletic programs and collegiate recreation programs on your campus. What titles do the directors of these programs hold? How many participants are involved in these programs and what activities are offered? How are these programs marketed and promoted? Do you have any suggestions for improving the program?
3. Access the Institute for Diversity and Ethics in Sport (https://www.tidesport.org/). Review the latest Race and Gender Report Cards. Discuss your findings relative to hiring practices and representation in different sport organizations.
4. Becoming an entrepreneur is one way to create your own business. In a small group, discuss some ideas that you have that you would be interested in pursuing.

GET CONNECTED

Athletic Business–allows free registration and access to archives of articles on a variety of sport issues pertaining to equity, management, coaching, fitness, and professionalism.

https://www.athleticbusiness.com/

North American Society for Sport Management–contains information about the organization, membership, publications, and conferences.

https://www.nassm.org/

NIRSA: Leaders in Collegiate Recreation–access to information about campus recreation, clubs, and competitions as well as job opportunities.

https://nirsa.net/nirsa/

The Institute for Diversity and Ethics in Sport–access to race and gender report cards reflecting hiring practices and representation in sport organizations.

https://www.tidesport.org/

Women's Sports Foundation–gives access to research, information about career opportunities in sport, articles on a variety of topics, and internships.

https://www.womenssportsfoundation.org/

Self-Assessment Activities

These activities are designed to help you determine if you have mastered the materials and competencies presented in this chapter.

1. Blogging is a popular way for professionals and fans to share news on what is happening in sports. Using a free blogging site, create a blog on a specific theme or sport, adding at least four posts on your topic. Share your blog with other people in your class and invite them to comment.
2. If possible, interview individuals working in sport management positions. Ask each person to define his or her responsibilities and the skills that are the most helpful in the performance of the job. Determine the entry-level positions in this area.

Ask each individual for suggestions about advancing to top-level managerial positions in the field.

3. Discuss the positive and negative aspects of pursuing a performance career. Since performance careers may be of short duration, how can individuals prepare for another career after the culmination of their performance career? Select one professional athlete in any sport and research his or her background. Trace the athlete's career path, starting from their beginning interest in the sport to the current time. Be sure to include information about the athlete's education.
4. Using the information provided in the Get Connected box, locate an article on a topic of interest related to sport management, sport media, dance, officiating, or athletics. Write a brief summary of the article, identifying five key points and what you have learned.
5. Select a game to watch, either live or on TV. Use Twitter or another microblogging site to follow a game, sending out regular updates to keep your classmates informed of the game's action.

REFERENCES

1. Research and Markets. (2021). Sports global market opportunities and strategies to 2030: COVID-19 impact and recovery.
2. The Institute for Diversity and Equity in Sport. (2021). Racial and gender report cards, 2021. Retrieved from https://www.tidesport.org/racial-gender-report-card.
3. DeSensi, J., Kelley, D., Blanton, M., & Beitel, P. (1990). Sport management curricular evaluation and needs assessment: A multifaceted approach. *Journal of Sport Management, 4*, 31–58.
4. Parkhouse, B. L., & Pitts, B. G. (2005). History of sport management. In B. L. Parkhouse (Ed.), *The management of sport: Its foundation and application* (4th ed.). New York, NY: McGraw Hill.
5. Blann, W. (2004, December 20). Four-factor analysis of sport management. Personal communication.
6. AAHPERD. (2000). NASPE-NASSM: *NASPE-NASSM sport management curriculum standards and program review*. AAHPERD: Reston, VA.
7. North American Society for Sport Management. (2014). Program accreditation. Retrieved April 3, 2019, from http://www.nassm.com/InfoAbout/NASSM/ProgramAccreditation.
8. Chelladurai, P. (2009). *Managing organizations for sport and physical activity: A systems perspective* (3rd ed.). Scottsdale, AZ: Holcomb Hathaway.
9. Masteralexis, L. P., Barr, C. A., & Hums, M. A. (2015). *Sport administration*. Burlington, MA: Jones & Bartlett.
10. Blann, W. (2004, December 20). Sport management career paths. Personal communication.
11. NIRSA. (n.d.). What is collegiate recreation? Retrieved from nirsa.net.
12. Young, J. (January 26, 2022). SportsTech, gambling and alcohol helped the NFL earn almost $2 billion in sponsorships this season. https://www.cnbc.com/2022/01/26/tech-gambling-alcohol-helped-nfl-earn-almost-2-billion-in-sponsorships.html.
13. Young, J. (June 29, 2021). Microsoft among deals that helped NBA set record $1.46 billion in sponsorship revenue. https://www.cnbc.com/2021/06/29/nba-set-record-1point46-billion-in-sponsorship-revenue-this-season.html.
14. Gharagozlou, L. (2018, July 14). The real World Cup final isn't France vs. Croatia, it's Nike vs. Adidas. Retrieved April 3, 2019, from https://www.cnbc.com/2018/07/13/the-real-world-cup-final-isnt-france-vs-belgium-its-nike-vs-adidas.html.
15. Gray, A. (2018, July 3). The explosive growth of eSports. World Economic Forum. Retrieved from https://www.weforum.org/agenda/2018/07/the-explosive-growth-of-esports/.
16. 2021 Global Esports Market Report. eSports market revenue worldwide from 2019 to 2024. (Retrieved from Statista, 26 March 2022).
17. Markets and Markets. (2016). Sports analytics market by type (solutions & services), by applications (player analysis, team performance analysis, health assessment, video analysis, data interpretation & analysis, fan engagement), by deployment type & by region–global forecast to 2021, May 2016. Retrieved April 4, 2019, from http://www.reportsnreports.com/reports/539529-sports-analytics-market-by-type-solutions-services-by-applications-player-analysis-

team-performance-analysis-health-assessment-video-analysis-data-interpretation-analysis-fan-engagement-by-deployment-type-by-region-global-forecast-to-2021.html.

18. Brousell, L. (2014, March 13). 8 ways big data and analytics will change sports. Retrieved April 4, 2019, from http://www.cio.com/article/2377954/data-management/data-management-8-ways-big-data-and-analytics-will-change-sports.html.

19. Dizikes, P. (2015, March 2). Six keys to sports analytics: Massive MIT Sloan Sports Analytics Conference reveals state of growing field. Retrieved April 4, 2019, from http://news.mit.edu/2015/mit-sloan-sports-analytics-conference-0302.

20. Sports TV Career Center. Retrieved from http://www.sportstvjobs.com/sports-careers/sports-tv-careers-landing-page.html.

21. Lee, S. (1984). Dance administrative opportunities. *Journal of Physical Education, Recreation & Dance, 55*(5), 74–75, 81.

22. NCAA. (n.d.) NCAA guide for the college-bound student-athlete. 2021–2022.

/ Saint James/Photodisc/Getty Images

Anthony Saint James/Photodisc/Getty Images

Mitch Hrdlicka/Photodisc/Getty Images

IV

Future Professionals as Leaders and Advocates

Physical educators, exercise scientists, and sport leaders need to be aware of the important role they face in promoting physical activity, fitness, and sport as future professionals in their respective disciplines.

In this final chapter, we emphasize the importance of professionals being leaders in the field and advocating on behalf of their programs and for the value of physical activity.

Polka Dot Images/Getty Images

CHAPTER 15

FUTURE PROFESSIONALS AS LEADERS AND ADVOCATES

OBJECTIVES

After reading this chapter, students should be able to–

- Discuss the importance of leadership relative to lifespan participation in physical activity, fitness, physical education, and sport.
- Describe how professionals can be leaders of physical activity, fitness, physical education, and sport.
- Explain the importance of advocacy in a variety of physical activity settings.
- Describe how professionals can be advocates of physical activity, fitness, physical education, and sport.
- Identify current and future trends that professionals will encounter in relation to physical activity, fitness, physical education, and sport.

As you enter a profession within the field of kinesiology, it will be important for you to provide leadership in physical activity to individuals across the lifespan. You now have the expertise and knowledge to educate others about physical activity, fitness, and sport and will be looked upon to take on a leadership role in encouraging and supporting others to engage in physical activity. As young professionals, it will also be important for you to advocate for your profession particularly for those with whom you work. In this final chapter, we will provide you with some specific strategies and suggestions on how you can demonstrate leadership and be an advocate within your respective profession.

LEADERSHIP IN PHYSICAL ACTIVITY

Physical education, exercise science, and sport professionals must step forward and assume a greater leadership role in the promotion of physical activity. Substantial evidence supports the positive contribution of physical activity to health and quality of life. Physical inactivity has been related to premature mortality and morbidity, which exert a tremendous toll on society, both in human terms and monetary costs. Individuals who engage in physical activity on a regular basis reduce their risk for many chronic diseases and increase their chances for living a long healthy life.

As professionals, we are in a unique position to take a more central, active role in responding to society's needs and engaging its members in physical activity so that they can realize the powerful concomitant health benefits. We have a responsibility to educate the public about the benefits of physical activity and fitness, and we must make a greater effort to disseminate a national message about the relationship between physical activity and health. It is very important that part of this includes the barriers and lack of opportunities offered to many depending on their social identities and living situation.

During the past five decades, we have witnessed dramatic increases in participation in fitness and physical activities by people of all ages and identities. There has been an unprecedented proliferation of programs and products designed to capitalize on these interests. Although many programs are sound in nature and products are safe and live up to their claims, there are some programs that are not reputable and the validity of claims for some products is highly questionable.

Commercial sports clubs, community fitness centers, health and fitness clubs, and health spas all offer opportunities for people to engage in physical activities. Some of the programs offered are highly reputable, meet the health and fitness industry standards, and are staffed by qualified personnel. On the other hand, there are programs that advertise their services as leading to quick and dramatic results, fail to meet industry standards, and are staffed by personnel hired more for their appearance than their credentials. And these beneficial physical activity opportunities are mostly available to those who can afford them. What about those who cannot?

Although some organizations, such as the International Health, Racquet, and Sportsclub Association (IHRSA), establish standards for clubs and others offer guidelines for exercise leaders and participants' safety, such as the American College of Sports Medicine (ACSM), there is no way to determine the number of programs that comply with accepted standards. For people who want to begin a physical activity program, where can they turn to find out whether the program meets industry standards or the staff is certified? What type of certification should the staff have? Is the program safe? Will it enable them to accomplish their goals?

Along with the proliferation of physical activity programs came the growth of fitness and health products, now a multibillion-dollar-a-year industry. The marketplace offers the consumer a wide choice of exercise equipment, websites sell diet products and fitness services, infomercials extol the merits of various types of ab machines, and magazine ads

Sport professionals in high school and college need to advocate for their players, so they are not exploited and taken advantaged of by the big business industry.
Purestock/SuperStock

exhort readers to try products that guarantee weight loss. Books, magazines, and periodicals concerned with health, fitness, self-improvement, and sport are best sellers. DVDs, apps, and Internet downloads of celebrity experts leading specially designed workout programs are popular purchases for those people who like to work out at home. How are consumers to know what works and what does not?

Given the wide range of programs and products relating to physical activity and fitness, it is important that the members of the public make an educated choice from among the services and goods available; participation in programs that fail to meet recognized standards of care or the use of products that are of questionable value can have harmful results. Professionals can play a critical role in educating consumers about physical activities and fitness.

Corbin[1] suggests that professionals can do several things to "lead the parade" and should actively seek leadership roles in the fitness movement. First, as experts, professionals should be cognizant of current findings in the field. Second, the public needs to be made aware that physical education, exercise science, and sport professionals are experts in this field and are a resource for potential answers and advice. Professionals should educate their students and the public to be wise consumers of exercise programs and products. Additionally, professionals should provide their clientele with the knowledge and the skills to solve their own exercise and physical activity problems and to evaluate their own fitness needs. As professionals, we must step forward and provide leadership for the physical activity movement because it falls within our domain. Collaborative, committed leadership is essential in reducing physical inactivity and promoting a physically active lifestyle.

Leadership in Physical Education and Youth Sport

As professionals, we realize that engaging children and youth in physical activity through physical education and, for many, through youth sport is an important step in promoting lifespan participation. Today, as professionals, we must promote high-quality physical education programs in the nation's schools that respect the uniqueness of each student. Furthermore, professionals should also provide all students with the skills and knowledge to be physically active and encourage the development of dispositions that value physical activity. As teachers, we must practice culturally relevant pedagogy to meet the needs of the increasingly diverse population of students. We hope that you are now more aware of the inequities and injustices experienced by many in our society. Our schools provide the best means to reach all children and youth with the hope that they will be advocates and leaders for justice and equity in our society.

Youth sport involves millions of children and youth and adult volunteers across a wide variety of levels of competition. Youth sport is often cited as contributing to the healthy physical, psychological, and social development of participants.

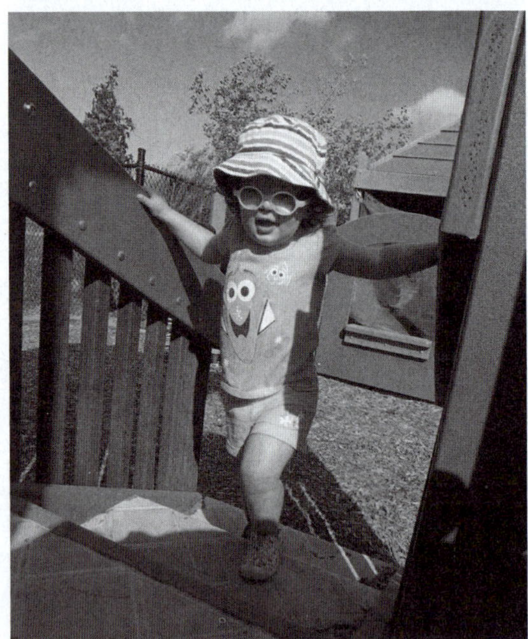

Physical activity and play experiences need to be provided to toddlers and young children to develop their gross motor movements and increase their confidence.
Jennifer Walton-Fisette

Additionally, a positive experience in youth sport can lay the foundation for a lifetime of participation in physical activity. While many participants have a positive experience in youth sport, others find the experience to be negative in nature. Youth sport programs have been severely criticized by educators, physical educators, physicians, parents, and the media for the manner in which many programs are conducted. Much of the criticism has been directed at the overemphasis on winning and competition, which makes it difficult to attain many of the stated developmental objectives. Concern has also been raised about the high dropout rate of program participants.

Professionals need to take a more active role in the conduct of youth sport programs. Professionals can play a greater role in the education of volunteer coaches, providing them with opportunities to develop competencies in how to promote skill acquisition, conduct meaningful practices, address the psychological needs of youth, and provide for their safety. Sound training programs for the millions of volunteers, conducted by qualified professionals, will help youth realize the physical, psychological, and social benefits of youth sport and "turn kids on to physical activity for a lifetime."[2]

Advocacy

Advocacy is an important responsibility of physical education, exercise science, and sport professionals. The decline of physical education programs in the schools, the increased privatization of sports resulting in decreasing opportunities for individuals with limited economic resources, and the growing need for health promotion and physical activity programs in the worksite, community, and medical settings make it important that each professional takes a role in promoting the value of our programs. Advocates need a strong voice to clearly articulate the benefits of participation in quality physical education, exercise science, and sport programs. Additionally, addressing the health disparities among population groups and inequities of opportunities for women, racial minorities, and people with disabilities in sport requires that we be willing to work as agents for social change and for social justice. We must assume more social responsibility and take a more active leadership role if we are to accomplish our mission of lifespan physical activity for all people.

The Advocacy Institute defines advocacy as the "pursuit of influencing outcomes–including public policy and resource allocation decisions within political, economic, and social systems and institutions–that directly affect people's lives."[3] Advocacy consists of organized efforts to change what is–to "highlight critical issues that have been ignored and submerged, to influence public attitudes, and to enact and implement law and public policies so that the vision of 'what should be' in a just, decent society becomes a reality."[3] The overarching framework for advocacy is human rights. Advocates seek to influence and play a role in the decision making of relevant institutions; they challenge the dominance of those with political, economic, or cultural power and through their efforts bring an improvement in people's lives.[3,4]

Advocacy is the use of communication to influence others and to have influence on the decision-making process. Activities can include researching an issue, writing press releases, presenting your case to a group, talking to a legislator, planning special events, securing a grant, maintaining a website, networking with individuals, forging new partnerships with organizations, or working to stay abreast of current issues. It is important that we communicate our message effectively via various formats and media to the public and decision makers if we are to bring about change.

Public relations is an important component of program promotion and advocacy efforts. Now is the time to capitalize on the widespread public interest in sport, physical fitness, and health. Professionals teaching in the school setting; instructing in community and recreational sport programs; working in commercial sport clubs, fitness centers, and health spas; and directing corporate and community fitness programs must use public relations techniques to market their programs. Professionals must inform the public and prospective clientele of the values that accrue from participation in a sound physical activity and exercise program.

In the school setting, where physical education is often regarded as an extra or is cut to make more time for other academic subjects, where budgetary cutbacks are becoming increasingly common, and where class sizes are expanding, teachers must be willing to advocate on behalf of their programs to gain the personal and budgetary support of school administrators, politicians, and parents. School boards at the local level and other legislative bodies and state education commissions must also be addressed because of the power they wield as decision making bodies.[5]

Advocacy is just as important in physical activity programs that are conducted outside of the school setting. Advocacy in these settings can take many different forms. Professionals may work to initiate programs, to expand services offered within programs, and to increase access to programs by undeserved populations. Additionally, professionals must work to promote and market their programs.

Prospective clientele for community and commercial programs must be aware of the nature of the programs offered and the benefits to be derived from participation in such programs. In the corporate fitness setting, professionals must promote the values and benefits to be derived from participation to management as well as to employees. Corporate management personnel will be reluctant to invest corporate resources, particularly money, to support these programs if they are not aware of their value or if the stated benefits are not achieved.

Active involvement by physical education, exercise science, and sport professionals is critical to attaining our goal of lifespan involvement in physical activity for all people. Every professional is urged to be an active member in their own community. Contact organizations that promote physical activity and health and "advocate that these organizations become more proactive in presenting the facts . . . to those decision makers who in turn can make policies to facilitate a more physically active lifestyle, and thereby play a direct part in facilitating a healthier and more prosperous America."[6] Active professional involvement will help us reduce the morbidity and mortality associated with chronic disease and help people of all social identities live healthier lives.

Increasing the amount of time physical educators spend teaching lifetime sports is important to lifespan involvement.

BananaStock/Alamy Stock Photo

Professionals must undertake a greater role as advocates for social justice. Inequities persist despite our professed societal value of equality and the passage of legislation such as the Civil Rights Act, Title IX, and the Americans with Disabilities Act. Much more needs to be done. We promote lifespan involvement in physical activity for all people as important to their health and well-being, yet there are tremendous disparities in physical activity and disease conditions according to race, ethnicity, gender, age, education, sexual orientation, ability/disability, and income. Sport participation for males and females of all ages has increased dramatically, yet opportunities at all levels of sport and within sport administration and the sport industry remain inequitable.

We view school physical education as the means to provide all children with the skills, knowledge, and dispositions to participate in lifelong physical activity. As Larry Locke points out, the public schools provide us with a means to reach across barriers of race, ethnicity, gender, social

The growth of community and commercial sport programs has enabled more children to receive instruction and develop a lifelong interest in sport and fitness activities.
Sarah Rich

class, and economic conditions to reach millions of children and youth.[7] In theory, the schools afford us the opportunity to ensure that all children learn what they need to know to be physically active for a lifetime. Yet, in reality, the physical education experience of children and youth in inner-city schools in Los Angeles is likely to be quite different from that of students in an upper class suburb of Chicago or those of students in a rural area of Maine.

As professionals, we must be ready and willing to work as agents of social change–as advocates to change public policies, to increase access for underrepresented populations, to provide services to those in need, and to empower people to make a difference in their own lives. We must be concerned not only with strengthening our programs, but also with increasing access to our services for all segments of our population.

CURRENT AND FUTURE TRENDS

It is tempting to look back on these past five decades, which have been a time of tremendous growth for physical education, exercise science, and sport, and bask in the glow of many accomplishments. However, if the potential of our field to enhance the lives of people of all identities is to be realized, we must take a more active role in creating our future and shaping our destiny. We must take

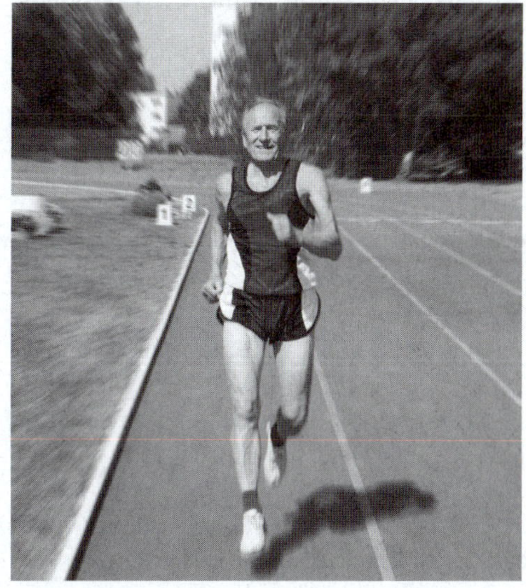

Many seniors enjoy an active lifestyle and participate in a wide range of activities such as bocci or running.
Left: Lawrence M. Sawyer/J&L Images/Photodisc/Getty Images; Right: Andrei Nekrassov/Alamy Stock Photo

a proactive, rather than reactive, stance in dealing with the issues and challenges that confront us. Furthermore, both individually and collectively, we must reflect more critically upon social issues related to physical education, exercise science, and sport and question long-held assumptions, sacrosanct beliefs, and traditional practices.[8] We must be introspective, engaging in a thoughtful examination of our actions and values. We also must look outward, beyond ourselves, and examine the broader societal issues and their impact on our lives, institutions, programs, and the people with whom we work. But we must move beyond reflection to consider alternatives to the problems that confront us. Personally and professionally, both individually and collectively, we must move toward solutions if the potential of our field is to be fulfilled.

Oberle,[9] in a discussion about the future directions for health, physical education, recreation and leisure, and dance, stressed the importance of exerting quality control within the profession. He suggested that each of the disciplines consider the following actions to enhance their effectiveness:

- Establish minimum standards of competency.
- Develop programs and services that are flexible to meet changing needs while accomplishing avowed disciplinary objectives.
- Provide meaningful programs that will meet needs today as well as tomorrow.
- Reduce ineffective programs.
- Establish minimum standards for entry into professional preparation programs.
- Provide high-quality experiences for professionals within the discipline, such as in-service education and graduate education.
- Develop a system for relicensure for all professionals, not just public school personnel.
- Establish professional accrediting agencies, as the American Medical Association has done, to ensure quality control.
- Develop high-quality model programs and build facilities that can serve as the standard for the profession.[9]

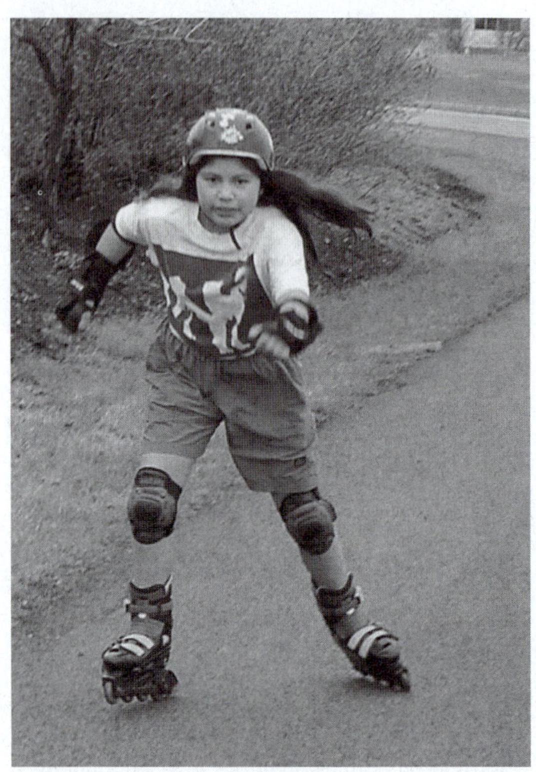

Let us remember to promote fun when we promote lifespan involvement in physical activity.

Deborah Wuest

Many challenges and opportunities await us this decade. The delivery of services within the disciplines in our field should reflect two trends: globalization and the lifespan involvement, from neonatal to geriatric.[10] The increased diversity of our population and a greater understanding of how race, ethnicity, gender, social class, and a host of other factors influence access and opportunities relative to physical activity and health must be considered as we move toward the future.

In addition to the growing diversity in our country, the number of people across all ages who are living a life with mental health issues and negative effects from traumatic events and traumatic or toxic stress is increasing. Because many of the educational programs within kinesiology do not prepare us to navigate individuals who are struggling in these ways, it is important that you obtain resources and professional development to best support, coach, teach, and train all individuals—including those who have mental health issues and/or have experienced trauma in their lives. The growing recognition from the general public and health professionals that physical activity is an essential ingredient of living at all ages provides us with the opportunity to contribute to the well-being of individuals throughout their lifespan.

At the end of each of the previous 14 chapters, we included a Current Trends box to highlight future trends related to the content in that chapter. We highly suggest that you return to the end of each chapter to become more informed of what tasks and challenges you will face when you begin your career as a professional in the field of kinesiology. All professionals are responsible for "changing to the times" and educating our students, players, patients, or clients on how to be physically active and successfully attaining their physical activity, fitness, and/or sport performance goals. It is up to us to be active agents of social and professional change, now and in the future.

The vision of lifespan involvement in physical activity for all people is a powerful one, but its achievement requires dedicated and committed professionals. Excellence must be present in all our professional endeavors. After you have read this text, we hope that you have an appreciation for the tremendous substance and worth of the field that you have chosen to study. Physical education, exercise science, and sport have a tremendous potential to enrich and enhance the health and quality of life of all people. Whether this potential is realized depends on each professional's willingness to make a personal commitment to achieving this goal.

Summary

Professionals in physical education, exercise science, and sport need to be leaders in their disciplines and advocates for change. As professionals, we are in a unique position to take an active role in responding to society's needs and engaging its members in physical activity so that they can realize the powerful health benefits. We have the responsibility to educate the public about the benefits of physical activity and fitness, and we must make a greater effort to disseminate a national message about the relationship between physical activity and health. Collaborative, committed leadership is essential in reducing physical inactivity and promoting a physically active lifestyle.

Advocacy is an important responsibility of physical education, exercise science, and sport professionals. As advocates, we need a strong voice to clearly articulate the benefits of participation in quality physical education, exercise science, and sport programs. We also need to work as agents for social change in reducing the health disparities and inequities experienced by individuals based on their gender, race, ethnicity, (dis) ability, sexual orientation, and social class within the physical education, exercise science, and sporting communities.

Discussion Questions

1. How can professionals demonstrate leadership in promoting lifespan participation in physical activity and fitness?
2. How can physical educators, exercise scientists, and sport leaders advocate for their profession at the local, state, and national levels?
3. What various strategies can be utilized to promote lifespan involvement of people of all ages, abilities, races and ethnicities, genders, and social class?

Self-Assessment Activities

These activities are designed to help you determine if you have mastered the materials and competencies presented in this chapter.

1. Discuss the role of the physical educator, exercise scientist, and sport leader in the physical activity movement. Formulate a list of strategies and next steps on what we can do to move the field forward.
2. Discuss the importance of advocacy programs in the physical education, exercise science, and sport setting of your choice. What local organizations exist in your current community that offer health promotion programs? How would you work to organize these groups into a coalition to promote physical activity?
3. Develop a plan for the upcoming 2020s that provides specific suggestions for improving the disciplines of physical education, exercise science, and sport.
4. Across activities 1–3, consider how social justice and equity issues are being addressed related to leadership, advocacy, and moving the field forward.

References

1. Corbin, C. B. (1984). Is the fitness bandwagon passing us by? *Journal of Physical Education, Recreation and Dance, 55*(9), 17.
2. Martens, R. (1996). Turning kids on to physical activity for a lifetime. *Quest, 46,* 303–310.
3. Advocacy Institute. (2001). What is advocacy? In D. Cohen (Ed.), *Part I: Reflections on advocacy.* West Hartford, CT: Kumarin Press.
4. DePauw, K. P. (1998). Futuristic perspectives for kinesiology and physical education. *Quest, 50,* 1–8.
5. Dunn, J. M. (1999). Communicating with school boards: Position, power, perseverance. *Quest, 51,* 157–163.
6. Booth, F. W., & Chakravarthy, M. V. (2002). Cost and consequences of sedentary living: New battleground for an old enemy. *President's Council on Physical Fitness and Sport Research Digest, 3*(16).
7. Locke, L. F. (1998). Advice, stories, and myths: The reactions of a cliff jumper. *Quest, 50,* 238–248.
8. Bain, L. L. (1988). Beginning the journey: Agenda for 2001. *Quest, 40,* 96–106.
9. Oberle, G. H. (1988). A future direction plan for our profession. *Journal of Physical Education, Recreation and Dance, 59*(1), 76–77.
10. Charles, J. M. (2005). Changes and challenges: A 20/20 vision of 2020. *Quest, 57,* 267–286.

INDEX

Note: Page numbers followed by *f* or *t* indicate figures or tables, respectively.

AAAPE; *see* American Association for the Advancement of Physical Education
AAPE; *see* Association for the Advancement of Physical Education
AASP; *see* Association for Applied Sport Psychology
ABL; *see* adventure-based learning
academic disciplines, 11, 98
academic performance
  in career preparation, 326-327
  cost of participation in, 227
  intercollegiate sports and, 226-230
  interscholastic sports and, 224-226
academic progress rate (APR), 228
Academic Search Premier, 21
acceleration
  defined, 155, 156*t*
  law of, 160
accountability
  and professionalism, 337
accountability, in physical education pedagogy, 297-300
accuracy
  in biomechanical analysis, 171
  in motor learning, 127-128
achievement, determination of, 46
ACL; *see* anterior cruciate ligament
action and reaction, law of, 161
activist approaches, 290, 295-296
adaptability, 119
adapted physical activity
  career opportunities within, 12*t*
  physical education
    areas of study, 12, 15
    career opportunities within, 12*t*
    defined, 15
adapted physical activity/physical education
  teaching of, 365-367, 379-380
Adapted Physical Education National Standards project, 366
administration
  career opportunities, 411
Adobe Connect, 21
adolescents; *see* children and adolescents
Adrian, M. J., 174
adults; *see also* older adults
  fitness and physical activity status of, 69
  obesity and overweight among, 58*f*
adventure-based learning (ABL), 290, 294-295
advertisement, 219
advocacy, 317, 336-337
advocacy, 439-441
Advocacy Institute, 439
aerobic, 186, 186*t*, 187
aerobic efficiency, 191
aerobic exercise, 191-192
aesthetics, 27, 28
affective learning domain, 35-36, 39-42
African Americans, 233-236
  history of sports participation by, 90, 233
  population of, 51
  women, 233
agents, sport, 428
agility, 182
Alaskan Natives, 51
allied fields, 16-18
Amateur Athletic Foundation of Los Angeles, 111
Amateur Sports Act, 107
American Academy of Kinesiology and Physical Education, 99
American Academy of Physical Education, 99
American Alliance for Health, Physical Education, Recreation, and Dance (AAHPERD), 77, 87, 99, 101, 342
American Association for Health, Physical Education, and Recreation, 95
American Association for the Advancement of Physical Education (AAAPE), 87-88, 99
American Athletic Union (AAU), 88
American Cancer Society, 55
American College Athletics (report), 94
American College of Sports Medicine (ACSM), 35, 99, 217, 341-342, 392, 398, 399, 406, 408, 437
  certifications offered by, 323
  certifications offered by, 398*t*
  on creatine, 214
  establishment of, 97
  exercise recommendations of, 192, 193
  website of, 23
  Well-coaches Certified Health and Wellness Coach, 394

American Council on Exercise (ACE), 398, 408
certifications offered by, 398*t*
American Dance Therapy Association (ADTA), 403
American Indians; *see* Native Americans
American Medical Association (AMA), 399
American Psychological Association Division of Exercise and Sport Psychology, 278
American Red Cross, 323
Americans with Disabilities Act (ADA) of 1990, 106, 107
American Therapeutic Recreation Association, 403
anabolic-androgenic steroids, 214-215
anaerobic system, 186-187, 186*t*
analytics, sport, 421
Anderson, A., 270
Anderson, D., 120
Anderson, L. W., 36
Anderson, William, 87, 89, 97
angular acceleration, 155-156, 156*t*
angular velocity, 155, 156*t*
anorexia nervosa, 197-198
Anshel, M. H., 258, 259, 262, 263
anterior cruciate ligament (ACL), 152
anthropometry, 166
anxiety, 275
and arousal, 261-264
intervention strategies for, 273
nature of, 261
and performance, 262-264
reducing, 263
signs of, 261
state, 262
trait, 262
APR; *see* academic progress rate
Aristotle, 148-149
arousal, physiological
anxiety and, 261-264
intervention strategies for, 273
nature of, 261
and performance, 261-264
reducing, 263
signs of, 261
articulation, 43
Asians, 52
assessment, 45-47, 357
defined, 45
formative, 297, 298
performance-based, 297, 298
in physical education pedagogy, 297-300
purposes of, 45-47
summative, 297, 298
types of, 297-300
Association for Applied Sport Psychology (AASP), 249, 278
Association for the Advancement of Physical Education (AAPE), 87, 88
Association of Intercollegiate Athletics for Women (AIAW), 103
associative stage of learning, 121-122, 121*t*
Athlete Project, 217
athletes
mental health of, 274-276
athletes, biomechanics used by, 167-168
athletic administration, 413-415
Athletic Business, 432
athletics, defined, 9
Athletics and Fitness Association of American (AFAA), 398
certifications offered by, 398*t*
athletic trainers (ATs), 399-401
defined, 399
employment opportunities for, 399
growth in opportunities, 386
rehabilitation, 11
responsibilities of, 12-13
responsibilities of, 400
salaries for, 401
athletic training; *see* sports medicine/athletic training
ATP (adenosine triphosphate), 186-187
at-risk employees, 390
at-risk youth, 70
attention, 362
goals setting and, 264
autonomous stage of learning, 121*t*, 122
axiology, 27, 28
axis, 159, 161

B

back squats, 152
Baggataway, 83
balance
in physical fitness, 182
ballistic stretching, 205
barefoot running, 153
Basedow, Johann Bernhard, 79-80, 83
basketball
intercollegiate, 96
National Basketball Association, 411, 420
origins of, 88
women's professional, 102, 231
Battle of the Systems, 87
Beck, Charles, 84, 89
Beecher, Catharine, 84, 89
behavior, motor; *see* motor behavior
behavioral risk factors, 183
behavior change
stages of, 253, 255
theories and models of, 252-256
Beitel, P., 411
bending, 137-138
bicycles, 90
Biles, S., 233, 275
bioelectrical impedance analysis, 199
biofeedback, 169
biomechanics, 146-175
analysis of, 165-175, 170*f*
applications of, 146-147
areas of study, 13, 149, 154-155
career opportunities within, 12*t*
clinical, 152
core concepts, 174
defined, 13, 148
future of, 174-175
growth of, 148-149
kinesiology and, 147-155
principles of, 158-165
reasons for studying, 150-154
terminology of, 155-158, 156*t*
Bird, Larry, 109
Black
population of, 51
Blacks, 52; *see* African Americans
Blann, W., 412, 413
Blanton, M., 411
blogging, 22
Bloom, B. S., 36
body composition
measurement of, 198-199
physical activity and, 196
in physical fitness, 182, 190, 195-199
body fat, 195-199
body issues, in physical education, 307
Body Mass Index (BMI), 141, 195-196
body-mind relationship, 31-32, 93
Bolt, U., 160
Boston Conference on Physical Training (1889), 87
bowling, 88
broadcasting career, 422-423
Brown, R. M., 150
Brown v. Board of Education, 233
bulimia, 197-198
Burden, J. W. Jr., 54
burnout, 377-379

C

caffeine, 211
caloric balance, 196, 197
caloric consumption and expenditure, 209
cameras, in biomechanical analysis, 165-167
cancer, 55-56
CAPE (Certified Adapted Physical Educator), 366
carbohydrates, 209
Cardinal, Bradley, 339
cardiopulmonary resuscitation (CPR) course, 396
cardiorespiratory endurance
  measurement of, 194-195
  in physical fitness, 182, 190, 191-195
cardiovascular disease, 55
career(s); *see also specific types*
  attaining a position, 330-335
  guidelines for choosing, 320-322
  list of examples of, 319
  preparation for, 322-330, 324-325*t*
career opportunities, in physical education, 5
career opportunities in
  career opportunities in, 413-421
Carter, M., 233
Cassidy, Rosalind, 93, 95
catching, 138
census, 2020, 52
center of gravity, 156-157, 156*t*, 158
Centers for Disease Control and Prevention (CDC), 55, 68, 73, 183
certifications, 323, 326
  ACE, 398*t*
  ACSM, 323, 398*t*
  AFAA, 398*t*
  career preparation, 397-398
  CPR, 323, 397
  NATA, 323
  NSCA, 323, 398*t*
  in specific sport, 323
  of teachers, 366, 367, 370-371, 380
Certified Mental Performance Consultant (CMPC), 249
challenge by choice, 295
change, behavior
  stages of, 253, 255
  theories and models of, 252-256
Chapman, Larry, 389
checklists, 297, 299
children and adolescents; *see also* interscholastic sports; youth sports
  at-risk, 70
  fitness and physical activity, 66-68
  obesity and overweight among, 56-58
  parents' role in physical activity of, 70
  population of, 50-52
  sociology of sport on, 237-239
  trauma among, 350-351
chiropractic care, 404-405
  holistic health, 404
Christianity, muscular, 82
chronic diseases
  as leading causes of death, 55, 56*f*
  risk factors for, 182-183
chronoscopes, 166
CIAR; *see* Cooper Institute for Aerobic Research
CIAR's Prudential Fitnessgram system, 101
Civil War, American, 85
clap skates, 152
Clark, J. E., 141
class, social; *see* socioeconomic status
classic learning theories of behavior change, 252-253, 254
classification, based on assessment, 46
class size, in physical education, 288
clinical biomechanics, 152
clinical sport psychologists, 248-249
closed motor skills, 126-127, 126*f*
clubs, sport; *see* sport clubs
CMPC; *see* Certified Mental Performance Consultant
coaches/coaching, 371-377
  anxiety and, 263
  and athletes' health, 275
  and biomechanical analysis, 171
  biomechanics used by, 150
  burnout in, 377-379
  certification, 376-377
  characteristics of effective, 374
  cultural competency of, 349
  cultural humility of, 349
  education of, 376-377
  health and wellness coaches, 394-395
  list of career opportunities in, 318
  marketability of, 379-382
  in nonschool settings, 371
  personal, 429
  position, securing, 375-376
  professional organizations for, 343
  reasons for choosing career in, 371-372
  responsibilities of, 374-375
  rewards/benefits/challenges of, 372-373
  role conflict problem with, 372-373
  salaries in, 372
  in school settings, 371
  sport psychology used by, 248
  standards, 376-377
  as teachers, 371-377
  in today's world, 350-351
  women, 232
Coakley, J., 220, 221, 223, 234, 235, 241
coeducational classes, 306
cognitive intervention strategies, 274
cognitive learning domain, 35-36
cognitive psychology, 260
cognitive stage of learning, 120-121, 121*t*
cold weather, 208
Collaborative for Academic, Social, and Emotional Learning (CASEL), 296
colleges and universities; *see* intercollegiate sports
  recreation programs of, 416-417
  worksite wellness programs in, 390
colonial period, US, 82-84
commercial sport clubs, teaching in, 368-369
Commission on Civil Rights, 236
Commission on Sport Management Accreditation (COSMA), 413
communication, 357-358
  online, 21
communication skills, teachers, 301-302
community centers, schools as, 59
community organizations, teaching in, 369-370
competition, 222
component sequences, 140
Comprehensive School and Physical Activity Program model (CSPAP), 358-360
computers; *see also* technology
  in biomechanical analysis, 165, 169-170
  professionals communicate, 21
concentric contraction, 201
consistency
  in biomechanical analysis, 171, 173
  in motor learning, 120
contemporary physical education, 4-5
  exercise science/sport programs, 5-16
contract-relax technique, 205
control
  motor; *see* motor control
  perceived, in behavior change, 253
controllability, in mental imagery, 271-272
Cooper, John M., 174
Cooper Institute for Aerobic Research (CIAR), 101

coordination, in physical fitness, 182
Corbin, C., 438
coronary heart disease, 183
corporations
  wellness programs, 389
Coubertin, Pierre de, 88
Counsilman, J., 150
countering, 269
COVID-19 pandemic, 350
  commercial/community fitness programs, 391
  employees comprehensive onsite health promotion programs, 6
  employment opportunities, for exercise and fitness specialists, 386
  employment opportunities, for professionals, 386
  global sports market, 410
  health and fitness clubs in pre-COVID conditions, 386
  national and global experiences, 2
  number of deaths, 52
  outdoors, in physical activity, 6
  severe symptoms, 7
  sport industry, 410, 411
  sport retailing, 418
  virtual training, 393
Cox, R. H., 258
CPR courses, 323
cramps, heat, 207
creatine, 214
CSPAP; *see* Comprehensive School and Physical Activity Program model
culminating events, in sport education model, 293
cultural competency, 317
  of coaches, 349
  of teachers, 349
cultural diversity, 51
cultural humility, 52-54, 53
  of coaches, 349
  and professionalism, 337
  of teachers, 349
curriculum, 356
  hidden, 304
curriculum development, 285-289, 286*f*, 287*f*
cynicism, 377

D

dance
  allied fields, 17
  careers in, 425-426
dance/movement therapy, 403
Dartfish Blog, 176
DASH Eating Plan, 210
databases, electronic, 21
Dave, R. H., 42
death, leading causes of, 55, 56*f*
decisional balance, 254
decision making, 117
demographic changes, 50-60
De Moto Animalium (Aristotle), 149
Denmark, history of physical education in, 81-82, 83
Department of Health and Human Services; *see* Health and Human Services (HHS), US Department of
depression, 275
DeSensi, J., 52, 411
DeSensi's broad, 52
developmental biomechanics, 151
developmental sequences approach to motor development, 139-140, 140*f*
Dewey, John, 30, 31, 93
DGWS; *see* Division for Girls' and Women's Sports
diagnosis, based on assessment, 45-46
Dieffenbach, K., 259
diet; *see also* nutrition
  and body composition, 196
  and eating disorders, 197-198
  nutrients in, 209
  and physical fitness, 209-211
Dietary Guidelines for Americans (USDA), 209-210
digital technologies, 410
diminishing returns, in fitness training, 188
disabilities, individuals
  adapted physical activity/physical education for, 15
  disease prevention, in national health goals, 56-59
disabilities, individuals with
  adapted physical activity/physical education for, 365-367, 379-380
  history of physical education of, 98
  legislation impacting, 105-108
  in Paralympics, 107, 110
  and physical education pedagogy, 305-306
  recent developments in physical education of, 105-108
  transitional services for, 105-106
disability, assumptions about term, 305
disciplinary movement, 98-99
disease prevention, 50
disease prevention, in national health goals, 99-100
Dishman, R. K., 252
diversification, 142
diversity, 351
  cultural, 51-52
  racial and ethnic, 51-52
Division for Girls' and Women's Sports (DGWS), 97
Docheff, D., 130
dose-response debate, 183-184
dramatic racial, 51
drinks, sports, 212-214
drives, in motivation, 123
drop jumps, 172, 173
drug abuse, 229
drugs
  performance-enhancing; *see* performance-enhancing drugs (PEDs)
  testing for, 241
dual-energy x-ray absorptiometry (DXA), 198-199
dualism, 31
dynamical systems model of motor learning, 118-119, 119*f*, 140, 141*f*
dynamic equilibrium, 158
dynamics, in biomechanics, 154-155
dynamic stretching, 205-206
dynamography, 168
dynamometer, 203

E

eating disorders, 197-198
eccentric contraction, 201
ecological approach to behavior change, 254, 256
education
  in career preparation, 322-327
  of coaches, 376-377
  contemporary physical education/exercise science/sport programs, 5-16
  funding for, 288
  modern, 30-31
  physical; *see* physical education
  progressive, 30-31
educational institutions; *see* intercollegiate sports; interscholastic sports
educational level, 5

Education Amendments of 1972, Title IX of, 102-105, 230-233
Education of All Handicapped Children Act of 1975, 105, 107
"education of the physical" approach, 32, 90
"education through the physical" approach, 32, 90
Effective Accommodation Test, 231
Eisenhower, Dwight, 96, 97
elderly; *see* older adults
electives, 322
electroencephalograph (EEG), 168
electrogoniometry, 166
electrolytes, 212-213
electromyography (EMG), 168
electronic databases, 21
elementary schools, physical education programs in, 361-363
e-mail, 21
emotion, in mental imagery, 271
emotional wellness, 54
employment opportunities
  to COVID-19 pandemic, for exercise and fitness specialists, 386
empowerment, in personal and social responsibility model, 291
endurance
  cardiorespiratory, 182, 190, 191-195
  muscular, 182, 190, 199-203, 202*f*
energy
  balance, and body composition, 196-197
  in biomechanics, 156*t*, 158
  production for physical activity, 186-187, 186*t*
entrepreneurship, 428-430
environment, in dynamical systems model of motor learning, 118-119, 140, 141*f*
environmental conditions, and physical fitness, 206-209
environmental health, 16
environmental risk factors, 182-183
environmental wellness, 54
epidemiologic shift, 55
epistemology, 27, 28
equilibrium, 158, 159
equipment
  biomechanics in design of, 152
  for physical education, 288
ESPN, 421
eSports, 410
  growth of, 420*f*
Estes, S. G., 78
ethics, 27, 28
  codes of, 338*t*
  performance-enhancing drugs and, 241
  and professionalism, 337-338, 338*t*
ethnical changes, 51
ethnically diverse learners, 54
ethnic diversity, 54
Europe, history of physical education and sport in, 79-82
evaluation; *see also* assessment
  of goals, 267
  measurement *vs.*, 45
Every Student Succeeds Act (ESSA), 284
exercise; *see also* physical activity; physical fitness
  biomechanics of, 151-152
  defined, 8
  designing programs for, 206
  preventative *vs.* rehabilitative exercise programs in, 387-389
  psychology of adherence to, 252-257
exercise physiology, 179-216; *see also* physical fitness
  areas of study, 12, 180-181
  career opportunities within, 12*t*
  defined, 11, 179, 180
  professional organizations and journals in, 216
exercise psychology; *see* psychology, sport and exercise
exercise-related careers; *see* fitness-related careers
exercise science, 9
  academic discipline of, 10-11, 12*t*
  allied fields of, 16-18
  assessment of learning in, 45-47
  career opportunities in, 317-320
  contemporary programs in, 4-5
  defined, 8
  evolution of, 4-5
  focus of, 4
  future trends, 441-443
  goals of, 35
  historical foundations of, 76-110
  in learning domains, 35-45
  professional development in, 18-22
  profession of, 10
  use of term, 98
exhaustion
  in burnout, 377
  heat, 207
existentialism, 30
expectations, in effective teaching, 302-303
experiential learning cycle, 295
Exploratorium, 176
external imagery, 271
extracurricular activities, in career preparation, 327, 329-330
extrinsic feedback, 130
extrinsic (external) motivation, 123, 223, 250-251

F

Facebook, 21
FaceTime, 21
facilities, for physical education, 288
facilities management, 416-418
fantasy sport, 410
fat, body, 195-199
fat, dietary, 209
feedback
  biofeedback, 169
  defined, 129
  in motor learning, 117-118
feedback sandwich, 130
fencing, 118
festivity, in sport education model, 293
field, of physical education, 10
fieldwork, 323
financial assistance, in intercollegiate sports, 227
first-class lever, 161
fitness; *see* physical fitness
fitness and physical activity movement, 60-72
  among adults, 70
  among children and youth, 66-68
  historical shift, 66
  implications of, 69-71
  recent developments in, 101
  women impacted by, 231
fitness education model, 290, 294
Fitnessgram, 101
fitness-related careers, 386-399
  certifications for, 398*t*
  preparation for, 396-397
  preventative *vs.* rehabilitative exercise programs in, 387-389
  salaries in, 389
  types of, 387-399
  in worksite wellness programs, 389-391
fitness training
  anaerobic *vs.* aerobic, 187
  careers in; *see* fitness-related careers
  FITT formula, 189-190, 192-194
  principles of, 187-189
  strength, 200-201

FITT formula, 189-190, 192-194
Fitts, P. M., 120
Fitz, George, 89
flexibility
  in physical fitness, 182, 190, 203-206
fluid replacement, 213, 214
focus; *see* attention; mental focus
Follen, Charles, 84, 89
follow-up, 334
Fontaine, K. R., 250
food; *see* diet; nutrition
football
  advertising during, 219
  National Football Leagues (NFL), 419
  professional ranks, 426
force, 156, 156*t*, 162-166
  absorption of, 164
  application of, 163-164
  production of, 163
force platforms, 168
formal competition, in sport education model, 292
formative assessment, 297, 298
Fosbury, D., 151
four Rs, 351
frequency, in fitness training, 192, 201, 202
friction, 156*t*, 157
front squats, 152
FS1, 421
fulcrum, 161
full value contract, 295
fundamental motor skills, 135-143
  defined, 44
  development of, 44, 133-134, 139-143
  types of, 135-139
funding, for physical education, 288

G

Gabbard, C., 141
Gallahue, G. L., 132-135
galloping, 137
Game Performance Assessment Instrument, 299
games, assessment of performance in, 299
Gatorade Sports Science Institute, 217
gender; *see also* women and girls
  and physical education pedagogy, 306-307
generalizability, 120
geographic location, 5
Germany
  history of physical education in, 79-81, 83
  influence on US physical education, 84, 87
  in Olympics, 108, 109
girls; *see also* women and girls
Gittings, Ina, 91
global wellness economy, pre-COVID, 401
glycogenic supercompensation, 212
goals
  defined, 33, 264
  outcome, 264
  performance, 264
  of physical education/exercise science/sport, 35
  process, 264
  setting, 264-267
  types of, 264
golf
  biomechanics in, 167-168
  history of, 88
  professional, 102
  professional opportunities, 426
goniometer, 168
Goodway, J. D., 132
Gould, D., 258, 259, 261
graduation rates, in intercollegiate sports, 228
graduation success rate (GSR), 228
gravity
  center of, 156-157, 156*t*, 158
  defined, 156, 156*t*
Great Britain, history of physical education in, 82, 83
Great Depression, 94-95, 96
Greece, ancient, 78-79
Greenleaf, C. A., 270, 271, 272
Grove City College v. Bell, 103, 104
Guidelines for Undergraduate Biomechanics, 149
Gulick, Luther, 86, 89, 90-91
Guts Muths, Johann Christoph Friedrich, 79, 80, 81, 83
gymnastics
  in ancient Greece, 79
  in Europe, 79-81
  in US, 84-87

H

Hamilton, N., 147
Hanna, Delphine, 86, 89
hardiness, psychological, 259
Harrison, L. Jr., 54
health
  allied fields, 16-17
  defined, 54
  holistic approach, 54, 404
  impact of physical activity on, 60, 181-185
  national goals for, 56-59
  in national health goals, 99-100
  traditional approach to, 54
  wellness approach to, 54-55
Health and Human Services (HHS), US Department of, 21, 23, 183
health and wellness coaches, 387-389, 394-395
health belief model of behavior change, 253, 254
health care, cost of, 58, 59
health clubs; *see also* sport clubs
  career opportunities in, 391-394, 401-402
  growth in, 412-413
  membership in, 5-6
  trends in, 392
health coaching, 392
health education, defined, 16
health fitness, 181, 364
health instruction, defined, 16
health promotion
  in national health goals, 56-59, 99-100
health-related careers, 399-402
  list of career opportunities in, 318
  types of, 399-402
health-related physical fitness, 101
Health-Related Physical Fitness Test, 101
Healthy People, 99-100
Healthy People 2030, 6, 34, 56
  goal/objectives of, 34
  physical activity objectives, 34
  website of, 73
heart rate, measurement of, 192-193
heart rate monitors, 381
heart rate reserve (HRR), 193, 194
heat cramps, 207
heat exhaustion, 207
heat stroke, 207
Hellison, D. R., 42
Hemenway, Mary, 87
Henry, F. M., 10, 11
Henry, Franklin, 98
Hetherington, Clark, 93, 95
HickokSports.com, 111
hidden curriculum, 304

higher education; *see also* colleges and universities
physical education programs in, 364-365
high jumping, 151
high schools, physical education programs in, 363-364; *see also* interscholastic sports
high-speed imaging, 166
Hispanics, 51, 52, 67, 69
historical foundations, 76-110; *see also* sport history
Hitchcock, Edward, 85, 87, 89
Hitler, Adolf, 93
Hodge, S. R., 54
holistic health, 54
chiropractic care, 404
in chiropractic care, 404-405
Homans, Amy Morris, 87, 89, 97
home exercise equipment, 391, 393
homeschooling, 8
hopping, 137
hot weather, 207-208
hourglass model of motor development, 132-135, 133*f*, 134*f*
Hudson, J. L., 173-174
humanism, 30, 31
human relations skills, teachers, 301, 303
humidity, 206, 207-208
humility, 52-54
hydrostatic weighing, 198
hypokinetic diseases, 182
hypothermia, 208

I

IAPS; *see* International Association for the Philosophy of Sport
idealism, 27-28, 31
imagery; *see* mental imagery
imitation, 39, 43
implicit messages, 304
improved performance, 120
inclusion approach, 106
income, 5
income, and physical activity, 70-71
individual, in dynamical systems model, 118-119, 119*f*, 140, 141*f*
individual differences
in fitness training, 188
motor learning influenced by, 124-125
Individuals with Disabilities Education Act (IDEA) of 1990, 105-106, 107
inertia, law of, 160
informational interviews, 321
information processing model, 117-118, 117*f*
injury prevention, athletic trainers and, 400
injury rehabilitation
athletic trainers and, 400
exercise adherence during, 257
input, in information processing model, 117
Instagram, 21
The Institute for Diversity and Ethics in Sport, 432
Institute for the Study of Youth Sports, 243
institutionalization, 222-223
institutional responsibilities
of coaches, 375
of teachers, 361
instruction, unit of, 286
instructional alignment, 297
instructional responsibilities
of coaches, 374
of teachers, 360
instructional skills, of teachers, 301, 302
instruments, in biomechanical analysis, 165-170
intangible reinforcers, 124
InTASC; *see* Interstate Teacher Assessment and Support Consortium
integration
gender, in physical education, 306-307
in personal and social responsibility model, 291
intensity, in fitness training, 189, 192-193, 202
intercollegiate sports, 6, 15, 226-230
academic performance and, 226-230
coaches in, 371, 375
diversity of, 226, 227
financial assistance in, 227
governance of, 103, 227
graduation rates in, 228
history of, 84-85, 88, 94, 96
influence of money on, 219-220
recent growth in participation in, 102, 223
sociology of, 226-230
women in, 88, 90, 102-105, 230-233
internal imagery, 271
International Association for the Philosophy of Sport (IAPS), 48, 343
International Health, Racquet, and Sportsclub Association (IHRSA), 391, 437
International Olympic Committee (IOC), 109, 110, 211, 241
International Sports Engineering Association, 176
Internet, 321
careers related to, 425
communication, 21
communication with professionals, 21
online courses/degrees, 22
and personal training, 394
professional development, 22
professional profiles on, 333
internships, 323
interscholastic sports, 223, 224-226
coaches in, 371
girls in, 102-105, 224*f*, 231
pros and cons of, 224-226
recent growth in participation in, 102, 223-224, 224*f*
sociology of, 224-226
specialization in one sport, 225
Title IX and, 102-105
Interstate Teacher Assessment and Support Consortium (InTASC), 354
intervention strategies, 273-274
interviews, job, 334
intrinsic feedback, 130
intrinsic (internal) motivation, 123, 223, 250, 251
IOC; *see* International Olympic Committee
Isaacs, L. D., 132
isokinetic exercises, 200, 201
isometric exercises, 200-201
isotonic exercises, 200, 201
"I-stroke" arm pull, 150

J

Jahn, Friedrich Ludwig, 80-81, 83, 84
job(s)
accepting, 334-335
applying for, 334
interviewing for, 334
searching for, 332, 333
job burnout, 377
job shadowing, 321
Johnson, Ben, 109
joint flexibility; *see* flexibility
Jones, G., 259

Jordan, Michael, 109
journal(s); *see also specific publications*
of biomechanics, 175
of exercise physiology, 216
of motor behavior, 142
of sport and exercise psychology, 273
of sport history, 110
of sport sociology, 242
of teaching and coaching, 380
used for formative assessment, 299
journalism, careers in, 422–423
Journal of Health, Physical Education, and Recreation, 96
Journal of Sport History, 78
journal(s); *see also specific publications*
of health, fitness, and sports medicine, 406
of sport management, media, and performance, 430
Joyner, F. G., 160
jumping, 137–138, 172–173
justice, equity, diversity, and inclusion (JEDI), 3

K

Kaepernick, C., 233
Karvonen equation, 193
Kelley, D., 411
Kelly, John P., 96
kicking, 139
Kim, C., 275
kinematics, 155, 156*t*
kinesiology, 436
areas of study, 147
and biomechanics, 147–155
defined, 147, 149
disciplines within, 11–16
diversity settings, 4
reasons for studying, 147
use of term, 99, 147
kinesiotherapists, 387, 403
kinetic energy, 158
kinetics, 155, 156*t*
Knight Commission on Intercollegiate Athletics, 229–230
knowledge of performance, 129
Knudson, D., 171
Kobasa, S. C., 259
Krathwohl, D. A., 36
Kraus-Weber Minimal Muscular Fitness Tests, 96–97
Krieg, N., 160

L

Landing Error Scoring System (LESS), 152
languages, 51
Lapchick, R., 233
Latino origin, 51
law; *see* legislation
law, sport, agency, 428
law of acceleration, 160
leadership, 335–336
in motor learning, 131
in physical education, 438–439
in promotion of physical activity, 436–441
in youth sports, 238–239, 438–439
leaping, 137
learning
assessment of, 45–47
motor; *see* motor learning
transfer of, 128–129
learning domain, 35–45
affective, 35, 39–42
cognitive, 36–39
psychomotor, 42–43
learning strategies, in goal setting, 264–265
least restrictive environment approach, 106
Lee, S., 426
Leffingwell, T. R., 267, 270
legislation
on individuals with disabilities, 105–107
on women in sports, 230
leisure; *see* recreation and leisure, as allied field
LESS; *see* Landing Error Scoring System
lesson plan, 287, 311
leverage, 161–162
Lewis, Carl, 109
Lewis, Dioclesian, 85, 89
liberal arts courses, 322
life expectancy, 34, 52, 54, 55
lifestyle, in motor development, 135
Lifetime Sports Foundation, 98
linear motion, 159
Ling, Hjalmar Frederik, 81, 83
Ling, Per Henrik, 81, 83
linguistically diverse learners, 54
LinkedIn, 21
live web conferencing programs, 21
Locke, L. F., 20, 440
locomotor skills, 135–137, 361
Logan, G. A., 156
logic, 28
Love, K., 275
love, pedagogies of, 297
Luttgens, K., 147

M

Maclaren, Archibald, 82, 83
Magill, R. A., 120
mainstreaming, 366
managerial responsibilities
of coaches, 375
of teachers, 360–361
manipulation, 43
manipulative skills, 135, 138–139
Manuel, S., 233
manufacturers' representatives, 418
marketability, increasing
professional, 405–406
in sport management, media, and performance, 430
for teachers and coache, 379–382
marketing
career opportunities, 411
Maslach, Christina, 377
mass, 156, 156*t*
maximal heart rate, 193, 194
McCloy, Charles, 95
McKenzie, Robert Tait, 91, 95
McKinney, W., 156
measurement
evaluation *vs.,* 45
in goal setting, 265
Mechikoff, R. A., 78
media, sport, career opportunities in, 318, 421–425
media coverage, 410
advertising in, 219
growth of, 219
medical fitness centers, 392–393
of professional sports, 219
sport events, 410
on sport violence, 239–240
mental focus; *see also* attention
imagery in, 272
mental health
of athletes, 274–276
literacy, 276
physical activity and, 185, 249–250
mental imagery, 270–273
nature of, 271–272
uses of, 272–273
mental skills, mental imagery and, 273

mental toughness, 259
mental well-being, 275-276
mental wellness, 54
metaphysics, 27, 28
Middelweerd, A., 257
middle school, physical education programs in, 363
mild traumatic brain injury (mTBI), biomechanics of, 152
military, teaching in, 370
mind-body relationship, 31-32, 93
minerals, 209
minorities, sociology of sport on, 233-236
minors, 323
moderate-intensity physical activity, 183
Moffatt, A., 259
money, influence in intercollegiate sports, 219-220
monism, 32
motion, 159-161
  laws of, 159-161
  linear, 159
  rotary, 159-160
motion capture, 165-166
motivation, 223, 250-252
  assessment and, 45-47
  defined, 123
  in effective teaching, 301
  intrinsic *vs.* extrinsic, 223, 250-251
  motor learning influenced by, 123-124
  psychology of, 250-252
motor behavior
  defined, 114
  professional organizations and journals in, 142
motor control, 115-131
  areas of study, 116-117
  defined, 116
motor cross
  professional opportunities, 426
motor development, 11, 12, 14, 131-143
  areas of study, 132
  career opportunities within, 12*t*
  defined, 14, 116, 132
  fundamental skills in, 135-143
  phases of, 132-135
  in psychomotor learning domain, 42-45
motor learning, 115-131
  additional concepts in, 125-131
  areas of study, 116-117
  career opportunities within, 12*t*
  defined, 115, 116
  factors influencing, 122-125
  models of, 117-119, 117*f*, 119*f*
  performance characteristics and, 119-120
  stages of, 120-122, 121*t*
motor skills
  acquisition of; *see* motor learning
  fundamental, 44, 135-143
  open *vs.* closed, 126-127, 126*f*
  in psychomotor learning domain, 42-45
Moving into the Future (NASPE), 100
Murray-Garcia, J., 337
muscular Christianity, 82
muscular endurance
  measurement of, 203
  in physical fitness, 182, 190, 199-203, 202*f*
muscular strength
  measurement of, 203
  in physical fitness, 182, 190, 199-203, 202*f*
MyPlate, 210, 211*f*

N

Nachtegall, Franz, 81, 83
NAIA; *see* National Association of Intercollegiate Athletes; National Association of Intercollegiate Athletics
Naismith, James, 88
names; *see* team names, Native Americans in
Napoleon, 80
Nash, Jay B., 93, 95
NASPSPA; *see* North American Society for Psychology of Sport and Physical Activity
NASSH; *see* North American Society for Sport History
NASSM; *see* North American Society for Sport Management
NASSS; *see* North American Society for the Sociology of Sport
NATA (National Athletic Trainers' Association), 97
National Alliance for Youth Sports, 243, 377
National Association for Sport and Physical Education (NASPE)
  Moving into the Future, 100
  on sport management, 411-413
National Association of Intercollegiate Athletes (NAIA), 96
National Association of Intercollegiate Athletics (NAIA), 102, 227
National Athletic Trainers' Association, 408
National Athletic Trainers' Association (NATA), 97, 99, 340, 342
  certifications offered by, 323
National Basketball Association, 411
National Collegiate Athletic Association (NCAA), 6, 53, 227, 241, 243, 415, 419, 420, 426
  on academic performance, 228
  on Native American imagery, 236
  on participation rates, 102, 223-224
  on professional athletes, 426-427
  revenues associated with, 102
  Title IX and, 103
  on women's participation, 231
National Conference on Program Planning in Game and Sports for Boys and Girls of Elementary School Age, 96, 98
National Consortium for Physical Education and Recreation for Individuals with Disabilities, 383
National Federation of State High School Associations (NFHS), 102, 103, 223, 383
  coach certification offered by, 377
National Health and Nutrition Examination Survey (NHANES), 56
National Health Interview Survey, 69
National Institutes of Health (NIH), 101
nationalism, in sport history, 79, 81
national period, US, 84-85
National Physical Activity Plan (NPAP), 70, 183
  strategies of, 61-63
National Recreation Association, 91
national standards, for physical education, 284-285, 356
National Standards and Grade Level Outcomes for K-12 Physical Education (SHAPE America), 284
National Standards for Sport Coaches (SHAPE America), 376
National Strength and Conditioning Association (NSCA), 398, 408
  certifications offered by, 323
  certifications offered by, 398*t*
Native Americans, 235-236
  history of sport among, 82-83, 235
  population of, 51
  in team names and images, 236

Native Hawaiian, 51
naturalism, 30
naturalization, 43
NCAA; *see* National Collegiate Athletic Association
needs, in motivation, 123
negative reinforcement, 124
negative self-talk, 267, 268, 269
negative transfer of learning, 128-129
networking, 333
Neuroscience for Kids, 144
"new physical education," 90
Newton, Isaac
  laws of motion, 159-161
Nike, 153, 169
Ning, 21
NIRSA: Leaders in Collegiate Recreation, 343, 432
Nissen, Hartvig, 86, 87
No Child Left Behind Act (NCLB), 284
non-Hispanic races, 51
non-Hispanics, 52
nonlocomotor skills, 135, 137-138
North American Society for Psychology of Sport and Physical Activity (NASPSPA), 144, 343
North American Society for Sport History, 111
North American Society for Sport History (NASSH), 78, 343
North American Society for Sport Management (NASSM), 343
North American Society for Sport Management (NASSM), 412, 413, 431, 432
North American Society for the Sociology of Sport (NASSS), 343
Northrip, J., 156
nutrients, categories of, 209
nutrition; *see also* diet
  and body composition, 196
  and physical fitness, 209-211
nutritional supplements, 214

O

Oberle, G. H., 442
obesity
  among adults, 56, 57
  among children and adolescents, 56, 57*f*
  biomechanics and, 175
  defined, 196
  health risks of, 58, 196
  prevalence of, 56, 58
objectives, 33-35
O'Bryant, C. P., 54
Occupational Outlook Handbook, 320, 346
Occupational socialization, 344
Office of Civil Rights, 103, 231
older adults
  coaching of, 371
  physical activity, 71
  population of, 51
  teaching of, 370
Olympic and Amateur Sports Act of 1998, 107
Olympic Games
  in ancient Greece, 78
  modern, establishment of, 88, 108
  personality of athletes in, 259
  recent history of, 108-110
  US participation in, 88
Om Yun-chol, 160
on-campus jobs, 329
on-demand virtual training, 386, 393
online courses/degrees, 22
On the Movement of Animals (Aristotle), 149
open motor skills, 126-127, 126*f*
organizational skills, teachers, 300, 301
organizations; *see* professional organizations
Osaka, N., 275
outcome goals, 264
outdoor education, 295
outdoor education model, 290
output, in information processing model, 117
overconformity, performance-enhancing drugs and, 241
overload, in fitness training, 187
overweight, 195
  among children and adolescents, 68
  defined, 196
  health risks of, 196
  prevalence of, 56, 68, 69
Owens, Jesse, 93, 108
oxygen consumption, measurement of, 194
Ozmun, J. L., 132

P

Pacific Islanders, 51, 52
Paralympics, 107, 110
Parkhouse, B. L., 411
part method of teaching motor skills, 127
Payne, V. G., 132
"pay-to-play" plans, 102, 226
Peace Corps, 366-367
PE Central, 311, 381, 381*f,* 383
pedagogical models, 289-297
pedagogies of affect, 296-297
pedagogy, physical education, 281-310
  areas of study, 15, 282-283
  assessment and accountability, 297-300
  career opportunities within, 12*t*
  characteristics of effective teaching, 300-303
  curriculum development, 285-289, 286*f,* 287*f*
  defined, 15, 282
  pedagogical models, 289-297
  social justice issues, 304-309
  standards-based education, 283-285
PELinks4U, 311
perceived control, in behavior change, 253
performance
  anxiety and, 262-264
  arousal and, 261-264
  characteristics of, 120
  defined, 119
  goal setting and, 265-267
  knowledge of, 129
  mental imagery and, 270-273
  personality and, 258-261
  self-talk and, 267-270
performance-based assessment, 297, 298
performance-enhancing drugs (PEDs), 211-215
  anabolic-androgenic steroids, 214-215
  caffeine, 211
  carbohydrate loading, 212
  creatine, 214
  in Olympics, 109
  in sports, 240-241
performance goals, 264
performance-related physical fitness, 101, 181
Perlman, D., 251
persistence, 120
personal and social responsibility model (PSRM), 289, 290, 291
personal coaching, 429
personal development, in career preparation, 327
personality, 257-261
  defined, 258
  nature of, 258
  and sport performance, 258-261

personal problems, and job burnout, 378
personal trainers, 393-394, 429
personal training, 386
Phelps, M., 274
philosophy, 25-48
  branches of, 27
  career opportunities within, 12*t*
  defined, 25, 26
  educational, 30-31
  existentialism, 30, 31
  humanism, 30, 31
  idealism, 31
  mind-body relationship, 31-32
  naturalism, 31
  pragmatism, 31
  professional, 26-27
  realism, 28-29, 31
  sport; *see* sport philosophy
phosphocreatine, 214
photography, sport, 424
physical activity, 5-7; *see also specific types*
  barriers, 70
  and body composition, 196
  defined, 8
  dose-response debate on, 183-184
  energy production for, 186-187, 186*t*
  future trends, 441-443
  guidelines for instruction, 131
  health benefits of, 184-185
  initiatives, 355
  leadership in promotion of, 436-441
  leadership promotion, 436-441
  moderate-to-vigorous physical activity, 64, 66
  movement, 50, 60-66
  objectives of, 7
  participation benefits, 16
  psychological benefits of, 249-250
  and public recognition, 6
  recommendations on, 64, 69
  sport psychologists, 248-249
Physical Activity and Health: The Surgeon General's Report, 60, 100
Physical Activity Guidelines for Americans (2018), 60, 70
physical activity pyramid, 183, 184*f*
Physical and Health Education America, 383
Physical Best, 101
physical culture, 222
physical education, 8, 438-439, 441-443
  academic discipline of, 10-11
  allied fields of, 16-18
  assessment of learning in, 45-47
  career opportunities in, 317-320
  career opportunities within, 12*t*
  components of, 356
  contemporary programs in, 4-5
  defined, 5-8
  in elementary school, 361-363
  focus of, 6
  goals of, 35
  in higher education, 364-365
  in high school, 363-364
  leadership in, 438-439
  in learning domains, 35-45
  meaningful, 296
  in middle school, 363
  name of field, 99
  national standards for, 284-285, 356
  professional development in, 18-22
  in professional preparation programs, 365
  profession of, 10
  quality programs, 355-358
  SHAPE America's education standards, 354
  social justice issues in, 304-309
  teachers, competencies for, 354-355
  use of term, 76
physical education and sport, as name of field, 99
physical education pedagogy; *see* pedagogy, physical education
  career opportunities within, 12*t*
Physical Education Public Information Project (PEPI), 100
physical fitness, 181-216
  body composition in, 182, 195-199
  cardiorespiratory endurance in, 182, 190, 191-195
  careers in; *see* fitness-related careers
  components, 182, 190-206
  defined, 8, 181
  designing programs for, 206
  development of, 44-45, 186-190
  environmental conditions and, 206-209
  flexibility in, 182, 190, 203-206
  health benefits of, 184-185
  health fitness, 181
  movement, 60-71, 101
  muscular endurance in, 182, 190, 199-203, 202*f*
  muscular strength in, 182, 190, 199-203, 202*f*
  nutrition in, 209-211
  performance-related *vs.* health-related, 181, 182
  in psychomotor learning domain, 44-45
physical therapists, 403-404
physical therapy, 403-404
physical wellness, 54-55
physiological readiness, 122
physiology; *see* exercise physiology
Pitts, B. G., 411
placement files, 332
planned behavior, theory of, 253, 254
plateaus, in motor learning, 130
play, 16-17
Playground Association of America, 91
population, US, demographic changes in, 50-54
portfolios, career, 332
positive reinforcement, 124
positive self-talk, 267-268
positive transfer of learning, 128, 129
Posner, M. J., 120
Posse, Baron Nils, 86, 89, 149
potential energy, 158
poverty, 51, 52
power
  in biomechanics, 156*t,* 158
  in physical fitness, 182
power movement, 199
practice sessions, in motor learning, 125
practicums, 323
practitioner-based research, 19
pragmatism, 29, 31
precision, 43
preperformance routines, 273
preschool, teaching in, 361
President's Council on Fitness, Sports, and Nutrition, 96, 97, 101, 217
pressure, 156, 156*t*
preventative exercise programs, 387
process goals, 264
profession, defined, 10
professional athletics
  careers in, 426-427
professional development, 18, 22
professional involvement, 330, 339
professionalism, 335-339
  accountability and, 337
  advocacy and, 336-337
  cultural humility and, 337
  ethics and, 337-338, 338*t*
  leadership and, 335-336
  role modeling in, 339
professional journals; *see* journal(s)
professional marketability, 405-407

professional organizations, 339–343, 346; *see also specific groups*
benefits of, 340
in biomechanics, 175
career opportunities in, 420–421
of exercise physiology, 216
in fitness-related careers, 398
in health, fitness, and sports medicine, 406
major, overview of, 341–343
of motor behavior, 142
reasons to join, 340–341
in sport and exercise psychology, 273
of sport history, 110
in sport management, media, and performance, 430
in sport sociology, 242
in teaching and coaching, 380
professional philosophy, 25–26, 32–33
professional preparation, 322–330, 324–325*t*
programs, teaching physical education in, 365
professional sports
careers in, 425–430
growth of, 102
media coverage of, 410
minorities in, 233
salaries, for athletic trainers, 401
women in, 102, 231
professional theory courses, 322
program evaluation, assessment and, 46
progression, in fitness training, 187–188
progressive education, 30–31
progressive part method of teaching motor skills, 127
progressive resistance exercise, 201
Project Adventure, 293
Promoting Health/Preventing Disease: Objectives for the Nation, 56
promotion
career opportunities, 411
ProQuest, 21
proteins, 209
psychological benefits of physical activity, 249–250
psychological hardiness, 259
psychological readiness, 122
psychology
cognitive, 260
psychology, sport and exercise, 246–276
on anxiety, 261–264
areas of study, 247–249
defined, 247
on exercise adherence, 252–257
on goals setting, 264–267
on mental imagery, 270–273
on motivation, 250–252
on personality, 258–261
professional organizations and journals in, 273
scope of, 247
psychology, sport and physical activity
areas of study, 11
career opportunities within, 12*t*
defined, 11
psychomotor learning domain, 42–45
pulling, 138
Puritans, 82, 84
pushing, 138

Q

qualitative biomechanical analysis, 170–174
qualitative research, 19
quality physical education program, 355–358
quantitative biomechanical analysis, 170
quantitative research, 19

R

race, in physical education pedagogy, 307
Racial and Gender Report Card (RGRC), 233
racial diversity, 51
racial segregation, 90
racism, 234–236
radar guns, 166
Ray, H. L., 83
reaction time, in physical fitness, 182
readiness
defined, 122
motor learning influenced by, 122–123
realism
in goal setting, 265
philosophy of, 28–29
Really Simple Syndication (RSS), 21
real-time communication, 21
reasoned action theory, 253, 254
record keeping, in sport education model, 292–293
recovery, in fitness training, 188
recreation
allied fields, 17
collegiate, 415–416
recreational therapy, 403
therapeutic, 17
therapeutic, 403
recreation and leisure, as allied field, 16
reduction of attention demand, 120
reflecting on, systems of meaning, 4*f*
reflexive movement phase, 132
reframing, 269–270
rehabilitation; *see also* injury rehabilitation
rehabilitation
career opportunities in, 387–399
Rehabilitation Act of 1973, 105, 107
rehabilitative exercise programs, 387, 389
rehearsing, 272
reinforcement
defined, 124
motor learning influenced by, 124
relationships, in personal and social responsibility model, 291
relationship skills, 296
repetition, 202
repetition maximum (RM), 202
research
practitioner-based, 19
qualitative, 19
quantitative, 19
reports, reading, 18–19
reports, steps to understand, 18
scientific, 197
Research Quarterly for Exercise and Sport, 94
resiliency, 351
resistance, 202
resorts, teaching of, 370
resumes, 330–332, 331*f*
retailing, sport, 418–419
reversibility, in fitness training, 188
Rezazadeh, H., 160
risk factors
behavioral, 183
environmental, 182–183
nonmodifiable, 55
RM; *see* repetition maximum (RM)
Robertson, R., 160
Robinson, David, 109
role conflict, 372–373
Rome, ancient, 78–79
Roosevelt, Franklin, 96
rotary motion, 159–160
rubrics, 299
rudimentary movement phase, 132
running, 153
as locomotor skill, 136

S

safety, in fitness training, 188-189
sales of sporting goods
careers in, 418-419
Salzmann, Christian Gotthilf, 80
same-sex physical education, 306
Sargent, Dudley, 85, 86, 89, 91
"S-arm" pull, 150
scholarships, athletic, 227
school physical education programs, 6
schools; *see also* elementary schools; high schools; middle schools
as community center, 59
contemporary physical education programs in, 4-5
fitness and physical activity movement, 70
recent developments in physical education, 100
teaching in, 361-367
wellness movement, 59-60
worksite wellness programs, 390
school sports; *see* intercollegiate sports; interscholastic sports
Science Friday, 176
The Science of Swimming (Counsilman), 150
scientific research, defined, 19
seasonal work, 367
seasons, in sport education model, 292
second-class lever, 161
segregation, racial, 90
self-analysis, in motor learning, 130-131
self-awareness, 296
Self-care, 344-345
self-compassion, 345
self-concept, 41
self-confidence, self-talk and, 269
self-efficacy, 253, 254
in behavior change, 253
defined, 253
motor development and, 141
self-management, 296
self-reflection process, 42
self-talk, 267-270
application of, 268-269
defined, 267
modification of, 269-270
nature of, 267-268
negative, 267, 268, 269
positive, 267-268
types of, 268
SEMs; *see* sport education models
Senior Olympics, 371
service, in professionalism, 339
sets, 202
sex discrimination, 102-105, 231
sexuality, in physical education pedagogy, 309
sexual orientation, and physical education pedagogy, 309
SHAPE America, 398, 406, 420
SHAPE (Society of Health and Physical Education) America, 88, 282, 283, 299, 311, 342, 383
education standards developed by, 354
National Standards and Grade Level Outcomes for K-12 Physical Education, 284, 356
National Standards for Sport Coaches, 376
Shape of the Nation survey, 100
Sheard, M., 259
Sherrill, Claudine, 339
Shinny, 84
shoes, running, 153
Siedentop, Daryl, 292
Silverman, S., 20
simulation, in biomechanical analysis, 165
ski jumping, 151, 153
skill learning
mental imagery in, 272
performance characteristics and, 119-120
skill-related physical fitness, 181, 182; *see also* performance-related physical fitness
skill themes approach, 289, 290
skipping, 137
Skype, 21
sliding, 137
Sloane, William, 88
SMART goal setting, 265-266
Smithsonian Museum, 111
smoking, and chronic disease, 55
soccer
professional opportunities, 426
women's professional, 102, 231
social and emotional learning, 296
social awareness, 296
social bookmarking sites, 22
social class; *see* socioeconomic status
social cognitive theory of behavior change, 253, 254
social identity, 3-4
social justice, 52-54
biomechanics, 147
career and professional development, 317
defined, 5
defining, 5
demographics changes, 51
exercise physiology, 181
fitness- and health-related careers, 387
historical foundations, 77
issues, in physical education, 304-309
motor behavior, 115
physical education pedagogy, 282
professional philosophy, 26
sociological foundations, 220
sport and exercise psychology, 247
sport-related careers, 411
teaching and coaching careers, 351
social learning domain, 35-36, 39-42
social media, 21, 425
careers related to, 425
in job searches, 333
omnipresence of, 425
in professional development, 21-22
social needs, 41
social support, 345
in exercise adherence, 256, 257
in goal setting, 267
social wellness, 54
society, significance of sports in, 219-220
Society for Neuroscience, 144
Society of Health and Physical Education (SHAPE) America, 48; *see* SHAPE (Society of Health and Physical Education) America
socioeconomic status, 7, 14, 51-52, 70, 82, 307-309
sociology, sports, 219-242
areas of study, 14-15, 221
career opportunities within, 12*t*
on children and youth, 237-239
defined, 14, 220-221
in educational institutions, 223-230
on girls and women, 230-233
goals of, 220-221
on minorities, 233-236
on performance-enhancing drugs, 240-241
professional organizations and journals in, 242
sports, defined, 221-223
on violence, 239-240
Soviet Union, in Olympics, 108-109
spas, career opportunities in, 401-402
specialization
in one sport, 225
opportunity, 412
specialized movement skills, 134
The Special Kinesiology of Educational Gymnastics (Posse), 149

Special Olympics, 98
specificity
  in fitness training, 187
  in goal setting, 264, 265
spectators
  violence by, 240
spectatorship
  career opportunities, 411
speed
  in motor learning, 127-128
speed, in physical fitness, 182
speed-accuracy trade-off, 128
Speedo, 153, 169
speed skating, biomechanics in, 152
Spessato, B. C., 141
Spiess, Adolph, 79, 81, 83
spinning, 388
Spirduso, W. W., 20
spiritual wellness, 54
sport(s); *see also specific types*
  careers in; *see* sport careers
  defined, 221-223
  girls and women in, 230-233
  history of; *see* sport history
  minorities in, 233-236
  motives for participation in, 223
  physical activities considered as, 222
  rates of participation in, 101-105
  social significance of, 219-220
  use of term, 76
  violence in, 239-240
sport analytics, 421
sport and exercise psychology; *see* psychology, sport and exercise
sport and recreation clubs, 416
Sport and Recreation Law Association, 431
sport biomechanics; *see also* biomechanics
  areas of study, 12*t,* 13
  defined, 13
  use of term, 149
sport broadcasting, 422-423
sport careers, 317-320, 410-431, 425-430
  list of career opportunities in, 318
  in management, 416-418
  in media, 421-425
  performance and other, 425-430
sport clubs, 365; *see also* health clubs
  teaching in, 368-369
SPORTDiscus, 21
sport education model (SEM), 289, 290, 292-294
sport historian
  career opportunities within, 12*t*
sport history, 77-78
  in ancient Greece and Rome, 78-79
  areas of study, 12*t,* 13, 78
  career opportunities within, 12*t*
  defined, 13, 77
  in Europe, 79-82
  historical development, 77-78
  professional organizations and journals in, 110
  recent developments in, 98-110
  in US, 82-98
sporting goods, sales of
  careers in, 418-419
sporting goods manufacturing
  career opportunities, 411
sport law, careers in, 428
sport management, 411-413
  areas of study, 15
  career opportunities in, 12*t,* 318
  career paths, 413, 414f
  conceptual analysis of, 412
  defined, 15
  defined, 411
sport medicine
  career opportunities within, 12*t*
sport officiating
  careers in, 427-428
sport participation
  career opportunities, 411
sport philosophy, 32
  areas of study, 13
  career opportunities within, 12*t*
  defined, 13
sport photography, careers in, 424
sport programs
  focus of, 4
sport retailing, 418-419
sport(s); *see also specific types*
  academic discipline of, 11-12, 12*t*
  allied fields of, 16-18
  assessment of learning in, 45-47
  careers in, 422-424
  contemporary programs in, 4-5
  defined, 8
  focus of, 6
  future trends, 441-443
  goals of, 33-35
  in learning domains, 35-45
  professional development in, 18-22
  profession of, 9
sportscasters, 422
sports drinks, 212-214
sports facilities management, 416-418
Sports Illustrated (magazine), 423
sports information directors, 424, 425
sports medicine/athletic training
  areas of study, 12-13
  career opportunities within, 12*t*
  defined, 12
  practice domains, 401
sport sociology; *see* sociology, sports
sports vision training, 118
sportswriting, 421
  careers in, 422-423
squat jumps, 172, 173
stability
  in biomechanics, 158-159
  in motor learning, 120
stacking, 234
state anxiety, 262
static contraction, 199
static equilibrium, 158
statics, 154
static stretching, 205
stereotypes
  gender, 306
  minority, 233-236
steroids, anabolic-androgenic, 214-215
strength and conditioning professionals, 395-396
strength training, 199-200
stretching, 137-138
striking, 139
stroke, heat, 207
Struna, N. L., 77
student(s); *see also* intercollegiate sports; interscholastic sports
  demographics of, 52-53
  well-being of, 358
student-athletes, 227
Substance Abuse and Mental Health Services Administration (SAMHSA), 350-351
summative assessment, 297, 298
Super Bowl, advertising during, 219
Supreme Court, US, on Title IX, 103
Surgeon General's Vision for a Healthy and Fit Nation, 100
Sweden
  history of physical education in, 81, 83
  influence on US physical education, 86-87
swimming, biomechanics in, 150, 153
swinging, 138

T

tactical games model (TGM), 289, 290, 291-292
tangible reinforcers, 124

Tapped In, 21
target heart rate (THR), 193
task, in motor learning
  dynamical systems model of, 118-119, 140, 141*f*
  learners' understanding of, 125-126
taxonomies, 36
teachers/teaching; *see also* pedagogy, physical education
  and biomechanical analysis, 171
  burnout in, 377
  careers, 361-370
  certifications for, 367, 370-371
  certifications of, 366, 367
  characteristics of effective, 300-303
  as coaches, 371-377
  competencies for, 354-355
  cultural competency of, 349
  cultural humility of, 349
  defined, 300
  list of career opportunities in, 318
  marketability of, 379-382
  in nonschool settings, 367-370
  reasons for choosing career in, 352
  responsibilities of, 361-362
  rewards/benefits/challenges of, 352-354
  role conflict problem with, 372-373
  salaries in, 353, 354
  in school setting, 361-367
  in today's world, 350-351
teaching games for understanding (TGfU), 289, 290, 291-292
team affiliation, in sport education model, 292-294
team names, Native Americans in, 235
technology; *see also* computers
  in biomechanical analysis, 165-170
  and physical activity promotion, 257
  staying up-to-date, 19-22
  in teaching and coaching careers, 302
  wearable, 421
telemetry, 169
televised sports; *see* media coverage
tennis
  history of, 88
  professional, 102
terminal feedback, 130
Tervalon, M., 337
testosterone, 215
TGfU; *see* teaching games for understanding
TGM; *see* tactical games model
The Institute for Diversity and Ethics in Sport (TIDES), 411
theory of reasoned action, 253, 254
therapeutic recreation/recreation therapy, 403
therapy-related careers, 402-405
  dance/movement therapy, 403
third-class lever, 161
Thomas, L., 231-232
Thorpe, J., 234
threshold of training, 189
throwing, 138
time
  in fitness training, 189, 193, 203
  in goal setting, 265, 266
time management, 379
timing devices, 166
Title IX of the Education Amendments of 1972, 102-105, 230-233, 306
tobacco, and chronic disease, 55
torque, 156*t,* 158
total body sequence approach, 140
TPSR Alliance, 311
training; *see* athletic trainers (ATs); fitness training
trait anxiety, 262
transferability, in personal and social responsibility model, 291
transferable skills, 328
transfer of learning, 128-129
transtheoretical model of behavior change, 253, 254
trauma, 350-351
trauma-informed practices, 296-297
Tumblr, 22
Turner, Anita J., 89
turning, 138
turnover rates, for coaches, 372
Turnplatz, 79, 80
Turnvereins, 80, 84, 87
twisting, 138
Twitter, 21
type of exercise, in fitness training, 189, 193, 194

U

ultramarathon runners (ultras), 260
United States
  demographic changes in, 50-54
  history of physical education and sport in, 82-98
  national health goals of, 56-59, 99-100
  recent developments in physical education and sport in, 98-110
United States Anti-Doping Agency, 241
United States Commission on Civil Rights, 236
United States Department of Agriculture (USDA), 209-210
United States Olympic Committee (USOC), 107
unit of instruction, 286
unit plan, 286-287
universities; *see* colleges and universities
University of Central Florida Institute for Diversity and Ethics in Sport, 243
U.S. Department of Health and Human Services, 21
USA.gov, 73
US Congress, on intercollegiate sports, 228
US National Physical Activity Plan (2016), 60
USOC; *see* United States Olympic Committee

V

Valentini, N., 141
variation, in fitness training, 188
Vealey, R. S., 247, 251, 258, 270, 271, 272
velocity, 155, 156*t*
video chat, 21
videography, 166
vigorous physical activity, 183
violence, in sport, 239-240
virtual training, 386, 393
  during COVID-19 pandemic, 393
vision
  and leadership, 335
  in motor learning, 118
Vision for a Healthy and Fit Nation (US Surgeon General), 100
vitamins, 209
vividness, of mental imagery, 271
volleyball
  professional opportunities, 426
volunteering, 329

walking, as locomotor skill, 136
Walton-Fisette, J. L., 351
water
  for fluid replacement, 213, 214
  as nutrient, 209
wearable technology, 421
weather, and physical fitness, 206, 207-208

web development, 421, 424, 425
Webinars, 22
weight loss, and eating disorders, 197
weight management, 389, 390, 392, 394, 402, 405
Weimar, W., 147
Weinberg, R. S., 258, 260, 261, 264
well-being of students, 358
Well-coaches Certified Health and Wellness Coach, 394
wellness
  aspects of, 54
  defined, 54
wellness, social, 54
Wellness Council of American, 408, 409
wellness movement, 54-60
  chronic disease and, 55
  implications of, 59-60
  national health goals and, 56-59
wellness programs; *see* worksite wellness programs
wellness programs, 387, 389
whole method of teaching motor skills, 127
Whole School, Whole Community, Whole Child (WSCC) model, 358-359
Wilkerson, J. D., 149, 175
Williams, J. M., 267, 270
Williams, Jesse F., 93, 95
wind tunnels, 169
winning, overemphasis on
  in interscholastic sports, 225
  in youth sports, 238
women and girls
  African Americans, 233
  body issues of, 307
  in coeducational classes, 306
  history of physical education of, 84-86, 88, 90
  in intercollegiate sports, 88, 90, 102-105, 230-233
  in interscholastic sports, 224*f*, 231
  in professional sports, 102, 231
  recent growth of participation by, 102-105
  in sport, 230-233
  Title IX of Education Amendments of 1972 and, 102-105, 230-233, 306
Women's National Basketball Association (WNBA), 102, 231, 234
Women's Sports Foundation, 243, 420, 432
Women's United Soccer Association (WUSA), 102
Wood, Thomas Dennison, 86, 91, 95
work, 156*t*, 157
work experience, in career preparation, 327, 329-330
Worksite
  health promotion programs, 59
  in schools, 59
  wellness movement, 59-60
worksite wellness programs, 389
  careers in, 389
  characteristics of, 390
  core components of, 390
  in schools, 391
World Anti-Doping Agency, 241
World Health Organization (WHO), 54
World War II, 90, 96
World Wide Web, 21
writing
  of goals, 265-266

Young Men's Christian Association (YMCA), 87, 369
youth
  fitness and physical activity, 66-68
youth, trauma among, 350-351
youth organizations, teaching in, 369-370
Youth Risk Behavior Surveillance System, 2019 (YRBSS), 67
youth sports
  leadership, 438-439
  participation levels in, 6, 101-102
  sociology of sport on, 237-239

Ziegler, E. F., 99
Zoom, 21